Charles Seale-Hayne Library
University of Plymouth
(01752) 588 588
LibraryandITenquiries@plymouth.ac.uk

TREC

Digital Libraries and Electronic Publishing
William Y. Arms, series editor

Gateways to Knowledge: The Role of Academic Libraries in Teaching, Learning, and Research, edited by Lawrence Dowler, 1997

Civic Space/Cyberspace: The American Public Library in the Information Age, Redmond Kathleen Molz and Phyllis Dain, 1999

Digital Libraries, William Y. Arms, 1999

From Gutenberg to the Global Information Infrastructure: Access to Information in the Networked World, Christine L. Borgman, 2000

The Intellectual Foundation of Information, Elaine Svenonius, 2000

Digital Library Use: Social Practice in Design and Evaluation, edited by Ann Peterson Bishop, Nancy A. Van House, and Barbara P. Buttenfield, 2003

TREC: Experiment and Evaluation in Information Retrieval, edited by Ellen M. Voorhees and Donna K. Harman, 2005

TREC
Experiment and Evaluation in Information Retrieval

Edited by Ellen M. Voorhees and Donna K. Harman

Contribution of the National Institute of Standards and Technology

The MIT Press
Cambridge, Massachusetts
London, England

MIT Press books may be purchased at special quantity discounts for business or sales promotional use. For information, please e-mail ⟨special_sales@mitpress.mit.edu⟩ or write to Special Sales Department, The MIT Press, 55 Hayward Street, Cambridge, MA 02142.

This book was set in Stone Serif and Stone Sans by Asco Typesetters, Hong Kong.
Printed and bound in the United States of America.

Library of Congress Cataloging-in-Publication Data

TREC : experiment and evaluation in information retrieval / edited by Ellen M. Voorhees and Donna K. Harman.
    p.   cm. — (Digital libraries and electronic publishing)
Includes bibliographical references and index.
ISBN 0-262-22073-3 (alk. paper)
1. Text processing (Computer science)—Congresses. 2. Information storage and retrieval systems—Congresses. 3. Text REtrieval Conference. I. Voorhees, E. II. Harman, D. K. (Donna K.) III. Series.
QA76.9.T48T74   2005
025.04—dc22   2005050466

10   9   8   7   6   5   4   3   2   1

Contents

Preface

Prior to 1992, research in information retrieval was limited to small test collections (on the order of several megabytes), and there was little transfer of research ideas into commercial systems. The Text REtrieval Conference (TREC) introduced the first large test collection of full-text documents, along with the idea that providing an open testing event, with common tasks and a standard evaluation scenario, would lead to the acceleration of research on a realistic scale. The ensuing twelve years of TREC have demonstrated the remarkable success of this vision. More than 225 academic, commercial, and government groups have participated in some TREC. Retrieval effectiveness on the initial task has doubled, and the paradigm has been expanded to additional tasks such as working in other languages or media. This book describes the history of TREC, including the test collections that have been built and the common evaluation methodology that has evolved. The book also includes chapters on the various tasks that have been run in TREC as well as perspectives from some of the TREC participants.

Like any large endeavor, TREC would not happen without many contributions. The program committee has been instrumental in providing solid guidance, the track coordinators have been critical in making the various tasks happen, and the contractors who have helped create the testing material over the years (the "assessors") deserve a major thanks from the research community. Last but certainly not least, all of us would like to thank John Prange of the Advance Research and Development Activity and Charles Wayne of the Defense Advanced Research Projects Agency; both have provided funding for TREC over the years.

Any opinions, findings, and conclusions or recommendations expressed in the individual chapters are the authors' own and do not necessarily reflect those of the sponsors. The inclusion or omission of a particular company or product implies neither endorsement nor criticism by the National Institute of Standards and Technology.

Conference Proceedings

Proceedings of the sixteenth annual international ACM SIGIR conference on research and development in information retrieval, 1993, ed. R. Korfage, E. Rasmussen, and P. Willett. New York: ACM Press.

Proceedings of the seventeenth annual international ACM SIGIR conference on research and development in information retrieval, 1994, ed. W. B. Croft and C. J. van Rijsbergen. Berlin: Springer-Verlag.

Proceedings of the eighteenth annual international ACM SIGIR conference on research and development in information retrieval, 1995, ed. E. A. Fox, P. Ingwersen, and R. Fidel. New York: ACM Press.

Proceedings of the nineteenth annual international ACM SIGIR conference on research and development in information retrieval, 1996, ed. H. P. Frei, D. K. Harman, P. Schäuble, and R. Wilkinson. New York: ACM Press.

Proceedings of the twentieth annual international ACM SIGIR conference on research and development in information retrieval, 1997, ed. N. J. Belkin, A. D. Narasimhalu, and P. Willett. New York: ACM Press.

Proceedings of the twenty-first annual international ACM SIGIR conference on research and development in information retrieval, 1998, ed. W. B. Croft, A. Moffat, C. J. van Rijsbergen, R. Wilkinson, and J. Zobel. New York: ACM Press.

Proceedings of the twenty-second annual international ACM SIGIR conference on research and development in information retrieval, 1999, ed. M. Hearst, F. Gey, and R. Tong. New York: ACM Press.

Proceedings of the twenty-third annual international ACM SIGIR conference on research and development in information retrieval, 2000, ed. N. J. Belkin, P. Ingwersen, and M.-K. Leong. New York: ACM Press.

Proceedings of the twenty-fourth annual international ACM SIGIR conference on research and development in information retrieval, 2001, ed. W. B. Croft, D. J. Harper, D. H. Kraft, and J. Zobel. New York: ACM Press.

Proceedings of the twenty-fifth annual international ACM SIGIR conference on research and development in information retrieval, 2002, ed. M. Beaulieu, R. Baeza-Yates, S. H. Myaeng, and K. Järvelin. New York: ACM Press.

Proceedings of the twenty-sixth annual international ACM SIGIR conference on research and development in information retrieval, 2003, ed. J. Callan, C. Cormack, C. Clarke, D. Hawking, and A. Smeaton. New York: ACM Press.

Proceedings of the twenty-seventh annual international ACM SIGIR conference on research and development in information retrieval, 2004, ed. K. Järvelin, J. Allan, P. Bruza, and M. Sanderson. New York: ACM Press.

TREC-1, Proceedings of the first text retrieval conference, ed. D. K. Harman. Gaithersburg, Maryland: National Institute of Standards and Technology Special Publication 500-207.

TREC-2, Proceedings of the second text retrieval conference, ed. D. K. Harman. Gaithersburg, Maryland: National Institute of Standards and Technology Special Publication 500-215.

TREC-3, Proceedings of the third text retrieval conference, ed. D. K. Harman. Gaithersburg, Maryland: National Institute of Standards and Technology Special Publication 500-225.

TREC-4, Proceedings of the fourth text retrieval conference, ed. D. K. Harman. Gaithersburg, Maryland: National Institute of Standards and Technology Special Publication 500-236.

TREC-5, Proceedings of the fifth text retrieval conference, ed. E. M. Voorhees and D. K. Harman. Gaithersburg, Maryland: National Institute of Standards and Technology Special Publication 500-238.

TREC-6, Proceedings of the sixth text retrieval conference, ed. E. M. Voorhees and D. K. Harman. Gaithersburg, Maryland: National Institute of Standards and Technology Special Publication 500-240.

TREC-7, Proceedings of the seventh text retrieval conference, ed. E. M. Voorhees and D. K. Harman. Gaithersburg, Maryland: National Institute of Standards and Technology Special Publication 500-242.

TREC-8, Proceedings of the eighth text retrieval conference, ed. E. M. Voorhees and D. K. Harman. Gaithersburg, Maryland: National Institute of Standards and Technology Special Publication 500-246.

TREC-9, Proceedings of the ninth text retrieval conference, ed. E. M. Voorhees and D. K. Harman. Gaithersburg, Maryland: National Institute of Standards and Technology Special Publication 500-249.

TREC 2001, Proceedings of the tenth text retrieval conference, ed. E. M. Voorhees and D. K. Harman. Gaithersburg, Maryland: National Institute of Standards and Technology Special Publication 500-250.

TREC 2002, Proceedings of the eleventh text retrieval conference, ed. E. M. Voorhees and L. P. Buckland. Gaithersburg, Maryland: National Institute of Standards and Technology Special Publication 500-251.

TREC 2003, Proceedings of the twelfth text retrieval conference, ed. E. M. Voorhees and L. P. Buckland. Gaithersburg, Maryland: National Institute of Standards and Technology Special Publication 500-255.

INTRODUCTION

1 The Text REtrieval Conference

Ellen M. Voorhees and Donna K. Harman

Text retrieval technology targets a problem that is all too familiar: finding relevant information in large stores of electronic documents. The problem is an old one, with the first research conference devoted to the subject held in 1958 [11]. Since then the problem has continued to grow as more information is created in electronic form and more people gain electronic access. The advent of the World Wide Web, where anyone can publish so everyone must search, is a graphic illustration of the need for effective retrieval technology.

The Text REtrieval Conference (TREC) is a workshop series designed to build the infrastructure necessary for the large-scale evaluation of text retrieval technology, thereby accelerating its transfer into the commercial sector. The series is sponsored by the U.S. National Institute of Standards and Technology (NIST) and the U.S. Department of Defense. At the time of this writing, there have been twelve TREC workshops and preparations for the thirteenth workshop are under way. Participants in the workshops have been drawn from the academic, commercial, and government sectors, and have included representatives from more than twenty different countries. These collective efforts have accomplished a great deal: a variety of large test collections have been built for both traditional ad hoc retrieval and related tasks such as cross-language retrieval, speech retrieval, and question answering; retrieval effectiveness has approximately doubled; and many commercial retrieval systems now contain technology first developed in TREC.

This book chronicles the evolution of retrieval systems over the course of TREC. To be sure, there has already been a wealth of information written about TREC. Each conference has produced a proceedings containing general overviews of the various tasks, papers written by the individual participants, and evaluation results.[1] Reports on expanded versions of TREC experiments frequently appear in the wider information retrieval literature. There also have been special issues of journals devoted to particular TRECs [3; 13] and particular TREC tasks [6; 4]. No single volume could hope to be a comprehensive record of all TREC-related research. Instead, this book looks to distill the overabundance of detail into a manageable whole that summarizes the main lessons learned from TREC.

The book consists of three main parts. The first part contains introductory and descriptive chapters on TREC's history, the major products of TREC (the test collections), and the retrieval evaluation methodology. Part II includes chapters describing the major TREC "tracks," evaluations of special subtopics such as cross-language retrieval and question answering. Part III contains contributions from research groups that have participated in TREC. The epilogue to the book is written by Karen Sparck Jones, who reflects on the impact TREC has had on the information retrieval field.

The structure of this introductory chapter is similar to that of the book as a whole. The chapter begins with a short history of TREC; expanded descriptions of specific aspects of the history are included in subsequent chapters to make those chapters self-contained. Section 1.2 describes TREC's track structure, which has been responsible for the growth of TREC and allows TREC to adapt to changing needs. The final section lists both the major accomplishments of TREC and some remaining challenges.

1.1 History of TREC

The Cranfield tests [1] performed by Cyril Cleverdon and his colleagues in the 1960s were an investigation of appropriate indexing languages for information retrieval. The conclusion from the tests was that using the words of the texts themselves was very effective—a conclusion that was highly controversial for suggesting that full-text automatic indexing was a viable option for retrieval systems. Today, full-text indexing is an accepted practice and the tests are better known for the experimental methodology they introduced. Cleverdon created a test collection—a set of 1,400 documents and 225 queries in the field of aerodynamics, with a list of which documents should be retrieved for each query—that he used to compare the effectiveness of the different indexing languages. The Cranfield test collection was subsequently used by other groups to compare other retrieval devices.

Many experiments followed in the twenty-five years after the Cranfield tests, and several other test collections were built. There were two missing elements in these experiments, however. First, although some research groups did use the same test collections, there was no concerted effort by groups to work with the same data, use the same evaluation measures, or compare results across systems. The importance of the comparisons is not to show any one particular system to be superior but to allow comparison across a much wider variety of techniques than any one research group could tackle. In 1981, Sparck Jones [8] commented:

Yet the most striking feature of the test history of the past two decades is its lack of consolidation. It is true that some very broad generalizations have been endorsed by successive tests ... but there has been a real failure at the detailed level to build one test on another. As a result there are no explanations for these generalizations, and hence no means of knowing whether improved systems could be designed. (245)

Consolidation is more likely if groups can compare results across the same data, using the same evaluation method, and can meet to discuss openly how methods differ.

The second missing element was the lack of realistically sized test collections. The largest of the generally available test collections at that time contained about twelve thousand documents and had fewer than a hundred queries. Evaluation results on such small collections did not convince the operators of commercial retrieval systems that the research results would scale to their vastly larger document sets, creating a significant barrier for the transfer of research results into the commercial sector. In addition, some techniques such as the use of phrases and the construction of automatic thesauri seemed intuitively workable, yet repeatedly failed to improve effectiveness on the small collections. It was thought that larger collections might better demonstrate the effectiveness of these procedures.

1.1.1   Program History

In 1990, NIST was asked to build a large test collection for use in evaluating text retrieval technology developed as part of the Defense Advanced Research Projects Agency (DARPA) TIPSTER project [5]. This collection was to be on the order of one million full-text documents: about a hundred times larger than the existing nonproprietary test collections. The following year, NIST proposed that this large test collection be made available to the full research community by the formation of TREC. The belief was that the two missing elements in information retrieval (IR) experimentation could be addressed by providing a large test collection, uniform scoring procedures, and a forum for organizations interested in comparing results. This belief was codified into the four main goals of TREC:

- To encourage research in text retrieval based on large test collections
- To increase communication among industry, academia, and government by creating an open forum for the exchange of research ideas
- To speed the transfer of technology from research labs into commercial products by demonstrating substantial improvements in retrieval methodologies on real-world problems
- To increase the availability of appropriate evaluation techniques for use by industry and academia, including the development of new evaluation techniques more applicable to current systems

The first conference took place in November 1992 with twenty-five participating groups, including most of the leading text retrieval research groups such as the Center for Intelligent Information Retrieval (CIIR) at the University of Massachusetts, the Okapi group from the City University, London, and the SMART group from Cornell University. Although scaling their research algorithms to handle near-operational amounts of text (for 1992) was a massive undertaking, groups joined TREC to get the test data and take part in the first major cross-system evaluation.

The central task in the early TRECs was called the ad hoc task. This task tests the ability of retrieval systems to retrieve accurate and complete ranked lists of documents in response to fifty information need statements, called "topics" in TREC. The document set used in the first TREC consisted of approximately two gigabytes of newspaper/newswire articles and government documents. The test topics were generally natural-language text describing the information need (for a more complete description of the collection and example topics, see chapter 2, this volume).

The retrieval results for the first TREC were preliminary since participants had spent their time addressing the engineering issues required to get their systems to handle TREC's two gigabytes of text instead of the two megabytes of text that the largest of the previous test collections contained. Nonetheless, two important findings were established from TREC-1: that statistical methods were capable of handling three orders of magnitude more text, and that research using the much larger test collections could lead to new insights in text retrieval.

TREC-2 was held just nine months later, in August 1993. A total of thirty-one different groups participated, twenty-two of which had participated in TREC-1. Most of the engineering issues had been resolved by this point, and system builders had had a chance to do some system tuning using the collection created in TREC-1. The researchers believed that their TREC-2 systems were more effective than the TREC-1 counterparts, but the TREC-2 test used a new set of fifty topics so a direct comparison of scores from the two years of TREC was not meaningful—scores could be better simply because the topics were easier. As explained in chapter 4, this volume, the SMART group kept a frozen copy of the version of SMART that was used in each TREC and ran each subsequent test set using all previous versions of SMART. This allows a direct comparison of the improvement in SMART each year and, by extension, the improvement in retrieval systems in general. The TREC-1 version of SMART had a mean average precision score (for a definition of this measure, see chapter 3, this volume) of 0.244 and 0.262, respectively, for the TREC-1 and TREC-2 test sets; for the TREC-2 version of SMART, the corresponding values were 0.306 and 0.334, approximately a 25 percent relative improvement. The availability of a single large test collection had significantly improved retrieval performance. Retrieval performance continued to improve in subsequent years. The TREC-7 version of SMART has an average relative improvement of more than 100 percent over the TREC-1 version, and an average relative improvement of about 75 percent over the more realistic baseline of the TREC-2 version.

A few additional exploratory tasks were added to TREC-3. These tasks were the precursors to the TREC tracks structure described in the next section. Participation in TREC continued to grow as a result of the new tasks (see table 1.1) such that the most recent TREC, TREC 2003, had ninety-three participating groups.

1.1.2   The Participants' Perspective

Part III of this book contains chapters contributed by groups who have participated in TREC. Each chapter gives a retrospective of that group's participation in TREC, and as such, offers a history of TREC as experienced by the group. Each chapter also provides a venue for the group to motivate and explain the experiments they performed in TREC from a long-term perspective—something that is not possible in the annual proceedings papers.

Four chapters are from groups that participated in the original TREC and all (or almost all) of the TRECs since then. These groups had already-established research programs in experimental IR before TREC began, and have used TREC to continue and extend those programs. The CIIR project (see chapter 11) used TREC in support of its research goals. Technology developed through this research includes now-standard techniques such as local context analysis (LCA) and cross-language retrieval models.

The Okapi project (see chapter 12), which later moved to Microsoft Research Cambridge, came to TREC with a system designed to allow online public access to a library catalog. The changes required to the system to provide effective access to a collection of full-text documents of widely varying lengths were the genesis of the "BM25" weighting scheme that has been widely adopted throughout the field. The SMART system (see chapter 13), which later moved to Sabir Research, has a history of IR experimentation dating back to the 1960s. The public version of SMART available in the early 1990s was one of the few systems at the time that was designed for large collections, and the community made good use of the system. About one-third of the groups submitting results to TREC-1 used some form of SMART for their processing. The probabilistic indexing and retrieval components system (PIRCS) (see chapter 14) from the City University of New York is a probabilistic system based on a spreading activation model. Like Okapi, PIRCS had difficulty with widely varying document lengths—a difficulty that was solved by breaking documents into fixed-size pieces called "subdocuments." Subdocuments had the additional benefit of being a much better unit to base feedback on than the original full-length documents, and were thus used by other groups for that reason.

The remaining three chapters are from groups that used TREC to validate their approaches to information retrieval. The MultiText system (see chapter 15) at the University of Waterloo was originally designed to retrieve extracts of structured documents (such as SGML-formatted documents) based on features of the text rather than rank documents based on similarity. Through its participation in TREC, the MultiText group extended the system to also perform ranked retrieval while maintaining the original functionality. Djoerd Hiemstra and Wessel Kraaij (see chapter 16) originally participated in TREC as part of the Twenty-One Consortium. Their chapter describes the use of language modeling as a retrieval model for various TREC tasks. The IBM chapter (see chapter 17) provides an industrial perspective of TREC. Several different research groups within IBM have participated in a variety of tracks over the years. While the groups had different goals for participating, each found TREC to be an effective tool for furthering their research agendas, and thus improving IBM's products and services.

Of course, these seven participants are only a small sample of all the groups that have participated in at least one TREC. Overall, approximately 225 groups have participated in TREC; the complete list of participants is given in table 1.2 at the end of this chapter. The diversity of the groups participating in TREC ensures that TREC represents many different approaches to retrieval, which in turn provides a more accurate assessment of the state of the art.

1.2   The TREC Tracks

The first two TRECs had two common tasks: the ad hoc task described above, and the routing task. The routing task investigates the performance of systems that use standing queries to search new streams of documents, such as in news clipping services and library profiling systems. Starting in TREC-3, a variety of other tasks, the "tracks," were

Table 1.1
Number of participants per track and total number of distinct participants in each TREC

Track	TREC											
	92	93	94	95	96	97	98	99	00	01	02	03
Ad hoc	18	24	26	23	28	31	42	41	—	—	—	—
Routing	16	25	25	15	16	21	—	—	—	—	—	—
Interactive	—	—	3	11	2	9	8	7	6	6	6	—
Spanish	—	—	4	10	7	—	—	—	—	—	—	—
Confusion	—	—	—	4	5	—	—	—	—	—	—	—
Database merging	—	—	—	3	3	—	—	—	—	—	—	—
filtering	—	—	—	4	7	10	12	14	15	19	21	—
Chinese	—	—	—	—	9	12	—	—	—	—	—	—
NLP	—	—	—	—	4	2	—	—	—	—	—	—
Speech	—	—	—	—	—	13	10	10	3	—	—	—
Cross-language	—	—	—	—	—	13	9	13	16	10	9	—
High precision	—	—	—	—	—	5	4	—	—	—	—	—
Very large corpus	—	—	—	—	—	—	7	6	—	—	—	—
Query	—	—	—	—	—	—	2	5	6	—	—	—
Question answering	—	—	—	—	—	—	—	20	28	36	34	33
Web	—	—	—	—	—	—	—	17	23	30	23	27
Video	—	—	—	—	—	—	—	—	—	12	19	—
Novelty	—	—	—	—	—	—	—	—	—	—	13	14
Genome	—	—	—	—	—	—	—	—	—	—	—	29
HARD	—	—	—	—	—	—	—	—	—	—	—	14
Robust	—	—	—	—	—	—	—	—	—	—	—	16
Total participants	25	31	33	36	38	51	56	66	69	87	93	93

introduced into TREC. The idea of the tracks was to extend the common evaluation paradigm that was successful for the ad hoc and routing tasks to other retrieval tasks.

The tracks invigorate TREC by focusing research on new areas or particular aspects of text retrieval. Frequently, a track has been the first large-scale evaluation in that area. In this case, the track established a research community and created the first specialized test collections to support research in the area. To the extent that the same retrieval techniques are used for the different tasks, the tracks also validate the findings of the ad hoc task.

Taken together, the tracks represent the majority of the work done in TREC. Table 1.1 lists all of the tracks that have been held in each TREC and gives the number of groups that participated in the track each year. The last row in the table provides the total number of distinct participants per TREC. The tasks within the tracks offered for a given TREC have diverged as TREC has progressed. This has helped fuel the growth in

Aspect		92	93	94	95	96	97	98	99	00	01	02	03	Track
Static text		■	■	■	■	■	■	■	■				■	Ad hoc, robust
Streamed text		■	■	■	■	■	■							Routing
				■	■	■	■	■	■	■	■			Filtering
Human				■	■	■	■	■	■	■	■	■	■	Interactive, HARD
Beyond just English				■	■	■								Spanish
						■	■							Chinese
							■	■	■	■	■	■		X→{X,Y,Z}
Beyond text				■	■									OCR
							■	■	■	■				Speech
										■	■			Video
Web searching							■	■	■	■				Very Large Corpus
									■	■	■	■	■	Web
Answers, not documents									■	■	■	■	■	Question answering
												■	■	Novelty
Domain													■	Genomics

Figure 1.1
Tasks performed in TREC

the number of participants, but has also created a smaller common base of experience among participants since each participant tends to submit runs to fewer tracks.

The set of tracks run in any particular TREC depends on the interests of the participants and sponsors as well as the suitability of the problem to the TREC environment. The decision about which tracks to include is made by the TREC program committee, a group of academic, industrial, and government researchers who have the responsibility for TREC oversight. Some initial tracks have been discontinued because the goals of the track were met. For example, the Spanish track, an ad hoc task in which both documents and topics are in Spanish, was discontinued when the results demonstrated that current retrieval systems can retrieve Spanish documents as effectively as English documents. Other tracks, such as the interactive one, were run for many years, but have changed focus in different years.

Figure 1.1 provides a different view of the track structure. As in table 1.1, the figure shows the years in which a particular track was run, but groups the tracks by the aspect that differentiates them from one another. These same groupings are used to organize the chapters in part 2. The aspects, listed on the left in the figure, show the breadth of the problems that TREC has addressed, while the individual tracks listed on the right show the progression of tasks within the given problem area.

1.2.1 Static Text

The ad hoc task is the prototypical document retrieval task. The document set is a static collection of text documents, and a subset of the documents are to be retrieved in response to a user's query. This was the core task in the first eight TRECs, though it was discontinued after TREC-8 to allow resources to be applied to building infrastructure for other tracks. Donna Harman summarizes the lessons that have been learned from this core task in chapter 4.

In TREC 2003, the robust retrieval track reintroduced an ad hoc task into TREC, though with a different evaluation focus. In the robust retrieval track, systems were evaluated over their worst-performing topics to focus attention on the consistency of a system's retrieval effectiveness.

1.2.2 Streaming Text

An important variant of the classic ad hoc task is to retrieve documents from a stream of text (for example, a newswire) rather than a static collection. The routing main task was one formulation of this basic task, and the filtering track has used successively more realistic (and more difficult) formulations. As Stephen Robertson and Jamie Callan explain in chapter 5, filtering requires a system to make an immediate decision as to whether a document should be retrieved. Such a decision is more difficult than simply ranking documents since it requires determining an appropriate threshold.

1.2.3 Human-in-the-Loop

The test collection abstraction represents the end users of retrieval systems by a static set of relevance judgments. While the abstraction is useful for comparing the quality of different system devices, it says nothing about how users are best supported in their information-seeking tasks. The interactive track was established to examine the process of user interaction with retrieval systems. In chapter 6, Susan T. Dumais and Nicholas J. Belkin describe the history of the track and the challenges presented by trying to isolate system effects from the larger of effects caused by different searchers.

The "high accuracy retrieval from documents" (HARD) track, introduced in TREC 2003, took a different approach to investigating how best to support end users. The goal of the track is to improve retrieval performance by targeting retrieval results to the specific user. Each topic used in the HARD track contained additional information about the (putative) user, including such items as biographical data about the user, information regarding the search context, and a statement of the expected type of a result.

1.2.4 Beyond Just English

In chapter 7, Harman describes the various tasks that involved searching in languages other than English. The monolingual Spanish and Chinese tracks used a basic ad hoc task, but both topics and documents were written in the given language. A variant of this task is cross-language retrieval where topics in one language are used to retrieve documents that may be written in one of a variety of different languages. For pairs of languages (for example, using English topics to retrieve documents written in Arabic), cross-language retrieval can be more effective than the corresponding monolingual results due to the expansion that naturally results from translating the query.

TREC no longer contains tasks involving languages other than English, not because the problem is regarded as unimportant, but because there are now other venues for this research. The NTCIR evaluations sponsored by the National Institute of Informatics in Japan and the Cross Language Evaluation Forum (CLEF) evaluations supported by the European Union offer a range of retrieval tasks with a multilingual focus.[2]

1.2.5 Beyond Text

Not all information is recorded in textual documents, and one series of tracks has looked at the problem of retrieving information when the target is not electronically prepared text. Ellen M. Voorhees and John S. Garofolo review retrieval methods for retrieving noisy text—namely, optical character recognition (OCR) or speech recognizer output—in chapter 8. While the output from these processes usually contains errors when compared to the author's original intent, natural language is redundant enough such that retrieval of error-filled text can be as effective as retrieving clean texts for error rates likely to be seen in real-life applications.

The video track fosters research on content-based access to digital video, completely eliminating reliance on text for retrieval. The video track was started as a TREC track in 2001. Interest in the track has been high, though there is little overlap in techniques for video and text retrieval. As a result, the track was spun off as a separate evaluation effort in 2003.

1.2.6 Web Searching

TREC in general has placed little emphasis on the efficiency of retrieval systems. An exception to this is the "very large collection" (VLC) track where part of the evaluation criteria was the speed at which results could be displayed. The track used a hundred-gigabyte static subset of the Web as its test set. This naturally led to a successor track to investigate searching on the Web. While the Web is similar in many respects to other large collections of text, it is different in a number of ways as well. The most notable differences include the massive link structure, the lack of editorial control, the wide variety of different uses of search on the Web (that is, not just to find information but to navigate the link structure or locate services), and the use of active content. In chapter 9, David Hawking and Nick Craswell review the findings of these two tracks and discuss the kinds of Web-based search tasks that are—and are not—appropriate for a forum such as TREC.

1.2.7 Answers, Not Documents

While a list of on-topic documents is undoubtedly useful, even that can be more information than a user wants to wade through. Another set of tracks investigates techniques for minimizing the amount of extraneous text that users must look at before their information needs are met. The novelty track approaches this problem by having systems return sentences that are both relevant and contain information that no previously returned sentence contains. Question-answering systems have the goal of returning exactly the answer in response to a question. The TREC question-answering track has tested systems' ability to retrieve short text snippets in response to factoid questions (for example, How many calories are in a Big Mac?). As Voorhees reports in chapter 10, the track has generated a resurgence of research on question answering, and has established a common task for the information retrieval and information extraction communities.

1.2.8   Searching in a Domain

The genomics track was introduced in TREC 2003 and is the first TREC track devoted to retrieval within a specific domain. A primary goal of the track is to see how exploiting domain-specific information can improve retrieval effectiveness.

1.2.9   Other Tracks

Four of the tracks that have been run in TREC are not included in figure 1.1 nor discussed in the chapters of part 2. These tracks were run for just a few years, and either accomplished their goals in that time or were discontinued due to low participation. The tracks are briefly described here for completeness.

The database merging track had the goal of investigating distributed retrieval methods, specifically techniques for selecting which collection(s) to search and how to merge multiple ranked lists into a single cohesive response. The track was run in TRECs 4–5. Unfortunately, the track appears to have been a bit ahead of its time as it did not attract much participation despite general interest in the problem. A distributed retrieval community formed outside of TREC a few years after the track was discontinued, and this community makes good use of the collections built in the track.

The natural-language processing (NLP) track was run in TRECs 5–6. Its goal was to explore whether the NLP techniques available at the time could offer any advantage over the more conventional statistical methods for document retrieval. While specific NLP is not essential to obtain effective document retrieval on TREC collections [9], it has been shown to be beneficial for more complex requirements such as question answering.

The high-precision track was run in TRECs 6–7. The task in the track was for a human searcher to retrieve ten to fifteen relevant documents for a topic within five minutes of wall clock time, an abstraction of the problem of quickly finding a few good documents to get a feel for a topic area. Unlike the interactive track where the searchers are not usually experts on the particular search systems, the assumption in the high-precision track was that the searchers were system experts. As such, the results represent best-case scenarios for the systems. The major finding of the track was that retrieving fifteen good documents is a simple enough task for current retrieval systems that disagreements between the searcher and the assessor regarding what constitutes a relevant document bounds performance.

The task in the query track was an ad hoc task using old TREC document and topic sets. Participants in the track created different query variants from the topic statements and then exchanged query sets so all participants ran all queries. While the track officially started in TREC-7, only two groups participated that year; the bulk of the query track work has involved forty-three query sets, twenty-one of which were created in TREC-8 and the remaining twenty-two in TREC-9. The focus in the track was not on absolute retrieval effectiveness but on the variability of retrieval effectiveness across topics. In particular, the track was designed as a means for creating a large set of different queries as a resource to investigate the topic effect. One conclusion from the track was confirmation of the wide variability in the effectiveness of different systems across and, to a lesser degree, within topics. Chapter 3 describes an experiment using the query track data to evaluate the stability of retrieval evaluation measures.

1.3   Conclusion

With the level of participation TREC has had and the number of different tasks that have been examined, the cumulative effort in TREC represents thousands of individual experiments and many hours of research effort. So what has been learned from this massive undertaking? This section looks at some of the conclusions that can be drawn from TREC as well as some remaining challenges.

1.3.1   TREC Impacts

TREC has had such a profound impact on the way information retrieval research is practiced that it is easy to forget the original questions TREC was developed to address. When TREC began, there was real doubt as to whether the statistical systems that had been developed in the research labs (as opposed to the operational systems that used Boolean searches on manually indexed collections) could effectively retrieve documents from "large" collections. Clearly they can. The effectiveness has not only been demonstrated in the laboratory on test collections but also by today's operational systems that incorporate the techniques. Further, the techniques are routinely used on collections far larger than what was considered large in 1992. Web search engines are a prime example of the power of the statistical techniques; the ability of search engines to point users to the information they seek has been fundamental to the success of the Web.

The second question TREC originally addressed was the viability of test collections and the associated evaluation methodology as a research method. While test collections had always had their critics [12; 2], even some experimenters were questioning whether test collections had outlived their usefulness [7] (see also chapter 12, this volume), and different groups were reporting scores for different, incomparable measures. TREC has both validated and standardized the evaluation methodology. The large number of retrieval results accumulated through the years has allowed investigations of the retrieval methodology not previously possible (see chapter 3, this volume), providing a means for characterizing the stability of different evaluation measures and the difficulty of particular test sets. The use of pooling to build large test collections was suggested by Karen Sparck Jones and Keith van Rijsbergen [10], but first demonstrated in TREC. The resulting test collections that have been built through the TREC tasks are used by many more groups than actually participate in TREC, including commercial search companies that use the collection for in-house testing of new products. The evaluation methodology has also been extended and adapted as appropriate for new tasks.

In addition to standardizing the evaluation methodology, TREC has provided a forum where a large community of researchers, each of whom have attempted the same task with the same data, openly discuss their retrieval techniques. This was one of the original goals of TREC, and it has proved to be extremely beneficial. By defining a common set of tasks, TREC focuses retrieval research on problems that have a significant impact throughout the community. The meeting itself provides a forum in which researchers can efficiently learn from one another and thus facilitates technology transfer. TREC also provides a forum in which methodological issues can be raised and discussed, resulting in improved retrieval research.

Finally, TREC has been an incubator for new technologies for new retrieval applications. Cross-language retrieval, retrieval of recordings of speech, and factoid question answering are all research communities that TREC established and that have produced systems that are effective enough for real use.

1.3.2   Best Practices

Indexing, the representation of the content of a text by a set of word forms or terms, is an important component of a retrieval system. The TREC results suggest the following best practices for indexing full-text documents of varying lengths:

• Tokenization that regularizes word forms is generally helpful. The most common form of regularization is stemming, but normalizing proper nouns to a standard format can also be helpful.
• Simple "phrasing" techniques are generally helpful. The most helpful part of phrasing is the identification of common collocations that are then treated as a single unit. More elaborate schemes have shown little benefit.
• Appropriate weighting of terms is critical. The best weighting schemes reflect the discrimination power of a term in the corpus and control for document length. There are several different weighting schemes that achieve these goals and are equivalently effective. Language-modeling techniques are both effective and provide a theoretical justification for the weights assigned.

Query expansion is a second technique that has been shown to improve retrieval effectiveness on average. Getting a better query from the user is one of the best ways to improve retrieval performance, but that is frequently not a realistic option. Query expansion is a method that can improve the query without relying on the user to supply it. The most common way of expanding the query is to use *pseudorelevance feedback*: retrieve a first set of documents using the original query; assume the first X documents are relevant; perform relevance feedback with that set of documents to create a new query (usually including both new terms and refined query weights); and return the results of searching with the new query to the user.

1.3.3 Challenges

Despite the advances in the retrieval effectiveness over the course of TREC, many challenges remain. Retrieval systems are good enough to be useful, even indispensable, but absolute effectiveness levels are still lower than desirable. Three particular challenges for the current state of the art in retrieval technology are listed here.

An important component of effectiveness for operational retrieval systems is the ability of the system to return reasonable results for every topic. Users remember abject failures. A relatively few such failures cause the user to mistrust the system and discontinue use. Yet the standard text retrieval evaluation paradigm looks only at average scores. The averages increase the reliability of the evaluation, but hide large variability in per topic effectiveness. Retrieval systems must improve their ability to get good per topic performance rather than just good average performance.

Effective ways of testing methods to support user interaction with retrieval systems continues to be an open problem. Getting a good initial query is one of the best ways to improve retrieval effectiveness, and yet little is known regarding what information is required from the user and how best to elicit the necessary information. Despite concerted efforts in the interactive track (see chapter 6, this volume), there has been little progress in developing an effective, relatively inexpensive evaluation methodology for user-based studies. The major problem is that the system effect—the amount of difference in retrieval scores that is attributable to the difference in systems—is small compared to both the topic effect and the user effect. Isolating the system effect requires many topics and searchers to be able to control for these variables. But such designs imply extremely large, and hence extremely expensive, studies. New methodologies that control for the appropriate variables while minimizing the number of users required would significantly advance the state of the art by allowing much more research to be done.

A final challenge for the field is to move toward true information retrieval. Systems must become better at integrating heterogeneous information sources including structured and nonstructured sources and different media types into a cohesive whole. Integration will require the system to determine the appropriate unit for a response (a factoid? a document set? a summary?) and select the correct component technology to produce such a response. Since many desirable component technologies are not yet well developed, new collaborations with other research communities will be required to realize these systems.

Table 1.2
Organizations participating in TREC

Advanced Decisions Systems	Dartmouth College
Ajou University	David Lewis
Apple Computer	Defense Evaluation and Research Agency
AT&T Labs Research	DSO National Laboratories
Alicante University	Dublin City University
Australian Computing and Communications Institute	Duke University
Australian National University	EC Wise, Inc.
Avignon CS Laboratory/Bertin	Environmental Research Institute of Michigan
Axontologic, Inc.	Erasmus MC
BBN Technologies	Eurospider Information Technology
Bellcore	Excalibur Technologies, Inc.
California State University, San Marcos	Fondazione Ugo Bordoni
Canadian Imperial Bank of Commerce	Fraunhofer Institute (SCAI)
Carnegie Mellon University	Fudan University
CEA	Fulcrum
Center for Computing Science	FS Consulting, Inc.
Center for Information Research, Russia	Fujitsu Laboratories, Ltd.
Chapman University	GE Research and Development Center
Chinese Academy of Sciences	George Mason University
Chinese Information Processing Center	Georgia Institute of Technology
Chinese University of Hong Kong	GSI-Erli
CITRI	GTE Laboratories
City University, London	Harbin Institute of Technology
City University of New York	Harris Corporation
CLARITECH Corporation	HNC, Inc.
Clairvoyance Corporation	Hummingbird Communications
CLIPS-IMAG	IBM Almaden Research Center
CL Research	IBM Haifa
Columbia University	IBM T. J. Watson Research Center
Commissariat à l'Energie Atomique	Illinois Institute of Technology
Computer Technology Institute	Imperial College of Science, Technology, and Medicine
Conexor Oy	Indian Institute of Technology, Bombay
ConQuest Software, Inc.	Indiana University
Copernic Research	Information Technology Institute
Cornell University	Informatique-CDC
CSIRO	InsightSoft-M
CWI, the Netherlands	Institut de Recherche en Informatique de Toulouse
Cymfony Inc.	
Daimler Benz Research Center Ulm	

Table 1.2
(continued)

Institut EURECOM	National Security Agency
Institute for Decision Systems Research	National Taiwan University
Institute of Systems Science	National University of Singapore
InText Systems	NEC Corporation
ITC-irst	NeurOK, LLC
Johns Hopkins University	New Mexico State University
Justsystems Corporation	New York University
KAIST	NexTrieve
Kasetsart University	NTT Communication Science Labs
Katholieke Universiteit, Nijmegen	NTT DATA Corporation
KCSL	OcE Technologies
KDD R&D Laboratories	Online Computer Library Center, Inc.
Keio University	Open Text Corporation
Kent Ridge Digital Labs	Oracle Corporation
KerMIT Consortium	Oregon Health and Science University
Korea University	Oslo College
Laboratory for Information Technology	Pam Wood
Language Computer Corporation	PARA Group
Lehigh University	Pohang University of Science and Technology
LexiClone, Inc.	
Lexis-Nexis	PRC, Inc.
LIMSI	Prous Science
Logicon Operating Systems	Queensland University of Technology
Los Alamos National Laboratory	RICOH Co., Ltd.
Macquarie University	Royal Melbourne Institute of Technology
Management Information Technologies, Inc.	Rutgers University
	Saarland University
Massachusetts Institute of Technology	Sabir Research
Mayo Clinic	Seoul National University
Mead Data Central	SER Technology Deutschland, GmbH
Meiji University	Sharp Laboratories of Europe, Ltd.
Microsoft Research	Siemens AG
Microsoft Research Asia	Siemens Corporate Research, Inc.
Microsoft Research, Ltd.	Southern Methodist University
MITRE	SRI International
Monash University	State University of New York at Buffalo
Moscow Medical Academy	StreamSage, Inc.
National Institute of Informatics	Sun Microsystems
National Library of Medicine	Swiss Federal Institute of Technology
National Research Council Canada	Syracuse University

Table 1.2
(continued)

Systems Environments Corporation	University of Illinois at Urbana-Champaign
Tampere University of Technology	University of Iowa
Tarragon Consulting Corporation	University of Kansas
TextWise, Inc.	University of Limerick
Thinking Machines Corporation	University of Maryland, Baltimore County
Tilburg University	University of Maryland, College Park
TNO-TPD TU-Delft	University of Massachusetts
Tokyo Institute of Technology	University of Melbourne
Tokyo University of Science	University of Michigan
Trans-EZ, Inc.	University of Minnesota
TRW Systems Development Division	University of North Carolina
Tsinghua University	University of North Texas
Twenty-One Consortium	University of Ottawa
Universitaet Dortmund	University of Oulu
Universitat Politecnica de Catalunya and Universitat de Girona	University of Padova
Université d'Angers	University of Pennsylvania
Université de Montréal	University of Pittsburgh
Université de Neuchatel	University of Pisa
University Hospital of Geneva	University of Sheffield
University of Alaska, Fairbanks	University of Southern California
University of Albany	University of Sunderland
University of Alberta	University of Surrey
University of Amsterdam	University of Tampere
University of Bremen	University of Tokyo
University of Buffalo	University of Toronto
University of California, Berkeley	University of Twente
University of California, Los Angeles	University of Virginia
University of California, San Diego	University of Wales, Bangor
University of Cambridge	University of Waterloo
University of Central Florida	University of York
University of Colorado	Verity, Inc.
University of Edinburgh	Virginia Tech
University of Glasgow	West Publishing Company
University of Helsinki	Xerox PARC
University of Hertfordshire	Xerox Research Centre Europe
University of Illinois at Chicago	Yonsei University and ETRI

Notes

1. Electronic versions of the proceedings are available on the TREC Web site, ⟨http://trec.nist.gov⟩.

2. For the NTCIR evaluations, see ⟨http://research.nii.ac.jp/ntcir⟩. For the CLEF evaluations, see ⟨http://clef.iei.pi.cnr.it⟩.

References

[1] Cleverdon, C. W. The Cranfield tests on index language devices. In vol. 19, *Aslib proceedings*, 173–192, 1967. (Reprinted in K. Sparck Jones and P. Willett, S., *Readings in information retrieval*, San Francisco: Morgan Kaufmann Publishers, 1997.)

[2] Cuadra, C. A., and R. V. Katter. Opening the black box of relevance. *Journal of Documentation* 23, no. 4 (1967): 291–303.

[3] Harman, D. K. The second text retrieval conference (TREC-2). Special issue, *Information Processing and Management* 31, no. 3 (May–June 1995).

[4] Hersh, W., and P. Over. Interactivity at the text retrieval conference (TREC). *Information Processing and Management* 37 (2001): 365–367.

[5] Merchant, R. H. TIPSTER program overview. In *Proceedings of TIPSTER text program (phase 1)*, R. Merchant, ed. 1–2. San Francisco: Morgan Kaufmann Publishers, September 1993.

[6] Robertson, S. E. Overview of the TREC routing and filtering tasks. Introd. to special issue, *Information Retrieval* 5 (2002): 127–137.

[7] Robertson, S. E., and M. M. Hancock-Beaulieu. On the evaluation of IR systems. *Information Processing and Management* 28, no. 4 (1992): 457–466.

[8] Sparck Jones, K. *Information Retrieval Experiment*. London: Butterworths, 1981.

[9] Sparck Jones, K. What is the role of NLP in text retrieval? In *Natural language information retrieval*, ed. Tomek Strzalkowski, 1–24. Dordecht: Kluwer, 1999.

[10] Sparck Jones, K., and C. van Rijsbergen. *Report on the need for and provision of an "ideal" information retrieval test collection*. British Library Research and Development report 5266. Cambridge: Computer Laboratory, University of Cambridge, 1975.

[11] Sparck Jones, K., and P. Willett, eds. Introd. to *Readings in information retrieval*. San Francisco: Morgan Kaufmann Publishers, 1997.

[12] Taube, M. A note on the pseudomathematics of relevance. *American Documentation* 16, no. 2 (April 1965): 69–72.

[13] Voorhees, E. M. The sixth text retrieval conference (TREC-6). Special issue, *Information Processing and Management* 36, no. 1 (January 2000).

2 The TREC Test Collections
Donna K. Harman

2.1 Introduction

The Cranfield studies (Cleverdon, Mills, and Keen 1966) emphasized the importance of creating test collections and using these for comparative evaluation. The Cranfield collection, created in the 1960s, contained approximately 1,400 abstracts and 225 requests, and was widely used by researchers. Subsequently, other collections have been built and used, such as the Communications of the Association of Computing Machinery (CACM) collection (Fox 1983) and the National Physical Laboratory (NPL) (UK) collection (Vaswani and Cameron 1970). Even though these collections were small (by today's standards), they were major computing challenges when first used. As hardware and information retrieval technology matured, however, it became critical to use more realistically sized collections. Evaluation using the small collections often does not reflect performance of systems in large full-text searching, and certainly does not demonstrate any proven abilities of these systems to operate in real-world information retrieval environments. This was a major barrier to the transfer of laboratory systems into the commercial world.

In the mid-1970s, Karen Sparck Jones and Keith van Rijsbergen (1975) proposed the creation of a large test collection. This collection was not only to be many magnitudes larger than the then-current test collections but was to be carefully designed to allow controlled experimentation. There were many factors to be considered in selecting the documents, selecting the test requests, and creating the relevance judgments, and these were discussed in detail in a later survey (Sparck Jones and van Rijsbergen 1976). They pointed out the need for different text populations (for example, various styles of writing), different document populations (for instance, general newspapers versus scientific articles), different request populations (for example, precise versus nonprecise requests), and so forth, all to be measured and controlled to allow the various factors of the retrieval environment to be correlated with the various search parameters used in retrieval systems.

Unfortunately, this ideal test collection was not built due to a lack of funding, forcing researchers to continue to use the small test collections. Not only were these collections too small for testing, but most of them had been designed and built in support of a specific experimental purpose, with specific design criteria and motivation. For example, the Cranfield collection was built to test hypotheses about the manual indexing of documents, with careful attention paid to the location of all relevant documents and the creation of multiple types of manual indexes. The CACM collection was built to investigate the interaction between textual and bibliographic data, with an emphasis on providing full bibliographic information, including citation links and manual categories, from a complete set of journal articles (*CACM* from the years 1958–1979).

As researchers eagerly tried to use any and all collections available, they were usually not aware of these design criteria or, more important, the factors that could influence the outcomes of their particular experiments. For example, the requests built for the Cranfield collection were not "natural" user requests but were specifically constructed around the documents in the collection. The document collection was also constructed such that there were sufficient numbers of relevant documents for each request. This interrelationship can have unknown effects on experiments that exploit the structure of the collection, such as those involving clustering. The CACM collection created sixty-four independent requests (gathered from Cornell faculty and students), and had an independent collection (assorted abstracts, titles, and bibliographic information for 3,204 articles), but almost 50 percent of the articles had only a title, and there was a highly variable number of relevant documents per request, including twelve with no relevant documents at all. Whereas these characteristics reflect a real operational system environment, they are likely to cause unpredictable effects in experiments if the researchers are unaware of these high variations.

It should be noted that these limitations are apparent only in hindsight. In the case of Cranfield, the design was correct for the specific experiment, but the reuse of the collection without recognizing the interaction of the design with aspects of a new experiment caused problems. For the CACM collection, the design was more general in order to reflect an operational situation, but limitations in the available documents caused a skew in the overall collection.

The design of a new test collection such as the one laid out in the 1970s' ideal collection work presents many challenges. The first is to build a collection that is realistic in that it mirrors some operational situation, but also is multifaceted enough that it can be reused in many different controlled experiments. The second challenge is to sufficiently document the motivation, design, and creation of this test collection such that researchers are aware of its limitations.

This chapter is the documentation for the very large TREC test collections, with an emphasis on the collections in English used in the TREC ad hoc tasks. It describes both the motivation for building the collections and the factors that were considered in designing them. The actual methods of creating the collections are also discussed, with the hope that researchers will recognize any potential experimental conflicts and be able to modify experiments to compensate. Some basic statistics of the collections are given, and some analysis of collection components is provided. The chapter ends with information on the non-English collections and other special collections, such as those produced from Web documents or for use in the question-answering task.

2.2 Overall Test Collection and Testing Design

In 1991, the DARPA TIPSTER project (Merchant 1994; Altomari and Currier 1996; Gee 1999) was launched in an effort to significantly advance the state of the art in effective document detection (information retrieval) and data extraction from large, real-world data collections. The first two-year phase of the program was concerned with the development of algorithms for document retrieval, document routing, and data extraction that were both domain and language independent. The users for this effort were to be intelligence analysts, but also any other type of user who works with information intensively, such as journalists, medical researchers, or legal staff.

The document detection part of the project required the retrieval of relevant documents from very large (two gigabyte) collections of documents. Whereas this project initially involved only four DARPA detection contractors, the TREC initiative (Harman 1993, 1994, 1995, 1996; Voorhees and Harman 1997, 1998, 1999, 2000, 2001, 2002; Voorhees 2003) opened the evaluation to the wider information retrieval research community, with twenty-five additional research groups taking part in 1992 and ninety-three groups by 2003.

The TIPSTER test design was based on traditional information retrieval testing models, involving a test collection of documents, user requests (called topics in TREC), and relevance judgments. The creation of an appropriate test collection was critical; in particular, it was important to match all three components (documents, topics, and relevance judgments) of the collection to the TIPSTER application. In general, the guidelines used in TIPSTER have also been followed in TREC so that results using the TREC collections measure at least one specific type of user searching needs.

The document collection needed to reflect the corpus seen by information analysts. This meant that a very large collection was needed to test the ability of the algorithms to handle huge numbers of full-text documents. The documents needed to cover many different subject areas in order to test the domain independence of the algorithms. Additionally, the documents needed to mirror the different types of documents used in the TIPSTER application; specifically, they had to be of varied length, writing style, level of editing, and vocabulary. As a final requirement, the documents had to cover information from different years to show the effects of document date.

The topics (requests) for the new test collection were also designed to model some of the needs of analysts. It was assumed that the typical user of these retrieval systems was a dedicated searcher, not a novice searcher, and that the model for the application was a task needing both the ability to do ad hoc searches on archived data for new topics and the monitoring of incoming data streams for information on specific topics of longer-term interest. It was also assumed that the users needed the ability to do both high-precision and high-recall searches, and were willing to look at many documents and repeatedly modify queries in order to get high recall. The topics therefore were created to be quite specific, but included both broad and narrow searching needs.

The relevance assessments were made by retired analysts who were asked to view the task as if they were addressing a real information need. The narrative section of the topic (described in more detail later) contains a clear definition of what makes a document relevant, and the assessors used this section as the definition of the information need. Documents retrieved for each topic were judged by a single assessor so that all documents screened would reflect the same user's interpretation of the topic.

This takes care of part of the design criteria for relevance assessments in that a true operational environment is being mimicked. In order to build a more general test collection, however, there is the additional requirement that the relevance assessments be as complete as possible. This became a critical piece of both the implementation of TREC and the later analysis of the collections (for details, see sections 2.5 and 2.6.3).

TIPSTER and the first eight TREC cycles centered around two main tasks based on traditional information retrieval modes: an ad hoc task, and a monitoring task (called routing in TREC). In the ad hoc task, it is assumed that new requests are being asked against a fixed set of data. This task is similar to how a researcher might use a library, where the collection is known, but where the requests likely to be asked are unknown. In the routing task, it is assumed that the same topics are always being followed, but that new data is being searched. This task is similar to that done by news clipping services.

The ad hoc task is represented by new topics for known documents. The routing task is represented by using known topics and known relevant documents for those topics, but new data for testing.

Table 2.1 shows the document sets used for testing in the first eight TRECs, along with the appropriate topic numbers used in each of the two main tasks. Fifty new topics were built for the ad hoc task each year. The fifty routing topics used for testing were a specific subset of the training topics (selected by NIST). Two different methods were used for selecting those routing topics. In TRECs 1–3, the routing topics

Table 2.1
Document and topics sets for the first eight TRECs

TREC	Task	Documents	Topics
TREC-1	ad hoc	disks 1 and 2	51–100
	routing	disk 2	1–50
TREC-2	ad hoc	disks 1 and 2	101–150
	routing	disk 3	51–100
TREC-3	ad hoc	disks 1 and 2	151–200
	routing	disk 3	101–150
TREC-4	ad hoc	disks 2 and 3	201–250
	routing	CS + FR	assorted
TREC-5	ad hoc	disks 2 and 4	251–300
	routing	FBIS-1	assorted
TREC-6	ad hoc	disks 4 and 5	301–350
	routing	FBIS-2	assorted
TREC-7	ad hoc	disks 4 and 5	351–400
TREC-8	ad hoc	disks 4 and 5	401–450

were the ad hoc topics used the previous year. Because of the difficulty in getting new data, starting in TREC-4 it was decided to select the new data first, and then select topics that matched the data. This was done for TRECs 4–6.

This was the task pattern for the first six TRECs. Starting in TREC-4, additional secondary tasks (called tracks) were introduced. These tracks either focused research on particular aspects of the original two tasks or provided the infrastructure for research on new areas of retrieval. An example of the first type of track would be the filtering track, which is the same basic task as the routing task, but uses various types of set value metrics for the evaluation. This track basically replaced the routing task starting in TREC-7, and therefore there is no routing work listed in table 2.1 beyond TREC-6. An example of the second type of track (new research areas) was the Spanish retrieval track started in TREC-4, where the task was similar to the ad hoc task, but the documents and topics were in Spanish. The use of the track structure has become an essential part of TREC, allowing for a major expansion of the types of research being pursued by the information retrieval community, and encouraging interaction with other communities such as speech recognition and natural-language processing.

2.3   The English Documents

The English documents, consisting of six disks, came from many different original sources (table 2.2). These sources were selected not only because of their suitability to the TIPSTER task but also because of their availability. The first three disks were produced as a joint effort by NIST and the Linguistic Data Consortium (LDC), for use in TREC and for (limited) public distribution for research purposes. Since these were developed specifically for the TIPSTER project, they are also known as the TIPSTER disks, even though they have been used in TREC. Disks 4, 5, and 6 were produced by NIST from donated data. Because most of the material is copyrighted, all users are required to sign a detailed agreement in order to protect the copyrighted source material.

A successful pattern for data source selection was established for disk 1, and was followed for disks 2 and 3. First, two sets of documents were obtained that contained articles from all domains. The first set of articles was from a newspaper (the *Wall Street Journal* on disks 1 and 2, the *San Jose Mercury News* on disk 3), and the second set of articles was from a newswire, Associated Press, on all three disks. In addition to covering all domains, these two sets provide a strong contrast in their format, style, and level of editing, and both were readily available. The third set of documents was selected to cover a particular domain more thoroughly. Partially because of availability, the particular set used was a subset of the *Computer Select* disks, from Ziff-Davis Publishing. These documents cover the subject area of computers and computer technology, but include many different sources of actual documents. This creates a set of documents in a single (broad) domain, but having a range of formatting and writing styles. The final set of documents (or final two sets in the first disk) were selected less for content than for the length of articles. Since the documents in the first three sets were of "medium" length (two to three hundred words), and were fairly uniform in length, the

Table 2.2
Document collection statistics (words are strings of alphanumeric characters; no stop words were removed and no stemming was performed)

	Size (megabytes)	No. of docs	Median no. of words/docs	Mean no. of words/docs
Disk 1				
Wall Street Journal, 1987–1989 (WSJ)	267	98,732	245	434.0
Associated Press newswire, 1989 (AP)	254	84,678	446	473.9
Computer Selects articles, Ziff-Davis (ZIFF)	242	75,180	200	473.0
Federal Register, 1989 (FR)	260	25,960	391	1315.9
Abstracts of U.S. Department of Energy publications (DOE)	184	226,087	111	120.4
Disk 2				
Wall Street Journal, 1990–1992	242	74,520	301	508.4
Associated Press newswire, 1988	237	79,919	438	468.7
Computer Selects articles, Ziff-Davis	175	56,920	182	451.9
Federal Register, 1988	209	19,860	396	1378.1
Disk 3				
San Jose Mercury News, 1991 (SJM)	287	90,257	379	453.0
Associated Press newswire, 1990	237	78,321	451	478.4
Computer Selects articles, Ziff-Davis	345	161,021	122	295.4
U.S. patents, 1993	243	6,711	4445	5391.0
Disk 4				
Financial Times, 1991–1994 (FT)	564	210,158	316	412.7
Federal Register, 1994 (FR94)	395	55,630	588	644.7
Congressional Record, 1993 (CR)	235	27,922	288	1373.5
Disk 5				
Foreign Broadcast Information Service (FBIS)	470	130,471	322	543.6
Los Angeles Times, 1989–1990 (LA)	475	131,896	351	526.5
Disk 6				
Foreign Broadcast Information Service (FBIS)	490	120,653	348	581.3
Los Angeles Times, 1994	475	131,896	351	526.5

final set of documents was picked to be especially long and of nonuniform length. Documents from the *Federal Register* were used for the first two disks, and some U.S. patents were used on disk 3. For disk 1, a large set of abstracts was obtained from the U.S. Department of Energy to further test the effects of document length.

Acknowledgment should be made to the companies that donated this data. The *Wall Street Journal* was provided to the LDC by Dow Jones and Company. Both the Department of Energy abstracts and the *Federal Register* documents came from old tapes of data that had been donated to the ACL/DCI initiative (the LDC's predecessor). The Associated Press newswire came from data that was automatically collected by Bell Labs and was given to the LDC after permission was obtained from the newswire company. Rights for the research use of the articles from *Computer Select* disks were purchased by the TIPSTER project from Ziff-Davis Publishing, and the LDC also purchased rights for the research use of the *San Jose Mercury News* (1991). The U.S. patents were donated by the U.S. Patent and Trademark Office.

All documents on disks 1, 2, and 3 were initially received at the University of Pennsylvania in various print-tape formats. These formats were converted to an SGML-like structure and sent to NIST. At NIST, the documents were assigned unique document identifiers and the formats were standardized. Figure 2.1 shows an abbreviated version of a typical document.

```
<DOC>
<DOCNO>FT911-3</DOCNO>
<PROFILE>AN-BEOA7AAIFT</PROFILE>
<DATE>910514
</DATE>
<HEADLINE>
FT 14 MAY 91 / International Company News: Contigas plans DM900m east
German project
</HEADLINE>
<BYLINE>
By DAVID GOODHART
</BYLINE>
<DATELINE>
BONN
</DATELINE>
<TEXT>
CONTIGAS, the German gas group 81 per cent owned by the utility Bayernwerk,
said yesterday that it intends to invest DM900m (Dollars 522m) in the next four
years to build a new gas distribution system in the east German state of Thuringia.
. . .
</TEXT>
</DOC>
```

Figure 2.1
A document extract from the *Financial Times*

All documents have beginning and end markers, and a unique DOCNO identification field. Additionally, other fields taken from the original data appear, but these vary widely across the different sources. The documents have differing amounts of errors, which were not checked or corrected. Not only would this have been an impossible task, but the errors in the data provide a better simulation of the TIPSTER task. Errors that would seriously impede evaluation, such as missing document separators or bad document numbers, were screened out.

Disks 4, 5, and 6 were produced at NIST from data donated directly to NIST. The choice of data was dictated by what was donated, but also by looking for data with specific characteristics. In particular, it was decided to get more domain-independent data and data with very long records, such as the *Federal Register*.

For disk 4, there was five hundred megabytes of the *Financial Times* that was donated to NIST by the Financial Times Limited (with the help of Keith van Rijsbergen and Mark Sanderson at the University of Glasgow). In addition, NIST was able to purchase more formatted *Federal Register* data, and Dean Wilder at the Library of Congress donated material from the *Congressional Record*.

Disks 5 and 6 also contain some major newspaper data: the *Los Angeles Times* was donated by the *Los Angeles Times*, and obtained with the help of Allen Lu and Rao Ashwin at Lexis-Nexis. And there is some data from the Foreign Broadcast Information Service, obtained with the help of Carmen Molino.

TREC documents are distributed on CD-ROMs with approximately one gigabyte of text on each, compressed to fit. Table 2.2 shows some basic document collection statistics. Note that although the collection sizes are roughly equivalent in terms of megabytes, there is a range of document lengths from very short documents (DOE) to very long (*Federal Register*). Also, the range of document lengths within a collection varies. For example, the documents from Associated Press are similar in length (the median and the mean length are quite close), but the *Wall Street Journal* and the *Computer Selects* documents have a wider range of lengths. The documents from the *Federal Register* have an extremely wide range of lengths.

It should be noted that all these various design criteria in the selection of the documents were with respect to the TIPSTER application. The genre is limited to mostly news-type information, with minimal scientific journals, books, or heavily structured information. Additionally, although there have been experiments with some of the field information contained in the documents, there was no attempt to create consistent detailed structural information for the collections.

2.4   The Topics

Information retrieval test collections have typically included sentence-length requests. These requests are usually automatically transformed into a machine version for searching, with only stop words removed (and possible stemming). In designing the TIPSTER/TREC tasks, there was a conscious decision made to provide user need statements rather than the more traditional requests. Three major issues were involved in this decision. First, there was a desire to allow a wide range of query construction methods by keeping the topic (the need statement) distinct from the query (the actual text submitted to the retrieval system). The second issue was the ability to increase the amount of information available about each topic—in particular, to include with each topic a clear statement of what criteria make a document relevant in order to improve the consistency of later relevance judgments. The third issue was the recognition that any future use of the test collections would need as much detailed information about the topics as possible to allow for different types of experiments.

All the topics were designed to mimic a real user's need, and were written by people who are actual users of a retrieval system. The actual topic writers, the topic format, and the method of construction have evolved over time, however. This evolution has had major effects on the results, and therefore care should be taken in selecting TREC topic sets for various experimental purposes. In particular, care should be taken in grouping topic sets to create larger collections of topics; not only is there a link between document sets and topic sets (see table 2.1) but individual topic sets were not created in the same manner, especially in the early years of TREC.

2.4.1 Topics for TREC-1 and TREC-2 (Numbers 1–150)

The topics for TREC-1 and TREC-2 had the same format and the same method of construction. Topics 1–25 and 51–80 were written by a variety of different users. Topics 26–50 were mostly written by a single user and cover the general domain of computers. Topics 81–150 were also written by a single user, but cover many domains.

Although the subject domain of the topics was diverse, some consideration was given to the documents to be searched. The initial ideas for topics were either generated spontaneously or by seeing interesting topic areas while doing other searches. These initial ideas were then used in trial searches against a sample of the document set, and those topics that had roughly twenty-five to one hundred hits in that sample were used as a final topic. This created a range of broader and narrower topics. After a topic idea was finalized, each topic was developed into a standardized format.

Figure 2.2 contains one of the topics used in TREC-1 and TREC-2, and shows the formatting.

Each topic is formatted in the same standard manner to allow easier automatic construction of the queries. Besides a beginning and an end marker, each topic has four major types of sections.

The first type of section is a short statement area, including the topic number, a domain, a title, a description, and a summary. The description was constructed during the topic creation as a one-sentence description of the information need. In contrast, the summary was retrofitted to topics 51–150 after TREC-2 to be used as a surrogate for the full topic. This was done in collaboration with the relevance assessors, who were asked to describe in one sentence the topic *as defined by the relevance assessments*. Unfortunately, this often resulted in a sentence that is similar to the description itself.

The second type of section, the narrative section, is meant to be a full description of the information need in terms of what separates a relevant document from

```
<num> Number: 053
<dom> Domain: International Economics
<title> Topic: Leveraged Buyouts

<desc> Description:

Document mentions a leveraged buyout valued at or above 200 million dollars.

<smry> Summary:
Document mentions a leveraged buyout valued at or above 200 million dollars.

<narr> Narrative:
A relevant document will cite a leveraged buyout (LBO) valued at or above 200
million dollars.   The LBO may be at any stage, e.g., considered, proposed,
pending, a fact. The company (being) taken private must be identi ed.   The offer
may be expressed in dollars a share.

<con> Concept(s):
1. leveraged buyout, LBO
2. take private, go private
3. management-led leveraged buyout

<fac> Factor(s):
<price> Price: >= 200 million dollars </fac>

<def> Definition(s):
Leveraged Buyout (LBO) - Takeover of a company using borrowed funds, with the
target company's assets serving as security for the loans taken out by the acquiring
firm, which repays the loans out of the cash flow of the acquired company or from
the sale of the assets of the acquired firm.
```

Figure 2.2
Sample topic statement from TREC-1 and TREC-2

a nonrelevant one. The narrative sections were constructed by looking at relevant documents in the trial sample and determining what kinds of information were needed to provide focus for the topic. These sections were primarily meant as instructions to the assessors, but could be used in building the queries either manually or automatically. The narratives often contain augmentations of the description, such as examples, or restrictions to focus the topic. Whereas the narratives do provide the type of clear direction needed by the human assessors, they also present a challenge for automatic query construction because of the unpredictability of what this section contains.

The third type of section, the concept section, was meant to reflect the "world knowledge" brought to the task by the users, and is the type of information that could be elicited by prompts from a good interface. The concept sections were constructed by the topic writers by locating useful terminology in some of the relevant documents in the trial sample. These terms were then grouped into conceptually related ideas, although these relationships vary widely across topics.

It should be noted that the number of concepts given, the organization of the concepts, and the usefulness of the concepts also vary widely across the topics. The concepts in general provide excellent keywords for retrieval systems, although this too varies.

The fourth type of section contains optional information. There were two different types of optional information: a factors section and a definition section, either of which appear only when necessary. The factors section was an attempt to codify some of the text in the narrative for easier use by automatic query construction algorithms. Such factors as time, location, and price were sometimes used here. The definition section contained one or two of the definitions critical to a human understanding of the topic. Although the definitions section was minimally used, it did provide definitions for some of the more unusual terminology.

2.4.2   Topics for TREC-3 (Numbers 151–200)

The topics used in TREC-3 reflect a major change in design, both in terms of format and topic creation. Note that the topics for TREC-1 and TREC-2 (topics 1–150) were not only extremely long but also contained complex structures. They were intended to represent long-standing information needs for which a user might be willing to create elaborate topics rather than the much shorter questions that a typical end user might ask. The topics used in TREC-3 (see figure 2.3) were not only much shorter but were missing the complex structure. In particular, the concepts field (containing a miniknowledge base about the topic) was removed because it was felt that real user questions would not contain this field, and because inclusion of the field discouraged research into techniques for expansion of "too short" user need expressions. (The summary field and optional information fields were also deleted, but this had a minimal affect on results.)

In addition to being shorter, the TREC-3 topics were written by the same group of users that did the relevance assessments. Specifically, each of the topics was developed from a genuine need for information brought in by the assessors. Each assessor constructed their own topics from some initial statements of interest, and performed all the relevance assessments on these topics (with a few exceptions).

2.4.3   Topics for TREC-4 (Numbers 201–250)

Participants in TREC-3 felt that the topics were still too long compared with what users normally submit to operational retrieval systems. Therefore, the TREC-4 topics were made even shorter. Only one field was used (that is, there was no title field and no narrative field). A second comment of the TREC-3 participants was that the TREC-3 topics had been constructed to fit the data rather than being natural topics. For this reason, the TREC-4 assessors were asked to bring in ten trial topics during the topic construction phase. These trial topics were to be completely written and not changed based on what was found using the NIST PRISE system during trial searches. The number of

<num> Number: 168
<title> Topic: Financing AMTRAK

<desc> Description:
A document will address the role of the Federal Government in nancing the operation of the National Railroad Transportation Corporation (AMTRAK).

<narr> Narrative:
A relevant document must provide information on the government's responsibility to make AMTRAK an economically viable entity. It could also discuss the privatization of AMTRAK as an alternative to continuing government subsidies. Documents comparing government subsidies given to air and bus transportation with those provided to AMTRAK would also be relevant.

<num> Number: 207

<desc> What are the prospects of the Quebec separatists achieving independence from the rest of Canada?

<num> Number: 312
<title> Hydroponics

<desc> Description:
Document will discuss the science of growing plants in water or some substance other than soil.

<narr> Narrative:
A relevant document will contain specific information on the necessary nutrients, experiments, types of substrates, and/or any other pertinent facts related to the science of hydroponics. Related information includes, but is not limited to, the history of hydroponics, advantages over standard soil agricultural practices, or the approach of suspending roots in a humid enclosure and spraying them periodically with a nutrient solution to promote plant growth.

Figure 2.3
Sample topic statement from TREC-3 (top), TREC-4 (middle), and TRECs 5–8 (bottom)

relevant documents found during those trial searches was used to predict the number of relevant documents likely to be found in TREC-4. NIST personnel selected the final fifty topics from among these candidates, based on having a reasonable range of estimated number of relevant documents across topics and balancing the load across assessors. In general, this method of topic creation worked successfully.

2.4.4   Topics for TREC-5, TREC-6, TREC-7, and TREC-8 (Numbers 251–450)
One of the conclusions reached in TREC-4 was that the much shorter topics caused both manual and automatic systems trouble, and that there were issues associated with using short topics in TREC that needed further investigation (Harman 1996). Accordingly, the TREC-5 ad hoc topics reintroduced the title and narrative fields, making

the topics similar in format to the TREC-3 topics. TREC-6, TREC-7, and TREC-8 topics used this same format, as shown in figure 2.3. While having the same format as the TREC-3 topics, the later topics are shorter (they contain fewer words on average) than the TREC-3 topics.

Although the topics were created in the full format as a result of the experience in TREC-4, different parts of the topic were used in various required experiments to investigate the effects of the topic length (for an analysis of this, see section 2.6.2).

Since TREC-3, the ad hoc topics have been created by the same person (assessor) who performed the relevance assessments for that topic. Each assessor comes to NIST with ideas for topics based on their own interests, and searches the ad hoc collection (looking at approximately a hundred documents per topic) to estimate the likely number of relevant documents per candidate topic. NIST personnel select the final fifty topics from among these candidates.

2.5   The Relevance Judgments

The relevance judgments are of critical importance to a test collection. For each topic, it is necessary to compile a list of relevant documents; this list needs to be as comprehensive as possible. For the TIPSTER/TREC task, three possible methods for finding the relevant documents could have been used. In the first method, full relevance judgments could have been made on over a million documents for each topic, resulting in over a hundred million judgments. This was clearly impossible. As a second approach, a random sample of the documents could have been taken, with relevance judgments done on that sample only. The problem with this approach is that a random sample that is large enough to find on the order of one hundred relevant documents per topic is a very large random sample, and is likely to result in insufficient numbers of relevant documents. The third method, the one used in building the collection, was to make relevance judgments on the sample of documents selected by the various participating systems. This is known as the pooling method, and it was the recommended method in the 1975 proposal to the British Library for building a very large test collection (Sparck Jones and van Rijsbergen 1975).

To construct the pool, the following was done:

- For each topic within a set of results, the top X-ranked documents were selected for input to the pool
- These results were merged across all systems and sorted by document numbers, and then duplicate documents were removed

The merged list of results was then shown to the human assessors, with each topic being judged by a single assessor to ensure the best consistency of judgments. Each topic pool was sorted by document number so that assessors could not tell if a document was highly ranked by some system or how many systems (or which systems) retrieved that document. Section 2.6.3 discusses several investigations into both the completeness and the bias of the relevance judgments that were made using this method.

The definition of relevance has always been problematic in building information retrieval test collections (Katter 1968; Cooper 1971; Bookstein 1979; Burgin 1992; Harter 1996). The TIPSTER task was defined to be a high-recall task where it is important not to miss information, and this heavily influenced the TIPSTER/TREC definition of relevance. Relevance was defined within the task of the information analyst, with TREC assessors instructed to judge a document relevant if information from that document would be used in some manner for the writing of a report on the subject of the topic. This also implies the use of binary relevance judgments; that is, a document either contains useful information and is therefore relevant, or it does not. Additionally, it has been part of the definition of the task that documents containing duplicate (but relevant) information were also to be included. This latter decision sprung from the difficulties in determining duplicate documents consistently across assessors.

2.6   Analysis of the Characteristics of TREC Test Collection

The ideal test collection proposed in the mid-1970s was carefully designed to allow controlled experimentation. Specific factors such as the type of document and the type of request (question) were to be built in with the goal being that researchers could test for how these factors affected results.

Some of this design was possible in TREC, but much was not. Some control was made on the document selection, but the availability for public distribution also played a large role. Because the emphasis of the TIPSTER program was on high recall, the requests (topics) were all narrowly focused, and in fact became more tightly focused over the years to enable more complete relevance judgments (for details, see section 2.6.3).

2.6.1   Analysis of the Documents
Since a major effort was made to get different sources and lengths of documents, an obvious question involves the effect of these on the system performance. Table 2.3 shows the distribution of retrieved documents, nonduplicate documents retrieved (and therefore judged), and relevant documents across the collections for the ad hoc task in TREC-2 and TREC-3. The columns labeled "retrieved" give the total number of documents from each document source that was contributed to the pooling for the systems in TREC-2 and TREC-3. The numbers are approximate for TREC-3 because the original pools have been lost and some data, in particular additional counts of retrieved documents for the *Wall Street Journal* data set, are missing. The other columns show how many of these documents were nonduplicate and therefore were judged, and how many of these judged documents were actually relevant.

This analysis shows that by far the largest number of relevant documents come from the document sources covering all domains: *Wall Street Journal* and Associated Press. Of the five document sources, these two had the overwhelmingly highest

Table 2.3
Distribution of retrieved documents across data sources

Database	TREC-2 ad hoc			TREC-3 ad hoc		
	Retrieved	Nonduplicate retrieved	Nonduplicate relevant	Retrieved	Nonduplicate retrieved	Nonduplicate relevant
WSJ	125,921	23,706 (19%)	4,556 (19%)	349,151	42,437 (12%)	3,913 (9%)
AP	96,135	16,530 (17%)	4,823 (29%)	376,410	23,567 (6%)	4,933 (20%)
FR	24,848	11,675 (48%)	406 (3%)	148,228	12,911 (9%)	336 (3%)
DOE	15,544	4,018 (26%)	678 (17%)	94,130	9,272 (10%)	305 (3%)
ZIFF	19,886	6,770 (34%)	1,183 (17%)	91,030	9,132 (10%)	318 (4%)

number of retrieved documents and the highest percentage of relevant documents found in the judged set. These two sources also had the lowest percentage of unique retrieved documents as many groups were able to hone in on the correct documents.

In contrast, the very long *Federal Register* documents had few relevant documents, but a high number of retrieved documents and a high percentage of unique documents for TREC-2. This demonstrates the difficulty most retrieval systems had in screening out long documents and the almost random nature of retrieval from this set of "noise" documents. It should be noted, however, that by TREC-3 this effect has disappeared and the statistics for the *Federal Register* look similar to the other data sources. Many of the systems made major corrections in their term-weighting algorithms between TREC-2 and TREC-3, and were thus able to cope with any length document.

The much shorter Department of Energy documents caused no problems in either TREC-2 or TREC-3, with the percentages of correctly retrieved documents resembling more the *Wall Street Journal* and Associated Press set. The lower percentage of unique documents for the Department of Energy documents as opposed to the *Federal Register* ones indicates that these short documents were being effectively handled by the systems. The single-domain *Computer Selects* document source also appears to be as effectively retrieved as the all-domain sources.

It is also interesting to note that while the number of relevant documents remains about constant for the *Wall Street Journal* and Associated Press from TREC-2 to TREC-3, the total number of relevant documents for the other data sources goes down. This is probably because the topics were constructed differently with no specific data source targeted.

Table 2.4 shows a different view of the effect of the document sources for TREC-2, TREC-3, TREC-7, and TREC-8. This table gives the number of topics that have zero, between one and ten, or more than ten relevant documents from a given source of data. It can be seen that the newspapers and newswires provide relevant documents for most of the topics. In particular, the *Wall Street Journal*, the Associated Press newswire, the *Los Angeles Times*, and the *Financial Times* seldom have zero relevant documents for a given topic, and also usually have more than ten relevant documents. Note that there were fewer relevant documents overall in TREC-7 and TREC-8 so that the higher numbers of topics with fewer than ten relevant documents for the *Los Angeles Times* and *Financial Times* data sources are consistent with those for the *Wall Street Journal* and the Associated Press.

The domain-specific data source (*Computer Selects*) was referenced by many fewer topics—that is, an average of over half the topics had no relevant documents from this source, and most of the topics had fewer than ten documents from this source. Whereas the *Wall Street Journal* and the *Financial Times* have large amounts of financial news, it is interesting to note that they have similar numbers of relevant documents to the *Los Angeles Times* data source. The Foreign Broadcast Information Service data source is not a general news source but tends to concentrate on issues of interest to various agencies in the U.S. government. About half of the topics had more than ten relevant documents from this data source.

Table 2.4
Distribution of topics/relevant documents across data sources

Document source	TREC-2 ad hoc			TREC-3 ad hoc			TREC-7 ad hoc			TREC-8 ad hoc		
	0 topics	1–10 topics	>10 topics	0 topics	1–10 topics	>10 topics	0 topics	1–10 topics	>10 topics	0 topics	1–10 topics	>10 topics
WSJ	0	6	44	0	7	43	—	—	—	—	—	—
AP	0	4	46	0	6	44	—	—	—	—	—	—
FR	17	22	11	19	22	9	21	21	8	31	15	4
DOE	31	10	9	32	12	6	—	—	—	—	—	—
ZIFF	18	23	9	29	14	7	—	—	—	—	—	—
LA	—	—	—	—	—	—	0	16	34	5	18	27
FT	—	—	—	—	—	—	2	18	30	1	15	34
FBIS	—	—	—	—	—	—	12	16	22	7	17	26

The very long *Federal Register* documents were not a major source of relevant documents. There is little "general" information in this data source, which deals mainly with issues related to U.S. government activities. The very short Department of Energy abstracts are quite narrowly focused on some scientific issue and therefore were seldom referenced by the topics. Both of these data sources were included in the collection as "noise" sources rather than as likely sources of relevant documents.

As a final comment on the documents, it should be pointed out that these collections have been used by many groups for experiments outside of TREC and provide useful corpora for different kinds of studies. The *Wall Street Journal* is heavily used by the natural-language processing community for parsing and other annotation studies. It was also used in the category B version of the ad hoc track that allowed groups to work with less data (the *Wall Street Journal* only) so that many more relevance judgments were made for this data source. Groups have studied the effects of hyphenation and effective retrieval of long, structured (the *Federal Register*) documents (Wilkinson 1994). Other characteristics of the data such as spelling errors (especially in newswires), duplication of information (again, mostly in newswires), British versus American English (the *Financial Times* versus the *Wall Street Journal*), evolution over time of news stories, and other areas invite further study. Additionally, some sources of documents provide fielded information ranging from titles and headlines, to manual-indexing terms, to the heavily structured data in the patent collection.

2.6.2 Analysis of Topics

The topics built for TREC underwent a major evolution across the first five TRECs. Part of this evolution came as a result of changes in the personnel constructing the topics, but most of the evolution was the result of deliberate changing of the topic specifications. Table 2.5 provides a summary of the various topic fields used in the first eight TRECs and includes the lengths of the various sections in the TREC topics as they have evolved. The effects of these changes in the topics and the methods of topic creation can be observed from this table, and are described in more detail below.

There is a length difference between the topics in TREC-1 and TREC-2 (topics 51–100 and 101–150). The narrative and concept fields are shorter on average for the TREC-1 topics due to the presence of many short topics. The TREC-1 topics were produced quickly, without guidelines, by several different people, whereas the TREC-2 topics were produced by a single person. This person constructed elaborate topics that are more standardized in length, and have longer narrative and concept fields.

The TREC-3 topics are missing the concept fields (by design) and were written by the ten TREC-3 assessors who made the relevance judgments for those topics. The lengths of the description and narrative fields are relatively similar to those of TREC-2, however, probably because the TREC-2 topics were used as examples of how to create these fields.

The TREC-4 topics are much shorter than the TREC-3 ones. Not only was the narrative field removed, but the title field is also gone. In addition, the description field turned out to be significantly shorter going from TREC-3 to TREC-4. This was not

Table 2.5
Topic length statistics by topic section (lengths count number of tokens in topic statement including stop words)

	Minimum	Maximum	Mean
TREC-1 (51–100)	44	250	107.4
Title	1	11	3.8
Description	5	41	17.9
Narrative	23	209	64.5
Concepts	4	111	21.2
TREC-2 (101–150)	54	231	130.8
Title	2	9	4.9
Description	6	41	18.7
Narrative	27	165	78.8
Concepts	3	88	28.5
TREC-3 (151–200)	49	180	103.4
Title	2	20	6.5
Description	9	42	22.3
Narrative	26	146	74.6
TREC-4 (201–250)	8	33	16.3
Description	8	33	16.3
TREC-5 (251–300)	29	213	82.7
Title	2	10	3.8
Description	6	40	15.7
Narrative	19	168	63.2
TREC-6 (301–350)	47	156	88.4
Title	1	5	2.7
Description	5	62	20.4
Narrative	17	142	65.3
TREC-7 (351–400)	31	114	57.6
Title	1	3	2.5
Description	5	34	14.3
Narrative	14	92	40.8
TREC-8 (401–450)	23	98	51.8
Title	1	4	2.5
Description	5	32	13.8
Narrative	14	75	35.5

expected, but resulted from a change in the way the topics were built. In TREC-3, the assessors brought in "seeds" of topics—that is, ideas of issues on which to build a topic. These seeds were then expanded by each assessor, based on looking at the items that were retrieved. To avoid this tuning in TREC-4, the assessors were asked to bring in completed topics—that is, one-sentence descriptions that were used for the actual searching. This different method of constructing topics resulted in the much shorter descriptions.

The topics for TRECs 5–8 were built using the same fields as the TREC-3 topics, but were constructed using the method developed in TREC-4, with the assessors bringing in the description field of the completed topic before looking at the data. The only major change since TREC-5 has been the decision to make the title no more than three words long, often more a set of keywords than a specific title. This was done for use in a titles-only ad hoc retrieval task.

Of course, the various changes in fields and construction methods affected much more than the length. The rest of this section examines some of the interactions between topic structure, method of topic construction, and system performance.

The complexity of the early TREC topics with four fields plus optional factors and definitions fields had diverse effects on system performance. Few systems were able to take advantage of the structure; one notable exception is the structured query work by the INQUERY system at the University of Massachusetts (Callan and Croft 1993) The INQUERY system allows for the use of various operators in the queries, and these operators were employed both to take advantage of the complex structure of these topics and as a method of automatically adding even more structure based on the terms in the topics.

Most groups either removed the topic structure and treated the topics as unstructured text, or performed individual experiments testing the usefulness of each field. Table 2.6 shows the results from experiments by the group from City University, London (the Okapi system) (Robertson et al. 1995).

It can be seen from this table that the use of the factors and definitions fields in an unstructured manner slightly hurt performance, but that the concepts field was by far the most valuable for systems to use in TREC-2. The generally high-quality key-

Table 2.6
Use of different fields of the TREC-2 topics by the Okapi system

Topic fields	Mean average precision
Full topic (including factors and definitions)	0.35
Title, concepts, description, and narrative	0.36
Title, concepts, and narrative	0.36
Title, concepts, and description	0.35
Title and concepts	0.34
Title, description, and narrative	0.28

words in the concepts section enabled systems that used the concept field as input to automatically build a query that did as well as systems that constructed a query manually.

Yet the use of the concepts field also masked any further improvements from techniques "known" to improve performance, such as relevance feedback. Therefore, when the topic-creation process moved to NIST, it was decided to build topics that did not contain this artificial keyword field.

The removal of the concepts field led to experiments by most groups into how to automatically create queries that would perform as well as ones using manually created keywords. These experiments used a query expansion based on an analysis of terms in the set of highly ranked documents (pseudorelevance feedback) (Buckley et al. 1995; Robertson et al. 1995) or an automatically constructed thesaurus (Jing and Croft 1994). Note that whereas this expansion did improve performance about 20 percent over no expansion, the automatically created queries did not outperform manually created queries in TREC-3.

This evolution in topic design also led to interest in how the length of an input query affects system performance. TREC-5, TREC-6, and TREC-7 saw a series of experiments working with shorter topics, usually either the title and description field only, or sometimes only the title. For example, several groups (Kwok 1996; Lu, Ayoub, and Dong 1997) devised improved weighting schemes that work with only the description field. Even so, results working only with the description field were about 30 percent lower than results using the full topic in TREC-5. By the end of TREC-7, however, results from the top groups had improved so much that the difference between using the full topic and only the title plus description fields was between 1 and 5 percent. It should be noted that the use of the title only did reduce performance by around 10 percent.

As a caution to experimenters, it should be mentioned that the description field of the TREC-6 topics often did *not* contain the same set of terms used in the title, and therefore results can be skewed in favor of using the title only for this collection.

A final issue about the topics relates to measuring the difficulty of a given topic. There has been no attempt in TREC to build topics to match any particular characteristics, partly because the emphasis was on real user topics, but also because it is not clear what particular characteristics would be appropriate. There have been efforts to analyze the effects of topic characteristics on system performance both in TREC-2 and TREC-5.

For these analyses, a measure called topic "hardness" was developed. The hardness of a topic is defined as an average over a given set of runs of the precision for each topic after all the relevant documents have been retrieved *or* after a hundred documents have been retrieved, if more than a hundred documents are relevant. This measure is thus oriented toward high-recall performance and how well systems do at finding all the relevant documents.

The hardness measure can be used to show correlations between some particular topic characteristic and system performance. In TREC-5, two specific topic characteristics were examined. The first is the length of the topic (the full topic in this case), and the second characteristic is the number of relevant documents found for that topic. A correlation coefficient using the Pearson product moment gives a correlation of 0.19 between the number of relevant documents and the hardness, and a correlation of 0.14 between the topic length and the hardness. This can be compared with a correlation of 0.20 between the topic number and the hardness, which is clearly a random correlation.

If the difficulty of a topic (as measured by hardness) is not related to either its broadness or its length, then what other characteristics are significant? This is currently a question with no answer. The performance of retrieval systems on a given topic depends on many items, including the specificity of the terms in the topic and how well they map to the document set being searched, or the likelihood that some relevant documents come easily to the top of the ranked list and therefore enable effective query expansion. A recent paper (Cronen-Townsend, Zhou, and Croft 2002) examines this area with the development of a "clarity" score to predict the performance of a given topic/document set combination. Additionally, there have been two workshops in 2003 (Harman and Buckley 2004a) and 2004 (Harman and Buckley 2004b) on this.

2.6.3 Analysis of Relevance Judgments

The third part of the test collection is the relevance judgments. The TREC relevance judgments were specifically designed to model users interested in high-recall tasks, and hence any analysis of them needs to take this into consideration. One obvious important characteristic is how complete the relevance judgments are; the more complete the relevance judgments are, the better the test collection models the high-recall needs of these users. Moreover, the more complete the test collection, the more likely that future systems using the collection for evaluation can trust that all/most of the relevant documents in the collection have been identified.

A test of the relevance judgment completeness assumption was made using TREC-2 results, and again during the TREC-3 evaluation. In both cases, a second set of one hundred documents was examined from each system, using only a sample of topics and systems in TREC-2, and using all topics and systems in TREC-3.

For the TREC-2 completeness tests, a median of twenty-one new relevant documents per topic was found (an 11 percent increase in total relevant documents). This averages to three new relevant documents found in the second hundred documents for each system, and this is a high estimate for all systems since the eight runs sampled for additional judgments were from the better systems. Lower numbers were found for the more complete TREC-3 testing, with a median of thirty new relevant documents per topic for the ad hoc task. This averages to less than one new relevant document per run, since forty-eight runs from all systems were used in this testing. (For more details on the specific tests, see Harman 1995).

These levels of completeness are quite acceptable; furthermore, it was demonstrated that there was no relationship between the number of new relevant documents found and the number of documents judged, implying that additional judgments are not necessary. Instead, the number of new relevant documents found was shown to

Table 2.7
Relationship between completeness in TREC-3 and the initial number of relevant documents

| | Number of relevant documents found between ranks one hundred and two hundred in TREC-3 | | |
Percent new relevant	Number of topics	Average initial relevant	Average new relevant
0	1	85	0
1–9	12	65	3
10–19	7	96	13
20–29	22	237	59
30–36	8	381	137
Average		196	50
Median		122	30

be correlated with the original number of relevant documents—that is, topics with many relevant documents are more likely to have additional ones that have not been found.

Table 2.7 shows the detailed breakdown for the fifty ad hoc topics in TREC-3. The median of 30 new relevant documents occurs for a topic with 122 original relevant documents. Topics with initially many more relevant documents tend to have more new ones found, and this has led to a greater emphasis on using topics with fewer relevant documents—that is, more tightly focused topics.

These findings were independently verified by Justin Zobel (1998) at the Royal Melbourne Institute of Technology. Additionally, Zobel found that any lack of completeness did not bias the results of particular systems and that systems that did not contribute documents to the pool can still be evaluated fairly using the pooled judgments.

Whereas it would have been ideal to have complete relevance judgments, it is important to recognize that the goal of the TREC collections is to allow comparisons of multiple runs, either across or within systems. So having the exact number of relevant documents, or having an exact recall number, is not as crucial as knowing that the judgments are complete enough to ensure that comparisons of two methods using the test collections will be accurate.

A second significant issue to any set of relevance judgments is their consistency—that is, how stable are the judgments, and how does their stability or lack thereof affect the comparison of the performance of systems using that test collection.

In each of the TREC evaluations, each topic was judged by a single assessor to ensure the best consistency of judgment. Some testing of this consistency was done after TREC-2, when a sample of the topics and the documents was rejudged by a second assessor. The results showed an average agreement between the two judges of about 80 percent. In TREC-4, all the ad hoc topics had samples rejudged by two additional assessors, with the results being about 72 percent agreement among all three judges, and 88 percent agreement between the initial judge and either one of the two additional judges. This is a remarkably high level of agreement in relevance assessment, and it is probably due to the similar background and training of the judges as well as a general lack of ambiguity in the topics as represented by the narrative section.

Looking more deeply into the inconsistencies, however, reveals that most of this agreement had to do with the large numbers of documents that are clearly non-relevant. On average, 30 percent of the documents judged relevant by the initial judge were marked as nonrelevant by both the additional judges, whereas less than 3 percent of the initial nonrelevant documents were marked as relevant by the secondary judges. This average hides a high variability across topics; for twelve of the fifty topics, the disagreement on documents initially marked relevant is higher than 50 percent. For four of the fifty topics, the second two judges declared that additional documents were relevant to the extent that the number of relevant documents would have increased by over 30 percent.

Whereas most of these disagreements are caused by human variation in judgment, this is often magnified by a mismatch between the topic statement, the task, and the document collection. For example, topic 234 is "What progress has been made in fuel cell technology?" If the stated task is to find documents that contain information that would be used in a report about this topic, then a lenient interpretation would declare relevant most documents that discuss fuel cells. A strict judge might require that relevant documents literally present a progress report on fuel cell technology. Additionally, some of the more problematic topics were either open to different interpretations (topic 245: "What are the trends and developments in retirement communities?") or so badly mismatched to the document collection that the initial assessor made extremely lenient relevance judgments (topic 249: "How has the depletion or destruction of the rain forest effected the world's weather?").

It should be noted, though, that all this topic and user variation is realistic, and should be accepted as part of any testing. Users come to retrieval systems with different expectations, and most of these expectations are unstated. If test collections do not reflect this noisy situation, then the systems that are built using these collections to test their algorithms will not work well in operational settings.

A critical question is how all this variation affects system comparisons. Ellen M. Voorhees (2000) investigated this by using different subsets of the relevance judgments from TREC-4. As her most stringent test, she used the intersection of the relevant document sets (where all judges had agreed), and the union of these judgments (where any judge had marked a document relevant). She found that although the mean average precision of a given set of system results did change, the changes were highly correlated across systems and the relative ranking of different system runs did not significantly change. Even when the two runs were from the same organization (and therefore are more likely to be similar), the two systems were ranked in the same order by all subsets of relevance judgments. This clearly demonstrates the stability of the TREC relevance judgments in the sense that groups can test two different algorithms and be reasonably assured that the results reflect a true difference between those algorithms.

These results were independently verified by the University of Waterloo's work in TREC-6. Waterloo personnel judged over thirteen thousand documents for relevance, and these judgments were used by Voorhees in a similar manner as the TREC-4 multiple judgments. Even though there was even less agreement between the NIST and Waterloo assessors (with their different backgrounds and training), the changes in the system rankings were still not significant. The one exception to this was the comparison between two same-system runs in which one run had used manual relevance feedback. In general, comparisons between automatic runs and runs with manual intervention, particularly manual relevance feedback that basically adds a third relevance judge, should be more carefully analyzed as they are the comparisons most likely to be affected by variations in relevance judgments.

The study by Voorhees additionally established a practical upper bound on retrieval system performance of 65 percent precision at 65 percent recall since that is the level at which humans agree with one another (based on the two sets of secondary judgments done in that study). It should be noted that system performance is still well below this upper bound. The best performances in the TREC-7 were 21 percent precision at 60 percent recall for the automatic systems and 30 percent precision at 60 percent recall for the manual systems.

As a final comment on the TREC relevance assessments, the relationship of the TREC definition of relevance to the wider area of relevance judgments needs be addressed. The TREC relevance judgments for the ad hoc task should be viewed as the broadest type of judgments—that is, the fact that a document contained *any* information about a topic/question was enough to make it relevant. This was important because of the perceived definition of the TREC task/user as that of a high-recall task. But it also was important in terms of creating the most complete set of relevance judgments possible. It is hoped that others will take the current judgments as the starting point for other types of relevance judgments, such as the removal of "duplicate" documents, the use of graded relevance judgments (Järvelin and Kekäläinen 2000; Sormunen 2002), or even the measurement of some type of learning effect. In the future, TREC may try these other approaches; graded relevance judgments have been used in the Web track (Voorhees 2001), where it is important to find highly relevant documents early, and issues dealing with the learning effect have been addressed in the TREC 2002 novelty track.

2.7   Further TREC Collections

The expansion of TREC into tracks in TREC-4 led to the design and building of many specialized test collections. None of these are as large or as heavily used as the ad hoc collections described earlier, but they demonstrate the wide range of test collections built for the TREC evaluations. This section gives an overview of the other collections, with an emphasis on how the design criteria had to change in each. Note that more details are provided in the other chapters in this book that deal specifically with the various tracks, and that details of how to obtain this data and the English ad hoc data are on the NIST Web site, ⟨http://trec.nist.gov/⟩, under the data section.

The test collections for the tracks all bear some resemblance to the ad hoc collections, ranging from slight modifications to major evolutions for tracks in the more recent TRECs. The subsections that follow are ordered by this resemblance and the years in which they were built.

2.7.1 Noisy Text

NIST built two collections for retrieval of OCR documents in TREC-4 and TREC-5. For TREC-4, the topics were the ad hoc topics, and the data was the *Wall Street Journal* data artificially degraded to reflect error rates of 10 and 20 percent character errors. For TREC-5, a more sophisticated method used actual OCR data from the 1994 *Federal Register*. A correct copy (electronic version) plus two scanned copies at 5 and 20 percent error rates were used. Additionally for TREC-5, the topics were changed to known item topics—that is, each topic was created to uniquely retrieve one document. This type of search is particularly useful in corrupted data, where a single corrupted term might cause a system to miss that document. For more details about these test collections, see the TREC Web site and chapter 8, this volume.

2.7.2 Spoken Document Retrieval Collections

A second type of noisy text is data coming from speech recognition systems. Two groups at NIST, the speech group and the retrieval group, collaborated to implement a test collection for broadcast news for TRECs 6–8. The documents for the test collections consisted of news transcriptions, both automatically and manually transcribed. TREC-6 used a 50-hour set of news; TREC-7 used 87 hours, and there were 557 hours for TREC-8. There were forty-seven known-item questions in TREC-6, with twenty-three and sixty ad hoc style questions for TREC-7 and TREC-8, respectively. For more information on these collections, see the TREC Web site and chapter 8, this volume.

2.7.3 Non-English Collections

TREC-3 began work in other languages than English. The first two languages were Spanish and Chinese. For both these languages, the test collections were created similar to the English ad hoc collections, but with Spanish and Chinese topics and documents, respectively. The Spanish collection consisted of the *El Norte* newspaper from Monterey, Mexico (200 megabytes) in TREC-3 and TREC-4, with the Spanish *Agence France Presse* (308 megabytes) added for TREC-5. There was a total of seventy-five topics developed for the Spanish collection (twenty-five each year). The Chinese collection was a 170-megabyte collection including the *Peoples Daily* and *Xinhua* newspapers with a total of fifty-eight topics built for TREC-5 and TREC-6.

Starting in TREC-6, TREC ran a cross-language retrieval track for three years. The documents for this were a Swiss newswire Schweizerische Depeschen Agentur in three languages (French, German, and Italian) and a set of English documents from the Associated Press newswire. There were twenty-five questions written in three languages at NIST for TREC-6, and an additional fifty-six written in four languages (English, French, German, and Italian) produced jointly by NIST and groups in Switzerland, Germany, and Italy for TREC-7 and TREC-8. It should be noted that this joint production of a test collection in four languages required distributed topic creation and relevance assessment, and there are more details on the motivation and design of this complex methodology in chapter 7, this volume. The CLIR track then moved to Europe to become a separate evaluation—Cross-Language Evaluation Forum (CLEF)—and information about the data is on its Web site, ⟨http://clef.iei.pi.cnr.it⟩.

TREC continued CLIR for three more years. In TREC-9, the task was English to Chinese, with 250 megabytes of Chinese from several 1994 Hong Kong newspapers, and twenty-five English topics built at NIST. In TREC-10 and TREC-11, the task was English to Arabic, with 869 megabytes of Arabic documents from the Arabic *Agence France Presse*, and seventy-five topics in total generated by the LDC. The Arabic document collection is available from the LDC. For more details on the non-English test collections, see the TREC Web site and chapter 7, this volume.

2.7.4   Very Large Corpus and Web Collections

David Hawking and his colleagues at CSIRO put together five large test collections to test efficiency and, more recently, Web applications. This work was piloted in TREC-6, with a document collection consisting of twenty gigabytes of assorted text (called VLC1). This collection was replaced by VLC2 with a hundred gigabytes of Web data from the Internet archive in TREC-7, and was used along with the TREC-7 ad hoc topics to test for differences in retrieval between regular text and the Web. Note that the pools for relevance assessment in the Web collection were very shallow (twenty-documents deep versus one hundred), and therefore this test collection would not meet any completeness test. For TREC-8, the VLC2 data were appropriately sampled to create a Web environment of two gigabytes (WT2g) and the TREC-8 ad hoc topics were used, with normal ad hoc relevance assessment done for both the text and Web collections.

TREC-9 saw the introduction of the WT10g collection, and finally TREC-10 used a new collection representing the eighteen-gigabyte collection created from material in the .gov domain. The topics for these Web collections evolved into more specialized topics such as home page locations and the locations of "authority" sites for a broad subject area. They were created in a similar manner to the ad hoc topics in that assessors brought in ideas, searched the appropriate Web collection, created the topics, and then made the relevance decisions for those topics. All these collections are available from CSIRO (see the TREC Web site), for more information, see chapter 9, this volume.

2.7.5   Routing and Filtering Collections

NIST built routing/filtering collections for eleven years. Some of these (for TRECs 1–8) used ad hoc topics, training data from the six TREC disks, and testing data also from those disks. In TREC-9, the OHSUMED collection plus some MeSH data were used. TREC-10 and TREC-11 used a new Reuters collection. The design and building of each of these latter filtering collections was unique; for further information, see chapter 5, this volume.

2.7.6   Question-Answering Collections

Starting in TREC-8, a completely new task was introduced to TREC. Instead of returning a ranked list of documents in response to a topic, systems were asked to return *the answer*. So whereas the document collections were the basic English ones used in the ad hoc task, the design of the topics (questions, in this case) had very different criteria. Initially, it was unclear what types of questions could be answered, and in TREC-8 the questions were mostly gathered from participants (198 fact-based/short-answer questions). It quickly became obvious, however, that a source of real questions was needed, and for TREC-9 and TREC-10, the questions were taken from the search logs of Excite and Encarta (693 questions for TREC-9) and from AskJeeves and MNSearch (500 questions for TREC-10). These questions were taken as is, but for TREC-9 all questions were checked to make sure there were documents that contained the answers (questions without answers were permitted in TREC-10). For TREC-11, the documents came from a new set of more recent newspapers and newswires on the AQUAINT disks. The 500 questions came from the same sources as TREC-10. For more details on these data, see the TREC Web page and chapter 10, this volume.

Note that the definition of a test collection had to be changed for this track. Whereas there are documents and questions (instead of topics), the answer set is not uniquely defined compared with the set of relevant documents for the ad hoc task. The scope of the answer that was judged correct was not fixed. In TREC-8, TREC-9, and TREC-10, passages of lengths 250 and 50 words respectively were accepted as correct. For TREC-11, only exact-answer strings were considered correct. These changes in design specifications were considered necessary in order to challenge the technology. The answer sets described above do not constitute a reusable test collection because the unit that is judged is the entire answer string. Different runs very seldom return exactly the same answer strings, and it is quite difficult to determine automatically whether the difference between a new string and a judged string is significant with respect to the correctness of the answer.

2.7.7   Video Retrieval Collections

In 2001, TREC started a video retrieval track. The data consisted of eleven hours of video, including one disk from NIST, data from the Open Video Project, and some stock shots from the BBC. The topics were known-item searches (seventy-four of them) contributed by the participants. In TREC-11, there was forty hours of video, again from the Open Video Project and the Internet Archive. There were twenty-five specially created topics from NIST. In 2003, the video retrieval task was split into its own evaluation, TRECVID. New data from news broadcasts were obtained, including 120 hours from ABC and CNN programs during 1998 and thirteen hours of C-SPAN programming. Information about these collections is available on the TREC Web site.

Once again, the classic test collection paradigm needed to be shifted. The topic needed to be expressed in a multimedia way—in particular, text had to be supplemented by video clips or bits of speech in order to handle multiple types of requests. The definition of documents needed to be extended to allow measurement at shot boundaries.

2.8 Conclusion

TREC has enabled the creation of a huge set of publicly available test collections for the English ad hoc task. These include six disks of documents, each containing two gigabytes of newspaper, newswire, and other data in English. The disks were carefully enough formatted so that researchers can easily access the documents, but with no content "correction" so that researchers have a realistic set of data for their experiments. There are also 9 sets of topics (450 in all), and comprehensive relevance judgments for those topics. This large English test collection has had a major impact on information retrieval research and is the collection of choice for most researchers today working in basic retrieval technologies.

Additionally, TREC allowed the creation of many other data sets for the various tracks. Data for other languages, such as Spanish, Chinese, and Arabic, have provided the first experiences for research in (non-English) monolingual and cross-lingual retrieval. Data from other media, such as speech and video, have allowed groups from areas related to information retrieval to extend retrieval methodologies into these new areas. Both the Web track and the filtering track have produced several different test collections as they have tackled new tasks over the years. The new question-answering task has also made pseudotest collections that have been quite useful to that community.

The test collections that have emerged from TREC have come a long way from the earlier Cranfield collection, thereby enabling information retrieval technologies to not only double in performance but operate in environments that previously were unexplored. Hopefully the careful attention that has been paid to appropriate design criteria has created test collections that will enable unanticipated use in further experiments to be successful.

References

Altomari, P. J., and P. A. Currier, eds. 1996. *The proceedings of the TIPSTER text program—Phase II*. San Francisco, CA: Morgan Kaufmann Publishing.

Bookstein, A. 1979. Relevance. *Journal of the American Society for Information Science* 30, no. 5:269–273.

Buckley, C., G. Salton, J. Allan, and A. Singhal. 1995. Automatic query expansion using SMART. In *TREC-3*, 69–80.

Burgin, R. 1992. Variations in relevance judgments and the evaluation of retrieval performance. *Information Processing and Management* 28, no. 5:619–627.

Callan, J. P., and W. B. Croft. 1993. An evaluation of query processing strategies using the TIPSTER collection. In *Proceedings of the sixteenth annual international ACM SIGIR conference*, 347–355.

Cleverdon, C., J. Mills, and E. Keen. 1966. *Factors determining the performance of indexing systems, vol. 1: Design, vol. 2: Test results*. Cranfield, UK: Aslib Cranfield Research Project.

Cooper, W. 1971. A definition of relevance for information retrieval. *Information Storage and Retrieval* 7:19–37.

Cronen-Townsend, S., Y. Zhou, and W. Croft. 2002. Predicting query performance. In *Proceedings of the twenty-fifth annual international ACM SIGIR conference*, 299–306.

Fox, E. 1983. *Characteristics of two new experimental collections in computer and information science containing textual and bibliographic concepts*. Technical report TR 83–561. Ithaca, NY: Computing Science Department, Cornell University.

Gee, F. R., ed. 1999. *The proceedings of the TIPSTER text program—Phase III*. San Francisco, CA: Morgan Kaufmann Publishing.

Harman, D. K. 1993. Overview of the first text retrieval conference (TREC-1). In *TREC-1*, 1–20.

Harman, D. K. 1994. Overview of the second text retrieval conference (TREC-2). In *TREC-2*, 1–20.

Harman, D. K. 1995. Overview of the third text retrieval conference (TREC-3). In *TREC-3*, 1–20.

Harman, D. K. 1996. Overview of the fourth text retrieval conference (TREC-4). In *TREC-4*, 1–23.

Harman, D. K., and C. Buckley. 2004a. The NRRC reliable information access (RIA) workshop. In *Proceedings of the twenty-seventh annual international ACM SIGIR conference*, 528–529.

Harman, D. K., and C. Buckley. 2004b. Ria and "where can IR go from here?" *SIGIR Forum* 38, no. 2.

Harter, S. P. 1996. Variations in relevance assessments and the measurement of retrieval effectiveness. *Journal of the American Society for Information Science* 47, no. 1:37–49.

Jarvelin, K., and J. Kekäläinen. 2000. IR evaluation methods for retrieving highly relevant documents. In *Proceedings of the twenty-third annual international ACM SIGIR conference*, 41–48.

Jing, Y., and W. B. Croft. 1994. An association thesaurus for information retrieval. In *Proceedings of RIAO94*, 146–160. Paris: Centre de Hautes Etudes Internationales d'Informatique Documentaire.

Katter, R. 1968. The influence of scale on relevance judgments. *Information Storage and Retrieval* 4:1–11.

Kwok, K. 1996. A new method of weighting query terms for ad-hoc retrieval. In *Proceedings of the nineteenth annual international ACM SIGIR conference*, 187–196.

Lu, A., M. Ayoub, and J. Dong. 1997. Ad hoc experiments using EUREKA. In *TREC-5*, 229–240.

Merchant, R., ed. 1994. *The proceedings of the TIPSTER text program—Phase I*. San Francisco, CA: Morgan Kaufmann Publishing.

Robertson, S., S. Walker, S. Jones, M. Hancock-Beaulieu, and M. Gatford. 1995. Okapi at TREC-3. In *TREC-3*, 109–126.

Sormunen, E. 2002. Liberal relevance criteria of TREC—Counting on negligible documents? In *Proceedings of the twenty-fifth annual international ACM SIGIR conference*, 324–330.

Sparck Jones, K., and K. van Rijsbergen. 1975. *Report on the need for and provision of an "ideal" information retrieval test collection*. British Library Research and Development report 5266. Cambridge: Computer Laboratory, University of Cambridge.

Sparck Jones, K., and K. van Rijsbergen. 1976. Information retrieval test collections. *Journal of Documentation 32*, no. 1:59–75.

Vaswani, P., and J. Cameron. 1970. *The national physical laboratory experiments in statistical word associations and their use in document indexing and retrieval*. Publication 42. Teddington, UK: Division of Computer Science, National Physical Laboratory.

Voorhees, E. M. 2000. Variations in relevance judgments and the measurement of retrieval effectiveness. *Information Processing and Management* 36, no. 5:697–716.

Voorhees, E. M. 2001. Evaluation by highly relevant documents. In *Proceedings of the twenty-fourth annual international ACM SIGIR conference*, 74–82.

Voorhees, E. M. 2003. Overview of TREC 2002. In *TREC 2002*, 1–16.

Voorhees, E. M., and D. K. Harman. 1997. Overview of the fifth text retrieval conference (TREC-5). In *TREC-5*, 1–28.

Voorhees, E. M., and D. K. Harman. 1998. Overview of the sixth text retrieval conference (TREC-6). In *TREC-6*, 1–24.

Voorhees, E. M., and D. K. Harman. 1999. Overview of the seventh text retrieval conference (TREC-7). In *TREC-7*, 1–24.

Voorhees, E. M., and D. K. Harman. 2000. Overview of the eighth text retrieval conference (TREC-8). In *TREC-8*, 1–24.

Voorhees, E. M., and D. K. Harman. 2001. Overview of the ninth text retrieval conference (TREC-9). In *TREC-9*, 1–14.

Voorhees, E. M., and D. K. Harman. 2002. Overview of TREC 2001. In *TREC 2001*, 1–15.

Wilkinson, R. 1994. Effective retrieval of structured documents. In *Proceedings of the seventeenth annual international ACM SIGIR conference*, 311–317.

Zobel, J. 1998. How reliable are the results of large-scale information retrieval experiments. In *Proceedings of the twenty-first annual international ACM SIGIR conference*, 307–314.

3 Retrieval System Evaluation
Chris Buckley and Ellen M. Voorhees

One of the primary motivations for TREC was to standardize retrieval system evaluation. While the Cranfield paradigm of using test collections (see chapter 2, this volume) had been introduced decades earlier, the particulars of how it was implemented —especially which evaluation measures to use—differed across researchers making evaluation results incomparable. The validity of test collections as a research tool was in question, not only from those who objected to the reliance on relevance judgments [6] but also from those who were concerned as to how they could scale to larger collections [9]. With the notable exception of Karen Sparck Jones and Keith van Rijsbergen's report on the need for larger, better test collections [12], there was little explicit discussion of what constituted a minimally acceptable experimental design and no hard evidence to support any position.

TREC has succeeded in standardizing and validating the use of test collections as a research tool for ad hoc retrieval, and has extended the use of test collections to other tasks. The trec_eval program written by Chris Buckley is publicly available and has become the primary method for evaluating retrieval results. TREC's scale, in terms of both the size of the test collections and the number of retrieval results, has provided the data necessary for studying the effect features of an IR experiment's design have on the conclusions that can be drawn from the experiment. Evaluation has also been a major focus of tracks such as the filtering track (see chapter 5, this volume) and the question answering track (see chapter 10, this volume) where the retrieval result is not a ranked list of documents, thus extending the paradigm to new areas.

This chapter recaps what has been learned about IR system evaluation over the course of TREC. The first section motivates the choice of evaluation measures now included in trec_eval by recounting the history of its development. The following section examines the variability of system performance across topics and the implications of such variability for system evaluation. Section 3.3 shows that comparative evaluations are stable despite changes in the relevance judgments, thus validating the collections as laboratory tools. The final section concludes with recommended best practices for IR system evaluation.

3.1 Test Collection Evaluation Measures

For an ad hoc retrieval task, a *run* is defined to be a ranked list of documents for each of the set of topics in a test collection. The documents in a list are sorted such that the document the system believes is most likely to match the topic is retrieved in the first rank. While in principle the entire collection may be ranked, in practice a *cutoff level*, λ, is defined such that documents in ranks greater than λ are considered not retrieved. The relevance judgments, called *qrels* for short, list which documents should be retrieved for each topic. In this chapter, relevance judgments are assumed to be binary (either a document is relevant to a topic or it is not), though others have looked at evaluation measures for nonbinary relevance judgments [7; 16].

The specific evaluation goal for the TREC ad hoc task is to compare how well systems can find relevant documents. This is deliberately distinct from evaluating a particular IR application. To successfully accomplish some real-world IR application, a system would need to do additional application-dependent processing of the retrieved set. Examples of such processing for a basic document retrieval task are:

- Finding the best single document
- Finding all relevant documents
- Finding documents with "different" relevant information
- Finding representative relevant documents

For each processing type, the system must be able to find the relevant documents as a first step. The basic assumption within TREC is that for most IR applications it is necessary, though not sufficient, that the underlying IR system be capable of doing well on the TREC ad hoc task.

There are dozens of evaluation measures that can be used for ad hoc retrieval; the current version of trec_eval calculates 108 evaluation numbers for a single run. A much small number of measures have been widely used for system evaluation, however. The remainder of this section provides a historical perspective on the theoretical and practical considerations in choosing the measures used in TREC.

3.1.1 Evaluation Measures Prior to TREC

In the three to four years immediately preceding TREC-1, test collection evaluation as seen in published papers had become increasingly chaotic. Computing resources had become cheap enough so that many more groups could perform retrieval experiments, but the groups did not agree on how to evaluate those experiments. Papers reported scores for only the authors' preferred measure, when each of the following was preferred by someone (most of these measures are defined below): precision at ten documents, recall measures, utility, full recall-precision curves, three-point averages from the recall-precision curves, ten-point averages, and eleven-point averages. Even when papers reported what they called the same measure—for example, a three-point average—the implementation of the measure often differed (see the discussion of interpolation below). Thus, it was unusual that the results presented in any two papers could legitimately be compared to each other, despite having used the same test collections. This was a major problem when trying to learn from papers of the era. The reader was never quite sure whether a single system evaluation comparison showed a poor system becoming mediocre or a good system actually demonstrating a technique that was generally useful.

3.1.2   Evaluation in TREC-1

Trec_eval was created for TREC-1 by repackaging the evaluation code contained within the SMART retrieval system from Cornell University [2]. SMART implemented most of the evaluation measures in widespread use at the time, making it a logical starting point. The input to trec_eval is a retrieval run and the set of relevance judgments. Trec_eval computes multiple evaluation scores for each topic (one score for each evaluation measure used) according to the placement of the relevant documents within the ranked list. It also computes an average score across all topics for each measure.

For TREC-1, a run consisted of the top two hundred (or fewer) documents retrieved by a system for each of fifty topics. Each document was assigned a numerical retrieval status value (RSV) by the system. Each document was also assigned a rank by the system, but this rank was deliberately ignored by trec_eval. Instead, trec_eval produced its own ranking of the top two hundred documents based on the RSV values to ensure consistent system-independent tie breaking among documents that a system considered equally likely to be relevant (the ordering of documents with tied RSV values was arbitrary yet consistent across runs). Breaking ties in an equitable fashion was an important feature at the time since many systems had large numbers of ties—Boolean and coordination-level retrieval models could produce hundreds of documents with the same RSV.

The major measures calculated by trec_eval for TREC-1 were:

Precision at Document Cutoff λ for $\lambda =$ (5, 15, 30, 100, 200)   The fraction of retrieved documents that are relevant assuming the retrieved set consists of the documents retrieved at ranks $\leq \lambda$. If r retrieved documents are relevant, precision is r/λ. For example, if five of the top fifteen documents are relevant, then precision at document cutoff fifteen or P(15) is $5/15 = 0.333$.

Recall at Document Cutoff λ for $\lambda =$ (5, 15, 30, 100, 200)   The fraction of relevant documents that have been retrieved by rank λ. If r retrieved documents are relevant and there are R relevant documents, recall is r/R. For example, if five out of the top fifteen documents are relevant and there are fifty relevant documents for that topic, then R(15) is $5/50 = 0.1$.

Interpolated Precision at Recall Point X for X = (0.0, 0.1, 0.2, 0.3, … 1.0)   The precision after the given fraction of the relevant documents has been retrieved. For example, if there are fifty relevant documents for a topic and the tenth relevant document has been retrieved at rank forty, then precision at recall point 0.2 is 0.25. Interpolation is discussed below.

Eleven-Point Average   The average of precision at recall point X for all eleven values of X.

Three-Point Average   The average of precision at recall point X for X = 0.2, X = .50, and X = 0.8. This is a slight variant of the three-point average used by Cornell and others in the late 1980s.

In addition to averages across all fifty topics for each of these measures, trec_eval also reported the total numbers of documents retrieved, relevant documents, and relevant documents that were retrieved summed across all topics.

Interpolation is an issue that attracts a lot of debate because there are several reasonable alternatives, but in practice it makes little difference when comparing systems. The major issue addressed by interpolation is that it rarely happens that any particular recall point is achieved. For example, if there are three relevant documents for a topic, then recall is 0 until the first relevant document is retrieved, at which point recall is 0.333. Nevertheless, precision needs to be defined at a set of standard recall points both to average the measure across topics and plot precision versus recall. The approach used by trec_eval is to define the interpolated precision at recall point X to be the maximum precision obtained at any recall point $\geq$ X. This is well defined at all points and has the side benefit that it reduces the volatility of the measure when there are few relevant documents. The volatility of the measure is not much of a problem with the number of relevant documents in a typical TREC collection, but it was a much larger problem with the extremely small test collections before TREC.

3.1.3   Analysis of the TREC-1 Measures

During the TREC-1 meeting, there was a lot of attention paid to the evaluation methodology, both in the talks by participants and during two 1.5-hour evaluation breakout sessions. The majority of the discussion related to the pooling process, but there were also problems identified with the measures themselves. Three months after TREC-1, Chris Buckley presented an analysis of the problems, proposing slight modifications to the evaluation procedures as well as introducing two new measures at the TIPSTER eighteen-month meeting [8]. The suggestions were adopted for both TIPSTER and TREC-2, and the methodology has remained basically unchanged since then.

The following problems with the TREC-1 measures were identified:

Precision at Document Cutoff λ for $\lambda = $ (5, 15, 30, 100, 200)   Precision at a given cutoff doesn't average well across topics since topics have different numbers of relevant documents. A topic with only 2 relevant documents has a maximum P(30) score of 0.06; the average P(30) score will not be affected much by this topic regardless of how well or poorly a system ranks the documents. On the other hand, another topic in the TREC-1 test set had 878 relevant documents; a cutoff of 30 barely scratches the surface of the relevant documents for this topic. The averaging problem is not nearly as important with the small pre-TREC collections since the range of the number of relevant documents is much smaller.

Recall at Document Cutoff λ for $\lambda = $ (5, 15, 30, 100, 200)   Recall at a given cutoff suffers from the same problems with averaging as precision. Recall is also less trustworthy than precision because of the pooling process: relevance judgments are known to be incomplete, and the amount of incompleteness is known to be topic dependent [18]. Further, recall at a cutoff is measuring the same thing as precision at that cutoff since both are a constant factor times the number of relevant documents retrieved for that topic. The only real difference between the two measures comes from averaging where recall treats topics with a large number of relevant documents as comparatively less important than does precision.

Interpolated Precision at Recall Point X for X = (0.0, 0.1, 0.2, 0.3, ... 1.0)   These measures were affected by the small number of documents returned for each topic. Since only 200 documents were evaluated per topic, the high-recall points could never be obtained for topics with more than 200 relevant documents. This caused the scores for all but the smallest recall points to be volatile in that a small difference in the retrieved set made a huge difference in the score. As an example, consider topic seventy-four with 499 relevant documents. If a system retrieved 149 relevant documents in the 200 documents returned, its interpolated precision score at recall point 0.3 is 0.0 since 0.3 recall is not reached. Yet if that system instead retrieved 150 relevant documents, its score at 0.3 recall is 0.75. This volatility made comparisons between runs unreliable.

Eleven-Point Average   As in the example above (since it includes the same values), there were several topics for which small retrieval differences for that topic could lead to large differences in the measure, even when averaged over fifty topics. Despite this flaw, this was the single measure that participants thought best characterized a run.

Three-Point Average   The same problems existed as with the eleven-point average.

One common problem noted in several of the measures above is that while the individual topic scores may be meaningful for a measure, averaging those scores across all topics is not reasonable. In particular, measures that use a fixed cutoff that is identical across all topics do not average well. The fixed cutoff may be appropriate for some topics, but wildly inappropriate for others.

A typical topic might have some easy-to-retrieve relevant documents (for instance, the documents use the same vocabulary as the topic), some harder-to-retrieve relevant documents (different vocabulary), some marginally relevant documents, and some nearly relevant documents. The existence of these last two categories was demonstrated when multiple assessors judged the same topic as described in section 3.3 below. For the TREC-4 collection, no pair of assessors completely agreed on the relevant document set for any of the forty-nine topics. For twenty-four of the forty-nine topics, the documents judged relevant by one assessor were a superset of the documents judged relevant by the other assessor. That is, for each of these twenty-four topics, more than 90 percent of the disputed judgments were caused by one assessor judging (almost) all of the other assessor's relevant documents as relevant, but also judging substantially more documents as relevant. These additional documents could be considered either marginally relevant (if they were included as relevant in the official judgments) or nearly relevant (if they were not), and they illustrate that the process of drawing the boundary between relevant and nonrelevant varies between users. As shown later in this chapter, however, these boundary documents do not have a large effect when comparing systems using good evaluation measures.

Measures that use a fixed cutoff for all topics may be measuring how well a system retrieves easy-to-retrieve relevant documents for some topics while measuring how well it retrieves boundary documents for others, simply because of the cutoff value. That may be fine for some end-user applications, but it is less useful for system comparisons. The average scores of such measures tend to be dominated by a small number of topics. For example, recall at low cutoffs such as ten is dominated by those topics with few relevant documents, while precision at high cutoffs such as one hundred is dominated by those topics with many relevant documents. Since the average score depends on a relatively few number of topics, its ability to accurately distinguish among systems is reduced.

Measures that evaluate systems at the same comparative point across topics have greater discriminatory power. Not only is the average score more reliable since it depends on more topics, but selecting different comparative points enables systems to be characterized as to their performance. Indeed, this is one of the strengths of the traditional recall-precision graph. Precision is measured after X percent of the relevant documents for a topic have been retrieved, and that number is averaged with all other topics for that same recall point. Systems can then be compared at different recall points to determine, for example, if one system does a better job at retrieving all relevant documents while another system does better at retrieving the first relevant documents very highly for each topic.

The large variance in the number of relevant documents in TREC-1 emphasized the problems with averaging scores for some of the traditional measures like precision(λ).

3.1.4 Changes for TREC-2

The most immediately obvious change to make for the TREC-2 evaluation was to increase the number of retrieved documents from two hundred to one thousand. The number of retrieved documents needs to be much greater than the number of relevant documents for any measure based on high recall to behave properly. Otherwise, the artificiality of the scores for topics that are still retrieving relevant documents when the end of the retrieved set is reached will generally dominate the true performance of the other topics in the averages. At the current levels of performance of IR systems, the number of retrieved documents for a topic should be at least three times greater than the number of relevant documents.

Another change was to add two new measures to address the deficiencies of the TREC-1 measures.

R-Precision Precision (or recall) after R documents have been retrieved, where R is the number of relevant documents for the topic. R-precision measures precision at a comparable point of the retrieval process for every topic. This makes the average R-precision score for a set of topics meaningful unlike averaging precision or recall at fixed document cutoffs. Note that at R retrieved documents, precision and recall are both the same value—namely, the number of relevant retrieved documents divided by the number of relevant documents. R-precision characterizes the complete retrieval for a topic by the performance at this designated single point. Thus, R-precision is a measure of overall system performance. This contrasts with precision(λ), which is much more of an application-oriented evaluation measure (where λ is chosen as appropriate for the application) than a system-oriented measure. Since TREC is a comparative evaluation of systems, precision(λ) is less appropriate.

Trec_eval computes variants of R-precision designed to give a more complete picture of the full retrieval process. In addition to R, multiplicative factors of R such as 0.5 or 2.0 are used. While theoretically useful, in practice the recall-precision graph provides much the same information.

Noninterpolated Average Precision   The precision at each relevant document, averaged over all relevant documents for a topic. If some relevant document is not retrieved, its contribution to the average is 0.0. This measure replaced the eleven-point average both theoretically and functionally. It has become the single measure most often used in IR research to represent the overall effectiveness performance of a system. When averaged over all the topics in a run, the measure is called the mean average precision (MAP).

Average precision has a number of nice properties that contribute to its attractiveness.
1. No thresholds or interpolation are needed.
2. Contributions to the score are consistent with intuitive notions of what is important. A relevant document ranked very highly contributes much more than a relevant document much further down in the ranked list.
3. It is relatively easy to explain.
4. It has a geometric interpretation as the area under the (noninterpolated) recall-precision curve.
5. It is separable. That is, the immediate contribution of each relevant document is known. Thus, average precision is quite useful for failure analysis and tuning systems.
6. It is extremely sensitive. Any change in the rank of a relevant document will result in a change in the score. This is not true of any other measure described so far. Again, this makes it a good measure for the incremental tuning of systems.
7. It has proved to be robust in practice as compared to other measures. MAP differences between systems for one collection tend to imply MAP differences between those systems for other collections.

Average precision also has its own weaknesses:
1. It is an overall system evaluation measure, not an application measure. There is no single user application that directly motivates MAP.
2. Statisticians don't like some aspects, in part because the same relevant document affects the score of all other relevant documents ranked below it (that is, if the document were removed, the precision of the other documents would change).

The addition of R-precision and MAP caused several of the TREC-1 measures to be dropped for TREC-2. The eleven-point and three-point averages were replaced by MAP, and recall at document cutoffs were dropped because of the various problems with it. Precision at document cutoffs were retained even though they are poor system evaluation measures when averaged. One reason for their continued use is that they are appealing user application measures for several applications—for example, P(10) is a good measure for how many relevant documents appear on the first page of a Web search. They also are among the oldest measures: people are comfortable with the measures, flaws and all.

3.1.5 Correlations among Measures

An obvious question with so many different evaluation measures is whether there are differences in the measures with respect to how they rank systems—in other words, whether they measure different things. NIST used the TREC-7 automatic ad hoc results to compute correlations between pairs of measures to investigate this question.

The correlations are given in table 3.1 and were computed in the following way. Each run was evaluated using each measure, where the score for a measure was its average score over the fifty topics (except for the total relevant retrieved measure). The runs were then ranked by score for each measure. The correlation between two different measures was defined as the Kendall's τ correlation between the respective rankings [13]. Kendall's τ computes the distance between two rankings as the minimum number of pairwise adjacent swaps to turn one ranking into the other. The distance is normalized by the number of items being ranked such that two identical rankings produce a correlation of 1.0, the correlation between a ranking and its perfect inverse is −1.0, and the expected correlation of two rankings chosen at random is 0.0.

Several measures shown in the table are not described above. The ".5 prec" measure is the recall obtained by the system when precision first dips below 0.5 and at least ten documents have been retrieved. This measure reflects the heuristic that users will keep looking at a result set while there are more relevant than nonrelevant

Table 3.1
Kendall's τ correlations between pairs of system rankings based on different evaluation measures

	P(30)	R-prec	MAP	.5 prec	R(1,000)	Rel ret	MRR
P(10)	0.88	0.81	0.79	0.78	0.78	0.77	0.77
P(30)		0.87	0.84	0.82	0.80	0.79	0.72
R-prec			0.93	0.87	0.83	0.83	0.67
MAP				0.88	0.85	0.85	0.64
.5 prec					0.77	0.78	0.63
R(1,000)						0.92	0.67
Rel ret							0.66

documents being retrieved. The total number of relevant documents retrieved, abbreviated as "rel ret" in the table, is the sum of the number of relevant documents retrieved across the fifty topics. The difference between this measure and R(1,000) is in the averaging. R(1,000) is averaged such that each topic is weighted equally, while the total number of relevant documents retrieved is dominated by topics that have many relevant documents. The mean reciprocal rank (MRR) is the average of the reciprocal of the rank at which the first relevant document was retrieved.

The correlations between the different measures are all at least 0.6, showing that each pair of measures is correlated. This is not surprising since all the measures were designed to reflect the quality of a retrieval run. The high correlation between R(1,000) and number of relevant documents retrieved is also not surprising, though the fact that the correlation is not 1.0 demonstrates that averaging does have an effect. The weakest correlations are between MRR and each of the others. This is mostly a reflection of the fact that the MRR measure is an unstable measure when used with as few as fifty topics. The measure is unstable because it is based on a single bit of information per topic so small changes in the ranking can cause large differences in the score (retrieving the first relevant document at rank two instead of rank one halves the score).

The highest correlation (0.93) is between R-precision and MAP, a much more surprising finding. R-precision evaluates at exactly one point in a retrieval ranking, while MAP represents the entire area underneath the recall-precision curve. The fact that the two measures rank systems as consistently with one another supports the designation of R-precision as an overall system performance measure. Precision at document level cutoffs do not share this property: the correlation between MAP and P(10) is only 0.79, for example.

One of the current debates in IR is whether recall is important outside a few specific applications such as patent searching. Those who question the utility of recall argue that users never look beyond the "first screen" of results, and therefore the only measure that matters is precision at some small cutoff level. Proponents of recall point out that a measure such as P(10) is too coarse-grained for system tuning, even when P(10) is the final measure of interest. The only change in a document ranking that affects P(10) is a relevant document entering or leaving the top ten, while the mean average precision measure is sensitive to the entire ranking. The correlation between P(10) and the mean average precision cannot answer which is a better measure but does show that they measure different things. (Note, though, that some part of this difference is likely caused by P(10) emphasizing a smaller number of topics in its average; how much of the difference can be attributed to this is unknown.)

3.2   Topic Variability

Test collections contain a set of topics and effectiveness is reported as an average over the set because retrieval system performance is known to vary widely depending on the topic. An analysis of variance model fitted to the TREC-3 results demonstrated that the topic and system effects, as well as the interaction between the topic and the system, were all highly significant, with the topic effect the largest [1]. In other words, retrieval effectiveness depends on the information need, the retrieval mechanism used, and how the retrieval mechanism deals with the topic type. On average, the topic has a bigger effect on effectiveness than the retrieval mechanism used, though different mechanisms work relatively better on different types.

This variability in topic performance has a profound effect on retrieval system evaluation. First, it makes it much more difficult to compare system performance because it is difficult to isolate the relatively small differences in performance that can be attributed to retrieval system differences. In addition, it complicates failure analysis because average effectiveness scores hide an enormous amount of variance. For instance, figure 3.1 shows a plot of precision at standard recall points for an example TREC run. The heavy solid line is the average recall-precision curve over the fifty topics in the test set, while the dotted lines are the curves for fifteen individual topics within the test set.

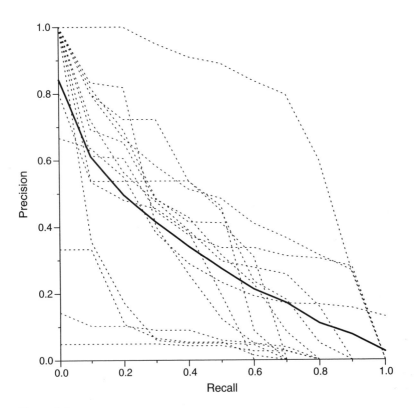

Figure 3.1
Recall-precision curves for individual topics and the average

The large number of different runs using a common collection that have been submitted to TREC provides the opportunity to empirically examine the effect of topic variability on the evaluation methodology. This section looks at two such investigations. The first investigation seeks to determine the minimum number of topics needed in a test set to be confident in the conclusions drawn from using the test collection [17]. The second investigation examines the stability of different evaluation measures [4].

3.2.1   Sensitivity Analysis

Since retrieval system effectiveness depends on the information need, the particular set of topics included in a test collection will influence evaluation results. The set of topics in a test collection is assumed to be a random sample of the universe of possible questions, so there is always some chance that a comparison of two systems using any given test set will lead to the wrong conclusion. The probability of an error can be made arbitrarily small by using arbitrarily many topics, but there are practical limits to the number of topics that can be included in a test collection. We used the runs submitted to TREC to estimate error rates: the likelihood of reaching a wrong conclusion from a single comparison as a function of the number of topics used in the comparison and the size of the difference of the evaluation scores (called Δ). Once established, the error rates can be used to derive the minimum difference in scores required for a certain level of confidence in the results given the number of topics used in the comparison.

The core of the procedure to estimate the error rates is comparing the effectiveness of a pair of runs on two disjoint topic sets of equal size to see if the two sets disagree as to which of the runs is better. The comparisons are repeated for many different pairs of runs and many different topic sets. The error rate is then the percentage of times that the two topic sets disagreed as to which is the better system. Since TREC runs contain fifty topics, this procedure can be used to directly compute error rates for topic set sizes up to twenty-five. By fitting curves to the observed error rates for sets up to twenty-five topics, we can extrapolate to get error rates for larger topic sets. Curves of the form $ErrorRate = A_1 e^{-A_2 S}$ where S is the size of the topic set have a good fit with the observed rates (χ^2 values ≤ 2.18 for all curves).

Figure 3.2 shows the extrapolated error rate curves computed from the TREC results and using MAP as the evaluation measure. Each curve plots the error rate for a different range of Δ values. For example, the solid triangle curve shows the error rate for $0.02 < \Delta \leq 0.03$. As expected, the error rates decrease as the number of topics increases.

As a way of gauging the importance of an experimental result, Sparck Jones proposed that differences in scores of 0.05 were noticeable and differences of 0.1 were material [11]. For topic set sizes of twenty-five, the error rate for a difference of .05 is approximately 13 percent. That is, if we know nothing about systems A and B except their MAP scores, which differ by 0.05, and if we repeat the experiment on a hundred different sets of twenty-five topics, then on average we can expect thirteen out of those hundred sets to favor one system and the remaining eighty-seven to favor the other.

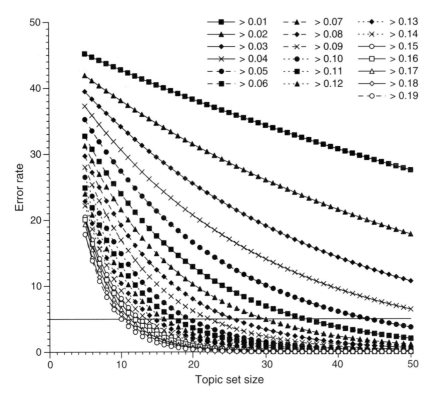

Figure 3.2
Extrapolated error rates for topic set sizes up to fifty topics

The error rate for a difference of 0.1 with twenty-five topics is much smaller at approximately 2.5 percent. The error rates are also much smaller for sets of fifty topics—3.7 and 0.15 percent, respectively. For topic sets of fifty topics, a difference of 0.05 is the smallest Δ with an error rate less than 5 percent (shown as the horizontal line in the figure).

Note that the differences in MAP scores used to compute the error rates are absolute differences, while much of the IR literature reports percentage differences. An absolute difference of 0.1 is a substantial difference, especially when the best MAP scores on the TREC collections are approximately 0.3. The percentage difference between a run with a 0.3 MAP score and a run with a 0.10 absolute difference is approximately 33 percent, and for a 0.05 absolute difference it is approximately 15 percent. These percentage differences are larger than has generally been used within TREC experiments to signify meaningful differences. This suggests researchers need to do a deeper analysis of how systems differ, rather than just compare MAP scores, before drawing conclusions.

3.2.2 Evaluation Measure Stability

Studies of the topic effect on system performance such as the one by David Banks, Paul Over, and Nien-Fan Zhang [1] necessarily conflate the effect of the *expression* of the information need on system performance and the effect of the information need itself since the retrieval results are returned only after the need has been expressed. In TREC, this is the distinction between a *topic*, the information need itself, and a *query*, the data structure given to the retrieval system to represent the information need. The TREC query track was designed to gather the data necessary to separate the topic and query effects on retrieval performance [3]. In particular, the track created a large set of different queries for each of topics 51–100, and also collected the retrieval results for different systems using each of the query variants.

One of the uses that can be made of the query track data is to calculate the error associated with an evaluation measure. Each query allows us to obtain a separate evaluation score for its topic, producing a set of scores for the exact same topic. While using different queries does affect retrieval behavior—some queries are better expressions of the topic than others—the effect of the number of relevant documents on system behavior is controlled because the number of relevant documents remains constant. Controlling this topic effect allows us to isolate the error inherent in the evaluation measure itself.

Let us call a *query set* a collection of fifty queries, one for each topic. Forty-three different query sets were produced over the course of the query track, though the experiment reported here used only the first twenty-one query sets. Each of the twenty-one query sets was run using nine different retrieval methods. This produced a data set consisting of nine sets of the top one thousand documents retrieved for each of 1,050 queries (twenty-one versions of fifty topics).

As in the sensitivity analysis experiment, we compute the error rate for an evaluation measure by comparing the scores obtained by different retrieval methods, but the particulars of how the error rate is defined differ. First, we choose an evaluation measure and a "fuzziness" value. The fuzziness value is the percentage difference between scores such that if the difference is smaller than the fuzziness value, the two scores are deemed equivalent. For example, if the fuzziness value is 5 percent, any scores within 5 percent of one another are counted as equal. We pick a query set and compute the mean of the evaluation measure over that query set for each of the nine retrieval methods. For each pair of retrieval methods, we compare whether the first method is better than, worse than, or equal to the second method with respect to the fuzziness value. We select another query set and repeat the comparison multiple times. This results in a 9×9 triangular matrix giving the number of times each retrieval method was better than, worse than, and equal to each other retrieval method over all query sets.

Because there are thirty-six different pairs of retrieval methods and twenty-one different query sets, there are $36 \times 21 = 756$ decisions regarding the relative effectiveness of the retrieval methods. If for each pair of methods we assume that the correct answer is given by the greater of the better-than and worse-than values, then the lesser of those two values is the number of times a test result is misleading or in error. We define the error rate to be the total number of errors across all method pairs divided by the total number of decisions:

$$Error\ rate = \frac{\sum Min(|A > B|, |B > A|)}{\sum(|A > B| + |A < B| + |A = B|)} \tag{1}$$

where $|A > B|$ is the number of times method A is better than method B for a single pair of methods. Note that the error rate can never be more than 50 percent, and random effects start dominating the calculation of the error rate if it exceeds approximately 25 percent.

The number of times that methods are deemed to be equivalent is also of interest because it reflects on the power of a measure to discriminate among systems. It is possible for a measure to have a low error rate simply because it rarely concludes that two methods are different. The proportion of ties, defined as the total number of equal-to counts across all method pairs divided by the total number of decisions, quantifies this effect.

To increase the reliability of the error rate computations, the error rate for a single measure was computed fifty times. For each of the fifty computations, the queries were randomly permuted among twenty-one new query sets such that each query for a topic was put in a different query set, but different topics used different permutations. Table 3.2 lists the mean error rate over the fifty different sets of permuted query sets for a variety of measures using a fuzziness value of 5 percent and ordered by decreasing error rate. The table also gives the standard deviation of the average error rate and the mean proportion of ties for each measure.

The error rates for the different measures are clearly different. Measures that depend on a relatively few highly ranked documents have higher error rates than

Table 3.2
Average error rate, standard deviation of the average error rate, and average proportion of ties for different evaluation measures using fifty topics and a fuzziness factor of 5%

Measure	Error rate (%)	Standard deviation (%)	Ties (%)
P(1)	14.3	1.3	23.4
P(10)	3.6	0.9	24.3
P(30)	2.9	0.8	23.8
P(100)	1.8	0.5	20.7
MAP	1.5	0.4	12.8
R-precision	1.3	0.4	19.1
P(1,000)	1.0	0.4	22.5
Recall(1,000)	0.6	0.2	20.8

measures that incorporate more documents. The proportion of ties for the various measures also differ substantially. Precision at the various cutoffs fails to distinguish between two systems from 20 to 24 percent of the time, while MAP fails to distinguish about 13 percent of the time.

Comparisons among TREC systems are most often made in terms of MAP, R-precision, or precision at a small document cutoff level such as P(10) or P(30). P(30) is clearly a less powerful measure than MAP: it has both twice the error rate and almost twice the number of ties. Precision at cutoffs less than fifty or so had the highest error rates of any of the measures tested, with smaller cutoffs having larger error rates. Much of this instability is due to the fact that precision does not average well. While R-precision and MAP have similar accuracy levels as one another, R-precision does not have as much discrimination power as MAP.

Of course, the error rate of an evaluation measure is only one of a measure's properties. Since different measures evaluate different aspects of retrieval behavior, it would be foolish to select an evaluation measure based on error rate alone. Instead, the evaluation measure to be used in a retrieval experiment should be selected based on the particular aspect of retrieval behavior that is of interest. Experimenters can increase their confidence in conclusions drawn from measures with relatively higher error rates by using larger topic sets or larger differences between scores before deciding two methods are different.

3.2.3 The Effect of Topic Variability on Retrieval Evaluation

As stated in the introduction to this section, topic variability has a profound effect on retrieval system evaluation because topic effects are generally larger than retrieval system effects. The sensitivity analysis shows that comparatively large differences—larger differences than are usually found between the top retrieval systems in a given TREC— are required to have confidence that a single comparison leads to the correct conclusion, when using fifty topics as is standard for TREC collections. Doesn't this imply that retrieval system evaluation using test collections is pointless? No, for at least two reasons.

First, the primary use of test collections is not cross-system comparison but optimizing the effectiveness of a single system. Experiments with variants of a single system require much smaller absolute differences in scores to yield meaningful results because most of the variance due to system-topic interaction is controlled.

Second, the confidence in a cross-system comparison can be significantly increased by repeating the comparison using multiple collections. Even a small difference that is consistently present in multiple collections is likely to represent a true difference among systems. The fact that it is difficult to distinguish among good systems using a single test explains why TREC does not crown "winners."

3.3 Validating the Cranfield Paradigm

All of the preceding analysis accepted the basic premise of the Cranfield paradigm: that comparing retrieval systems on test collections is a reliable indicator of system effectiveness in operational environments. If this basic premise is not true, the rest does not matter. Chapter 2 already described how the TREC test collections were built and briefly summarized experiments to validate the collections as laboratory tools. This section discusses those experiments in more detail.

The Cranfield paradigm makes a number of simplifying assumptions:

• Judges can assess the relevance of a document from the document's content.
• All relevant documents are equally desirable.
• The relevance of one document is independent of the relevance of any other document.
• The user information need is static.
• A set of topics with corresponding judgment sets is representative of the user population.
• The list of relevant documents for each topic is complete (that is, all relevant documents are known).

While none of the assumptions is strictly true, this does not invalidate the Cranfield paradigm. A test collection is a viable tool provided it reliably ranks better retrieval methods ahead of worse retrieval methods. In other words, the only requirement for a test collection is that it fairly compare two methods.

There are two main issues: inconsistency and incompleteness. Inconsistency refers to the fact that relevance is known to be highly personal. The critics question how valid conclusions can be drawn when the evaluation process is based on something as volatile as relevance [6; 14; 5]. Incompleteness reflects the fact that document collections built through pooling have many documents that were never judged for any given topic. The concern is that systems that retrieve unjudged documents cannot be evaluated fairly because some of those documents might be relevant.

3.3.1 Inconsistency

Inconsistency is the primary criticism of the Cranfield paradigm. Relevance judgments are known to differ across judges and for the same judge at different times [10]. Furthermore, a set of static, binary relevance judgments makes no provision for the fact that a real user's perception of relevance changes as one interacts with the retrieved documents. If the conclusions of a retrieval experiment change as these opinions change, then the test collection abstraction is not reliable.

Tests using the TREC results indicate that the relative performance of retrieval systems is extremely stable despite changes to the relevance judgments [15]. In these tests, the topics in a TREC collection are independently judged by different assessors. Different relevance judgment sets (*qrels*) are produced by randomly choosing which assessor's judgments to use for each topic. Each TREC run is then evaluated using the current qrels set, and the set of runs is ranked by the evaluation score (this is called a *system ranking*). Kendall τ correlations are computed for different system rankings as was done for the test of evaluation measure differences.

Two special qrels sets can be produced from the different judgments. In the union qrels, a document is considered to be relevant to a topic if any assessor judged it relevant to that topic. In the intersection qrels, a document is considered to be relevant to a topic if all three assessors judged it relevant to that topic.

Figure 3.3 shows a plot of MAP scores for the set of TREC-4 runs when evaluated by different qrels. The point plotted as a circle is the average score as computed over 100,000 randomly permuted qrels; the error bars on that point show the minimum and maximum MAP scores within the 100,000 qrels set. The point plotted as a square is the score using the official qrels as published for the TREC-4 collection. The triangle plots the score when using the union qrels, and the diamond plots the score for the intersection qrels. The systems are ordered by the mean score over the 100,000 qrels. The plot shows that the absolute value of the MAP score does change depending on which qrels is used to perform the evaluation. The difference between the minimum

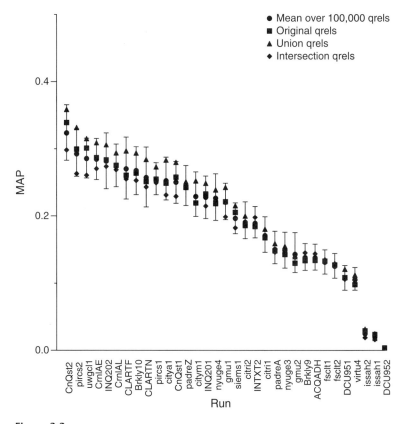

Figure 3.3
MAP scores for TREC-4 runs evaluated using different qrels

Table 3.3
Kendall correlation of system rankings

	Mean	Minimum	Maximum
With official	.9380	.8712	.9962
In subsample	.9382	.8409	.9962

and maximum MAP values is greater than .05 for most systems. The changes are highly correlated across systems, however. That is, if a particular system gets a relatively high score with a particular qrels, then it is quite likely that the other systems will also get a relatively high score with that qrels. The union qrels (the triangle in figure 3.3) is close to the top of the range for each system, for example.

The Kendall τ scores quantify this correlation. Mean correlations among the system rankings produced from the 100,000 qrels were computed in two different ways. In the first case, the mean is the average correlation between the ranking produced by the official qrels and the rankings produced by each of the random 100,000 qrels. In the second case, the mean is the average across all pairs in a random subsample of 1,000 qrels. The mean, minimum, and maximum Kendall correlations for both methods are given in table 3.3.

The correlations are extremely strong. On average it takes only sixteen pairwise, adjacent swaps to turn one ranking into another ranking. The swaps that do occur take place between systems whose MAP scores are close: no swap took place for systems whose MAP scores differed by at least 0.05, the smallest difference sensitivity analysis showed to have an error rate of less than 5 percent when using topic set sizes of fifty topics.

The basic experiment to test the effect of changes to the relevance judgments was repeated for multiple conditions: different kinds of relevance assessors (topic authors versus nonauthors, NIST assessors versus students, group judgments versus single assessor judgments); different test collections; and different evaluation measures. In all cases, the relative performance of the retrieval runs was almost always the same, excepting only those runs whose difference in scores suggests they should be considered equivalent.

3.3.2 Incompleteness

The relevance judgments in early retrieval test collections were complete. That is, a relevance decision was made for every document in the collection for every topic. The size of the TREC document sets makes complete judgments utterly infeasible—with 800,000 documents, it would take over 6,500 hours to judge the entire document set for one topic, assuming each document could be judged in just 30 seconds. Instead, TREC uses pooling to create a subset of the documents to judge for a topic. Unjudged documents are assumed to be not relevant.

The use of pooling to produce a test collection has been questioned because unjudged documents are assumed to be not relevant. Critics argue that evaluation scores for methods that did not contribute to the pools will be deflated relative to methods that did contribute because the noncontributors will have highly ranked unjudged documents.

Justin Zobel demonstrated that the quality of the pools (the number and the diversity of runs contributing to the pools, and the depth to which those runs are judged) does affect the quality of the final collection [18]. He also found that the TREC collections were not biased against unjudged runs. In this test, he evaluated each run that contributed to the pools using both the official set of relevant documents published for that collection and the set of relevant documents produced by removing the relevant documents uniquely retrieved by the run being evaluated. For the TREC-5 ad hoc collection, he found that using the unique relevant documents increased a run's eleven-point average precision score by an average of 0.5 percent. The maximum increase for any run was 3.5 percent. The average increase for the TREC-3 ad hoc collection was somewhat higher at 2.2 percent.

A similar but more stringent test has been applied to the TREC ad hoc collections built since Zobel's investigation. For each run that contributed to the pool, we compute the MAP scores of the run using the standard relevance judgments and the set of relevance judgments produced by removing the relevant documents uniquely retrieved by that run's group (that is, instead of just removing the unique relevant documents contributed by the single run being evaluated, the unique relevant documents contributed by any run submitted by that participant are removed). For the TREC-8 collection, the mean percentage difference in MAP scores over the seventy-one runs that contributed to the pool was 0.78 percent, with a maximum difference of 9.9 percent. Not surprisingly, manual groups that had the largest number of unique relevant documents also had the largest percentage differences in MAP. But given that the manual runs' contributions are in the pool, the difference in evaluation results for automatic runs is negligible. For automatic runs, the largest percentage difference in MAP scores was 3.85 percent, which corresponded to an absolute difference of only .0001. Every automatic run that had a MAP score of at least 0.1 had a percentage difference of less than 1 percent.

Figure 3.4 shows the absolute difference in MAP scores for TREC-8 automatic runs plotted against the number of unique relevant documents contributed by that run's group. The runs are sorted by increasing difference and then by the number of unique relevant documents. The two obvious outliers in the number of unique relevant documents (for runs GE8ATDN1 and iit99au1) reflect organizations that submitted manual runs in addition to automatic runs; the vast majority of their unique relevant documents were contributed by their manual run.

While the lack of any appreciable difference in the scores of submitted runs is not a guarantee that all relevant documents have been found, it is strong evidence that the test collection is reliable for comparative evaluations of retrieval runs. The

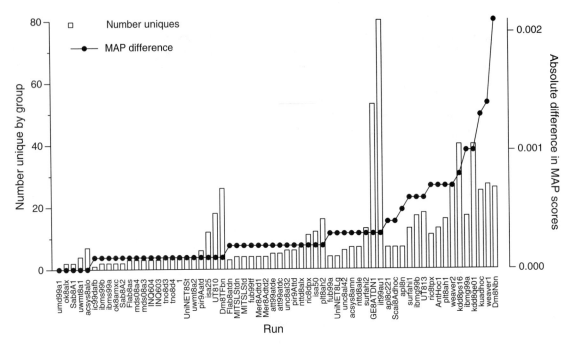

Figure 3.4
Absolute difference in MAP scores when a run is evaluated using relevance pools with and without that group's unique relevant documents. Also plotted is the number of unique relevant documents contributed to the pools by that group

differences in scores resulting from incomplete pools observed in TREC are smaller than the differences that result from using different relevance assessors, which in turn are smaller than using a different topic set.

3.4 Other Retrieval Tasks

Some retrieval tasks do not result in a ranked list of documents returned for a topic. For example, the result for a filtering task is a(n unordered) set of documents, and the result for a question answering task is a set of answer strings. Interactive retrieval, where the task is to evaluate the effect of the user in the loop, must accommodate differences among human searchers.

Defining an appropriate evaluation methodology has been a primary concern of TREC tracks that cannot use the standard methodology developed for ad hoc tasks. The details of the problems and approaches each task faces are provided in the corresponding chapter in part II.

3.5   Conclusion

TREC was founded on the belief that the Cranfield paradigm of using test collections as laboratory tools to compare the effectiveness of different retrieval methods was fundamentally sound, though in need of updating with regard to collection size and standardization of evaluation metrics. Research using TREC results in the intervening years has resoundingly confirmed this belief. TREC has standardized ad hoc retrieval evaluation, validated the reliability of experiments based on test collections, and empirically determined bounds on the sensitivity of test collection comparisons. A focus on evaluation in tracks where the result is not a ranked list of documents has extended the paradigm to new tasks.

Test collections are research tools that provide a means for researchers to explore the relative benefits of different retrieval strategies in a laboratory setting. As such, they are abstractions of an operational retrieval environment. Test collections are useful because they allow researchers to control some of the variables that affect retrieval performance, increasing the power of comparative experiments while drastically decreasing the cost as compared to user-based evaluations. But because the assumptions on which the Cranfield paradigm is based are not strictly true, the evaluation of retrieval systems is a noisy process. The primary consequence of the noise is the fact that evaluation scores computed from a test collection are *relative* scores only. The only valid use for such scores is to compare them to scores computed for other runs using the exact same collection.

A second consequence of the noise is that there is an (unknown) amount of error when comparing two systems on the same collection. There are three interrelated components of the experimental design that can be manipulated to minimize this error: the number of topics used in the comparison, the evaluation measure used to assess retrieval effectiveness, and the size of the difference in the effectiveness score used to decide two runs are different. The number of topics used in a comparison has the biggest effect, though this is often outside the experimenter's control since the test collection will have a given number of topics. Set sizes smaller than twenty-five topics have high error rates. That is, the decision as to which system is better may change simply by changing the topic set even for relatively large differences in evaluation scores. Set sizes of fifty topics, the norm in TREC, also require larger differences between systems than are commonly used to have confidence that the comparison is reliable.

Different evaluation measures measure different aspects of retrieval behavior and have different properties. Precision at small document cutoffs is an intuitively appealing application-oriented measure for some applications, but does not average well, and thus is much less stable than other measures such as MAP. MAP is the preferred measure for system tuning: it is sensitive to the location of all the relevant documents in the document ranking, it is well behaved, and it has good discrimination power.

Increasing the size of the difference between scores used to decide whether two runs are different will increase the reliability of the comparison for all evaluation measures. The cost associated with increasing the difference is that fewer conclusions can be drawn since more techniques will be considered equivalent.

The error rates computed for each of these factors all assumed a single comparison. In practice, IR researchers often use multiple test collections to compare the same techniques, and this is an excellent way to increase the confidence in a conclusion.

References

[1] Banks, D., P. Over, and N.-F. Zhang. Blind men and elephants: Six approaches to TREC data. *Information Retrieval* 1 (1999): 7–34.

[2] Buckley, C. *Implementation of the SMART information retrieval system*. Technical report 85–686. Ithaca, NY: Computer Science Department, Cornell University, May 1985.

[3] Buckley, C. The TREC-9 query track. In *TREC-9*, 81–85, 2001.

[4] Buckley, C., and E. M. Voorhees. Evaluating evaluation measure stability. In *Proceedings of the twenty-third annual international ACM SIGIR conference*, 33–40, 2000.

[5] Cuadra, C. A., and R. V. Katter. Opening the black box of relevance. *Journal of Documentation* 23, no. 4 (1967): 291–303.

[6] Harter, S. P. Variations in relevance assessments and the measurement of retrieval effectiveness. *Journal of the American Society for Information Science* 47, no. 1 (1996): 37–49.

[7] Järvelin, K., and J. Kekäläinen. IR evaluation methods for retrieving highly relevant documents. In *Proceedings of the twenty-third annual international ACM SIGIR conference*, 41–48, 2000.

[8] Merchant, R. H. TIPSTER program overview. In *Proceedings of TIPSTER text program (phase 1)*, ed. R. Merchant, 1–2. San Francisco: Morgan Kaufmann Publishers, September 1993.

[9] Robertson, S. E., and M. M. Hancock-Beaulieu. On the evaluation of IR systems. *Information Processing and Management* 28, no. 4 (1992): 457–466.

[10] Schamber, L. Relevance and information behavior. *Annual Review of Information Science and Technology* 29 (1994): 3–48.

[11] Sparck Jones, K. Automatic indexing. *Journal of Documentation* 30 (1974): 393–432.

[12] Sparck Jones, K., and C. J. van Rijsbergen. Information retrieval test collections. *Journal of Documentation* 32, no. 1 (1976): 59–75.

[13] Stuart, A. Kendall's tau. In vol. 4, *Encyclopedia of statistical sciences*, ed. S. Kotz and N. L. Johnson, 367–369. New York: John Wiley and Sons, 1983.

[14] Taube, M. A note on the pseudomathematics of relevance. *American Documentation* 16, no. 2 (April 1965): 69–72.

[15] Voorhees, E. M. Variations in relevance judgments and the measurement of retrieval effectiveness. *Information Processing and Management* 36 (2000): 697–716.

[16] Voorhees, E. M. Evaluation by highly relevant documents. In *Proceedings of the twenty-fourth annual international ACM SIGIR conference*, 74–82, 2001.

[17] Voorhees, E. M., and C. Buckley. The effect of topic set size on retrieval experiment error. In *Proceedings of the twenty-fifth annual international ACM SIGIR conference*, 316–323, 2002.

[18] Zobel, J. How reliable are the results of large-scale information retrieval experiments? In *Proceedings of the twenty-first annual international ACM SIGIR conference*, 307–314, 1998.

II SELECTED TRACK REPORTS

4 The TREC Ad Hoc Experiments
Donna K. Harman

4.1 Introduction

The ad hoc line of research started with experiments in indexing languages, such as the Cranfield I tests (Cleverdon 1962), and has continued with over forty years of experimentation with the retrieval engines themselves. The Cranfield II studies (Cleverdon, Mills, and Keen 1966) showed that automatic indexing was comparable to manual indexing; this and the availability of computers created a major interest in the automatic indexing and searching of texts. By the 1980s this interest had spread to a large research community, and with more powerful computers and huge amounts of digitized full text, this community was ready to move to much bigger test collections.

With the advent of the new TREC collections (see chapter 2, this volume), research in ad hoc retrieval suddenly became much more interesting. These new collections were not only much larger (by a factor of almost one thousand) but contained the full text for documents as opposed to only the abstracts. The ad hoc task was the first of two tasks tackled in TREC and was run for eight years, representing hundreds of experiments. The graph in figure 4.1 shows that retrieval effectiveness approximately doubled during those eight years. The figure plots retrieval effectiveness for one well-known retrieval engine, the SMART system of Cornell University. The SMART system has consistently been one of the more effective systems in TREC, but other systems are comparable with it, so the graph is representative of the increase in effectiveness for the field as a whole.

Researchers at Cornell ran the version of SMART used in each of the eight TREC conferences against each of the eight ad hoc test sets (Buckley and Walz 2000). Each line in the graph connects the mean average precision scores produced by each version of the system for a single test. For each test, the TREC-8 system has a markedly higher mean average precision than the TREC-1 system. The recent decline in the absolute scores reflects the evolution toward more realistic, and difficult, test questions, and also possibly a dilution of effort because of the many tracks being run in TRECs 5–8 (plus the failure of a new method tried by Cornell in TREC-8).

This chapter highlights some of the experiments run during the eight years of the ad hoc task. It examines some of the trends and analyzes some of the resulting data. Readers are referred in each instance to the papers in the proceedings of each TREC for more details on the experiments, and to later journal or conference papers that provide even more detail and analysis of the individual experiments.

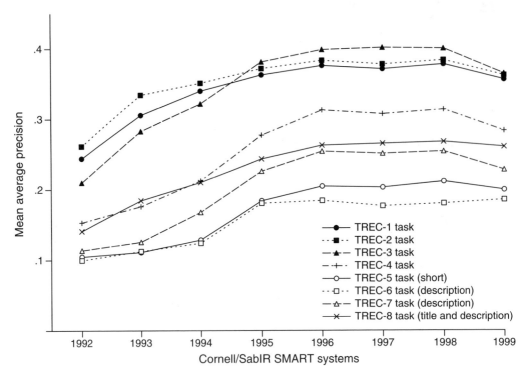

Figure 4.1
Retrieval effectiveness improvement for Cornell's SMART system, TRECs 1–8

4.2 The TREC Ad Hoc Task

The ad hoc task investigates the performance of systems that search a fixed set of documents using new questions (called topics in TREC). This task is similar to how a researcher might use a library—the collection is known, but the questions likely to be asked are not known. Participants were given a document collection consisting of approximately two gigabytes of text and fifty topics for testing purposes. The set of relevant documents for these topics in the document set was not known at the time the participants received the topics. Participants then produced a query set, in a manner consistent with their experimental aims, from the ad hoc topics and ran those queries against the ad hoc documents. The output from this run is the official test result for the ad hoc task.

The production of this query set has been governed by various guidelines, which have changed over successive TRECs.

4.2.1 Task Guidelines

In addition to the task definitions, TREC participants were given a set of guidelines outlining acceptable methods of indexing, knowledge-base construction, and generating queries from the supplied topics. In general, the guidelines were constructed to reflect an actual operational environment and to allow fair comparisons among the diverse query construction approaches.

Initially (TRECs 1–3), there were three allowable query construction methods. The queries could be constructed completely automatically from the topics, with no manual modifications or interventions. Alternatively, the queries could be constructed manually, but then submitted to the system with no further manual intervention. The third method allowed any type of human intervention, such as allowing users to look at individual documents retrieved by the ad hoc queries and then reformulate the queries based on the documents retrieved.

By TREC-4, the retrieval methods had become more sophisticated and it was decided to merge the two manual methods as it was increasingly difficult to separate the two. So the later ad hoc experiments in TREC were separated into only two types: those queries constructed *completely* automatically, and those experiments where there was *any* type of manual involvement.

4.2.2 The Ad Hoc Test Collections

Like most traditional retrieval test collections, there were three distinct parts to the collections used in TREC: the documents, the questions or topics, and the relevance judgments or "right answers." Details of these test collections were given in chapter 2, this volume, but are summarized here.

The English documents, consisting of six disks (only five of which were used in the ad hoc task), came from many different original sources, including the *Wall Street Journal*, the Associated Press, *Computer Selects* documents from Ziff-Davis, the *Federal Register*, abstracts of U.S. Department of Energy publications, the *San Jose Mercury News*, U.S. patents, the *Financial Times*, the *Congressional Record*, the Foreign Broadcast Information Service, and the *Los Angeles Times*. They were distributed on CD-ROMs with approximately one gigabyte of text on each, compressed to fit. There is a range of document lengths from very short (the Department of Energy abstracts) to very long (the *Federal Register*). The documents are in a standard format with unique document numbers.

All topics were designed to mimic a real user's need, and were written by people who are actual users of a retrieval system. The actual topic writers, the topic format, and the method of construction have evolved over time, however. This evolution has had major effects on results, and therefore care should be taken in selecting TREC topic sets for various experimental purposes. Table 4.1 shows which disks and topic numbers are associated with each TREC.

Since TREC-3, the ad hoc topics have been created by the same person (assessor) who performed the relevance assessments for that topic. Each assessor came to NIST with ideas for topics based on their own interests, and searched the ad hoc collection

Table 4.1
Document and topic sets for the first eight TRECs

TREC	Task	Documents	Topics
TREC-1	ad hoc	disks 1 and 2	51–100
TREC-2	ad hoc	disks 1 and 2	101–150
TREC-3	ad hoc	disks 1 and 2	151–200
TREC-4	ad hoc	disks 2 and 3	201–250
TREC-5	ad hoc	disks 2 and 4	251–300
TREC-6	ad hoc	disks 4 and 5	301–350
TREC-7	ad hoc	disks 4 and 5	351–400
TREC-8	ad hoc	disks 4 and 5	401–450

(looking at approximately a hundred documents per topic) to estimate the likely number of relevant documents per candidate topic. NIST personnel selected the final fifty topics from among these candidates.

The relevance assessments were made by a pooling method.

• For each topic within a set of results, the top X-ranked documents were selected for input to the pool.
• These results were merged across all systems and sorted by document numbers, and duplicate documents were then removed.

The merged list of results was then shown to the human assessors, with each topic being judged by a single assessor to ensure the best consistency of judgments. The topics had around one hundred relevant documents each, although there is a wide variation across topics.

4.2.3 Evaluation
An important element of TREC is to provide a common evaluation for the systems. TREC reports a variety of recall- and precision-based evaluation measures for each run to give a broad picture of the run. A standard evaluation package, called trec_eval, has been used to evaluate each of the submitted runs. For more information on TREC evaluation, see chapter 3, this volume.

4.3 The Ad Hoc Results

The basic TREC ad hoc paradigm has presented three major challenges to search engine technology from the beginning. The first was the vast scale-up in terms of the number of documents to be searched, from several megabytes to two gigabytes of documents. This system engineering problem occupied most systems in TREC-1, and has continued to be the initial work for most new groups entering TREC. The second challenge was that these documents are mostly full-text and thus much longer than most algorithms in TREC-1 were designed to handle. The document-length issue has resulted in major changes to the basic term-weighting algorithms, starting in TREC-2. The third challenge has been the idea that a test question or topic contains multiple fields, each representing either facets of a user's question or the various lengths of text that question could be represented in. The particular fields, and the lengths of these fields, have changed across the various TRECs, resulting in different research issues as the basic environment has changed.

4.3.1   TREC-1

Because TREC-1 required significant system rebuilding by most participating groups due to the huge increase in the size of the document collection, the TREC-1 results should be viewed as only preliminary due to severe time constraints. A second reason these results are preliminary is that groups were working blindly as to what constitutes a relevant document. There were no reliable relevance judgments for training and the use of the long topics was completely new. Groups often had to make primitive adjustments to their basic algorithms in order to get results, with little evidence of how well these adjustments were working.

Despite all this, thirty-three sets of results were submitted for judgment; thirteen of these used a smaller subset of the data (25 percent), but the rest used the full data set (all two gigabytes). Of these twenty groups, thirteen used an automatic construction of queries and seven used some type of manual involvement. One of the interesting results of TREC-1 was that there was little performance difference between the automatic and manual systems, with most topics showing equal performance in terms of both overall average precision and the percentage of relevant documents retrieved by rank one hundred. This was encouraging for the automatic system builders, and probably occurred because the TREC topics were long, complex, and often difficult to express manually.

4.3.2   TREC-2

TREC-2 occurred in August 1993, less than ten months after the first conference, and the TREC-2 results can be seen as both a validation of the earlier experiments on the smaller test collections of the 1980s and an excellent baseline for the more complex experimentation that has taken part in later TRECs. There were forty-four sets of results, with thirty-eight of them based on the full data set. Of these, twenty-four used an automatic construction of queries, with fourteen using some type of manual construction.

It should not be surprising that the top systems were all "veterans." The INQUERY system, from the University of Massachusetts at Amherst (Croft, Callan, and Broglio 1994), was not only well established in 1993 but used a probabilistic inference net to combine various topic and document features. This allowed it to easily adjust to the long topics and documents being used in TREC. Three of the other systems were all based on the Cornell SMART system (another long-established system)

(Buckley, Allan, and Salton 1994). SMART itself had long been able to handle longer documents as it both normalized for length and used term-frequency information from within each document. Two variations of this system were built on top of the publicly distributed SMART system. One, from the University of California, Berkeley (Cooper, Chen, and Gey 1994), developed a completely new weighting scheme by performing logistic regression analysis to learn optimal weighting for various term-frequency measures. The other, from the University of Dortmund (Fuhr et al. 1994), used polynomial regression to find weights for various preset term features. The fifth top automatic system was from the CLARIT Corporation (Evans and Lefferts 1994), which expanded each topic with noun phrases found in a thesaurus that is automatically generated for each topic.

The systems that used manual query construction tried many different things. Three of them simply manually modified their automatic queries, either modifying the terms (based on a strict rule set) or reweighting them. In general, this modification did not improve results. One group from Virginia Tech (Fox and Shaw 1994) tried merging results from automatic queries and manually constructed Boolean queries. Two companies, ConQuest Software (Nelson 1994) and Verity (Lehman and Reid 1994), submitted completely manually built queries. These results once again did not beat the automatically generated results.

By TREC-2, however, it was becoming obvious that the topics being used were quite rich. In particular, they contained a "concepts" field that was providing excellent keywords for the automatic systems. This field was removed for TREC-3, and as a consequence the automatic systems no longer had results better than the manual systems.

4.4   Trends in Later TRECs

Table 4.2 summarizes the ad hoc task across TRECs 2–7. It illustrates some of the common issues that have affected all groups, and also shows the initial use and subsequent spread of some of the now-standard techniques that have emerged from TREC.

The rest of this chapter is organized around these themes in order to show progress across the TRECs rather than simply report work in each TREC. Five different research areas are shown in the table, with research in many of these areas triggered by changes in the TREC evaluation environment. For example, the use of subdocuments or passages was caused by the initial difficulties in handling full text documents, particularly excessively long ones. The use of better term weighting, including correct length normalization procedures, made this technique less used in TREC-4 and TREC-5, but it resurfaced in TREC-6 to facilitate better input to relevance feedback.

4.4.1   Term Weighting
The first research area shown in table 4.2 is that of term weighting. Most of the initial participants in TREC used term weighting that had been developed and tested on very small test collections with short documents (abstracts). Many of these algorithms were modified to handle longer documents in simple ways; however, some algorithms were

Table 4.2
Use of new techniques in the ad hoc task

	TREC-2	TREC-3	TREC-4	TREC-5	TREC-6	TREC-7
Term weighting	Baseline for most systems Beginning of Okapi weighting experiments	Okapi perfects BM25 algorithm	New weighting algorithms in SMART, INQUERY, and PIRCS systems	Use of Okapi/SMART weighting algorithms by other groups	Adaptations of Okapi/SMART algorithms in most systems	New retrieval models by TNO and BBN
Passages	Use of sub-documents by PIRCS system	Heavy use of passages/subdocuments	Decline in use of passages	Decline in use of passages	Use of passages in relevance feedback	Multiple uses of passages
Automatic query expansion		Beginning of expansion using top X documents	Heavy use of expansion using top X documents	Beginning of more complex expansion schemes	More sophisticated expansion experiments by many groups	
Manual query modification		Beginning of manual expansion using other sources	Major experiments in manual editing, user-in-the-loop	Extensive user-in-the-loop experiments	Simpler user-specific strategies tested	
Other new areas		Initial use of "data fusion"		Start of more concentration on initial topic	More complex use of data fusion Continued focus on initial topic, especially the title	

not amenable to this approach, resulting in some new fundamental research. The group from the Okapi system, City University, London (Robertson and Walker 1994), decided to experiment with a completely new term-weighting algorithm that was both theoretically and practically based on term distribution within longer documents. By TREC-3, this algorithm had been "perfected" into the BM25 algorithm in use by many of the systems in TRECs 5–7. Continuing along this same row in table 4.2, three other systems (the SMART system from Cornell [Singhal, Buckley, and Mitra 1996], the PIRCS system from the City University of New York [Kwok 1996], and the INQUERY system from the University of Massachusetts [Allan et al. 1996]) changed their weighting algorithms in TREC-4 based on analysis comparing their old algorithms to the new BM25 algorithm. By TREC-5, many of the groups had adopted these new weighting algorithms, with the early adopters being those systems with similar structural models.

TREC-6 saw even further expansion of the use of these new weighting algorithms (alternatively called the Okapi/SMART algorithm, or the Cornell implementation of the Okapi algorithm). In particular, many groups adapted these algorithms to new models, often involving considerable experimentation to find the correct fit. For example, IRIT (Boughanem and Soulé-Dupuy 1998) modified the Okapi algorithm to fit a spreading activation model, IBM (Brown and Chong 1998) modified it to deal with unigrams and trigrams, and the Australian National University (Hawking, Thistlewaite, and Craswell 1998) and the University of Waterloo (Cormack 1998) used it in conjunction with various types of proximity measures. Of major note is the fact that the City University, London, also ran major experiments (Walker et al. 1998) with the BM25 weighting algorithm in TREC-6, including the extensive exploration of the various existing parameters, and the addition of some new ones involving the use of nonrelevant documents.

It could be expected that six years of term-weighting experiments would lead to a convergence of the algorithms. Yet a snapshot of the top eight systems in TREC-7 (see table 4.3) shows that these systems are derived from many models, and use different term-weighting algorithms and similarity measures. Of particular interest here is that new models and term-weighting algorithms are still being developed, and that these are competitive with the more established methods. This applies both to new variations on old weighting algorithms, such as the double-log term-frequency weighting from AT&T (Singhal et al. 1999), and to more major variations, such as the two new language modeling algorithms from TNO (Hiemstra and Kraaij 1999) and BBN (Miller, Leek, and Schwartz 1999). Note that the column in table 4.3 labeled "Phrase improvement." shows improvements from the use of phrases and is discussed in section 4.4.6.

4.4.2 Subdocuments and Passages
The second new technique started back in TREC-2 (the second line of table 4.2) was the use of smaller sections of documents, called subdocuments or passages, by the PIRCS system at the City University of New York (Kwok and Grunfeld 1994). Again, this issue

Table 4.3
Models and term weighting in TREC-7

Organization	Model	Weighting/ similarity	Phrase improvement	Comments
Okapi group	Probabilistic	BM25	minimal*	*Last reported in TREC-5
AT&T Labs Research	Vector	Pivot*		*Byte normalization
INQUERY group	Inference net	Belief function	3.6%	
RMIT/UM/CSIRO	Vector	BM25/cosine		Phrases used
BBN	HMM	Probabilistic	2%	Bigram phrases
Twenty-One	Vector	New probabilistic		No phrases used
CUNY	Spreading activation	Avtf/RSV	2%	Phrases used for reranking
Cornell/SabIR	Vector	Pivot		

was forced by the difficulty of using the PIRCS spreading activation model for documents having a wide variety of lengths. By TREC-3, many of the groups were also using passages to help with retrieval. But as mentioned before, TREC-4 and TREC-5 saw far less use of this technique as many groups dropped the use of passages due to minimal added improvements in performance.

TREC-6 saw a revival in the use of passages, but generally only for specific uses. Whereas the PIRCS system continued to use 550-word subdocuments for all its processing, most systems used passages only in the topic expansion phase. The Australian National University (Hawking, Thistlewaite, and Craswell 1998) worked with "hot spots" of five hundred characters surrounding the original topic terms to locate new expansion terms. AT&T (Singhal 1998) used overlapping windows of fifty words to help rerank the top fifty documents before selecting the final documents for use in expansion. The University of Waterloo (Cormack et al. 1998) used passages of a maximum length of sixty-four words to select expansion terms, whereas Verity (Pedersen, Silverstein, and Vogt 1998) used its automatic summarizer for this purpose. Two groups, Lexis-Nexis (Lu et al. 1998) and RMIT (Fuller et al. 1998), performed major experiments in the use of passages, particularly when employed in conjunction with other methods as input to data fusion. This diverse use of passages continued in TREC-7, with passages clearly becoming one of the standard tools for experimentation.

4.4.3 Query Expansion

The query expansion/modification techniques shown in the third and fourth lines of table 4.2 were started when the topics were substantially shortened in TREC-3. As described earlier in chapter 2, the format of the topics was modified to remove a valuable source of keywords: the concept section. In the search for some technique that would automatically expand the topic, several groups revived an old technique of assuming that the top retrieved documents are relevant, and then using them in relevance feedback. This technique, which had not worked on smaller collections, turned out to work quite well in the TREC environment.

By TREC-6, almost all groups were using variations on expanding queries utilizing information from the top retrieved documents (often called *pseudorelevance feedback* or *blind feedback*). There are many parameters needed for success here, such as how many top documents to use for mining terms, how many terms to select, and how to weight those terms. There has been general convergence on some of these parameters. Table 4.4 shows the characteristics of the expansion tools used in the top eight systems in TREC-7. The second column gives the basic expansion model, with the vector-based systems using the Rocchio expansion and other systems using expansion models more suitable to their retrieval model. For example, the local context analysis (LCA) method developed by the INQUERY group (Xu and Croft 1996) has been successfully used by other groups. The third column shows the number of top-ranked documents used (P if passages used), and the number of terms added from these documents. It should be noted that these numbers are more similar than in earlier TRECs, although they are still being investigated by new systems adopting these techniques

Table 4.4
Characterization of query expansion used in best automatic ad hoc TREC-7 runs

Organization	Expansion/ feedback	Top documents/ terms added	Disks used	Comments
Okapi group	Probabilistic	Full—15/30 T + D—10/30 T only—6/20 + title	1–5	
AT&T Labs Research	Rocchio	10/20 + 5 phrases	1–5	Conservative enrichment
INQUERY group	LCA	30P/50	1–5	Reranking using title terms before expansion
RMIT/UM/CSIRO	Rocchio	10/40 + 5 phrases	Unknown	Additional experiments with passages
BBN	HMM-based	6/unknown	Unknown	Differential weighting on topic parts
Twenty-One	Rocchio	3/200	Unknown	
CUNY	LCA	200P/unknown	1–5	
Cornell/SabIR	Rocchio	30/25	4–5	Clustering, reranking

as there can be subtle differences between systems that strongly influence parameter selection. The fourth column shows the source of the documents being mined for terms, which has generally moved to the use of as much information as possible—that is, all the TREC disks as opposed to only those being used for testing purposes or even use of non-TREC documents such as those from the Web.

TRECs 5–7 saw many additional experiments in the query expansion area. The Open Text Corporation (Fitzpatrick and Dent 1997) gathered terms for expansion by looking at relevant documents from past topics that were loosely similar to the TREC-5 topics. Several groups (Lu, Ayoub, and Dong 1997; Namba et al. 1999) have tried clustering the top retrieved documents in order to more accurately select expansion terms, and in TREC-6 three groups (the City University London, AT&T, and IRIT) successfully got information from negative feedback—that is, using nonrelevant documents to modify the expansion process.

TREC-7 contained even more experiments in automatic query expansion, such as the group (Mandala et al. 1999) that compared the use of three different thesauri for expansion (WordNet, a simple co-occurrence thesaurus, and an automatically built thesaurus using predicate-argument structures). Of particular note is the AT&T (Singhal et al. 1999) investigation into "conservative enrichment" to avoid the additional noise caused by using larger corpora (all five disks) for query expansion.

4.4.4 Manual Experimentation

Groups that build their queries manually also looked into better query expansion techniques starting in TREC-3 (see the fourth line of table 4.2). At first, these expansions involved using other sources to manually expand the initial query. The rules governing manual query building changed in TREC-5, however, to allow unrestricted interactions with the systems. This change caused a major evolution in the manual query expansion, with most systems not only manually expanding the initial queries but then looking at retrieved documents in order to further expand the queries, much in the manner that users of these systems could operate. Two types of experiments were notable in TREC-5: those that could be labeled as "manual exploration" runs, and those that involved a more complex type of human-machine interaction. The first type is exemplified by the General Electric group (Strzalkowski et al. 1997), where the group's task was to ask users to pick out phrases and sentences from the retrieved documents to add to the query, in hopes that this process could be imitated by automatic methods. The CLARITECH group's project (Milic-Frayling et al. 1997) is a good example of the second type of manual TREC-5 runs. This group examined a multistage process of query construction, where the goal was to investigate better sets of tools that allow users to improve their queries, including different sources for suggestions of expansion terms and also various levels of user-added constraints to the expansion process.

Many of the manual experiments seen in both TREC-6 and TREC-7, however, hark back to the simpler scenario of having users either edit the automatically generated query or select documents to be used in automatic relevance feedback. Several of the groups had specific user strategies that they tested.

• The General Electric Corporate R&D/Rutgers University (Strzalkowski, Lin, and Perez-Carballo 1998) teams used automatically generated summaries of the top thirty documents retrieved as sources of manually selected terms and phrases.
• The CLARITECH Corporation (Evans et al. 1999) performed a user experiment measuring the difference in performance between two presentation modes: a ranked list versus a clustered set of documents.
• The University of Toronto (Bodner and Chignell 1999) group used its dynamic hypertext model to build the queries.
• Lexis-Nexis (Rao et al. 1999) experimented with human relevance feedback as opposed to automatic feedback from the top twenty documents.

4.4.5   Data Fusion

The final line in table 4.2 shows some of the other areas that have seen concentrated research in the ad hoc task. Data fusion has been used in TREC by many groups in various ways, but it has increased in complexity over the years. For example, a project involving four teams led by Tomek Strzalkowski has continued the investigation of merging results from multiple streams of input using different indexing methods (Strzalkowski et al. 1997, 1999; Strzalkowski, Lin, and Perez-Carballo 1998). In TREC-6, several groups such as Lexis-Nexis (Lu et al. 1998) and MDS (Fuller et al. 1998) used multiple stages of data fusion, including merging results from different term-weighting schemes, various mixtures of documents and passages, and different query expansion schemes.

The INQUERY system from the University of Massachusetts has worked in all TRECs to automatically build more structure into their queries, based on information they have "mined" from the topics (Brown 1995). Starting in TREC-5, there have been experiments by other groups to use more information from the initial topic. Lexis-Nexis (Lu, Ayoub, and Dong 1997) used the interterm distance between nouns in the topic. Several other groups have made use of term-proximity features (the Australian National University [Hawking, Thistlewaite, and Bailey 1997], the University of Waterloo [Clarke and Cormack 1997], and IBM [Chan, Garcia, and Roukos 1997]) to improve retrieval scores, while others (the City University of New York [Kwok and Grunfeld 1997], AT&T [Singhal 1998], and INQUERY [Allan et al. 1999]) have used the initial topic to look for clues that would suggest a need for more emphasis on certain topic terms. TREC-7 had two additional groups working with the use of term co-occurrence and proximity as alternative methods for ranking (see Braschler et al. 1999; Nakajima et al. 1999).

4.4.6   The Use of Phrases

A final theme that has continued throughout all the TRECs has been the investigation of the use of phrases in addition to single terms. This has long been a topic for research in the information retrieval community, with generally unsuccessful results. Initially, however, there was hope that the use of phrases in these much larger collections would become critical, and almost all groups have experimented with phrases. In general, these experiments have been equally unsuccessful. It is important to note that TREC is defined as a high-recall task; the use of phrases in a high-precision task involving huge amounts of data such as Web searching has been more successful.

The fourth column of table 4.3 shows the widespread use of phrases in addition to single terms in TREC-7, but the minimal improvement from their use. The biggest improvement reported in the papers was 3.6 percent from the INQUERY group at the University of Massachusetts (Allan et al. 1999). Whereas most of the other groups are also using phrases, many did not bother to test for differences due to the minimal results in earlier years. Cornell/SabIR reported a 7.7 percent improvement in TREC-6, but this is the improvement on top of the initial baseline, not the improvement after expansion. Private conversations with several of these groups indicate that these improvements are likely to be much less if measured after expansion. As is often the case, these minimal changes in the averages cover a wide variation in phrase performance across topics. A special run by the Okapi group showed less than a 1 percent average difference in performance, but nineteen topics helped by phrases, fourteen hurt, and the rest unchanged. Whereas the benefit of phrases is not proven, phrases are likely to remain a permanent tool in the retrieval systems in a manner similar to the earlier adoption of stemming.

It is interesting to note that many of these groups are using different phrase "gathering" techniques. The Okapi group has a manually built phrase list with synonym classes that has slowly grown over the years based on mostly past TREC topics. The automatically produced INQUERY phrase list was new for TREC-6 (Allan et al. 1998), the Cornell list was basically unchanged from early TRECs (where it had been created using the co-occurrence of terms), and the BBN list was based on a new bigram model.

4.4.7 The Effects of Topic Length

The creation of two formal topic lengths in TREC-5 has inspired many experiments comparing results using those different topic lengths, and the addition of a formal "title" in TREC-6 increased these investigations. Table 4.5 lists the results (official and unofficial as reported in the papers) of the top eight TREC-7 groups showing their use of different topic parts. The second column gives the various topic parts used by each group (T = title, D = description, and N = narrative). The third column gives the average precision using only the description and the title. The fourth and fifth columns give the corresponding performance of the systems using either only the title or the full topic (all topic parts).

Note that most of the best runs use the full topic. Yet there is a smaller performance difference between runs that use the full topic and those that use only the title and description sections than was seen in earlier TRECs. This is most likely due to improved query expansion methods, but could be due to variations across topic sets as well. The improvement going to the full topic is only 1 percent for several groups; the decrease in performance using only the title is more marked, ranging from 4 to 22 percent. The TREC-7 title results should be a truer measure of the effects of using the

Table 4.5
TREC-7 performance using variations in topic length

Organization	Topic parts	D + T	T only	Full topic	Comments
Okapi group	T,D,N	0.281	0.253 (−10%)	0.284 (1%)	fused run—0.296
AT&T Labs Research	T,D	0.296	0.249 (−16%)		
INQUERY group	T,D,N	0.252		0.274 (9%)	title-filtered run—0.282
RMIT/UM/CSIRO	T,D	0.281	0.220 (−22%)	0.285 (1%)	
BBN	T,D,N			0.280	
Twenty-One	T,D,N			0.279	
CUNY	T,D,N	0.254	0.243 (−4%)	0.266 (5%)	with phrases—0.272
Cornell/SabIR	T,D,N	0.254*	0.239 (−6%)	0.267 (5%)	*description only

Table 4.6
Number of TREC-7 topics performing best by topic length

	Long	Description only	Title
Okapi	28	13	9
CUNY	27	10	13
Cornell	22	17	11

title only than TREC-6, where the descriptions were often missing key terms. Still, it is not clear how representative these titles are with respect to very short user inputs, and therefore title results should best be viewed as how well these systems could perform on extremely short, but extremely good user input.

Looking at individual topic results shows a less consistent picture. Table 4.6 shows the number of topics that had the best performance from among a group's three runs using different input lengths. Not only is there a wide variation across topics, there is also a wide variation across systems in that topics that work best at a particular length for one group, did not necessarily work best at that length for the other groups.

4.5   Conclusions and the Future of Ad Hoc in TREC

The TREC ad hoc track ran for eight years, producing hundreds of runs and allowing veteran groups like Cornell, the University of Massachusetts at Amherst, the City University, London, and Queens College, CUNY, to engage in major experiments with their algorithms on realistically sized test collections. Equally important, it allowed many groups new to information retrieval to build their own systems. By TREC-8, there were forty-one groups doing the ad hoc task. Many were small groups from universities, but several large companies had also joined.

The ad hoc track also generated eight large test collections, which were all made publicly available. These have become the collections of choice for many experiments outside of TREC, both in terms of companies using them for developing new systems and in terms of universities performing continual experiments with them.

The wide range of experiments tackled across the years in the ad hoc task provide a rich store of ideas. Many of these ideas were picked up by other groups and have become part of the accepted information retrieval set of algorithms. Others either were not successful enough or were simply not used by others and have been forgotten. As new efforts start up in the ad hoc area, either at TREC or individual sites, these ideas should be retested and analyzed.

A final note about the ad hoc task is that it allowed the community to validate and extend the Cranfield paradigm started in the late 1960s. The extensions necessary to the paradigm, such as the use of pooling and the modified metrics, worked well. The very large document collection, containing full documents rather than just abstracts, enabled groups to verify that algorithms generally scaled up to this challenge, and to better understand where to modify them if necessary. The wide range of document lengths ensured that the new algorithms were insensitive to document length. The large number of relevant documents per topic allowed ideas that had not worked in the past (such as pseudorelevance feedback) to be retested in a more realistic environment. The consistently sized versions of the topics led to investigations into how topic (request) length affects results and, in particular, how to best expand very short topics.

Following TREC-7, a decision was made by the TREC program committee to run the ad hoc task only one more year in order to build a final test collection with 150 topics using the same topic set. It was generally felt that there was no further point in running the task because the community was not learning much compared to the effort needed to run the task. Much of the problem came from using averages across fifty topics; as with many issues in the past, certain techniques work for some topics but not for others. More work needs to be done on customizing methods for each topic, and this work needs be taken up in later TRECs.

References

Allan, J., L. Ballesteros, J. Callan, B. Croft, and Z. Lu. 1996. Recent experiments with INQUERY. In *TREC-4*, 49–63.

Allan, J., J. Callan, W. B. Croft, L. Ballesteros, D. Byrd, R. Swan, and J. Xu. 1998. INQUERY does battle with TREC-6. In *TREC-6*, 169–206.

Allan, J., J. Callan, M. Sanderson, J. Xu, and S. Wegmann. 1999. INQUERY and TREC-7. In *TREC-7*, 201–216.

Bodner, R., and M. Chignell. 1999. ClickIR: Text retrieval using a dynamic hypertext interface. In *TREC-7*, 573–582.

Boughanem, M., and C. Soulé-Dupuy. 1998. Mercure at TREC-6. In *TREC-6*, 321–328.

Braschler, M., M. Wechsler, B. Mateev, E. Mittendorf, and P. Schäuble. 1999. SPIDER retrieval system at TREC-7. In *TREC-7*, 509–518.

Brown, E. 1995. Fast evaluation of structured queries for information retrieval. In *Proceedings of the eighteenth annual international ACM SIGIR conference*, 30–38.

Brown, E. W., and H. A. Chong. 1998. The GURU system in TREC-6. In *TREC-6*, 535–540.

Buckley, C., J. Allan, and G. Salton. 1994. Automatic routing and ad-hoc retrieval using SMART: TREC-2. In *TREC-2*, 45–56.

Buckley, C., and J. Walz. 2000. SMART at TREC-8. In *TREC-8*, 577–582.

Chan, E., S. Garcia, and S. Roukos. 1997. TREC-5 ad-hoc retrieval using K nearest-neighbors re-scoring. In *TREC-5*, 415–426.

Clarke, C. L., and G. V. Cormack. 1997. Interactive substring retrieval (MultiText experiments for TREC-5). In *TREC-5*, 267–278.

Cleverdon, C. 1962. *Report on the testing and analysis of an investigation into the comparative efficiency of indexing systems*. Cranfield, UK: Cranfield Research Project.

Cleverdon, C., J. Mills, and E. Keen. 1966. *Factors determining the performance of indexing systems, vol. 1: Design, vol. 2: Test results*. Cranfield, UK: Aslib Cranfield Research Project.

Cooper, W., A. Chen, and F. Gey. 1994. Full text retrieval based on probabilistic equations with coefficients fitted by logistic regression. In *TREC-2*, 57–66.

Cormack, G. V., C. L. Clarke, C. R. Palmer, and S. S. L. To. 1998. Passage-based refinement (MultiText) experiments for TREC-6. In *TREC-6*, 303–319.

Croft, W., J. Callan, and J. Broglio. 1994. TREC-2 routing and ad-hoc retrieval evaluation using the INQUERY system. In *TREC-2*, 75–84.

Evans, D., A. Huettner, X. Tong, P. Jansen, and J. Bennett. 1999. Effectiveness of clustering in ad hoc retrieval. In *TREC-7*, 143–148.

Evans, D., and R. Lefferts. 1994. Design and evaluation of the CLARIT-TREC-2 system. In *TREC-2*, 137–150.

Fitzpatrick, L., and M. Dent. 1997. Automatic feedback using past queries: Social searching? In *Proceedings of the twentieth annual international ACM SIGIR conference*, 306–313.

Fox, E. 1983. *Characteristics of two new experimental collections in computer and information science containing textual and bibliographic concepts*. Technical report TR 83–561. Ithaca, NY: Computing Science Department, Cornell University.

Fox, E., and J. Shaw. 1994. Combination of multiple searches. In *TREC-2*, 243–252.

Fuhr, N., U. Pfeifer, C. Bremkamp, and M. Pollmann. 1994. Probabilistic learning approaches for indexing and retrieval with the TREC-2 collection. In *TREC-2*, 67–76.

Fuller, M., M. Kaszkiel, C. L. Ng, P. Vines, R. Wilkinson, and J. Zobel. 1998. MDS TREC-6 report. In *TREC-6*, 241–257.

Hawking, D., P. Thistlewaite, and P. Bailey. 1997. ANU/ACSys TREC-5 experiments. In *TREC-5*, 359–376.

Hawking, D., P. Thistlewaite, and N. Craswell. 1998. ANU/ACSys TREC-6 experiments. In *TREC-6*, 275–290.

Hiemstra, D., and W. Kraaij. 1999. Twenty-One at TREC-7: Ad-hoc and cross-language track. In *TREC-7*, 227–238.

Kwok, K. 1996. A new method of weighting query terms. In *Proceedings of the nineteenth annual international ACM SIGIR conference*, 187–196.

Kwok, K., and L. Grunfeld. 1994. TREC-2 document retrieval experiments using PIRCS. In *TREC-2*, 233–242.

Kwok, K., and L. Grunfeld. 1997. TREC-5 English and Chinese retrieval experiments using PIRCS. In *TREC-5*, 133–142.

Lehman, J., and C. Reid. 1994. Knowledge-based searching with TOPIC. In *TREC-2*, 209–222.

Lu, A., M. Ayoub, and J. Dong. 1997. Ad hoc experiments using EUREKA. In *TREC-5*, 229–240.

Lu, A., E. Meier, A. Rao, D. Miller, and D. Pliske. 1998. Query processing in TREC-6. In *TREC-6*, 567–576.

Mandala, R., T. Tokunaga, H. Tanaka, A. Okumura, and K. Satoh. 1999. Ad hoc retrieval experiments using WordNet and automatically constructed thesauri. In *TREC-7*, 475–480.

Milic-Frayling, N., D. Evans, X. Tong, and C. Zhai. 1997. CLARIT compound queries and constraint-controlled feedback in TREC-5. In *TREC-5*, 315–334.

Miller, D., T. Leek, and R. Schwartz. 1999. A hidden Markov model information retrieval system. In *Proceedings of the twenty-second annual international ACM SIGIR conference*, 214–221.

Nakajima, H., T. Takaki, T. Hirao, and A. Kitauchi. 1999. NTT DATA at TREC-7: System approach for ad hoc and filtering. In *TREC-7*, 481–490.

Namba, I., N. Igata, H. Horai, K. Nitta, and K. Matsui. 1999. Fujitsu Laboratories TREC-7 report. In *TREC-7*, 383–392.

Nelson, P. 1994. The ConQuest system. In *TREC-2*, 265–270.

Pedersen, J. O., C. Silverstein, and C. C. Vogt. 1998. Verity at TREC-6: Out-of-the-box and beyond. In *TREC-6*, 259–273.

Rao, A., T. Humphrey, A. Parhizgar, C. Wilson, and D. Pliske. 1999. Experiments in query processing at Lexis-Nexis for TREC-7. In *TREC-7*, 451–460.

Robertson, S., and S. Walker. 1994. Some simple effective approximations to the 2-poisson model for probabilistic weighted retrieval. In *Proceedings of the seventeenth annual international ACM SIGIR conference*, 232–241.

Singhal, A. 1998. AT&T at TREC-6. In *TREC-6*, 215–225.

Singhal, A., C. Buckley, and M. Mitra. 1996. Pivoted document length normalization. In *Proceedings of the nineteenth annual international ACM SIGIR conference*, 21–29.

Singhal, A., J. Choi, D. Hindle, D. Lewis, and F. Pereira. 1999. AT&T at TREC-7. In *TREC-7*, 239–252.

Strzalkowski, T., F. Lin, and J. Perez-Carballo. 1998. Natural language information retrieval: TREC-6 report. In *TREC-6*, 347–366.

Strzalkowski, T., F. Lin, J. Wang, L. Guthrie, J. Leistensnider, J. Wilding, J. Karlgren, T. Straszheim, and J. Perez-Carballo. 1997. Natural language information retrieval: TREC-5 report. In *TREC-5*, 291–314.

Strzalkowski, T., G. Stein, G. B. Wise, J. Perez-Carballo, P. Tapananinen, T. Jarvinen, A. Voutilainen, and J. Karlgren. 1999. Natural language information retrieval: TREC-7 report. In *TREC-7*, 217–226.

Vaswani, P., and J. Cameron. 1970. *The national physical laboratory experiments in statistical word associations and their use in document indexing and retrieval.* Publication 42. Teddington, UK: Division of Computer Science, National Physical Laboratory.

Walker, S., S. Robertson, M. Boughanem, G. Jones, and K. Sparck Jones. 1998. Okapi at TREC-6: Automatic ad hoc, VLC, routing, filtering, and QSDR. In *TREC-6*, 125–136.

Xu, J., and W. Croft. 1996. Query expansion using local and global document analysis. In *Proceedings of the nineteenth annual international ACM SIGIR conference*, 4–11.

5 Routing and Filtering
Stephen Robertson and Jamie Callan

5.1 Introduction

During the first eleven years of TREC, the routing and filtering tracks studied online, time-critical, text-filtering applications, where the value of a document decays rapidly with time. Routing and filtering were the only tasks to be studied every year, in one form or another, during this period. This chapter attempts an overview of this eleven-year history.

5.2 Overview of Filtering at TREC

A text-filtering system sifts through a stream of incoming information to find documents relevant to a set of user needs represented by "profiles." Filtering differs from the traditional ad hoc or retrospective search in that documents arrive sequentially over time. This means that potentially relevant documents must be presented immediately to the user. There is no time to accumulate and rank a set of documents. On the other hand, user profiles are persistent, and tend to reflect a long-term information need. With feedback from the user, the system can learn a better profile and improve its performance over time.

In this chapter, as generally in the filtering literature, we use the word *profile* to refer to all of the information the system has acquired about a specific information need, and the system's current operational specification of the information need (for instance, a conventional query and a dissemination threshold). When we say that profiles are persistent, we mean that a person may remain interested (have the same need for information) for some (long) period of time; for example, the authors have tracked the information-filtering literature for many years. A single person may have many profiles, each representing a different interest or information need.

To some extent, the routing/filtering tasks can be seen as similar to the task of text categorization, and like that task, susceptible to approaches taken from machine learning. This is particularly appropriate to the degree that routing and filtering use feedback (documents identified by the user as relevant). There are also some significant differences between routing/filtering and text categorization, however. Some of the issues are discussed toward the end of this chapter.

5.2.1 Initial Description
This section provides a brief overview of the various tasks covered in this chapter. It may also be read as a history of the TREC effort in this area.

The routing task, which was one of the two core tasks from the very beginning of TREC and remained a subtask in the final TREC filtering track, takes a simple view of the filtering situation as described above. In effect, the simulation is located at a particular, fixed point in time, with some history (the training set) and some future incoming documents (the test set); one can see it as a form of text categorization. The history includes some original text form of the topic, together with all available relevance judgments on the training set documents. These relevance judgments are generally assumed to be more or less complete, although in practice they were made (only) on all those documents retrieved for this topic by any system in some previous TREC experiment. The test involves representing each topic as a profile, improving or optimizing this profile by making use of the relevance judgments on the training set, and running it against the complete test set of documents. In fact, despite the above comment about ranking, evaluation of this routing task has relied on the usual ranked-output-based measures of retrieval performance on the complete test set.

A filtering track was introduced at TREC-4. Between TREC-4 and TREC-6, the task was a nonadaptive form of filtering, but from TREC-7 on, routing ceased to be a core task and became part of the filtering track, and the range of tasks was expanded. The primary task was adaptive filtering, which attempted a more realistic simulation of the real filtering situation. In this task, after some initialization stage (discussed in more detail below), the passage of time is simulated by processing a test set of documents in date order. For each profile and each document, a binary decision is taken by the system: to refer the document to the user (the owner of the profile) or not. When a document is referred to the user, the user is assumed to provide (instantly) a relevance judgment. A document not referred to the user is assumed to be unjudged as far as the system is concerned, though not of course for the eventual evaluation of the system. No backtracking or revisiting of rejected documents is allowed. Nevertheless, the system can make use of any kind of information derived from previously processed documents—for example, in modifying a profile for new documents.

This time-based simulation is clearly more realistic than the routing task, though equally clearly it has several oversimplifications or unrealistic assumptions. The one that stands out most is the assumption of instant feedback, and perhaps also the assumption of no backtracking and batching of documents or ranking of small sets. One could perfectly well imagine a situation, at least for some document streams and/ or user groups, where the system maintains a ranked list of the documents matched over, say, the past week, which might be modified during feedback, with the user potentially providing feedback at any time or not at all. The complications of simulating such a situation, however, are considerable; the TREC filtering assumptions combine the advantages of relative simplicity and implementability in a laboratory with some reasonable degree of realism.

Another oversimplification is that the user's interest remains the same over the period. We might imagine that even if the user identifies a continuing need, any aspect of the user's view, perception, or understanding of the need may drift over time. Although drift is an important issue, it greatly complicates the evaluation methodology and so is usually ignored in filtering research (although see Allan 1996). TREC participants were allowed to design systems that modeled any drift present in topic vocabulary or relevance assessments during the filtering period, though the design of the TREC filtering tasks did not explicitly attempt to simulate such drift.

Yet the filtering tasks do introduce, in contrast to the routing task, one substantial complication: the need to evaluate on the basis of binary retrieval decisions rather than ranking. This matter is discussed further below.

5.2.2 TREC Reports

The history and development of the TREC routing and filtering tasks can be traced by reading the yearly final reports: TREC 2002 (Robertson and Soboroff 2003), TREC 2001 (Robertson and Soboroff 2002), TREC-9 (Robertson and Hull 2001), TREC-8 (Hull and Robertson 2000), TREC-7 (Hull 1999), TREC-6 (routing: Voorhees and Harman 1998; filtering: Hull 1998), TREC-5 (routing: Voorhees and Harman 1997; filtering: Lewis 1997), TREC-4 (routing: Harman 1996; filtering: Lewis 1996), TREC-3 (routing only: Harman 1995), TREC-2 (routing only: Harman 1994), and TREC-1 (routing only: Harman 1993).

In addition, in every TREC proceedings, the participants make their own reports of their experiments.

In the sections that follow, we describe the various data sets and tasks as defined for the different TRECs.

5.3 Data

The particular set of documents and topics used is not central to this discussion, but it is useful to give a brief description as a basis for the task definitions. More detail is given about the data sets used most recently.

5.3.1 TREC-1

The first TREC did not have the advantage of a history of collection building behind it. Only two TREC tasks were defined—ad hoc and routing. The document collection, about 740,000 documents altogether, was divided into training and testing subsets (for example, the test subset was about 230,000 documents), and similarly there were two sets of topics, fifty in each set. For routing, the fifty training topics were used. It was necessary to have some relevance data for the training process, so the NIST assessors who constructed the training topics also did searches on the training set of documents, using whatever internal systems they could, to identify as many as possible of the relevant documents. It was clear that the resulting sets of relevant documents were by no means complete, but it served to both start the collection-building process and encourage participants to work further on routing methods. Also, despite the time-based conception of the task, the training and test documents covered a diverse set of sources and date ranges.

5.3.2   TREC-2 to TREC-5

After the initialization of TREC-1, the pattern for the next few rounds was that each year a new document collection and a new set of fifty ad hoc topics were added to the set. The previous year's fifty ad hoc topics were used as routing topics in the current round. The relevance judgments made for the previous year's ad hoc task provided the training material for routing. Since these relevance judgments had been made on the pooled output of the ad hoc searches from all participating systems, they could be assumed to be sufficiently complete.

We began to depart from this model with TREC-4 and TREC-5. In these two rounds, document collections were added specifically for the routing test. In both cases, topics had to be selected from the accumulated topics previously used at TREC, to fit with the new collections. Several new problems arose—for example, with topics that turned out to have few relevant documents in the test set.

In TREC-2 and TREC-3, the training collection of documents was the entire 740,000 document collection from TREC-1, with an additional set of 335,000 documents—the same both years—for testing. In TREC-4, the training set was 570,000 documents taken from parts of the old collection, and testing was 330,000 documents, a mixture of old and new data from different sources. In TREC-5, training was 525,000 mixed documents, while testing was, for the first time, a single-source collection of 130,000 Foreign Broadcast Information Service documents.

5.3.3   TREC-6

To allow for the changing definition of the filtering task, a specific source (the Foreign Broadcast Information Service) was chosen for the documents—the existing Foreign Broadcast collection from TREC-5, 130,000 documents, from 1993 and 1994, was used for training, and a new Foreign Broadcast collection, 120,000 from 1994 and 1995, was obtained for testing. The filtering task now required time-stamped documents—a requirement partially satisfied by the Foreign Broadcast collections (unfortunately, the time-division between training and test data was not clean). Most of the fifty topics were old TREC topics with existing relevance judgments on the training data; however, some new topics were added, which required assessors to do their own searches in the training data to provide training material, resulting in a somewhat limited set of judgments for those topics.

5.3.4   TREC-7

Again, a specific source was chosen for the filtering track, the Associated Press newswire data from 1988 to 1990, consisting of about 240,000 documents, which had been included in earlier TREC collections. For routing and batch filtering, the 1988 data, about 80,000 documents, was used for training, and the rest for test. The adaptive-filtering task had no training data; the entire Associated Press collection was the test set. The topics were the first fifty TREC topics, as used for the routing task in TREC-1—which had relevance judgments of different degrees of completeness on different parts of the document set.

5.3.5 TREC-8

The TREC-8 filtering experiments used the *Financial Times* document collection, again from an earlier test collection, which consists of slightly more than three years of newspaper articles covering part of 1991 and most of 1992–1994. The 210,000 documents were ordered roughly as a function of time, and all systems were required to process the documents in the same order. All tasks used TREC topics 351–400, which were constructed for the TREC-7 ad hoc experiments. Relevance judgments were available from TREC-7; however, a small number of additional documents, which had not been judged for TREC-7 but were retrieved by participants in the TREC-8 filtering track, were judged for TREC-8.

The training-test split was similar to TREC-7: for the main adaptive-filtering task, the entire *Financial Times* collection was the test set, but for batch filtering and routing, the 1992 data, about 65,000 documents, was treated as a training set and the remainder as the test set.

5.3.6 TREC-9

The TREC-9 filtering experiments went outside the usual TREC collections and used the OHSUMED test collection compiled by, and available from, William Hersh (Hersh et al. 1994). This consists of Medline documents from the years 1987–1991 as well as a set of requests (topics) and relevance judgments. A slightly modified version of this data set was put together for the task.

The entire collection contains about 350,000 documents. Actually, these are bibliographic records containing the usual fields including abstract, although only about two-thirds of the records contain abstracts; there were no full texts. They also have a field containing MeSH headings—that is, human-assigned index terms from the Medical Subject Headings thesaurus. These are assumed to arrive in identifier order, at a rate of approximately 6,000 documents per month. The 1987 data, equivalent to about nine months' worth, was extracted from the data set to provide training material, as discussed below; the test set is therefore the 1988–1991 data. Sixty-three of the original OHSUMED topics—those with a minimum of two definitely relevant documents in the training set—were selected.[1] These sixty-three topics form the OHSU set.

An additional set of topics was constructed from the MeSH headings described above. Each MeSH heading was assumed to represent a topic: the text of the topic was taken from the scope notes available for MeSH headings, and assignments of headings to documents were regarded as relevance judgments. Again, they were selected to have a minimum of four relevant documents in the training set and at least one in the final year; also, rare and frequent headings were excluded.[2] The remaining 4,903 MeSH headings formed the MSH topic set. Finally, because of the size of this topic set—

which made it difficult for some research systems to process it in its entirety—a random sample of five hundred of these was made, to form the MSH-SMP set.

The MeSH field of the records could not be used for the MSH or MSH-SMP topic sets since they contain headings representing the topics directly.

5.3.7 TREC 2001

For the second time, a source outside the usual TREC documents was sought for the TREC 2001 filtering track. This was the then newly available Reuters corpus, volume 1 (Reuters n.d.), made available to the research community by Reuters. It consists of about 800,000 Reuters newswire reports, or all of the regular English-language Reuters wires for a year (August 20, 1996 to August 19, 1997). The documents from August 1996 (twelve days, 23,000 documents) were taken as the training set.

No TREC-style topics or relevance judgments were available for this corpus; instead, the subject codes assigned by Reuters to the stories were used as filtering topics (rather like the MeSH headings used in TREC-9). The assignments of codes to the documents were taken as the relevance judgments so it could be assumed that the relevance judgments were more or less complete. Codes were selected according to their occurrence in the training set: they had to have at least two documents, but no more than 5 percent of the training set, and this gave eighty-four topics. The text of each topic was taken from the code label, generally a short phrase.

5.3.8 TREC 2002

The same Reuters documents were used, but with a different set of topics and a different training/test split, for TREC 2002. A new set of fifty TREC-style topics was constructed for the TREC 2002 filtering track, by the usual processes involving NIST assessors; in addition, the assessors conducted an extensive series of searches to establish an adequate base of relevant documents for each topic. These searches were made using a variety of different systems, and multiple searches were made on each system, incorporating relevance feedback based on relevant documents identified by the assessors from earlier searches. A further set of fifty topics was constructed from the conjunction of pairs of Reuters subject codes. Any document assigned both codes was taken as relevant. Documents from August and September 1996 (about 84,000) were taken as the training set, and the remainder (about 720,000) were taken as the test set.

5.4 Relevance Judgments

As can be seen from the above discussion of data sets, the availability of relevance judgments was a major issue for routing and filtering tasks.

A characteristic of the methods described is that they make use of data sets where the relevance judgments have already been made. In the early TREC routing experiments, it was possible to work with a data set in which judgments had been made on the training set, but not on the test set; these last could be made after the participants had submitted their runs to NIST as part of the evaluation stage. This method does raise the issue that an assessor may be judging new documents for relevance to a given topic long after that topic was first formulated or the original assessments were made. (Unfortunately, we cannot use this fact to simulate user drift since the time distribution of the documents has no correspondence at all to the dates on which the assessments were made.) Such assessor drift may well have reduced the reliability of the judgments.

In any case, this is no longer a possible scenario for adaptive filtering (see below), where the system is expected to modify the profile on the fly as documents are retrieved and judged for relevance. Such an experiment requires "canned" relevance judgments to be available.

In the usual TREC style, relevance judgments for each topic have been made in past TRECs on the pooled output of a number of searches. Attempts have been made to ensure that a wide range of different systems are represented, to maximize the chance that most relevant documents have been found, but of course some relevant documents will have been missed. It may well be that the routing or filtering searches throw up documents that were not originally judged because of not appearing in any output in the original pooled searches.

For the TREC-8 experiment, some of the newly retrieved documents for each topic were judged for relevance. This process did indeed throw up a small number of previously unknown relevant documents, which were then treated as relevant for evaluation purposes. The process was not repeated in TREC-9 because of a lack of resources at NIST and because there were no suitable judges available for the medical topics; it would in any case have been out of the question to attempt such judgments on the topics based on MeSH headings. This may be seen as a limitation of this form of experiment. In TREC 2001, the assignment of subject codes by Reuters staff was assumed to be complete, and no further judgments were made; however, it might have been interesting to attempt some further judgments for at least some topics. Nevertheless, a major problem with Reuters subject codes for this purpose was that they were in general quite broad—sometimes assigned to thousands of documents in the test set. In TREC 2002, for the first set of topics (conventional TREC topics constructed by assessors), further relevance judgments were made on some unjudged documents retrieved by the various systems. The second set of topics (constructed from intersections of Reuters categories) turned out to be problematic. (For a fuller discussion of the methods used in building the TREC 2002 collection, see Soboroff and Robertson 2003.)

5.4.1 Pools and Samples

Another issue that arises here is the choice of documents to judge. In the ad hoc task, the usual procedure was to pool, say, the top one hundred ranked documents from each submitted search; this is obviously an efficient procedure for finding many relevant documents without a huge judgment task. When filtering systems produce unranked document sets of arbitrary size, this issue is much less easy to resolve. In the early runs of the filtering track, much effort went into developing methods for sampling and pooling the output (Lewis 1996).

The problem actually has two components:

• Providing a fair evaluation of the performance of each system
• Contributing to a pool of relevance judgments that may be used for other experiments

One way to deal with the first problem is to sample the output of each system, make relevance judgments on the sample, and then estimate the performance of that system only from the items sampled from it. (Of course, in practice one would pool the various samples for relevance assessment, but each system would be evaluated only on the basis of its sample.) Some measures of performance—for example, linear utility as defined below—can in principle be estimated in an unbiased fashion from sampling; what is more, strong statements can be made about confidence limits for the true value. Other performance measures, essentially those that depend on recall, cannot be estimated in this way.

An alternative is to treat the pooled output in a similar way to that used for the TREC ad hoc assessments—that is, to use all documents in the pool to evaluate any system and to assume that any document not in the pool is not relevant. In the case of sampled output from filtering, though, this will normally give a lower bound on effectiveness rather than an unbiased value.

The experience suggests that on the whole, the unbiased sample estimates and the lower-bound pool estimates are not usually too far apart. Yet it is clear that the pool estimates are improved by a good pool, which should ideally be built from the output of traditional ranking systems as well as filtering systems. In general in TREC, the parallel routing experiments on the same data have indeed meant that this condition is satisfied.

5.5 Tasks

Careful decisions need to be made about what data can be made available to a system, for whatever purpose, at any stage in the process. Clearly, no system should see any aspect of the "future" documents before they are processed; therefore, for example, the test documents should not be used to set initial idf-based weights. These must be based on some other collection. Nor could anything relating to the test topics be used, except as precisely specified.

The descriptions that follow combine a current view of the task with some historical notes on its development. The order in which the tasks are discussed takes the most realistic task first; in effect, they are taken in the reverse order in which they were introduced into TREC, where the starting point was the somewhat unrealistic task of routing, which was modified in stages into the present adaptive filtering task.

5.5.1 Adaptive Filtering with Positive Examples

The adaptive-filtering task is designed to model the text-filtering process from the moment of profile construction, with at least moderately realistic restrictions on the use of relevance information. This version of the adaptive-filtering task was first introduced in TREC-9.

It is assumed that the user arrives with a small number of known positive examples (relevant documents). Thus, for the adaptive-filtering task, the initial specification of the profile consists of a text topic and the specified number of positive examples: two, three, or four, depending on the year and topic set, usually chosen in some random or arbitrary way from the known relevant documents in the training set. This is an attempt at representing a realistic possible starting point—we assume that a user might initiate a filtering profile by providing a text description and also a small number of examples of what that user would like the system to provide. These examples might come from the user's knowledge of the field and/or from an ad hoc search on a retrospective document collection. It may be argued that a random choice of positive examples does not simulate this situation well, in that items known to or found by the user are probably highly correlated with any text description of the topic that the user provides. This issue has not been addressed in the TREC track.

Subsequently, once a document is retrieved, the relevance assessment (when one exists) is immediately made available to the system. Judgments for unretrieved documents are never revealed to the system. Once the system makes a decision about whether or not to retrieve a document, that decision is final. No backtracking or temporary caching of documents is allowed.

Evaluation is based on set retrieval, discussed below.

5.5.2 Adaptive Filtering, Text Topic Only

This version of the task, which ran from TREC-6 to TREC-8, is similar to the task just described, except that the only information available at the start is the text topic, with no positive examples. In all other respects, though, the specification of the task is the same as above.

Evaluation is based on set retrieval, discussed below.

5.5.3 Batch-Adaptive Filtering

In this task, introduced in TREC-6 with the first version of adaptive filtering, the initialization of the profile is allowed to use the complete relevance judgments for that topic from some training set of documents. In TREC-8, this was the 1992 *Financial Times* collection; in TREC-9, it was the 1987 OHSUMED collection. When searching the test set (1993–1994 *Financial Times* or 1988–1991 OHSUMED), the same rules applied as for adaptive filtering: the relevance judgment on any document retrieved for a topic could be used to modify the profile for matching against future documents. The task was abandoned after TREC-9.

This task is considered to be realistic in its adaptive setup, but somewhat unrealistic in respect to the initial data, which included more or less complete relevance judgments on the training set. Some participants have made it a little more realistic by restricting themselves to using those relevant documents in the training set that would have been retrieved by an initial search in, say, the top one hundred ranked documents.

Evaluation is based on set retrieval, discussed below.

5.5.4 Batch Filtering (nonadaptive)

A batch-filtering task was first introduced at TREC-4. At this point, the basic model was still one of optimizing profiles at a single time point, with no explicit timeline over the future documents. Thus no adaptation was considered. Initialization was the same as for batch-adaptive filtering for TREC-8 and TREC-9. In TREC 2001, the August 1996 Reuters documents were used for training, and in TREC 2002, those from August and September 1996. The only difference between batch filtering and routing was that for filtering, the output was assumed to be an unranked set of documents: the system function was seen as a binary decision on each document rather than a ranking operation.

This task represents a minimal implementation of the realistic requirement that a filtering system should make a yes/no retrieval decision on each arriving document. The initialization is unrealistic for batch adaptive filtering. The lack of adaptation, however, may be more realistic for some user environments—expecting a substantial volume of relevance feedback from the user might be seen as unrealistic.

Evaluation is again based on set retrieval.

5.5.5 Routing

This task is still seen essentially as it was defined for TREC-1: to devise optimal profiles for each topic, based on some accumulated history and applied to some future test set. The search part was treated exactly as the ad hoc task in that the output was expected to be a ranked list, with no absolute cutoff or threshold.

In the present view, initialization is the same as for batch and batch-adaptive filtering. Yet the complete test set is searched in one go, the output is ranked, and the top one thousand documents are returned for evaluation. Evaluation is based on the measures used for TREC ad hoc tasks, as implemented in the trec_eval package, such as mean average precision, R-precision (the precision when the number of documents retrieved is equal to the number relevant in the collection), and precision at n documents for various n. Thus, no threshold or other mechanism for binary retrieval is required, and no adaptation is possible.

The ability to optimize a profile based on some extensive training data is seen as a valid objective—informative about the nature of information retrieval, but not necessarily as a realistic representation of any real-world task. (Though as indicated above, there may be some environments in which limited batching and ranking rather than a yes/no decision on each document is a plausible scenario.) Together with the batch-filtering tasks, it remains of interest to some TREC participants, and has continued to generate useful results.

5.5.6 Recap

Hence, the distribution of tasks over eleven TRECs was as follows:

TREC	1	2	3	4	5	6	7	8	9	10	11
Routing	m	m	m	m	m	m	t	t	t	t	t
Batch (nonadaptive)	—	—	—	—	t	t	t	t	t	t	t
Batch adaptive	—	—	—	—	—	t	t	t	t	—	—
Adaptive (no initial positives)	—	—	—	—	—	t	t	t	—	—	—
Adaptive (with initial positives)	—	—	—	—	—	—	—	—	t	t	t

m = main task; t = track

In general, the object has been to improve the realism of the tasks over successive TRECs. Still, the earlier and less realistic tasks have continued to be of interest to some TREC participants. Decisions on which tasks to include each year reflect this fact, but also the fact that too many tasks tends to dilute the participant effort applied to each one, while increasing the effort required centrally to run the track. Note also that different evaluation measures generate different tasks, as discussed in the next section, and different topic sets, as in TREC-9 (see above), have the same effect. Thus, the total number of tasks defined in the routing/filtering category has been considerably in excess of the twenty-eight identified in the above table.

5.6 Evaluation Measures

As discussed, filtering systems are expected to make a binary decision to accept or reject a document for each profile. Therefore, the retrieved set consists of an unranked list of documents. This fact has implications for evaluation in that it demands a measure of effectiveness that can be applied to such an unranked set. Many of the standard measures used in the evaluation of ranked retrieval, such as average precision or precision at a fixed document cutoff, are not applicable.

Furthermore, the choice of evaluation measure has strong implications for the system itself, specifically in the area of thresholding. This matter is discussed further in section 5.7.1, but it has the consequence that for each task, a specific single measure of performance, the primary measure, must be identified in advance. Systems are then likely to be tuned to that measure, and a submitted run will therefore expect to be evaluated according to the measure for which it is tuned. The usual practice in TREC, particularly in the ad hoc task, of always evaluating runs on an entire portfolio of measures is not applicable in the same way to filtering. Also, the obvious traditional measures of recall and precision, although designed for set retrieval rather than ranked retrieval, do not serve this purpose because they must be taken as a pair.

Nevertheless, it is often useful and informative—for instance, for diagnostic reasons—to present various other evaluation measures for any run. Thus, TREC filtering runs tend to be reported using the primary measure for which each run was optimized and a small number of additional measures.

Through most of the TREC filtering experiments, the main primary measures of performance have been based on the concept of utility. In TREC-9, a different measure, described as precision oriented, was introduced in addition to utility. In TREC-10 and TREC-11, the precision-oriented measure was dropped, but a version of the F measure commonly used in text categorization was added.

In this section, the notation is taken from the following table of outcomes from a set-retrieval process:

	Relevant	Not relevant
Retrieved	R^+	N^+
Not retrieved	R^-	N^-
Total	R	N

5.6.1 Utility

Utility measures essentially assume that the desirable outcomes of a binary retrieval decision may be given credits that accumulate in some fashion, while the undesirable outcomes are given corresponding debits, which count against the credits. A fuller discussion of utility measures can be found in the various reports of the TREC filtering track or Robertson 2002b.

Most TREC evaluations have been based on *linear* utility, and the TREC linear utility measures have all taken the form

$$\text{Utility} = AR^+ + BN^+ \tag{1}$$

with positive A and negative B. The exact values of A and B have varied from year to year (some years more than one pair of values was used), but for example the measure used in TRECs 9–11 had $A = 2$ and $B = -1$. Any linear utility measure can be equated to defining a minimum probability of relevance—in other words, optimizing linear utility is equivalent to a retrieval rule that states that a document should be retrieved if and only if its probability of relevance exceeds a certain threshold. If the utility measure is defined by equation (1), the rule is

$$\text{retrieve if } P(\text{document relevant}) > \frac{-B}{A - B},$$

which gives a threshold probability of 33 percent for TRECs 9–11.

For TREC-8, we experimented with a *nonlinear* utility measure. The idea is that successive relevant documents retrieved lose value—later documents (after many have already been retrieved) are of less value than earlier ones. This is achieved by raising R^+ to a fractional power in equation (1). The nonlinear measure was thought to be difficult to interpret, however, and was abandoned for later TRECs.

One problem with a utility measure is that for any given topic it has a maximum (AR where R is the total relevant), but it can go negative and is effectively unbounded below. This has some consequences for averaging. In particular, a straightforward mean of utility across topics can easily be dominated by an especially poor performance on a single topic. In earlier TRECs, no average was calculated—systems were compared on the basis of counting topics for which each system did well. From TREC-7 on, various attempts were made to average utilities fairly. A somewhat complex scheme was tried in TREC-8 in which utilities for each topic were scaled between the maximum and some notional minimum, which could be varied. A much simpler method was used in TREC-9: large negative utilities were simply truncated to some minimum value. In fact, many of the systems were sufficiently well adapted and successfully avoided large negative utilities; for all the top-scoring systems, this truncation rule was never activated. TREC 2001 reverted to the TREC-8 scheme, and TREC 2002 modified it somewhat, following a suggestion by, Tom Ault and Yiming Yang (2002).

Yet it remains the case that mean utility is a somewhat tricky concept. This is seen as a disadvantage of the utility measure.

5.6.2 Precision-Oriented Measure

One particular issue that emerged with the use of the utility measure was the baseline. By definition, a system that retrieves nothing gets zero utility (under equation [1]). In some TREC filtering experiments, even the best systems have failed to reach an average utility above zero—in other words, under this measure they perform worse than a system that retrieves nothing. This issue is discussed further in section 5.7.2 below.

The precision-oriented measure, used in TREC-9, was an attempt to address this problem directly. The basic idea behind this measure is that the user may set a target number of documents to be retrieved over the period of the simulation. This situation might be said to correspond roughly with cases where the user indicates what sort of volume of material they expect, are prepared for, are able to deal with, and/or would like to see. In TREC-9, a fixed target was used: fifty documents over the test period. Clearly, a fixed target is a simplification of such cases, each of which is a little different from the others, but may be seen as an acceptable simplification for experimental purposes.

The measure is essentially precision, but with a penalty for not reaching the target:

$$\text{Target precision} = \frac{R^+}{\max(\text{Target}, (R^+ + N^+))} \tag{2}$$

This may be regarded as something akin to a "precision at (target) documents" measure. It provided some opportunity for comparisons between filtering and ad hoc retrieval performance (Robertson 2002a). It was not used again after TREC-9, however.

5.6.3 The FBeta Measure

Filtering with a binary decision rule may be compared to categorization, a task that has been extensively studied (each filtering topic must be regarded as a single, self-contained categorization task—for this topic, documents must be categorized as relevant or not, independently of any other topics). One of the measures commonly used in text-categorization evaluation is the F1 measure, which is based on Keith van Rijsbergen's E measure of retrieval performance, a single-figure combination of recall and precision. The E measure has a balancing parameter β that determines the balance of recall and precision; in the F1 measure, this parameter is set to one, which in effect puts equal weight on recall and precision.

It was decided for TREC 2001 to introduce this measure as an alternative to utility. Nevertheless, the filtering requirement is generally assumed to be fairly high precision, so the beta parameter was set to reflect this. The formula is

$$\text{FBeta} = \frac{(1+\beta)R^+}{\beta R^- + N^+ + (1+\beta)R^+},$$ \hfill (3)

with $\beta = 0.25$.

5.6.4 Additional Measures

As indicated above, and for reasons discussed further in the next section, each filtering task at each TREC had one specific performance measure as the target measure—that is, systems were expected to be optimized against this one measure, which would serve as the primary measure for evaluation. A number of other measures are normally calculated, though, particularly the usual recall and precision:

$$\text{Recall} = \frac{R^+}{R^+ + R^-}$$

$$\text{Precision} = \frac{R^+}{R^+ + N^+}$$

Routing is normally evaluated in the same way as ad hoc retrieval, using the trec_eval program: measures include the usual average precision, R-precision, precision at n documents retrieved, and so forth.

5.7 Some Issues Arising in Filtering

5.7.1 Thresholding and Optimization

In traditional ranked retrieval for an ad hoc task, as mentioned above, a range of measures are commonly used, particularly those evaluated by the trec_eval program used in the TREC experiments. These measures include precision at fixed document cutoffs (five, ten, twenty, ... documents), precision at fixed recall levels (10 percent, 20 percent, 30 percent, ... recall), various forms of uninterpolated or interpolated average precision, R-precision (precision at the point at which the number of documents retrieved equals the number relevant for this topic), and so on. It is of course possible to tune an ad hoc retrieval system to give good results on a specific measure; in general, however, it appears that ranking systems are relatively robust across these measures. Some measures appear more stable than others (Buckley and Voorhees 2000; chapter 3, this volume), but a system that is tuned to perform well on one of the more stable measures is likely to perform well on all the other measures in the list above.

This is not at all the case for the set-based filtering measures. Tuning of a filtering system has to be closely based on the specific measure it is intended to optimize. Thus, typically a filtering system should know the measure under which it will be evaluated, and the methods for both initializing a profile and adapting it to feedback need to be explicitly aimed at this measure.

The necessity for this measure-specific tuning is perhaps most in evidence in filtering systems that are based on traditional ranked-retrieval systems. In such a system, the profile would typically consist of a traditional query formulation—for example, terms and weights—to be used in a traditional matching method, resulting in a score for each document—together with a nontraditional threshold. This threshold would be used to turn the document score into a binary decision: a document whose score exceeds the threshold is retrieved and any other is rejected for this profile.

The initial query formulation and scoring in such a system can be identical to those functions in ad hoc retrieval: a scoring method that produces ad hoc rankings that perform well on the above ranking measures is in general good for filtering as well. The subsequent modification of the query formulation based on relevance feedback may also be similar to that used in feedback on an ad hoc search. Still, the nontraditional part of the process, the thresholding, is quite different: the threshold must be set and adapted with the optimization measure in mind. A good threshold for a certain utility measure will likely be bad for a different utility measure—that is, a different pair of credit-debit parameters—let alone another measure altogether.

Table 5.1 illustrates how the optimal threshold depends on the utility function. In this example, documents are ordered by their scores, thereby making it easier to see the effect of setting thresholds at different values. The cumulative utility, based on different utility functions, is shown after each document is disseminated (columns 4–7). A system optimized for $A = 3$, $B = -1$ (a "high-recall" scenario) might set its threshold at 0.485, allowing it to deliver as many relevant documents as possible while achieving a cumulative utility of 10. Often several different thresholds achieve a maximal cumulative utility; for example, a threshold of 0.515 also maximizes cumulative utility for $A = 3$, $B = -1$, but yields lower recall (document 873 is not delivered). Other thresholds are required to maximize other utility functions.

Thus, an experimental evaluation of filtering systems needs to be performed on the basis of a specific evaluation measure. Typically, all runs being compared will be tuned to that measure.

Table 5.1
The optimal threshold varies with the utility function. If the utility function is $A = 3$, $B = -1$ (a "high-recall" scenario), the cumulative utility is maximized by setting the threshold between 0.51 and 0.52, or between 0.48 and 0.49 (column 4). If the utility function is $A = 1$, $B = -2$ (a "high-precision" scenario), the cumulative utility is maximized by setting the threshold between 0.63 and 0.67, or between 0.55 and 0.57 (column 7)

DocId	Score	Relevance	Cumulative utility for different utility functions (A, B)			
			$(3, -1)$	$(2, -1)$	$(1, -1)$	$(1, -2)$
1043	0.67	+	3	2	1	1
1743	0.63	−	2	1	0	−1
692	0.60	+	5	3	1	0
584	0.57	+	8	5	2	1
1521	0.55	−	7	4	1	−1
982	0.52	+	10	6	2	0
482	0.51	−	9	5	1	−2
212	0.51	−	8	4	0	−4
1321	0.50	−	7	3	−1	−6
873	0.49	+	10	5	0	−5
1672	0.48	−	9	4	−1	−7
323	0.47	−	8	3	−2	−9

5.7.2 Utility, Target Precision, and Overall Performance

If the measure chosen is one of the utility ones, a system that retrieves nothing in response to any given topic scores zero on that topic. Since utility may in general be positive or negative, scoring zero may be preferable to scoring negatively, so a conservative strategy (don't retrieve anything) may be a relatively good one for a particular measure.

One of the conclusions of some experiments in TREC-7 and TREC-8 was indeed that a conservative strategy was a good one to follow. On one of the utility measures in TREC-7, the best "system" overall was a notional baseline system that retrieved nothing for any topic. This was seen as a rather discouraging conclusion. To put it another way, the task as set, with the specific utility measure, seemed to be simply too hard.

The hardness of the task may be due to, or alleviated by, a number of factors. One response in TREC-9 was to provide a few positive examples as well as the text topic for query initialization. It is also the case that the number of relevant documents per topic in the TREC-7 and TREC-8 data sets was low—systems did not have much opportunity to adapt.

Yet another response was to introduce the target precision measure as an alternative to utility. This turned out to be an extremely informative measure because it allowed some performance comparisons between ranked retrieval and set retrieval by comparing target precision based on a target of fifty documents with the traditional precision at fifty documents for ranked retrieval (Robertson 2002a). Although there are several qualifications to such a comparison, it appears that the better filtering systems are indeed performing comparably with the better ranked-retrieval systems.

Also, some of the systems using the utility measure in later TRECs achieved average utilities substantially above zero.

Nevertheless, thresholding is crucial. The performance of a system can be completely destroyed by a poor thresholding mechanism, however good its weighting and scoring. In this sense, filtering *is* a harder task than ranked retrieval.

5.7.3   Adaptation

The filtering task presents, in principle, opportunities for adaptation based on feedback that are far greater than those normally open in ad hoc retrieval.

In the old routing task, without the thresholding complication, the best-performing TREC systems on the whole were ones that did fairly heavy-duty query optimization. That is, given a substantial training set for a given topic, an almost unlimited number of queries could be tried out by successively reducing or expanding the term set and/or adjusting weights up or down. Although the space of possible queries is far too large to be explored completely, a reasonably well-designed heuristic program could be expected to find, given time, a very good query. Some later work on batch filtering (for example, Lewis 2002) showed that a reasonable machine-learning approach such as SVM could give quite good results in the batch-filtering task, with thresholding but without adaptation.

Still, both heuristic optimization and many machine-learning approaches are computationally demanding, and do not translate well to the filtering environment. Most of the filtering systems used at TREC do not attempt such iterative query reoptimization at each stage of adaptation: query term selection and weighting are normally done by rule. Some limited iterative threshold optimization might be used: this is, after all, a problem in only one dimension. Questions of computational load and efficiency are discussed further below.

Some of the systems represented at TREC do in fact show substantial benefit from adaptation.

5.8   Summary and Conclusions

Given the length of time that the filtering/routing task/track ran, and the range and variety of methods used by participants over that time, it is hard (if not impossible) to summarize the results obtained in any reasonable way. What we attempt here is a strictly bird's-eye view. It depends heavily on the impressions, and therefore also on the biases, of the authors.

For this bird's-eye view, we make one strong distinction: although the filtering track, and in particular adaptive filtering, grew out of the old routing task and has some similarities to it, in terms of methods used and results obtained it looks very different indeed. We divide the discussion accordingly.

5.8.1 Routing

From the beginning of the routing task, the emphasis was on the fact that we had large amounts of relevance information to use. It became apparent early on that the original text topic was not important in this context—it was possible to do just as well, or almost, by ignoring the text topic as by taking it into account. The crucial thing was to learn by example from the known relevant documents. Successive TRECs have seen successively more sophisticated learning methods, some of them originating in the information retrieval field (referred to below as "homegrown") and some brought in from areas of machine learning, perhaps via adoption in the text-categorization community. Many of the homegrown methods involve essentially iterating through a large number of possible query formulations, testing them all on the training data. The space of possible query formulations is far too big to explore in its entirety, but progress was made from year to year by both thinking of clever heuristics to explore more of the space more effectively and simply throwing more computing power at the problem. Some of the methods imported from machine learning have similar characteristics, even though they may be based on stronger models of what the space looks like, how it may be treated mathematically, and how an optimal solution may be found. An example of such a method would be support-vector machines. In this case, it is not at all clear even how one might use the original text topic—the obvious way to use such a learning method is exactly to ignore the text topic and learn entirely from examples.

It also became clear early on in TREC, when some groups were using manual or partially manual methods, that in routing at least, automatic systems easily outperformed manual ones. Whatever skills a human may bring to searching, they are no match for the raw statistical power of learning from sufficient examples. In some sense, the routing task is exactly what machines are good at.

5.8.2 Adaptive Filtering

Four things combine to make the case of adaptive filtering very different indeed from routing: the starting point, adaptation, thresholding, and the efficiency problem.

Starting and Adapting As regards the starting point (a text topic with few or no known relevant documents) and the adaptation, homegrown methods have a significant advantage. In the case of the starting point, this is not surprising—we know how to make good use of the text topic in information retrieval since for many tasks this is all we have. What is perhaps not quite so obvious is that homegrown methods also have an advantage when it comes to smooth adaptation from the text topic, using the few relevant examples given in later versions of the task, and then using each relevant document as it is retrieved. Query expansion/modification methods such as Rocchio are designed for such a situation. Many methods native to a machine-learning environment have difficulty with both starting from a text topic and adapting smoothly to each new relevant document.

Thresholding   The major problem area for the homegrown methods has been thresholding since absolute thresholding has not generally been required in information retrieval tasks. Thresholding has turned out to be a seriously hard task, and it may well be what distinguishes the different systems more than anything else. The result observed in several TRECs that for utility, the best system was one that retrieved nothing, is a good indication of this problem. Although later TRECs regularly got systems that performed better than this baseline, this was partly the result of having made the task easier, by providing some initial example relevant documents and by having enough relevant in the test set to give the adaptation a serious chance. Neither of these changes seems badly unrealistic, but then the earlier tasks did not seem unrealistic either.

It is of some interest to compare the TREC filtering task with TDT (the topic detection and tracking evaluation) and in particular the topic tracking task, which has some similarities to filtering (Allan 2002). Participants in this task seem to have had less difficulty with thresholding. One possible reason for this is that the utility function used for topic detection and tracking has generally been much more recall oriented than the one used in TREC filtering (for instance, 10:1 instead of 2:1).

Efficiency   The problem of designing filtering systems that run efficiently is severe. Adaptive-filtering systems are in principle extremely heavy computationally—much more so than ad hoc retrieval systems. At the beginning of TREC, it seemed quite a challenge to deal with two gigabytes of text data; however, the basic ad hoc retrieval technology, dating from the 1970s and based on inverted files, was completely adequate for the task. The off-line indexing process might take a long time, but once done, searching could be made very fast. TREC has never tackled the problem of maintaining up-to-date indexes for ad hoc searching when documents are added or modified, which would have prefigured some of the problems of efficient adaptive filtering.

We may describe the process of filtering as follows: each document, as it arrives, is parsed and matched against each profile. Potentially, following this process, each profile may be revised to take account of this new document. This modification may involve either or both query modification and threshold modification. Either or both of these may mean going back to any part of the accumulating collection of documents that have already been processed for information deriving from any or all of the entire accumulated collection (for example, term statistics for weighting), the list of documents that would be retrieved if the current version of the profile were run against the collection (for instance, for quantitative thresholding), the set of documents previously retrieved against this profile (say, for calibration of some quantity that requires known relevance), and the set of documents previously retrieved and judged relevant (for example, as a source of new terms). In principle, this process must be repeated for every profile before the next document is processed.

Of course, there are many ways in which this can be simplified. We may restrict profile modification to the situation where the document just processed has been both retrieved for this profile and judged relevant to it. This might reduce the load by several orders of magnitude, but still leave it very heavy indeed—and leave the problem that a profile that never retrieves a relevant document, never gets modified.

For many commonly used methods of machine learning, the natural desire would be to reoptimize the profile every time the information about it changes. Since profile optimization is likely to be a heavy process, such an approach is probably out of the question. Even homegrown methods, where relevance feedback may be a simple single-vector operation involving known relevant documents, might have difficulty with this volume of activity. It should also be noted that the dimensionality of the problem is potentially huge (the total size of the vocabulary, or more if phrases are considered), and a machine-learning method that uses the full space is likely to be heavy indeed. Computational load issues were particularly evident with the MSH topic set in TREC-9—processing five thousand topics was seriously hard or even impossible for some systems.

It is of course the case that the situation changes—computational activities that were regarded as too heavy in 1999 may now be feasible, for all the usual reasons. Nevertheless, such changes will not be sufficient (in the foreseeable future) to allow *any* optimization to be repeated at *every* possible time.

For all these reasons, the filtering track at TREC has encouraged the investigation and use of efficient algorithms. In ad hoc, the efficiency question is relatively simple—if your algorithm can be coded as merge operations on inverted lists, it can be made efficient. There is no such simple equation in the case of adaptive filtering, and participants have had to consider efficiency explicitly in their choice of methods.

5.8.3 Overview

The research community's view of information routing and filtering changed considerably during the 1990s, due in large part to TREC. In 1992, when TREC began, most of the research on these topics was done with what might now be viewed as an unrealistic experimental methodology. The resulting research taught the community much about creating accurate profiles for batch-oriented environments, but it also allowed important problems such as thresholding to be overlooked. A decade later, the situation had changed completely. The research community was focused on modeling "real" information-filtering environments and producing highly responsive systems that adapt quickly to changing conditions. This healthy change can be attributed to NIST's support of routing and filtering tasks over an eleven-year period.

One impression from looking at the track over the years is that while routing with a significant quantity of training data is a relatively easy task, adaptive filtering with a realistic starting point is seriously hard, and progress toward better systems has been slow. We have certainly not had the experience of some of the other tracks, a major advance that might take us to new heights of performance. We may take a positive view of this situation, and conclude that the area is a fertile and fruitful one for continued research.

One important challenge for future adaptive information-filtering research is to better model people and their information needs. In theory, current information-filtering systems model a person's information need, but it is usually done with crude models—for instance, a linear classifier on a unigram text representation, and numerical thresholds. This area is ripe for a broader approach to user profiles because it is one of the few areas in information retrieval where regular, long-term sustained interaction with the user is inherent in the task. Interaction over a period of years is realistic for today's computer users. A major obstacle to research in this direction is that the experimental methodology, and especially the test corpora, will need to be redesigned again. For example, current methods cannot address the issue of drift in a user's information need over time—the assumption of persistent profiles should not imply an assumption of static information needs. Thus, we still face the challenge of increasing the realism of our experiments, as well as that of raising our utility targets from the current P(relevant) ≥ 0.33 to a more respectable number.

Looking ahead, it seems likely that information routing and filtering will continue their evolution from "marginal" to "mainstream" technologies. In 1992, information routing and filtering were important mostly to large-scale information providers, large-scale subscription services, and large-scale information consumers. Today, these technologies are becoming more mainstream. Small businesses and consumers can easily create medium-sized, private document streams using subscription services, Web crawlers, and agent-based systems. The information-filtering solutions developed in forums such as TREC may soon be software that many people use on a regular basis.

Acknowledgments

This chapter draws extensively from the introduction to a special issue on filtering (Robertson 2002b), as well as from the track reports variously authored, but built on the foundations of early reports by David Lewis and David Hull. We also thank Ian Soboroff and a referee for their helpful comments.

Notes

1. Relevance judgments for OHSUMED topics were made on a three-point scale: not relevant, possibly relevant, and definitely relevant. The training documents for adaptive filtering were definitely relevant. Systems were free to make use of the graded relevance judgments in any way they saw fit, but the final evaluation was based on treating both possibly relevant and definitely relevant as relevant.

2. The reason for excluding those MeSH headings not represented in the final year was to avoid headings that had been dropped out of MeSH (which undergoes continual modification) during the period.

References

Allan, J. 1996. Incremental relevance feedback for information. In *Proceedings of the nineteenth ACM SIGIR conference*, 270–278.

Allan, J. 2002. *Topic detection and tracking: Event-based information organization*. Boston: Kluwer Academic Publishers.

Ault, T., and Y. Yang. 2002. KNN, Rocchio, and metrics for information filtering at TREC-10. In *TREC 2001*, 84–93.

Buckley, C., and E. M. Voorhees. 2000. Evaluating evaluation measure stability. In *Proceedings of the twenty-third annual international ACM SIGIR conference*, 33–40.

Harman, D. K. 1993. Overview of the first text retrieval conference, TREC-1. In *TREC-1*, 1–20.

Harman, D. K. 1994. Overview of the second text retrieval conference, TREC-2. In *TREC-2*, 1–20.

Harman, D. K. 1995. Overview of the third text retrieval conference, TREC-3. In *TREC-3*, 1–20.

Harman, D. K. 1996. Overview of the fourth text retrieval conference, TREC-4. In *TREC-4*, 1–24.

Hersh, W. R., C. Buckley, T. J. Leone, and D. H. Hickam. 1994. OHSUMED: An interactive retrieval evaluation and new large test collection for research. In *Proceedings of the seventeenth annual international ACM SIGIR conference*, 192–201.

Hull, D. A. 1998. The TREC-6 filtering track: Description and analysis. In *TREC-6*, 45–68.

Hull, D. A. 1999. The TREC-7 filtering track: Description and analysis. In *TREC-7*, 33–56.

Hull, D. A., and S. Robertson. 2000. The TREC-8 filtering track final report. In *TREC-8*, 35–56.

Lewis, D. D. 1996. The TREC-4 filtering track. In *TREC-4*, 165–180.

Lewis, D. D. 1997. The TREC-5 filtering track. In *TREC-5*, 75–96.

Lewis, D. D. 2002. Applying support vector machines to the TREC 2001 batch filtering and routing tasks. In *TREC 2001*, 286–292.

Reuters. n.d. Reuters corpus, volume 1. ⟨http://about.reuters.com/researchandstandards/corpus/⟩ (visited September 26, 2002).

Robertson, S. E. 2002a. Comparing the performance of adaptive filtering and ranked output systems. *Information Retrieval* 5:257–268.

Robertson, S. E. 2002b. Introduction to the special issue: Overview of the TREC routing and filtering tasks. *Information Retrieval* 5:127–137.

Robertson, S., and D. A. Hull. 2001. The TREC-9 filtering track final report. In *TREC-9*, 25–40.

Robertson, S., and I. Soboroff. 2002. The TREC 2001 filtering track report. In *TREC 2001*, 26–37.

Robertson, S., and I. Soboroff. 2003. The TREC 2002 filtering track report. In *TREC 2002*, 27–39.

Soboroff, I., and S. Robertson. 2003. Building a filtering test collection for TREC 2002. In *Proceedings of the 26th annual international ACM SIGIR conference*, 243–250.

Voorhees, E. M., and D. K. Harman. 1997. Overview of the fifth text retrieval conference, TREC-5. In *TREC-5*, 1–28.

Voorhees, E. M., and D. K. Harman. 1998. Overview of the sixth text retrieval conference, TREC-6. In *TREC-6*, 1–28.

6   The TREC Interactive Tracks: Putting the User into Search

Susan T. Dumais and Nicholas J. Belkin

6.1   Introduction

The study of interactive information retrieval has been a consistent part of TREC from the beginning. The main arena for such work has been the interactive track (TRECs 3–11), although other activities have also explored how users interact with information retrieval systems (for instance, the interactive and manual query modes in TRECs 1–8, a subtrack of the Web track in TREC-12 and the HARD track introduced in TREC-12). This chapter presents an overview of those efforts together with a summary of the evolving experimental framework within which studies of interaction have taken place.

During the course of the core interactive track's nine-year life, there were fifty-six contributions, from twenty-two different groups, exploring a wide range of questions ranging from different presentation and visualization techniques to individual differences in search processes and effectiveness. Paul Over (2001), in a paper published as part of a special issue of *Information Processing and Management*, provides a brief history of the development of the interactive track during TRECs 3–8. He also includes an annotated bibliography, indicating the major characteristics of the tasks, the names of the participants, and the participants' general approaches to the task. In addition to Over's bibliography, the annual overviews of the interactive track (published as part of the general TREC overviews for TRECs 3–4 and as a separate paper in the proceedings of TRECs 5–12) provide a complete history of the goals and development of the interactive track through its life span. In this chapter, we highlight some of the key developments, briefly summarize and synthesize these developments, and outline some opportunities and challenges in evaluating interactive information retrieval systems in the context of TREC.

Information retrieval is naturally an interactive and iterative process, which is interleaved with other activities. People have information needs; they express these needs using some query interface, then evaluate and interpret the results, and are either satisfied with the results or continue the process. This process is rich and complex, with information needs and understanding evolving over time (see, for example, Bates 1989; Belkin, Oddy, and Brooks 1982). Marti Hearst (1999) provides a nice overview of a wide range of user interface and visualization techniques that have been developed to support the information retrieval process.

The majority of TREC tracks have been concerned with the evaluation of matching and ranking algorithms as isolated system components, and this has led to a number of important developments in the field. In general, TREC evaluations operate in a static batch mode with fixed document collections, queries, and relevance assessments. This has been crucial in developing a reusable set of resources and systematically comparing different retrieval algorithms. Even under these well-controlled circumstances, system comparisons are not as straightforward as it may seem at first glance. There are a number of small differences such as stemming algorithms, stopword selection, term-weighting heuristics, named-entity identification and weighting, automatic thesaurus construction, automatic query expansion, and so on, that influence the performance of algorithms of interest and must be specified in sufficient detail to allow for meaningful comparisons. When one considers the broader challenge of evaluating interactive retrieval systems, a number of additional challenges not present in other TREC tracks arise.

A significant difference between the interactive track and other TREC tracks is that performance in interactive retrieval is greatly influenced by the searchers as well as the topics and the systems. Searchers vary in their expertise in the topic under consideration, their skills in searching in general, and their experience with specific interface or interaction features of the system under study. All of these factors are known to influence the performance of the end-to-end retrieval systems, oftentimes in complex ways (for overviews of individual differences in interactive search, see Egan 1988; Bhavnani 2002; and for an alternative perspective, see Saracevic and Kantor 1988). These individual differences and the potential of complex interactions among searcher, topic, and system make it especially challenging to compare different interactive retrieval systems. One way to overcome the known variability in performance across topics is to use a large sample of topics, and fifty or more topics have been used in most TREC tracks. When one adds to that the differences among searchers, and possibly searcher-topic interactions, the number of combinations needed for reducing variability and effectively comparing across systems increases correspondingly. Careful experimental design is required to tease apart the effects of searcher, topic, and systems (see Lagergren and Over 1998). In order to obtain good experimental power, large numbers of searchers and topics are required.

Interactive systems also pose important challenges from the evaluation perspective. TREC has typically required a single query to be submitted and the top K results examined for accuracy (precision and recall). When users are involved in the process, it can be difficult to identify a single-"best" query since information is acquired from many different queries and results. Indeed, it is not clear that the notion of a single-best query makes sense in an interactive retrieval environment. The differences in judgments of relevance between searchers and TREC assessors is especially noticeable in interactive evaluation. Although there are well-documented interrater differences in relevance, the use of the authoritative relevance judgments of TREC assessors provides a useful benchmark for fully automatic systems (see, for example, Voorhees 1998). When "real" searchers are added, however, there will be differences between their judgments and those of the assessors, and these differences will be compounded by iteration. Thus, some kinds of interaction between the user and the system, like relevance feedback, are difficult to evaluate in an interactive setting. The precision and recall of interactive runs reflects not only the quality of the underlying ranking engine but also the degree of overlap between the searcher's and the assessor's relevance judgments.

In addition to these key evaluation issues, interactive retrieval also raises a number of pragmatic issues. First, there has to be at least one (and preferably more) user interface for query specification, results presentation and exploration, feedback, and so forth. This in and of itself represents a substantial development effort. In addition, any system that is evaluated with people in the loop needs to be fast, robust to the wide range of boundary conditions that users will uncover, and allow for logging of details of user interaction, again increasing system development costs. Finally, testing human participants is time-consuming and expensive. For example, if there are fifty topics and each topic takes thirty minutes to complete, a total of twenty-five hours is required for a single participant using a single system variant. A not-so-mythical person-month is required just to conduct the user tests themselves (without counting the time for algorithm and system development) for two systems with fifteen participants using each. Typically, the number of topics, participants, or task complexity is decreased to reduce the time requirements, at the cost of greater experimental variability and the need for large system differences to be discovered. All of these issues introduce additional challenges in evaluating highly interactive information retrieval systems.

A fundamental problem with the interactive track that was not encountered by either the main tasks or other tracks, is that the basic TREC structure is not well suited to the investigation of interactive IR. There are two reasons for this. One is that the general evaluation schema of TREC is designed for evaluating and comparing batch searching, and does not transfer well to the interactive environment. The other is that TREC is designed to compare the performance of systems at different sites with one another. Unfortunate (from this point of view) characteristics of interactive IR experiments are that performance in interactive IR is highly influenced by characteristics of the searchers, and that searchers in such experiments generally cannot search on a large number of topics. The former means that it becomes difficult, if not impossible, to compare the performance of different systems at different sites since the searching at each site is done by different people. The latter means that it is difficult, if not impossible, to take into account the well-known influence of the topic that is being searched on performance. The situation is further complicated by interaction effects among searcher, topic, and system that cannot be easily accounted for in any cross-site comparison. If it is possible to have several leitmotifs, then the continuing attempt to get around these problems is the second one that characterized the interactive track throughout its history.

The history of the TREC interactive track can be viewed as the progressive evolution of a methodology for conducting experiments in interactive IR, together with the specification of realistic IR tasks and the development of measures for evaluation of the performance of systems in support of these tasks. Although the tasks and measures initially conformed to the standard TREC model, it soon became clear that there were problems with evaluation of interactive IR within this model, and that the initial ideas about the ability to compare performance between different systems at different sites needed to be drastically revised. In this chapter, we provide an overview of these evaluation challenges and how they were addressed.

6.2   Overview of Interactive Tracks at TREC

6.2.1   TRECs 1–8, Manual and Interactive Query Modes
From the beginning, the TREC guidelines attempted to accommodate a simple kind of interactive search, allowing both automatic and manual input in the query construction process. Three general categories of query construction were defined for the ad hoc and routing tasks, based on the amount and the kind of manual intervention used.

Method one involved completely automatic initial query construction. For the ad hoc task, systems had to automatically generate a query from the topic provided by NIST. For the routing task, systems had to automatically construct a query using the training topics, the training relevance judgments, and the training documents.

Method two used manual intervention in the initial query construction. For the ad hoc task, systems had to construct the query in some manner from the topic, using some combination of manual and automatic input. The techniques used were identified, along with the human expertise (both domain expertise and computer expertise) needed to construct a query. For the routing task, the queries were constructed in the same manner as the ad hoc queries for method two, but using the training topics, relevance judgments, and training documents.

Method three used automatic or manual query construction along with interactive feedback and query modification. For the ad hoc task, a subset of the retrieved documents is used for manual relevance feedback. These judgments could be used to automatically modify the query, or the human could simply choose to modify the query itself. In either case, the expertise of the person or persons examining the documents were described (both their domain expertise and their experience in online searching), and the manner of system feedback reported (that is, automatic system modification of the query or human modification). At some point, feedback should end and the query should be accepted as final. Two results sets were to be provided to NIST, one based on the initial query and the other based on iteration, to be used in computing frozen rank evaluation measures.

This fully automatic method was the most popular method from the outset, but several groups tried experiments using manual or interactive query modification. In TREC-1 ad hoc, thirteen runs used automatic construction, six used manual construction, and one used interactive feedback. In TREC-1 routing, eight runs used the automatic construction of routing queries and eight used manual construction. In TREC-2 ad hoc, twenty-three runs used the automatic construction of queries, nine used manual construction, and two used interactive feedback. In TREC-2 routing, twenty-three runs used the automatic construction of queries and nine used manual construction. In TREC-3 ad hoc, twenty-eight runs used the automatic construction of queries, twelve used manual construction, and two used interactive feedback for construction. In

TREC-3 routing, twenty-four runs used the automatic construction of queries, eighteen used manual construction, and four used interactive query construction. The four interactive groups represent the first attempt at studying interactive retrieval and will be discussed in more detail in the next section.

In general, there were no advantages to the manual or interactive modification of queries in the routing tasks. This is not surprising given that the automatic baseline systems used solid machine-learning techniques operating over large amounts of training data. Human searchers are not as effective at exploiting large amounts of training data. The ad hoc runs, in contrast, produced two interesting types of results. The first has to do with conditions under which manual query construction can improve on automatic query construction, and the second concerns the diversity of documents produced by the two approaches.

In TREC-1 and TREC-2, performance for the best automatic and manual runs was about the same. This was probably the result of rich topics, consisting of title, description, narrative, and concept fields, and averaging 149 words in TREC-1 and 178 words in TREC-2. The TREC-3 topics omitted the concept field, and were "only" 119 words long. In TREC-3 ad hoc, the best manual runs were 10 to 15 percent better than the best automatic runs, and within system comparisons showed even larger improvements. The University of Massachusetts group's INQUERY system used passage retrieval techniques in combination with automatic query expansion using thirty phrases that were automatically selected from a phrase thesaurus, which was automatically constructed from the text collection (the INQ101 run is described in Broglio et al. 1995). Their manual run (INQ102) used some simple modifications of the resulting queries to remove words or phrases, modify term weights, or add proximity restrictions. The manual run showed a 15 percent improvement in average precision, although it is not clear which of the manual modifications was the most effective. The University of California at Berkeley group's manual run (Brkly7 is described in Cooper, Chen, and Gey 1995) expanded the automatically generated queries by using synonyms, more general terms, and more specific terms found in external resources, including the searchers' domain knowledge. This manual run showed a 34 percent gain in average precision compared to Berkeley's automatic run, which did not include any automatic expansion. These results suggest that the reworking of automatically generated requests can enhance a system's retrieval effectiveness. It is important to note that the searchers in these experiments were often trained intermediaries or the system developers, and they sometimes spent ten or more minutes modifying each query. In TREC-4, the topics were further reduced to include only descriptions and averaged sixteen words in length. Again, there were advantages observed for manual query construction. Manual query modification continued to be examined in subsequent TRECs with much the same result. The best manual runs often outperform the best automatic runs using short queries (titles and/or descriptions)—for the TREC-8 results, see, for instance, Voorhees and Harman 2000, figures 6 and 7. Detailed comparisons are difficult because of the different amounts of effort and the external resources involved in the manual runs, but searchers who expend effort are rewarded with improved results. In addition to modifications based on term removal, term reweighting, the use of proximity operators, and the introduction of synonyms from external sources, some groups (for example, Claritech, Conquest, Management Information Technologies, and Oracle) used commercial systems with support for richer types of user interaction. This highlights the significance of user interaction as a process with important products along the way—something that is not well captured in the TREC model where a single-best query is required.

The second interesting contribution of the manual query runs was in introducing a greater diversity of relevant documents into the document pool. Ellen M. Voorhees and Donna K. Harman's (2000) overview summarizes the number of documents and relevant documents contributed by the various ad hoc runs (automatic, manual, both automatic and manual, other) for TRECs 4–8. For example, for TREC-8, 72 percent of the document pool came from automatic runs, 14 percent from manual runs, and 14 percent from both. The proportions are quite different for relevant documents; 17 percent of the relevant documents are from automatic runs, 24 percent from manual runs, and 59 percent from both. Manual runs consistently retrieve a higher percentage of relevant documents than they contribute to the overall judgment pool.

Even within the ad hoc track, there are some indications that manual intervention in query construction can provide substantial retrieval benefits. Manual runs have been useful in identifying diverse documents for test collection construction and, more important, in illustrating that even the best automatic systems have room for improvement. The interactive track takes this a step further by trying to elucidate the process of retrieval (in addition to its end results), and the best places and methods for human intervention.

6.2.2   TREC-3

Participants and Approaches

City University, London—human intervention to generate routing queries consisting mostly of the addition of phrases as query terms, some relevance judgments, and the ability to delete candidate terms from the expansion list (Robertson et al. 1995)

Rutgers University—characteristics of ten professional searchers' behavior in transitioning from Boolean systems to a best-match ranked retrieval system; individual differences in performance and the search process including the use of operators and relevance feedback for query expansion and term reweighting (Koenemann et al. 1995)

University of Toronto—mixed graphic and text interface to a simple Boolean retrieval system (Charoenkitkarn, Chignell, and Golovchinsky 1995)

Verity, Inc.—building complex query structures using commercially available concept modeling tools; effects of searcher expertise and query difficulty (Tong 1995)

Task and Methods The TREC-3 interactive task was a translation of the standard routing task into an interactive setting. The searcher's task was to generate an optimal routing query. The topics were the fifty standard routing topics, including the title, narrative, and description fields. The required output was a ranked list of the top one thousand documents returned from the final routing query, and the standard routing evaluation metrics (precision and recall) were reported.

Searchers developed their queries using the database, the topics, and the relevance judgments supplied for training in the routing task. In keeping with the goals of understanding and influencing interactive IR behavior, the participating groups investigated the influence of different system features on searcher behaviors, and attempted as well to relate the features and characteristics of searchers and topics to performance. The general procedure that participating sites were to follow was simply that there should be at least one search carried out by at least one human searcher (*subject*) on each of the fifty routing topics. There was no standard protocol for how the investigations at each site would be carried out, there was no standard set of features for each site to investigate, there were no restrictions on who the subjects could be or how many of them there should be, and the only data that participants were required to submit were the final queries that the subjects constructed and the top one thousand documents retrieved by these queries from the test database. Individual sites, in order to investigate the issues that they were concerned with, each collected substantial data concerning the subjects and the searches, but these were not required to be reported, nor was there any stipulation about data that all sites should collect.

Observations The goals at the outset were to gain some experience in interactive evaluation, to compare human performance in the task with automatic performance, and to compare performance in different interactive systems at different sites to one another. As with any new track, many lessons were learned. None of the interactive systems performed as well as the automatic systems. In retrospect, this is not surprising. Sophisticated machine-learning techniques allow automatic systems to take advantage of the large amounts of training data in ways that are impossible for people to do. In addition, routing is not a typical search task and thus it is something that participants found difficult to do. Finally, the descriptions of the systems, experimental manipulations, searchers, and the search process were not standardized across sites, making it difficult to compare across sites.

6.2.3 TREC-4

Participants and Approaches

City University, London—graphic interface for interactive feedback and passage retrieval for relevance feedback (Robertson 1996)

Claritech Corporation—searcher effectiveness and behavior using their commercial retrieval system and graphic user interface focusing on the use of relevance feedback (Milic-Frayling et al. 1996)

Cornell University—varied the time spent judging documents (shallow versus deep reading) for standard relevance feedback using a simple textual user interface (Buckley et al. 1996)

Georgia Institute of Technology—visualization showing the distribution of query terms in a set of documents (Veerasamy 1996)

Lexis-Nexis Group—commercial Boolean system with top-performing ranked retrieval systems from other TREC-4 groups (Lu, Holt, and Miller 1996)

Rutgers University—relation between previous experience and the use of ranking and relevance feedback functions in a ranked retrieval system (Belkin et al. 1996)

University of Toronto—searcher strategies as function of interface style (markup or type-in) (Charoenkitkarn, Chignell, and Golovchinsky 1996)

U.S. Department of Defense—interface for document clustering, visualization, and labeling (Huffman 1996)

ETH-Zurich—effect of fast query evaluation and passage highlighting in retrieved documents (Knaus et al. 1996)

Xerox Corporation—three techniques (standard ranked retrieval, Scatter/Gather document clustering, and TileBars to display the distribution of terms within documents) were all available to searchers (Hearst et al. 1996)

Task and Methods   The TREC-3 interactive task experience led to a number of changes in how the TREC-4 interactive track was defined and evaluated. One result of the TREC-3 interactive task was that it seemed that the routing task was not a realistic one for human beings. The participants treated it more as an ad hoc task, and had difficulty with the concept of constructing a query on one data base that would then be used to search on another data base. Furthermore, to the extent that comparisons with fully automatic systems are of interest, it is difficult for people to exploit the large amounts of labeled training data given limited interaction time (and possibly even with infinite time). So, to improve the realism of the task, the TREC-4 interactive track was set to be roughly equivalent to the main ad hoc task. From TREC-3, it was also clear that reducing the number of topics on which subjects searched would ease the burden on the subjects and make it possible to have multiple searches on the same topics.

Therefore, for TREC-4, twenty-five of the fifty ad hoc topics were chosen for use in the interactive track. The searchers were given two tasks. The primary task was to find and save as many relevant documents as possible in up to thirty minutes. They were told to "find as many good documents as you can for a topic, in around thirty minutes, without collecting too much rubbish." The secondary task was to construct a so-called final query that they thought would be the best-single query for the ad hoc topic. Results submitted for evaluation were the saved documents (for the primary task) and the top one thousand documents retrieved by the final query, with the saved documents at the top of the list (for the secondary task). Placing the saved documents at the top of the list is a kind of "frozen rank" evaluation; the more-standard frozen rank procedure places all seen documents (both saved and unsaved) at the top of the list. Standard precision and recall measures were reported for both primary and secondary tasks.

Again, an aim of the track was to compare the results of interactive ad hoc searching with automatic searching, but much more emphasis was placed on analysis of the search process and user behavior. Therefore, some substantial changes were made in TREC-4 in the specification of what data were to be collected, and under what conditions. This was done primarily in order to enhance the study of behavior in interactive IR, by making publicly available the data concerning the subjects' searching behaviors. Participating sites were asked to log each search; to provide (among others) summary data about the time taken per search, the number of queries (iterations) per search, and the use of system features; and to provide an annotated log of one complete search on a prespecified topic. As in TREC-3, there was no standard protocol for conducting the experiment, other than that each topic had to have a search by at least one user, and there were no constraints on the number of subjects or their characteristics.

Observations The ad hoc environment was a more natural one than routing. The use of two tasks—one focused on a kind of productivity measure (the number of relevant documents per unit time) and the other on a more TREC-like single-best query—was an attempt to explore different measures that are easy to summarize and compare across sites, and also to reflect directly how easy it is for searchers to accomplish their tasks.

The difference between individual searcher's and TREC assessor's notions of what constituted relevant documents was immediately obvious. (This has also been noted in studies of interrater reliability, but in the interactive environment the effect is compounded by iteration.) For the primary task, the precision (and recall) of interactive runs reflects the overlap between the searchers and the assessors in addition to the quality of the underlying ranking engine. For the secondary task, frozen ranks measures were necessary to accommodate the fact that searchers had viewed and judged many documents. Using frozen ranks for only relevant documents makes it difficult to compare the average precision between different participants. Chris Buckley, Amit Singhal, Mandar Mitra, and Gerard Salton (1996) offer some discussion of alternative frozen rank techniques, but all such techniques focus comparisons on a subset of documents—namely, those that were not retrieved by initial queries and iterations. The task of identifying a single-best query seems at odds with what happens in interactive retrieval, where relevant documents are accumulated using a variety of different search and navigation techniques.

A larger number of sites participated in exploring techniques for improving the ease with which users could make relevance judgments, using clustering and visualizations to organize search results, and beginning to examine details of the search process as well as individual differences. There were several promising results and directions, but additional work is required in evaluation methods.

6.2.4 TREC-5

Participants and Approaches

City University, London—task-specific functions to allow actions to be reversed; automatic and incremental addition of query terms based on relevance feedback (Beaulieu et al. 1997)

Rutgers University—searchers' understanding and use of relevance feedback and ranked retrieval; effects of topic characterization, searcher, and order (Belkin et al. 1997)

Task and Methods   One main result of the TREC-4 interactive track was the realization that the TREC model of evaluating performance on the basis of relevance judgments on the pooled retrieved documents by the NIST assessors was not working as intended in evaluating interactive IR. In the evaluation of automatic IR, it is assumed that if a document is judged relevant (or not) by the assessor, and the system has not retrieved it (or has), then the system has made an error, and this is an appropriate basis for evaluating the system itself. But in the TREC-4 interactive track, human searchers, and not the systems with which they searched, were making the judgments about whether a document was relevant or not. If their judgments were not in agreement with those of the assessors, then the degree of agreement between the two humans is what was being measured by precision and recall (at least with respect to the saved documents), not some characteristic of the interactive IR system itself. This suggested that for the TREC-5 interactive track, some other evaluation measures, or some other task, that were not subject to this problem should be explored.

Three other related issues that became clear from the TREC-4 results were that: the standard ad hoc task of retrieval of one thousand documents was not the kind of task in which searchers in interactive IR systems would normally engage; there seemed to be little point in comparing automatic and interactive IR within the TREC context; and there should be a concerted attempt to develop a method for comparing the performance of different interactive IR systems at different sites. All these factors led to several changes in how the interactive track was to be carried out.

For TREC-5, a new task was designed, which did not correspond to either of the main TREC tasks. The new task, called *aspectual recall* (or in later TRECs, *instance recall*), was thought to be representative of a realistic interactive retrieval task, and capable of being evaluated without the problems found in TREC-4. This task sought to emulate the situation where an information seeker does not require all of the relevant documents on a topic but rather just those that discuss or identify the different aspects of a topic. A typical such situation would be a person who was interested in knowing what the different types of treatments are for high blood pressure. Thus, this task asked subjects to identify documents that discussed one or more aspects of the topic; once an aspect had been identified, no further documents dealing with that aspect should be saved. Searchers were asked to "retrieve as many relevant documents as possible in twenty minutes, so that taken together they cover as many difference 'aspects' of the task as possible." The individual topics were a subset of previous ad hoc topics, modified to suit the new task. Twelve topics were used. Subjects were allowed a maximum of twenty minutes for each topic search.

Participating sites returned the list of documents saved by searchers, not the list of aspects. In addition, event logs for all searches and a detailed narrative account of one search were to be submitted. Event logs consisted of key events in the interaction such as query terms, documents seen, documents judged relevant, and so on. The primary evaluation measure for the task was aspectual or instance recall. The documents saved by the searchers at all sites for each topic were pooled, and NIST assessors then went through this pool, compiled a list of unique aspects, and generated a matrix indicating which aspects appeared in which documents. The determination of what counted as an instance or aspect was left up to the assessors. Searches were scored at the document level, for any aspects identified by the NIST assessors. This presumably mitigated to some extent the differences in granularity of aspects that different searchers may have. Aspectual recall was the number of aspects discussed in the documents saved by a searcher, divided by the number of aspects identified by the assessor. A secondary measure was standard precision, the number of relevant documents saved, divided by the total number of documents saved. Although searchers were instructed not to save documents that discussed aspects of the topic that had already been identified, there was no penalty for saving documents that duplicated aspects already saved.

A new experimental design was also instituted for the TREC-5 interactive track to reflect a shift to more tightly designed experiments with fewer topics. The design grew out of a desire to be able to compare systems across sites, and to systematically isolate the effects of topic, searcher, and system. Each site was to implement two retrieval systems: one system common to all sites to act as a baseline (this was a version of ZPRISE, a ranking system developed at NIST), and another system of the site's own choosing. Topics were divided into four *blocks* of three topics each. Subjects searched on the topics in one block on one of the two retrieval systems, and then on the topics in a second block using the other system. The design stipulated that the order of the topics within a block was constant, as was the order of searching the blocks. Thus, in order to have each block of topics searched by at least one searcher in each system, four subjects were required for one iteration of the design. Comparability between the different experimental systems at the various sites was to be achieved by measuring the difference in subjects' performance at each site using the common baseline system and their performance using the site's experimental system. The idea was that the direction and magnitude of the differences between the baseline and the experimental systems could then be directly compared across sites since this design would presumably factor out subject variability across the sites.

Observations   A number of factors—the definition of a new task, a new experimental design, the development and installation of the common control system, and the need to provide more detailed logs from searches—contributed to delays in carrying out the TREC-5 interactive task as planned. Only two sites were able to participate in the TREC-5 interactive track, and even those two were unable to complete the experiment as designed, so the results by definition are not comparable across sites. In effect, TREC-5 became a pilot study for the TREC-6 interactive track.

The change toward more tightly designed experiments on fewer topics was highly debated among track members, with many participants worrying that there were too few topics to allow a comfortable basis for generalization. The preliminary results showed that there were strong searcher effects, strong topic effects, and a strong searcher-topic interaction, highlighting the need to have experimental designs that allow these factors to be teased apart. Another important lesson was that the assumed agreement between a document's relevance and its coverage of topic aspects was mistaken. There were also some unexpected inconsistencies between aspectual recall and relevance that arose from using aspectual recall, but standard precision for assessing performance. Searchers were asked to find relevant documents that covered various aspects. Yet there were some differences in relevance and aspect retrieval—some documents contained aspects, but were not relevant, and a larger number of documents were relevant, but covered no aspects.

6.2.5   TREC-6

Participants and Approaches

City University, London—two versions of relevance feedback (Beaulieu and Gatford 1998)

IBM—information retrieval prototype system exploring four user interface issues (Schmidt-Wesche, Mack, and Cesar 1998)

New Mexico State University at Las Cruces—use of Pathfinder networks to help query generation (McDonald, Ogden, and Foltz 1998)

Oregon Health Sciences University—Boolean searching versus natural-language searching (Hersh and Day 1998)

RMIT—use of clustering and feedback to group and reorder documents dynamically (Fuller et al. 1998)

Rutgers University—positive and negative relevance feedback (Belkin et al. 1998)

University of California at Berkeley—baseline study after some task-specific modifications of their Cheshire system (Larson and McDonough 1998)

University of Massachusetts at Amherst—two results visualizations; expert and non-expert users (Allan et al. 1998)

University of North Carolina at Chapel Hill—use of linear adaptive and probabilistic models; nonbinary relevance judgments (Sumner et al. 1998)

Task and Methods   TREC-6 was largely a repeat of TREC-5, with some modifications to improve the consistency of scoring. Six topics were selected from those prepared for the TREC-6 ad hoc task for use in the interactive track. The aspectual retrieval task was maintained, and searchers were allowed a maximum of twenty minutes per search. There were changes in both the explicit directions for completing the aspectual retrieval task and assessing the documents at NIST. Participants were now required to name the aspect(s) that each document they saved discussed. The documents saved by all subjects at all sites for each topic were pooled, and the pooled documents were assessed at NIST. The assessment process asked the evaluators to read the documents from the pool, create a set of aspects of the topic, select a name for each aspect, and then indicate which documents addressed which aspects, and where in the document this occurred. There was no separate judgment of relevance, and it was hoped that by asking both subjects and assessors to name the aspects, it would be possible to address the issue of agreement on aspects between subjects and NIST assessors.

The evaluation measures for TREC-6 were aspectual recall (as in TREC-5) and aspectual precision, which is the fraction of saved documents that contain one or more aspects. Participating sites returned a list of saved documents and elapsed clock time for each search. In addition, detailed event logs for all searches, a full narrative description for at least one interactive session using the experimental system (for a topic common to all sites), and any further guidance given to searchers were reported. Given the experimental design, a typical experimental session consisted of introductory material, prequestionnaires, a tutorial for system one, a post–system one questionnaire, a tutorial for system two, a post–system two questionnaire, and any additional feedback gathered at the end of the entire session.

For the TREC-6 interactive track, the goal of comparing performance between systems at different sites (as well as different systems at the same site) was maintained. The means for doing this was the comparison of the subjects' performance using the ZPRISE control system common to all sites as well as the particular site's experimental system. Having just six topics allowed a Latin square experimental design, in which all subjects at all sites searched on all six topics in the same (random) order. Half of the subjects searched on the first three topics using the experimental system and the last three topics using the control system; the other half of the subjects used the control system first followed by the experimental system. In order to control for interaction effects, each site had to have a minimum of four subjects.

Nine sites participated in the TREC-6 interactive track, a substantial increase over the previous year.

Observations   TREC-6 represents the first true cross-site comparisons in the interactive track. An analysis of variance model was used to assess the contributions of topic, searcher, system, and the system-topic and system-searcher interactions. The topic and the searcher are modeled as random effects and the system as a fixed effect (control/experimental). Eric Lagergren and Paul Over (1998) provide a detailed discussion of the experimental design and statistical evaluation. For all sites, there were significant effects of topic, searcher, and system. The topic effects were the largest, and the searcher effects were present in six of the ten comparisons. Some interactions were also reliable, although which ones varied by site. Using the best model for each site, a cross-site analysis was run. There was a system effect (comparing the experimental and control systems), but multiple comparisons to identify sites that differed from each other did not substantiate the global differences.

This work represents a solid step forward in comparing interactive retrieval systems both within and between sites. An important methodological question remains, however. The experimental design *assumes* that the common control system is effective in eliminating site-related differences. Some preliminary attempts to validate this assumption by comparing results obtained by directly comparing two systems or comparing them indirectly via a common control were not successful (see, for instance, Swan and Allan 1998). In addition, there were pragmatic concerns about the costs of design. To accomplish all of the controls, each searcher was required to complete all six tasks. This along with training and questionnaires took roughly three hours, which is a challenge to accomplish in a single sitting. Participants were also concerned that half of the experimental effort was expended on a control condition that was not of interest to most of them. Groups would have preferred running their own comparisons and controls to better focus effort on interface or interaction techniques of interest to them.

6.2.6   TREC-7

Participants and Approaches

New Mexico State University at Las Cruces—thumbnail-document visualization showing the distribution of matching search terms in the document (Ogden, Davis, and Rice 1999)

Oregon Health Sciences University—Boolean versus natural-language searching for experienced information retrieval professionals; additional individual difference measures (Hersh et al. 1999)

Okapi group (City University, London, and Microsoft Research Ltd.)—comparisons of Okapi with and without relevance feedback and ZPRISE without feedback (Robertson, Walker, and Beaulieu 1999)

RMIT—cluster-based versus list-based organization of search results (Fuller et al. 1999)

Rutgers University—use of negative relevance feedback; relevance feedback implemented as a term-suggestion method (Belkin et al. 1999)

University of California at Berkeley—baseline study after some task-specific modifications of the Cheshire system with more searchers and background information about the searchers (Gey et al. 1999)

University of North Carolina at Chapel Hill—modification of term weights; passage versus document-level relevance feedback (Yang et al. 1999)

University of Toronto—system that blends querying and browsing versus common Web-like interface (Bodner and Chignell 1999)

Task and Methods   The experience and results of the TREC-6 interactive track led to some changes in the design of the TREC-7 experimental protocol. Foremost among these was the decision to drop the comparison of performance of systems between different sites. Although this concept is a central tenet of TREC, the members of the interactive track decided that based on the TREC-5 and TREC-6 experience, this could not be accomplished without imposing inordinately stringent conditions on the participants and decreasing participation in future evaluations. The same experimental design as TREC-6 was used, but groups substituted a control system appropriate to their own research goals.

In TREC-7, as in TREC-5 and TREC-6, the task was aspectual retrieval. The instructions were changed slightly to use the term instance in hopes of clarifying confusions that had arisen, and searchers were given fifteen minutes for each topic. Eight ad hoc topics tailored for the aspectual task were used, and the narrative section of the topic was removed to simplify the judgment process for searchers and assessors. A minimum of eight searchers were required.

Participating sites returned a list of saved documents and elapsed clock time for each search. Detailed event logs for all searches, a full narrative description for at least one interactive session using the experimental system, and any further guidance given to searchers were reported. A test of verbal fluency (Educational Testing Service's FA–1, Controlled Associations) for each searcher and previously recommended data about searcher characteristics were added as requirements. The evaluation measures for TREC-7 were aspectual recall, aspectual precision, and elapsed time.

Observations   Given the experimental design, direct cross-site comparisons are not possible, so the main comparisons of interest are between different systems within a site. Groups conducted several interesting experiments on novel interface and interaction techniques. Although the differences between each group's experimental and control systems were small (and generally nonsignificant), there were still some interesting observations. The Oregon and Rutgers groups identified some individual differences in search performance. A browsing interface explored by the Toronto group tended to promote recall at the expense of precision. And the New Mexico group noted an important caveat in studying visualizations. Their thumbnail visualization technique was intended to help users more quickly identify potentially new aspects. But the time that searchers spend in this component process is dwarfed by the time they spend reading the articles, so improvements in this subcomponent may not be seen in overall speed or accuracy measures.

6.2.7 TREC-8

Participants and Approaches

New Mexico State University at Las Cruces—visualization showing the distribution of query terms, extracted names of people, and locations (Ogden et al. 2000)

Oregon Health Sciences University—compared results from interactive versus batch evaluations (Hersh et al. 2000)

University of California at Berkeley—basic Boolean Cheshire system with new capabilities for negation as well as new ways of navigating results and selecting relevant items (Larson 2000)

RMIT/Commonwealth Scientific and Industrial Research Organisation (CSIRO)—user organization of results (Fuller et al. 2000)

Rutgers University—term suggestion via user controlled relevance feedback versus automatic local context analysis (Belkin et al. 2000)

University of North Carolina at Chapel Hill—several levels of relevance feedback (Yang and Maglaughlin 2000)

University of Sheffield—system with document ranking, best-passage retrieval, and query expansion (Beaulieu et al. 2000)

Task and Methods The TREC-8 interactive track followed the TREC-7 evaluation framework very closely. The task again was the aspectual/instance retrieval task that had been used since TREC-5. Six ad hoc topics tailored for the aspectual task were used, again with the narrative section omitted. The searchers had a maximum of twenty minutes per topic (compared with fifteen in TREC-7). A minimum of twelve searchers were required.

Participating sites returned a list of saved documents and elapsed clock time for each search. Detailed event logs for all searches, a full narrative description for at least one interactive session using the experimental system, and a required set of question-naire data were reported. The verbal fluency test was omitted since no site found any significant relationship between scores on this test and searching behavior or perfor-mance on TREC-7. The evaluation measures for TREC-8 were aspectual recall, aspectual precision, and elapsed time.

Observations   Given the experimental design, direct cross-site comparisons are not possible. Thus, the main comparisons of interest are between different systems within a site. As was the case for TREC-7, most of the differences between each group's control and experimental systems were small and generally nonsignificant. This is true for novel visualization techniques (such as those reported by New Mexico State University and RMIT) as well as techniques like relevance feedback and term weighting that have been shown to be effective in batch evaluations (for example, Oregon Health Sciences University's term-weighting experiment and Sheffield's relevance feedback experi-ment). Either there are really no differences for these different techniques or the experi-ments lack the statistical power to detect differences. With only six topics, it is quite likely that experimental error is still sufficiently large to preclude the detection of all but the largest differences. In some cases, subjective preferences favored alternative in-teraction techniques, suggesting that additional measures can usefully supplement the precision, recall, and time measures.

6.2.8   TREC-9

Participants and Approaches

Chapman University—use of a rich transcript of user actions to predict relevance (Vogt 2001)

Oregon Health Sciences University—compared results from interactive versus batch evaluations (Hersh et al. 2001)

RMIT/Commonwealth Scientific and Industrial Research Organisation (CSIRO)—differ-ent document summaries, title plus first twenty words from document versus title plus the three best-matching sentences (D'Souza et al. 2001)

Rutgers University—different results presentation techniques; ten titles plus the text of the top document versus six scrollable documents showing the best-matching passage (Belkin et al. 2001)

University of Glasgow—different document summaries, query-biased summaries versus full-text of documents (Alexander et al. 2001)

University of Sheffield—use of a known Okapi-based system on a new task (Beaulieu, Fowkes, and Joho 2001)

Task and Methods   The general experimental framework was based on that used in previous interactive tracks, but there were several important changes. There was a desire among the participants to reduce the time required for each search (twenty minutes in TREC-8), reduce the overall length of a search session for each searcher (more than three hours in TREC-8), and explore different tasks and test collections. All of these goals were accomplished by using a fact-finding task (instead of an aspectual retrieval, an ad hoc, or a routing task). Questions from the TREC-8 question-answering track were considered, but they proved to be too easy for the interactive track. Eight more challenging fact-finding tasks that required searchers to look in multiple documents to find the answers were constructed. There were four *n-answer* tasks (for instance, "Name three U.S. senators on nuclear regulatory committees") and four *specific-comparison* tasks (for example, "Do more people graduate with an MBA from Harvard Business School or MIT Sloan?"). A minimum of sixteen searchers were required, and a maximum of five minutes was allowed for each question.

The searcher's task was to answer each question and provide a minimal set of documents that support the answer. Participating sites returned a list of answer parts, their associated documents, and elapsed clock time for each search. Detailed event logs for all searches, a full narrative description for at least one interactive session using the experimental system, and a required set of questionnaire data were reported.

The assessment procedure checked each question to see whether or not it was fully answered, and whether the answers were supported by the document(s) cited. Fully answered and supported questions were assigned a score of one; otherwise a score of zero was assigned to the question. Thus, the evaluation measures for TREC-9 were zero or one answer scores along with the elapsed time.

Observations   Given the experimental design, direct cross-site comparisons are not possible. Hence, the main comparisons of interest are between different systems within a site. There were some reliable differences within sites (for example, RMIT's accuracy and subjective preference advantage for summaries consisting of the three best sentences) as well as several qualitative observations of interest. Again, though, most groups reported no significant differences in accuracy or time for their experimental and control systems. The five-minute time limit proved problematic for some searchers and some topics, especially given the requirement of both providing answers and justifying documents.

Based on the results of the TREC-9 track and a workshop held at SIGIR 2000, several suggestions for improvements in the interactive track were proposed for exploration. An important decision was to reduce some of the time pressures on participants by going to a two-year cycle. The first year (TREC-10) would be used for focused observational studies of Web searching (to identify key issues and define a new task), and the second year (TREC-11) would be used for more detailed metrics-based evaluations. Some candidate recommendations included focusing on more realistic Web searching, including characteristics such as redundant information, authority, heterogeneity and recency, identifying a small number of domains based on popular Web usage, and adding more topics.

6.2.9   TREC-10/2001

Participants and Approaches

Commonwealth Scientific and Industrial Research Organisation (CSIRO)—three interfaces for results presentation (ranked list, clustered results, and a combination); two searching tasks (individual documents or sets of documents) (Craswell et al. 2002)

Oregon Health Sciences University—searchers allowed to choose search engine and other resources; measured the time taken for searching, the number of pages viewed, user satisfaction, and choice of topics (Hersh, Sacherek, and Olson 2002)

Rutgers University—explored differences in query length, encouraged by different instructions (enter complete sentences or words) and interfaces (line or box) (Belkin et al. 2002)

University of Glasgow—investigated the extent to which implicit feedback based on user interactions can substitute for explicit feedback (White, Jose, and Ruthven 2002)

University of Michigan—differences in search expertise (expert or nonexpert searchers) and domain expertise (shopping, medicine) (Bhavnani 2002)

University of Toronto—explored query versus browsing interfaces, and query length (Toms et al. 2002)

Task and Methods   Six groups participated in these observational studies. Important goals of the observations were to increase the realism of the tasks by allowing searchers to use publicly available Web search systems and tools, and to propose a testable hypothesis for TREC-11. To focus the observations somewhat, eight topics were used. These represented four common search tasks (finding consumer medical information, buying an item, planning travel, and collecting materials for a research project) and two levels of specification (full and partial specification—for example, identify three categories of people who should or should not get flu shots and why versus identify the pros and cons of taking large doses of ⟨some drug⟩). The second level of specification was intended to make searches more interesting to the searchers. A target number of twenty-four searchers were recommended, and each searcher was to carry out four searches—two fully specified and two partially specified. Although there was no formal reporting required, sites were encouraged to collect a list of all URLs visited along with a minimal set of effectiveness and efficiency measures as well as searcher characteristics and satisfaction.

Observations   Observational studies can complement the more tightly controlled experimental ones that had previously been used in the interactive track. The six groups explored quite different search scenarios than had previously been tackled in the more controlled TREC settings. The lessons learned from exploratory studies are often difficult to summarize. One theme that emerged at several of the participating sites (for instance, Michigan, Oregon, and Toronto) was that domain expertise can influence the search strategies, although not always the final search outcome.

6.2.10   TREC-11

Participants and Approaches

Commonwealth Scientific and Industrial Research Organisation (CSIRO)—continued explorations of structuring returned results; compared ranked lists with an organizational structure that grouped results by their two-level domain name (Craswell et al. 2003)

Oregon Health Sciences University—explorations of searcher differences in spatial visualization ability and presearch confidence on search (Hersh et al. 2003)

Rutgers University—investigated effects of query length and amount of interaction required (Belkin et al. 2003)

University of Glasgow—ranked lists versus automatically clustering results into a navigable hierarchy; summarization techniques to represent groups of multiple documents (Osdin, Ounis, and White 2003)

University of North Carolina at Chapel Hill—3-d results visualization compared to standard results list; used their own search system instead of the Panoptic search engine (Newby 2003)

University of Toronto—techniques for restricting queries and augmenting queries (Toms, Freund, and Li 2003)

Task and Methods   The tasks were similar to those explored in TREC-10. More experimental control was added by using a common collection, the .gov collection that was used in the TREC-11 Web track, and a common index using the Panoptic search engine (Hawking, Bailey, and Craswell 2000) was available if sites wanted to use it. Eight search topics representing four common search tasks were used (finding personal health information, seeking regulatory information, making travel plans, and collecting materials for a research project), and topics were formulated to require either short answers or the identification of Web sites that address the information need. An example topic is the following: "You are interested in learning more about what measures the U.S. government has taken since 2001 to prevent mad-cow disease. Identify three such measures." The searchers were allotted a minimum of ten minutes per task. The results were to be reported at the end of ten minutes, and optionally at five and fifteen minutes.

The experimental design followed that developed for the TREC-9 interactive track. A minimum of sixteen searchers were required, and each searcher performed all eight search tasks—four using one system and four using another system. Each site performed its own determination of relevant documents, and its relevant documents were then pooled with those of other sites for the final scoring of the tasks. The searches were evaluated for effectiveness (whether the task was successfully completed or not) and efficiency (the elapsed time). In addition, calibration queries were executed, and the time between when the search button was pushed and the result appeared was reported. Standard instruments for collecting background information about the searchers and subjective satisfaction were available, and their use was encouraged.

Observations   As was the case for TREC-7, TREC-8, and TREC-9, the main comparisons of interest are between different systems within a site. There were some reliable performance differences within sites (for example, the Royal Melbourne Institute of Technology found some advantages for its categorization interface at the end of fifteen minutes, although not in the first five minutes; Rutgers found that an interface displaying multiple documents at the same time resulted in less interaction and greater satisfaction, and that longer queries resulted in better performance) and several preference measures supporting various experimental systems. There were some questions about the quality of the baseline search engine and the difficulty of the task for participants.

6.2.11   TREC-12, Interactive Subtrack of the Web Track

Participants and Approaches

Commonwealth Scientific and Industrial Research Organisation (CSIRO)—interface tailored to assist searchers in evaluating and selecting key resources by showing site summaries and site maps (Craswell et al. 2004)

Rutgers University—the role of hierarchical layout of search results in supporting searchers in the topic distillation task compared with a standard ranked list; informal comparisons of query length (Belkin et al. 2004)

Task and Methods   The TREC-12 interactive track was a subset of the Web track focusing on human participation in the topic distillation task. The searchers were asked to construct a resource list (that is, a list of good resources for a topic) on a broad topic by interacting with one or more retrieval systems. Eight topics were selected from the Web topic distillation task and then modified to accommodate searcher interactions. An example distillation task topic is the following: "Assume that you are an art teacher in a high school. You are about to introduce your students to U.S. folk art and folk music. Prepare a list of bookmarks for your students for study materials." A good resource page was defined as one that is principally on the topic, provides credible information on the topic, and is not part of a larger site also principally devoted to the same topic, and examples were provided to the searchers. This task requires searchers to make judgments about the relevance, scope, and diversity of aspects (relative to previously saved searches).

For comparability to the TREC-12 Web track, the .gov collection was used. NIST provided two versions of the Panoptic search engine (Hawking, Bailey, and Craswell

2000). One version of the system was optimized for the topic distillation task by balancing relevance and home pageness, and the other version simply returned pages in decreasing order of relevance. The goals of the track were to investigate whether automatic topic distillation features assisted searchers in performing their task, see if humans could achieve better results than fully automatic systems, and explore whether observed user behaviors could provide insights about improving topic distillation algorithms.

Sixteen searchers were required to balance the eight topics into two blocks that varied the order of two systems. Participating sites sent a list of URLs for each search task to NIST for assessment. Assessors completed a five-point Likert scale for four evaluation criteria: relevance, depth, coverage, and repetition. In the automatic topic distillation task, systems were judged according to the relevance of the answers produced in the top ten results, and the same figure of merit can be computed for the interactive task. Additional information about the search process and the searcher characteristics was also recommended, although not required.

Observations   Only two sites participated in the track, so it is difficult to draw any strong conclusions about the experimental method or results. Both groups, for different reasons, compared a linear presentation of search results with some form of hierarchical structuring of results. The Rutgers group found differences in preference and ease of learning for a hierarchical experimental system compared with a linear control. The hierarchical system required less effort as measured by the number of iterations, the number of documents seen, selected, and reviewed, and the shorter search times. There were some tendencies for linear displays to improve coverage and hierarchical displays to reduce overlap, although the effects are not reliable statistically. The Commonwealth Scientific and Industrial Research Organisation (CSIRO) group also found that searchers preferred the experimental system, and there were some indications that it required less effort, but there were no significant effects of the experimental and control interfaces in terms of relevance, depth, coverage, or repetition measures. There were significant improvements, however, compared to the fully automatic system in terms of relevance, depth, and precision. This suggests that a searcher's effort has a positive effect on system performance (much as it did in early manual query runs) and that there is room for improvement of the automatic algorithms.

6.2.12   TREC-12, HARD Track

Historically, information retrieval systems treat all users the same; if two users provide the same query, they will get the same results. The HARD track has the goal of trying to understand and accommodate some kinds of user differences. A structured technique for obtaining and acting on user information was adopted, consisting of two different processes. Both processes begin with an initial search constructed by someone interested in that topic, who will also be the eventual assessor of the search results. Associated with each search topic was a set of *user metadata*, with values representing aspects of the searcher's context. For instance, the user's familiarity with the topic, the genre of document that the user is interested in, and so on, were encoded as metadata about the topic. Participating sites were initially given the search topic without the metadata and required to submit a ranked list of documents to the track organizers. After this list was submitted, two things happened. The metadata were distributed to the participating sites, to be used as they wished to modify queries and/or results lists. In addition, participating sites were allowed to enter into a limited clarification dialogue with the searcher. Clarification questions could include a request for information about the searcher and that searcher's information need (for instance, the purpose of the query, the genre of document of interest, or the searcher's familiarity with the topic) or about the query and results (say, providing relevance judgments or selecting clarifying terms). Clarification dialogues were limited in the size and the time required to complete them. They were sent to the TREC assessors to complete in a batch fashion. The results of the dialogue then could be used by the sites to modify the queries or search results. The sites then submitted new lists of documents for each of the search topics, which were pooled with the original search results for relevance assessment. Each site's performance in the two runs (the original list and the modified one) was compared in order to measure the effect of taking into account the metadata or the dialogue.

The goal of understanding and accommodating different search and searcher characteristics is similar in some respects to the interactive track, but the batch nature of the interaction makes it quite different in scope. The HARD track is just in its first year (as of this writing), so it is difficult to know how it will evolve, and how its goals and evaluation methods will overlap with those of earlier interactive tracks. Some changes are already being considered, including a reconsideration of passage-level scoring, and more interestingly, the identification of a collection with richer and more interesting metadata.

6.3   Interactive Track Summary and Speculations

Over the course of nine years, the TREC interactive track has changed in significant ways. In TREC-3 and TREC-4, interactive systems (consisting primarily of human modification of queries) were compared with fully automatic systems on the standard routing and ad hoc retrieval tasks. The routing task was especially difficult for searchers both conceptually and pragmatically. The ad hoc task was more natural, but even in this task the notion of constructing a single-best query was not something that is common in interactive retrieval systems. In TREC-5 and TREC-6, an experimental framework for comparing systems (both across and within sites), topics, and searchers was developed. An aspectual retrieval task was developed with interactive searching in mind. The task goes beyond retrieving relevant documents to a type of focused question answering. In addition to the new task, the data on which the summary measures are based has been supplemented with qualitative and quantitative data on searcher characteristics, user satisfaction, and the search process. This data includes system logs, detailed search descriptions, video recording, and think-aloud protocols, all of which support the rich microanalysis of the search process. In TREC-7, TREC-8, and

TREC-9, the emphasis on cross-site comparisons was dropped in order to focus experimental effort on questions of interest for each group. The framework still allowed groups to estimate the effect of their experimental manipulation independent of the effects of the searcher and the topic as well as the order of experimental systems and topics. In TREC-9, the aspectual retrieval task was replaced with a fact-finding task in order to reduce the time required for a session, and to examine a different task and test collection. A two-year cycle was explored in TREC-10 and TREC-11, resulting in more realistic Web-based searches focusing on some common search tasks.

A major result of the TREC interactive track has been the development of a standard methodology for studying interactive IR and comparing the performance of interactive IR systems. Starting with TREC-5, a within-subject experimental design that allows for systems, topic, and searcher main effects and interactions to be identified has been used. The number of searchers and searches per topic has increased from four to sixteen (and more than thirty searchers have been used in some cases). This experimental rigor has come at the cost of long experimental sessions. To mitigate this, the number of topics used is smaller than it was in early years (less than a dozen in TRECs 5–12 compared to fifty in TREC-3).

In addition to improved experimental designs, standard techniques for reporting event logs and detailed narrative descriptions of the search process have been developed, as have instruments for reporting searcher characteristics. This rich data is difficult to analyze, but some innovative techniques like those reported by Suresh Bhavnani (2002) provide some interesting insights into the richness of the interactive search process.

The interactive track, as it has evolved, shares little with other TREC tracks in terms of cross-system comparisons and the development of reusable test collections. Nevertheless, it still shares the important function of encouraging groups to develop and share resources (common tasks, topics, document collections, and assessment methods), and more generally serving as a focal point for work in interactive retrieval systems.

Although there have been several interesting systems developed in the interactive track to support interactive query specification and modification as well as results presentation and exploration, and to look at individual differences in the search process, many of the effects that have been reported over the years have been small, variable, and often not significant statistically. It is always difficult to interpret the failure to find significant effects—it could mean that there are no effects or that there is still sufficiently high variability, making it difficult to detect all but the strongest effects. The continuing, strong desire for more experimental power to find significant effects, when they exist, requires a reduction in the variability or an increase in the number of searches. This might be accomplished by either increasing the number of tasks per searcher or focusing on subtasks. Experimental designs that include significantly more topics (perhaps by focusing on simple searches that participants can accomplish quickly) might be considered as a way to improve experimental power and the generalizability of the results. An alternative is to focus on individual subtasks rather than the end-to-end search process, as is sometimes done in the human-computer interaction and visualization communities. Yet we must be careful not to delude ourselves into thinking that all the ideas suggested by system designers and/or users are good ones, and that simply increasing the experimental power will validate them. There are many reasons why seemingly good ideas are not useful in practice—they may be implemented poorly or inefficiently, there may be usability issues, and the techniques may not be as useful as anticipated.

The interactive track continues to bring to the surface a number of important theoretical and pragmatic issues in conducting experiments with human participants. Such experiments are expensive to run from many perspectives (system development, iterative design of interfaces, and even simply the execution of the experiments of interest), making it difficult to iterate quickly. The idea of going to a longer cycle that mixes less structured observations with more controlled experiments is a good compromise worth pursuing, although it may be difficult to maintain momentum using this format. One of the added advantages of looking at new interaction environments from time to time is that it may increase the realism of the search tasks explored. Using common tasks, topics, collections, and judgments has a number of advantages, yet it is limiting in many ways as well. For example: common tasks are often defined generically to appeal to many researchers, but wind up being of real interest to no one; common topics and collections are not generated by the end user, and may be of limited interest to them; and as noted earlier, there are issues with shared relevance judgments. A renewed exploratory examination of search tasks (perhaps including the development of a taxonomy of search tasks or tactics along the lines of those proposed by Marcia Bates [1979, 1989], Nicholas Belkin, Robert Oddy, and Helen Brooks [1982], and more recently Andrei Broder [2002] for Web search) might also be useful in identifying interesting new research directions.

People are the ultimate consumers of results from information retrieval systems, and it is thus critical to understand their needs and develop systems to support them. In spite of the importance of information retrieval systems in a wide variety of business and government settings, the human-computer interaction aspects of search systems are quite primitive. The most common search experience (on the Web and in many commercial systems) is an impoverished one—a searcher types words into a small box, sees a long list of results, and if they don't succeed they try again. The TREC interactive track has been crucial in developing shared methods for evaluating interactive information retrieval systems. By continuing to explore new evaluation methods and tasks, and by reaching out to other communities, the track can continue to provide a focal point for work in designing and evaluating interactive retrieval systems.

Note

The interactive track is the product of many individuals engaged in spirited discussion over the last decade. The evolution of the track and the prospects for future work have been the subject of a great deal of discussion among TREC organizers, participating groups, attendees in workshops held at SIGIR and SIGCHI conferences, and generally interested observers.

These contributors are too numerous to cite individually, but four groups that participated in six or more of the nine interactive tracks and led one or more of them deserve special mention. One group from Rutgers University participated in all nine of the tracks; a second group, variously from the City University, London, the University of Sheffield, and Microsoft Research Cambridge, participated in the interactive track of TRECs 3–9; another group, from the Royal Melbourne Institute of Technology and Commonwealth Scientific and Industrial Research Organisation (CSIRO), participated in the track in TRECs 5–11; and a fourth group, from the Oregon Health Services University, participated in the track in TRECs 6–11. The full list of participating groups is listed in the summary for each TREC above.

References

Alexander, N., C. Brown, J. Jose, I. Ruthven, and A. Tombros. 2001. Question answering, relevance feedback, and summarisation: TREC-9 interactive track report. In *TREC-9*, 523–532.

Allan, J., J. Callan, W. B. Croft, L. Ballesteros, D. Byrd, R. Swan, and J. Xu. 1998. INQUERY does battle with TREC-6. In *TREC-6*, 169–206.

Bates, M. J. 1979. Information search tactics. *Journal of the American Society for Information Science* 30:205–214.

Bates, M. J. 1989. The design of browsing and berrypicking techniques for online search. *Online Review* 13 (October 1989): 407–424.

Beaulieu, M. M., H. Fowkes, N. Alemayehu, and M. Sanderson. 2000. Interactive Okapi at Sheffield—TREC-8. In *TREC-8*, 689–698.

Beaulieu, M. M., H. Fowkes, and H. Joho. 2001. Sheffield interactive experiment at TREC-9. In *TREC-9*, 645–654.

Beaulieu, M. M., and M. J. Gatford. 1998. Interactive Okapi at TREC-6. In *TREC-6*, 143–167.

Beaulieu, M. M., M. Gatford, X. Huang, S. E. Robertson, S. Walker, and P. Williams. 1997. Okapi at TREC-5. In *TREC-5*, 143–165.

Belkin, N. J., A. Cabezas, C. Cool, K. Kim, K. B. Ng, S. Park, R. Pressman, S. Rieh, P. Savage, and H. Xie. 1997. Rutgers interactive track at TREC-5. In *TREC-5*, 257–265.

Belkin, N. J., C. Cool, J. Jeng, A. Keller, D. Kelly, J. Kim, H.-J. Lee, M.-C. Tang, and X.-J. Yuan. 2002. Rutgers' TREC 2001 interactive track experience. In *TREC 2001*, 465–472.

Belkin, N. J., C. Cool, J. Koenemann, K. B. Ng, and S. Park. 1996. Using relevance feedback and ranking in interactive searching. In *TREC-4*, 181–210.

Belkin, N. J., J. Head, J. Jeng, D. Kelly, S. Lin, S. Y. Park, C. Cool, P. Savage-Knepshield, and C. Sikora. 2000. Relevance feedback versus local context analysis as term suggestion devices: Rutgers' TREC-8 interactive track experience. In *TREC-8*, 565–574.

Belkin, N. J., A. Keller, D. Kelly, J. Perez-Carballo, C. Sikora, and Y. Sun. 2001. Support for question-answering in interactive information retrieval: Rutgers TREC-9 interactive track experience. In *TREC-9*, 463–474.

Belkin, N. J., D. Kelly, G. Kim, J.-Y. Kim, H.-J. Lee, G. Muresan, M.-C. Tang, X.-J. Yuan, and C. Cool. 2003. Rutgers interactive track at TREC 2002. In *TREC 2002*, 539–548.

Belkin, N. J., D. Kelly, H.-J. Lee, Y.-L. Li, G. Muresan, M.-C. Tang, X.-J. Yuan, and X.-M. Zhang. 2004. Rutgers' HARD and Web interactive track experiments at TREC 2003. In *TREC 2003*, 532–543.

Belkin, N. J., R. N. Oddy, and H. M. Brooks. 1982. ASK for information retrieval: Part I: Background and theory. *Journal of Documentation* 38, no. 2:61–71.

Belkin, N. J., J. Perez Carballo, C. Cool, D. Kelly, S. Lin, S. Y. Park, S. Y. Rieh, P. Savage-Knepsheild, and C. Sokora. 1999. Rutgers' TREC-7 interactive track experience. In *TREC-7*, 275–284.

Belkin, N. J., J. Perez Carballo, C. Cool, S. Lin, S. Y. Park, S. Y. Rieh, P. Savage, C. Sikora, H. Xie, and J. Allan. 1998. Rutgers' TREC-6 interactive track experience. In *TREC-6*, 597–610.

Bhavnani, S. K. 2002. Important cognitive components of domain-specific search knowledge. In *TREC 2001*, 571–578.

Bodner, R. C., and M. H. Chignell. 1999. ClickIR: Text retrieval using a dynamic hypertext interface. In *TREC-7*, 573–582.

Broder, A. 2002. A taxonomy of Web search. *SIGIR Forum* 36, no. 2:3–10.

Broglio, J., J. P. Callan, W. B. Croft, and D. W. Nachbar. 1995. Document retrieval and routing using the INQUERY system. In *TREC-3*, 29–38.

Buckley, C., A. Singhal, M. Mitra, and G. Salton. 1996. New retrieval approaches using SMART: TREC-4. In *TREC-4*, 25–48.

Charoenkitkarn, N., M. Chignell, and G. Golovchinsky. 1995. Interactive exploration as formal text retrieval method: How well can interactivity compensate for unsophisticated retrieval algorithms? In *TREC-3*, 179–199.

Charoenkitkarn, N., M. H. Chignell, and G. Golovchinsky. 1996. Is recall relevant? An analysis of how user interface conditions affect strategies and performance in large-scale text retrieval. In *TREC-4*, 211–231.

Cooper, W., A. Chen, and F. C. Gey. 1995. Experiments in the probabilistic retrieval of full text documents. In *TREC-3*, 127–134.

Craswell, N., D. Hawking, T. Upstill, A. McLean, R. Wilkinson, and M. Wu. 2004. TREC-12 Web and interactive tracks at CSIRO. In *TREC 2003*, 193–204.

Craswell, N., D. Hawking, R. Wilkinson, and M. Wu. 2002. TREC-10 Web and interactive tracks at CSIRO. In *TREC 2001*, 151–158.

Craswell, N., D. Hawking, R. Wilkinson, and M. Wu. 2003. TREC 11 Web and interactive tracks at CSIRO. In *TREC 2002*, 197–206.

D'Souza, D., M. Fuller, J. Thorn, P. Vines, J. Zobel, and O. de Krester. 2001. Melbourne TREC-9 experiments. In *TREC-9*, 437–452.

Egan, D. 1988. Individual differences in human-computer interaction. In *Handbook of human-computer interaction*, ed. M. Helander, 543–568. North Holland, Netherlands: Elsevier.

Fuller, M., M. Kaszkiel, D. Kim, C. Ng, J. Robertson, R. Wilkinson, M. Wu, and J. Zobel. 1999. In *TREC-7*, 465–474.

Fuller, M., M. Kaszkiel, S. Kimberley, J. Zobel, C. Ng, R. Wilkinson, and M. Wu. 2000. The RMIT/CSIRO ad hoc, Q & A, Web, interactive, and speech experiments at TREC-8. In *TREC-8*, 549–564.

Fuller, M., C. L. Kaszkiel, P. Ng, P. Vines, R. Wilkinson, and J. Zobel. 1998. MDS TREC-6 report. In *TREC-6*, 241–257.

Gey, F., H. Jiang, A. Chen, and R. R. Larson. 1999. Manual queries and machine translation in cross-language retrieval and interactive retrieval with Cheshire II at TREC-7. In *TREC-7*, 527–540.

Hawking, D., P. Bailey, and N. Craswell. 2000. Efficient and flexible search using text and metadata. In *CSIRO mathematical and information sciences Technical Report 2000–83*. Panoptic system available at ⟨http://www.panopticsearch.com⟩.

Hearst, M. 1999. User interfaces and visualization. In *Modern Information Retrieval*, ed. R. Baeza-Yates and B. Ribeiro-Neto, 257–323.

Hearst, M., J. Pedersen, P. Pirolli, H. Schuetze, G. Grefenstette, and D. Hull. 1996. Xerox site report: Four TREC-4 tracks. In *TREC-4*, 97–119.

Hersh, W., and B. Day. 1998. A comparison of Boolean and natural language searching for the TREC-6 interactive task. In *TREC-6*, 585–596.

Hersh, W., S. Moy, D. Kraemer, L. Sacherek, and D. Olson. 2003. More statistical power needed: The OHSU TREC 2002 interactive track experiments. In *TREC 2002*, 505–511.

Hersh, W., S. Price, D. Kraemer, B. Chan, L. Sacherek, and D. Olson. 1999. A large-scale comparison of Boolean versus natural language searching for TREC-7 interactive. In *TREC-7*, 491–500.

Hersh, W., L. Sacherek, and D. Olson. 2002. Observations of searchers: OHSU TREC 2001 interactive track. In *TREC 2001*, 434–441.

Hersh, W., A. Turpin, S. Price, D. Kraemer, B. Chan, L. Sacherek, and D. Olson. 2000. Do batch and user evaluations give the same results? An analysis from the TREC-8 interactive track. In *TREC-8*, 531–540.

Hersh, W., A. Turpin, L. Sacherek, D. Olson, S. Price, B. Chan, and D. Kraemer. 2001. Further analysis of whether batch and user evaluations give the same results with a question answering task. In *TREC-9*, 407–416.

Huffman, S. 1996. Acquaintance: Language independent document categorization by n-grams. In *TREC-4*, 359–371.

Knaus, D., E. Mittendorf, P. Schauble, and P. Sheridan. 1996. Highlighting relevant passages for users of the interactive SPIDER retrieval system. In *TREC-4*, 233–243.

Koenemann, J., R. Quatrain, C. Cool, and N. Belkin. 1995. New tools and old habits: The interactive searching behavior of expert online searchers using INQUERY. In *TREC-3*, 145–177.

Lagergren, E., and P. Over. 1998. Comparing interactive information retrieval systems across sites: The TREC-6 interactive track matrix experiment. In *Proceedings of the twenty-first Annual International ACM SIGIR conference*, 164–172.

Larson, R. R. 2000. Berkeley's TREC-8 interactive track entry: Cheshire and ZPRISE. In *TREC-8*, 613–622.

Larson, R. R., and J. McDonough. 1998. Cheshire II at TREC-6: Interactive probabilistic retrieval. In *TREC-6*, 649–659.

Lu, X. A., D. J. Holt, and D. J. Miller. 1996. Boolean system revisited: Its performance and its behavior. In *TREC-4*, 459–473.

McDonald, J., W. Ogden, and P. Foltz. 1998. Interactive information retrieval using term relationship networks. In *TREC-6*, 379–383.

Milic-Frayling, N., C. X. Zhai, X. Tong, M. P. Mastrioanni, D. E. Evans, and R. G. Lefferts. 1996. CLARIT TREC-4 interactive experiments. In *TREC-4*, 323–357.

Newby, G. B. 2003. Progress in general-purpose IR software. In *TREC 2002*, 758–764.

Ogden, B., J. Cowie, E. Ludovik, H. Molina-Salgado, S. Nirenburg, N. Sharples, and S. Sheremtyeva. 2000. CRL's TREC-8 systems cross-lingual IR and Q&A. In *TREC-8*, 513–523.

Ogden, W., M. Davis, and S. Rice. 1999. Document thumbnail visualizations for rapid relevance judgments: When do they pay off? In *TREC-7*, online version only.

Osdin, R., I. Ounis, and R. W. White. 2003. Using hierarchical clustering and summarization approaches for Web retrieval: Glasgow at the TREC 2002 interactive track. In *TREC 2002*, 640–644.

Over, P. 2001. The TREC interactive track: An annotated bibliography. *Information Processing and Management* 37, no. 3:369–381.

Robertson, S. E., S. Walker, and M. M. Beaulieu. 1999. Okapi at TREC-7: Automatic ad hoc, filtering, VLC, and interactive track. In *TREC-7*, 253–264.

Robertson, S. E., S. Walker, M. M. Beaulieu, M. Gatford, and A. Payne. 1996. Okapi at TREC-4. In *TREC-4*, 253–264.

Robertson, S. E., S. Walker, S. Jones, M. M. Hancock-Beaulieu, and M. Gatford. 1995. Okapi at TREC-3. In *TREC-3*, 109–126.

Saracevic, T., and P. Kantor. 1988. A study of information seeking and retrieving. III. Searchers, searching, and overlap. *Journal of the American Society for Information Science* 39, no. 3:197–216.

Schmidt-Wesche, B., R. Mack, and C. L. Cesar. 1998. IBM search UI prototype evaluation at the interactive track of TREC-6. In *TREC-6*, 517–534.

Sumner, R. G., Jr., K. Yang, R. Akers, and M. W. Shaw Jr. 1998. Interactive retrieval using IRIS: TREC-6 experiments. In *TREC-6*, 711–734.

Swan, R. C., and J. Allan. 1998. Aspect windows, 3-D visualizations, and indirect comparisons of information retrieval systems. In *Proceedings of the twenty-first annual international ACM SIGIR conference*, 173–181.

Toms, E. G., L. Freund, and C. Li. 2003. Augmenting and limiting search queries. In *TREC 2002*, 813–822.

Toms, E. G., R. W. Kopak, J. Bartlett, and L. Freund. 2002. Selecting versus describing: A preliminary analysis of the efficacy of categories in exploring the Web. In *TREC 2001*, 653–662.

Tong, R. 1995. Interactive document retrieval using TOPIC: A report on the TREC-3 experiment. In *TREC-3*, 201–209.

Veerasamy, A. 1996. Interactive TREC-4 at Georgia Tech. In *TREC-4*, 421–431.

Vogt, C. 2001. Passive feedback collection—An attempt to debunk the myth of clickthroughs. In *TREC-9*, 141–150.

Voorhees, E. M. 1998. Variations in relevance judgments and the measurement of retrieval effectiveness. In *Proceedings of the twenty-first annual international ACM SIGIR conference*, 315–323.

Voorhees, E. M., and D. K. Harman. 2000. Overview of the eighth text retrieval conference. In *TREC-8*, 1–23.

White, R. W., J. M. Jose, and I. Ruthven. 2002. Comparing explicit and implicit feedback techniques for Web retrieval: TREC-10 interactive track report. In *TREC* 2001, 534–538.

Yang, K., and K. Maglaughlin. 2000. IRIS at TREC-8. In *TREC-8*, 645–656.

Yang, K., K. Maglaughlin, L. Meho, and R. G. Sumner Jr. 1999. IRIS at TREC-7. In *TREC-7*, 555–566.

7   Beyond English
Donna K. Harman

7.1   Introduction

The investigation into the retrieval for languages other than English started in TREC-3. In particular, it was decided to do the ad hoc task in Spanish, and this task continued for three years (TRECs 3–5). In TREC-5, a second language was added and the ad hoc task was done in Chinese for two years. TREC-6 added a much more challenging task: cross-language retrieval. Here the idea is to start with a question in one language, and then retrieve documents in a second language. The task was first done with European languages (for three years), then one year of Chinese, and finally two years of Arabic (English questions against Arabic documents).

This chapter summarizes the work done in all these tasks. The TREC proceedings for each year (available online at ⟨http://trec.nist.gov⟩) contain overviews of the tracks, plus papers from all groups participating in the tracks that year. The rest of this chapter summarizes the work done, with those summaries derived from the various track overviews (Smeaton and Wilkinson 1997; Wilkinson 1998; Schäuble and Sheridan 1998; Braschler et al. 1999; Braschler, Schäuble, and Peters 2000; Gey and Chen 2001; Gey and Oard 2002; Oard and Gey 2003). To conserve space, the numerous individual papers mentioned in this chapter are not included in the references but can be found in the overview for the track in the appropriate TREC proceedings. Note that there are additional publications from these groups, including further results and analyses, and the references in the track overviews should be checked to obtain these.

Each section in this chapter reviews one of the tasks. For the monolingual tasks (Spanish and Chinese), both the task and the evaluations were similar to the English ad hoc task, and the sections mainly review what was done and summarize what was learned. The cross-language tasks were more complex, and the sections for these tasks contain the design (and redesign) of the tasks and discuss the various issues in evaluation.

7.2   Spanish in TRECs 3–5

Note that the track overviews were not separate from the main TREC overview in TREC-3 and TREC-4, and readers are referred to those overviews (Harman 1995, 1996) for references and details. TREC-5 has a separate track report (Smeaton and Wilkinson 1997).

In TREC-3, four groups worked with twenty-five topics in Spanish, using a document collection consisting of about two hundred megabytes (58,000 records) of a Mexican newspaper from Monterey called *El Norte*. Since there was no training data for testing (similar to the start-up problems for TREC-1), the groups used simple techniques in TREC-3. But these techniques grew more complex once training data were available.

Two of the four groups simply ported their TREC-3 ad hoc systems to Spanish. Cornell University built a simple stemmer and a stop-word list of 342 terms, and then used its SMART system for Spanish. The University of Massachusetts at Amherst found that a new Spanish stemmer produced a 12 percent improvement in later experiments.

The other two groups used n-grams. Dublin City University used a trigram retrieval model, weighting the trigrams from traditional frequency weighting, and built a simple stemmer based on the Porter algorithms. The Environmental Research Institute of Michigan used a quad-gram retrieval model with some of the traditional weighting mechanisms.

The major result from the preliminary TREC-3 experiment in a second language was the ease of porting the retrieval techniques across languages. Cornell reported that only five to six hours of system changes were necessary (beyond the creation of any stemmers or stop-word lists).

The Spanish track in TREC-4 used the same documents as TREC-3, but twenty-five new topics were built. In addition to three of the groups from TREC-3, there were seven new groups. In TREC-4, there were training data (the results of TREC-3), and groups were able to do more elaborate testing.

Cornell and the University of Massachusetts at Amherst continued their strategy of porting their ad hoc systems. Both groups performed query expansion experiments, with Cornell expanding by fifty terms in the top twenty documents and the University of Massachusetts using a Spanish version of its query expansion tool InFinder.

Dublin City University abandoned n-grams to try the New Mexico State University (NMSU) part-of-speech tagger (at New Mexico State University) as an input to the SMART system. This method also produced the base forms. The traditional tf $*$ IDF weighting was used, but adjectives were double weighted.

The University of Central Florida used semantic modeling of the topics. A profile (entity-relationship schema) was manually built for each topic using the TREC-3 topics as training. Lists of synonyms were constructed and an automatic Spanish verb form generator was built. The synonym and domain lists (instances of entities) were carefully created by Sara Abbott as part of a student summer project. The results for this were spectacular in the sense that it gave an indication of what could be done with lots of manual effort.

Xerox Research Center tested several Spanish-language analysis tools, including a finite-state morphological analyzer and a hidden-Markov part-of-speech tagger to produce correct stemmed forms as well as to identify verbs and noun phrases. The SMART system was used as the basic search engine. Expansion was done using the top twenty retrieved documents.

George Mason University tried combinations of three, four, and five grams, at different thresholds of retrieval, using a vector-space type system for ranking. The best results were obtained using five grams and a hundred terms. A Spanish stop-word list was constructed using a Spanish linguist to prune a list of the most frequent five hundred terms in the text.

The University of California at Berkeley trained its logistic regression method on the Spanish results from TREC-3. This group also built a rule-based Spanish stemmer, including a borrowed file of all verb forms for irregular verbs. The queries were formed manually by translating them into English, searching the university's news database from the MELVYL electronic catalog to reformulate the English queries based on these searches, and then translating the queries back into Spanish.

The Royal Melbourne Institute of Technology (RMIT), Australia, tried the combination methods used for its English results. A stop list of 316 words was created, along with a Spanish stemmer that principally removed regular verb suffixes. Experiments were done using combinations of stopped and stemmed results.

The U.S. Department of Defense used a five-gram method that normalizes the resulting document vectors by subtracting a "collection" centroid vector. Minimal topic expansion was done.

New Mexico State University investigated five different methods of query translation. The Spanish topics were first manually translated into English for use in these tests. Then five different methods were used to automatically translate the topics into Spanish. The five methods were a term-by-term translation using a bilingual dictionary, the use of the parallel corpus (the United Nations corpus) for high-frequency terms, the use of a parallel corpus to locate statistically significant terms, optimization of the second method, and finally a latent semantic indexing (LSI) technique on the parallel corpus.

Figure 7.1 shows the results of the evaluation.

In general, the groups participating in the TREC-4 Spanish task were using the same techniques as for English. This is consistent with the philosophy that the basic search engine techniques are language independent. Only the auxiliary techniques, such as stop-word lists and stemmers, need to be language dependent. Several of the groups did major linguistic work on these auxiliary files, such as the noun-phrase identifier necessary for expansion using InFinder (part of the University of Massachusetts INQUERY system) and the several new Spanish stemmers that were built. Two groups used n-gram methods, as had two of the groups in TREC-3.

Several other issues unique to the TREC-4 track should be mentioned. First, the outstanding results from the University of Central Florida indicate the benefits of very careful building of the manual queries, in this case by building extensive synonym sets and other such lists. The utility of this technique outside the rather limited domain of the TREC-4 topic set is an open question, however. The group from Xerox did extensive work with Spanish-language tools, but the effort had the same type of minimal effects generally seen in English. As a final point, the query translation experiments by New Mexico State University demonstrated an interesting approach to the problem of multilingual retrieval.

The Spanish retrieval track in TREC-5 should be seen as the concluding event for Spanish ad hoc task. One reason it was run for the third year is that there had

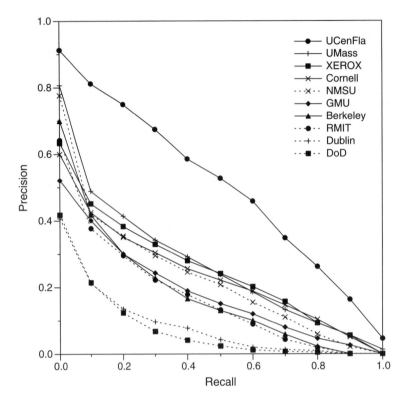

Figure 7.1
Spanish retrieval results in TREC-4

been some concern that the Spanish task was being done only with Mexican news-papers. For TREC-5, a 173,950 document collection from the *Agence France Press* 1994 newswire from Spain was added to the task, along with twenty-five new topics.

Note that most of the groups continued to use their TREC ad hoc systems, with minor modifications for Spanish. Groups that had used n-grams moved back to using their more traditional systems in TREC-5. Two groups, Xerox and New Mexico State University, continued their more complex experiments, although their results did not surpass those groups that simply ported their English ad hoc systems.

Figure 7.2 shows the results of the evaluation.

7.3   Chinese

It was decided to try a new and quite different language in TREC-5 along with the final round of Spanish. Chinese was chosen because it was completely unlike Spanish in that a simple port, using a stemmer and a new stop-word list, would not suffice for re-

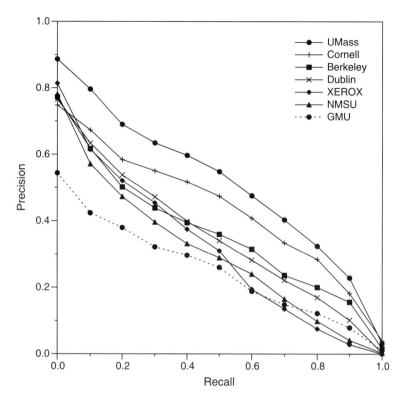

Figure 7.2
Spanish retrieval results in TREC-5

trieval. Chinese has no word separation, and is composed of characters that represent at least one complete syllable rather than a word. Whereas the retrieval task was the same as for the Spanish (monolingual ad hoc), it was expected that the task would be much harder. The data were a collection of 164,811 documents taken from both the *People's Daily* and the *Xinhua News Agency*. The twenty-eight topics were built outside NIST by a nonnative speaker of Chinese.

Ten groups took part in this first Chinese track (for details, see the track overview in Smeaton and Wilkinson 1997). Three of the groups (Cornell University, George Mason University, and the Swiss Federal Institute of Technology (ETH)) tried the simplest method, which was to use their standard retrieval system and treat the characters as if they were words. This worked reasonably well (for the results of the evaluation, see figure 7.3). Note that the Swiss Federal Institute of Technology (ETH) results are not included since its run arrived late and was therefore unofficial.

Other groups, particularly those with a knowledge of Chinese (the City University of New York (CUNY); the University of California at Berkeley, and the Information

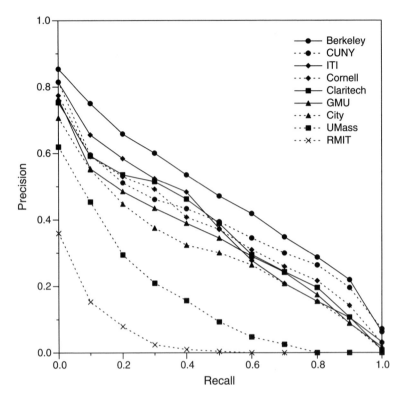

Figure 7.3
Chinese retrieval results in TREC-5

Technology Institute, Singapore), worked on segmenting the characters into words before processing using their standard methods. They used different methods for that segmentation, with the City University of New York using dictionary and statistical techniques to detect 2-, 3-, and occasionally 4-character words, and the group from Berkeley building a dictionary of 140,000 words to automatically segment the text.

There were four groups that tried both word- and character-based retrieval. The University of Massachusetts at Amherst used a hidden-Markov model to segment the text, and utilized characters, groups of characters, and words to retrieve. The Royal Melbourne Institute of Technology (RMIT) used both characters and words (found by dictionary methods) in various combinations. Claritech Corporation utilized n-gram character and word-based approaches, with the segmentation done using dynamic programming algorithms and heuristics to segment the text into minimal numbers of words via a 100,000-word dictionary. And finally, the City University, London, used both characters and words, with those words found using a greedy algorithm approach with a 70,000-word dictionary.

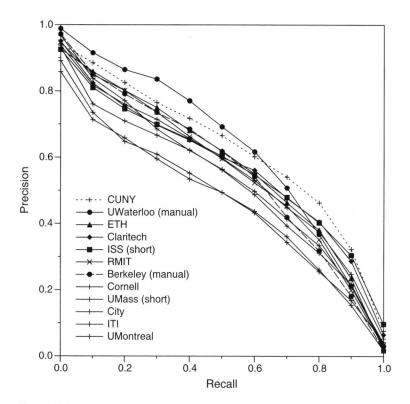

Figure 7.4
Chinese retrieval results in TREC-6

Almost all groups tried query expansion using characters and/or words. Expansion generally worked well for everyone. Many groups also tried manual corrections to the queries, and this also improved the results. It should be noted from figure 7.3 that the results are generally quite high compared with English.

The Chinese track was rerun in TREC-6 (Wilkinson 1998), using the same documents but with twenty-six new topics. Twelve groups took part, and major effort was put into comparing the use of words versus character n-grams. Additionally, there was work in phrases by the City University, London, investigation of n-grams (n = 2, 3, and 4) by the Institute of Systems Science, new techniques for identifying names by the University of California at Berkeley, and various combining techniques for others. Many groups chose to manually edit the topics, again getting improvements from this.

Figure 7.4 shows the best run for each group. Two things should be noted from these results. First, the manual runs are marked as manual since there were many groups doing this. And second, the results are not only high; the curves also do not have the usual recall/precision curve shapes. Both the participants and NIST felt that something was wrong with either the topics or the data: possibly the topics were too easy and/or the data too small. For this reason, it was decided to stop monolingual Chinese retrieval in TREC until more analysis could be done. In TREC-9, both monolingual and cross-language versions of Chinese were evaluated (see section 7.6).

7.4   The European Cross-Language Track

A paper (Sheridan, Ballerini, and Schäuble 1998) given at the workshop on cross-language retrieval at the Nineteenth Annual International ACM–SIGIR Conference on Research and Development in Information Retrieval in 1996 (Grefenstette 1998) led to the formation of a cross-language information retrieval (CLIR) track in TREC-6. This track was done in cooperation with the Swiss Federal Institute of Technology, which not only obtained permission for TREC to use stories from the Swiss news agency Schweizerische Depeschen Agentur (SDA) but also provided considerable guidance and leadership to the track. There were CLIR tracks for European languages in TREC-6, TREC-7, and TREC-8.

7.4.1   TREC-6 CLIR

The TREC-6 CLIR track (Schäuble and Sheridan 1998) required the retrieval of either English, German, or French documents that are relevant to topics written in a different language. Participating groups could choose any cross-language combination—for example, English topics against German documents or French topics against English documents. In order to have a baseline retrieval performance measurement for each group, the results of a monolingual retrieval experimental run in the document language were also to be submitted. For instance, if a cross-language experiment was run with English topics retrieving German documents, then the result of an equivalent experiment where German topics retrieve German documents must also have been submitted. These results would be considered comparable since the topics are assumed to be proper translations across the languages.

The different document collections used for each language are outlined in table 7.1. The Associated Press collection consists of newswire stories in English, while the

Table 7.1
Document collections used in the CLIR track

Document language	Source	Number of documents	Size
English	AP news, 1988–1990	242,918	760MB
German	SDA news, 1988–1990	185,099	330MB
	NZZ articles, 1994	66,741	200MB
French	SDA news, 1988–1990	141,656	250MB
Italian	SDA news, 1989–1990	62,359	90MB

French Schweizerische Depeschen Agentur collection is a similar collection of newswire stories from the Swiss news agency of the same name. The German document collection has two parts: the first is composed of further newswire stories from the Swiss news agency while the second part consists of newspaper articles from a Swiss newspaper, the *Neue Zuercher Zeitung* (NZZ).

The Italian data are included in this table for completeness, although they were not used in TREC-6.

The newswire collections in English, French, and German were chosen to overlap in time frame (1988 to 1990) for two reasons. First, since a single set of topics had to be formulated to cover all three document languages, having the same time frame for newswire stories increased the likelihood of finding a greater number of relevant documents in all languages. The second reason for the overlapping time frame was to allow groups that use corpus-based approaches for CLIR to investigate what useful corpus information they could extract from the *comparable* document collections being used. One of the resources provided to the CLIR track participants was a list of 83,698 news documents in the French and German Schweizerische Depeschen Agentur collections that were likely to be comparable based on an alignment of stories using news descriptors assigned manually by the news agency reporters, the dates of the stories, and common cognates in the texts of the stories.

The twenty-five test topic descriptions were provided by NIST in English, French, and German, using translations of topics originally written mostly in English (for an example topic, including all its translations, see figure 7.5). Participating groups that wished to test other topic languages were permitted to create translations of the topics in their own language and use these in their tests, as long as the translated topics were made publicly available to the rest of the track participants. The final topic set therefore also had translations of the twenty-five topics in Spanish, provided by the University of Massachusetts, and Dutch, provided by TNO in the Netherlands.

Although not strictly within the definition of the cross-language task, participation by groups that wanted to run monolingual retrieval experiments in either French or German using the CLIR data was also permitted. Since the CLIR track was run for the first time in TREC-6, this was intended to encourage new IR groups working with either German or French to participate. The participation of these groups also helped to ensure that there would be a sufficient number of different system submissions to provide the pool of results needed for relevance judgments.

The evaluation of CLIR track results was based on the standard TREC evaluation measures used in the ad hoc task. Participating groups were free to use different topic fields (lengths) and to submit either automatic or manual experiments according to the definitions used for the main TREC ad hoc task.

7.4.2   TREC-6 Results

A total of thirteen groups, representing six different countries, participated in the TREC-6 CLIR track. Participating groups were encouraged to run as many experiments as possible, both with different kinds of approaches to CLIR and different language

<num> Number: CL9
<*E*-title> Effects of logging

<E-desc> Description:
What effects has logging had on desertification?

<E-narr> Narrative:
Documents with specific mention of local government's or international agencies' efforts to stop deforestation are relevant. Also relevant are documents containing information on desertification and its side effects such as climate change, soil depletion, flooding, and hurricanes caused by excessive logging.

<num> Number: CL9
<F-title> Les effets de la déforestation

<F-desc> Description:
Quels sont les effets de la déforestation sur la désertification?

<F-narr> Narrative:
Tous les documents qui donnent des analyses spéci ques sur les mesures des gouverments locaux ou des agences internationales pour frêner la déforestation sont pertinants.   Les articles qui contiennent des renseignements sur la déserti cation et ses effets secondaires comme les changements de climat, l'épuisement de la terre, les inondations et les ouragans sont également applicables.

<num> Number: CL9
<G-title> Auswirkungen von Abholzung

<G-desc> Description:
Welche Auswirkungen hat das Abholzen auf die Ausbreitung der Wüste?

<G-narr> Narrative:
Alle Artikel über Bemühungen von Regierungen ebenso wie von internationalen Agenturen die Wüstenausbreitung zu bremsen, sind wesentlich. Ebenso relevant sind Artikel über Ausbreitung der Wüsten und ihre Mitwirkungen, wie zum Beispiel Klimawechsel, Verarmung der Erde und Orkane die auf übermässige Abholzung zurückzuführen sind.

Figure 7.5
Sample CLIR topic statement from TREC-6, showing all languages

Table 7.2
Overview of submissions to CLIR track

Language combinations

Document language	Query language					
	English	German	French	Spanish	Dutch	Total
English	7	15	10	2	6	40
German	12	10	4	—	—	26
French	10	4	15	—	—	29
Total	29	29	29	2	6	95

combinations. An overview of the submitted runs is given in table 7.2 and shows that the main topic languages were used equally (each were used in twenty-nine experiments), whereas English was somewhat more popular than German or French as the choice for the document language to be retrieved. This is in part because the groups that used the query translations in Spanish and Dutch only evaluated those queries against English documents. In total, ninety-five result sets were submitted for evaluation in the CLIR track.

An important contribution to the track was made by a collaboration between the University of Maryland and the LOGOS Corporation, which provided a machine translation of German documents into English. Only the German Schweizerische Depeschen Agentur documents were prepared and translated in time for the submission deadline. This machine-translation output was provided to all participants as a resource, and was used to support experiments run at ETH, Duke University, Cornell University, the University of California at Berkeley, and the University of Maryland.

Cross-language retrieval using dictionary resources was the approach taken in experiments submitted by groups at New Mexico State University, the University of Massachusetts, the Commissariat à l'Energie Atomique of France, the Xerox Research Centre Europe, and TNO in the Netherlands. Machine-readable dictionaries were obtained from various sources, including the Internet, for different combinations of languages, and used in different ways by the various groups.

The corpus-based approach to CLIR was evaluated by ETH, using similarity thesauri, and the collaborative group of Duke University, the University of Colorado, and Bellcore, which used latent semantic indexing. An innovative approach for cross-language retrieval between English and French was tested at Cornell University. This approach was based on the assumption that there are many similar-looking words (near cognates) between English and French, and that with some simple matching rules, relevant documents could be found without a full translation of queries or documents.

An overview of results for each participating group is presented in figure 7.6. This figure represents the results based on only twenty-one of the twenty-five test

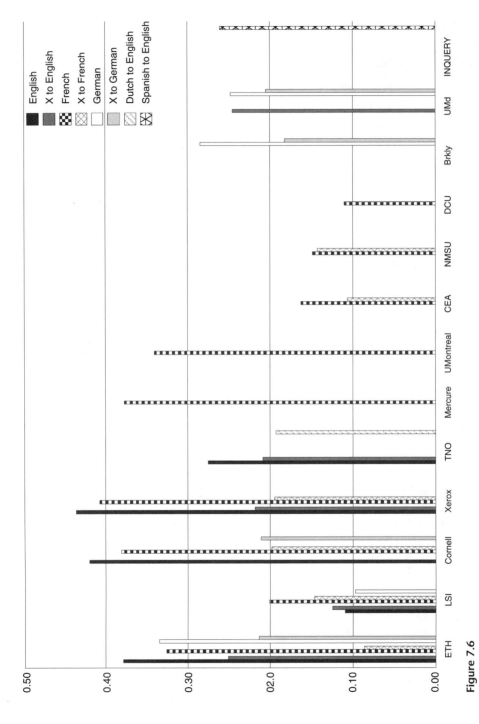

Figure 7.6
TREC-6 CLIR track results (average precision, best run)

topics, but the results from all twenty-five are not significantly different. The figure shows results for each group and each document language for which experiments were submitted. The y axis represents the average precision achieved for the *best* experiment submitted by each group and each document language. Cross-language experiments are denoted by, for example, "X to French," whereas the corresponding monolingual experiments are denoted "French." For instance, the figure shows that the best experiment submitted by Cornell University performing cross-language retrieval of French documents achieved an average precision of 0.2.

Note that the presentation of results in figure 7.6 does not distinguish between fully automatic cross-language retrieval, and those groups that included some interactive aspect and user involvement in their experiments. The groups at Xerox, Berkeley, and Dublin City University submitted experiments that involved manual interaction. Also, some groups participated only in a monolingual capacity: Dublin City University, the University of Montreal, and IRIT France (labeled Mercure in figure 7.6).

Although figure 7.6 does not provide a sound basis for between-group comparisons, some general comments can be made on the overall results. Comparing cross-language results to the corresponding monolingual experiments, it seems that cross-language retrieval is performing in a range of roughly 50 to 75 percent of the equivalent monolingual case. Many different approaches to cross-language retrieval were tried and evaluated, and groups using each of the different approaches have achieved good results. For example, the corpus-based method used by ETH to perform cross-language retrieval for German documents worked as well as the machine-translation-based methods used by the University of Maryland and Cornell. The dictionary-based method used by Xerox for cross-language retrieval to French did about the same as the use of cognate overlap by Cornell.

7.5   TREC-6 Evaluation Issues

In general, the testing paradigm and test collection used in the TREC-6 CLIR track worked well, but there were two issues that caused concern. First, the many possible language pairs used by the various participants made it difficult to compare across systems, and presented a somewhat unrealistic evaluation in that many situations require the retrieval of documents irregardless of the language of those documents. This would suggest that an improved task would be the retrieval of a ranked list of documents in all three languages—that is, a merged list—and this task was implemented in TREC-7.

The second issue was more difficult to solve. The TREC-6 topics were created at NIST by two persons who were native English speakers, but had strong skills in French and German. Because these people were new to TREC and because the NIST staff was unable to provide much guidance due to a lack of language skills, the TREC-6 CLIR topics are more simplistic than TREC topics normally done in English, and this may have allowed the simpler CLIR techniques to work better than would be expected. Additionally, there were some problems with the translations produced for the topics at NIST, and corrections needed to be made by native speakers before the topics could be released. As a final problem, NIST assessors working in nonnative languages tend to be much slower in making relevance judgments, and this became considerably worse when working in three languages. Only thirteen out of twenty-five topics were evaluated in time for any analysis before TREC, with the rest not finished until several months later. This problem with nonnative speakers led to forming collaborative partnerships for the evaluation effort in TREC-7.

7.5.1   TREC-7 and TREC-8 CLIR Track

In TREC-7 (Braschler et al. 1999), the task was changed slightly and participants were asked to retrieve documents from a multilingual pool. They were able to choose the topic language, and then had to find relevant documents in the pool regardless of the languages the texts were formulated in. As a side effect, this meant that most groups had to solve the additional task of merging results from various bilingual runs. The languages present in the pool were English, German, French, and Italian, with Italian being a new language introduced for TREC-7. There were twenty-eight topics distributed, each topic being translated into four languages. To allow for participation of groups that did not have the resources to work in all four languages, a secondary evaluation was provided that permitted such groups to send in runs using English topics to retrieve documents from a subset of the pool just containing texts in English and French. There were no monolingual runs as part of the cross-language track in TREC-7.

The TREC-7 task description also defined a subtask (GIRT), working with a second data collection containing documents from a structured database in the field of social science. Unfortunately, the introduction of these data were probably premature since no groups were able to work with these data in TREC-7. The data were used again in TREC-8 (for more information on these data, see task description in TREC-8).

The document collection for the main task contained the same documents used in TREC-6, with an extension to Italian texts from the Schweizerische Depeschen Agentur (see table 7.1). Note that Italian texts were only available for 1989 and 1990, and therefore the Italian Schweizerische Depeschen Agentur collection is considerably smaller than the one for French or the English Associated Press texts.

There were significant changes in the way the topics were created for TREC-7 because of the problems in TREC-6. Four different sites, each located in an area where one of the topic languages is natively spoken, worked on both topic creation and relevance judgments.

The four sites were:

- English: NIST, Gaithersburg, Maryland, United States (Ellen M. Voorhees)
- French: EPFL Lausanne, Switzerland (Afzal Ballim)
- German: IZ Sozialwissenschaften, Berlin, Germany (Jürgen Krause and Michael Kluck)
- Italian: CNR, Pisa, Italy (Carol Peters)

Seven topics were chosen from each site to be included in the topic set. The twenty-one topics from the other sites were then translated, and this ultimately led to a collection of twenty-eight topics, each available in all four languages. Relevance judgments were made at all four sites for all twenty-eight topics, with each site examining only the pool of documents in its native language.

How well did this distributed manner of creating topics and making relevance judgments work?

Topic development is clearly subjective and depends on the creator's own particular background. Additionally, for CLIR it must be presumed that both the language and the cultural background also impact the choice and phrasing of topics. A close examination of the topics would probably permit an astute observer to group them fairly accurately according to source language and creation site. This should not be considered negative, nor should it affect the validity of the results. Nevertheless, it causes some problems both in the translation of the topics and their assessment.

Topic translation raises the typical problems involved in any translation: a total understanding of the source is necessary in order to achieve a perfect rendering of the target. But this is complicated in CLIR by the need to find an acceptable balance between precision with respect to the source and naturalness with respect to the target language. Ideally, the translations should reflect how a native speaker would phrase a search for that topic in one's own language and culture.

An accurate assessment of relevance for retrieved documents for a given topic implies a good understanding of the topic. The fact that the CLIR track used a distributed scenario for building topics and making relevance judgments meant that relevance judgments were usually not done by the creators of the topics. In addition to general problems of judgment consistency when this occurs, there is the influence of the multilingual/multicultural characteristics of the task. The way a particular topic is discussed in one language will not necessarily be reproduced in the documents in other languages. Therefore, a topic that did not appear to raise problems of interpretation in the language used for its preparation may be much more difficult to assess against documents in another language.

There were no problems reported by the participants with either the topic creation, the translations, or the relevance judgments. Nevertheless, it was decided to work on closer coordination between the four groups in TREC-8, and to get a fifth group that specializes in translations to check all final topic translations for both accuracy and naturalness. The effect of the distributed method of relevance judgments on results is probably small since the distribution was across languages, not topics. As long as results are compared within the same language—that is, pairs of results on German documents—and not across languages—that is, results on English documents versus German documents—there are unlikely to be issues here. Comparing results from retrieving documents in different languages is equivalent to the comparison of results using two different human judges, and therefore this comparison should be avoided.

For TREC-8 (Braschler, Schäuble, and Peters 2000), each site first formulated an initial ten topics. At a topic selection meeting, the seven topics from each site that were felt to be best suited for the multilingual retrieval setting were selected. Each site then translated the twenty-one topics formulated by the others into the local language. This ultimately led to a pool of twenty-eight topics, each available in all four languages. It was decided that roughly one-third of the topics should address national/regional, European, and international issues, respectively. To ensure that topics were not too broad or too narrow and were easily interpretable against all document collections, monolingual test searches were conducted. As a final check on the translations, Professor Christa Womser-Hacker from the University of Hildesheim volunteered her students to review all topic translations.

7.5.2   TREC-7 and TREC-8 CLIR Results

A total of nine groups from five different countries submitted results for the TREC-7 CLIR track. The participants submitted twenty-seven runs: seventeen for the main task, and ten for the secondary English to French/English evaluation. Five groups (Berkeley, Eurospider, IBM, Twenty-One, and Maryland) tackled the main task. English was, not surprisingly, the most popular topic language, with German coming in a strong second. Every language was used by at least one group.

Figure 7.7 shows a comparison of runs for the main task. The best automatic runs against the full document pool are depicted for each of the five groups that worked on the main task. As can be seen, most participants performed in a fairly narrow band. This is interesting given the extremely different approaches of the individual participants: IBM used translation models automatically trained on parallel and comparable corpora, Twenty-One used sophisticated dictionary lookup and a "Boolean-flavored" weighting scheme; Eurospider employed corpus-based techniques, using similarity thesauri and pseudorelevance feedback on aligned documents; and the Berkeley and Maryland groups used off-the-shelf machine-translation systems.

A particularly interesting aspect of the TREC-7 CLIR track was how participants approached the merging problem. Again, many interesting methods were used. Among the solutions tried were: Twenty-One compared the averages of similarity values of individual runs, Eurospider used document alignments to map runs to comparable score ranges through linear regression, and IBM used the modeling of systemwide probabilities of relevance. But it was also possible to avoid the merging problem—for example, the Berkeley group expanded the topics to all languages and then ran them against an index containing documents from all languages, therefore directly retrieving a multilingual result list.

A total of twelve groups from six different countries submitted results for the TREC-8 CLIR track. Eight participants tackled the full task (up from five in TREC-7), submitting twenty-seven runs (up from seventeen). The remainder of the participants either submitted runs using a subset of languages or concentrated on the GIRT subtask only. English was the dominant topic language, although each language was used by at least one group as the topic language.

Figure 7.8 shows a comparison of runs for the main task. The graph shows the best runs against the full document pool for each of the eight groups. Because of the diversity of the experiments conducted, the figures are best compared on the basis of the specific features of the individual runs, details of which can be found in the track

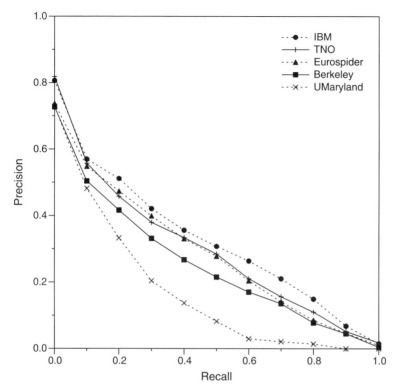

Figure 7.7
TREC-7 CLIR results, X to English/German/French/Italian

papers. For example, New Mexico State runs use manually translated queries, which are the result of a monolingual user interactively picking good terms. This is clearly an experiment that is different from the runs of some other groups that are essentially doing ad hoc–style cross-language retrieval, using no manual intervention whatever.

Approaches employed in TREC-8 by individual groups include:

- Statistical machine translation by IBM
- Combinations of n-grams and words by the Applied Physics Lab at Johns Hopkins University
- Query translation using bilingual dictionaries by Twenty-One
- Experiments using pseudorelevance feedback by Claritech
- Transaction models derived from parallel text by the University of Montreal
- Similarity thesaurus-based translation by Eurospider
- Evaluation of the Pirkola measure by the University of Maryland
- Manually translated queries using interactive testing

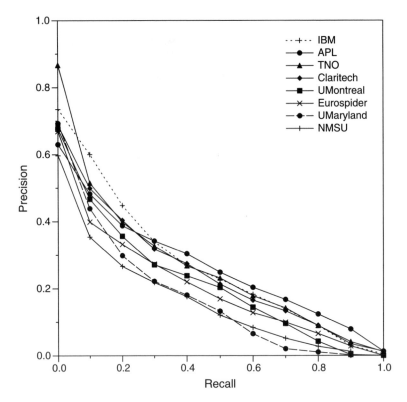

Figure 7.8
TREC-8 CLIR results, X to English/German/French/Italian

Merging remained an important issue for most participants. The University of Maryland tried to circumvent the problem by using an unified index in some of its runs, but the other groups working on the main task all had to rely on merging of some sort to combine their individual, bilingual cross-language runs. Some of the approaches that year included: merging based on probabilities that were calculated using log (rank) by various groups including IBM, merging using linear regression on document alignments by Eurospider, linear combinations of scores by the Applied Physics Laboratory, and of course, straight, score-based merging.

Two groups submitted runs for the GIRT subtask. The University of California at Berkeley participated in that subtask only, and did some extremely comprehensive experiments using both the English titles of the documents and the English/German thesaurus supplied with the collection. These runs show some of the interesting properties of GIRT. It is also possible to do ad hoc–style runs on GIRT, ignoring controlled vocabulary, English titles, and the thesaurus. This approach was taken by Eurospider.

7.5.3   Summary of European CLIR in TREC

Part of the reason for the heavy use of English as the topic language is that 75 percent of the TREC-8 participants were from English-speaking countries. But an additional factor is the lack of resources that do not use English as the source language—for example, dictionaries for German to Italian. Both of these reasons contributed to the decision to move the European cross-language task to Europe in 2000 within the new CLEF evaluation (⟨http://www.clef-campaign.org⟩). It was generally felt that more Europeans would join such an activity and that these groups would bring with them increased knowledge of non-English resources.

The three years of European cross-language evaluation done at NIST not only achieved the initial goals but laid the foundation for continued CLIR evaluation in the CLEF workshop in Europe and the NTCIR (⟨http://research.nii.ac.jp/ntcir/workshop/⟩) workshop in Asia. A technique to produce the necessary topics and relevance judgments for the test collections in a distributed manner such that the collection properly reflects its multilingual and multicultural origins was devised in TREC-7 and TREC-8, and this method is currently being used in both these non-NIST CLIR evaluations. Twenty-two groups took part in the NIST evaluations, cumulatively reporting over one hundred experiments on diverse methods of cross-language retrieval, and these early experiments serve as the basis for continued research in CLIR.

7.6   Chinese CLIR

A different cross-language evaluation was held in TREC-9—that of using English topics against Chinese documents (Gey and Chen 2001). The new corpus was 188 megabytes (126,937 documents), from 1998–1999 Hong Kong newspapers. Note that these newspapers use a different encoding scheme (BIG5) than the newspapers used in the TREC-4 Chinese track, which used Chinese from mainland China (GB encoding), and it is likely that the newspapers used in this track had less duplication of exact documents than those used earlier.

This time the twenty-five topics were built at NIST, although not with native speakers. This gave NIST more control over the topics, in that the English version could be checked. A native Chinese speaker at NIST did check the translations.

Sixteen groups took part in the TREC-9 evaluation, including three from China. The majority of the approaches used word or phrase translation from English to Chinese by lookup in bilingual dictionaries or word lists. The most-used dictionary was the English-Mandarin word list of approximately 120,000 word pairs that had been generated by the Linguistic Data Consortium (LDC). Other dictionaries included the CETA dictionary and the KingSoft online bilingual dictionary, with some of the groups also using local or proprietary dictionaries.

Because only one language is involved in this cross-language task (unlike the European one), it was decided to ask all groups for both cross-lingual and monolingual runs. (Note that the terms *cross-language* and *cross-lingual* are being used interchangeably here and in general in the CLIR community.)

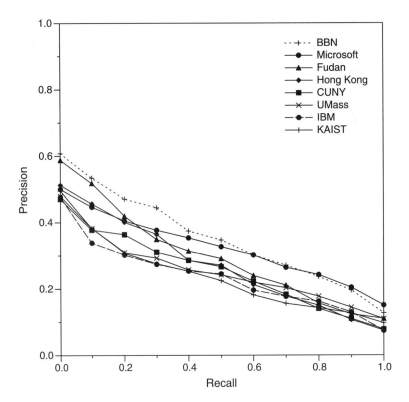

Figure 7.9
TREC-9 Chinese cross-lingual retrieval results

Figure 7.9 gives the results for the best eight systems for the cross-language task. In general, these systems are more complex than those seen in the earlier European cross-language task. The top system (BBN) modeled the word-translation probabilities using a hidden-Markov method, utilizing some of the lexica mentioned earlier and also two parallel corpora for the translations. It used both pre- and post-translation expansion, but using words only.

Another of the systems, Microsoft Research, China, used a modified SMART system, but did many experiments using both words and characters. This system also used parallel text from the Web, bilingual lexica, and a statistical translation model that is a variant of the IBM models. Additionally, it heavily investigated translation disambiguation and the correct location and translation of phrases.

Fudan University, China, used translation resources available only locally, including three different dictionaries and a Chinese thesaurus with 70,000 entries. It also worked on rule-based named-entity extractors for the words not included in the dictionaries.

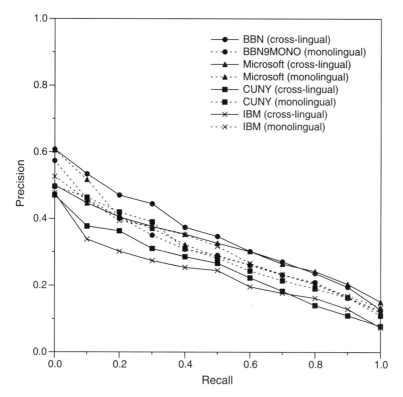

Figure 7.10
TREC-9 Chinese monolingual versus cross-lingual retrieval results

Two groups, IBM and the City University of New York, tried a combination of techniques, with the City University combining the results of commercial translation software with a run using dictionary-translated queries based on the LDC word list. IBM combined three runs based on statistical query translation, a commercial translation, and statistical document translation. Both groups not only used the LDC word list but mined additional terms out of the parallel corpus of the Hong Kong laws.

This short summary of some of the groups illustrates the different methods that were tried. For more information, see the track overview (Gey and Chen 2001) and also the full papers in the TREC-9 proceedings.

Figure 7.10 compares the cross-lingual results with the monolingual ones. It should be noted that the performance of the monolingual systems are "normal" compared to the Chinese monolingual runs in TREC-4. This is probably due to both better data and better topics, and confirms that this test collection is much better than the older one. The second item to note is that there is little difference between monolingual and cross-lingual results, with the cross-lingual run from BBN actually better than the monolingual run. This was quite unexpected as the monolingual results are usually regarded as the "ceiling" for the cross-language runs. One fact is that BBN simply did less work on the monolingual runs, but more important, this difference was also seen in the later Arabic cross-language evaluations. This phenomena shows that there is something interesting about the methods used in CLIR; in particular, it is speculated that the various expansion techniques when used across languages are actually improving performance over monolingual. One possibility is that by providing multiple sources of evidence, there is both better term disambiguation and better coverage of multiple aspects of terms in the original query.

Since the NTCIR workshop in Asia had started to include Chinese CLIR, it was decided to do a different language in TREC-10 to avoid the duplication of efforts. To see later work in Chinese CLIR, go to the NTCIR Web site (⟨http://research.nii.ac.jp/ntcir/workshop/⟩).

7.7   Arabic CLIR

TREC 2001 (TREC-10) and TREC 2002 (TREC-11) had evaluations of cross-language English to Arabic (Gey and Oard 2002; Oard and Gey 2003). The design of the test collection and evaluation were similar to the Chinese CLIR, but unlike the Chinese, there was no earlier test collection to train on in TREC 2001. Ten groups took part, most using a simple bag-of-words approach.

The document collection was the Arabic *Agence France Press* newswire from the years 1994–2000. There were 383,872 newswire stories in Unicode and encoded in UTF-8, for a 896 megabyte collection. There were twenty-five topics built at the LDC using native speakers of Arabic. The topics were built in English, but then translated to Arabic. Additionally, there was a French translation donated by the French Ministry of Defense. Participants could do cross-lingual (from English or French) or monolingual runs.

Although there are word separators in Arabic (unlike Chinese), one of the main known difficulties about Arabic is its rich morphology, and therefore the importance of properly dealing with this. The various groups tried different ways of indexing the terms, including sometimes combining these indexes:

- Using the words as they occurred (seven groups tried this)
- Using a stemmer that removes suffixes and prefixes (seven groups also did this); there were three stemmers developed—by the Illinois Institute of Technology (IIT), New Mexico State University, and the University of Maryland—plus two stemmers from nonparticipants (Tim Buckwalter and Shereen Khoja)
- Using the root (a further "stemming" operation), which allows words with related meaning to cluster (two groups did this)
- Using character n-grams (three groups tried this)

There was additional normalization done by many of the groups such as the deleting of characters that are "optional" in Arabic or normalizing alternative Unicode representations of an Arabic letter. Stop words were also removed, where those stop words were usually the stemmed version of a word.

All of the nine groups that did cross-language retrieval translated the query to Arabic. There were four different types of resources used, with two heavily used and two used by only one group:

· Machine-translation systems, where there were two different commercial systems used, either to do the direct translation or to provide a source of evidence to construct the query
· Translation lexica, where two different commercial lexica plus one locally constructed by New Mexico State University were used
· Parallel corpora; BBN used the parallel set of United Nations documents, aligning these documents statistically and locating useful word pairs
· Transliteration; the University of Maryland used pronunciation-based transliteration to Arabic for "unknown" English terms in the query

In addition to various indexing methods and resources, groups did experiments automatically selecting from multiple possible translations, and pretranslation and/or post-translation query expansion using pseudorelevance feedback.

Figures 7.11 and 7.12 show the results of the evaluation. Figure 7.11 portrays the cross-lingual results of the evaluation, with a comparison of the best of these to their monolingual version shown in figure 7.12. It should be noted that the results for monolingual and cross-lingual are not much different for some systems, and at least one system had higher CLIR results. This is the phenomena glimpsed in the Chinese CLIR and illustrated here once again.

In a cautionary note, this first cross-language Arabic test collection should be used carefully for later runs. Because it was the first time that Arabic had been run in TREC, there were diverse approaches that unfortunately led to little overlap in the retrieved document list. This meant that the pooling for relevance judgments could take fewer documents from each list (only seventy as opposed to the normal one hundred), and this is likely to lead to missed relevant documents. The fact that the topics used were fairly broad, with many (an average of 165) relevant documents, will also lead to missed relevant documents. So the collection does not pass the normal "completeness" tests of TREC as defined in chapter 2, this volume. Whereas this does not affect the results of the TREC 2001 evaluation, it does indicate that this collection is flawed as far as future use by other systems, and thus care needs to be taken.

The second year of Arabic cross-language retrieval drew nine participants and allowed more complex experiments (Oard and Gey 2003). Besides individual experiments on both monolingual and cross-lingual Arabic retrieval, the groups did a separate experiment to measure the effect of resources on results. A set of standard

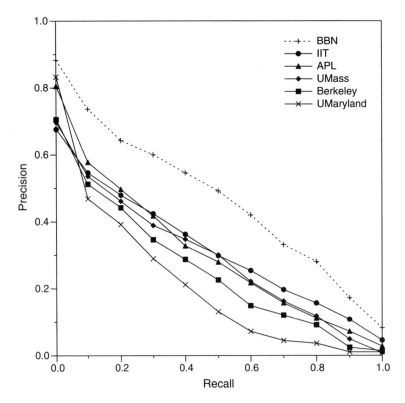

Figure 7.11
TREC 2001 Arabic cross-lingual retrieval results

linguistic resources was made available and runs were made to compare results using only this set to those using all available information.

The documents were the same as for TREC 2001, and fifty new topics were created by the LDC. These topics were generally seen as improved from the first year in that they were less broad (the average number of relevant documents came down from 165 to 118). There was more overlap between the returned document sets, and therefore the relevance judgments could be based on the full pooling of the top one hundred documents from each group. Various tests showed that this test collection is likely to be complete and stable for later use, unlike the TREC 2001 collection.

Because the groups had training data for this second year, they were able to tackle more complex algorithms. Five of the nine groups concentrated on monolingual Arabic retrieval; of these five, three groups then did the cross-language task by translating the topic into Arabic in order to repeat their monolingual task.

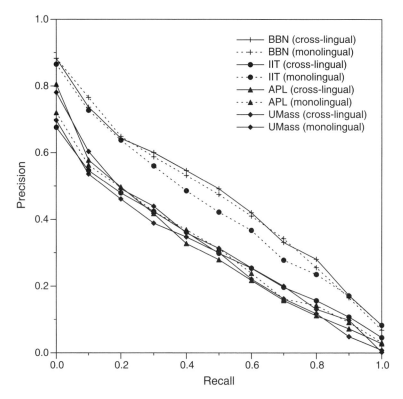

Figure 7.12
TREC 2001 Arabic monolingual versus cross-lingual retrieval results

• Hummingbird Technologies did monolingual only, using the same system as in TREC 2001.

• The University of Neuchatel indexed words and trigrams, performed their monolingual retrieval, and then merged those retrieval runs. It also tried query expansion with both types of indexes.

• The University of California at Berkeley focused on stemming and stop words using a fully translated version of the Arabic data to build two different stemmers and a 3,447-entry stop-word list. These were used for monolingual retrieval utilizing the standard Berkeley system, including query expansion. The CLIR was performed by using machine translation from the English topics to Arabic.

• The Illinois Institute of Technology also worked with different stemming approaches—one that used rule-based stemming, and one that used patterns. It also used a machine translation of the topic to Arabic for the CLIR runs.

• The Applied Physics Laboratory at Johns Hopkins University has traditionally worked with n-grams. For TREC 2002, it tested three, four, and five-grams, using a combination of these for its monolingual runs. The CLIR was performed using machine translation to Arabic for the topics.

The other four groups worked mainly on the CLIR task.

• The University of Maryland created translation probabilities using input from several different sources (two machine-translation systems, a bilingual dictionary, and the BBN translation probability tables). These translations were then used with five different CLIR methods.
• IBM Research used its machine-translation capabilities for the CLIR task. Two different systems were tried—one that translated the documents to English (for retrieval using the English topic), and one that looked at the probability of generating the English query stem based on Arabic words or morphemes.
• The University of Massachusetts did an extensive set of experiments from the information retrieval viewpoint. For translation, it built a bilingual lexicon using a proper-name dictionary and machine-translation systems. Both pre- and post-translation query expansion was used, along with a series of morphological normalization techniques. Its final runs were combinations of variants using these different pieces.
• BBN continued its work with probabilistic translation and retrieval, generating a new bilingual translation lexicon using the United Nations corpus. It tried several stemmers, and performed both English and Arabic query expansion.

The cross-lingual and monolingual results are shown in figures 7.13 and 7.14. The monolingual results are somewhat higher, reflecting the concentration on monolingual Arabic retrieval by many groups. For the groups that did both, however, there are cross-language runs that are better than the monolingual. Once again, this verifies that there is something unusual going on in cross-language expansion that needs further investigation in terms of applications to monolingual expansion principles.

The use of standard resources was a unique contribution of this track. These resources were contributed by several groups for use by all, and included an Arabic "light" stemmer built in collaboration between the University of Massachusetts and the University of Maryland. BBN also contributed its table of translation probabilities based on the United Nations corpus. These, and two resources from nonparticipants, were used in a standard run by five groups. The maximum improvement from using additional resources ranged from 4 to 11 percent.

7.8   Conclusions

The search engines used in TREC are mostly language independent. For a language similar to English, such as Spanish, a simple port of the system, and a Spanish stemmer and stop-word list, will do an adequate job. Better results can be obtained with knowl-

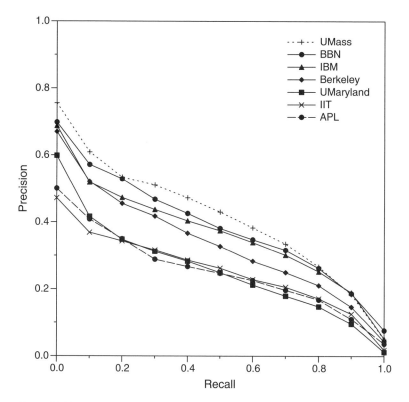

Figure 7.13
TREC 2002 Arabic cross-lingual retrieval results

edge of the language, and further work, such as seen in the European CLEF campaign, shows that adapting general-purpose information retrieval tools to specific languages has some payoff (Savoy 2003). Yet in general, most of the tools developed for English, such as pseudorelevance feedback or other query expansion methods, also work in these other languages. When looking at heavily agglutinative languages, such as German, an n-gram system such as the Applied Physics Laboratory system could improve results, but even there the simple English tools work adequately.

Languages that are extremely different from English, such as Chinese, require extra steps. For Chinese, segmentation into words or work with bigram indexing is necessary in order to take advantage of the English tools. Again, improved results can be obtained using more sophisticated methods (some of the work done in TREC-9 illustrates that), but adequate results can be obtained using language-independent retrieval on segmented words or character bigrams. For Arabic, the morphology poses a problem, but again, once this was "solved," the standard tools such as query expansion worked.

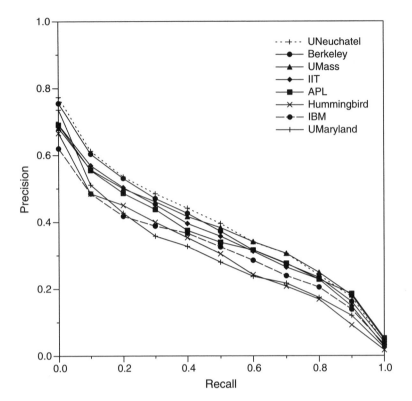

Figure 7.14
TREC 2002 Arabic monolingual retrieval results

For cross-language work, reasonable resources are necessary to allow the translation of the topic into the target language. For example, many groups in TREC worked on monolingual Arabic retrieval, and then used the two commercial Arabic translation systems to transform the English topic into Arabic.

The TREC work in non-English has left behind a good set of test collections, all available to the public. A new distributed method of building test collections for multiple languages has been created, and is currently being used both in the European CLEF project and the Asian NTCIR project. Equally important, the TREC work has created a community of researchers interested in working with other languages, either in a monolingual or a cross-lingual mode.

References

Braschler, M., J. Krause, C. Peters, and P. Schäuble. 1999. Cross-language information retrieval (CLIR) track overview. In *TREC-7*, 25–32.

Braschler, M., P. Schäuble, and C. Peters. 2000. Cross-language information retrieval (CLIR) track overview. In *TREC-8*, 25–34.

Gey, F., and A. Chen. 2001. TREC-9 cross-language information retrieval (English-Chinese) overview. In *TREC-9*, 15–24.

Gey, F., and D. Oard. 2002. The TREC 2001 cross-language information retrieval track: Searching Arabic using English, French, or Arabic queries. In *TREC 2001*, 16–25.

Grefenstette, G., ed. 1998. *Cross-language information retrieval*. Boston: Kluwer Academic Publishers.

Harman, D. K. 1995. Overview of the third text retrieval conference (TREC-3). In *TREC-3*, 1–20.

Harman, D. K. 1996. Overview of the fourth text retrieval conference (TREC-4). In *TREC-4*, 1–23.

Oard, D., and F. Gey. 2003. The TREC 2002 Arabic/English CLIR track. In *TREC 2002*, 17–26.

Savoy, J. 2003. Cross-language information retrieval: Experiments based on the CLEF 2000 corpora. *Information Processing and Management* 39, no. 1:75–115.

Schäuble, P., and P. Sheridan. 1998. Cross-language information retrieval (CLIR) track overview. In *TREC-6*, 31–44.

Sheridan, P., J. P. Ballerini, and P. Schäuble. 1998. Building a large multilingual test collection from comparable news documents. In *Cross-language information retrieval*, ed. G. Grefenstette, 137–180. Boston: Kluwer Academic Publishers.

Smeaton, A., and R. Wilkinson. 1997. Spanish and Chinese document retrieval at TREC-5. In *TREC-5*, 57–64.

Wilkinson, R. 1998. Chinese document retrieval at TREC-6. In *TREC-6*, 25–30.

8 Retrieving Noisy Text

Ellen M. Voorhees and John S. Garofolo

Much of the text available today is created in electronic form. The widespread availability of word processors, computer-based typesetting equipment, and Web page authoring packages means that the full text of documents are readily available as input for retrieval systems. Such documents are not necessarily error free—they may contain misspellings and grammatical errors, for example, and formatting commands for structural elements such as tables may be intermixed with the text—but they are generally a faithful representation of the author's content. Given the ubiquitousness of such text, most retrieval tasks assume faithful representations. Nevertheless, applications such as retrieving text that has been garbled in transmission require methods for retrieving noisy or "confused" text.

The TREC confusion and spoken-document retrieval (SDR) tracks were investigations into retrieval methods that are robust in the face of systematic errors in the document text. The confusion track was motivated by the need to provide electronic access to legacy documents by scanning originals and capturing the output of the optical character recognition (OCR) process. Since OCR processing can have substantial error rates for poor-quality originals, retrieval methods that can accommodate OCR errors are required. The focus in the SDR track was to provide access to spoken documents (recordings of speech) by retrieving the output of automatic speech recognition (ASR) systems. Once again, the ASR process is likely to introduce errors into the textual representation of the document, so robust retrieval methods are required.

This chapter reviews the findings of the two tracks, with the confusion track described in the next section and the SDR track in the following one. Both tracks found that the systematic errors introduced by the earlier processing can be compensated for. With appropriate compensation, ad hoc retrieval from noisy text can be as effective as retrieval from clean text for a broad range of error rates.

8.1 The Confusion Track

The confusion track was run in both TREC-4 and TREC-5. In TREC-4, the baseline "truth" document set was corrupted at NIST by randomly selecting characters to be deleted, substituted, or added to create two new documents sets with 10 and 20 percent error rates, respectively (that is, 10 and 20 percent of the original characters were affected). The random selection of characters to corrupt was intentionally neutral in that it did not try to model any particular type of error-producing process; the hope was that if the noise was not specific to one kind of noise, the results would apply to any kind of noisy data. Random noise does not map well to actual applications where the errors are systematic, however. The TREC-5 confusion track, therefore, concentrated specifically on the problem of retrieving scanned documents [10]. The remainder of this section describes the TREC-5 version of the confusion track.

8.1.1   The Task

The TREC-5 confusion track studied a particular type of retrieval problem called *known-item searching*. A known-item search simulates a user seeking a particular, partially remembered document in the collection. In contrast to the more standard ad hoc search task where the goal is to retrieve and rank the entire set of documents that pertain to a given subject of interest, the goal in a known-item search is to retrieve just that one particular document. Known-item searching is well suited to the problem of retrieving noisy data because it stresses those parts of a retrieval system that are most affected by noise. OCR techniques generally misinterpret low-frequency words such as proper nouns and technical terms more often than common words. Yet low-frequency words are high content-bearing words, and are precisely the words likely to be used to locate a specific document.

8.1.2   The Data

Table 8.1 provides examples of the known-item questions used in the track. The questions were created by five NIST staff members who developed ten questions each (one question needed to be dropped from the test set so only forty-nine topics were actually used in the test). Each question was designed to target one specific document from the *1994 Federal Register*, the corpus used in the track. Different topic authors used different techniques to construct their questions—such as using an index of the collection to find unique words, or starting with "interesting" documents and adding conditions to the question to ensure uniqueness—but the authors did not specifically pick documents that they thought would be difficult for the OCR process.

The *Federal Register* is printed by the U.S. Government Printing Office as a record of the transactions of the government. One issue is published each business day, and it contains notices to federal agencies and organizations, executive orders and proclamations, proposed rules and regulations, and so forth. The *Federal Register* was selected for these experiments because it is a large collection for which both hard-copy and elec-

Table 8.1
Examples of known-item questions from the TREC-5 confusion track

- Use of solar power by the Florida energy office
- Excessive markup of zero-coupon treasury bonds
- I am looking for a document about the dismissal of a lawsuit involving Adventist Health Systems
- I am looking for theft data on the Chevrolet Corsica
- Efforts to establish cooperative breeding programs for the yellow-crowned amazon parrot
- Morphological similarities between different populations of saltwater crocodiles

tronic versions are readily available. The corpus contains 395 megabytes of text divided into approximately 55,600 documents.

Participants in the track were given three different text versions of the *Federal Register* corpus. The first version was derived from the typesetting files provided by the Government Printing Office; this was regarded as the ground-truth text version of the collection and was used to design the questions. The second version was the output obtained by scanning the hard-copy version of the corpus. The estimated character error rate of this version of the corpus is 5 percent. The final version of the corpus was obtained by down sampling the original page images produced above and scanning the new images. The estimated character error rate of the down-sampled images is 20 percent.

8.1.3 Evaluation

The task in the track was to locate the target story for each question in each of the three versions of the corpus. Participants submitted to NIST a ranking of the top one thousand candidates per question per corpus. They were free to use any retrieval approach they desired, provided no information from one version of the corpus was used to search another version of the corpus. For example, this restriction prohibited groups from expanding queries using the clean collection and running those expanded queries on a degraded version of the corpus. The design of the track permits the study of how individual retrieval approaches deal with OCR character error rates, and also provides a comparison of the effectiveness of different retrieval approaches when using noisy data.

The most basic evaluation of how well a retrieval system performs a known-item search is to look at the rank at which the target document is retrieved. Summary measures are also needed to facilitate comparison. The most commonly used comparative measure is the "mean-reciprocal-rank." The mean-reciprocal-rank is the mean of the reciprocal of the rank at which the known item was found, averaged over all the queries, and using zero as the reciprocal for queries that did not retrieve the known document.

As a measure, the mean of the reciprocals of the ranks has several advantages compared to the mean of the ranks themselves. The mean reciprocal is bounded between zero and one (with one representing perfect retrieval), so its value is interpretable without knowing how many documents were ranked. Furthermore, the mean rank is greatly influenced by target documents that are retrieved at large ranks, which does not reflect the importance of those documents in practice. In contrast, the mean reciprocal still penalizes runs that do not retrieve a known item, but minimizes the difference between, say, retrieving a known item at rank 750 and retrieving it at rank 900. An additional benefit is that since there is only one target document, the mean reciprocal is mathematically equivalent to the summary measure most commonly used to report ranked retrieval results, mean average precision, and is also equal to precision at 100 percent recall. This gives researchers familiar with ranked retrieval evaluation a feel for the known-item search results.

Table 8.2
Mean reciprocal rank scores for runs submitted to the TREC-5 confusion track

Run name	Submitter	Baseline	5%	20%
rutcf	Rutgers	—	.2041	.1174
anu5con	ANU	.3635	.2992	—
gmu961	GMU	.3856	.3135	.2221
gmu962	GMU	.2039	.1900	.1524
CLCON	CLARIT	.7293	.4024	.2138
CLCONF	CLARIT	.7293	.2297	.1898
ETHFR94N	ETH	.7353	.5737	.3218
ETHFR94P	ETH	.7353	.3720	.4978

8.1.4 Retrieval Results

Track participants were permitted to submit one or two run sets to NIST, where each set consisted of a run on the three different versions of the corpus (though not all participants ran complete sets). A run on the true version of the corpus was considered a baseline run, and results from the degraded versions of the corpus were compared to the corresponding baseline. Different sets from the same participant used different methods to compensate for the corruption and/or different retrieval methods. Five groups submitted a total of eight run sets as listed in table 8.2.

For specific details about how a run was produced, see the appropriate paper in the TREC-5 proceedings (Rutgers University [12], the Australian National University (ANU) [9], George Mason University (GMU) [8], CLARITECH Corporation (CLARIT) [17], and the Swiss Federal Institute of Technology (ETH) [2]). Here, we simply highlight the main differences among the methods.

The different approaches used by the participants varied in their treatment of both the query and the corrupted texts. Three participants used different ways to expand the query in an effort to include or match corrupted forms in the document.

• Rutgers University expanded the terms appearing in the query by a five-gram sliding window with each character replaced with any set of zero, one, or two characters. The five-grams did not cross word boundaries. Retrieval ranking was based on the average number of hits per line of text (a ranking method found to discriminate much too strongly against long documents).
• The Australian National University expanded queries based on corruption errors found likely in a study of a sample of corrupted text. Thus additional terms, which might in principle be words in a lexicon, were added to the query.
• George Mason University resolved both query and documents into overlapping four-grams (assumed to be more resistant to corruption) and required an exact match. Special stop lists of four-grams were constructed. Queries were expanded by a method based on preliminary retrieval from the corpus, resulting in the addition of new four-grams.

In contrast, the remaining two participants sought to "clarify" the corrupted texts.

• CLARITECH Corporation used statistical methods to replace each token that did not occur in the lexicon by a word that makes the entire resulting sentence most likely in a well-defined sense. Each nonword is replaced by exactly one word.
• The Swiss Federal Institute of Technology, in effect, replaced each slot (word or non-word) by a vector of candidate words, each of which is permitted to contribute to the computed similarity to the question. This is, in principle, a wider expansion of the corrupted text since the second-ranked candidate can enter the computation in the ETH method, but not in the CLARIT method.

8.1.5 Discussion

All runs but one show a noticeable drop in effectiveness as the noise in the documents increases. (The lone exception, the ETHFR94P 5 percent run whose effectiveness was worse than the corresponding 20 percent run, had a mistake in the weighting function used so that a relatively large number of terms were given negative weights.) These results thus demonstrate that retrieval effectiveness in a known-item task can be depressed by recognition errors.

Yet additional research suggests that the TREC-5 known-item task was particularly challenging. Kazem Taghva and his colleagues have consistently found that the errors arising from OCR processing of high-quality images have little impact on the average retrieval effectiveness for an ad hoc retrieval task [4; 16; 14; 15]. Mandar Mitra and Bidyut Chaudhuri explain this result in their survey of IR techniques for document images [11]. Since natural-language text is redundant, and it is rare for a word to be misrecognized repeatedly, the set of index terms for an OCR document is generally a superset of the index terms assigned to a clean version of the document. The additional terms can cause changes to the term weights relative to the clean version, but the retrieval effectiveness was generally within 2 percent of the effectiveness of clean text in Taghva's experiments. A noticeable degradation in the retrieval effectiveness was observed when lower-quality images were used (since the character error rate increased) and when the collection contained many short documents (since the redundancy was reduced).

The lack of redundancy is likely to be the cause of the degradation in retrieval results observed for the known-item task. Query statements for a known-item task focus on the unique aspects of the target document—a focus that differs from normal text-usage patterns.

8.2 The SDR Track

The SDR track was a successor to the confusion track and was run four times in TRECs 6–9 [6]. The goal of the track was to foster research on technology that provides content-based access to recordings of speech. There are many large stores of speech audio such as legacy radio and television broadcasts or recordings of meetings and classes that are not manually transcribed or indexed. For all practical purposes, the content in such archives is lost in the absence of successful SDR technology.

SDR is accomplished by using a combination of ASR and information retrieval technologies. A speech recognizer is applied to an audio stream and generates a time-marked transcription of the speech. The transcript, which is likely to contain recognition errors, becomes the input to a retrieval system. The result returned for a query is a list of temporal pointers to the audio stream ordered by decreasing similarity between the content of the speech being pointed to and the query. In TREC, the SDR task was assumed to be that of a user searching an archive of prerecorded news broadcasts. The user submits a textual query, which the system then uses to perform a retrospective, ad hoc search of the entire collection of transcripts.

This section reviews the findings of the SDR track, with particular emphasis on the later tracks since the tasks within the track were progressively more realistic, and more difficult, in each successive year. The detailed test specifications and documentation for the tasks are archived at ⟨http://www.nist.gov/speech/tests/index.htm⟩. The overview paper for each year of the track and the participants' papers giving the details of their systems can be found in the appropriate TREC proceedings at ⟨http://trec.nist.gov/pubs.html⟩.

8.2.1 SDR Track Design

The audio recordings used in the track were subsets of the radio and television news broadcasts collected by the LDC (see ⟨http://www.ldc.upenn.edu⟩) for use by the DARPA speech community [7]. The broadcast recordings were digitally sampled (sixteen-bit samples, linear-PCM encoded, sixteen-KHz. sampling rate) using a monophonic channel and stored in NIST SPHERE-formatted files. To facilitate the evaluation of component technologies as well as end-to-end SDR performance, three different types of transcripts were produced from the audio files.

Reference: a "perfect" human-produced transcript. While human-produced transcripts are not really perfect, they were assumed to be so for the purposes of the evaluation.
Baseline: a common transcript produced by a single, selected ASR system.
Speech: a transcript produced by an ASR system of the participant's choosing.

The reference transcripts, contributed by the LDC, were filtered to remove commercials, sports summaries, and weather reports; filler segments, nontopical transitional material such as "Coming up next," were retained. The baseline transcript was a one-best, word-based transcript (that is, the output of the ASR system was words rather than phones and the particular word selected at any given time was the word the recognizer deemed most probable). Participants were free to use other kinds of transcripts (for example, to use phones rather than words, or to use lattices or n-best lists rather than forced one-best) for the individual speech transcripts. The baseline and other

ASR-produced one-best word transcripts were stored as SGML-formatted files that included the (human-determined) story boundaries plus a record for each word with its start and end times.

This componentized approach allowed different ASR and IR sites to join together to create pipelined systems in which the components could be mixed, matched, and separately evaluated. Runs on the reference transcript permitted the evaluation of the overall effectiveness of the retrieval algorithms on a spoken-language collection while removing ASR as a factor. Baseline runs permitted the comparison of the effectiveness of retrieval algorithms on the same errorful ASR-produced transcripts, while speech runs permitted the evaluation of end-to-end SDR performance. Speech runs also provided a venue where a single site with both ASR and IR capabilities could test hybrid SDR technology rather than simple stovepipe combinations. Retrieval sites without access to ASR systems could participate in a limited way by performing the reference and baseline runs.

Retrieval runs on each of the types of transcripts used the same textual topics and were required to use completely automatic processing. For all runs, the systems were given the human-annotated story boundaries with story identifiers. This is artificial in that an operational SDR system must also segment the audio signal into stories. Nevertheless, providing a common set of boundaries allowed the traditional IR document-based evaluation paradigm to be used unchanged. A test of retrieval using unknown story boundaries was also included in the later SDR tracks.

The tasks that were performed in each year of the SDR track are summarized in table 8.3. The tasks and the special conditions that were tested each year will be more fully explained in the next section. The remainder of the table describes the data collections used. The last two columns give the size of the document collection both in the number of hours of audio and the number of stories contained in the audio. While the initial document sets contain orders of magnitude fewer stories than other TREC text retrieval test collections, the amount of speech to be recognized was a significant increase over previous speech collections. Prior to the TREC-6 SDR track, all of the speech collections contained fewer than three hours of audio, and recognition rates of

Table 8.3
Tasks and associated data used in the TREC SDR track

Year	Task	Number of topics	Document set size	
			Hours	Number of stories
TREC-6	known-item retrieval	47	43	1,451
TREC-7	ad hoc retrieval	23	87	2,866
TREC-8	ad hoc retrieval	49	557	21,754
TREC-9	ad hoc retrieval	50	612	28,509

Table 8.4
Participants in the TREC SDR track

TREC-6 (1997)	TREC-7 (1998)
AT&T	AT&T
Carnegie Mellon University	Carnegie Mellon University (two groups)
City University, London	Cambridge University
CLARITECH	DERA
Dublin City University	National Security Agency
ETH Zurich	RMIT
Glasgow University	University of Sheffield
IBM	TPD TU-Delft
National Security Agency	University of Maryland
RMIT	University of Massachusetts
University of Sheffield	
University of Maryland	
University of Massachusetts	
TREC-8 (1999)	**TREC-9 (2000)**
AT&T	Cambridge University
Carnegie Mellon University	LIMSI
Cambridge University	University of Sheffield
IBM	
LIMSI	
RMIT	
University of Sheffield	
SUNY Buffalo	
Twenty-One Consortium	
University of Massachusetts	

forty times real time were the norm. One of the major accomplishments of the SDR track was fostering improvement in ASR technology such that comparable word error rates can now be obtained at near real-time recognition rates.

8.2.2 The SDR Tracks
This section describes the tasks that were performed in each of the SDR tracks and highlights the main results from that year. The groups that participated in each year are listed in table 8.4.

TREC-6   The TREC-6 SDR track was the first formal evaluation of SDR technology. The task in the TREC-6 track was a known-item search task like the confusion track had used. Forty-nine known-item topics were created by NIST staff. Approximately one-quarter of the topics targeted documents that had easy-to-recognize speech, another quarter of the topics targeted documents that had difficult-to-recognize speech (for example, nonnative speakers, unscripted speech, or speech with noise in the background), and the remaining half of the topics targeted documents that had retrieval challenges such as vocabulary mismatches between the topic and the target. The document collection consisted of fifty hours of audio, seven hours of which had to be discarded for a variety of reasons. The forty-three hours of audio resulted in 1,451 stories. The baseline transcript was produced by IBM [5] and had a mean story word error rate of 50 percent.

Because of the small size of the document set, the retrieval results from the first track can only be regarded as indicative. The results did demonstrate that speech recognition and IR technologies were sufficiently advanced to do a credible job of retrieving specific documents. The better systems were able to retrieve the target document at rank one over 70 percent of the time using their own speech transcript, compared to the best performance on the reference transcript of 79 percent. The results also provided the first evidence of two key themes of the track over the years: that retrieval performance is the limiting factor in overall SDR effectiveness, and that the primary negative effect from faulty recognition is the loss of recall caused when out-of-vocabulary words cannot be recognized.

Retrieval performance as the limiting factor was demonstrated by the average effectiveness scores computed over the three different types of topics: easily recognized speech, difficult-to-recognize speech, and difficult-retrieval content. For all three forms of the document text (reference, baseline, and speech), the set of topics that targeted easy-to-recognize speech documents had the best average effectiveness score. The average effectiveness for the topics that targeted difficult-to-recognize speech was noticeably worse, even for the reference text where there was no recognition effect. This indicates that factors in transcribed speech other than recognition errors influence retrieval effectiveness. The average effectiveness for the topics that presented retrieval challenges was worse still.

The disastrous effect of missing vocabulary was illustrated by topic SDR18, "Has DNA evidence been used in the Unabomber case?" All thirteen systems retrieved the target document when using the reference transcript, but only two systems retrieved it using the baseline transcript, and only three of eight systems retrieved the target when using their own transcript. The key content word, Unabomber, was not in the lexicon of the recognizers and so it could never be correctly recognized.

TREC-7   The TREC-7 SDR track used the standard ad hoc retrieval task and an eighty-seven-hour, 2,866-story broadcast news corpus. Two baseline transcripts with different error rates were produced at NIST using the CMU SPHINX-III recognizer: the first baseline had a word error rate of 33.8 percent and the second had a word error rate of 46.6 percent. A team of three NIST assessors created twenty-three test topics and judged the retrieved documents for relevance after the retrieval results were submitted to NIST. A new category of transcripts, *cross-recognizer transcripts*, was added as an optional condition in the track. Participants who created their own one-best word transcripts were encouraged to submit them to NIST so that groups could run the retrieval portion of the task on a wider variety of ASR output.

Once again, the overall performance of the systems was quite good. The most effective system, from the University of Massachusetts, had a mean average precision (MAP) score of 0.567 using the reference transcripts and 0.508 using its speech transcript (which was produced by Dragon Systems). The AT&T group had a higher MAP score for its speech transcript (0.512) than for the reference transcript (0.499). AT&T attributed this surprising finding to the use of contemporaneous newswire text to expand the documents in the case of the speech transcripts, but not expanding the reference transcript documents [13].

The main problem with the TREC-7 track was that both the number of documents and the number of topics were too small to have confidence in the conclusions about retrieval behavior. This deficiency was addressed in the TREC-8 track.

TREC-8   The TREC-8 SDR track was designed to determine if the SDR technology demonstrated in TREC-7 scaled for realistically large spoken-document collections. To do so, the track used a subset of the TDT-2 corpus consisting of 557 hours and almost 22,000 stories. The entire TDT-2 corpus was collected to support the Topic Tracking and Detection (TDT) program and contains news recordings from ABC, CNN, Public Radio International, and the Voice of America, plus a contemporaneous newswire collection containing articles from the *New York Times* and the Associated Press [3]. While the collection was too large to have high-quality reference transcripts produced for it, it did contain closed-caption transcripts that were used as the reference transcript. Two baseline transcripts were produced at NIST using BBN's BYBLOS Rough 'N Ready recognizer; the baselines had similar word error rates of 27.5 and 26.7 percent. NIST assessors created forty-nine test topics for the track.

The amount of audio was large enough that it required recognition algorithms that worked in close to real time, as opposed to the forty or even three hundred times real-time algorithms that were common in other speech recognition evaluations. To better mimic a real SDR task, participants were permitted to use "rolling" language models in their recognizer rather than the traditional pretrained recognizer. Traditional recognizers train a language model once from a training set and then use that model to recognize all of the incoming speech. In a real application, the language in the incoming news and the language encoded in a fixed model would diverge, resulting in increasing error rates over time. A rolling language model is one that is periodically retrained using recent material. TREC-8 participants were permitted to use either a traditional pretrained recognition system or a continuously adaptive recognition system that used the contemporaneous newswire text from days prior to the day being recognized for adaptation. Groups were free to choose whatever retraining period or strategy they liked as long as they didn't look ahead in time as they performed recognition.

In addition to the test conditions supported in TREC-7, an optional story-boundaries-unknown condition was added to the TREC-8 task to provide a more realistic picture of how systems could perform if given a set of continuous, unsegmented

Table 8.5
MAP scores for selected TREC-8 SDR track runs

Participant	Reference	Story boundaries known		Story boundaries unknown	
		Baseline	Speech	Baseline	Speech
AT&T	0.560	0.554	0.543	—	—
University of Sheffield	0.560	0.530	0.526	0.430	0.425
LIMSI	0.541	0.483	0.507	—	—
Carnegie Mellon University	0.538	0.502	0.265	—	—
Cambridge University	0.523	0.496	0.553	0.386	0.415

recording streams to recognize and search. The scoring procedure needed to change for this condition since it was not document based—the natural unit of retrieval for audio recordings is time rather than documents or words, so systems returned a ranked list of time pointers in response to a topic. For evaluation, the times returned by the systems were first mapped to known stories and then scored using traditional document-based measures.

Despite the fact that recognition needed to be much faster to process the larger test corpus, recognition error rates improved as compared to TREC-7 error rates. The retrieval results were comparable to TREC-7, suggesting that the technology scaled for a collection almost an order of magnitude larger with no loss in accuracy. Table 8.5 gives the MAP scores for five groups for the reference, baseline, and speech transcripts in both the story-boundary-known and story-boundary-unknown conditions.

As is common in retrieval tasks, the MAP scores given in table 8.5 hide a large variance in scores for different topics. Three example topics illustrate the range:

Topic 105: "How and where is nuclear waste stored in New Mexico?" Seven relevant stories with an average MAP score of 0.85 across all runs for all conditions.
Topic 117: "If we get more income, will we save more or spend more?" Twenty-eight relevant stories and an average MAP score of 0.34 across all runs for all conditions.
Topic 94: "What percentage of the population is in prison in the U.S.A. and in the E.C. countries?" Seven relevant stories and an average MAP score of 0.01 across all runs for all conditions.

The retrieval effectiveness when the story boundaries were not given was always worse than the corresponding run when the story boundaries were known. Part of this degradation was an evaluation effect: the scoring method used for the task overly penalized systems that returned more than one time pointer for the same story. The unknown-boundaries condition was also intrinsically harder than the known-boundaries condition, however, since in the unknown-boundary case the systems had to avoid commercials and other filler that the story boundaries automatically

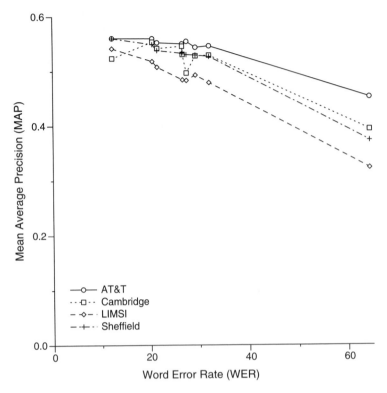

Figure 8.1
Retrieval effectiveness versus recognition error for TREC-8 cross-recognizer runs

eliminate. The University of Sheffield group, whose system performed the best in the boundaries-unknown condition, noted that while automatic segmentation led to approximately a 10 percent absolute degradation in MAP scores, it was still the case that more than half of the top ten stories were relevant for most topics [1].

TREC-8 repeated the cross-recognizer condition that was introduced in TREC-7. Four groups—AT&T, Cambridge University, LIMSI, and University of Sheffield—participated in the story-boundaries-known, cross-recognizer task by performing a retrieval run using each of eight-submitted recognizer transcripts. Figure 8.1 shows a plot of MAP score versus word error rate using the cross-recognizer data. Each of the four retrieval systems shows a slight decrease in MAP scores as the word error rate increases. The inverse correlation between MAP and word error rate scores is consistent enough to be statistically significant, but slight enough to be unimportant in practice (for a word error rate less than 50 percent). The degradation in MAP scores for the recognizer with more than a 60 percent word error rate was definitely significant, but systems with such large recognition error rates are unlikely to be used in operational systems. As is true with retrieving OCR documents, the natural redundancy of content words in spoken documents permits relevant documents to be retrieved even when a substantial number of words are misrecognized.

TREC-9   The TREC-9 SDR track was largely a confirmation of the findings from the TREC-8 track. The same portion of the TDT-2 corpus that was used for TREC-8 SDR was used as the corpus. The number of stories in the collection increased because only the story-boundary-unknown condition was used in TREC-9, so commercials and fillers were counted as stories. The reference transcript was a combination of high-quality human reference transcripts, closed-caption transcripts, and automatically combined (using NIST's ROVER algorithm) automatic transcripts. Two different versions of fifty new topics were created by NIST assessors. The "standard" version of the topics was a one-sentence description, while the "terse" version of the topics was just a few words.

Three groups participated in the track. Overall, the retrieval results were excellent: the systems could find relevant passages produced by a variety of recognizers on the full unsegmented news broadcasts, using either the terse or longer standard queries. For each of the participants, retrieval from the transcript created by their own recognizer was comparable to the retrieval from the reference transcript.

8.2.3   Discussion

One of the research questions when the SDR track began was whether hybrid SDR approaches were more effective than simple stovepipe combinations of recognition and retrieval technology. In the end, the successful SDR systems tended to be stovepipe combinations of good retrieval technology applied to good one-best word transcripts. All three of the systems that participated in the TREC-9 track used standard text-normalization procedures such as tokenization, stop-word removal, stemming, and good weighting on the ASR transcript. All used some form of query expansion, generally using both expansion from contemporaneous newswire data and blind feedback on the target corpus. Expansion from newswire data helps retrieval by adding relevant words that are known to not be recognition errors. Using newswire to adapt the recognizer's language model also helps avoid problems with out-of-vocabulary proper nouns.

The main alternative to word-based transcripts is phone sequences. In all of the TREC SDR tasks, systems based on word-based transcripts were more effective than those based on phone sequences. However, the SDR tasks used textual topics, which are more difficult for phone sequences since the text of the topic must be transformed into a phone sequence for matching against the corpus. A phone-based system might fare better with a task in which spoken queries were used to retrieve the recordings, or in cases when recognition accuracy is extremely poor.

The SDR track clearly met its goal of fostering research on retrieval from spoken audio recordings. Over the course of the track, researchers developed systems that achieved retrieval effectiveness on ASR transcripts that was comparable to its effectiveness on reference transcripts. The results from the track demonstrated that the technology is robust across a wide range of recognition accuracy. The worst effect of poor recognition, out-of-vocabulary words, can be compensated for by using adaptive language models to limit the number of out-of-vocabulary words encountered and by expanding by related clean texts to include out-of-vocabulary words in the documents and queries [18]. The track also contributed to the development of techniques for near-real-time recognition of open-vocabulary speech under a variety of nonideal conditions including spontaneous speech, nonnative speakers, and background noise.

8.3 Conclusion

While the majority of text created today is initially developed electronically, legacy documents and alternate media types such as audio and video require automatic processing to produce searchable text. Such processing frequently introduces errors into the text to be searched. Fortunately, since the errors are a result of the kind of processing being done, they are not random, and thus can be modeled and compensated for. With appropriate compensation, retrieval from the errorful texts can be as effective as retrieving from clean texts at error rates likely to be seen in real-life applications.

References

[1] Abberley, D., S. Renals, D. Ellis, and T. Robinson. The THISL SDR system at TREC-8. In *TREC-8*, 699–706.

[2] Ballerini, J.-P., M. Büchel, R. Domenig, D. Knaus, B. Mateev, E. Mittendorf, P. Schäuble, P. Sheridan, and M. Wechsler. SPIDER retrieval system at TREC-5. In *TREC-5*, 217–228.

[3] Cieri, C., D. Graff, M. Liberman, N. Martey, and S. Strassel. TDT-2 text and speech corpus. In *Proceedings of the DARPA broadcast news workshop*, 57–60. San Francisco: Morgan Kaufmann Publishers, February 1999.

[4] Croft, W. B., S. Harding, K. Taghva, and J. Borsack. An evaluation of information retrieval accuracy with simulated OCR output. In *Proceedings of the third annual symposium on document analysis and information retrieval*, 115–126. University of Nevada, Las Vegas: April 1994.

[5] Dharanipragada, S., M. Franz, and S. Roukos. Audio-indexing for broadcast news. In *TREC-7*, 115–119.

[6] Garofolo, J. S., C. G. P. Auzanne, and E. M. Voorhees. The TREC spoken document retrieval track: A success story. In *Proceedings of RIAO 2000*, 1:1–20. Paris: Centre de Hautes Etudes Internationales d'Informatique Documentaire (CID) 2000.

[7] Graff, D. The 1996 broadcast news speech and language-model corpus. In *Proceedings of the speech recognition workshop*, 11–14. San Francisco: Morgan Kaufmann Publishers, Inc., February 1997.

[8] Grossman, D. A., C. Lundquist, J. Reichart, D. Holmes, A. Chowdhury, and O. Frieder. Using relevance feedback within the relational model for TREC-5. In *TREC-5*, 405–414.

[9] Hawking, D., P. Thistlewaite, and P. Bailey. ANU/ACSys TREC-5 experiments. In *TREC-5*, 359–375.

[10] Kantor, P. B., and E. M. Voorhees. The TREC-5 confusion track: Comparing retrieval methods for scanned text. *Information Retrieval* 2, nos. 2/3 (May 2000): 165–176.

[11] Mitra, M., and B. B. Chaudhuri. Information retrieval from documents. *Information Retrieval* 2 (2000): 141–163.

[12] Ng, K. B., D. Loewenstern, C. Basu, H. Hirsh, and P. B. Kantor. Data fusion of machine-learning methods for the TREC-5 routing task (and other work). In *TREC-5*, 477–487.

[13] Singhal, A., J. Choi, D. Hindle, D. D. Lewis, and F. Pereira. AT&T at TREC-7. In *TREC-7*, 239–251.

[14] Taghva, K., J. Borsack, and A. Condit. Effects of OCR errors on ranking and feedback using the vector space model. *Information Processing and Management* 32, no. 3 (1996): 317–327.

[15] Taghva, K., J. Borsack, and A. Condit. Information retrieval and OCR. In *Handbook of character recognition and document image analysis*, ed. H. Bunke and P. Wang, 755–777. Singapore: World Scientific Publishing Co., 1997.

[16] Taghva, K., J. Borsack, and A. Condit. Results of applying probabilistic IR to OCR text. In *Proceedings of the seventeenth international ACM SIGIR conference*, 202–211.

[17] Tong, X., C. X. Zhai, N. Milić-Frayling, and D. A. Evans. OCR correction and query expansion for retrieval on OCR data—CLARIT TREC-5 confusion track report. In *TREC-5*, 341–345.

[18] Woodland, P. C., S. E. Johnson, P. Jourlin, and K. Sparck Jones. Effects of out of vocabulary words in spoken document retrieval. In *Proceedings of the twenty-third annual international ACM SIGIR conference*, 372–374.

9 The Very Large Collection and Web Tracks
David Hawking and Nick Craswell

9.1 Introduction

Together, the TREC very large collection (VLC) track and its successor the Web track have run for seven years, after an initial VLC pretrack. During that time, five new test collections have been created, five different types of retrieval task have been studied, a large number of important issues have been addressed, and new methods have been tried, not only for retrieval, but also for test collection construction.

Since the Web track was a natural evolutionary step from the VLC track, from here on we will refer to them as a single VLC/Web track.

The corpora created in support of the track have been distributed to more than 120 organizations worldwide; they are clearly being used for evaluation and research purposes well beyond the confines of TREC. The Web track model has also been adopted for similar Japanese-language evaluations within the context of NTCIR (NII–NACSIS test collection for IR systems, ⟨http://research.nii.ac.jp/ntcir/index-en.html⟩).

Each edition of the VLC/Web track (except the 1996 VLC pretrack) has already been described in a track overview paper in the appropriate TREC proceedings [29; 26; 30; 21; 22; 23; 16]. This chapter:

· Provides a layperson's guide to the track
· Briefly summarizes the history of the track and consolidates key information
· Documents the VLC/Web resources that are available for ongoing experimentation and how to obtain them
· Discusses the contributions of the track to achieving stated TREC goals
· Lists the questions that have been addressed by the track over the years and outlines the current state of knowledge with respect to them
· Discusses the impact that the track has had outside TREC
· Reflects on what has been achieved by the track and what has not
· Recognizes the limitations on what can possibly be achieved by the track
· Indicates directions for future work in the area
· Acknowledges contributions

9.2 A Layperson's Guide to the Track

The initial VLC track evaluations were similar to those in the ad hoc task described in chapter 4, this volume, and used the same NIST-constructed topics. As time went by, the track focused more on web search and diverged further from the ad hoc formula.

Web search is different from the retrieval modeled by TREC ad hoc because of the size of the data sets (up to five billion documents or more), the type of document, the presence and the nature of interlinking between documents, the volume of queries submitted (around five hundred million queries per day to Web search engines), the length of typical queries (a little over two words on average), and the types of search activity undertaken.

9.2.1   Web Terminology

Some web-specific terms deserve explanation. We use the term *Web* to refer to the World Wide Web, and *web* to refer to any hyperlinked collection of documents served by web protocols, particularly the HyperText Transfer Protocol (HTTP) [33]. The Web is an example of a web, and a web may or may not be a subset of the Web.

Generally, web documents are encoded in HyperText Markup Language (HTML; see ⟨http://www.w3.org/MarkUp/Overview.html⟩), though they may also link to images and documents in other formats. Conventionally, web documents are addressable via a unique address in the form of a Uniform Resource Identifier (URI), more commonly known as a Uniform Resource Locator (URL) [43]. An HTML document accessible by this means is usually called a *web page* or just a *page*. Within an HTML document, certain groups of words serve as the *anchors* of outgoing links. These words are normally highlighted when the document is displayed in a browser.

The collection of text from the anchors of all links targeting a particular page is called its *referring anchor text*.

As well as the structure imposed by the hyperlink graph, a web possesses structure because of the relationship between URLs. This gives rise to the concept of *web site* or just *site*. For example, all the pages whose URL start with trec.nist.gov may be considered to be on the "TREC site" regardless of links. Those pages that start with trec.nist.gov/pubs/ may be considered to be on the "TREC publications" site. Sites usually have an *entry page*, which can also be called a *home page*. The URL of a home page is likely to end with a slash (trec.nist.gov/pubs/) or in one of a small number of names such as index.html or default.htm.

The Web is highly dynamic and, due to automatic page generators, infinite. Pages that are not linked to by any other page are discoverable only by knowing or guessing the URL. Such pages may or may not be considered part of the Web (depending on the definition). It is not possible to take a complete snapshot of the Web because the only way of identifying "all" the pages is to use a *crawler* (also known as a robot or a spider). Crawling can never discover all the pages and it takes weeks, during which time the structure and the content of the Web will have changed significantly.

A crawler starts with a list of to-visit URLs (perhaps just yahoo.com). It operates by taking a URL off the list, adding it to a list of URLs that have been visited, and fetching the page at that URL. Once a page is fetched, its links are extracted and any previously unseen URLs are added to the to-visit list. This process continues until the to-visit list is empty. The collection of pages fetched by a crawler is referred to as *a crawl*. Corpora used in the Web track are crawls or selections from them.

Sometimes crawlers are configured to fetch only URLs within a specified Internet domain (or set of domains) in order to provide an enterprise-level search. For example, an outward-facing local search engine for Sony might crawl only the publicly accessible pages within sony.com. Behind the Sony firewall may be another *enterprise web*, inaccessible to the outside world, but searchable by the company's *enterprise search engine*. In general, an enterprise search engine must search not only internal web documents but e-mail, database records, the contents of document management systems, and files on shared hard drives.

Other crawlers may visit pages determined to be more likely relevant to a particular topic. This is called *focused crawling* and it may find application in a *subject portal*, providing a single search interface to Web resources on a topic such as chemistry or mental health.

Web *search engines* include a crawler as well as a conventional text retrieval system. *Metasearchers* are brokers that broadcast queries to a set of primary search engines and merge the results.

9.2.2 Typical Tasks in the Track

A typical Web track experiment proceeds as follows:

1. Documents and Query Topics: Participants are provided with a set of Web documents and a set of fifty or more query topics. Each query topic supplies a user's query ("Qantas") and either states or implies an underlying need ("find me the Qantas home page," "find me all pages about Qantas," or "find me a short list of the most important Qantas pages").

2. Submitting Runs: Participants run the queries over the documents and submit the top n results to NIST. The value of n depends on the task.

3. Judging (Informational/Transactional): NIST creates a document pool for each query, based on the results of all participants. Assessors are employed to judge which pooled documents would satisfy the user's underlying need. In the case of a known-item (or a suspected-item) search, the correct answer is determined in advance and the only requirement for human judging may be to identify effective duplicates of it.

4. Judging (Navigational): Assessors are employed to locate target items such as home pages. Judging is then only required to identify duplicates of the target items within the submitted runs.

5. Evaluation: The set of documents judged to satisfy each query is made available. Based on these judgments, effectiveness can be measured in a number of ways. Typical Web track measures are:

• Precision at n (P@n): Proportion of the top n documents that are satisfactory. P@10 = .4 means that four of the top ten documents were satisfactory. A run of fifty queries would be measured according to mean P@n.

• Success at n (S@n): The proportion of queries for which a correct answer was within the top n. S@1 = .5 means that for half the queries, the correct answer was at rank one.

• Mean reciprocal rank of first correct answer (MRR1).

• Mean average precision (MAP).

If method A is significantly better than method B over a large enough number of queries (and even better, over multiple TRECs), then we believe that method A is superior for this task. For example, home-page-finding effectiveness has been improved in a number of experiments using anchor text propagation [15] or URL-type classification [32] so we believe these are useful techniques for home page finding.

It is understood by VLC/Web track organizers and participants that a real web search is a complex and dynamic human activity usually undertaken as part of some broader task. Nevertheless, the VLC/Web track has mostly focused on trying to maximize the value of each individual query-response transaction between a searcher and the search engine. In 2003, this focus was broadened with the incorporation of former interactive track activities as a subtrack.

VLC/Web track evaluations are conducted in order to learn things that will help make more useful search systems for use in the real world. Each of the ingredients of a Web track experiment should therefore be representative of a real-world application. The documents should represent a real document set. For example, a crawl of .gov as might be used by a U.S. government search engine. The query topics and the assessors should be representative of real user needs and preferences. Evaluation measures should accurately reflect real user requirements and behavior. For instance, P@1000 isn't a realistic measure in a Web search because few Web searchers look at more than the first five or ten results.

9.2.3 A Potted History of the Track

Table 9.1 provides a summary of dates, collections, tasks, and participation for the VLC/Web track. The following brief history offers some explanation and context for the events.

In November 1995, David Hawking and the late Paul Thistlewaite proposed the creation of a VLC track in order to ensure that TREC kept pace with the burgeoning text collections, particularly the Web. The track was intended to provide a focus within TREC for the study of scalability, efficiency, and the applications of parallelism.

Two new corpora were created to serve these objectives. The first was the twenty-gigabytes VLC, released in 1997. It included large quantities of newspaper and government data, many gigabytes of USENET news, and a small amount of Web data. The second was the hundred-gigabytes VLC2, a truncated Internet Archive [31] Web crawl from February 1997. It was released in 1998 and represented a fifty-fold increase in data size over the TREC ad hoc task. Both VLC and VLC2 contained too many documents to justify the assumption made in TREC pooling of *sufficiently complete* relevance judgments. Accordingly, the evaluation focus with these collections was necessarily, and appropriately, given the nature of a typical Web search, on early precision.

In 1999, the attention shifted away from efficiency and scalability, and toward conducting evaluations that simulated more of the features of a Web search. The large Web task in 1999 required the processing of ten thousand queries extracted from real Web search logs, of which fifty were selected post hoc for judgment.

The 1999 small Web task addressed the question of whether hyperlink information could be used to improve ad hoc retrieval effectiveness. The small Web task used a

Table 9.1
Summary of VLC and Web track evaluations, 1996–2003

Year	No.	Track/task	Collection	Topics	No. of participants
1996	TREC-5	Pre-VLC	CDs 1–4	251–300 (from ad hoc)	4
1997	TREC-6	VLC	VLC	301–350 (from ad hoc)	7
1998	TREC-7	VLC	VLC2	351–400 (from ad hoc)	7
1999	TREC-8	Large Web	VLC2	50/10,000 (from search engine NLQ logs)	8
2000		Small Web	WT2g	401–450 (joint with ad hoc)	17
	TREC-9	Large Web (online services)	VLC2	50/10,000 (from search engine NLQ logs)	5
		Main Web	WT10g	451–500 (Reverse engineered from search engine query logs)	19
2001	TREC 2001	Web topic relevance	WT10g	501–550 (Reverse engineered from search engine query logs)	29
		Home-page finding	WT10g	EP1–145 (random target selection)	16
2002	TREC 2002	Topic distillation	.GOV	551–600 (NIST engineered)	17
		Named-page finding	.GOV	NP1–150 (NIST engineered)	18
2003	TREC 2003	Topic distillation	.GOV	TD1–TD50 (NIST engineered)	23
		Mixed named/home page	.GOV	NP151–450 (NIST engineered)	19
		Interactive (topic distillation)	.GOV		2

subset of VLC2 documents small enough to allow easy participation and enable sufficiently complete relevance judgments.

At the Infonortics Search Engines meeting in April 2000 (⟨www.infonortics
.com/searchengines/sh00/boston2000pro.html⟩), Chris Buckley and David Hawking
argued the case for the application of TREC evaluation methodology to the development of Web search engines. A spirited debate between the TRECers and a panel comprising Larry Page (Google), Eric Brewer (Inktomi), Marc Krellenstein (Northern Light),
Andrei Broder (Alta Vista), and Jan Pedersen (recently of InfoSeek) was (in the opinion
of a fully engaged participant) quite valuable to both sides. The search engine representatives contended that the bulk of Web searches did not correspond to the *seeking a
range of relevant information* task model assumed in TREC ad hoc (and in the Web track
at that time). They also maintained that "relevance" judgments should record multiple
levels and use judging criteria appropriate to the task. The Web track responded quickly
to these suggestions.

In 2000, queries were selected for judgment in the large Web task on the basis
of whether they seemed to be attempts to locate an online service, such as download-
ing MP3 files or sending flowers. Documents were judged to be *useful* if and only if
they provided direct access to the desired service (their relevance was not sufficient).

Also in 2000, three-level relevance judgments were used for the first time in the
main Web task. Contrary to her own expectations, Ellen M. Voorhees [44] showed that
the ranking of runs did depend on whether they were evaluated using all relevant
documents or highly relevant documents only. The topics used in the main Web task
were reverse engineered by NIST assessors. The assessors chose queries of interest from
a Web log and used those as the titles of topics. They then decided on an interpretation
of the need behind the query, and filled in description and narrative fields accordingly.
In 2000, some of the titles deliberately included misspellings.

The 2000 main Web task used a new, carefully engineered selection from VLC2,
called WT10g [5]. It was selected to ensure a high proportion of interserver links. Despite this, the participants did not report major gains in ad hoc effectiveness through
the use of links.

In 2001, the use of the VLC2 corpus was suspended because it was felt that
more could be learned from WT10g. The previous year's Topic Relevance Task was repeated with a similar methodology, but spelling errors were not included this time. In
addition, a new type of search (home page finding) was introduced. The judging criterion in this case was whether a document was the home page (site entry page) of the
entity named in the query. In this type of search, both the URL and the link structure
were found to be highly beneficial.

In 2002, two further types of search were introduced and evaluated in the
context of the .GOV collection, named-page finding, and topic distillation. Unlike the
WT2g and WT10g collections, which were artificial selections from a large whole-of-
Web crawl, .GOV is a natural (albeit truncated) crawl of a limited but interesting Internet domain; .GOV is a 1.25 million–page crawl of the .gov Internet domain collected
in early 2002.

Note that home pages constitute the only correct answers in navigational searches, but are also quite valuable in informational searches—if someone is searching for information about NIST, they will be happy to see NIST's home page at the top of the list.

The named-page-finding task was a simple variation of the home-page-finding task. For each query, the desired result is a single important document, but it was not in general the entry page of a web site.

Both named-page finding and home-page finding are related to a known-item search in that in each case, a single answer is sought. There are crucial differences, however. The usual scenario underlying a known-item search is that the searcher wishes to re-locate a document they have seen before. In home-page finding, it is frequently the case that the searcher has never visited the target document before and merely suspects that it exists—a *suspected-item search*. Furthermore, the home page may not contain any text that matches the query or indeed any text at all. It is also possible that a named page has not been visited previously (for instance, a bus timetable for service 359) and may sometimes be graphic rather than textual (say, an A–Z map of London SE1).

The topic distillation task introduced in 2002 was related to earlier topic relevance tasks, but was intended to identify key resources on a topic. The task proved difficult to explain precisely to both participants and assessors. In essence, a perfect topic distillation system would, when given a broad topic, make a short list of key resources that would closely match the list a human might create as a bookmark file or give to students of the topic. The definition of the ideal list is, like relevance, in the mind of the human judge. Unfortunately, the documents identified by the 2002 judges as being key resources did not accord very well with what the participants were expecting.

Consequently in 2003, the topic distillation task was simplified. Key resources were constrained to be web sites, represented by their entry pages. Thus, the topic distillation task became a type of home page finding, with the important distinction that the query is not generally the name of the entity represented by the web site, and there will usually be several good home pages for a topic.

In 2003, a combined home page/named-page task was set with a total of three hundred topics. Also in 2003, the interactive track administratively became a subtrack of the Web track and studied human performance on topic distillation.

9.3   The Relation to TREC Goals

The VLC/Web track has contributed significantly in achieving TREC's four goals [36].

9.3.1   Goal 1: To Encourage Research in Information Retrieval Based on Large Test Collections

We interpret *large test collections* as meaning "large enough to be confident that the results obtained will apply in the majority of current retrieval applications of that type." We consider it risky to extrapolate results from a test collection of a particular type to real collections more than an order of magnitude larger. The definition of what qualifies as a large test collection has needed frequent review because the lifetime of TREC has coincided with phenomenal growth, not only in the scale of real search applications, but also in the volume of searches conducted.

In 1992, the scale of the TREC-1 ad hoc collection reflected that of CD-ROMs, electronic newspaper archives, collections of legislation, parliamentary transcripts, and the electronic text holdings of government agencies and certain enterprises. Library catalogs were of a similar scale, and so were information sources on the Internet such as FTP and Gopher servers as well as USENET news collections. The total amount of electronic text spread across these types of collection was of course enormous, but in 1992, there was no effective means to combine them.

Even at the time of TREC-1, powerful forces were at work that would inexorably increase the scale of text collections over which people wanted to search. Even a steady rate of accumulation of new material resulted in high proportional growth because many organizations had only recently started to store their text electronically. In addition, the number of organizations and individuals producing and publishing electronic text was increasing, and means were being developed by which collections could be aggregated for the purpose of a unified search.

The Wide Area Information Service (WAIS) was released by Thinking Machines Corporation in 1991 [46], and by February 1993, there were approximately four hundred WAIS servers (⟨http://www.upenn.edu/computing/printout/archive/v09/4/navigation.html⟩). The University of Nevada's VERONICA tool for searching multiple Gopher sites was first released in November 1992, and that same year saw the first implementations of the Z39.50 protocol [35]. By far the most significant development, however, was the advent of the World Wide Web.

In early 1992 [8], the first Web browser was released, and late in that year there were twenty-six generally accessible Web servers [6]. Within the lifetime of TREC, that number has grown to an estimated 150 million [46]. Furthermore, the world has come to expect that all of those sites will be searchable via a single interface.

The Lycos search engine was launched in May 1994 by Michael Mauldin of CMU (⟨http://www.clubi.ie/webserch/engines/lycos/index.htm⟩), and Alta Vista followed in December 1995. The subsequent growth in the amount of Web data indexed by commercial search engines was so rapid that TREC could not keep up.

At the time it was first distributed (1998), the 18.5 million–page VLC2 collection was comparable to the coverage of Lycos, though much smaller than that of Alta Vista. Five years later, in 2003, major search engines were indexing two hundred times as many documents as are in VLC2.

Given that the average size of Web pages in 2004 is (at the time of writing) of the order of twenty kilobytes, the data size of the collections indexed by Google and Yahoo! search engines is of the order of sixty to one hundred terabytes, not including images and other binary data. Distributing that quantity of data as a test collection would be logistically infeasible. Not only that, but few if any TREC participants would be able to deploy the hardware resources and advanced engineering capability necessary to deal with it.

While TREC is constrained to operate with test collections a couple of orders of magnitude smaller than the Web, Web search engine companies are unlikely to look to it for advice on scalability or efficiency techniques. Moreover, results obtained using WT10g or .gov scale data sets and link graphs should be extrapolated with great caution to the Web as a whole. Despite this, the VLC/Web track does offer a collaborative environment in which methods and hypotheses can be proposed and tested.

Retrieval within the webs operated by organizations is both commercially important and scientifically interesting. The scale of VLC/Web evaluations is well matched to this type of problem. The amount of text data held by large organizations is growing, but it remains true that few individual organizations hold more than 18.5 million documents.

The Diminishing Difficulties Posed by Large Test Collections   In 1992, the two gigabyte data size of the TREC-1 collection set a difficult indexing hurdle that some participants were unable to surmount [19]. Yet hardware and indexing advances over the next few years dramatically reduced the challenge.

At TREC-7 (November 1998), David Hawking showed that it was possible to index the ad hoc collection and process fifty queries within a one-hour conference slot, using only a midrange laptop computer (266-megahertz Pentium II, 128-megabyte RAM, and 6-gigabyte internal disk). The following November, he demonstrated that with the addition of a second 10-gigabyte disk, the same laptop could process queries at a reasonable rate over prebuilt indexes for the full VLC2 collection.

In TREC-2002, twenty-three groups succeeded in indexing the 18-gigabyte .gov collection and submitting runs.

9.3.2   Goal 2: To Increase Communication among Industry, Academia, and Government by Creating an Open Forum for the Exchange of Research Ideas

The Web track attracted more than ten commercial participants in 2001. Nevertheless, endeavors to persuade [27] and later provoke [24] Web search engine companies to join in have so far been unsuccessful.

Despite this, employees of commercial search engine companies such as Jack Xu (Excite); Andrei Broder, Monika Henzinger and Michael Moricz, Peter Anick and Bob Travis (Alta Vista); Knut Magne Risvik and Per Gunnar Auran (Fast/AlltheWeb); Edwin Cooper (the Electric Monk), Krishna Bharat, Amit Singhal, Larry Page and Ron Dolin (Google); Raman Chandrasekhar and Bill Bliss (MSN Search); and Andy MacFarlane (Omsee) have contributed to the planning of track activities and the interpretation of results (the affiliations shown are those applicable at the time).

An invited talk by Andrei Broder (then chief scientist at Alta Vista) during the Web plenary session at TREC-9 (2000) [7] in which he proposed the classification of search types into informational, navigational, and transactional, and expanded on his search engines 2000 coining of the term *adversarial information retrieval*, was well received by the TREC audience.

A number of attempts have been made to highlight the relevance of TREC results and methodology to the search engine companies by comparing the performance of TREC systems with that of public search engines (without their cooperation). These are summarized in the section 9.4.6 below.

It is now clear that the major search engine companies take scientific evaluation of their search quality very seriously, even if they do not publish the results of their evaluations.

9.3.3   Goal 3: To Speed the Transfer of Technology from Research Labs into Commercial Products by Demonstrating Substantial Improvements in Retrieval Methodologies on Real-World Problems

It is difficult to estimate the rate of technology transfer between TREC and the Web (and enterprise) search industry because commercial companies are free to adopt directions, algorithms, and methodologies published in TREC, and are under no obligation to disclose the extent to which they do so.

As mentioned above, there are significant limits on how much the VLC/Web track can influence the engineering of whole-of-Web search engines. It is quite clear that major search engine companies are a long way ahead of academic research laboratories in these areas. They have accumulated substantial experience with crawling and indexing quantities of data orders of magnitude beyond the scope of TREC.

Furthermore, *crawl quality* and *spam rejection* are essential to high-quality Web searches, and neither are amenable to study within a static test collection. The quality of a crawl refers to its recency and coverage, and the extent to which low-value and duplicate or near-duplicate pages are excluded. Spam refers to artificial Web pages and structures designed to inappropriately promote certain pages in search engine result lists. To be successful, spam technology must and does adapt rapidly to changes in search engine algorithms. Any countermeasure developed to defeat one type of spam would in reality be immediately subject to a counter-countermeasure, but this cannot happen in a static test collection.

As previously noted, the web search industry is much broader than a whole-of-Web search, and the VLC/Web evaluations have direct bearing on enterprise and portal search. It is known that technologies based on VLC/Web track results do make their way into products in these areas (see section 9.6).

9.3.4   Goal 4: To Increase the Availability of Appropriate Evaluation Techniques for Use by Industry and Academia, including Development of New Evaluation Techniques More Applicable to Current Systems

This is an area in which major progress has been made by, and in conjunction with, the VLC/Web track. As noted in the introduction, five test corpora (see table 9.2) have been created and evaluation methodologies for five different types of search (topic

Table 9.2
Summary of test collections used in VLC and Web tracks from 1997 onward (CSIRO-distributed collections are accessible via ⟨http://es.csiro.au/TRECWeb/⟩)

Collection	Data	Number of documents	Average document size	Collection size	Availability	Notes
VLC	Mixed, ad hoc, and Web	7,492,048	2.8 KB	20 GB	—	No longer distributed
VLC2 (WT100g)	Web	18,571,671	5.7 KB	100 GB	CSIRO	From Internet Archive 1997 crawl 1 and 10 percent samples defined and distributed
WT2g	Web	247,491	8.9 KB	2.1 GB	CSIRO	Subset of VLC2 (with doc. renaming)
WT10g	Web	1,692,096	6.2 KB	10 GB	CSIRO	Subset of VLC2 (with doc. renaming)
.GOV	Web	1,247,753	15.2 KB	18 GB	CSIRO	UWaterloo 2002 crawl of .gov domain; in crawl order; early termination; images and so forth saved
.GOV2	Web	27 M	15 KB	400 GB	CSIRO	NIST/UWaterloo 2004 more complete crawl of .gov domain; under construction

relevance, online service finding, home page finding, named-page finding, and topic distillation) have been developed.

Judgments involving WT2g, WT10g, and .GOV are for most purposes reusable. Although past judgments involving VLC and VLC2 are incomplete and therefore not reusable, the cost of rejudging sufficient documents to make P@20 (precision at twenty documents retrieved) comparisons is low, even if assessors are paid.

Home page finding and named-page finding judgments are both cheap to create and reusable as, potentially, are those for topic distillation. Manual judging may be required to identify answers that are duplicates of the listed one or automatically redirect to it, but judging whether two pages are identical is far simpler than assessing whether their content is relevant to a topic. In any case, the judging process is largely capable of automation.

9.4   Issues Addressed by the VLC/Web Track

Rather than repeating TREC-by-TREC material from the VLC/Web track overviews and participant reports, we draw out the issues that were addressed and summarize the findings.

9.4.1   Scalability
The TREC-6 and TREC-7 VLC tracks investigated the scalability of retrieval systems on various dimensions including query-processing time, index size, and index-building time. Unsurprisingly, index size tended to grow linearly with collection size, but the scalability of the time measures was dependent on the nature of the particular system and the hardware employed.

9.4.2   Engineering Issues
Well-known principles apply in engineering IR systems for high performance:

1. Use RAM rather than disk (design data structures to ensure high memory-reference locality; use compact structures and compression to make the best use of limited RAM resources)
2. Use cache rather than RAM (use tight loops in frequently executed code)
3. Use efficient algorithms
4. Consider potentially lossy optimizations, such as early termination
5. If applicable, minimize communication between processors

As with the scalability, though, the question of which engineering issues are most important is system and hardware dependent.

In the TREC-7 VLC track, the ACSys VLC Medal was awarded to the University of Waterloo group for indexing the VLC2 in less than ten hours (8.53) and processing queries in an average of under two seconds (0.882), while achieving median P@20 or better. The group used a cluster of four personal computers costing a total of around US$8,500.

In the TREC-8 large Web task, an attempt was made to explore the trade-offs made by the participating systems across five key measures:

1. Speed of indexing
2. Size of indexes
3. Speed of query processing
4. Query-processing effectiveness
5. Cost

Kiviat diagrams were chosen to communicate the trade-offs. Figure 9.1 shows five-axis Kiviat diagrams summarizing the performance on each of these dimensions of several TREC-8 runs. On each axis, the best performance is represented by a point on the circumference. For effectiveness, the best performance corresponds to the maximum P@20 score, whereas in each other case the best performance corresponds to the minimum score.

To illustrate the scaling process, the smallest index size was achieved by Fujitsu at 3.9 gigabytes. (It preprocessed the data to remove binary and non-English data.) This minimum was divided by the actual index size for each run to give a scaled score of 1 for Fujitsu and a score of 0.1 for a hypothetical index of 39 gigabytes. Scaled scores of less than 0.05 are shown as 0.05 to prevent the creation of spikes that are too narrow to see.

In TREC-8, the University of Waterloo team demonstrated subsecond query processing over VLC2 on a pair of cheap personal computers that they brought along to the conference. In TREC-9, Fujitsu Laboratories set a new mark for the cheapest system used to run the large Web task. With a US$1,700 dual-Celeron system (648-megabytes RAM, and 3×40–gigabyte disks), it indexed the data in just over twelve hours (including decompression) and was able to process queries in an average of 0.31 seconds.

9.4.3   The Effect of Collection Size on Effectiveness

Contrary to the expectations of many—for example, Gerard Salton and Michael J. McGill [38, 173]—the observation of all participants in the TREC-7 VLC track was that P@20 was considerably greater for retrieval over the full VLC collection compared with retrieval over a 10 percent sample of it. Various hypotheses were advanced as to why this might be so, and these have been analyzed in considerable detail by David Hawking and Stephen Robertson [28], who found that observed behavior could be well described by a signal detection model with due allowance for discreteness.

9.4.4   How Does Web Data Differ from Ad Hoc Data?

In TREC-8, the question of whether the effectiveness of retrieval systems was dependent on the type of data was studied in the small Web task. The same topics were used in both the ad hoc track and the small Web, and they had been developed with both collections in mind. The TREC-8 Web track overview compares the MAP for each of ten matched pairs of runs across small Web and ad hoc. For convenience, the

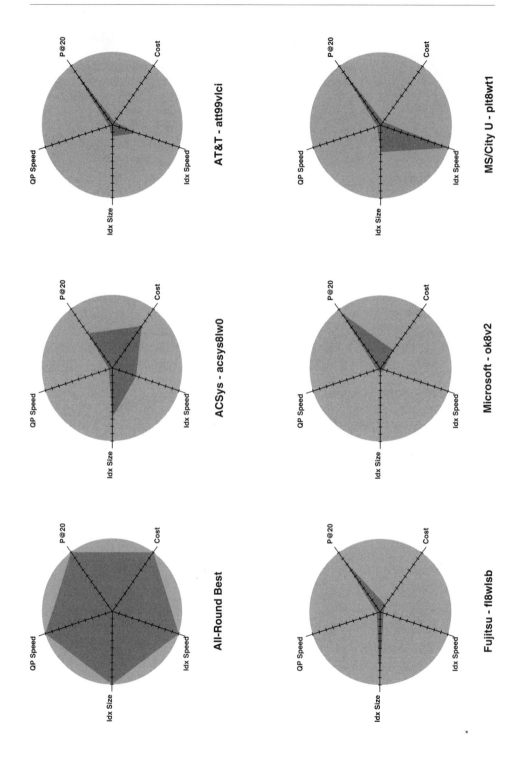

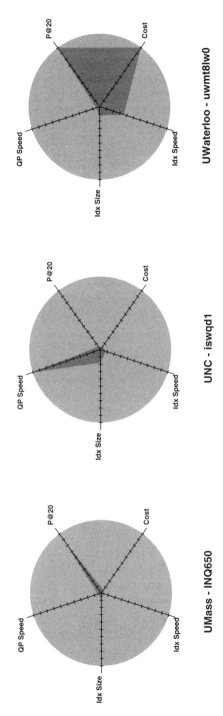

UMass - INQ650

UNC - iswqd1

UWaterloo - uwmt8lw0

Figure 9.1

Composite results for illustrative runs submitted in the TREC-8 large Web task. Note that the University of North Carolina at Chapel Hill runs were submitted after the deadline and consequently included a high percentage of unjudged documents. Accordingly, their precision result is quite low. Their query processing, however, was two orders of magnitude faster that the next fastest, scaling other speed results into oblivion. The AT&T run was also unjudged due to a formatting problem. The all-around best is a hypothetical composition of the best-achieved result on each dimension. Finally, because ACSys coordinated the track, employed the assessors, and tabulated the results, the ACSys results should be regarded as unofficial

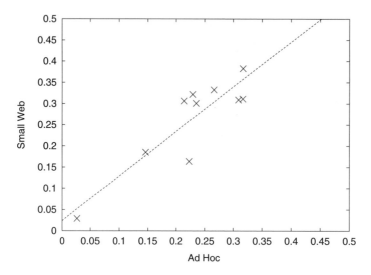

Figure 9.2
Average precision on the TREC-8 small Web task plotted against average precision on the TREC-8 ad hoc task for pairs of runs believed to correspond closely. Also shown is the line of best (least-squares) fit.

resulting scatter plot is reproduced in figure 9.2. The Pearson R coefficient of correlation is 0.884, which is significant at the 0.05 level (two-tailed).

9.4.5   Are Hyperlinks Useful in Topic Relevance Tasks?
Quite a few groups have attempted to demonstrate a benefit of using link information in topic relevance tasks (that is, the well-known TREC ad hoc task in which the goal is to "find as many documents as possible providing information relevant to a topic").

In TREC-8, twenty out of forty-four runs in the small Web task (WT2g) attempted to exploit link evidence. The methods employed included sibling pages, Kleinberg hub and authority (and variants) [49], PageRank [50], spreading activation [48], probabilistic argumentation systems [51], and indegree and outdegree. The differences between content-plus-link runs and the corresponding baseline were mostly small and usually negative. The few large differences were all negative. Both the University of Neuchatel and Fujitsu Laboratories reported that they could find no correlation between relevance on the TREC-8 topics and link-based measures. ACSys found no benefit in the large Web task from the use of PageRank scores.

A strong motivation in the replacement of WT2g with WT10g in TREC-9 was the low number of interserver links within the former collection and the possibility that this was responsible for the negative results of the link trials. Yet the proportion of TREC-9 main Web task submissions that attempted to exploit links dropped to 27 out of 105. Once again, despite the richness of the hyperlink graph in this artificial

Web subset, gains, if any, due to link methods (including anchor text) were inconsistent and at best quite small. This was true even when highly relevant documents were valued highly.

The exploration of link methods within the TREC 2001 topic relevance task was less vigorously pursued. Once again, it was shown to be possible to achieve top results using only document content.

To many, this is a surprising outcome—one that challenges the Web track's claim to be doing interesting work. Many find it beyond question that hyperlink methods work because Google uses hyperlink methods and Google produces good results.

The resolution of this apparent dilemma is straightforward:

Hyperlink and other web evidence is highly valuable for some types of search task, but not for others. Because binary judgments were employed and judges looked only at the text of the retrieved pages, the TREC-8 small Web task and the TREC-9 main Web task did not accurately model typical Web search.

In the next section, we cite evidence that, using TREC ad hoc evaluation methodology, TREC systems (without hyperlink evidence) actually outperform well-known Web search engines on a whole-of-Web search. But this is a relatively meaningless victory since, as was forcefully stated by the panel of Web search experts at the 2000 Infonortics Search Engines meeting (⟨http://www.infonortics.com/searchengines/sh00/boston2000pro.html⟩), the TREC ad hoc search task (see chapter 4, this volume) is not at all typical of a search on the Web.

In prototypical TREC ad hoc methodology, the task presupposes a desire to read text relevant to a fairly precisely defined topic, and documents are judged on their own text content alone as either relevant or not relevant.

By contrast, Web searchers typically prefer the entry page of a well-known topical site to an isolated piece of text, no matter how relevant. For example, the NASA home page would be considered a more valuable answer to the query "space exploration" than newswire articles about Jupiter probes or NASA funding cuts. As a further example, there are estimated to be around forty million web pages matching the query Microsoft, but web searchers expect that the entry page to the official Microsoft site will be ranked first.

People search on the Web for a variety of reasons in which a long unordered list of matching documents is not useful. They may wish to visit a site where they can browse or perform local searches, they may wish to find contact details or answer a question, they may wish to buy something, or alternatively, they may wish to access an online service.

A number of types of search task (listed below) modeled within the Web track show that web evidence such as anchor text, URL structure, and hyperlink measures brings dramatic benefits. The measures used in these tasks reflect the fact that certain pages, particularly site-entry pages, are much more valuable than isolated matching pages.

Web measures are effective at ranking on likely value to the searcher, within the set of relevant documents. Note that in Web search literature the term *value* is not typically used. Instead, people have written about importance, popularity, authority, and so forth.

9.4.6   How Do TREC Systems Compare to Web Search Engines?

Two studies involving the present authors [26; 27; 25] showed a significant superiority of TREC systems over commercial Web search engines on a topic relevance task. In these comparisons, retrieval systems in the TREC-7 VLC track were considered to be search engines all sharing the same incomplete and out-of-date crawl. The same queries were fed to a number of public search engines, and the results were pooled and judged by the same judges who evaluated the VLC submissions.

We also collected the data necessary to compare TREC systems with public search engines on the TREC-9 online service location task, but did not publish the comparison. That oversight is rectified here in figure 9.3. The mean precision of the search engines (0.4932) is about 9 percent higher than the mean for the best runs from each group. The victory to the search engines, however, is hardly decisive as the decision to evaluate online service finding for the TREC systems was made post hoc, after runs had been submitted.

By contrast, Amit Singhal and Marcin Kaszkiel [41] compared a well-qualified TREC system against public search engines on a home-page-finding task and found that the latter were greatly superior.

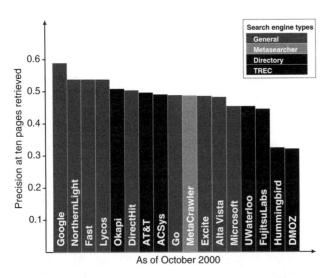

Figure 9.3
P@10 for eighty-four online service queries, comparing TREC large Web systems with public search engines

The difference in outcome of these four studies highlights to us the importance of modeling different types of searches. At the time of the Singhal and Kaszkiel study, TREC systems were not oriented toward home-page finding, and did not make use of link and URL evidence later found to be highly beneficial on this task.

9.4.7 Different Types of Search

As noted above, web search takes many forms. The VLC/Web track has explored quite a few.

Online Service Finding   Online service finding is obviously a commercially important type of search that is not well understood. As noted earlier, the adoption of this task in TREC-9 large Web was decided postsubmission, and there was no opportunity to tune systems or compare methods. Furthermore, it is not at all clear that VLC2 was a good test bed for this type of search.

Future work in this area may well involve a specially constructed corpus comprising commerce sites as well as appropriate reviews and referral agencies.

Home-Page Finding   On the home-page-finding task in TREC 2001, web-specific methods, specifically link anchor text and URL structure, came into their own. Referring anchor text was shown to be highly beneficial. The teams of Nick Craswell, David Hawking, and Stephen Robertson [15] as well as Trystan Upstill, Nick Craswell, and David Hawking [42] have confirmed this on several different collections. Attempts to use link graph measures such as inlink counts and PageRank were not as successful. The best results on the TREC task were achieved by TNO/UTwente, which calculated prior probabilities of different categories of URL (root, subroot, directory default, and file) [45; 32]. This was a previously unpublished method and, as far as we know, is not widely used by search engine companies.

Named-Page Finding   Named-page finding was proposed as a task to see if significant pages that were not site-entry pages also tended to attract links or to be distinguished by the nature of their URLs. The two top performing runs in the TREC 2002 task used a fusion of different methods, including anchor text, but did not gain benefit from URL structure, URL length, or inlink count [47; 13].

Mixed Named Page/Home Page   In TREC 2003, three hundred navigational queries were generated by NIST, comprising a fifty-fifty mixture of home pages and named pages. Overall, it seemed useful to consider different document representations or surrogates (such as referring anchor text) and to fuse results. The link structure gave mixed benefit. A number of attempts to switch retrieval methods based on automatic classification of query type showed promise, but it didn't surpass the best other methods.

Topic Distillation   Topic distillation was proposed as a task to see if Web-specific features such as links and URL structure could be used to distinguish key resources from among the set of pages relevant to a topic. By key resources, we meant the type of resources that a human editor might list under a subject category in the Open Directory Project, Yahoo! or LookSmart online Web directories.

If a purely automatic system could produce a high-quality DMOZ-like directory in response to a subject category as the query, not only would there be a major potential saving in human effort, but searchers would not be restricted to categories previously identified.

Unfortunately, in TREC 2002, the intended nature of topic distillation was not effectively communicated by the organizers to assessors and participants. As a result, the topics chosen sometimes corresponded to no key sites within .GOV. Indeed, the lists of key resources were qualitatively different to DMOZ lists and tended to be isolated pages that the assessors felt were highly significant.

Topics were defined in standard TREC format and included a description—for example:

```
<top>
<num> Number: TD26
<title>Nuclear power plants</title>
<desc>Description:
Operational and safety information associated
with nuclear power plants.
</top>
```

Sometimes, as in the example shown, the description tended to narrow the definition of the topic, encouraging the choice of single documents rather than sites.

Results for 2002 were inconclusive due to confusion about the task definition. Participants who developed algorithms biased in favor of retrieving sites rather than individual pages were unable to say whether their methods were effective.

In TREC 2003, the topic distillation task was redefined. This time, systems were required to find entry pages to web sites devoted to specified broad topics. This definition no doubt excluded some key single-page resources, but was well understood by participants and assessors, and enabled participants to focus on web-specific attributes of the problem.

By way of illustration, the official answers to the topic "cotton industry" included home pages for the Cotton Pathology Research Unit, the Foreign Agricultural Service (FAS) Cotton Group, the Western Cotton Research Laboratory, and the U.S. Department of Agriculture Cotton Program.

For details of experiments and conclusions, readers are referred to [16]. In general, referring anchor text was found to be useful, and URL structure and link counts were also helpful.

A number of participants noted that the TREC 2003 topic distillation task was quite representative of real Web search.

9.5 The Evaluation Methodology for Web Retrieval

Many of the methodological decisions taken in the Web track are relatively uncontroversial, but some questions have not been fully resolved. Issues in the evaluation of public search engines are addressed in [18; 14; 25]. The key issue of using measures and judging instructions appropriate to the type of search applies equally in test collection evaluations.

9.5.1 Evaluating the Effectiveness of Navigational Search

Home page and named-page finding tasks are easy to judge, introducing only the minor complication of multiple URLs for the same page. The judging criterion is, "Is this the page I wanted?"—that is, the home page of the entity I was thinking of or the page I named.

For navigational tasks, success at n documents retrieved (that is, did the right answer appear in the first n results) or mean reciprocal rank of the first right answer are suitable measures. An even better measure might weight the ranks according to relative prominence within the result list.

For example, the first item in the list is more prominent than the rest; items "above the fold" (that is, those that can be seen without scrolling) are more prominent than those below it; and items on the first page of results are more prominent than the second. Yet these weightings depend on the formatting of the results page, the number of results presented per page, and the size of the browser window in which the searcher is viewing the results.

9.5.2 Evaluating the Effectiveness of Informational Search

Three types of informational search may be identified: TREC ad hoc, topic distillation, and Q&A.

TREC Ad Hoc   Find me a selection of documents relevant to this topic. For example, "I'm writing a paper on this topic and I need background information on all aspects, plus references." The TREC ad hoc methodology is generally applicable apart from the presentational issues discussed below, and the greater prevalence of duplicate and near-duplicate documents.

A further methodological issue considered by the track is that of indirect relevance—whether documents that link directly to a relevant page should be considered partly useful. There is no simple answer because the usefulness of a link depends on how many other outgoing links there are from that page, how prominent the link is on that page, and how easy it would be for a searcher to tell that the link was likely to lead to relevant content.

Topic Distillation   Make a list of the key resources on some broad topic, similar to those compiled by human editors at DMOZ, Yahoo! or LookSmart.

It is vital to understand, but difficult to explain, how very different this type of search is from that which we have just labeled TREC ad hoc. Unlike the newspaper archives represented in TREC ad hoc, the Web (like many other webs):

- Is organized into sites, each of which typically provides an entry page giving an overview of the site, navigational links to subsites, and a local search capability
- Is extensively interlinked
- Provides services as well as information
- Can instantaneously generate customized documents in response to requests (such as theater seating availability)

These characteristics allow webs to be used for different purposes and encourage the use of the "search-and-browse" paradigm in which the searcher types a broad query, gets a list of prominent web sites, goes to one or more of the sites, and browses (or searches) locally. By visiting the site-entry pages, the searcher quickly acquires an understanding of how the topic is organized, what vocabulary is used, and so forth.

To illustrate this, imagine a prospective computer science PhD student has heard of the information retrieval discipline and would like to know more about it: read an introductory textbook, find out who are the leading researchers, list some active departments, know which are the main conferences, and so on.

If we pretended that the Web were a structureless, unlinked, source-anonymized newspaper archive, then the query "information retrieval" would return huge numbers of matching documents (as of May 18, 2004, Google estimated 2.7 million, and Yahoo! 4.6 million) and the ranking would be based on the similarity of the text to that of the query (essentially the density of references to those terms). If someone had created a document containing nothing but a hundred repetitions of the phrase "information retrieval," that document would almost certainly rank first. Such a ranking is unlikely to provide quick access to the sort of understanding the PhD candidate wanted and it is almost certain that a chain of queries would ensue, trying to narrow down to the valuable information expected to be there.

By contrast, rankings produced by the two large-coverage Web search services at the time of this writing (Google and Yahoo!) do an impressive job of presenting a list of key resources on the first page: the home page of the Keith van Rijsbergen textbook, an IR bibliography, the home page for CIIR at the University of Massachusetts, a site devoted to the Ricardo Baeza-Yates and Berthier Ribeiro-Neto textbook, the SIGIR information server, the home page of the *Information Retrieval* journal, key sites on chemical IR and music IR, and an IR research directory on Searchtools.com. One may argue that certain sites deserved to be ranked above others, but for the hypothetical student with their hypothetical requirement, these results are a gold mine at the price of a query so obvious that any such student is able to think of it, and no student is too lazy to type it.

Several desirable features of both the Google and Yahoo! rankings for this query are immediately apparent (try it for yourself):

1. The results are at the right level in the site hierarchy: The CIIR home page ciir.cs .umass.edu is presented ahead of its parent cs.umass.edu and its estimated 10,500 children; the van Rijsbergen textbook is represented by its entry (preface) rather than by arbitrary individual chapters; Hearst's site on the Baeza-Yates and Ribeiro-Neto textbook is represented as www.sims.berkeley.edu/~hearst/irbook/ rather than www.sims .berkeley.edu/~hearst/ because the parent site is not restricted to information retrieval.
2. No single source (publisher) of information dominates the ranking. Additional results from the same sites are hidden behind a "more results from this site" link.
3. The listed resources are generally well-known and reputable.
4. There is a diversity of resource types.

These positive attributes informed the TREC 2003 methodology for evaluating topic distillation. Key resources were constrained to be site-entry pages that:

- Were principally devoted to the topic
- Provided credible information on the topic
- Were not part of a larger site also principally devoted to the topic

No reward was given for diversity among the results returned, but the three criteria adopted prevent credit being given for multiple results from the same source.

Systems were compared on the basis of their ability to retrieve as many key resources as possible early in the ranking. The first ten results were judged and R-precision (that is, precision when R documents have been retrieved, where R is the number of known key resources) or MAP measures were calculated. No reward was given for diversity of resource types, and all key resources were judged to have the same value.

Note that finding the appropriate level (within XML elements and subelements) for an answer is also a major issue in XML retrieval [52].

Q&A   What is the answer to this question? For example, I'm competing on *Who Wants to Be a Millionaire* and I need help. Q&A tasks have been shown to be well suited to a Web environment (see, for example, [37]), but have not yet been evaluated within the Web track. For a discussion of the methodological issues, readers are referred to chapter 10, this volume.

9.5.3   Evaluating the Effectiveness of Transactional Search

It seems appropriate to evaluate online service finding in a similar fashion to an informational search, varying only the judging instructions. Measures such as P@n and average precision seem appropriate because it is likely that the searcher wants to see a selection of sites providing the service, in order to be able to compare prices and service details.

The definition of a suitable test collection, including a wide range of e-commerce sites plus useful review and directory pages, would be essential to a meaningful evaluation.

9.5.4   Evaluating the Effectiveness of Exhaustive Search

Recall-oriented search may be important on the Web or within an enterprise (for instance, Enron) for legal reasons or for creating lists that need to be complete. For example, "find all web pages that mention my name," "find the home pages of every computer science department in the United States," "find all the pages that link to the W3C web site," "find all pages that contain erroneous JavaScript," or "find every page on the web that makes a claim that eating brand-X hamburgers leads to obesity."

An exhaustive search might seek pages that could also be valid targets of a navigational, transactional, or informational search, but often the motivation is different. I might compile a list of all pages where I can buy MP3 players, but not because I want to buy one.

The challenge for future evaluations of exhaustive search is to find reliable techniques for estimating the full set of matching answers for nontrivial requests. A comparison of systems can be done quite easily, but in an exhaustive search, absolute recall is also of interest.

Finding all documents containing the word TREC is an example of a trivial request—the population of relevant documents is easily determined, yet it is also to be expected that any bug-free retrieval system should be capable of achieving perfect recall within a fixed text collection. (On the Web itself, incomplete recall could result from deficiencies in crawling.) By contrast, finding precedents for a particular legal issue is fraught with difficulty because no single term can actually capture what is required.

The problem of exhaustive search evaluation is superficially similar to that of estimating animal populations, where mark-recapture methods [40] can be effective. Unfortunately, such methods make assumptions that are not easily satisfied in document retrieval. In particular, relevant documents have unequal probabilities of being "captured" by a particular retrieval run, and exactly the same set of relevant documents will be captured by a subsequent retrieval run with the same parameters.

One possible approach might be to seed the test collection with a set of K known relevant documents chosen in such a way as to be representative of the complete population of possible relevant documents. A retrieval run over the test collection (plus seeds) that retrieved k of the seeds and r other documents judged to be relevant could be used to infer that the number of relevant documents in the original test collection was $R = rK/k$. Multiple heterogeneous retrieval runs could be used to derive and compare a variety of estimates of R.

In estimating populations of relevant documents, there may be value in stratifying by degree of relevance—say, on a seven-point scale. Intuitively, estimates of the population of highly relevant documents may be more reliable than estimates for the population of those that are peripherally relevant. Furthermore, when rating the usefulness of retrieval tools in exhaustive retrieval applications, the recall of highly relevant documents should weigh more heavily.

Note that the density of relevant documents in large collections is too low to permit effective estimation by random sampling.

9.5.5 Presentational Issues in Web Search Evaluation

The way in which documents are presented to Web track assessors is far more signifi-cant than was the presentation of text-only documents such as newswire reports in the TREC ad hoc task. For example, if a book about "estimating animal populations" were published on the web, it might be represented as a number of separate pages: an entry page, a table of contents, a page for each chapter, and an index. If the entry page con-sisted only of a scanned image of the front cover with a link to the table of contents, it would be judged irrelevant (in TREC ad hoc) to the topic of "animal populations," if the judge saw only the (empty) text content, even though it is arguably the best entry to the hyperbook.

Ideally, assessors should experience exactly what a real Web searcher would ex-perience if they were carrying out the task in question.

The logistics of presenting pages in a static collection as though they were live pages is fraught with difficulty. If the judging interface allows the viewing of images and the following of links on the live Web, there is the risk that the images and the target pages will have disappeared or changed since the corpus was gathered. On the other hand, if a proxy server is used to serve images and linked pages from within the corpus, many links will be dead because they lead outside the corpus.

Two Web-specific presentational issues are worthy of mention. If one page au-tomatically *redirects* to another via standard HTTP or HTML mechanisms, both pages should be regarded as correct since what the searcher experiences is more or less the same regardless of which URL they select. This is another source of duplicate content. There are additional difficulties in the case of *frame sets*:

- The document that specifies the frame set may have no content at all, but may be the appropriate answer to a transactional or an informational query because of the useful content in its subsidiary frames (which will be seen by the searcher when the container page is displayed).
- Retrieval systems may retrieve individual frames that are not designed to be displayed in isolation. How should these be displayed for the purpose of judging?

In early VLC and Web evaluations, assessors saw only the rendered text of the page being judged. They could not see images or follow links. This may mean that cer-tain pages that would be considered useful in a real search are judged useless.

When the .GOV collection was crawled, images and PDF files, and so on, within .gov were saved. Nevertheless, logistics dictated that they be separated from the text version of the collection and not distributed to participants. This was done because the nontext data size was about four times that of the text—too large to conveniently distribute via CD-ROM. CSIRO, however, has recently started distributing test collec-tions on large capacity hard drives.

The TREC 2002 interactive track made use of the .GOV collection via a search engine (Panoptic, ⟨http://www.panopticsearch.com⟩) operated by CSIRO. In 2003, the interactive track became a subtrack within the Web track and studied topic distillation tasks within the .GOV collection. This time, the Panoptic search engine was operated by NIST (⟨http://ir.nist.gov⟩), and a mechanism was set up by Ian Soboroff by which images and links were mapped to targets within the original crawl, rather than on the live Web.

9.6   VLC/Web Track Influence outside TREC

A cursory survey of recent conference proceedings and journal issues reveals that the resources created by the VLC/Web track are being used quite routinely in studies reported outside TREC. For example, during the years 2000–2002, eight SIGIR papers [34; 2; 44; 15; 32; 3; 4; 39] and four *Transactions on Information Systems* articles [12; 11; 10; 9] made use of VLC/Web data, and several others referred to the track or its methodology. A glance at the same forums for 2003 suggests that the usage of VLC/Web track resources and results is increasing still further.

It is clear that the VLC/Web collections are being used quite widely for tuning, developing, and evaluating commercial systems. Examples for which information is available include:

- Copernic Enterprise Search, a commercial search engine specially designed for small and midsize enterprises (typically having five thousand to two million documents).
- IXE, a C++ class library for indexing and search that is being commercialized by Ideare SpA. The product has been used to build several search services, including an on-line search facility at www.repubblica.it, one of the major Italian newspapers.
- Microsoft is using Web track data (among other corpora) to prototype search algorithms that are intended for future product releases.
- Panoptic, CSIRO's metadata-plus-content enterprise search engine with over thirty commercial customers.
- TechRoute Chinese-language search engine, which is already used in many organizations.

The collections have been distributed to more than 120 organizations worldwide. Many of these groups have not yet participated in TREC.

9.6.1   The Limitations of the VLC/Web Track

The VLC/Web track draws on admirable TREC traditions of building test collections and encouraging group experiments. These are strengths, but they also impose limitations:

- It is not feasible to work with collections whose size and link graph complexity even approaches that of the Web. The logistics of distribution are too difficult, and too few participants would be able to work with the data. The track can have little to say to Web search engine companies about scalability, efficiency, or large-scale graph algorithms.

- The static nature of test collections makes it difficult to use them to explore problems in the areas of crawling or spam rejection.

Evaluation methodologies applicable to the whole of the Web can be explored in smaller collections, however. New methods and ideas may also be prototyped and tested on the TREC collections, provided results are not extrapolated to the whole Web without appropriate validation.

Furthermore, enterprise-level search (such as modeled by .GOV) is commercially and scientifically interesting in its own right. Experimental findings at this scale are applicable in large numbers of search products, potentially affecting a huge number of enterprise/intranet search services.

9.7   Resources for Ongoing Experimentation

Table 9.2 details the test collections that have been created in the course of the VLC/Web track. Table 9.3 details server and connectivity properties for the web collections. Table 9.4 details the breakdown of the .GOV collection by mime type. Images and the original forms of PDF, MSWord, and so on (around sixty gigabytes) were collected and saved. As previously noted, they have been used to provide a frozen context for the .GOV collection in the 2003 interactive experiments.

Table 9.3
Link and server statistics for the Web collections. The link density is calculated by dividing the total number of within-collection links (either inlinks or outlinks) by the total number of pages. The cross-server link density is calculated by dividing the total number of within-collection cross-server links (either inlinks or outlinks) by the total number of servers. In the case of WT10g and .GOV, connectivity files are distributed on CD-ROM with the data. The same information is available for WT2g from the Web track web site

Collection	Servers	Pages/ server	Link density	Cross-server link density	Connectivity data
VLC2	117,101	159	—	—	On tape
WT2g	—	—	4.71	—	Web site
WT10g	11,680	144	4.77	14.7	On CD-ROM
.GOV	7794	160	8.95	317	On CD-ROM

Table 9.4
Types of document (mime type) within the .GOV collection (excluding nontext documents)

Text/HTML	Appl/PDF	Text/plain	Appl/msword	Appl/postscript	Other
1,053,110	131,333	43,753	13,842	5,673	42

9.8   Likely Future Directions

At the time of this writing, guidelines for the TREC 2004 Web track activities are being finalized. Activities are likely to include a mixed home page/named-page/topic distillation task on the existing .GOV collection, and some exploratory search tasks within a single-enterprise collection consisting of both web sites and e-mail messages.

Enterprise search is economically important, and there is a strong incentive for the Web track to move in this direction, though the challenges are considerable [1; 17; 20].

Also in TREC 2004, a preliminary version of a new terabyte track will revive the tradition of larger-scale retrieval within TREC. A new, deeper crawl of the .gov domain has been made, resulting in a collection of approximately four hundred gigabytes and twenty-seven million documents. It will be distributed by CSIRO on a single ATA hard drive.

9.9   Conclusions

The VLC/Web track has shown that in appropriately constituted web search evaluations, retrieval methods based entirely on document content can be substantially outperformed by others that make use of "web evidence," such as anchor text, link measures, and URL or site structure. This has been demonstrated for both informational (topic distillation) and navigational (home page finding and named-page finding) tasks. It is probable that web evidence will in the future be found to be similarly important in transactional tasks. It is also possible that page popularity measures (such as click-through data) may be useful in a web search.

This conclusion is unsurprising as commercial search companies have known for years that web evidence was invaluable when searching the whole Web. Yet the track has shown that the nature of the task is important, and has contributed an understanding of the relative merits of many different types of web evidence. Anchor-text evidence is highly effective on a range of tasks and in many different webs. Query-independent evidence is harder to exploit because of the necessity to combine with query-dependent scores. URL structure is highly effective when web sites are static, but less so when sites are dynamically generated and URLs have the same form. In enterprise-scale webs where spam is not an issue, simple inlink counts seem to work as well as more sophisticated variants such as PageRank.

The discovery, within the track, that URL structure could be exploited effectively was a novel contribution.

Another significant outcome of VLC/Web track (and related) experiments has been to demonstrate that web evidence can strongly contribute to effectiveness even in relatively tiny webs. Significant effectiveness gains due to anchor text and other web evidence have been documented in search tasks over .GOV (1.25 million pages) and even over the artificially constructed WT2g collection (0.25 million pages). Within enterprise webs of only a few thousand pages, anchor text and other web evidence can be used to identify key sites from within large numbers of "relevant" pages.

Many participants and onlookers were shocked when initial Web track experiments using TREC ad hoc methodology showed no benefit whatever from the use of web evidence. In hindsight, the explanation is breathtakingly simple: the evaluation methodology did not accurately represent the major phenomenon (typical web search) we were purporting to study.

The reality is that many web searchers regard entry pages of authoritative relevant sites as more valuable than are isolated pieces of relevant text. They have come to expect that entry pages of key relevant sites will appear at the top of search engine rankings.

An effective web search tool must be able to support the search-and-browse paradigm by bringing the most valuable matching resources (frequently site home pages) to the top, while preventing the list from being flooded by pages from a single source. Our early evaluations failed to recognize this, and we scored individual pages on their text content only, using only a binary scale. For searchers prepared to treat the Web as a newspaper archive and scan thousands of relevant documents, this was acceptable, but on the Web such people are a rare breed.

More recent evaluation methodologies adopted by the track, such as home page and named-page finding and the 2003 topic distillation task, have rectified the methodology problem by considering only the most valuable web sites (or specific named pages) on a topic. This approach automatically penalizes multiple results from the same source and gives infinitely higher value to the most valuable resources than to individual relevant documents.

A more subtle evaluation methodology seems possible in which retrieved documents are given scores (across a wide range, not just a few degrees of text match) commensurate with the value they have to the prototypical Web searcher. The formulation of such a scoring function would have to address the issues of duplicate documents and source diversity, and would probably score zero for duplicates and fractions for subsequent documents from the same source. Such a methodology could largely avoid the need for segregating tasks into search types (for example, topic relevance, home page finding, topic distillation) as topics for which there were no key web sites or other extra valuable resources would automatically fall back to evaluation in standard TREC ad hoc fashion.

Acknowledgments

The late Paul Thistlewaite was a driving force behind the VLC/Web track, and Donna K. Harman, Ellen M. Voorhees, and Ian Soboroff at NIST have been extremely supportive of it. The many individual donors of data to the VLC collection have been thanked in the appropriate TREC proceedings, but are acknowledged again here. John Ritchie and Mark Sanderson, of the University of Glasgow at the time of creating the VLC collection, provided great assistance in negotiating permission to use some of this data. John O'Callaghan and Darrell Williamson showed vision in agreeing to let ACSys distribute data sets, as did Murray Cameron in agreeing that CSIRO should continue the work. A large number of relevance assessors from ACSys, CSIRO, and NIST were employed over the years, and their work was indispensable.

The willingness of Brewster Kahle of the Internet Archive to supply what was at the time a huge crawl was instrumental in the success of the track. Edward King (CSIRO) provided data conversion facilities, and Peter Bailey (of Australian National University at the time of creation of WT10g) did a great job in planning and creating WT10g. Edwin Cooper (the Electric Monk) and Michael Moricz (Alta Vista) provided query sets that formed the basis of many evaluations. Charlie Clarke (the University of Waterloo), Ed Fox (Virginia Tech), and Ian Soboroff made possible the .GOV collection.

Many ACSys administrative staff assisted in the distribution of test collections, and since CSIRO took on the role, all aspects of distribution have been capably looked after by Daphne Bruce.

We are grateful for the cooperation and assistance of the large number of people who have helped build the infrastructure of the track and support its operation. We also acknowledge the many groups that have participated in VLC/Web track evaluations, thereby contributing to the advancement of knowledge in this important area.

References

[1] Abrol, M., N. Latarche, U. Mahadevan, J. Mao, R. Mukherjee, P. Raghavan, M. Tourn, J. Wang, and G. Zhang. Navigating large-scale semi-structured data in business portals. In *Proceedings of the twenty-seventh VLDB conference*, 663–666, Rome, Italy, 2001. Available at ⟨http://www.vldb.org/conf/2001/P663.pdf⟩.

[2] Anh, V. N., O. de Kretser, and A. Moffat. Vector-space ranking with effective early termination. In *Proceedings of the twenty-fourth annual ACM SIGIR Conference*, 35–42.

[3] Anh, V. N., and A. Moffat. Impact transformation: Effective and efficient Web retrieval. In *Proceedings of the twenty-fifth annual ACM SIGIR conference*, 3–10.

[4] Bahle, D., H. E. Williams, and J. Zobel. Efficient phrase querying with an auxiliary index. In *Proceedings of the twenty-fifth annual ACM SIGIR conference*, 215–221.

[5] Bailey, P., N. Craswell, and D. Hawking. Engineering a multi-purpose test collection for Web retrieval experiments. *Information Processing and Management* 39, no. 6 (2003): 853–871.

[6] Berners-Lee, T. *List of WWW servers*. 1992. ⟨http://www.w3.org/History/19921103-hypertext/hypertext/DataSources/WWW/Servers%.html⟩.

[7] Broder, A. A taxonomy of Web search. *ACM SIGIR Forum* 36, no. 2 (2002): 3–10.

[8] Calliau, R. *A little history of the World Wide Web*. 1995. ⟨http://www.w3.org/History.html⟩.

[9] Cannane, A., and H. E. Williams. A general-purpose compression scheme for large collections. *ACM Transactions on Information Systems* 20, no. 3 (2002): 329–355.

[10] Carpineto, C., G. Romano, and V. Giannini. Improving retrieval feedback with multiple term-ranking function combination. *ACM Transactions on Information Systems* 20, no. 3 (2002): 259–290.

[11] Chowdhury, A., O. Frieder, D. Grossman, and M. C. McCabe. Collection statistics for fast duplicate document detection. *ACM Transactions on Information Systems* 20, no. 2 (2002): 171–191.

[12] Clarke, C. L. A., and G. V. Cormack. Shortest-substring retrieval and ranking. *ACM Transactions on Information Systems* 18, no. 1 (2000): 44–78.

[13] Collins-Thompson, K., P. Ogilvie, Y. Zhang, and J. Callan. Information filtering, novelty detection, and named-page finding. In *Proceedings of TREC 2002*, 107–118.

[14] Craswell, N., P. Bailey, and D. Hawking. *Is it fair to evaluate Web systems using TREC ad hoc methods? ACM SIGIR '99 workshop on Web retrieval.* 1999. ⟨http://pastime.anu.edu.au/nick/pubs/sigir99ws.ps.gz⟩.

[15] Craswell, N., D. Hawking, and S. Robertson. Effective site finding using link anchor information. In *Proceedings of the twenty-fourth annual ACM SIGIR conference*, 250–257.

[16] Craswell, N., D. Hawking, R. Wilkinson, and M. Wu. Overview of the TREC 2003 Web track. In *TREC 2003*, 78–92.

[17] Fagin, R., R. Kumar, K. S. McCurley, J. Novak, D. Sivakumar, J. A. Tomlin, and D. P. Williamson. Searching the workplace Web. In *Proceedings of WWW2003*. Budapest, May 2003. Available at ⟨http://www2003.org/cdrom/papers/refereed/p641/xhtml/p641-mccurley.html⟩.

[18] Gordon, M., and P. Pathak. Finding information on the World Wide Web: The retrieval effectiveness of search engines. *Information Processing and Management* 35, no. 2 (March 1999): 141–180.

[19] Harman, D. K., ed. *Proceedings of TREC-1.*

[20] Hawking, D. Challenges in enterprise search. In *Proceedings of the Australasian Databases Conference ADC2004*, Dunedin, New Zealand, 15–26. Australian Computer Society, January 2004.

[21] Hawking, D. Overview of the TREC-9 Web track. In *TREC-9*, 87–102.

[22] Hawking, D., and N. Craswell. Overview of TREC 2001 Web track. In *TREC 2001*, 61–67.

[23] Hawking, D., and N. Craswell. Overview of TREC 2002 Web track. In *TREC 2002*, 86–95.

[24] Hawking, D., N. Craswell, P. Bailey, and K. Griffiths. *Measuring the quality of public search engines.* 2000. ⟨http://pastime.anu.edu.au/TAR/Search_Engines_Conf/⟩.

[25] Hawking, D., N. Craswell, P. Bailey, and K. Griffiths. Measuring search engine quality. *Information Retrieval* 4, no. 1 (2001): 33–59. Preprint at ⟨http://www.ted.cmis.csiro.au/~dave/INRT83-00.ps.gz⟩.

[26] Hawking, D., N. Craswell, and P. Thistlewaite. Overview of TREC-7 very large collection track. In *TREC-7*, 91–104.

[27] Hawking, D., N. Craswell, P. Thistlewaite, and D. K. Harman. Results and challenges in Web search evaluation. *Proceedings of WWW8* 31 (1999): 1321–1330. Available at ⟨http://www8.org/w8-papers/2c-search-discover/results/results.html⟩.

[28] Hawking, D., and S. Robertson. On collection size and retrieval effectiveness. *Information Retrieval* 6, no. 1 (2003): 99–150.

[29] Hawking, D., and P. Thistlewaite. Overview of TREC-6 very large collection track. In *Proceedings of TREC-6*, 93–106.

[30] Hawking, D., E. M. Voorhees, N. Craswell, and P. Bailey. Overview of TREC-8 Web track. In *TREC-8*, 131–150.

[31] Internet Archive. *Building a digital library for the future.* August 1997. ⟨http://www.archive.org/⟩.

[32] Kraaij, W., T. Westerveld, and D. Hiemstra. The importance of prior probabilities for entry page search. In *Proceedings of the twenty-fifth annual international ACM SIGIR conference*, 27–34.

[33] Lafon, Y. *HTTP—Hypertext transfer protocol.* ⟨http://www.w3.org/Protocols/⟩ (accessed September 2002).

[34] Lu, Z., and K. S. McKinley. Partial replica selection based on relevance for information retrieval. In *Proceedings of the twenty-third annual international ACM SIGIR conference*, 248–255.

[35] Lynch, C. A. The Z39.50 information retrieval standard, part 1. *D-Lib Magazine*, April 1997. Available at ⟨http://mirrored.ukoln.ac.uk/lis-journals/dlib/dlib/dlib/april97/04lynch.html⟩.

[36] NIST. *TREC overview.* ⟨http://trec.nist.gov/overview.html⟩ (accessed September 2002).

[37] Radev, D. R., K. Libner, and W. Fan. Getting answers to natural language questions on the Web. *JASIST* 53, no. 5 (2002): 359–364. Available at ⟨http://www.asis.org/Publications/JASIS/vol53n05.html⟩.

[38] Salton, G., and M. J. McGill. *Introduction to Modern Information Retrieval.* New York: McGraw-Hill, 1983.

[39] Scholer, F., H. E. Williams, J. Yiannis, and J. Zobel. Compression of inverted indexes for fast query evaluation. In *Proceedings of the twenty-fifth annual international ACM SIGIR conference*, 222–229.

[40] Seber, G. A. F. *The estimation of animal abundance and related parameters.* 2nd ed. London: Charles Griffin and Co., 1982.

[41] Singhal, A., and M. Kaszkiel. A case study in Web search using TREC algorithms. In *Proceedings of WWW10*, Hong Kong, 2001, 708–716. Available at ⟨http://www.www10.org/cdrom/papers/pdf/p317.pdf⟩.

[42] Upstill, T., N. Craswell, and D. Hawking. Query-independent evidence in home page finding. *ACM Transactions on Information Systems* 21, no. 3 (2003): 286–313.

[43] URL. *RFC1738: Uniform resource locators*. T. Berners-Lee, L. Masinter, and M. McCahill. Available at ⟨http://rfc.net/rfc1738.html⟩.

[44] Voorhees, E. M. Evaluation by highly relevant documents. In *Proceedings of the twenty-fourth annual international ACM SIGIR conference*, 74–82.

[45] Westerveld, T., W. Kraaij, and D. Hiemstra. Retrieving Web pages using content, links, URLs, and anchors. In *TREC 2001*, 663–672.

[46] Zakon, R. *Hobbes' Internet timeline*. 2002. ⟨http://www.zakon.org/robert/internet/timeline/⟩.

[47] Zhang, M., R. Song, C. Lin, S. Ma, Z. Jiang, Y. Jin, Y. Liu, and L. Zhao. The TREC 2002 Web experiments. In *TREC 2002*, 591–594.

Additional References

[48] Cohen, P. R., and R. Kjeldsen. Information retrieval by constrained spreading activation in semantic networks. *Information Processing and Management*, 23, no. 4 (1987): 255–268.

[49] Kleinberg, J. Authorative sources in a hyperlinked environment. *Journal of the ACM*, 46, no. 5 (1999): 604–632.

[50] Page, L., S. Brin, R. Motwani, and T. Winograd. The pagerank citation ranking: Bringing order to the web. Technical report, Stanford, Santa Barbara, CA 93106, January 1998. www-db.stanford.edu/~backrub/pageranksub.ps.

[51] Picard, J. Modelling and combining evidence provided by document relationships using probabilistic argumentation systems. In *Proceedings of the twenty-first annual international ACM SIGIR conference*, 182–189.

[52] Kazai, G., M. Lalmas, and A. P. de Vries. The overlap problem in content-oriented xml retrieval evaluation. In *Proceedings of the twenty-seventh annual international ACM SIGIR conference*, 72–79.

10 Question Answering in TREC
Ellen M. Voorhees

Question answering covers a broad range of activities. In its most general interpretation, question answering is an AI-complete problem: the automated assistant that is able to comprehend and respond to arbitrary questions on arbitrary subjects. Since such systems remain well beyond the current state of the art, researchers have limited the scope of the general question-answering problem to concentrate on more manageable tasks. This has resulted in different kinds of systems that can all be seen as types of question-answering systems. Database systems return exact answers with respect to highly structured data in response to questions posed in query languages such as SQL that have precise semantics; document retrieval systems return unstructured texts related to queries posed as sets of query words with optional structural connectives; and reading comprehension systems demonstrate proficiency with natural language by responding to questions pertaining to a specific natural-language text. In TREC, question answering is used to distinguish systems that return an answer itself rather than a ranked list of documents in response to a natural-language question.

The motivation for the TREC question-answering (QA) track is the belief that users would prefer to be given answers to their questions rather than find the answer for themselves by reading an entire document. The time savings to be realized by not reading documents are greatest when the answer is a simple fact that does not require explanation or detailed background knowledge to be understood. In addition, fact-based, short-answer questions are the easiest type of question to answer. The original task in the QA track was therefore defined similar to the task that Julien Kupiec's MURAX [11] system was designed to perform, retrieving answers to *closed-class* questions from a set of natural-language texts. Kupiec defined a closed-class question as "a question stated in natural language, which assumes some definite answer typified by a noun phrase rather than a procedural answer." Whereas MURAX used an encyclopedia as the source of answers, TREC QA systems use the TREC document collections. That is, the focus of the TREC QA track has been extracting answers to fact-based, short-answer questions from large collections of open-domain, natural-language text. The most recent tracks incorporated additional tasks to increase the kinds of questions that systems can answer.

This chapter provides an overview of the TREC QA track, from its inception in TREC-8 (1999) through TREC 2003. The next section offers a summary of the track for each of its five years, chronicling how the tasks and the systems have evolved. Since there was no generally accepted evaluation protocol for question-answering systems, the following section assesses the quality of the evaluations themselves. The final section looks toward the future of the QA track.

10.1   The TREC QA Tracks

Question answering as a research endeavor has a history that long predates TREC. Question-answering systems generally fall into two broad categories: natural-language-understanding systems and systems that target text extracts with no attempt to understand the meaning of the question. In the first category are natural-language front ends to database and knowledge-base systems, reading comprehension systems, and dialogue systems. The second category is represented by passage retrieval systems, and systems such as FAQ Finder [1] and help-desk systems that respond to incoming questions with cached answers to similar questions. Lynette Hirschman and Rob Gaizauskas provide a summary of QA research in their introduction to a special issue of *Natural Language Engineering* devoted to question answering [12].

One of the motivations for the TREC QA track was to define a common task for the IR and information extraction (IE) communities. IE systems—such as those used at the Message Understanding Conferences (see ⟨http://www.itl.nist.gov/iad/894.02/related_projects/muc/⟩)—recognize particular kinds of entities and relationships among those entities in running text. While not strictly QA systems, the goal of IE systems is to populate database-like tables with the extracted data to facilitate future tasks such as data mining, summarization, or question answering. A task similar to the MURAX system's task seemed ideal as a common task. Targeting small extracts from a large, open-domain text source was familiar to the IR community as a passage retrieval task, while the IE community was familiar with recognizing the named entities that are the usual answers to closed-class questions.

10.1.1   TREC-8: The Original Task

In TREC-8, the participants were given a document collection and a test set of questions. The document set consisted of the set of documents on TREC disks four and five (approximately 1,900 megabytes of text and 528,000 documents mostly drawn from newswires/newspapers). The question set contained two hundred fact-based, short-answer questions such as the ones shown in figure 10.1. Most of the questions were created expressly for the track, and each question was guaranteed to have at least one document in the collection that explicitly answered it.

Participating systems returned a ranked list of five [*document-id*, *answer-string*] pairs per question such that each answer string was believed to contain an answer to the question. The test was blind: the participants were not allowed to change their systems once they received the questions, and the answers were required to be produced completely automatically. Answer strings were limited to either 50 or 250 bytes depending on the run type, and could either be extracted from the corresponding document or automatically generated from information contained in the document.

All of the [*document-id*, *answer-string*] pairs for a single question for all runs were gathered into a single pool file. Human assessors read each string and made a binary decision as to whether the string actually did contain an answer to the question in the context provided by the document (see section 10.2.1). Taking document context

• How many calories are there in a Big Mac?

• What two US biochemists won the Nobel Prize in medicine in 1992?

• Who is the voice of Miss Piggy?

• Where is the Taj Mahal?

• What costume designer decided that Michael Jackson should only wear one glove?

• In what year did Joe DiMaggio compile his 56-game hitting streak?

• What language is commonly used in Bombay?

• Where is Rider College located?

• Name a film in which Jude Law acted.

Figure 10.1
Example questions used in the QA track

Table 10.1
MRR and number of questions for which no correct response was found (number not found) for top TREC-8 submissions

Run name	Participant	MRR	Number not found
textract9908	Cymfony, Inc.	0.66	54 (27%)
SMUNLP1	Southern Methodist University	0.56	63 (32%)
attqa50e	AT&T Research Labs	0.36	109 (55%)
IBMDR995	IBM (Prager)	0.32	110 (56%)
xeroxQA8sC	Xerox Research Centre Europe	0.32	111 (56%)

into account allowed a system that correctly derived a response from a document that was in error (for example, a typographic error or a misreported fact such as an incorrect number of casualties) to be given full credit for its response. The pool file was sorted by the document identifiers so that the assessor could not tell which systems returned which strings or the ranks at which the different strings were returned.

Given a set of judgments for the strings, the score computed for a submission was the mean reciprocal rank (MRR). An individual question received a score equal to the reciprocal of the rank at which the first correct response was returned, or zero if none of the five responses contained a correct answer. The score for a submission was then the mean of the individual questions' reciprocal ranks.

Twenty participants submitted a total of forty-five runs to the track. Table 10.1 gives both the MRR and the number of questions for which no answer was found for the top five TREC-8 runs. Only runs that used the fifty-byte limit on answer strings are considered, and only the best run for a given participant is included (participants were allowed to submit two fifty-byte runs). Note that the cutoff of five runs was chosen for convenience; there were other runs submitted to the tracks whose scores are close to the ones listed here.

Allowing 250 bytes in a response is an easier task than limiting responses to 50 byte•: though not shown in the results table, participants' 250-byte-limit runs had a higher MRR than the same group's 50-byte run. The submissions from AT&T Research Labs demonstrate that existing passage retrieval techniques can be successful for 250-byte runs, but are not suitable for 50-byte runs [17]. AT&T's question-answering system used a traditional vector-based retrieval system to select fifty documents and then scored each sentence within those documents by the number of question words in the surrounding context. In one set of runs (its "passage-based" runs), the highest-scoring sentences were returned as the response. In a second set (its "entity-based" runs), high-scoring sentences were further processed by a linguistic module. The passage-based method was quite competitive for the 250-byte limit, but was not nearly as successful when restricted to just 50 bytes. These results suggest that the relatively simple bag-of-words approaches that are successfully used in document retrieval are not sufficient for extracting specific, fact-based answers.

Most systems used a version of the following general approach to answer the questions. The system first attempted to classify a question according to the type of its answer as suggested by its question word. For example, a question that begins with "who" implies a person or an organization is being sought, and a question beginning with "when" implies a time designation is needed. Next, the system retrieved a small portion of the document collection using standard text retrieval technology and the question as the query. The system performed a shallow parse of the returned documents to detect entities of the same type as the answer. If an entity of the required type was found sufficiently close to the question's words, the system returned that entity as the response. If no appropriate answer type was found, the system fell back to best-matching-passage techniques.

This approach worked well provided the query types recognized by the system had broad enough coverage and the system was able to classify questions sufficiently accurately. Most systems could answer "who" questions such as "Who invented the paper clip?" very accurately. Questions that sought a person yet did not actually begin with "who" ("Name the first private citizen to fly in space." "What Nobel laureate was expelled from the Philippines before the conference on East Timor?") were much more difficult, however. More difficult still were questions whose answers were not an entity of a specific type ("Why did David Koresh ask the FBI for a word processor?"). Of course, pattern matching on expected answer types was not foolproof even when "good" matches were found. One response to the question "Who was the first American in space?" was Jerry Brown, taken from a document that says, "As for Wilson himself, he became a senator by defeating Jerry Brown, who has been called the first American in space."

10.1.2 TREC-9: Using "Real" Questions

The task in the TREC-9 track was identical to the TREC-8 task. For TREC-9, the document set was expanded to include all of the newspaper and newswire articles from the first five TREC disks, which amounts to approximately 979,000 documents and 3,033 megabytes of text. The question set consisted of 693 questions: 500 questions drawn from log files, and 193 question variants, described below. The use of naturally occurring questions gathered from logs, rather than questions created for the task, had a large impact on the task in that these "real" questions were much more difficult than the constructed ones.

The questions were selected from an Encarta (⟨http://encarta.msn.com⟩) log that contained actual questions, and a raw Excite (⟨http://excite.com⟩) log. Since the raw Excite log did not contain many grammatically well-formed questions, question authors used the Excite log as a source of ideas for actual questions, and created questions without referring to test documents. To guarantee that a question had an answer in the document collection, assessors searched for answers to the candidate questions; only those candidates with answers in the test corpus were included in the final test set. Because the TREC-8 questions were constructed for the track, many of them were back formulations of sentences in the test documents. This meant the vocabulary used in the question and in the answer passage was extremely similar, and extracting the answer passage was thus easier. But vocabulary differences were not the main reason why the naturally occurring questions were more difficult. The TREC-9 set contained many more high-level questions such as "Who is Colin Powell?" than did the constructed set, and this increased ambiguity was the main difficulty.

The 193 question variants included in the test set of questions were syntactic variants of some other question in the test set. The purpose of the syntactic variants was to investigate whether QA systems are robust to the variety of different ways a question can be phrased. Once the first five hundred questions were selected, NIST assessors were given a subset of the questions and asked to create "natural" variants of the question. The intent was that the variant should have the same semantic meaning of the original as well as be phrased in a way that a native English speaker might ask the question. For example, the test set contained four variants for the question "What is the tallest mountain?": "What is the world's highest peak?" "What is the highest mountain in the world?" "Name the highest mountain," and "What is the name of the tallest mountain in the world?" The 193 variants included variants for fifty-four different original questions, with a range of one to seven new questions per original.

The final difference between the TREC-8 and TREC-9 tracks was a change in the way answers were scored. In TREC-8, assessors judged a string as either right or wrong. Yet there were a number of instances during the TREC-8 judging when an answer string contained the correct answer, but that answer could not possibly have been determined from the document returned. For example, the correct answer for "Who is the sixteenth President of the United States?" is Abraham Lincoln. One of the answer strings returned contained Abraham Lincoln, but the associated document discussed

Table 10.2
MRR and number of questions for which no correct response was found (number not found) for top TREC-9 submissions

Run name	Participant	MRR	Number not found
LCCSMU2	Southern Methodist University	0.58	229 (34%)
uwmt9qas0	MultiText, University of Waterloo	0.32	395 (58%)
ISI0A50	Information Sciences Institute, University of Southern California	0.32	385 (57%)
IBMKR50	IBM (Prager)	0.32	402 (59%)
ibmhlt0050	IBM (Ittycheriah)	0.29	394 (58%)

Lincoln's Gettysburg Address. The document does not even mention that Lincoln was president, let alone that he was the sixteenth president. Since the TREC-8 task did not specifically require that the document returned with the answer string support the string as the answer, these cases were judged as correct even though the assessors were uncomfortable doing so. In subsequent tracks, the track guidelines required that the document returned with the answer string actually support the answer contained in the string. If the answer string did not contain a correct answer, the response was judged incorrect. If the string did contain a correct answer, but the document did not support that answer (such as the Lincoln/Gettysburg Address example above), the response was judged unsupported. Otherwise, the response was judged correct. Two MRR scores were thus computed for runs submitted to later tracks: a *strict* score in which unsupported answers are considered incorrect, and a *lenient* score in which unsupported answers are considered correct.

Twenty-eight participants submitted a total of seventy-eight runs to the TREC-9 track. The scores for the top five runs are given in table 10.2. As in table 10.1, the second table gives the MRR and the number of questions for which no answer was found using only fifty-byte-limit runs, the best run for each participant, and strict MRR scores.

Despite the drop in the absolute value of the evaluation scores, the performance of the TREC-9 systems represents a significant improvement in question-answering technology over the TREC-8 systems given that the TREC-9 question set was much more difficult than the TREC-8 set. The improvement in QA systems between TREC-8 and TREC-9 came from refinements to the individual steps of the general processing strategy introduced in TREC-8 rather than an entirely new approach. TREC-9 systems were better at classifying questions as to the expected answer type, and used a wider variety of methods for finding the entailed answer types in retrieved passages. Many systems used WordNet [5] as a source of related words for the initial query and as a means of determining whether an entity extracted from a passage matched the required answer type.

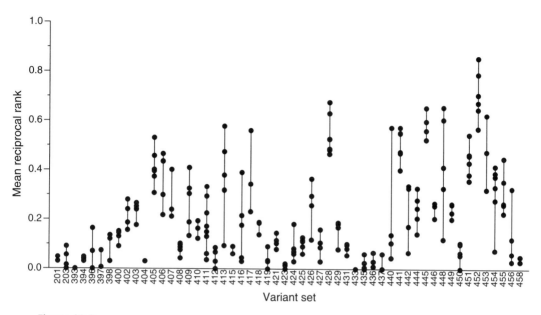

Figure 10.2
Average reciprocal rank for question variants

Figure 10.2 shows a plot of the average score for each question in a variant set. The average score for a question is the mean of the reciprocal rank scores averaged over the thirty-three runs that used the fifty-byte limit on responses and using strict evaluation. The y-axis in the plot is the average score, and the x-axis represents the different variant sets. The variant sets are identified by the question number of the original question that was used to generate the variants.

While the intent had been for each variant to have identical semantics, assessment demonstrated that this was not always the case. Sometimes, rewording a question caused the focus of the question to change slightly so that some answer strings were acceptable for some variants but not others. For example, the assessor accepted "November 29" as a correct response for "What is Dick Clark's birthday?" but required the year as well for "When was Dick Clark born?"

Many variant sets show little variability in the average score. Generally, the average score for each of these variants is low, indicating that the underlying information being sought was difficult to obtain no matter how the question was phrased. A few variant sets did have a wide range of average scores. Frequently, the difference was caused by different word choices in the variants. For instance, the variant set generated from question 413 asked for the location of the U.S. headquarters of Proctor and Gamble. The variant with the lowest-average score used "corporate offices" instead of "headquarters." For the variant set generated from question 440, the original question was "Where was Poe born?" which had a much higher score than any of the variants that all asked for Edgar Allan Poe's birthplace. The unintentional change in focus of some variants also made differences in average scores. "New Jersey" was an acceptable (and common) answer to question 448, "Where is Rider College located?" but it was not acceptable for the variant "Rider College is located in what city?"

10.1.3 TREC 2001: List Questions

The TREC 2001 track contained two tasks. The main task was similar to the TREC-9 task, except there was no longer any guarantee that an answer was contained in the document collection. The list task introduced a new type of question processing into TREC.

The main task used the same document collection as in TREC-9 and a new set of five hundred questions. The source of the questions was a set of filtered MSNSearch (⟨http://www.msn.com⟩) and AskJeeves (⟨http://www.ask.com⟩) logs. Raw logs were automatically filtered (at Microsoft and AskJeeves) to select queries that contained a question word (for example, what, when, where, which, and so on) anywhere in the query; that began with modals or the verb *to be* (for instance, are, can, could, define, describe, does, do, and so forth); or that ended with a question mark. Additional human filtering of the logs then removed queries that were not appropriate for the TREC task. The spelling, punctuation, and occasionally the grammar of the queries selected to be in the final question set were manually corrected, but except for a few questions, the content of the question was precisely as it appeared in the log. Those few changes that were made consisted of substituting a closely related concept for a concept in the question in the log (say, substituting one Greek god for another) so the question had an answer in the document collection. To test whether systems can recognize when there is no answer in the document set, forty-nine of the test questions have no known correct answer in the document collection. A system returned "NIL" as a response to indicate its belief that the corpus did not contain an answer.

NIST made no attempt to control the relative number of different types of questions (for instance, who versus where versus when) in the test set from year to year. Instead, the distribution of question types in the final test set reflected the distribution in the source of questions. Definition questions ("Who is . . ." and "What is . . .") appear frequently in the query logs, and thus approximately one-quarter of the questions in the TREC 2001 test set are definition questions. This resulted in a challenging test set: definition questions are particularly difficult for a system to return short answers to since the system has no context in which to frame a suitable response.

Thirty-six participants submitted sixty-seven main task runs to the track. All of the runs were required to use a 50-byte limit since the results of both the TREC-8 and TREC-9 tracks demonstrated that passage retrieval techniques were satisfactory when a 250-byte limit was allowed. Table 10.3 gives the scores for the top five main task runs. Once again, only the best run from each participant is included and strict scoring was used. In addition to the MRR score and the number of questions for which no answer was found, the table also reports the number of questions for which the system

Table 10.3

MRR, number of questions for which no correct response was found (number not found), and number of questions for which NIL was returned (NIL returned) and correct (NIL correct) for top TREC 2001 main task submissions

Run name	Participant	MRR	Number not found	NIL Returned	NIL Correct
insight	InsightSoft-M	0.68	152 (31%)	120	38
LCC1	Language Computer Corporation	0.57	171 (35%)	41	31
orcl1	Oracle	0.48	193 (39%)	82	35
isi1a50	Information Sciences Institute, University of Southern California	0.43	205 (42%)	407	33
uwmta1	MultiText, University of Waterloo	0.43	212 (43%)	492	49

returned NIL as a response (NIL returned) and the number of questions for which NIL was correctly returned as a response (NIL correct).

The best scoring system was able find an answer to 70 percent of the test questions—about the same percentage of questions answered by the best systems in the TREC-8 task. As noted above, the difficulty of the TREC 2001 test set was much greater than that of the TREC-8 test set, so this represents a large increase in the effectiveness of QA systems in three years' time. Detecting whether or not an answer exists in the collection was feasible—the LCC1 run had an accuracy of 31/41 or 0.76—but apparently difficult as only five runs had an accuracy greater than 0.25. (Accuracy is computed as the number of questions for which NIL was correctly returned divided by the total number of questions for which NIL was returned.)

There were two general categories of QA systems represented in the TREC 2001 track. The first category continued to refine the general strategy of earlier years by applying sophisticated language processing for question categorization and answer finding. The second category relied on simpler pattern-matching methods using very large corpora (generally the Web) instead of the language processing. The idea exploited in the massive data approach is the fact that in a large enough data source, a correct answer will usually be repeated often enough to distinguish it from the noise that happens to occasionally match simple patterns.

Examples of sophisticated language processing QA systems are PowerAnswer from the Language Computer Corporation (the successor to the Southern Methodist University systems) [8], Webclopedia from the Information Sciences Institute at the University of Southern California [10], and the QALC system from LIMSI [3]. The PowerAnswer system includes successive feedback loops that try progressively larger modifications to the original question until it finds an answer that can be justified as an abductive proof. The system first parses the question and recognizes entities contained in it to create a question semantic form. The semantic form of the question is used to determine the expected answer type by finding the phrase that is most connected to other concepts in the question. The system uses an answer taxonomy that contains WordNet subhierarchies and thus has broad coverage. PowerAnswer next retrieves paragraphs from the corpus using Boolean queries and terms drawn from the original question, related concepts from WordNet, and an indication of the expected answer type. The paragraph retrieval is repeated using different term combinations until the query returns a number of paragraphs in a predetermined range. The retrieved paragraphs are parsed into their semantic forms, and a unification procedure is run between the question semantic form and each paragraph semantic form. If the unification fails for all paragraphs, a new set of paragraphs is retrieved using synonyms and morphological derivations of the previous query. When the unification procedure succeeds, the semantic forms are translated into logical forms, and a logical proof in the form of an abductive backchaining from the answer to the question is attempted. If the proof succeeds, the answer from the proof is returned as the answer string. Otherwise, terms that are semantically related to important question concepts are drawn from WordNet and a new set of paragraphs is retrieved.

The system from InsightSoft-M [18] is a pattern-based QA system, though in this case the patterns were built by hand by the system's architects using a create/test/modify cycle on large amounts of text. The main idea of the system is to extend the template matching used to determine a question's type to be the core of the system. Patterns are modular structures that allow complex patterns to be built from simpler components. A pattern may contain free variables that represent items from predefined lists. For example, "[country name]'s [term from a list of posts] [term from a list of titles] [two capitalized words]" is one pattern for detecting a person who is the head of a government. An important part of a pattern's specification is an associated set of rules that describe appropriate contexts for a good match. To process a question, the system determines the expected answer type and retrieves passages using the question words. The system then attempts to match patterns associated with the expected answer type to the passages, starting with the most complex pattern first. This ordering of the patterns reflects the fact that complex patterns are usually quite reliable when they match, but they match infrequently. To qualify as a match, the rules contained in the pattern definition must be satisfied. These rules encode semantics and are responsible for the high-quality results that the InsightSoft-M system obtains. Attempts to automatically mine patterns from large corpora have not included these "context check" rules [16] and to date have not been as successful.

A more typical pattern approach that relies on the redundancy in extremely large corpora is the AskMSR system [4]. Instead of doing sophisticated language processing to determine all the various ways a given concept may be expressed in any given document, the system searches the Web looking for a small number of simple, highly indicative patterns. For example, for the question "Who killed $\langle X \rangle$?" the system looks for the string "$\langle X \rangle$ was killed by $\langle Y \rangle$." While the system may miss many

- Name 4 U.S. cities that have a "Shubert" theater.

- Name 30 individuals who served as a cabinet officer under Ronald Reagan.

- Who are 6 actors who have played Tevye in "Fiddler on the Roof"?

- Name 4 countries that can produce synthetic diamonds.

- What are 9 novels written by John Updike?

Figure 10.3
Example list task questions

documents that contain the answer because the answer is expressed differently in that document, with a big enough corpus it will find the answer expressed just the way it is looking for it sufficiently often to distinguish the correct answer from serendipitous matches. Once the answer is determined from the Web, it is mapped back into the target document collection to return a supporting document. Other systems that rely on redundancy in the data source to select answers include the system from the University of Waterloo that gives more frequent answers a boost in the score computed for them [2], and the system from ITC-irst that finds the answer in the target corpus, but then validates that answer on the Web using mutual information-like measures [13].

The second task included in the TREC 2001 track was the list task. The list task requires systems to assemble an answer from information located in multiple documents. Such questions are harder to answer than the questions used in the main task since information duplicated in the documents must be detected and reported only once.

Each question used in the list task specified the number of instances of a particular kind of information to be retrieved, such as in the example questions shown in figure 10.3. Each instance was guaranteed to obey the same constraints as an individual answer in the main task and was judged in the same manner as a response in the main task. The document collection was guaranteed to contain at least the target number of instances. Systems returned an unordered list of [*document-id, answer-string*] pairs where each pair represented a single instance. The list could contain no more than the target number of instances.

The questions used as the list task test set were constructed by NIST assessors and staff since there were not enough appropriate questions in search engine logs. The assessors were instructed to construct questions whose answers would be a list of entities (people, places, dates, numbers) such that the list would not likely be found in a reference work such as a gazetteer or an almanac. The target number of instances ranged from three to forty. The assessors searched the document collection to find as complete a list of instances as possible. The target was then set to a value less than the total number of instances the assessor found, but greater than the number of instances that could be found in any one document. A single document could contain multiple instances, and the same instance might be repeated in multiple documents.

Judgments of correct, incorrect, or not supported were made individually for each [*document-id, answer-string*] pair. The assessor was given one list at a time, and while judging for correctness the assessor also marked a set of responses as distinct. The assessor arbitrarily chose any one of a set of equivalent responses to mark as the distinct one, and marked the remainder as not distinct. Incorrect responses were always marked as not distinct (the assessment software enforced this), but unsupported responses could be marked distinct.

List results were evaluated using accuracy, the number of distinct responses divided by the target number of instances. Since unsupported responses could be marked distinct, the reported accuracy is a lenient evaluation.

Ten groups submitted eighteen list task runs in TREC 2001. The run from the Language Computer Corporation had the best average accuracy at 76 percent. This was significantly more accurate than any of the other submissions. Most systems found at least one instance for most questions. Duplication was not a major source of error for any of the runs since each run contained many more wrong responses than duplicate ones. There was not enough participation in the list task to know whether the lack of duplication is because systems are capable of recognizing and eliminating duplicate responses, or if there simply wasn't much duplication in the document set.

10.1.4   TREC 2002: Exact Answers

The TREC 2002 track continued to use closed-class questions, but made two major departures from earlier tracks. The first difference was that systems were to return exact answers rather than the text snippets containing an answer that were accepted previously. The second difference was that systems were required to return exactly one response per question and the questions were to be ranked by the system's confidence in the answer it had found.

The change to exact answers was motivated by the belief that a system's ability to recognize the precise extent of the answer is crucial to improving question-answering technology. The problems with using text snippets as responses are illustrated in figure 10.4, which shows answer strings that were judged correct for the question "What river in the US is known as the Big Muddy?" Strings listed closer to the top are clearly better responses than strings listed closer to the bottom. Accepting only exact answers as correct forces systems to demonstrate that they know precisely where the answer lies in the snippets.

The second change, ranking questions by confidence in the answer, tested a system's ability to recognize when it has found a correct answer. Systems must be able to recognize when they do not know the answer to avoid returning incorrect responses. In many applications, returning a wrong answer is much worse than returning a "don't know" response.

The document collection used as the source of answers was the the *AQUAINT Corpus of English News Text* (LDC catalog number LDC2002T31), another collection of newswire articles. The test set of questions was drawn from MSNSearch and AskJeeves logs. NIST did not include any definition questions in the test set, but otherwise made

the Mississippi
Known as Big Muddy, the Mississippi is the longest
as Big Muddy , the Mississippi is the longest
messed with . Known as Big Muddy , the Mississip
Mississippi is the longest river in the US
the Mississippi is the longest river in the US,
the Mississippi is the longest river(Mississippi)
has brought the Mississippi to its lowest
ipes.In Life on the Mississippi, Mark Twain wrote t
Southeast;Mississippi;Mark Twain;officials began
Known; Mississippi; US,; Minnesota;Gulf Mexico
Mud Island,;Mississippi;"The;– history,;Memphis

Figure 10.4
Correct text snippets for "What river in the US is know as the Big Muddy?"

no attempt to control the relative number of different types of questions in the test set.

A system response consisting of a [*document-id*, *answer-string*] pair was assigned exactly one judgment by the assessor as follows:

Wrong   the answer string does not contain a correct answer or the answer is not responsive.

Not Supported   the answer string contains a correct answer, but the document returned does not support that answer.

Not Exact   the answer string contains a correct answer and the document supports that answer, but the string contains more than just the answer (or is missing bits of the answer).

Right   the answer string consists of exactly a correct answer and that answer is supported by the document returned.

Only responses judged right were counted as correct in the final scoring. A NIL response was counted as correct if there is no known answer in the document collection for that question. Forty-six questions have no known answer in the collection.

The scoring metric used, called the confidence-weighted score, was chosen to emphasize the system's ability to correctly rank its responses. The metric was inspired by document retrieval's uninterpolated average precision, though the confidence-weighted score requires *questions* to be ranked while average precision is computed for a single topic. The confidence-weighted score rewards a system for a correct answer early in the ranking more than it rewards for a correct answer later in the ranking. More formally, if there are Q questions in the test set, the confidence-weighted score is defined as

Table 10.4
Evaluation scores for TREC 2002 runs

Run name	Participant	Score	Judged right	
			Number	Percentage
LCCmain2002	Language Computer Corporation	0.856	415	83.0
exactanswer	InsightSoft-M	0.691	271	54.2
pris2002	National University of Singapore (Hui)	0.610	290	58.0
IRST02D1	ITC-irst	0.589	192	38.4
IBMPQSQACYC	IBM (Prager)	0.588	179	35.8

$$\frac{1}{Q}\sum_{i=1}^{Q}\frac{\text{number correct in first } i \text{ ranks}}{i}.$$

Thirty-four groups submitted sixty-seven runs to the TREC 2002 task. Table 10.4 gives evaluation results for the top-scoring runs. The table includes one run each from the top five groups. The run shown in the table is the run with the best confidence-weighted score. Also shown is the number of questions that were judged as "right." (Note that this table reports the percentage of correct responses whereas the table for earlier TRECs reports the percentage judged incorrect. Incorrect is a fuzzier concept in TREC 2002 since it incorporates wrong, unsupported, and inexact judgments.)

Since the test set of questions did not contain any definition questions, the TREC 2002 questions are most likely easier to answer than the TREC-9 and TREC 2001 sets. The overall task is harder, however, since systems had only one chance to respond correctly, not five, and were required to return exact answers. Three groups were able to answer more than half the questions correctly under these more stringent conditions, with the top-scoring Language Computer Corporation run answering more than 80 percent of the questions correctly. Across all participants, there was a marked increase in the use of name lists, gazetteers, and the like to answer specific question types, and continued reliance on the Web as a system component.

The results in table 10.4 also illustrate that the confidence-weighted score does indeed emphasize a system's ability to rank correctly answered questions before incorrectly answered ones. For example, the *exactanswer* run has a greater confidence-weighted score than the *pris2002* run despite answering nineteen fewer questions correctly. The systems used a variety of approaches to create their question rankings. Almost all systems used question type as a factor since some question types are easier to answer than others. Some systems use a score to rank candidate answers for a question. When that score is comparable across questions, it can also be used to rank questions. A few groups used a training set of previous years' questions and answers to learn a good feature set and corresponding weights to predict confidence. Many systems used NIL as an indicator that the system couldn't find an answer (rather than the system was sure there was no answer) and thus ranked NIL responses last.

10.1.5   TREC 2003: A Combined Task

The list task was run as a separate task in both TRECs 2001 and 2002, but not many groups participated in them as they concentrated on the main task. To encourage broader participation for different question types, the main task in the TREC 2003 track was a single combined task that included closed-class, list, and definition questions. Each question was tagged as to its type, and the response formats and evaluation methods differed for each type, but the final score for a run was a weighted average of the scores for the three component tasks.

The closed-class portion of the task was the same as the main task in TREC 2001 except confidence-weighted scoring was not used. Instead, the final score for the closed-class portion of the task was the fraction of questions that were answered correctly.

The list portion of the task was also similar to previous years' tasks. However, the target number of responses was not included in the question: systems were expected to return all of the correct, distinct answers contained in the document collection. The list portion was then evaluated using the average F measure score based on instance precision (IP) and instance recall (IRe). Let S be the size of the final answer list (that is, the number of known answers), D the number of correct, distinct responses returned by the system, and N the total number of responses returned by the system. Then $IP = D/N$ and $IRe = D/S$. Precision and recall were then combined using the F measure with equal weight given to recall and precision:

$$F = \frac{2 * IP * IRe}{(IP + IRe)}$$

The definition portion of the task was a new task for TREC. The definition question test set contained fifty questions drawn from search engine logs. Assessors selected a question from the log, and searched the document collection for information about the target. The final set of questions contained thirty questions for which the target was a (perhaps fictional) person (for example, Vlad the Impaler, Andrea Bocceli, Ben Hur), ten questions for which the target was an organization (say, Bausch and Lomb, Friends of the Earth, Freddie Mac), and ten questions for which the target was some other thing (a golden parachute, feng shui, TB). If the question had a qualification in the log, the qualification remained in the test set (for instance, "What is Ph in biology?"). The following scenario was assumed to provide context:

The questioner is an adult, a native speaker of English, and an "average" reader of U.S. newspapers. In reading an article, the user has come across a term that they would like to find out more about. They may have some basic idea of what the term means either from the context of the article (for example, a bandicoot must be a type of animal) or basic background knowledge (Ulysses S. Grant was a U.S. president). They are not experts in the domain of the target, and therefore are not seeking esoteric details (for example, not a zoologist looking to distinguish the different species in genus *Perameles*).

A system returned an unordered set of [*document-id, answer-string*] pairs as a response for a definition question. Each string was presumed to be a facet in the definition of the target. There were no limits placed on either the length of an individual answer string or the number of pairs in the list, though systems were penalized for retrieving extraneous information.

Judging the quality of the systems' responses was done in two steps. In the first step, all of the answer strings from all responses were presented to the assessor in a single (long) list. Using these responses and the assessor's own research done during question development, the assessor first created a list of "information nuggets" about the target. An information nugget was defined as a fact for which the assessor could make a binary decision as to whether a response contained the nugget. At the end of this step, the assessor decided which nuggets were vital—nuggets that must appear in a definition for that definition to be good. The assessor went on to the second step once the nugget list was created. In this step, the assessor went through each of the system responses in turn and marked where each nugget appeared in the response. If a system returned a particular nugget more than once, it was marked only once.

Figure 10.5 shows an example of how one response was judged for the question "What is a golden parachute?" The top of the figure shows the nugget list developed by the assessor with the vital nuggets indicated. The bottom of the figure shows a system response with the nugget identifiers of the nuggets that were assigned to the response to the left of the individual strings that match the nugget. For example, the assessor matched nugget 1 to item b, and nugget 4 to item i.

Given the judgments as described above, it is straightforward to compute the nugget recall of a response: it is simply the ratio between the number of correctly retrieved nuggets to the number of nuggets on the assessor's list. But the corresponding measure of nugget precision, the ratio between the number of nuggets correctly retrieved to the total number of nuggets retrieved, is problematic since the correct value for the denominator is unknown. A trial evaluation prior to the track showed that assessors found enumerating *all* concepts represented in a response to be so difficult as to be unworkable. For example, how many information units are contained in the string "Oh, Eaton also has a new golden parachute clause in his contract?" Using only nugget recall as a final score is untenable since systems would not be rewarded for being selective. Retrieving the entire document collection is guaranteed to give a perfect recall score for every question. Borrowing from the evaluation of summarization systems [9], length was used as a crude approximation to precision. A length-based measure captures the intuition that users would prefer the shorter of two definitions that contain the same concepts. The particular length-based measure used gives a system an allowance of one hundred (nonwhite-space) characters for each correct nugget it retrieved. The precision score is set to one if the response is no longer than this

1	vital	Agreement between companies and top executives
2	vital	Provides remuneration to executives who lose jobs
3	vital	Remuneration is usually very generous
4		Encourages execs not to resist takeover beneficial to shareholders
5		Incentive for execs to join companies
6		Arrangement for which IRS can impose excise tax

a) nugget list

Nuggets		Answer Strings
2, 3	a.	The arrangement, which includes lucrative stock options, a hefty salary, and a "golden parachute" if Gifford is fired,
1	b.	Oh, Eaton also has a new golden parachute clause in his contract.
	c.	But some, including many of BofA's top executives, joined the 216 and cashed in their "golden parachute" severance packages.
	d.	The big payment that Eyler received in January was intended as a "golden parachute"
	e.	Cotsakos' contract included a golden parachute big enough to make a future sale of the company more likely
	f.	syndication, the golden parachute for production companies
6	g.	But if he quits or is dismissed during the two years after the merger, he will be paid $24.4 million, with DaimlerChrysler paying the "golden parachute" tax for him and the taxes on the compensation paid to cover the tax.
	h.	If he left, On leaving, O'Neill could would be able to collect a golden parachute package providing three years of salary and bonuses, stock and other benefits.
4	i.	After the takeover, as jobs disappeared and BofA's stock tumbled, many saw him as a bumbler who had sold out his bank, walking away with a golden parachute that gives him $5 million a year for the rest of his life.
	j.	And after BofA disclosed that he had a golden parachute agreement giving him some $50 million to $100 million if he left following the merger, he sent a voice mail message to bank employees that he intended to stay.

b) system response

Figure 10.5
Assessor annotation of a sample response for definition question 1905, "What is a golden parachute?"

Let r be the number of vital nuggets returned in a response;

 a be the number of acceptable (nonvital but on the list) nuggets returned in a response;

 R be the total number of vital nuggets in the assessor's list; and

len be the number of nonwhite-space characters in an answer string summed over all answer strings in the response.

Then,

$$\text{recall} = r/R$$
$$\text{allowance} = 100 * (r + a)$$
$$\text{precision} = \begin{cases} 1 & \text{if len} < \text{allowance} \\ 1 - \dfrac{\text{len} - \text{allowance}}{\text{len}} & \text{otherwise} \end{cases}$$
$$F(\beta = 5) = \frac{26*\text{precision} * \text{recall}}{25*\text{precision} + \text{recall}}$$

Figure 10.6
Computation of the F ($\beta = 5$) score for a definition question

allowance. If the response is longer than the allowance, the precision score is downgraded using the function

$$\text{precision} = 1 - \frac{\text{length} - \text{allowance}}{\text{length}}.$$

Remember that the assessors marked some nuggets as vital and the remainder are not vital. The nonvital nuggets act as a "don't care" condition. That is, systems should be penalized for not retrieving vital nuggets and for retrieving items that are not on the assessor's nugget list at all, but should be neither penalized nor rewarded for retrieving a nonvital nugget. To implement the don't care condition, nugget recall was computed only over vital nuggets, while the character allowance in the precision computation was based on both vital and nonvital nuggets. The recall for the example in figure 10.5 is thus 3/3, and the character allowance is five hundred.

The final score for a definition response was computed using the F measure with recall five times as important as precision, known as F($\beta = 5$). The value of five is arbitrary, but it both reflects the emphasis given to recall by the assessors and acknowledges the crudeness of the length approximation to true precision. Figure 10.6 shows the complete computation of the F($\beta = 5$) score for a single definition question. The score for the definition component was the average F($\beta = 5$) score over the fifty definition questions.

Fifty-four runs from twenty-five different groups were submitted for the combined task. Table 10.5 shows the individual component scores plus the combined

Table 10.5
Component scores and final combined scores for top TREC 2003 runs

Run tag	Submitter	Component score			Final score
		Closed-class	List	Defi-nition	
LCCmainS03	Language Computer Corporation	0.700	0.396	0.442	0.559
nusmml03r2	National University of Singapore (Yang)	0.562	0.319	0.473	0.479
lexiclone92	LexiClone	0.622	0.048	0.159	0.363
isi03a	Information Sciences Institute, University of Southern California	0.337	0.118	0.461	0.313
BBN2003C	BBN	0.206	0.097	0.555	0.266

scores for the best run for each of the top five groups. The best run was selected on the basis of the final combined score, and the table is sorted by this same measure.

The best-scoring run for closed-class questions, the LCCmainS03 run, was able to answer 70 percent of the closed-class questions. This is a somewhat lower percentage than in TREC 2002, indicating that the test set was probably more difficult. The overall approach taken for answering closed-class questions remained essentially unchanged from previous years. Systems determine the expected answer type of the question, retrieve documents or passages likely to contain answers to the question using important question words and related terms as the query, and then perform a match between the question words and the retrieved passages to extract the answer. While this overall approach remains the same, individual groups did continue to refine their techniques for these three steps, increasing the coverage and accuracy of their systems.

The top two systems obtained average F scores above 0.3 for the list component, but in general the systems had difficulty with the list task. Only eleven of the fifty-four runs had an average score for the list component that was greater than 0.1 (the top two systems accounted for five of these eleven runs), and only nine of the thirty-seven questions had a median F score greater than 0.0. Most groups used exactly the same system for closed-class and list questions, changing only the number of responses returned as the answer. The main challenge for the list task was determining the number of responses to return. Systems whose matching phase creates a question-independent score for each passage returned all answers whose score was above an empirically determined threshold. Other systems returned all answers whose scores were within an empirically determined fraction of the top result's score.

The best-scoring run for the definition component was the BBN2003C run with a $F(\beta = 5)$ score of .555. The relative effectiveness of different runs changed as the relative importance between recall and precision changed, demonstrating that different systems have different emphases. Answering definition questions generally involved using different techniques than those used for closed-class questions. Since the definition task emphasized nugget recall and did not require "exact" answers, most systems first retrieved passages about the target using a recall-oriented search. Subsequent processing reduced the amount of material returned. Many systems used pattern matching to locate definition content in text. These patterns, such as looking for copular constructions and appositives, were either hand constructed or learned from a training corpus. Systems also looked to eliminate redundant information, using either word overlap measures or document summarization techniques. The output from this step was then returned as the definition of the target.

10.1.6 Summary

The TREC QA track has offered a series of tasks that have challenged systems to find answers in open-domain text. Systems have progressed to the point that the best systems can provide exact answers for 70 to 80 percent of a set of closed-class questions. The ability to answer closed-class questions provides a basis for answering more demanding question types.

By definition, there are a limited number of different kinds of closed-class questions. This allows relatively simple pattern-based methods to be successful when large corpora are available: in large corpora, answers exist in simple forms frequently enough to be recognized. Systems that do more sophisticated language processing are necessary when operating in more restrictive environments.

10.2   Validating Closed-Class Question Evaluations

The particular evaluation methodology adopted to measure the effectiveness of a technology can have a profound effect on how the technology develops. The Cranfield paradigm described in chapter 3, this volume, was already well established for document retrieval when TREC began, but there was no similarly accepted evaluation methodology for question-answering systems at the beginning of TREC-8. An important part of NIST's role in the track has been assessing the quality of the evaluations themselves as the tasks in the track evolve. In this section, we validate the QA evaluation methodology using techniques similar to those used for document retrieval.

10.2.1   The Stability of Evaluation Results

The rationale for using human assessors to evaluate a task is to incorporate the perceptions of the end users of the technology to the greatest extent possible. To investigate the effect of using human judges as the basis of a QA evaluation, each TREC-8 question was independently judged by three different assessors. The separate judgments were combined into a single judgment set through adjudication for the official track evaluation, but the individual judgments were used to measure the effect of differences in judgments on systems' scores.

Assessors were trained for the QA task before they did any judging. The purpose of the training was to motivate the assessors' task and provide general guidance on the issues that would arise during assessing rather than to drill the assessors on a specific set of assessment rules. To begin, each assessor was given the following instructions:

Assume there is a user who trusts the answering system completely, and therefore does not require that the system provide justification in its answer strings. Your job is to take each answer string in turn and judge if this answer string alone were returned to the trustful user, would the user be able to get the correct answer to the question from the string.

Assessors then judged four sample questions whose response strings were concocted by NIST staff to illustrate various fundamentals of QA judging, including the fact that document context must be taken into account and that the string must be responsive to the question. Document context is vital for questions whose answers change over time. For example, responses to questions phrased in the present tense ("Who is the prime minister of Japan?") were judged as correct or incorrect based on the time of the document associated with the response. Requiring that the answer string be responsive to the question addressed a variety of issues. Answer strings that contained multiple entities of the same semantic category as the correct answer, but did not indicate which of those entities was the actual answer (for instance, a list of names in response to a who question), were judged as incorrect. Certain punctuation and units were also required. Thus, "5 5 billion" was not an acceptable substitute for "5.5 billion," nor was "500" acceptable when the correct answer was "$500." Finally, unless the question specifically stated otherwise, correct responses for questions about a famous entity had to refer to *the* famous entity and not to imitations, copies, and so on. For example, two separate questions asked for the height of the Matterhorn (that is, the Alp) and the replica of the Matterhorn at Disneyland. Correct responses for one of these questions were incorrect for the other.

The results of the assessment process demonstrated that assessors do have legitimate differences of opinion as to what constitutes an acceptable answer even for the deliberately constrained questions used in TREC-8 [21]. Two prime examples of where such differences arise are the completeness of names and the granularity of dates and locations. For instance, for the question "When did French revolutionaries storm the Bastille?" some assessors accepted "July 14," others accepted "1789," and everyone accepted "July 14, 1789." Assumed context also mattered, and differed among assessors. For the question "Where is the Taj Mahal?" one of the three assessors accepted "Atlantic City, NJ" (home of the Taj Mahal casino) as an acceptable response even in light of the guidelines that stated replicas and imitations should not be used as answers for questions about a famous entity. For this assessor, the casino was sufficiently well-known to be an entity in its own right, perhaps because mentions of the casino outnumbered mentions of the mausoleum by about five to one in the document collection.

In TREC 2002, the assessors were asked to judge whether an answer string was exact rather than whether it simply contained a correct answer. Since there was concern that "exactness" might mean too many different things to different assessors, once again each question was independently judged by three different assessors. And once again, there was disagreement. Half of all the responses that were not obviously wrong (that is, at least one assessor judged the response as something other than wrong) had some disagreement among the three judges, with a third of those disagreements involving differences between right and inexact judgments. While these numbers seem frightening at first glance, closer inspection of the right-inexact disagreements reveals that they do not in general represent a new category of disagreement. Instead, the same granularity differences observed in TREC-8 are now reflected in the right-inexact distinction. For example, for assessors who want a full name as an answer, a response of last name only was now marked as inexact rather than wrong.

Fortunately, as with document retrieval systems, the relative scores between QA systems remain stable despite differences in the judgments used to evaluate them. The procedure to verify this is the same as for document retrieval: rank systems by effectiveness score using each of a set of judgments and compute the average distance among the system rankings. The distance measure used is Kendall's τ, which computes the distance between two rankings as the minimum number of pairwise adjacent swaps to turn one ranking into the other. The distance is normalized by the number of items being ranked such that two identical rankings produce a correlation of 1.0, the correlation between a ranking and its perfect inverse is -1.0, and the expected correlation of two rankings chosen at random is 0.0.

Three different judgment sets were produced by combining the judgments from the first assessor who judged the question for all questions ("Set 1"), the second assessor who judged the question for all questions ("Set 2"), and finally the third assessor's judgments ("Set 3"). The pairwise Kendall τ scores among these sets and the final adjudicated judgment set are shown in table 10.6 for both TREC-8 and TREC 2002. For TREC 2002, the system rankings were produced using both the confidence-weighted score as the evaluation metric and the raw count of the number of questions correctly

Table 10.6
Kendall τ correlations between system rankings

	TREC-8, MMR			TREC 2002, CWS			TREC 2002, raw count		
	Set 1	Set 2	Set 3	Set 1	Set 2	Set 3	Set 1	Set 2	Set 3
Adjudicated	0.968	0.951	0.961	0.954	0.941	0.944	0.958	0.949	0.960
Set 1	—	0.954	0.963	—	0.920	0.917	—	0.933	0.944
Set 2	—	—	0.951	—	—	0.906	—	—	0.926
Mean		0.958			0.930			0.945	

Note: CWS = confidence-weighted score

answered as the evaluation metric. The last row of the table gives the mean τ of the corresponding six pairwise τs. All of the correlations are greater than 0.9, indicating that all three evaluations are sufficiently stable [20].

10.2.2 Sensitivity Analysis

Human judgments are not the only source of variability when evaluating QA systems. QA system effectiveness depends on the questions that are asked, so the particular set of questions included in a test set will affect evaluation results. Since the test set of questions is assumed to be a random sample of the universe of possible questions, there is always some chance that a comparison of two systems using any given test set will lead to the wrong conclusion. The probability of an error can be made arbitrarily small by using arbitrarily many questions, but there are practical limits to the number of questions that can be included in an evaluation. We can use the runs submitted to a QA track to empirically determine the relationship between the number of questions in a test set, the observed difference in scores (δ), and the likelihood that a single comparison of two QA runs leads to the correct conclusion. Once established, the relationship can be used to derive the minimum difference in scores required for a certain level of confidence in the results given the number of questions in the test set.

We performed this analysis for the TREC 2002 track using the confidence-weighted score as the evaluation measure [19]. The error curves show that to obtain an error rate no greater than 5 percent, there needs to be an absolute difference of at least 0.07 in the confidence-weighted scores of the runs being compared. Using this standard, the *pris2002*, *IRST02D1*, and *IBMPQSQACYC* runs shown in table 10.4 should be considered equivalently effective. When comparing the effect of using different human assessors to evaluate QA systems, the differences in the system rankings that did occur involved systems whose scores were extremely similar when using the adjudicated judgment set. In fact, for all 177 cases when a pair of systems evaluated differently depending on which judgments were used, the difference in the scores of the two systems was less than 0.07. Since the sensitivity analysis suggests that these systems should be considered equivalently effective, some reordering of the systems when judgments are changed is to be expected.

10.3 Conclusion

The TREC QA track has fostered a resurgence in question-answering research, which in turn has produced new question-answering technology. Question answering has also become a focus task in multilingual evaluations with the introduction of the question-answering challenge at NTCIR Workshop 3 [6] and a QA task at the 2003 Cross-Language Evaluation Forum [14]. Nonetheless, much work remains to be done. The tracks to date have examined only a small portion of the possible question-answering tasks. Future TREC tracks will continue to incorporate new tasks to increase the complexity of the types of questions that can be answered and the diversity of sources from which the answers can be drawn.

Which tasks to add to the track will be determined by the research community, guided by the various road maps that have been prepared [7; 15]. Pilot evaluations done in the context of the ARDA AQUAINT program (see ⟨http://www.ic-arda.org⟩) will also inform track decisions. In addition to fostering research on better question-answering technology, the track will continue to examine the appropriate dimensions along which such technology can be usefully evaluated.

Acknowledgments

The original coordinators of the TREC QA track were Amit Singhal and Tomek Strzal-kowski; together with Donna K. Harman at NIST, they defined the original TREC QA task.

References

[1] Burke, R. D., K. J. Hammond, V. A. Kulyukin, S. L. Lytinen, N. Tomuro, and S. Schoenberg. Question answering from frequently-asked question files: Experiences with the FAQ Finder system. Technical report TR-97-05, Computer Science Department, University of Chicago, June 1997.

[2] Clarke, C. L. A., G. V. Cormack, and T. R. Lynam. Exploiting redundancy in question answering. In *Proceedings of the twenty-fourth annual international ACM SIGIR conference*, 358–365.

[3] de Chalendar, G., T. Dalmas, F. Elkateb-Gara, O. Ferret, B. Grau, M. Hurault-Plantet, G. Illouz, L. Monceaux, I. Robba, and A. Vilnat. The question answering system QALC and LIMSI: Experiments in using Web and WordNet. In *TREC 2002*, 407–416.

[4] Dumais, S., M. Banko, E. Brill, J. Lin, and A. Ng. Web question answering: Is more always better? In *Proceedings of the twenty-fifth annual international ACM SIGIR conference*, 291–298.

[5] Fellbaum, C., ed. *WordNet: An electronic lexical database*. Cambridge: MIT Press, 1998.

[6] Fukumoto, J., T. Kato, and F. Masui. Question answering challenge (QAC-1): An evaluation of question answering task at NTCIR Workshop 3. In *Proceedings of the third NTCIR workshop*, ed. K. Oyama, E. Ishida, and N. Kando. Tokyo: National Institute of Informatics, 2003, 77–86.

[7] Harabagiu, S., J. Burger, C. Cardie, V. Chaudhri, R. Gaizauskas, D. Israel, C. Jacquemin, C.-Y. Lin, S. Maiorano, G. Miller, D. Moldovan, B. Ogden, J. Prager, E. Riloff, A. Singhal, R. Shrihari, T. Strzalkowski, E. M. Voorhees, and R. Weishedel. *Issues, tasks, and program structures to road map research in question and answering (Q&A)*. October 2000. ⟨http://www-nlpir.nist.gov/projects/duc/roadmapping.html⟩.

[8] Harabagiu, S., D. Moldovan, M. Paşca, R. Mihalcea, M. Surdeanu, R. Bunescu, R. Gîrju, V. Rus, and P. Morărescu. The role of lexico-semantic feedback in open-domain textual question-answering. In *Proceedings of the association for computational linguistics*, 274–281. July 2001. San Francisco: Morgan Kaufmann.

[9] Harman, D. K., and P. Over. The DUC summarization evaluations. In *Proceedings of the second international conference on human language technology research*, 44–51, ed. M. Marcus. San Francisco: Morgan Kaufmann, 2002.

[10] Hovy, E., L. Gerber, U. Hermjakob, C.-Y. Lin, and D. Ravichandran. Toward semantics-based answer pinpointing. In *Proceedings of human language technologies conference*, 339–345, ed. J. Allan. San Francisco: Morgan Kaufmann, March 2001.

[11] Kupiec, J. MURAX: A robust linguistic approach for question answering using an on-line encyclopedia. In *Proceedings of the sixteenth annual international ACM SIGIR conference*, 181–190.

[12] Hirschman, L., and R. Gaizauskas. Natural language question answering: The view from here. *Natural Language Engineering* 7, no. 4 (2001): 275–300.

[13] Magnini, B., M. Negri, R. Prevete, and H. Tanev. Is it the right answer? Exploiting Web redundancy for answer validation. In *Proceedings of ACL 2002*, 425–432. San Francisco: Morgan Kaufmann, 2002.

[14] Magnini, B., S. Romagnoli, A. Vallin, J. Herrera, A. Peñas, V. Peinado, F. Verdejo, and M. de Rijke. The multiple language question answering track at CLEF 2003. In *Working notes for the CLEF 2003 workshop*, ed. C. Peters, 21–22 August. Trondheim, Norway, 2003.

[15] Maybury, M. T. *Toward a question answering road map*. 2002. ⟨http://www.mitre.org/work/tech_papers/tech_papers_02/maybury_toward/may%bury_toward_qa.pdf⟩.

[16] Ravichandran, D., and E. Hovy. Learning surface text patterns for a question answering system. In *Proceedings of ACL–2002*, 41–47. San Francisco: Morgan Kaufmann, 2002.

[17] Singhal, A., S. Abney, M. Bacciani, M. Collins, D. Hindle, and F. Pereira. AT&T at TREC-8. In *TREC-8*, 317–330.

[18] Soubbotin, M. M., and S. M. Soubbotin. Use of patterns for detection of answer strings: A systematic approach. In *TREC 2002*, 325–331.

[19] Voorhees, E. M. Evaluating the evaluation: A case study using the TREC 2002 question answering track. In *Proceedings of the human language technology conference of the North American chapter of the association for computational linguistics (HLT–NAACL)*, 260–267. East Stroudsburg, PA: The Association for Computational Linguistics, 2003.

[20] Voorhees, E. M. Evaluation by highly relevant documents. In *Proceedings of the twenty-fourth annual international ACM SIGIR conference*, 74–82.

[21] Voorhees, E. M., and D. M. Tice. The TREC-8 question answering track evaluation. In *TREC-8*, 83–105.

III SELECTED PARTICIPANT REPORTS

11 The University of Massachusetts and a Dozen TRECs
James Allan, W. Bruce Croft, and Jamie Callan

The Center for Intelligent Information Retrieval (CIIR) at the University of Massa-chusetts at Amherst participated in every TREC from TREC-1 to TREC 2003. The level of involvement varied widely, ranging from a single track to eight tracks in a single year, and a total of forty-three tracks in the course of a dozen years of participation. Table 11.1 provides a complete list.

In the first several years of TREC, the CIIR's research interests strongly matched the topics addressed by the tracks, such as ad hoc retrieval, multilingual access, docu-ment routing and filtering, distributed and large-scale collections, and the application of IR techniques to other media. In the late 1990s, however, the CIIR participated in large numbers of TREC tracks even though its research was focused on only a few. The motivation for participating was to provide additional data that were important for comparing a range of systems and creating sufficiently large pools of relevant docu-ments. For example, the CIIR submissions to the TREC-7 and TREC-8 ad hoc track involved only minimal changes to the TREC-6 system, which itself was not dramati-cally different from earlier versions.

In the early 2000s, the CIIR's focus began to coincide more closely with the TREC tracks again, and it used the tracks as an integral part of its research program. Some of the research areas include multi- and cross-language retrieval, question answering, novelty, and high accuracy retrieval.

This chapter discusses the CIIR's involvement in TREC over a dozen years. Al-though the CIIR participated in a large number of tracks during this time, the chapter focuses on the tracks that received most of our research effort: the ad hoc, routing/filtering, and multilingual/cross-lingual tracks. It also briefly surveys our work on other tracks, to show how proven techniques were adapted to new problems and to illustrate the range of research done at the CIIR during this period. The chapter concludes with a brief discussion of the impact that TREC has had on CIIR research.

11.1 Ad Hoc Retrieval

The CIIR participated in the ad hoc retrieval track (see chapter 4, this volume) from its inception at TREC-1 until TREC-8.[1] All of the CIIR's ad hoc retrieval research during this time used INQUERY. The CIIR's ad hoc retrieval research during this period was characterized by improvements to the basic retrieval model, the indexing of named entities, sophisticated query processing, and large-scale query expansion. Each of these topics is covered in some detail below.

Table 11.1
All TREC tracks in which the CIIR has participated

Track	TREC 1	2	3	4	5	6	7	8	9	2001	2002	2003
Ad hoc	×	×	×	×	×	×	×	×				
Routing	×	×	×	×	×	×						
Filtering					×	×	×	×				
Spanish		×	×	×								
Chinese					×	×						
Spanish CLIR						×						
Chinese CLIR									×			
Arabic CLIR										×	×	
Database merging				×								
Very large corpus						×	×					
Web								×				
Interactive						×						
Spoken documents						×	×	×				
Query								×	×			
Question answering								×	×			×
Novelty											×	
High accuracy												×

11.1.1 INQUERY

Although INQUERY evolved over the years, the core ideas and system remained the same from TREC-1 to TREC-8. INQUERY is a realization of a retrieval model based on Bayesian inference networks [63, 61, 62, 25]. An inference network is a directed acyclic graph where the nodes represent propositions and the edges represent dependencies: a node's value is a function of the nodes on which it depends. In INQUERY, the network is realized in two components. The first, the document network, expresses the relationship between documents (even permitting different representations of the same document) and the concepts that they contain. The second component is the query network. It shows the relationships between the searcher's information need, the query or queries that express it, and query concepts. The two networks are linked by a relationship between the document and query concepts.

Because inference networks allow complex combinations of evidence, the model admits a powerful query language. Entirely within the framework of the model, INQUERY supports proximity operators, probabilistic and strict Boolean operators, phrase and passage operators, field operators, synonym operators, and so forth. The flexibility of this language enabled researchers of the CIIR to incorporate a wide variety of retrieval operations.

One of the more pronounced changes in INQUERY over the many years of TREC was its underlying weighting function. In the same way that a vector-space model needs to assign weights to terms, INQUERY needs a mechanism for estimating the probability that a concept (term) represents a document. At the beginning of the TIPSTER/TREC era, the function was based on probabilistic IR techniques that had been used for a decade or more [32; 62; 63]:

$$bel_{term}(Q) = d_b + (1 - d_b) \cdot \left(d_t + (1 - d_t) \cdot \frac{tf}{max\_tf} \right) \cdot \frac{\log(C/df)}{\log(C)},$$

where tf is the frequency of term t in the document, max_tf is the frequency of the most frequent term in the document, df is the number of documents in which term t occurs, C is the number of documents in the collection, d_t is the minimum term frequency component when a term occurs in a document, and d_b is the minimum belief component when a term occurs in a document. Here, d_t and d_b were set to 0.5, representing a 50 percent belief that a document was about term t if the term did not occur in the document.

An early technology transfer experience with West Publishing and experience with the first TREC collection revealed a previously unknown length bias in the INQUERY belief estimation formula: it favored long documents. The formula used in the TREC-1 ad hoc experiments was adjusted heuristically to compensate for this bias: d_t and d_b were reduced from 0.5 to 0.4, log normalization was applied to the tf weight, and a strong penalty was applied to long documents. The formula used in TREC-1 was:

$$bel_{term}(Q) = d_b + (1 - d_b) \cdot \left(d_t \cdot H + (1 - d_t) \cdot \frac{\log(tf + 0.5)}{\log(max\_tf + 1.0)} \right) \cdot \frac{\log(C/df)}{\log(C)},$$

where

$$H = \begin{cases} 1.0 & \text{if } max\_tf \leq 200 \\ 200/max\_tf & \text{otherwise.} \end{cases}$$

Over the course of TRECs 1–4, the formula was shifted several times in an attempt to address length biases. For TREC-3, the H penalty was dropped by setting H to 1.0, and the penalties were moved into the d_t and d_b parameters:

$$d_t = 0.3 \cdot \left(1.0 - \frac{df}{C} \right) 2$$

$$d_b = \begin{cases} 0.4 - \frac{L}{1,000,000} & \text{if } L < 400,000 \\ 0.0 & \text{otherwise.} \end{cases}$$

None of these approaches to length normalization were consistently effective, however.

The CIIR's most effective method of length normalization was the passage operator, introduced at TREC-3 [23; 13]. The passage operator divided each document into a set of overlapping passages of fixed length, ranked each passage using the document-ranking algorithm, and returned the highest passage score. For TREC-3, documents were ranked by the query #wsum (2.0 #passage200 [query], 1.0 #sum [query]), which increased precision at all levels of recall (a 15.7 percent increase in average precision).

Also in TREC-3, the Okapi system (see chapter 12, this volume) demonstrated a highly effective way of incorporating the term frequency using a formula of the form $tf/(tf + K)$ where K was a "constant" that depended on the length tf of the document [59]. For TREC-4, INQUERY adopted the Okapi function to cope with the length bias, but it was combined with the previous weighting function to result in a complex measure [3]. Specifically, the term-frequency component was a mixture of the Okapi function and INQUERY's original term-frequency function:

$$idf \cdot \text{INQUERY tf} + (1 - idf)\text{Okapi tf},$$

where idf is the normalized IDF value that has always been used by INQUERY: $\log\left(\frac{C+0.5}{df}\right)\big/\log(C + 1.0)$. This combination means that for low-IDF (rare) terms, the Okapi function dominated, whereas for common terms the INQUERY function took over.

The "max tf normalized" term-frequency function was effective on many evaluations, but experiments showed that it was sensitive to small changes in stop-word lists and stemming algorithms. As research moved to other languages where stopping and stemming were less stable, the "max tf" factor hurt effectiveness and stability. By TREC-6, it was gone from INQUERY, leaving the belief-estimation formula as a combination of Okapi's tf formula and INQUERY's normalized IDF:

$$bel_{term}(Q) = d_b + (1 - d_b) \cdot \left(d_t + (1 - d_t) \cdot \frac{tf}{tf + 0.5 + 1.5 \cdot \text{doclen/avg\_doclen}}\right) \cdot \frac{\log(C/df)}{\log(C)}.$$

The estimation function was unchanged throughout the rest of the CIIR's involvement in TREC.

The passage operator was also dropped from most CIIR experiments after TREC-4. Experiments at TREC-4 and afterward revealed that one of the main contributions of passage retrieval in TREC-3 was that it controlled the length bias in the early INQUERY belief functions. Okapi-style term weighting was a simpler and more effective approach to length normalization; adding the passage operator to Okapi-style term weighting reduced accuracy.

11.1.2 Entity Recognition

Information extraction is the subdiscipline of natural-language processing that scans text to find mentions of named entities—for example, people, places, organizations, dates, and so on. Information extraction has value in a range of applications, one of which is document retrieval. For some types of document retrieval tasks, it can be useful to know that a string of words represents the name of a person or a company. Early TREC topics, in particular, had the property that finding names could be helpful.

Before information extraction really existed as a separate field, the CIIR built "special recognizers" to help with document retrieval. The recognizers leveraged hand-built rules and lengthy lists of names to find previously unseen names in text. When a recognizer matched a sequence of tokens, it stored the individual tokens (for instance, "Ronald" and "Reagan") and a feature-class token (say, "#person") in the index. The query language supported both types of index terms—for example, #uw20 (bribe #person)—which retrieved every twenty-word passage that contained the word *bribe* and a person's name. These techniques were in use for the TIPSTER experiments that predated TREC-1.

The CIIR focused primarily on company names (#company), person names (#person), country names (#foreigncountry), references to the United States (#usa), and dates (converted to a normalized form).

Over the years, the country names (including references to the United States) ended up being the most useful in the context of TREC. In particular, we found that effectiveness increased if we added "#not #foreigncountry" to any query that had a specific mention of the United States. Amusingly enough, adding "#usa" to such queries hurt performance because the United States was more commonly mentioned in documents about other countries.

Our use of entity tokens in the index and the queries provided improvements in effectiveness, but they were small for ad hoc retrieval [24], in part because few queries in the early TRECs required named-entity retrieval. Although we ultimately dropped them for that reason, they reemerged later on a widely used scale as predictive annotation for question-answering systems [58]. By that time, however, much more effective named-entity recognizers such as BBN's IdentiFinder [12] were available from the information extraction research community, so the CIIR's rule-based approaches were not used again.

11.1.3   Query Processing

Prior research on I^3R demonstrated that providing a search system with a detailed description of an information need greatly improved retrieval accuracy [33]. The first TREC information needs ("topics") were rich in detail, and INQUERY's Bayesian inference network architecture provided a powerful query language in which to express information needs, so it was natural for the CIIR to put much of its early research energy into automatically transforming TREC topics into complex ad hoc queries.

As a TIPSTER contractor, the CIIR had worked with the TREC training corpora well before the TREC-1 evaluation began. For reasons of "fairness," TIPSTER contractors had their results suppressed before the conference, so the CIIR both did and did not participate in TREC-1. The TIPSTER work was reported at TREC, though [30].

The CIIR's ad hoc work in TIPSTER included treating different parts of the complex TREC topics differently; recognizing phrases in queries; recognizing and leveraging "factors" such as locations, dates, and companies; and the use of a synonym operator to handle factors such as "developing countries" that had a set of possible values. In addition, we did extra runs to explore the value of minimal human involvement by having a searcher tweak the automatically generated queries by the deletion and the structuring of terms.

In TREC-1, the automatic transformation of TREC topics into structured queries yielded significant improvements over just using the topic words themselves [30; 24]. Small manual modifications to automatically generated queries improved average case effectiveness by a further 10 to 20 percent.

For TREC-2, the CIIR developed elaborate query processing techniques for identifying important concepts [31]. Specifically, part-of-speech tagging was used to find candidate search phrases, domain-dependent features (for example, company, date, foreign country, USA) were used to resolve some types of ambiguity, simple grammar rules were employed to find relationships between query concepts that should be preserved in documents, stop phrases (for instance, "Find a document that describes") in queries were stripped because they provided no meaningful content, and time expressions were recognized and processed appropriately. Figure 11.1 illustrates some of these capabilities.

```
#WSUM ( 1.0
!Terms from <title> field:
2.0 #UW50 (Control of Insider Trading)
2.0 #PHRASE (#USA Control) 5.0 #PHRASE (Insider Trading)
! Terms from <con> field:
2.0 #PHRASE (securities law) 2.0 bill 2.0 legislation 2.0 regulation
2.0 rule
2.0 #3 (Insider Trading Sanctions Act)
2.0 #3 (Insider Trading and Securities Fraud Enforcement Act)
2.0 #3 (Securities and Exchange Commission) 2.0 SEC
2.0 #3 (Commodity Futures Trading Commission) 2.0 CFTC
2.0 #3 (National Association of Securities Dealers) 2.0 NASD
! Terms from <desc> field:
1.0 proposed 1.0 enacted 1.0 changes 1.0 #PHRASE (#USA laws)
1.0 regulations 1.0 designed 1.0 prevent
! Terms from <fac> field:
2.0 #NOT(#FOREIGNCOUNTRY) )
```

Figure 11.1
The query created automatically for TREC topic 106. The #3 proximity operator requires the words to occur in order, no more than three words apart. The #UW50 proximity operator requires all of the words to occur, in any order, within a window of fifty words. The #PHRASE operator transformed itself into either #3 or #SUM depending on the frequency and mutual information of the terms. The #FOREIGNCOUNTRY matched any non-U.S. country name recognized by a named-entity detector [24]

The topics used in TREC-1 and TREC-2 were quite detailed, which favored systems like INQUERY that could exploit their contents effectively. Starting at TREC-3, and continuing for the next several years, the TREC topics were progressively simplified to better match "the real world." These changes eroded the effectiveness of complex TREC topic transformation techniques, and shifted attention to techniques that could infer the information need from limited information.

In TREC-3, the CIIR deployed its own part-of-speech tagger called JTAG [64; 13]. Query processing became slightly simpler: prepositional phrases were no longer specially considered and phrases with more than two words were broken into overlapping sequences of two-word phrases. The global association thesaurus made its TREC debut as PhraseFinder. Queries were expanded by adding thirty related concepts. The PhraseFinder terms resulted in a 10 percent improvement in effectiveness.

In TREC-4 [3], the CIIR made only minor changes for the ad hoc track. Again, user modification of queries had a pronounced impact on effectiveness (a 20 percent improvement), but query expansion did not help much, and incorporating passage-level information actually reduced accuracy (because of incompatibility with Okapi term weighting, as discussed in section 11.1.1).

For TREC-5, we replaced PhraseFinder with local context analysis (LCA) (see below). This approach resulted in similar gains in effectiveness, but when it did not work for a query, generally had little impact rather than the dramatically negative impact more common with global techniques such as InFinder.

We also worked toward finding key concepts in TREC topics. For example, consider the topic "What research is ongoing to reduce the effects of osteoporosis in existing patients as well as prevent the disease occurring in those unafflicted at this time?" It turns out that the only query word of great significance in that topic is *osteoporosis*, and recognizing its importance can cause substantial gains in effectiveness, in part because of the improved focus of documents retrieved for query expansion.

For the ad hoc track, we created three types of queries: the basic query using our traditional query processing, a query that isolated the core concepts, and a query that incorporated expanded LCA concepts (discussed in the next section). We found that core concept identification helped, but not consistently enough to be broadly useful, and that the combination of three forms of query was decidedly useful.

There were few changes in the CIIR query processing from TREC-6 through TREC-8. By this time, TREC topics had shifted from the lengthy, detailed descriptions of user information needs envisioned by I^3R to the brief, somewhat general descriptions of information needs seen in Web queries, where little is known about the individual user. There was little to be gained by complex automatic query-processing techniques, and so the CIIR's research interests shifted to other tracks. Our ad hoc track participation in TREC-6 through TREC-8 was done largely as a community service to broaden the pool of relevance assessments. Our interest in ad hoc retrieval reemerged in later TRECs, with the creation of the high accuracy retrieval of documents (HARD) track, which provided more detail about the individual user and their information need (see section 11.4.8).

11.1.4   Query Expansion

Query expansion was an important component of the CIIR ad hoc retrieval research. The CIIR experimented with two distinct approaches to query expansion: InFinder (also called WordFinder and PhraseFinder), and Local Context Analysis (LCA).

InFinder   As early as TREC-2, the CIIR was investigating techniques for expanding the user's query using a corpus-based association thesaurus.[2] The idea of such an approach is to find words in the corpus that are strongly associated with the user's query words. If those words are added to the query, then the retrieval is likely to be more successful because it more closely matches the vocabulary of the corpus and it incorporates synonyms that the user did not think to include.

From TREC-2 through TREC-4, the CIIR employed an association thesaurus that recognized "concepts" that occurred together. Called variously WordFinder, Phrase-Finder, and InFinder, the system worked as follows [40]. First, a corpus was scanned to find noun phrases that occurred at least a few times. Then, for each of those noun phrase "concepts," the system located all occurrences of the phrase and extracted a snippet of text surrounding the phrase (for example, twenty-five words on each side). The concept was then represented by a "pseudodocument" that was the union of all its snippets of text. The pseudodocuments were indexed by INQUERY.

When a query was run against the collection of pseudodocuments, the result would be a set of noun phrase concepts whose pseudodocuments were similar to the query. Since the pseudodocuments were built from snippets of text surrounding the noun phrase, a concept would only be retrieved if the query words were near the concept—and the more often a query word occurred near a concept, the more likely the concept would be to appear at the top of the list.

The InFinder expansion concepts were used like most automatic query expansion methods: an original query was augmented by adding those concepts—appropriately weighted with respect to the original query—and the resulting rich query was used to return a ranked list. Such techniques were quite effective and extremely fast, but suffered when a query contained a rare combination of words. The thesaurus would then retrieve concepts that were related to part of the query rather than the query as a whole. To solve this problem, we moved to a more computationally expensive query-time approach. InFinder continued to be faster (because all information was indexed in advance), but it was less effective on average.

LCA   At TREC-5, the CIIR introduced a query expansion device called local context analysis (LCA) [68]. The technique was inspired by query expansion techniques from much earlier [8], and demonstrated by Cornell University's SMART system in TREC-3 [17] and TREC-4 [18]. Those techniques are most commonly referred to as pseudorelevance feedback now, but were called "ad hoc query expansion" or "local feedback" at the time. The approach of such techniques is to retrieve a few dozen documents in response to a query and then apply relevance feedback as if those documents were relevant. The result is a new query that includes vocabulary from top-ranked documents.

LCA modified that approach in two ways. First, it retrieved *passages* of text that matched the query rather than entire documents. As a result, the vocabulary that is "fed back" into the query is only that which occurs near the query terms—for instance, spurious words from a very long document would not be included. The second modification was the term-selection function. Whereas earlier techniques used standard relevance feedback formulas, LCA used a much more elaborate function that strongly preferred terms that occurred in close proximity to query terms and that were more likely to be useful in query expansion.

On average, LCA proved to be more effective than classic feedback methods. The difference was that LCA was less prone to making a mistake and expanding the query in entirely the wrong way: an all-too-common problem with pseudorelevance feedback is that poor initial retrieval can result in the system "assuming" that nonrelevant documents are relevant. LCA appeared to reduce that problem by focusing on passages.

LCA was widely adopted for a range of purposes by the CIIR. It was used to expand the query in ad hoc retrieval, help minimize the translation problems in cross-language retrieval, compensate for recognizer errors in spoken-document retrieval, and identify candidate expansion terms in interactive retrieval. It was also incorporated into other tracks (for example, routing and filtering) where some sort of query processing is needed.

11.2   Multilingual IR

Prior to TREC, the standard, generally available IR test collections were not only small, they were in English (only). There were scattered efforts to apply standard IR techniques to other languages—for example, the CIIR's experiments with Japanese corpora done as part of the TIPSTER program [38], which suggested that standard IR techniques were effective on a variety of languages—but these results were often based on tiny corpora or were difficult to reproduce due to the limited availability of the corpora.

The TREC-3 Spanish track was the first large-scale study of the effectiveness of standard IR techniques in languages other than English. Success on Spanish led to the study of other languages, such as Chinese and Arabic. It also led to the study of cross-language information retrieval (CLIR), in which queries in one language are used to retrieve documents in another language.

The CIIR's efforts in these tracks is discussed below. The discussion of the earlier monolingual efforts is brief because, as the research community now knows, few changes are required to apply standard IR techniques to these languages.

11.2.1   Spanish IR
Earlier research at the CIIR on the indexing and the retrieval of Japanese documents [38] had convinced us that INQUERY would also work well with Spanish. Our TREC-3 Spanish track submissions consisted of creating a Spanish stop-word list (one week of effort) and a Spanish stemmer (five weeks of effort). The system performed quite well.

For TREC-4, we extended our work on Spanish retrieval, continuing to transfer query processing ideas that worked well in English to our Spanish track work. For example, we built a simple noun recognizer, developed a Spanish PhraseFinder, and incorporated passage retrieval. The results in Spanish were the opposite of those in English: passage retrieval definitely helped, but manual query adjustments did not. The Spanish PhraseFinder expansion hurt effectiveness. These results identified two areas of instability in the CIIR's research techniques: document-length normalization in the core retrieval algorithm, and query expansion. Both were replaced after TREC-4.

Spanish-language query processing and retrieval continued to converge with English-language query processing in the CIIR's TREC-5 experiments. Like the English ad hoc experiments, the Spanish ad hoc experiments used LCA for query expansion. The main difference was that phrases in the original query and LCA phrases that contained query terms were given special emphasis (that is higher query weights). This focus on phrases was partly due to our group's long-term interest in the use of phrases (see, for example, [34; 24]), and partly to our emerging research on cross-language information retrieval (CLIR).

11.2.2   Chinese IR

In TREC-5, research on multilingual ("not English") IR included Chinese. Our approach was similar to that used in our Japanese work around the time of TREC-1 [38]. Chinese characters in documents were indexed individually ("character-based indexing"). At retrieval time, a trainable text segmenter [56] divided the sequence of Chinese query characters into words; in the resulting query, each segmented Chinese word was represented by a proximity operator that only matched a document when the characters occurred adjacent and in order. To compensate for segmentation errors, sequences of single characters were grouped with the phrase operator, which transforms automatically into a proximity operator when the sequence is common in the corpus (and which does nothing if it is not). As with English and Chinese retrieval, LCA was used for automatic query expansion.

The same techniques were used for TREC-6, but we found that better results were achieved by *not* segmenting the query into words. Instead, we extracted overlapping character bigrams from the query and looked for documents that contained the bigrams. This result—that bigrams work as well or better than automatically segmented words—has continued to prove true since.

11.2.3   Cross-Language IR

The dominant approach to cross-lingual IR over the years has been to translate the query into the same language as the documents, and then to use the translated query with standard search techniques to retrieve documents in the target language. The CIIR was among the first groups to explore cross-language information retrieval (CLIR) and one of the first to publish extensive evaluations of its effectiveness [10; 11].

One of the simplest ways to translate a query is to use a bilingual dictionary to do the translation: each query word or phrase is found in the dictionary and replaced with one or more of its translations. The advantage of dictionary-based methods is that bilingual dictionaries are often readily available. The disadvantages are that they don't include many useful words and phrases (for example, idioms, common expressions, and company names), and that it can be difficult to select the correct translation from among several alternatives.

An alternative approach to translating a query is to find possible translations using a parallel corpus [53; 70]. This approach uses automatic sentence alignment of parallel corpora to construct a probabilistic dictionary, providing the likelihood of each possible translation rather than just an unordered list of words. The advantage of parallel corpus methods is that they cover the language as it is actually used. The disadvantages are that parallel corpora may not be available for a given language pair and that probabilistic dictionaries necessarily include some degree of error.

The TREC-6 cross-lingual track used Spanish queries to retrieve English documents. The CIIR system used a bilingual dictionary to find English translations of Spanish query words, part-of-speech tags to disambiguate some translations, a parallel corpus to select the most likely translation, and LCA-based query expansion to help find strongly related words both before and after translation. The result was a translated query that had the same structure as the original query and could be handled using the query processing techniques originally developed for English (for instance, parsing and query expansion) (see section 11.1). Results were 60 to 70 percent of monolingual performance (that is, using manually generated English translations of the queries).

The CIIR didn't participate in the CLIR tracks for TREC-7 and TREC-8.

When the CIIR resumed the CLIR track in TREC-9, the approach was similar, though the translation now included *all* possible translations for each query word [4]. To keep words with many translations from swamping the query, the translations were wrapped in INQUERY's synonym operator. The #syn operator causes INQUERY to behave as if all of its operands are instances of the same word: for example, "#syn(child children)" causes term statistics (for example, tf or idf) to be calculated as if those two words were the same word. This same approach was developed independently by Ari Pirkola [55].

The TREC-9 CLIR track used English queries to retrieve Chinese documents, just as in TREC-8. Still using dictionary translation and LCA expansion before and after translation, we were able to achieve cross-language performance that was about 90 percent of monolingual performance (that is, Chinese queries against Chinese documents).

The next two years, when TREC CLIR switched to Arabic documents, saw the introduction of techniques based on language modeling.

In TREC 2001, the CIIR used a language-modeling approach for the monolingual Arabic runs, but not for cross-language runs [43]. The cross-language system still used INQUERY and its structured operators. Our approach was to create a large dictionary by consolidating multiple dictionaries, and to utilize a lexicon of place and people names to ensure they were properly translated. The result was that cross-language performance was, again, about 90 percent of monolingual performance.

Post hoc experiments showed that our cross-language system could have actually beaten the monolingual system. The result was not as surprising as it might have been because BBN Technologies demonstrated that effect in its official submitted runs [69].

Language-modeling approaches were adopted more broadly for TREC 2002 [42].

• A cross-language statistical relevance modeling (CLRM) approach was developed [46] based on a form of query expansion called relevance models [47].
• A probabilistic dictionary was obtained from BBN Technologies. The dictionary was used by the CLRM to determine the probability that English and Arabic words are translations of each other.

Lexical processing was also improved. We constructed (and made available) a light stemmer for Arabic—one that did minimal collapsing of morphological variants—and developed a method for expanding acronyms into their component words since acronyms are rarely translated directly.

The final runs that were used for TREC 2002 were a combination of four variations on the CLRM technique and two variations of INQUERY processing (as described earlier).

We found our best results by combining the language modeling and the structured queries from INQUERY. In the end, our cross-language system outperformed the monolingual system. Acronym expansion turned out to be of little value for these queries.

Our more recent CLIR research [42] has more directly incorporated translation probabilities derived from a parallel corpus. Simple translation dictionaries are still sometimes useful to provide better vocabulary coverage. But parallel corpora provide more up-to-date word senses and avoid the rare translation possibilities that a dictionary needs to include—for example, translations that have not been used in a hundred years. We have explored techniques for integrating multiple dictionaries of varying quality, both probabilistic and not, to create a better bilingual lexicon.

Recent experiments by DARPA-funded researchers [52; 5; 44] explored the development of language technology for a "surprise" language. For the two languages tried, large amounts of parallel data were difficult to obtain, even though one of the languages, Hindi, had vast amounts of online information available. It may be that if the need is sufficiently great, humans can be found to provide the parallel text. For other situations, techniques like the original CLIR techniques we used—dictionary translation with optional parallel corpus improvements—may be the best that is possible.

11.2.4 Summary

One of TREC's most lasting contributions was its role in extending IR to languages other than English. TREC created the first large, generally available corpora in languages other than English. The successes of standard IR techniques on Spanish and Chinese as well as CLIR at TREC were directly responsible for the creation of the European Cross Language Evaluation Forum (CLEF) [54] and Asian NII–NACSIS Test Collection for IR Systems (NTCIR) [41] evaluation efforts.

Prior to TREC, it was unclear whether standard IR techniques were based on quirks of English or something fundamental about how humans use language. Today, in large part due to the evaluations begun at TREC, it is now generally accepted that many standard IR techniques are language independent.

More information on the multi- and cross-language information retrieval tracks can be found in chapter 7, this volume.

11.3   Routing and Filtering

TREC began with a focus on two tasks: ad hoc search (covered above) and routing. The routing task was intended to study the effectiveness of information retrieval systems at satisfying information needs that remained constant over time (for details, see chapter 5, this volume). When information needs don't change often, there is an opportunity to acquire training data (that is, relevance assessments for some documents) in addition to the original statement of the information need (that is, the TREC topic).

In its original form, the routing task was essentially a text-categorization task. Systems were given the TREC topic that described the information need as well as a set of documents that an assessor had judged relevant or nonrelevant. This information was used to learn a query that was tested against a new set of documents using an ad hoc retrieval methodology.

The CIIR initially approached the routing task as a case of classic relevance feedback. Prior relevance feedback research in interactive environments had shown that the best combination of stability and effectiveness was achieved by adding just a few additional terms to the query. In TREC-1, the CIIR employed a variation on classic relevance feedback techniques, adding up to five terms that were highly ranked using their expected mutual information [39], but relevance feedback did not help much.

The next several TRECs were characterized by a growing recognition that the large amount of training data available for routing was an important difference from classic relevance feedback. The TREC-2 query expansion used thirty terms rather than just five—and did so successfully. The TREC-3 experiments added co-occurrence features—that is, pairs of words that co-occurred in relevant documents in windows of five or fifty words—which was a highly successful technique (figure 11.2). The TREC-4 routing experiments continued the growth of features by adding terms, phrases, and word pairs that co-occurred frequently in windows of varying size (that is, five, twenty, and fifty); this too was successful. The TREC-4 experiments also adopted a variant of *dynamic feedback optimization* (DFO) [16] to improve the term and phrase weights provided by the Rocchio algorithm, but the variant DFO algorithm overfit the training data, which hurt accuracy on the test data. The TREC-4 approach was used again in TREC-5, except that the published DFO algorithm [16] was used instead of our variant DFO algorithm.

The routing track during the first five TRECs emphasized using large amounts of training data to develop accurate queries, and the results were generally successful.

#WSUM(1.000000 .433963 dougla 30.622835 subsid 14.105722
mcdonnel 2.856207 spain 22.664160 boe 30.620134 european
5.776313 g.m.b.h.   8.629494 340 14.828697 messerschmit
24.899202 industri 7.524240 jet 28.518532 aerospac 6.187950
unfair 34.157051 aircraft 5.245394 construccion 5.942457 330
12.249618 boelkow 5.435017 west 5.136472 franc 8.268916
aerospatial 5.439325 aeronautica 6.971968 jetlin 11.957228 blohm
9.611669 german 10.252533 mbb 25.656782 consortium 16.704779
british 138.805618 airbu 10.874762 plane 2.533194 plc 2.73149
#UW5(#company #foreigncountry) 6.74627 #UW50(330 airbu)
6.36442 #UW50(aid airbu) 6.03555 #UW50(airbu messerschmit
) 8.87131 #UW50(aircraft subsid) 7.39724 #UW5(british aerospac
) 11.1438 #UW50(british airbu) 3.45497 #UW50(competitor airbu
) 6.27218 #UW50(cost airbu) 20.7534 #UW50(european airbu)
4.8756 #UW50(g.m.b.h. airbu) 14.6286 #UW50(german airbu)
23.6137 #UW50(govern airbu) 4.41921 #UW5(govern european
) p3.63681 #UW50(help airbu) 4.04575 #UW5(mcdonnel boe)
8.33751 #UW5(mcdonnel dougla) 3.19623 #UW5(offic u.s.)
8.1083 #UW50(partner airbu) 4.9825 #UW50(price airbu) 6.19649
#UW50(project airbu) 10.3209 #UW50(say airbu) 18.1742 #UW50(
subsid airbu) 15.8317 #UW50(trade airbu) 25.5183 #UW50(u.s.
airbu) 5.23789 #UW5(u.s. trade) 2.04795 #UW5(wall street)
11.3886 #UW50(west airbu) 6.19697 #UW5(west german))

Figure 11.2
Routing profile created automatically from relevant documents for TREC topic 51. Note
the use of #UW5 and #UW50 operators to represent phase-level and paragraph-level co-
occurrence constraints. Terms were stemmed with the Porter stemmer

Routing systems became considerably more accurate during this five-year time
span.

In TREC-5, the CIIR also began participating in the filtering track, where the
goal was to retrieve a *set* of relevant documents, not an arbitrarily long ranked list.
The early filtering tracks were essentially routing track experiments with an additional
requirement that systems make a binary decision about whether or not to disseminate
a document. The CIIR, like most participants, used its routing track system for the filtering track, with the addition of a simple module that learned static dissemination
thresholds from training data. Our results, although not especially good, were among
the best reported that year.

Still, when the CIIR tried to apply its TREC-5 filtering algorithms in technology
transfer projects with commercial and government organizations interested in deploy-
ing "clipping" services, we discovered that systems developed for the routing and filtering tracks were only a partial solution to adaptive information filtering. Our algorithms
could create accurate queries, but they were not efficient enough to use with dynamic
information streams (say, newswires), and their decisions about whether to disseminate documents to the user were not sufficiently accurate for "real-world" use.

In TREC-6, the CIIR deployed a new adaptive information filtering system called InRoute [21]. InRoute was based on the same Bayesian inference network model used in INQUERY, and used the same approaches to lexical processing (stopping, stemming, and so forth). Yet InRoute was built to be a *true* filtering system that actually processed the arriving documents individually, in contrast to most research systems, which indexed all documents in advance and simulated their streamed appearance. InRoute used dynamic, profile-specific thresholds to decide whether to disseminate each document before processing the next one. It was arguably the first adaptive-filtering system tested at TREC.

The TREC-6 experiments showed that an incremental, dynamic approach to learning queries could be as successful as the large-scale updating used in earlier years. The TREC-6 experiments also tested adaptive dissemination thresholds, rather than a single threshold selected before the data arrived [22]. We found that the largest problem in filtering is determining the right threshold because it was too easy to be overly restrictive and end up retrieving nothing at all. Results from later TRECs confirmed that setting dissemination thresholds is one of the key information-filtering problems, and that disseminating nothing at all is more effective than having a bad threshold.

The TREC-7 system was essentially similar to the TREC-6 one. The focus for TREC-8 was on new methods for better threshold selection using a retrospective corpus and allowing the thresholds to automatically adjust depending on the characteristics of arriving documents. Like other groups, we found it was important to monitor query performance in order to "shut off" any queries that were performing poorly. Those changes were sufficient to achieve excellent performance in the track.

The CIIR's participation in the filtering track ended after TREC-8 due to Jamie Callan's move to Carnegie Mellon University (CMU). The CMU group continued to focus on better methods of setting dissemination thresholds [72; 71; 29] until the filtering track was ended.

11.4   Other Tracks

Over the years, the CIIR participated in a variety of tracks beyond those already discussed. We comment briefly on them here, to give a sense of the variety of the CIIR research program during this period.

11.4.1   Database Merging

The TREC-4 database merging track was an attempt to study federated search in the TREC environment. The task was to search ten separate collections as if they were a single collection: the query was fanned out to each collection, and the ten ranked lists were merged into a single list. The best results of this track were not substantially worse than the results would have been if all the documents were in a single collection. A key result from this work was that systems could search some parts of a collection, ignore others, and not sacrifice much accuracy.

The track continued in TREC-5, but the CIIR was unable to participate.

In hindsight, one might conclude that this track was slightly ahead of its time. It had a short life in part because it attracted few participants. Nevertheless, it laid the foundation for a range of distributed IR work outside of TREC [26; 45; 57; 20; 36; 66; 65] that continues as of this writing. Federated search, as the topic is now known, has attracted considerable research since TREC-4, much of it done with TREC data.

11.4.2 Very Large Corpus (VLC)

The database merging track was replaced by the Very Large Corpus (VLC) track in TREC-6 (see chapter 9, this volume). The "very large" corpus was twenty gigabytes of Web data—considerably more data than INQUERY had ever been run on prior to that time. Consequently, we focused more on efficiency than effectiveness. Our efficiency results showed that INQUERY's query processing time scaled linearly with query length. We introduced a "top docs" optimization [14] that halved the time to process queries and did not harm effectiveness. Roughly speaking, the top docs technique kept track of only the most highly weighted one thousand (or so) occurrences of each term.

One pleasant surprise was that we, like others, obtained better early precision (that is, precision at ranks one through thirty) with the same queries on the twenty-gigabyte database than on the two-gigabyte subset. It had been assumed that larger databases would be harder to search. The VLC track results were perhaps the first demonstration that searching larger databases can actually be easier, when measured by early precision, because there are more relevant documents to be found.

The TREC-7 VLC track required a hundred-gigabyte collection. At the time, that was a major stretch for an academic search engine and much of our effort was spent in the engineering needed to run queries. We approached the problem as a simple database merging problem, by splitting the corpus into five subsets of about twenty gigabytes each, running the queries on each, and merging the results.

11.4.3 Spoken-Document Retrieval (SDR)

The spoken document retrieval (SDR) track was created for TREC-6 (see chapter 8, this volume). In this case, the collection of documents was the output of a speech recognition system, so documents contained recognizer errors. We collaborated with Dragon Systems, which produced the recognizer output. The queries were known-item queries, so only a single document in the collection was relevant. We did some processing of the query (removing stop phrases and identifying useful phrases), but most of our gains were from expanding the query using LCA. Our goal was to broaden the query to include strongly related words, hoping that the speech recognition errors would not have corrupted *all* of the words associated with the query. We expanded using the target corpus and from an external corpus, finding that the latter was more useful than the former.

For TREC-7, our major focus was to explore how the quality of speech recognizer output impacted retrieval effectiveness. To that end, we obtained versions of the test collection from numerous participating sites and ran our system on all of them. Recognizer errors ranged from 0 percent (for the true transcript baseline) to over 50 percent (for a system that was mistuned). The results made it clear that even with speech recognition error rates of around 35 percent, the effectiveness of document retrieval was only marginally impacted.

At this point, the task of retrieving spoken documents was essentially "solved"—in the sense that retrieval accuracy was the same for SDR and clean text documents—though it took TREC-8 and TREC-9 for the community to be sufficiently confident to make such a claim. (The CIIR did not participate in the track in TREC-9.)

11.4.4   Interactive

The interactive track began in TREC-3, but the CIIR did not begin to participate until TREC-6. The task that year was to deploy an interactive IR system for finding instances of relevance rather than just finding all relevant documents. For example, a query about ferry sinkings would require finding mentions of any ferry that sank killing more than some number of people. Finding multiple mentions of the same ferry sinking was fine, but not useful.

We constructed a special-purpose interface for INQUERY that was intended to make this instance-finding problem easier for a user. It provided a space where the user could store documents and note which instances were mentioned. We also included an optional 3-D visualization of interdocument similarities. The visualization used colors and position to reflect the degree to which documents were similar to each of the instances. The hope was that a user could look for documents that seemed related to other relevant documents, but sufficiently different that they might discuss another instance.

We ran the largest TREC interactive track controlled user study to date (at the time), having twenty users try our system with or without the visualization as well as a control system provided by NIST. We found that the visualization *was* helpful, though despite using a relatively large number of users in the study, the significance of that result was marginal.

Our experiments (which were extended to twenty-four users slightly later [60]) showed that experienced users (librarians) were faster at completing searches, and just as accurate; spatial reasoning ability was less useful than past experience with a computer to predict whether someone would use a 3-D interface; spatial reasoning ability *did* predict whether someone would find the interface helpful; our special-purpose interface improved searchers' ability to find instances; and there was no evidence that the 3-D visualization increased recall of instances.

Chapter 6, this volume, provides more details about the interactive track.

11.4.5   Query

The goal of the query track (TREC-8 and TREC-9) was to explore the impact of query formulation on retrieval effectiveness. So rather than having a single statement of each topic, the track sought numerous ways of describing the same topic and then examined whether there were traits of queries that could be used to predict success or failure.

Our primary involvement in this track both years was to provide large numbers of alternate formulations of the queries. In both cases, students in an undergraduate database class were asked to create the queries as part of a homework problem. We provided fifteen forms for each of fifty queries for TREC-8 and another fifteen forms of those same queries for TREC-9. The queries included spelling errors, problems with people failing to include a critical word, and other oddities. Only a small number of duplicate queries occurred throughout the entire set, confirming the wide range of ways that an information need can be stated.

In TREC-8, we were only able to provide the query variants. For TREC-9, we carried out more detailed analysis of the impact of query formation. We focused on query expansion, finding that it generally compensated for the variant forms of the query—that is, after expansion most formulations of the same query performed comparably. There were, of course, usually a few ways of expressing a query that were disastrous.

The query track only lasted two years, but provided a rich source of information about query variation. It includes forty-three different ways of phrasing each of fifty queries. It has been used to explore evaluation stability [19] and provide a larger set of data (over 1,800 unique queries after stemming and stopping) for examining issues such as query expansion [35].

11.4.6   Question Answering (QA)

The question answering (QA) track was introduced in TREC-8, and the CIIR participated by providing a simple passage retrieval system. Because the evaluation at this time only measured the ability of a system to identify passages that contained the answer, this approach was viable. Although the QA task has since shifted to require a specific answer (for example, a few words), high-quality "answer passage" retrieval continues to be an important component technology and an active area of research at the CIIR, including the subtrack of TREC 2003 that addressed precisely that issue [1].

We continued our work in question answering during TREC-9 [4] by extending the query engineering to be more useful for the type of focused questions the track included. We also used query expansion in an effort to do a better job of finding passages that were likely to contain an answer. This approach was quite effective, but caused an unintended result that the NIST annotators did not like: we would occasionally retrieve passages that contained the answer, yet did not contain any support for the answer. For example, the question "Who was the sixteenth president of the United States?" requires the answer "Abraham Lincoln." Our system's top-ranking passage talked about Abraham Lincoln, but only about the animatronic Lincoln at Disneyland and how it was being replaced by Muppets. Our query expansion had added *abraham* and *lincoln* to the query, so that passage was highly ranked, even though it no longer matched any of the other query words. The track was amended the following year to disallow that situation.

Our participation in the QA track stopped after TREC-9 and did not resume until TREC 2003. Our focus has been on retrieving high-quality passages that are likely to contain an answer, a subtask of most QA systems that was not evaluated by the QA track in those years.

More information about the QA track is in chapter 10, this volume.

11.4.7   Novelty

The purpose of TREC 2002's novelty track was to integrate the goal of finding relevant material with that of avoiding redundant material. Participants were charged with selecting a set of relevant sentences from some documents that were related to a query, and then to identify which of those sentences contain new (novel) information. Because it was a new track, NIST was able to provide only four training topics. The CIIR built an additional forty-eight training topics so that we could understand the problem better. We were pleased that the statistical characteristics of our training topics were a reasonable match to the test topics that were eventually created.

The results of the track showed that almost all sentences were nonrelevant—only 2 to 3 percent on the training data and about 5 percent on the test data—and that almost all relevant sentences were novel—over 80 percent of them. As a result, randomly ordering the relevant sentences would do well for novelty, so it was far more important for a system to find relevant sentences than to recognize novelty. Novelty itself ended up being an unimportant aspect of the task.

One simplifying assumption that the novelty track made was to provide sites with a set of relevant documents to work from. In follow-on work [6], we showed that this assumption is dangerous: algorithms that detect novelty accurately when handed relevant documents fail—sometimes spectacularly—when relevance is not guaranteed; and algorithms that fail given relevance sometimes perform admirably when it is not. We believe that this casts suspicion on any results from the track.

For TREC 2003, the document sets were constructed to minize the problems found in the first year—that is, there were fewer sentences that were relevant and a larger proportion of those were novel. The CIIR did not participate in the 2003 evaluation.

11.4.8   High Accuracy Retrieval of Documents (HARD)

The goal of HARD is to achieve high accuracy retrieval from documents by leveraging additional information about the searcher and/or the search context, through techniques such as passage retrieval, and using targeted interaction with the searcher. The HARD track is a variant of the ad hoc retrieval task from the past. It was a "pilot track" in TREC 2003 because of the substantial extension on past evaluation—that is, it was not clear how best to evaluate some of the aspects of the track, so it was intended to be open ended. HARD will be running in TREC 2004 also, with most parameters of the task better specified.

The CIIR participated in all aspects of the track, including its management. In the first phase of the track, sites were given fifty topics that looked like "ad hoc" topics, and were expected to return a ranked list of one thousand documents for each query. The CIIR used a simple language-modeling system for this baseline run.

For the second phase, we generated several "clarification forms" for each of the topics. These forms were filled out (manually) by the person who created the topic, and provide a way for systems to request focused, single-interaction feedback from the searcher to help clarify intent, disambiguate concepts, and so on. We used three different approaches: providing a list of concepts (words and phrases) that appeared in top-ranked documents and asking whether they were pertinent, supplying a list of passages from top-ranking documents to get relevance feedback on those, and offering a list of document clusters that seemed relevant and asking for feedback on their relevance.

For the third phase, we used the response to the clarification forms to improve the queries and return an "improved" ranked list. We found that none of our techniques was particularly successful—in fact, our baseline run was the best of the runs that we submitted. This result was largely because of poor training data (four queries) in the track's first year: it was difficult to know how to tune a system.

We also carried out experiments on passage retrieval since pinpointed retrieval is another form of accurate retrieval. Unlike past uses of passage retrieval, we were actually identifying passages that were relevant rather than just using passage ranking to improve full document retrieval (as discussed in section 11.1.1). The evaluation of passage retrieval was a variation of average precision that accommodated overlapping passages. Again, the lack of training data meant that results of passage retrieval were inconclusive.

The HARD track will continue in TREC 2004. The second year is being designed to include more training data, beyond those developed during TREC 2003.

11.5   Impact of TREC on CIIR Research

A dozen years of TREC participation has left its mark on the CIIR. TREC has also certainly made its mark on the research community as a whole—for example, research papers are rarely viewed as meaningful if they do not include evaluation results on TREC or TREC-like corpora. The CIIR has felt the impact in numerous ways, including:

• Large-scale test corpora   Almost all experiments at the CIIR are now done with corpora that contain several gigabytes of text and/or hundreds of thousands of documents. There are certainly exceptions—the Topic Detection and Tracking (TDT) corpora include only fifty to eighty thousand documents apiece [27]—but those corpora are used only when there is little choice. The large-scale corpora have encouraged us to consider efficiency shortcuts [15], distributed information retrieval ("federated search") [26; 45; 57; 20; 65], and score merging [50; 51; 49].
• Retrieval accuracy   The large collections of TREC moved the CIIR's belief-estimation function from one that worked on small corpora to one that was more flexible for a wider range of corpora. The change that was discovered immediately was that tf grew too fast, forcing INQUERY to switch to a log tf model instead. In the course of TREC, experiments showed that the Okapi tf function was even better and it was adopted.

Accuracy also involved complex query processing—for instance, removing stop structure, recognizing phrases, looking for core concepts—and extracting names of people, places, and companies. We also developed global and local query expansion techniques that were broadly useful and developed better stemming approaches [67]. We explored the usefulness of passage retrieval [23], though found that improved ranking functions made passages less useful.

• Foreign languages   The CIIR's research has integrated foreign- and cross-language retrieval throughout its research program. We have constructed TDT systems that work with English, Arabic, and Chinese [2]; worked on Japanese [37] and Spanish retrieval [9]; built Chinese and cross-language question-answering systems [48]; and been involved in efforts to construct language technology for unusual languages [5; 44].

The TREC experiments have been an important catalyst for moving information retrieval research from "toy" collections to "real-world" problems with large-scale collections.

One of the great successes of TREC has been the ability to define a set of problems interesting to a broad set of researchers, provide resources not available elsewhere, and conduct comparative evaluations. This style of evaluation did not exist in IR prior to TREC and is now common throughout the field. As part of that process, TREC has been an exercise in community building around specific research problems—CLIR, filtering, distributed search, and so forth.

TREC also showed the power of making resources available at little or no cost. The resources have been critical in advancing the field and have been used widely outside of TREC itself—by the CIIR for a wide range of other experiments, by countless other researchers for their own problems, and often for work that was not foreseen when the collections were created. As one small example, large collections of results from different systems have been the mainstay of metasearch investigations [51; 50; 7]—something that was certainly not anticipated at the time the runs were archived.

The importance of shared resources had been known long before TREC—for example, the Cranfield studies [28]—but TREC has had a huge impact by making relatively real-world resources available for free. Little of what the CIIR (or any other researchers) did in the last decade would have been possible with only the CACM, CISI, MEDLINE, and NPL collections that were the norm prior to TREC.

Nonetheless, despite significant advances in the last dozen years, information retrieval is still not a "solved problem." Accuracy on document retrieval (only one of the IR tasks) still hovers around 40 to 50 percent for most well-behaved collections, whereas speech recognition and OCR technologies generally achieve 90 to 95 percent of what is possible (in well-behaved environments). IR is still extremely useful even at that level of effectiveness, and it is not necessarily the case that 100 percent accuracy is even required. Yet there is plenty of room between 40 and 100 percent for dramatic improvements.

Recent TREC tracks such as HARD or the robust retrieval track are exploring methods for greatly improving the average capabilities of systems. Web search engines have demonstrated the power available by harnessing "judgments" of millions of users to find important documents. There is increasing interest in leveraging such implicit and explicit collaborative activity, and in treating search as an interactive process that incorporates context and other world knowledge. It may be that these approaches will provide the next boost in effectiveness.

By the standards of the time, TREC brought mammoth collections to the IR research community. That, combined with cheap disks and the Web, catalyzed a decade of exciting research in the field. Collaboration and interactive computing, made possible by powerful desktop and mobile computers, may be the beginning of the next decade of advances.

Notes

1. Although the CIIR participated in TREC-1, its results were suppressed because it had been using similar data before TREC as part of the TIPSTER program.

2. The CIIR discussed its first version of a statistical association thesaurus in its TREC-2 paper [31], but did not use it for the TREC-2 tasks.

References

[1] AbdulJaleel, N., A. Corrada-Emmanuel, Q. Li, X. Liu, C. Wade, and J. Allan. UMass at TREC 2003: HARD and QA. In *TREC 2003*, 715–725.

[2] Allan, J., ed. *Topic detection and tracking: Event-based information organization*. Boston: Kluwer Academic Publishers, 2002.

[3] Allan, J., L. Ballesteros, J. Callan, W. B. Croft, and Z. Lu. Recent experiments with INQUERY. In *TREC-4*, 49–64.

[4] Allan, J., M. Connell, W. B. Croft, F. Feng, D. Fisher, and X. Li. INQUERY and TREC-9. In *TREC-9*, 551–577.

[5] Allan, J., V. Lavrenko, and M. E. Connell. A month to topic detection and tracking in Hindi. *ACM Transactions on Asian Language Information Processing* 2, no. 2 (2003): 85–100.

[6] Allan, J., C. Wade, and A. Bolivar. Retrieval and novelty detection at the sentence level. In *Proceedings of the twenty-sixth annual international ACM SIGIR conference*, 314–321.

[7] Aslam, J. A., and M. Montague. Models for metasearch. In *Proceedings of the twenty-fourth annual international ACM SIGIR conference*, 276–284.

[8] Attar, R., and A. S. Fraenkel. Local feedback in full-text retrieval systems. *Journal of the Association for Computing Machinery* 24, no. 3 (1977): 397–417.

[9] Ballesteros, L. Resolving ambiguity for cross-language information retrieval: A dictionary approach. PhD diss., University of Massachusetts, 2001.

[10] Ballesteros, L., and W. B. Croft. Dictionary methods for cross-lingual information retrieval. In *Proceedings of the DEXA conference on database and expert systems*, ed. R. Wagner and H. Thoma, 791–801. 1996

[11] Ballesteros, L., and W. B. Croft. Statistical methods for cross-language information retrieval. Paper presented at a SIGIR workshop, Zurich, 1996.

[12] Bikel, D., S. Miller, R. Schwartz, and R. Weischedel. Nymble: A high-performance learning name-finder. In *Fifth conference on applied natural language processing*, ed. R. Grishman, 194–201. San Francisco: ACL, 1997.

[13] Broglio, J., J. P. Callan, W. B. Croft, and D. W. Nachbar. Document retrieval and routing using the INQUERY system. In *TREC-3*, 29.

[14] Brown, E. Execution performance issues in full-text information retrieval. PhD diss., University of Massachusetts Computer Science, Technical Report TR95-81. 1995.

[15] Brown, E. Fast evaluation of structured queries for information retrieval. In *Proceedings of the eighteenth annual international ACM SIGIR conference*, 30–38.

[16] Buckley, C., and G. Salton. Optimization of relevance feedback weights. In *Proceedings of the eighteenth annual international ACM SIGIR conference*, 351–357.

[17] Buckley, C., G. Salton, J. Allan, and A. Singhal. Automatic query expansion using SMART: TREC-3. In *TREC-3*, 69.

[18] Buckley, C., A. Singhal, M. Mitra, and G. Salton. New retrieval approaches using SMART: TREC-4. In *TREC-4*, 25–48.

[19] Buckley, C., and E. M. Voorhees. Evaluating evaluation measure stability. In *Proceedings of the twenty-third annual international ACM SIGIR conference*, 33–40.

[20] Callan, J. Distributed information retrieval. In *Advances in information retrieval: Recent research from the CIIR*, ed. W. B. Croft, 127–150. Boston: Kluwer Academic Publishers, 2000.

[21] Callan, J. Document filtering with inference networks. In *Proceedings of the nineteenth annual international ACM SIGIR conference*, 262–269.

[22] Callan, J. Learning while filtering documents. In *Proceedings of the twenty-first annual international ACM SIGIR conference*, 224–231.

[23] Callan, J. P. Passage-level evidence in document retrieval. In *Proceedings of the seventeenth annual international ACM SIGIR conference*, 302–310.

[24] Callan, J. P., and W. B. Croft. An evaluation of query processing strategies using the TIPSTER collection. In *Proceedings of the sixteenth annual international ACM SIGIR conference*, 347–356.

[25] Callan, J. P., W. B. Croft, and S. M. Harding. The INQUERY retrieval system. In *Proceedings of the third international conference on database and expert systems application*, 78–83.

[26] Callan, J. P., Z. Lu, and W. B. Croft. Searching distributed collections with inference networks. In *Proceedings of the eighteenth annual international ACM SIGIR conference*, 21–28.

[27] Cieri, C., S. Strassel, D. Graff, N. Martey, K. Rennert, and M. Liberman. Corpora for topic detection and tracking. In *Topic detection and tracking: Event-based information organization*, ed. J. Allan, 33–66. Boston: Kluwer Academic Publishers, 2002.

[28] Cleverdon, C. The Cranfield tests on index language devices. In *Readings in information retrieval*, ed. K. Sparck Jones and P. Willett, 47–57. San Francisco: Morgan Kaufmann, 1997. Originally appeared in *Aslib Proceedings* 19 (1967): 173–192.

[29] Collins-Thompson, K., P. Ogilvie, Y. Zhang, and J. Callan. Information filtering, novelty detection, and named-page finding. In *TREC 2002*, 107–118.

[30] Croft, W. B. TIPSTER panel: The University of Massachusetts TIPSTER project. In *TREC-1*, 101.

[31] Croft, W. B., J. Callan, and J. Broglio. TREC-2 routing and ad hoc retrieval evaluation using the INQUERY system. In *TREC-2*, 75–84.

[32] Croft, W. B., and D. J. Harper. Using probabilistic models of document retrieval without relevance in formation. *Journal of Documentation* 35 (1979): 285–295.

[33] Croft, W. B., and R. H. Thompson. I^3R: A new approach to the design of document retrieval systems. *Journal of the American Society for Information Science* 38, no. 6 (November 1987): 389–404.

[34] Croft, W. B., H. R. Turtle, and D. D. Lewis. The use of phrases and structured queries in information retrieval. In *Proceedings of the fourteenth annual international ACM SIGIR conference*, 32–45.

[35] Cronen-Townsend, S., Y. Zhou, and W. B. Croft. Predicting query performance. In *Proceedings of the twenty-fifth annual international ACM SIGIR conference*, 299–306.

[36] French, J., A. Powell, J. Callan, C. Viles, T. Emmitt, K. Prey, and Y. Mou. Comparing the performance of database selection algorithms. In *Proceedings of the twenty-second annual international ACM SIGIR conference*, 238–245.

[37] Fujii, H. An investigation of the linguistic characteristics of Japanese information retrieval. PhD diss., University of Massachusetts, Computer Science Dept., 1997.

[38] Fujii, H., and W. B. Croft. A comparison of indexing techniques for Japanese text retrieval. In *Proceedings of the sixteenth annual international ACM SIGIR conference*, 237–247.

[39] Haines, D., and W. B. Croft. Relevance feedback and inference networks. In *Proceedings of the sixteenth annual international ACM SIGIR conference*, 2–11.

[40] Jing, Y., and W. B. Croft. *An association thesaurus for information retrieval*. Technical report 94-17. Amherst, MA: Computer Science Department, University of Massachusetts, 1994.

[41] Kando, N., ed. *NTCIR workshop 1: Proceedings of the first NTCIR workshop on research in Japanese text retrieval and term recognition*. Japan: National Center for Science Information Systems, 1999.

[42] Larkey, L., J. Allan, M. Connell, A. Bolivar, and C. Wade. UMass at TREC 2002: Cross language and novelty tracks. In *TREC 2002*, 43–55.

[43] Larkey, L., and M. Connell. Arabic information retrieval at UMass in TREC-10. In *TREC-10*, 562–570.

[44] Larkey, L., M. Connell, and N. Abdul Jaleel. Hindi CLIR in thirty days. *ACM Transactions on Asian Language Information Processing*, ed. D. W. Oard. Special issue IR-312, 2, no. 2 (2003): 130–142.

[45] Larkey, L. S., M. Connell, and J. Callan. Collection selection and results merging with topically organized U.S. patents and TREC data. In *Proceedings of the ninth international conference on information and knowledge management*, 282–289.

[46] Lavrenko, V., M. Choquette, and W. B. Croft. Cross-lingual relevance models. In *Proceedings of the twenty-fifth annual international ACM SIGIR conference*, 175–182.

[47] Lavrenko, V., and W. B. Croft. Relevance-based language models. In *Proceedings of the twenty-fourth annual international ACM SIGIR conference*, 120–127.

[48] Li, X., and W. B. Croft. Evaluating question answering techniques in Chinese. In *Proceedings of human language technology conference 2001*, ed. J. Allan, 201–206. San Francisco: Morgan Kaufman, 2001.

[49] Manmatha, R. Applications of score distributions in information retrieval. In *Language modeling for information retrieval*, ed. W. B. Croft and J. Lafferty, 167–188. Boston: Kluwer Academic Publishers, 2003.

[50] Manmatha, R., T. Rath, and F. Feng. Modeling score distributions for combining the outputs of search engines. In *Proceedings of the twenty-fourth annual international ACM SIGIR conference*, 267–275.

[51] Manmatha, R., and H. Sever. A formal approach to score normalization for metasearch. In *Proceedings of human language technology conference 2002*, ed. J. Allan, 88–93. San Francisco: Morgan Kaufman, 2002.

[52] Oard, D. W., ed. *Rapid development of language capabilities: The surprise languages*. New York: ACM Press, 2003.

[53] Och, F. J., and H. Ney. Statistical machine translation. In *Proceedings of EAMT workshop*, 39–46. Zurich: Springer, Available at ⟨http://www-i6.informatik-.rwth-aachen.de/Colleagues/och/EAMT00.ps⟩.

[54] Peters, C., ed. *Cross-language information retrieval and evaluation: Workshop of cross-language evaluation forum, CLEF 2000*. Lecture notes in computer science. Lisbon: Springer, 2001.

[55] Pirkola, A. The effects of query structure and dictionary setups in dictionary-based cross-language information retrieval. In *Proceedings of the twentieth annual international ACM SIGIR conference*, 55–63.

[56] Ponte, J., and W. B. Croft. USeg: A retargetable word segmentation procedure for information retrieval. In *Proceedings of the symposium on document analysis and information retrieval*, Las Vegas, 1996.

[57] Powell, A., J. French, J. Callan, M. Connell, and C. Viles. The impact of database selection on distributed searching. In *Proceedings of the twenty-third annual international ACM SIGIR conference*, 232–239.

[58] Prager, J., D. Radev, E. Brown, A. Coden, and V. Samn. The use of predictive annotation for question answering in TREC. In *TREC-8*, 399–410.

[59] Robertson, S. E., S. Walker, S. Jones, M. M. Hancock-Beaulieu, and M. Gatford. Okapi at TREC-3. In *TREC-3*, 109–126.

[60] Swan, R., and J. Allan. Aspect windows, 3-D visualizations, and indirect comparisons of information retrieval systems. In *Proceedings of the twenty-first annual international ACM SIGIR conference*.

[61] Turtle, H. R. Inference networks for document retrieval. PhD diss., University of Massachusetts, Computer Science Dept., 1991.

[62] Turtle, H. R., and W. B. Croft. Efficient probabilistic inference for text retrieval. In *Proceedings of RIAO*, ed. A. Lichnerowicz, 644–661. Conde-sur-Noireau, France: Corlet Imprimeur, 1991.

[63] Turtle, H. R., and W. B. Croft. Evaluation of an inference network-based retrieval model. *ACM Transactions on Information System* 9, no. 3 (1991): 187–222.

[64] Xu, J., J. Broglio, and W. B. Croft. *The design and implementation of a part of speech tagger for English*. Technical report IR-52. Center for Intelligent Information Retrieval, University of Massachusetts, Amherst, 1994.

[65] Xu, J., and J. Callan. Effective retrieval with distributed collections. In *Proceedings of the twenty-first annual international ACM SIGIR conference*, 112–120.

[66] Xu, J., and W. B. Croft. Cluster-based language models for distributed retrieval. In *Proceedings of the twenty-second annual international ACM SIGIR conference*, 254–262.

[67] Xu, J., and W. B. Croft. Corpus-based stemming using co-occurrence of word variants. *Transactions on Information Systems* 16, no. 1 (1998): 61–81.

[68] Xu, J., and W. B. Croft. Query expansion using local and global document analysis. In *Proceedings of the nineteenth annual international ACM SIGIR conference*, 4–11.

[69] Xu, J., A. Fraser, and R. Weischedel. TREC 2001 cross-lingual retrieval at BBN. In *TREC 2002*, 68.

[70] Yarowsky, D., G. Ngai, and R. Wicentowski. Inducing multilingual text analysis tools via robust projection across aligned corpora. In *Proceedings of human language technology conference 2001*, ed. J. Allan, 161–168, 2001.

[71] Zhang, Y., and J. Callan. The bias problem and language models in adaptive filtering. In *TREC 2001*, 78–83.

[72] Zhang, Y., and J. Callan. YFilter at TREC-9. In *TREC-9*, 135–140.

12 How Okapi Came to TREC
Stephen Robertson

12.1 Historical Background

In 1976, Karen Sparck Jones and I (Robertson and Sparck Jones 1976) published a paper on the relevance weighting of search terms, applying a probabilistic model to help devise a term-weighting and document-scoring function for ranked retrieval. Since relevance feedback was an explicit component of the model, it might be described as a statistical learning method; more specifically (in current terminology), because of its independence assumptions, it may be termed a naive Bayes model. In common with many other naive Bayes models in different application areas, this model and its term-weighting formula (referred to below as RSJ) were surprisingly successful.

It was not the first probabilistic model for information retrieval—that claim goes to a paper published by Bill Maron and J. L. Kuhns (1960), some sixteen years earlier. It took a rather different approach, though, partly because Maron and Kuhns were not concerned with multiple search terms, and later work (Robertson, Maron, and Cooper 1982, 1983) revealed fundamental differences in the viewpoints of the two models. Nevertheless, the RSJ model was in part inspired by earlier work by Miller (1971), Barkla (1969), and others (in fact, for a long time we referred to the weighting scheme as "miller4").

12.1.1 Early Experiments on RSJ

Sparck Jones ran the initial tests on the model (Sparck Jones 1979a, 1979b, 1980), with software designed for batch experiments on test collections. Keith van Rijsbergen, Martin Porter, and I (Robertson, van Rijsbergen, and Porter 1981) conducted some experiments with some variations on the model, including a version making use of the two-Poisson model of within-document term frequencies, due to Bookstein and Swanson (1974) as well as Harter (1975). Porter (1980) wrote the well-known Porter stemmer as part of this project, and also an interactive search program that became the basis for the commercial Muscat system.

In the mid-1980s, I conducted a live-user experiment with CIRT, the RSJ model implemented as a front end to a commercial Boolean system with the MEDLINE database (scientific abstracts and index terms) (Robertson, Thompson, Macaskill, and Bovey 1986). At the same time, Stephen Walker was beginning the development of an online public access library catalog called Okapi. Toward the end of the 1980s, Walker and the Okapi project joined me at the City University, London, and with Micheline Beaulieu we ran some live-user experiments using the library catalog (very short records) and the Inspec database (scientific abstracts) (Hancock-Beaulieu and Walker 1992).

Thus when TREC was announced, we had a system in place, albeit one designed for interactive, live-user experiments, not for batch experiments with test collections. The first task was to develop Okapi into something that could be used efficiently for such batch experiments, in the style of SMART or INQUERY. The second was to develop the model to make it better able to deal with full-text documents.

Before describing these activities, however, it is worth exploring why TREC was so obviously something that we should pursue.

12.1.2   The Test Collection Paradigm

The Cranfield experiments of the 1960s (Cleverdon, Mills, and Keen 1966) had defined the model of laboratory experiments in information retrieval: the document collection, the set of requests, the relevance judgments (whether by a genuine user or a substitute such as an independent expert), and the basic measures of performance. They had also provided a test corpus, a portable collection of documents, requests, and relevance judgments for other researchers to use for their own laboratory experiments. Given such a collection, experiments could be made entirely in vitro. The Cranfield collection was the first such corpus, but a succession of experiments from the 1960s on created a number of corpora of this kind.

Throughout the 1970s and into the 1980s, many experiments had been conducted on these test corpora. But corpora like Cranfield had been designed for particular experiments; they were mostly quite small, or else they had other problems like extremely inadequate relevance judgments. In the 1970s, a group of researchers in the United Kingdom began to consider setting up a new, large, general-purpose test collection, under the name of the "ideal" test collection (Sparck Jones and Bates 1977). Although the word "ideal" was in quotes, it was nevertheless a serious attempt to come up with a design that would satisfy a wide variety of needs of IR researchers.

Unfortunately, the project never came to fruition. It would have cost more than the U.K. research community at the time could afford, and so the plan was shelved. Beaulieu and I, having spent the 1980s trying to get away from the test collection paradigm by doing live-user experiments and having seen the failure of the "ideal" test collection project, wrote a paper in 1991 (Robertson and Hancock-Beaulieu 1992) in which we argued that the test collection paradigm had in effect run out of steam.

We could not have been more wrong. In between the writing and the publication of this paper in 1992, TREC was announced. TREC was the "ideal" test collection writ large, underwritten by U.S. funds and planned on a grand scale. While we did not abandon our commitment to live-user experiments, TREC was too good an opportunity to miss, and the Okapi team jumped in with both feet.

12.2   Okapi: The Basic Search System (BSS)

When we started on TREC, Okapi was a single program containing a range of search functionality and a user interface for searching, together with library routines for indexing. The necessity to do batch-searching experiments for TREC led us to separate out the search engine functionality from the user interface; the result was the BSS with which we have done all subsequent TREC experiments. The old user interface, a VT100 terminal system that was probably already obsolete (although interesting and the basis for some very informative experiments), eventually disappeared altogether. Subsequent user experiments, including those in the TREC interactive track, were done with graphic user interfaces written on top of the BSS.

Despite its batch orientation, the design of the BSS owes something to the old command-line Boolean search systems of the 1970s and the 1980s. In particular, a search session with the BSS has a session-based flavor: in a sequence of interactions, the BSS remembers search results and can reuse them in a subsequent interaction. Even more particularly, a search defines a result set—similar to the old Boolean results sets—that has essentially the same properties as a raw postings set from an inverted file. That is, in principle, a set resulting from a previous search (of any degree of complexity) has the same status as the set of postings for a single term read from the inverted file.

While it is capable of all the usual "Boolean" operations, though, including position-based operations such as adjacency, the BSS is oriented to weighted searching. This requirement has some consequences for the set-operation paradigm. Clearly each set of document postings may also have, in addition to term-position information, a score associated with each document, by which items can be ranked. But it is also the case that the set resulting from one operation may not be suitable for the application of another operation. In fact, the same statement applies to the "Boolean" systems, in the case of adjacency: for example, it makes sense to apply an *adj* to the result set of an *or* operation, but not to the result set of an *and* operation. Other constraints appear when we add in weighted search operations.

Nevertheless, the session-based, set-operation paradigm was retained. This puts Okapi in contrast with many current search engines (including virtually all those developed for Web searching), which generally operate in a stateless mode.

Over the course of eleven TRECs, clearly the BSS has evolved in a number of ways, though perhaps not in any fundamental way since the first two years. Yet as a result of work for the last few years on the adaptive-filtering task, the BSS has recently undergone some major changes—a suitable architecture for experiments on an essentially static collection has many differences from one that is suitable for an evolving collection and searches against new documents. One architecture currently being explored is to make an index/inverted file of profiles and search each incoming document against them. This presents a whole new set of problems.

12.3   BM25

The most important single change made in Okapi in the first three years of TREC, which turned out to be one of the most influential TREC-instigated results outside our own system, was the development of a new term-weighting and document-scoring function. This is currently known as (Okapi) BM25, and also quite commonly now as Okapi weights. A brief description of the function is given in the appendix to this chapter, but much more detailed accounts are given elsewhere (Robertson and Sparck Jones 1996; Sparck Jones, Walker, and Robertson 2000). It is worth recounting the reasons the development was necessary and the motivation behind it.

The RSJ model takes account only of term presence and absence, not of term frequency within a document, nor of document length. While it seemed to work reasonably well on short library catalog records and scientific abstracts (not quite so short, but fairly consistent in length), it seemed likely that it would not work so well on documents of extremely variable length. And indeed, our results in TREC-1 were mediocre and would have been considerably worse but for an implementation accident.[1]

So the challenge was to develop a new weighting/scoring scheme, consistent with the general ideas of the RSJ model, that would overcome this limitation. The work already done in the early 1980s (Robertson, van Rijsbergen, and Porter 1981) using the two-Poisson model seemed to have the potential to help, although the specific formulation in that work required the estimation of a large number of parameters and was not very successful, probably for that reason.

The analysis suggested that an approximation to the full complex weighting formula based on the two-Poisson model, which gave a simple although nonlinear *tf* weighting, combined with a simple although nonlinear document-length normalization, might work. Versions of both were introduced for TREC-2, but unfortunately we had one of those bad years that most veteran TREC participants have experienced, as a result of a succession of hardware problems. Although we noted much better runs in our report, our official results for TREC-2 were not very good. By TREC-3, however, we were easily among the best-performing systems.

Subsequently BM25 itself, variations on it, and ideas inspired by it (such as the pivoted document-length normalization in the SMART system (Singhal, Buckley, and Mitra 1996) have been widely adopted by other researchers in the field.

12.3.1 Relevance Feedback

BM25 retains the characteristic of the RSJ model: that it specifically allows for relevance feedback in the term weighting. That is, given no relevance information, the term-weighting scheme in BM25 might be described as a form of $tf * idf$ weight. Given some known-relevant documents, these are specifically taken into account in the weighting, which now becomes a measure of how much evidence for relevance the term provides.

Relevance feedback as usually practiced involves, in addition to term reweighting, query expansion (the addition of new terms to the query). Although in principle any term in the dictionary could be given a weight, we had accumulated evidence from a number of experiments that the model worked much better under conditions of strictly limited expansion. An exploration of this phenomenon in the early 1980s (Robertson and Bovey 1982) had provided some degree of theoretical justification for this conclusion. We had by the time of TREC a moderately effective term-selection algorithm, which incidentally does *not* choose terms on the basis of their weight alone (Robertson 1990).[2]

12.4   TREC Tasks

In successive TRECs, the Okapi team took part in a number of tasks. Not all of these were in fact done with the Okapi system, for a variety of reasons; some of them represented interests of particular members of the team, but stand somewhat apart from the main body. In this section, I will discuss a selection of the experiments performed, mainly those that seem in retrospect to be part of the main body. Again, detailed results are not in general given here; the reader is referred to other sources for these.

12.4.1   Ad Hoc, VLC, and Web

The main concern initially with the ad hoc task, as for many other TREC participants, was simply whether we could deal with collections of that size. It is hard to realize at this distance in time how difficult it could be to process two gigabytes of text.

The next important concern in ad hoc searching, including some experiments done as part of the VLC or Web tracks, as well as the official ad hoc task, was the weighting function described above. Thus the BM25 function, with different values for its various parameters (tuning constants) and various variants on it, was the subject of a number of experiments. Another substantial concern was with pseudorelevance or "blind" feedback. This is the method of performing an initial search on the query terms, assuming the top-ranked documents are relevant, and making use of them in a relevance feedback loop. We were among the first groups to attempt this procedure (at TREC-2), although some other groups have since used it more successfully. We remain a little skeptical of its value—although it is certainly possible to get performance gains from it, it is clear that it damages some queries, on the whole those that performed worst in the initial search.

12.4.2   Routing/Filtering

Our general interest in relevance feedback made the routing task a natural for us. Under the conditions of the routing task as developed in the early TRECs, however, we moved rapidly past the simple application of term-selection and term-weighting algorithms, toward iterative optimization methods. TREC routing assumes a substantial existing training corpus, with relevance judgments for each topic. This allows alternative query formulations to be tried out on the training set; although it is absolutely impossible to try out all possible query formulations, a heuristic exploration of the space of possibilities may be made. Given our understanding of the importance of term selection, we started only with that, and indeed with a simple version: take the terms in order of a term-selection function, start with the first three, and add each successive term to the query if and only if it increases performance on the training set. In successive TRECs, we made successively more complex algorithms covering successively larger subsets of the whole space. Okapi results were consistently among the best routing performances reported.

The adaptive-filtering task gave us new challenges. The existing program structure did not translate cleanly to adaptive filtering; the approach was to take documents in batches, make a small indexed database out of each batch, and search all profiles against it. The finer the granularity of the batches, the longer the program would take. Work on a more efficient implementation of filtering is currently under way.

The more serious challenge of filtering is the setting of thresholds. In the adaptive-filtering task as defined for TREC, and in some form at least in any reasonable definition of a filtering task, the system is required to make a binary decision on each document. Thus, a document-ranking function is not sufficient; a threshold or cutoff rule is required. Furthermore, this threshold needs to take into account the exact measure of performance to be used.

Most of the filtering tasks defined for successive TRECs have involved a linear utility measure of performance: each relevant document retrieved is given a certain credit, and each nonrelevant retrieved a certain debit (negative credit) value. The overall performance on a topic is the sum of credits. Such a measure can be translated into a threshold probability rule—retrieve if the probability of relevance exceeds a certain value, dependent on the relative debit and credit values. Hence, if we can assess realistically the probability of relevance of any given document, the threshold probability rule can be applied directly to optimize utility.

One might expect that a retrieval system based on a probabilistic model (as RSJ or BM25) would have no problem in assigning a probability of relevance to each document. Nevertheless, the various transformations involved in constructing the RSJ or BM25 weighting functions actually take the resulting score far from realistic probabilities. Although some of the transformations are reversible, some of them involve removing other unknown parameters that do not affect the ranking task but have a strong influence on the absolute probability values. For example, the full probability function includes a component based on the unconditional probability of relevance of a random document; we simply leave that out of the usual score since it is the same for all documents and therefore does not affect the ranking. But since we do not know that probability for an arbitrary query (it will vary vastly between queries), we cannot put it back in to improve the probability estimate. Thus, it is not simply a question of reversing the transformations.

The approach taken by the Okapi team was to attempt an empirical calibration of the score as a probability of relevance. This was accomplished by performing a logistic regression on some of the older TREC data (Robertson and Walker 2000b). Despite the fact that the test data are somewhat different, the calibration originally made has been remarkably successful. It is interesting, however, to contrast this calibration approach, in effect modeling the probability of relevance as a function of score, with the approach taken by some other participants (for example, Arampatzis and van Hameren 2001). This latter involves modeling and fitting the distributions of scores of relevant and nonrelevant documents, respectively. The relation between score and probability of relevance is implicit in such a distributional model. This is a parametric approach requiring assumptions about the generic shapes of the distributions, but it may be better at dealing with different topics with widely varying numbers of relevant documents.

12.4.3   Interactive

Prior to TREC-1, as indicated above, the Okapi team had undertaken a range of user experiments with interactive versions of the system. These experiments continued in parallel with TREC. It was therefore an obvious step for us to take part in TREC interactive tasks. Initially, however, TREC did not offer much in the way of interactive tasks. It was possible to perform manual runs as part of the ad hoc task, but these did not come close to simulating a truly interactive environment. One of the early concerns in TREC was with a formalization of interactive searching as a sequence of iterations, with each iteration explicitly delimited and formally evaluated. There are several problems with such an approach, and it was abandoned after TREC-2.

Subsequent work on interactive user experiments took place mainly in the context of the interactive track. The Okapi team took part in the early interactive track experiments and helped to formulate the principle of examining the process of interaction as well as the outcome of an interactive session. Again, the main focus of much of our work (within and without TREC) was the use of relevance feedback in interaction.

To provide some further detail on the purposes of these experiments, it is appropriate to start with the pre-TREC work with a VT100 interface.[3] This interface provided a text box for a query, a display of the top nine titles (usually truncated), a full-record display—and very little else. The relevance feedback function involved a relevance question at the bottom of the full-record display ("Is this the kind of thing you want?") and an option on the search screen to "Type M for more like the ones you have chosen." This option would only appear after the user had answered "yes" to the relevance question at least twice. The user could not exit from the full-record display without answering the relevance question, though—a degree of control on the part of the system designer that is both hard to achieve and probably unacceptable to users with present-day window-based interfaces.

Users were not instructed in the use of the system in any way. Nevertheless, in our real-user observations, many users discovered and used the "more" function, and subsequently found new documents that they marked as relevant. We thus acquired some evidence that a user relevance feedback function could be both used and useful. At the same time, users did sometimes express unhappiness with their lack of control. Apart from having to answer the relevance question every time, they also had no control over the way the feedback worked—all term selection was automatic, behind the scenes, and users often found it difficult to understand why a particular term had been selected or a specific document found.

In parallel with the early years of TREC, then, we undertook some user experiments with GUI interfaces to Okapi (Hancock-Beaulieu 1997). These were designed to give the user more control over the feedback process, by allowing them not to provide feedback on every document seen, and to reject terms that the system had selected. Unfortunately, it proved difficult to recover the same level of uptake and effectiveness achieved with the VT100 system—users often did not provide feedback, and if they got to the stage of a revised query, they would often reject most of the terms suggested by the system.

The TREC interactive track offered an opportunity for somewhat more controlled experiments. For these, the "users" were students recruited for the experiment and given set tasks. We could afford to supply them with a minimal amount of training, and introduce them to the idea and the practice of relevance feedback. Nevertheless, the general problem of reconciling the constraints of a laboratory experiment such as TREC with the requirements of a user experiment are considerable. TREC interactive experiments provided us with some new information about interactive relevance feedback, but in a rather limited way.

12.4.4   Other Related Experiments

Over the course of the Okapi team's participation in TREC, a number of experiments were conducted without using the Okapi software as such. These projects involved students and other researchers who were associated with the team, but for one reason or another preferred to write their own software rather than use Okapi. Often they made use of the Okapi algorithms. These include experiments on the Chinese-language material in TREC-5 and TREC-6 (Huang and Robertson 1998), the spoken-document material in TREC-6 (Walker et al. 1998), and ad hoc and Web track experiments with parallel software (MacFarlane, Robertson, and McCann 1999). The Okapi software itself has also been used by other researchers, sometimes as a back-end search engine for some other task such as question answering.

These researchers benefited in various other ways from the close involvement of the team with TREC work. It is without doubt easier to break into TREC if you can easily call on the advice and the experience of old TREC hands.

12.5   Final Comments

Looking back, it is hard to imagine the directions we would have taken if TREC had not happened when it did.

12.5.1   The Effects of TREC on Okapi

It will be apparent from all the above discussion that the experience of taking part in TREC, over an extended period, had a huge impact on the Okapi project. It stimulated a wide variety of different experiments, encouraged the interchange of ideas with other research groups, and at the same time provided a much more serious series of tests than any previous experiments of the value of the various ideas being explored.

It could be argued, however, that the Okapi team's concentration on TREC experiments has come at the expense of the user orientation that was such a dominant feature of the team's pre-TREC work. The team did continue live-user experiments, but undoubtedly the effort in that direction was affected by our TREC participation.

12.5.2   Laboratories and Users

Indeed, this last comment might be taken as a microcosm of a larger issue. The laboratory-experimental paradigm of Cranfield and TREC is certainly a wonderful discipline and a highly fruitful way of working. The longevity of TREC provides a significant component of this benefit: a single round of TREC would have done little for us or the world, but the cumulative effect of multiple rounds is much greater than the sum of the parts. The entire continuing TREC program has allowed and encouraged a tremendous range of good work on those aspects of IR that can best be investigated in a laboratory.

Nevertheless, it is clear that good user evaluation is a *much* more difficult task than laboratory-based evaluation and much less susceptible to the scale effect of a large cooperative approach such as TREC. Despite the interactive track, the success of TREC in general might be seen as having discouraged strongly user-based research. The problems of evaluating user-oriented interactive systems and researching those many aspects of IR that can only be revealed in a user-interaction context remain as open as they were in 1990.

12.5.3   The Effects of Okapi on TREC

Having built Okapi for other purposes, the task of making it do TREC was somewhat greater for us than for some of the groups with established experimental systems (such as SMART or INQUERY). This problem concerned not only the technology but also the models underlying the methods. This concern led directly to the development of the BM25 ranking algorithm.

It is probably fair to say that several of the ideas developed initially by the Okapi team were subsequently used by others, both within and outside of TREC—as well as the reverse form of influence. Still, it is clear that the single dominant contribution of the team to the wider community has been BM25. The algorithm will of course be replaced by something better eventually, but in the meantime it feels good to have made that contribution to TREC and the world.

Appendix: The BM25 Weighting and Scoring Function

The BM25 function defines both how individual terms in the query are weighted and how the weights are combined to give a document score. It derives rather indirectly from a two-Poisson model of term frequencies in documents, which might be described (in modern terminology) as an elementary form of language model.

The "query" may consist of any terms taken from a text topic, and/or terms selected as a result of a relevance feedback operation or any other query expansion method (BM25 does not directly determine which terms to select in a relevance feedback process; this is a separate function in Okapi, as indicated in the text of this chapter). The term weight has a component based on RSJ, which in the absence of relevance information is effectively an *idf* function, or in the presence of relevance information is determined by the occurrence characteristics of the term in relevant documents as well as in the collection as a whole. There is also a document-specific component, depending on term frequency in the document and document length, and a topic-text-specific component, depending on term frequency in the topic text (only appropriate for verbose or discursive forms of topic). The document-specific component ensures that a term absent from a document contributes nothing to the score.

Although there have been some variations in the exact formula for BM25 over the period of TREC, the following represents the now more or less standard form of BM25:

$$\text{Document score} = \sum_{T \in \mathcal{Q}} \log \frac{(r+0.5)/(R-r+0.5)}{(n-r+0.5)/(N-n-R+r+0.5)} \frac{(k_1+1)tf}{K+tf} \frac{(k_3+1)qtf}{k_3+qtf},$$

where

$\mathcal{Q}$ is a query, containing terms T;
tf is the frequency of occurrence of the term within a specific document;
qtf is the frequency of the term within the topic from which Q was derived;
dl and $avdl$ are the document length and average document length (arbitrary units), respectively;
N is the number of items (documents) in the collection;
n is the number of documents containing the term;
R is the number of documents known to be relevant to a specific topic (set to zero if there is no relevance information);
r is the number of relevant documents containing the term (ditto);
$K = k_1\left((1-b) + b * \frac{dl}{avdl}\right)$; and
$k_1 \geq 0$, $0 \leq b \leq 1$, $k_3 \geq 0$ are tuning parameters, for which optimal values may depend on the nature of the queries and possibly on the database.

The tuning parameters define various relationships between the term weight and other parameters. The tf component is essentially a function that starts at zero (for $tf = 0$), rises steeply at first, and then flattens out to reach an asymptotic limit. The speed with which it approaches the limit is controlled by k_1: a low value means it reaches it quickly, and larger tfs have little affect on the term weight—a value of zero would make the weight binary, giving no effect to tf values greater than one. A large value of k_1 would cause the effect of tf on the weight to be almost linear. The K in the denominator is k_1 modified by a document-length factor controlled by b: a b value of one means the term weight is fully normalized by the document length, whereas zero means no normalization. Also, k_3 relates to qtf as k_1 to tf, except that there is no length normalization.

For most of the TREC-7 experiments, the following values were used for the tuning parameters:

$k_1 = 1.2$
$b = 0.75$
$k_3 = $ anything from 0 to 1000

Notes

In 1998, Micheline Beaulieu, Stephen Walker, and myself all left the City University, London. Walker and I continued to work with Okapi from Microsoft Research, in cooperation with the City University.

The following are the main reports of the Okapi team (at the City University and then Microsoft) in successive TREC proceedings: Robertson et al. 1993, 1994, 1995; Robertson 1996; Beaulieu et al. 1997; Walker et al. 1998; Beaulieu and Gatford 1998; Robertson, Walker, and Beaulieu 1999; Robertson and Walker 2000a; Robertson and Walker 2001; Robertson, Walker, and Zaragoza 2002; Robertson, Walker, Zaragoza, and Herbrich 2003. Other related reports have been cited elsewhere in this chapter.

1. The system had a built-in document length limit—included in the days when "documents" (records) were all short—and it simply truncated anything longer. Without this bug/feature, our submitted results would have been totally dominated by the longest documents, notably the notorious *Federal Register* component of the early TREC collections.

2. The basic argument is that a term's contribution to the overall effectiveness of the search is not the same as the evidence it gives about an individual document. For example, a term occurring in only one document may be a strong indicator for that document, and therefore invite a high weight, but have little effect overall. A "term-selection value" is computed to estimate this overall effect and used to rank candidate terms, and the top n terms are chosen; n may be comparatively small (say, twenty).

3. For those readers who are too young to have come across VT100, it is a protocol for control of a text display terminal of (normally) eighty characters wide and twenty-five lines high. Extremely simple graphics can be constructed by means of some of the keyboard characters and control sequences to locate the cursor in any position, but 80×25 character positions does not give much scope. No mouse is involved—all interaction is via the keyboard.

References

Arampatzis, A., and A. van Hameren. 2001. The score-distributional threshold optimization for adaptive binary classification tasks. In *Proceedings of the twenty-fourth annual international ACM SIGIR conference*, 285–293.

Barkla, J. K. 1969. Construction of weighted term profiles by measuring frequency and specificity in relevant items. Presented at Second international Cranfield conference on mechanised information storage and retrieval systems.

Beaulieu, M., and M. Gatford. 1998. Interactive Okapi at TREC-6. In *TREC-6*, 143–167.

Beaulieu, M. M., et al. 1997. Okapi at TREC-5. In *TREC-5*, 143–165.

Bookstein, A., and D. R. Swanson. 1974. Probabilistic models for automatic indexing. *Journal of the American Society for Information Science* 25:312–319.

Cleverdon, C. W., J. Mills, and E. M. Keen. 1966. *Factors determining the performance of indexing systems*. 2 vols. Cranfield, UK: Aslib Cranfield Research Project, College of Aeronautics.

Hancock-Beaulieu, M. 1997. Experiments on interfaces to support query expansion. *Journal of Documentation* 53:8–19.

Hancock-Beaulieu, M., and S. Walker. 1992. An evaluation of automatic query expansion in an online library catalogue. *Journal of Documentation* 48:406–421.

Harter, S. P. 1975. A probabilistic approach to automatic keyword indexing (parts 1 and 2). *Journal of the American Society for Information Science* 26:197–206, 280–289.

Huang, X., and S. Robertson. 1998. Okapi Chinese text retrieval experiments at TREC-6. In *TREC-6*, 137–142.

MacFarlane, A., S. E. Robertson, and J. A. McCann. 1999. PLIERS at VLC2. In *TREC-7*, 327–335.

Maron, M. E., and J. L. Kuhns. 1960. On relevance, probabilistic indexing, and information retrieval. *Journal of the ACM* 7:216–244.

Miller, W. L. 1971. Probabilistic search strategy for medlars. *Journal of Documentation* 27:254–266.

Porter, M. F. 1980. An algorithm for suffix stripping. *Program* 14:130–137.

Robertson, S. E. 1990. On term selection for query expansion. *Journal of Documentation* 46:359–364.

Robertson, S. E., and J. D. Bovey. 1982. *Statistical problems in the application of probabilistic models to information retrieval*. Technical report no. 5739, London: British Library Research and Development Department.

Robertson, S. E., and M. Hancock-Beaulieu. 1992. On the evaluation of IR systems. *Information Processing and Management* 28:457–466.

Robertson, S. E., M. E. Maron, and W. S. Cooper. 1982. Probability of relevance: A unification of two competing models for information retrieval. *Information Technology—Research and Development* 1:1–21.

Robertson, S. E., M. E. Maron, and W. S. Cooper. 1983. The unified probabilistic model for IR. In *Research and development in information retrieval*, ed. G. Salton and H.-J. Schneider, 108–117. Berlin: Springer-Verlag.

Robertson, S. E., and K. Sparck Jones. 1976. Relevance weighting of search terms. *Journal of the American Society for Information Science* 27:129–146.

Robertson, S. E., and K. Sparck Jones. 1996. *Simple, proven approaches to text retrieval*. Rev. ed. Technical report no. 356. Cambridge, UK: Computer Laboratory. Available at ⟨http://www.cl.cam.ac.uk/ftp/papers/index.html⟩.

Robertson, S. E., C. L. Thompson, M. J. Macaskill, and J. D. Bovey. 1986. Weighting, ranking, and relevance feedback in a front-end system. *Journal of Information Science* 12:71–75.

Robertson, S. E., C. J. van Rijsbergen, and M. F. Porter. 1981. Probabilistic models of indexing and searching. In *Information retrieval research*, ed. R. Oddy, S. Robertson, C. J. van Rijsbergen, and P. Williams, 35–56. London: Butterworths.

Robertson, S. E., and S. Walker. 2000a. Okapi/Keenbow at TREC-8. In *TREC-8*, 151–162.

Robertson, S. E., and S. Walker. 2000b. Threshold setting in adaptive filtering. *Journal of Documentation* 56:312–331.

Robertson, S. E., and S. Walker. 2001. Microsoft Cambridge at TREC-9: Filtering track. In *TREC-9*, 361–368.

Robertson, S. E., S. Walker, and M. Beaulieu. 1999. Okapi at TREC-7: Automatic ad hoc, filtering, VLC, and interactive track. In *TREC-7*, 253–264.

Robertson, S. E., S. Walker, and H. Zaragoza. 2002. Microsoft Cambridge at TREC-10: Filtering and Web tracks. In *TREC 2001*, 378–383.

Robertson, S. E., S. Walker, H. Zaragoza, and R. Herbrich. 2003. Microsoft Cambridge at TREC 2002: Filtering track. In *TREC 2002*, 439–446.

Robertson, S. E., et al. 1993. Okapi at TREC. In *TREC-1*, 21–30.

Robertson, S. E., et al. 1994. Okapi at TREC-2. In *TREC-2*, 21–34.

Robertson, S. E., et al. 1995. Okapi at TREC-3. In *TREC-3*, 109–126.

Robertson, S. E., et al. 1996. Okapi at TREC-4. In *TREC-4*, 73–96.

Singhal, A., C. Buckley, and M. Mitra. 1996. Pivoted document length normalization. In *Proceedings of the nineteenth ACM SIGIR conference*, 21–29.

Sparck Jones, K. 1979a. Experiments in relevance weighting of search terms. *Information Processing and Management* 15:133–144.

Sparck Jones, K. 1979b. Search term relevance weighting given little relevance information. *Journal of Documentation* 35:30–48.

Sparck Jones, K. 1980. Search term relevance weighting—some recent results. *Journal of Information Science* 1:325–332.

Sparck Jones, K., and R. G. Bates. 1977. *Report on a design study for the "ideal" information retrieval test collection*. Cambridge: Computing Laboratory, University of Cambridge.

Sparck Jones, K., S. Walker, and S. E. Robertson. 2000. A probabilistic model of information retrieval: Development and comparative experiments. *Information Processing and Management* 36:779–808, 809–840.

Walker, S., et al. 1998. Okapi at TREC-6. In *TREC-6*, 125–136.

13 The SMART Project at TREC
Chris Buckley

13.1 Introduction

The SMART Project, at Cornell University and then an offshoot at Sabir Research, has been a major participant in TREC since the beginning. SMART is a statistical IR system, based on the work of Gerard Salton, that has proven to be effective, efficient, and robust in the application to many different information-related tasks.

The structure of this chapter is as follows. First, the theory and underlying algorithms of SMART are discussed. The implementation of SMART used in the initial TREC-1 is then described in some detail, not only for the historical background but also because it served (and still does) as a general resource for the TREC community. Next, the history of SMART participation in the major TREC tasks and tracks is described, year by year within each task. The ad hoc section covers the TREC main task, including a description of a yearly improvement chart giving a sense of how the entire field of TREC participants were progressing from year to year. Later sections then cover the routing task, foreign-language tasks, and other shorter-lived tasks.

The presentation of the historical sections is deliberately informal. The goal is not so much to describe what was done each year but to give a sense of why certain problems were attacked, how successful the attacks were, and how ideas flowed from year to year and group to group. Readers are encouraged to read the original reports for the actual details of what was done. I want to convey some of the excitement of the early years when every year introduced major improvements in IR systems. TREC changed the way IR was done, with an environment supporting realistic test collections and a comparative experimental methodology. It came along at the right time to have an enormous impact on both the research and the application of IR; the lessons learned from TREC affect hundreds of millions of people every day as they search for information.

13.2 The Algorithmic Underpinnings of SMART

Starting in the 1960s and through the 1990s, the SMART project at Cornell under the direction of Salton has been interested in the analysis, search, and retrieval of heterogeneous text databases, where the vocabulary is allowed to vary widely and the subject matter is unrestricted. In such an environment, complete theories of knowledge representation do not exist, and it is unclear what concepts, concept relationships, and inference rules may be needed to understand particular texts [18].

Accordingly, a text analysis and retrieval component must necessarily be based primarily on a study of the available texts themselves. Fortunately, very large text databases are now available in machine-readable form, and a substantial amount of information is automatically derivable about the occurrence properties of words and expressions in natural-language texts, and about the contexts in which the words are used. This information can help in determining whether a query and a text are semantically homogeneous—that is, whether they cover similar subject areas. When that is the case, the text can be retrieved in response to the query.

In the SMART system, the vector-processing model of retrieval is used to transform both the available information requests as well as the stored documents into vectors of the form:

$$D_i = (w_{i1}, w_{i2}, \ldots, w_{it}),$$

where D_i represents a document (or query) text and w_{ik} is the weight of some feature T_k in document D_i. A weight of zero is used for features that are absent from a particular document, and positive weights characterize features actually assigned.

Once feature vectors are available for the documents and queries, all subsequent processing can be based on vector manipulations. For example, the similarity between a query and a document might be defined as the inner product between the two vectors, or alternatively, might be defined as a measure of the angle between the vectors ("cosine similarity"). If there are some documents that are known to be responsive, or relevant, to a query, then a new query might be formed by taking the vector addition of the known-relevant documents and the original query ("relevance feedback").

In general in SMART, the features of a vector representing some text (document, document piece, or query) are taken as the individual terms and phrases occurring in the text. These terms are derived by a text transformation of the following kind [17]:

- Recognize individual text words
- Use a stop list to eliminate unwanted function words like "and" or "the"
- Perform suffix removal and root transformations to generate word stems
- Optionally use term-grouping methods based on statistical word co-occurrence or word adjacency computations to form term phrases (alternatively, syntactic analysis computations can be used)
- Assign term weights to all remaining word and/or phrase stems to form the term vector for all information items

In choosing a term-weighting system, low weights should be assigned to high-frequency terms that occur in many documents of a collection and high weights to terms that are important in particular documents, but unimportant in the remainder of the collection. The weight of terms that occur rarely in a collection is relatively unimportant because such terms contribute little to the needed similarity computation between different texts.

A well-known term-weighting system following that prescription assigns weight w_{ik} to term T_k in document D_i in proportion to the frequency of occurrence of the term in D_i, and in inverse proportion to the number of documents to which the term is assigned [20; 17]. Such a weighting system is known as a tf × idf (term frequency times inverse document frequency) weighting system. In practice the document lengths, and hence the number of nonzero term weights assigned to a document, vary widely. To allow a meaningful final retrieval similarity, it is convenient to use a length-normalization factor as part of the term-weighting formula. One particular high-quality term-weighting formula experimented with in TREC-1 for w_{ik}, the weight of term T_k in document D_i, is

$$w_{ik} = \frac{(\log(f_{ik}) + 1.0) * \log(N/n_k)}{\sqrt{\sum_{k=1}^{t}[(\log(f_{ik}) + 1.0) * \log(N/n_k)]^2}}, \tag{1}$$

where f_{ik} is the occurrence frequency of T_k in D_i, N is the collection size, and n_k the number of documents with term T_k assigned. The factor $\log(N/n_k)$ is an inverse collection frequency ("idf") factor that decreases as terms are used widely in a collection, and the denominator in expression (1) is used for weight normalization. This particular form is called "ltc" weighting. The weights assigned to terms in *queries* are much the same.

One important point that permeates SMART processing is that it is not assumed that all features assigned to a text representation vector are necessarily good, unambiguous features giving good semantic insights into the text's meaning. The state of the art in natural-language processing is not advanced enough to assume good features. Instead, vector features are regarded as evidence that some semantic feature exists, and the weight of a vector feature is the importance of that evidence. The similarity between two vectors is calculated as the totality of the evidence that the two vectors match. The notion is that the similarity between two semantically close texts will be comparatively high due to lots of pieces of evidence matching. The similarity between two semantically different texts may be nonzero because of random matches of poor pieces of evidence, but it will not be nearly as high as the match between semantically close texts. The entire system is designed to be tolerant of false matches, often by considering only comparative similarities rather than the actual values of similarities.

Thus, SMART processing is aggressive at adding and consolidating features that possibly represent some semantic idea of a text, much more so than most other statistical IR systems. This approach has weaknesses; one obvious weakness is that it is difficult to set overall thresholds or interpretations for similarity values. In general, though, the approach has proven itself useful in many different environments, as will be seen throughout this chapter.

13.3 SMART Version 11.0

There have been a large number of implementations of SMART over the almost forty years since the project began, though only a couple have been publicly released. There were several versions on IBM mainframes throughout the 1960s and 1970s, with new versions being written when minicomputers became available in the late 1970s. Ed Fox wrote a couple of versions in the early 1980s; afterward, I [1] started rewriting SMART—a process that continues to this day. SMART Version 11.0, my third reasonably complete rewrite, was released in early 1992.

SMART Version 11.0 was specifically designed for the general community to use for TREC; it could handle the large collections (a factor of a hundred larger than previous test collections), and was both efficient and flexible. It had been clear that scaling up to the large collections was going to be a barrier to participation in TREC for many groups; SMART 11 offered the ability for groups to implement their own retrieval algorithms on top of the base SMART system. About one-third of the groups submitting runs in TREC-1 used some form of SMART for a major part of their processing. In the early years of TREC, four to five groups typically used SMART directly, and another two to four groups used SMART for some part of their processing. There are still groups that are currently using modified versions of SMART 11 for part of their processing in TREC; an example would be the Language Computer Corporation (LCC) question-answering system.

Some of the features of SMART Version 11.0 are:

• Aggressive stemming. The reason for the aggressiveness was (and remains) better a false match due to inappropriately stemming two unrelated words to the same stem than missing a good match due to related words not being stemmed to the same stem.
• Large stop-word list of 570 items. This was done for efficiency's sake.
• Hyphenated words broken at the hyphen into two separate words. Again, this allowed more good matches to occur at the cost of having some inappropriate matches.
• Phrasing of adjacent word pairs possible. Note that the individual components of phrases are always also included as features, and that phrases were stemmed and order independent ("information retrieval" matches "retrieving information"). Again, the reason is to match as many features as possible.
• Extremely fast (for the time). Basic indexing took five and a half hours for TREC-1 with basic retrieval speed being one to two seconds per query.
• Flexible. Complete run-time choice of using any variant of any procedure implemented within SMART. Thus, there were several indexing approaches, dozens of weighting methods, and several retrieval approaches possible. Since new code could be added rather than replacing old code, comparisons against older experiments remained possible.

SMART Version 11.0 was quite successful and helpful in its time. Unless otherwise indicated, all the features of SMART Version 11.0 were used in subsequent TRECs in the descriptions that follow, along with whatever modifications were part of that year's experiment.

13.4   SMART and the TREC Ad Hoc Task

The ad hoc task of TREC was the major focus of TREC and TREC participants in the early years. It provides a direct test of pure test collection retrieval performance: how well systems can retrieve relevant documents. Groups are given a set of documents, normally between a half million and one million, with the majority being newspaper articles. The groups are then given a set of fifty user need topics and asked to retrieve a ranked list of documents for each topic that are their system's best guess at being documents relevant to the user's need. There are two main subcategories within the ad hoc task: the *automatic* runs where the systems retrieve documents without any human intervention at all, and the *manual* runs where a human looks at the original topic and aids the system in finding good documents. The SMART runs described here are all automatic runs.

13.4.1   TREC-1: Ad Hoc

There were three main aspects of this brand-new environment of TREC-1 that were different from any previous test collection that the SMART group had dealt with.

1. There were many more documents in the collection, by a factor of one hundred.
2. Each document was a full text document, potentially quite long (the longest document in the TREC-1 collection was as long as an eight-hundred-page book). Most previous test collections included only abstracts or extremely short documents.
3. Each topic was a full description of the user's need, including background material and definitions.

At the time, there were no statistics from large collections we could take advantage of, so the size of the collection was not something we could directly address yet. The topics were very long and different from anything we had dealt with, so again there was little we could address without experience. Nevertheless, we had been extensively working with full text documents in other work. So our official runs for TREC-1 [6] used the local-global approach we had developed for looking at similarities between long articles in encyclopedias.

Our basic approach was to compute the global similarity of each document to the topic. Then, for the five hundred documents with the highest global similarity, we computed the local similarity between each sentence in the topic with each sentence in the document. The final score for a document was a combination of the global similarity and the best sentence-sentence local match.

We did take some advantage of the collection's size by producing a list of statistical phrases or adjacent word pairs. We defined a valid phrase as being a pair of adjacent nonstop words that were stemmed and unordered, and that occurred in at least twenty-five documents in the first TREC volume. Previous experiments like this had not worked well for us on the small test collections, but the size of TREC offered an opportunity to try again.

The two official SMART runs for the TREC-1 ad hoc task were both local-global runs. One used single terms, and the other used single terms plus phrases. In general, both runs did very well compared with other groups. The phrase run was noticeably better than the single-term run. The local-global algorithm was a disappointment; it did only marginally better than just using a global similarity.

We also presented a set of other unofficial runs during our TREC-1 workshop talk. This was the first test collection of this size any of the research systems had been able to work with. We did a set of experiments involving trade-offs that previously worked on small test collections, but that we felt needed to be verified on large collections, especially with regard to efficiency. Some of the results from that include:

· The number of stop words has a significant effect on retrieval speed, but some common words are useful for retrieval even on large collections.
· The method of stemming is not important for effectiveness, though it has retrieval speed implications.
· The retrieval speed can be greatly increased by ending the search early, at a cost of a small decrease in effectiveness.
· Query and document weighting is extremely important.

By making two simple changes to our weighting strategy, without a local-global match, we were able to get a 17 percent improvement over our best official run—about 14 percent above any group's official run. The first change was to de-emphasize our idf component to our weighting. Idf weights varied much more on a large collection than the previous small test collections. It's important to include idf, but including it in the just the topic weighting worked much better. The second change was to de-emphasize the term-frequency component in both topic and document weighting. Long documents and topics gave too much variability in the term-frequency values. Taking the log of the term frequency worked well.

Overall, we were tremendously pleased with our results. We had gone into TREC-1 with some trepidation; this was the first large-scale test comparing statistical information retrieval against manual Boolean retrieval and other techniques. The SMART project had been arguing for decades that statistical approaches were superior, but the small size of the test collections meant our contentions were not convincing. TREC-1 validated the entire statistical approach.

13.4.2 TREC-2: Ad Hoc

In TREC-2, we spent most of our ad hoc effort trying to learn variations and parameters of our local-global approach that actually helped retrieval [2]. Our basic global vector similarity was the changed weighting strategy as described above. We constructed a training set from the *Wall Street Journal* subset of the TREC-1 collection. For every document, we calculated nineteen different local similarity values and tried various learning techniques to optimize the combination of global similarity with the local values.

Our final approach used only one local similarity and got a modest improvement over the global similarity on our training collection.

We submitted two official ad hoc runs—one using the global vector similarity only, and the other with the learned combination of local and global similarities. The local-global approach was slightly worse than the simple vector approach, despite all the learning effort. The improvements we got on the training collection were overly collection specific and did not carry over to the TREC-2 task. In particular, paragraph length was very different among the TREC subcollections and our local similarities were strongly affected.

One additional lesson learned in the TREC-2 ad hoc task was how easy it is to make a blunder when actually performing the runs to be submitted. We misnamed one of the inverted files and it turned out to include idf-weighted documents when the name indicated it did not. Thus, we unexpectedly had both idf-weighted documents and idf-weighted queries, and as our work in TREC-1 suggested, we suffered about a 10 percent penalty.

13.4.3   TREC-3: Ad Hoc

For TREC-3, we branched off and explored two different approaches for our two main official runs [7]. The first was a continuation of our local-global investigations of TREC-2, and the second was attempting to expand the initial query.

For TREC-3, we defined a local passage to be of fixed size instead of sentences or paragraphs. This addressed our TREC-2 problem of varying paragraph length affecting results. This gave us our first real improvements (16 percent) of local-global matching over a straight global vector similarity in our official run. Further analysis of the results showed that, as we had hoped, we were finally getting a precision-oriented run out of our local-global matching.

In TREC-3, the TREC committee started to reduce the size of the original topic. In particular, it got rid of the "concept" field, which tended to give good terms related to the information need. In reaction to this, we investigated methods of bringing additional terms into the query. We settled on pseudorelevance feedback as our main approach. This had been used successfully in TREC-2 by CLARITECH [12] and the University of California at Los Angeles [11]. We had some experience with it from the mid-1980s when we tried it on the small collections, where it proved noticeably unsuccessful.

For our pseudorelevance feedback, an initial retrieval was performed. The top thirty documents were assumed to be relevant, and a standard relevance feedback algorithm was used to expand and reweight the query. In fact, the same Rocchio algorithm that had been and was continuing to be used for the TREC routing task (described below) worked quite well. Our official expansion run improved the base vector run by over 20 percent. Unlike the local-global run, this improvement was a recall-oriented improvement; we retrieved many more relevant documents, though not at the highest ranks.

13.4.4 TREC-4: Ad Hoc

In TREC-4, the SMART project made a fundamental change in its similarity-ranking algorithms [9]. It had become increasingly obvious over the previous two years that cosine document-length normalization had problems. Until we examined the issue directly, we hadn't realized how major those problems were.

Document-length normalization is necessary for any weighted statistical system. We had used cosine normalization for over twenty years with good success. But cosine normalization was developed in an era when documents were short and about a single topic. It emphasizes the relationship between the query and the entire document. This is not appropriate for TREC documents—a fact that we realized and were trying to accommodate with our local-global matching.

By directly comparing the probability of retrieval of a cosine-normalized document as a function of document length and the probability of relevance of a document as a function of document length, we discovered an enormous gap. Cosine retrieval strongly favors short documents while the probability of relevance is low for short documents and increases monotonically as document length increases. Amit Singhal came up with a length-normalization scheme that directly attacked the problem: pivoted document-length normalization [21].

This fundamentally changed every approach we had been taking. For example, we discovered:

• Our TREC-3 improvements due to local-global matching were almost entirely an artifact of normalization. Once the global similarity was properly normalized, there was no need for our (nonnormalized) local matching.
• The fact that we could expand by several hundred terms and still be improving retrieval was a normalization effect. Adding random terms unassociated with the query simply increased the likelihood that long documents would be retrieved. Since cosine normalization unduly favored short documents, anything that randomly increased the likelihood of long documents being retrieved would help.
• The importance of nonrelevant documents in our routing-run Rocchio formula suddenly increased. The importance had been set at near zero, but that was in part due to the fact that long documents were more likely to be negatively affected than short ones.

In TREC-4, the lengths of ad hoc topics were drastically reduced. Topics were targeted at being a single sentence, without a narrative or a title as in TREC-3. Obviously, query expansion would play a crucial role in good performance in TREC-4. Given our lack of experience with our new weighting functions, we decided to expand cautiously, adding about 12 percent of the terms we had added in TREC-3. This turned out to be a mild mistake for TREC-4. Our overall approach still favors adding any term that has a reasonable chance of being associated with relevance.

Our official expansion run was the same algorithm as used for TREC-3, but with the new weighting scheme and with the number of expansion terms changed from

510 terms down to 60. This run did extremely well; it was strongly the best automatic run of TREC-4.

We also continued our tradition of experimenting with one of our official runs. We used a local similarity measure based around finding the best single point in the document with surrounding terms occurring in the query. This ended up hurting performance by about 5 percent.

13.4.5 TREC-5: Ad Hoc

The major effort for TREC-5 ad hoc task was to determine a set of good documents from which to draw expansion terms in a pseudorelevance feedback process [8]. We tried a number of approaches; the one that worked best was to rerank the top fifty documents according to how well some short passage in the document "covers" the query—that is, has a high number of independent query terms occurring in the document passage. The claim is that such documents are more likely to either be relevant themselves or at least contain good expansion terms.

We also defined query zones—for example, ranks 501–1,000—from which we could take documents that contained query terms, but that we did not expect to be relevant. The goal was to examine how terms occurred within this nonrelevant query zone as opposed to a relevant query zone composed of the top twenty reranked documents. Xerox, in its TREC-4 work [14], had pointed out that the nonrelevant documents in this "local region" are going to have different, and possibly more useful, occurrence characteristics than a typical nonrelevant document.

Our official run and later experimental ones got mild consistent improvement from including this fairly complicated apparatus. Unfortunately, it is hard to base new work on complicated algorithms with as many parameters as we find here. There is no real understanding of how the parameter settings are related to each other and in what environments particular settings may be appropriate. We attempted to simplify the approach from TREC-5, but without notable success.

13.4.6 TREC-6: Ad Hoc

In TREC-6, we continued our process of trying more and more complicated approaches, without much success [4]. We tried clustering the top documents and ensured that each top cluster was represented in the expansion process. This attacked the problem that often a topic has several aspects to it, and expansion frequently emphasizes only one aspect. If different aspects are represented in different clusters, then expansion by different clusters should be helpful. Unfortunately, our results were slightly worse using this.

Our other major attack also addressed the same problem of single aspects dominating in a multiple aspect topic. We defined SuperConcepts that had as seeds the original query terms. Every expansion term was assigned to one or more Super-Concepts depending on the occurrence correlation of the expansion term and the SuperConcept.

Again, the problem being addressed is important, but our results showed no improvement.

Overall, the TREC-6 results seemed to be disappointing for all groups. Query expansion itself was only marginally useful on the TREC-6 topics. But in general, the ad hoc algorithms of all groups became complicated enough so there were no real explanations of why this might be the case.

13.4.7   TREC-7 and TREC-8: Ad Hoc

In TREC-7 and TREC-8, we tried modest changes to our existing algorithms in an attempt to understand what was happening [3; 10].

There was a definite lack of success in this endeavor.

In TREC-8, we concentrated on the TREC-6 task, inventing new weighting approaches to improve performance. Unfortunately, while we were able to mildly improve performance on the TREC-6 task, we hurt performance on all other tasks, including TREC-8.

13.4.8   Yearly Improvement Chart

It is difficult to determine how much systems are improving from TREC to TREC since the queries and the documents are changing. For example, in TREC-3 the "concept" field of the queries was removed. These terms proved to be good ones for retrieval effectiveness in TREC-1 and TREC-2; thus, the TREC-3 task without them is a harder task than previous TRECs. The TREC-4 task was more difficult since so much more of the text was removed from the queries.

To examine both how much SMART has improved over the years of TREC and how much harder the TREC ad hoc tasks have gotten, we ran our eight TREC SMART systems against each of the eight TREC ad hoc tasks. Given the design of SMART, all procedures that have been used for some experiment utilizing SMART remain within SMART, they just remain unused as the focus of our SMART work changes. Only extremely rarely have there been changes that affect the backward compatibility of experiment results.

Table 13.1 gives results of running each system on each task, evaluated using MAP. Note that the indexing of the collections has changed slightly over the years (for example, hyphenation) so results may not be exactly what got reported in previous years. For simplicity, we only indexed each collection once per TREC task and kept the indexing constant across all TREC approaches. These results are all consistent with each other.

Comparing the table's columns gives an indication of how task difficulty has changed throughout the years, especially as queries have gotten shorter and shorter. In particular, the TREC-6 task seemed to be difficult for all participants, though nobody has a good explanation for it.

Comparing the table's rows gives an indication of how SMART has improved over the years. There were solid increases each year up through TREC-5, though note that a major part of the TREC-5 increase is due to the tuning of the TREC-4 algorithms

Table 13.1
Comparisons of SMART TREC-1 through TREC-8 ad hoc approaches

Methodology and run	TREC-1 task	TREC-2 task	TREC-3 task	TREC-4 task	TREC-5 short	TREC-6 desc	TREC-7 desc	TREC-8 ti-desc
TREC-1: ntc.ntc	.2442	.2615	.2099	.1533	.1048	.0997	.1137	.1412
TREC-2: lnc.ltc	.3056	.3344	.2828	.1762	.1111	.1125	.1258	.1846
TREC-3: lnc.ltc-Exp	.3400	.3512	.3219	.2124	.1287	.1242	.1679	.2102
TREC-4: Lnu.ltu-Exp	.3628	.3718	.3812	.2773	.1842	.1807	.2262	.2436
TREC-5: Exp-rerank	.3759	.3832	.3985	.3128	.2047	.1844	.2543	.2629
TREC-6: Rrk-clust	.3711	.3779	.4014	.3037	.2031	.1768	.2512	.2654
TREC-7: Rrk-clust	.3779	.3837	.4002	.3137	.2116	.1804	.2543	.2679
TREC-8: Lnb	.3563	.3623	.3647	.2836	.1997	.1857	.2282	.2608

rather than the TREC-5 approach. Since TREC-5, there's only been minor improvements in SMART.

Overall, SMART performance improved over 100 percent in MAP score during the first eight years of TREC. While MAP is an excellent measure for evaluating IR system performance for many reasons, it's not an intuitive measure. It is surprisingly difficult to come up with a measure of performance improvement that is meaningful, accurate, and intuitively understandable. One measure a bit more intuitive than MAP is the expected nonrelevant ratio (ENRR), which compares the number of nonrelevant documents retrieved before each relevant document given two retrieval runs.

The ENRR is calculated by the following algorithm, comparing the rankings from retrieval run A (the base run) and retrieval run B over T topics:

1. Construct a list L_A of all triples $\{t, r, n\}$ from the results of run A where:
- t is a topic number;
- r is the document id for a document relevant to topic t; and
- n is the number of nonrelevant documents retrieved before r in the retrieval ranking for topic t for run A.
2. Construct a similar list L_B of triples for run B.
3. Discard from L_A all triples of the form $\{t, r, 0\}$ where the corresponding triple in L_B (same t and r) also has an n value of 0.
4. Construct a list R of ratios n_A/n_B, one for each triple $\{t_A, r_A, n_A\}$ in L_A, where n_B is taken from the corresponding triple in L_B. If there is no corresponding triple in L_B, set n_B to be some large value (much larger than any entry in L_B) to give a very small value for the ratio. If n_B from the triple in L_B is 0, set n_B to .0001, to give a very large value for the ratio.
5. The ENRR (run A, run B) is the median value from the list R. Note that the ENRR is the median value and not the mean value.

When comparing the SMART TREC-1 run against the SMART TREC-8 run, the scores for the ENRR vary between 2.0 and 2.5 for the eight tasks. A score of 2.0 means for an average relevant document, you have to look through twice as many nonrelevant documents to find it using the TREC-1 version of SMART as opposed to the TREC-8 version of SMART. The ENRR gives intuitively satisfying support to the claim that SMART performance has doubled on the ad hoc task since the beginning of TREC.

Since SMART has been one of the leading research groups throughout this period, we can conclude that the IR research field as a whole has dramatically improved as well. We can also conclude that the improvement since TREC-6 or so has gotten much less. Other systems have caught up to SMART and surpassed it by 10 percent or so, but no system has been able to show solid improvement on the basic ad hoc task in recent years.

That claim applies even today. Systems have found applications in which they have shown great improvements—for example, question answering—but the performance on the basic information-seeking retrieval task has not changed much during the past seven years.

13.5   SMART and the TREC Routing Task

The routing task within TREC (described in detail in chapter 5, this volume) differs from the ad hoc task in that in addition to a topic, the systems are given a set of documents that are known to be relevant to the topic. The particular application that the routing task (and its filtering task successor) is aimed at is that of a user with a long-standing information need. The user wishes to see all new documents coming in that are relevant to their need and not see other new documents. Evaluation of the routing task is done in a batch form. There is a single collection of documents for which relevance information is known (the past documents already seen by the user) and a separate collection of documents with unknown relevance information (the new documents the user has not yet seen). Systems rank documents from the new collection for each topic, and the document ranking is evaluated using standard evaluation measures.

The routing task is much more important to general IR research than just the specific user application it is targeted at. It's the one environment where systems attempt to learn why a document is relevant and then apply what they learn to other documents. If systems can do the routing task well and synthesize the reasons why documents are relevant to a topic, then they've taken a major step toward understanding the topic and how to approach it. My personal opinion is that the next major advances in the IR ad hoc task will come from analysis and experimentation done on the routing task that determines how different topics should be handled differently.

13.5.1   TREC-1: Routing
We had no idea what to expect from the routing task in TREC-1 [6]. It was not something that was easy to duplicate on the small collections preceding TREC; the collec-

tions weren't large enough and didn't have enough relevant documents to be able to split them well. We decided to just use our normal Ide [15] relevance feedback algorithm to produce the routing query that was then run on the test collection. Each routing query was composed of the original query terms plus the best thirty terms from the relevant documents in the learning set. The weight of each routing query term was the sum of the weights in the original query plus the weights in the relevant documents minus the weight in a single nonrelevant document.

The effectiveness turned out reasonably, substantially above average, but not spectacularly so—about 20 percent less than the best routing system. The best routing system was from the University of Dortmund, and was based on SMART and actually run at Cornell, implementing Norbert Fuhr's feedback weights [13].

Overall, it was good to see that automatic systems were substantially better than manual ones at routing. By TREC-3, there were no groups even trying manual routing. But the SMART approach within TREC-1 had several problems, ranging from the choice of terms to the poor weighting of the original query terms. In addition, the training data were sketchy.

13.5.2   TREC-2: Routing

In TREC-2, there were many more training data available for each topic [2]. It was no longer appropriate to use the Ide relevance feedback algorithm because the original query would almost completely disappear. Instead, we chose Joseph Rocchio's feedback approach [16; 19], which we have used ever since. Expressed in vector-space terms, the final query vector is the initial query vector moved in toward the centroid of the relevant documents and away from the centroid of the nonrelevant documents.

$$Q_{\text{new}} = A * Q_{\text{old}} + B * \text{average\_wt\_in\_rel\_docs} - C * \text{average\_wt\_nonrel\_docs}$$

With Rocchio, there are now parameters that need to be estimated. Thus, before TREC-2, we split the training data in half and performed extensive testing of Rocchio parameter settings as well as choosing the number of terms to expand by. There was a core set of 158 training/test runs done.

One of the key ideas that we kept trying throughout the early TRECs is that topics are different, and we should be able to improve performance by using optimal approaches or parameters for each topic separately. In our retrospective training data experiments here, we were able to get over 10 percent improvement if we used the optimal setting on each topic.

There were two official runs. In the first, three hundred single terms were added along with fifty phrases. The values for A, B, and C were set to eight, sixteen, and four, respectively. In the second run, we chose parameters on a per topic basis, choosing the best of the 158 runs for each topic.

The algorithms performed well. The second run had the highest average among TREC-2 systems and for every topic was above the median score among systems. It was somewhat disappointing in that it actually only did less than 3 percent better than our first run, though. We were not able to get big improvements by altering parameters on a per topic basis.

One interesting fact that we'll come back to is that the massive expansion of 350 terms worked well for us, but other groups were expanding by significantly less, on the order of 20 terms. Massive expansion did not work as well for other groups.

13.5.3   TREC-3: Routing

Just as in TREC-2, for TREC-3 we did two official runs: the first run used the same fixed parameters as in TREC-2, and the second run attempted to vary the approach on a per topic basis [7]. Instead of just varying parameters of our Rocchio algorithm as in TREC-2, in TREC-3 we varied the entire algorithm, implementing seven different variants of expansion and weighting from several groups. All variants were again evaluated on half of the learning collection after learning on the other half.

Once again, the retrospective results on just the learning set did well, but the official run on the test set improved only mildly over the fixed parameter run. The topics that did improve, though, improved mostly by using a different Rocchio variant with greater expansion.

This was a disappointing result, and was the last time we tried varying routing approach by topic. Yet it should probably be looked at again in light of the changes that good document-length normalization make (as was done starting in the TREC-4 ad hoc task).

13.5.4   TREC-4: Routing

There were two major changes in TREC-4 routing as compared to TREC-3 [9]. The first was the document-length normalization as described previously in the ad hoc section. All of a sudden, our basic similarity function was no longer unduly biased toward short documents.

The second change was that a phase of dynamic feedback optimization (DFO) was added after our normal feedback query formulation. We had developed and presented DFO during the preceding SIGIR conference [5], and it had proven to be an effective weight-modification technique.

The DFO algorithm further tweaks the weights assigned each query term after Rocchio feedback, according to whether an increase or decrease in the weight will change effectiveness of the resulting query on the learning set of documents (those documents already seen and used in coming up with the feedback query). Several rounds of weight tweaking can be done; we used six in TREC-4, possibly increasing the weight of an expansion term by as much as a factor of five.

We decided to be conservative in the number of expansion terms being added, given the lack of experience with the interaction of the new document-weighting schemes, Rocchio feedback, and DFO. We expanded by only 60 terms instead of 330 terms.

Our basic result was good but not great. We did not get as much of an improvement due to DFO as we had been expecting. After the TREC-4 workshop, we performed some more experiments looking at proper parameter settings. We discovered if we increased the number of added terms back up to 330 and increased the negative weights due to terms occurring in nonrelevant documents, then we increased effectiveness by almost 15 percent. Note that with our previous weighting approach (cosine), we did not want to have high negative weights on nonrelevant terms since that tended to decrease the chance of long documents being retrieved.

Once again, this shows that all factors in a retrieval approach need to be balanced. A change in one factor will probably imply that the other factors need to be changed also.

13.5.5   TREC-5 and TREC-6: Routing

The changes in TREC-5 for routing [8] concentrated in three areas:

1. Adjust routing parameters to the more accurate weights developed in the TREC-4 ad hoc task.
2. Explore the concept of a "query zone." The properties of nonrelevant documents somehow related to the query (not having low similarity) are different from those of the general nonrelevant documents.
3. Examine co-occurrence of pairs of terms to see if pairs commonly occurring in the relevant documents can improve retrieval.

The query zone approach used for both routing and ad hoc in TREC-5 was an attempt to distinguish terms that are associated with the domain or general area of the query from terms that indicate relevance. The goal is to down weight those terms that occur in a large set of related documents, but not just in the relevant documents.

Pair co-occurrence has been looked at by the SMART project for at least the past twenty years, but it has never been successful. The major problem in the past has been weighting of the pairs of terms. In the routing task using DFO, initial weights are substantially less critical since DFO will adjust the weights according to whether the terms are useful in practice on the learning set.

Here is a summary of the steps used in routing, given a learning set L with judgments:

1. Create the initial vector query with ltu weighting from L.
2. Find the top five thousand documents to the query in L.
3. Expand the query with single terms and phrases occurring in more than 5 or 10 percent of the relevant documents.
4. Weight the expanded query using nonrelevant documents from the query zone (the top five thousand documents) within the Rocchio formula.

$$Q_{new} = 8 * Q_{old} + 64 * average\_wt\_in\_rel\_docs - 64 * average\_wt\_nonrel\_docs$$

5. Add pairs of co-occurring terms, one of which must be an original query term, occurring in more than 7 percent of the relevant documents.

6. Weight pairs according to Rocchio weights.

7. Restrict the expanded query to one hundred terms, ten phrases, and fifty pairs, using those concepts with the highest weights.

8. Perform a three-pass DFO to fine-tune the weights.

The approach above worked extremely well, within 1 percent of being the best routing run. It also performed 23 percent better than using the TREC-4 algorithm on the TREC-5 task—a notable improvement.

This algorithm was the final routing algorithm used by the SMART project for TREC tasks. It was used in TREC-6, performing well [4]. Then routing disappeared from TREC, to be replaced by the filtering task. In recent years, the filtering task has included a routing component, but the SMART project has not participated.

13.6 Confusion Track

The TREC-4 confusion track is another case where doing simple things on a solid basic approach works well [9]. In the confusion track, the characters in the document text were made artificially unreliable, attempting to mimic the degradation expected in a collection with, for example, massive OCR errors.

Our simple approach was query expansion by artificially degrading the query in the same manner in all possible ways. That included adding all terms that were the same as a query term except some letter has been added, deleted, or substituted. A typical twenty-term query might expand to over two thousand terms. Each of those terms might occur in only a few degraded documents.

Our results were quite good. At a text degradation level of 10 percent, which is pretty massive, there was only a retrieval degradation of about 20 percent. Our performance was solidly better than any other group.

13.7 Foreign Language

We participated in several foreign language TREC tracks, starting in TREC-3. We concentrated on the use of our basic retrieval algorithms, rather than on the features of any particular language. This was true even in tracks that would seem to require some knowledge of the language, such as the cross-lingual track of TREC-6, described later.

13.7.1 TREC-3, TREC-4, and TREC-5: Spanish

The TREC-3 Spanish track was the first time that the SMART project tried test collection retrieval on a foreign language [7]. SMART is a statistical system, with very little natural-language insights used. We spent a total of between five and six hours on the following:

- Making SMART eight-bit clean (to handle accents)
- Very simple stemming rules
- Constructing a list of the most common words to treat as stop words

Other than those simple changes, we used exactly the same procedures for Spanish as for the TREC-3 ad hoc runs. Our official results were extremely good, with average precision figures above .53. We feel those figures are artificially high due to the easy queries and low participation in the track. Nonetheless, it shows that a solid retrieval approach works quite well.

In TREC-4, again we duplicated our TREC-4 ad hoc runs in the TREC-4 Spanish track, but did no other work for the track [9]. Once again, we were one of the top three automatic Spanish groups, doing considerably better than many other groups that tried to incorporate more knowledge of Spanish into their system.

Again in TREC-5, we duplicated our TREC-5 ad hoc runs in the TREC-5 Spanish track, but did no other work for the track [8]. Once again, we were one of the top automatic Spanish groups.

In a nonofficial run, we examined whether the use of statistical phrases in Spanish would help. In both English and Spanish runs in TREC-5, phrases had basically no effect on the results. This was surprising considering the previous successes of phrases.

13.7.2   TREC-5 and TREC-6: Chinese

The Chinese language tracks in TREC-5 and TREC-6 were a true test of how well basic retrieval algorithms work without any linguistic understanding [8; 4]. There were no people involved at Cornell who understood anything about the Chinese language. We knew that Chinese characters occupied two bytes, and we could detect punctuation—that was the extent of our Chinese understanding.

There were no changes to SMART needed for Chinese other than thirty lines in the tokenizer to accommodate two-byte characters and two lines in the phraser to handle phrase components that are not separated by white space. Other than those two changes, we used our standard retrieval algorithms, including weighting and query expansion.

We performed exceptionally well in the TREC-5 results, being less than 1 percent away from the top run and doing better than the median system on every single topic. This was much better than many other systems that understood Chinese much better, but had a harder time adapting their algorithms to their understanding of Chinese.

Again in TREC-6 we did very well, being one of the top groups, though several other groups had comparable performances. Overall in TREC-6, the level of performance was at a remarkable .55 average precision. It's unclear whether this is because Chinese retrieval is inherently easier or because the task happened to have easy topics that year.

13.7.3   TREC-6: Cross-Lingual French

In TREC-6, we did both monolingual French runs and a simple English-topic, French-documents, cross-lingual run [4].

The monolingual French run was done with our usual minimalistic attention to the target language. A simple stemmer was implemented and frequently occurring words were added to a stop-word list. Our performance was quite good—one of the top French systems with a level of performance almost as good as our monolingual English run on the same basic topics.

The cross-lingual English-French run was more interesting. We had no expertise in foreign-language runs or resources, and no time to develop expertise, so we decided to treat French as being just misspelled English. There are a large number of cognates or almost cognates in the two languages; we hoped that with query expansion, we would hit enough of those cognates to get a reasonable performance.

We applied basically the same algorithms to the cross-lingual task as we did to the confusion track in TREC-4 (see above). We expanded the English query by adding French words that slightly differed from an English query term. We then ran the expanded query against the French document corpus, retrieving the top twenty documents. We used these documents as another expansion term source, just as we do in our standard English run.

We did amazingly well with this, on the face of it, ridiculous algorithm. On the original thirteen topics that had been judged by the time of the TREC-6 workshop, we were overall the best system by a substantial margin. Once the complete set of twenty-one topics was judged, we were still one of the top groups. The overall performance was about 50 percent of the monolingual performance, which was the general level of the best performance in TREC-6.

In more recent years, cross-lingual performance using various language resources has improved to be almost as good as monolingual performance, leaving our approach far behind. But there are still serious implications to the level of performance we were able to achieve. If you have a language without language resources, but you have a related language (as English and French are related) with language resources, then you may be able to get decent retrieval performance using our approach.

13.8   Conclusion

The SMART project has been an extremely active participant throughout most of the history of TREC—being one of the leaders in innovation and effectiveness. The overall philosophy of SMART has been that a solid statistical system without much dependency on linguistic information will be applicable to many information retrieval tasks and can serve as a springboard for quite complicated experimental investigations.

We've demonstrated that the entire IR experimental field has substantially improved since TREC has begun. This improvement is due to the collection resources provided by TREC and the substantial cross-fertilization between research groups as they work on common tasks.

The improvements in basic IR performance as evaluated in the TREC ad hoc task has dwindled in the last few years, though. There seems to be much room for improvement in the future, hopefully within the TREC framework.

References

[1] Buckley, C., Implementation of the SMART information retrieval system. Technical report 85-686. Computer Science Department, Cornell University, Ithaca, New York, May 1985.

[2] Buckley, C., J. Allan, and G. Salton. Automatic routing and ad-hoc retrieval using SMART: TREC-2. In *TREC-2*, 45–55.

[3] Buckley, C., M. Mitra, J. Walz, and C. Cardie. SMART high precision: TREC-7. In *TREC-7*, 285–298.

[4] Buckley, C., M. Mitra, J. Walz, and C. Cardie. Using clustering and SuperConcepts within SMART: TREC-6. In *TREC-6*, 107–124.

[5] Buckley, C., and G. Salton. Optimization of relevance feedback weights. In *Proceedings of the eighteenth annual international ACM SIGIR conference*, 351–357.

[6] Buckley, C., G. Salton, and J. Allan. Automatic retrieval with locality information using SMART. In *TREC-1*, 59–72.

[7] Buckley, C., G. Salton, J. Allan, and A. Singhal. Automatic query expansion using SMART: TREC-3. In *TREC-3*, 69–80.

[8] Buckley, C., A. Singhal, and M. Mitra. Using query zoning and correlation within SMART: TREC-5. In *TREC-5*, 105–118.

[9] Buckley, C., A. Singhal, M. Mitra, and G. Salton. New retrieval approaches using SMART: TREC-4. In *TREC-4*, 25–48.

[10] Buckley, C., and J. Walz. SMART in TREC-8. In *TREC-8*, 577–582.

[11] Efthimiadis, E., and P. Biron. UCLA–Okapi at TREC-2: Query expansion experiments. In *TREC-2*, 279–290.

[12] Evans, D., and R. Lefferts. Design and evaluation of the CLARIT-TREC-2 system. In *TREC-2*, 137–151.

[13] Fuhr, N., and C. Buckley. Optimizing document indexing and search term weighting based on probabilistic models. In *TREC-1*, 89–99.

[14] Hearst, M., J. Pedarson, P. Pirolli, H. Schutze, G. Grefenstette, and D. Hull. Xerox site report: Four TREC-4 tracks. In *TREC-4*, 97–120.

[15] Ide, E. New experiments in relevance feedback. In *The SMART retrieval system: Experiments in automatic document processing*, ed. G. Salton, 337–354. Englewood Cliffs, NJ: Prentice Hall, 1971.

[16] Rocchio, J. J. Relevance feedback in information retrieval. In *The SMART retrieval system: Experiments in automatic document processing*, ed. G. Salton, 313–323. Englewood Cliffs, NJ: Prentice Hall, 1971.

[17] Salton, G. *Automatic text processing: The transformation, analysis, and retrieval of information by computer*. Reading, MA: Addison-Wesley Publishing Co., 1989.

[18] Salton, G. Developments in automatic text retrieval. *Science* 253 (August 1991): 974–980.

[19] Salton, G., and C. Buckley. Improving retrieval performance by relevance feedback. *Journal of the American Society for Information Science* 41, no. 4 (1990): 288–297.

[20] Salton, G., and C. Buckley. Term-weighting approaches in automatic text retrieval. *Information Processing and Management* 24, no. 5 (1988): 513–523.

[21] Singhal, A., C. Buckley, and M. Mitra. Pivoted document length normalization. In *Proceedings of the nineteenth annual international ACM SIGIR conference*, 21–29.

14 Ten Years of Ad Hoc Retrieval at TREC Using PIRCS
Kui-Lam Kwok

14.1 Introduction

It is generally recognized that when a user searches for documents to satisfy information needs, one has several possible operational modes such as browsing, ad hoc, interactive, routing/filtering retrieval, and so on. Browsing (Campos and de Figuerriedo 2001; Cove and Walsh 1988) generally means probing a store of documents in a random or explorative fashion, and involves serendipity to discover what may be of interest. This does work sometimes, but it would be quite difficult to evaluate in a controlled fashion. This has not been studied in TREC, although the other modes were explored. Ad hoc is the one-shot retrieval where a user issues an unrehearsed query against a static document collection (see chapter 4, this volume). The interactive mode may be viewed as the multiple-cycle version of ad hoc with presentation and feedback techniques (see chapter 6). This involves the active participation of users in modifying their query for each cycle by consulting retrieved results from the target collection (or perhaps including a thesaurus) to try to satisfy needs. These are classified as "pull" operations. On the other hand, routing/filtering involves more investment at the beginning in designing an effective profile for a user's needs (see chapter 5). After that, the system would automatically alert the user of interesting items in a stream of incoming documents. This is a "push" operation (Cerami 1998; Garfield 2001) in that the user is generally inert and the profile is generally static, except for periodic adjustment manually when results become unsatisfactory. In theory, automatic adaptive filtering would delegate the profile adjustment operation to the machine as well.

One-shot ad hoc retrieval is considered to be the fundamental operation in IR. Improving it can also mean improvements in other retrieval modes and downstream processing such as question answering, extraction, and so forth. In this chapter, I concentrate on the approaches and the results of ad hoc experiments—including monolingual English, Chinese, and English-Chinese cross-language—based on the Probabilistic Indexing and Retrieval-Components-System (PIRCS).

14.2 Ad Hoc Retrieval

Ad hoc retrieval may be viewed as a user with a need who tries to obtain the right documents to satisfy this information need from a static document collection. Traditionally, this is the function of a library. Nowadays, a better example may be a user issuing a search question over the Web. It is probably the most difficult retrieval mode because the system has no prior knowledge of what kind of query content is issued or what type of document the user wants. During retrieval, the only clue the system has is the query statement formed by the user to represent his needs. This statement may be composed carefully or carelessly. Often, it is quite short—one or two words only, according to Web statistics. (If a user has their default interests, search history, and so on, stored as a profile, the system could employ this profile to augment the current query statement for a more personalized service [see, for example, Pitkow et al. 2002]. This enhancement to an IR system is not considered in this chapter.)

Over the past forty to fifty years of IR research, investigators have proposed various models as well as techniques that may enhance ad hoc retrieval effectiveness. We call the latter "factors that may influence ad hoc results." Determining what works and what doesn't work becomes the crucial objective for this difficult ad hoc retrieval environment. Although there were several theoretical models for retrieval proposed in the past, they require many approximations to be used in real environments. The experimental evaluation of retrieval results therefore becomes unavoidable. TREC has become the standard practice for these evaluations (see chapter 1).

The importance of the TREC ad hoc task is that it provides:

- Realistic large-scale collections of two gigabytes or more for participants to work with
- A blind environment where results are unknown during experimentation
- A uniform manual relevance judgment for queries against these collections
- The central and comparable evaluation of results for all participants
- A timely platform for retrieval evaluation just when Internet searching becomes popular

After ten years, TREC is still the premier conference for evaluating various types of retrieval-related tasks from the Web or document collections. The City University of New York has participated in the ad hoc track every year (and most of the routing/filtering experiments) using its PIRCS. Except for TREC-1 when our resources limited us to the smaller-scale category B tasks, the other years all involved the standard category A large-scale experiments. My experience and thoughts during these ten years with the City University group will form the content of this chapter.

14.3 PIRCS

The basis of my participation in TREC involves PIRCS (for a description of this system, see Kwok 1995, 2000). For completeness, I will summarize the salient properties of PIRCS and also define the meaning of some symbols for later use. Given a query q and a document d from a collection, the basic PIRCS assigns retrieval status value (RSV) for d in two ways:

$$\text{document focused: } \text{RSV}d(q,d) = \Sigma_k S(q_k/L_q) * w_{dk} \tag{1}$$

$$\text{query focused: } \quad \text{RSV}q(q,d) = \Sigma_k S'(d_k/L_d) * w_{qk} \tag{2}$$

Here, q_k and d_k are the within-item (query or document) frequency of term k, L_q and L_d are the lengths of the respective item, and $S(.)$ and $S'(.)$ (the two need not be the same) are sigmoid functions that flatten variation at the low and high end of the argument value. Also,

$$w_{dk} = \log[d_k/(L_d - d_k) * (N_w - L_d - F_k + d_k)/(F_k - d_k)] \qquad (3)$$

$$w_{qk} = \log[q_k/(L_q - q_k) * (N_w - F_k)/F_k] \qquad (4)$$

Here, N_w is the total number of content tokens in the collection, and $F_k = \Sigma_j d_j$ is the collection frequency of term k. If we use x_j to count only the presence and absence of a term in a document as one or zero (ignoring frequency), then the document frequency of term k is $D_k = \Sigma_j x_j$.

The RSV formulas are obtained based on the probabilistic retrieval considerations (Robertson and Sparck Jones 1976) and the following assumptions:

- Each item (document or query) is constituted from conceptual components that are independent, and each can be approximated by a content term of the item.
- The totality of document components defines a universe from which usage statistics of the concepts can be obtained.
- Each set of conceptual components of an item is self-relevant to the item.

If we temporarily imagine each item (document or query) as a "query" to retrieve against the collection of components, the last assumption automatically provides a relevant component set and an irrelevant set (approximated as the rest of the universe) for this "query" even at the initial stage when no feedback information is available. This approach allows us to define the weight of the conceptual features for each item (w_{dk} and w_{qk}) using the probabilistic retrieval formalism. When an actual query q is present to retrieve against the collection, the query-focused approach considers each conceptual component of d to pick up the corresponding weighted feature in q, summed and averaged over all the L_d document components. This results in RSVq(d). Analogously, the document-focused approach considers each component of q to pick up the corresponding weighted feature in a document, summed and averaged over the L_q components. In practice, a combination of these two RSVs,

$$\mathrm{RSV}(q, d) = \alpha * \mathrm{RSV}d(q, d) + (1 - \alpha) * \mathrm{RSV}q(q, d) \qquad (5)$$

(α is a constant chosen as 0.5 to 0.7), has been found to be more stable and often more effective than each of them alone, and is the default formula. The advantage of PIRCS is that it can bootstrap itself (that is, it defines weights for features) even at the initial stage without relevance information and can account naturally for nonbinary features in the probabilistic retrieval framework. It has been shown that the document-focused

RSVd is similar to that of a simple language model for IR (see chapter 16, this volume; Kwok 2000). Thus, PIRCS' approach can also be viewed as combining probabilistic retrieval with a language model and is the basis of our PIRCS ranking formula.

14.4 Factors Influencing Ad Hoc Retrieval

In addition to a retrieval model, there are other heuristic considerations based on empirical studies that may lead to better retrieval results on average. Many such methods and techniques—listed in the following subsections—have been employed by PIRCS. These factors may or may not work depending on the query set and the collection. There is usually no theoretical basis that guides the choice of parameters. They may also work because of synergy among the factors.

14.4.1 Factors Related to Representation

Manual and Statistical Stop-Word Removal   Generally, stop words are function words such as "the," "of," and "in," needed to compose a document into a grammatical, readable form. They may be quite important in carrying relationship semantics for words in a sentence. For example, "library science" is quite different from "library of science." In this bag-of-words approach without relationship information, however, stop words are considered to be noncontent bearing and are eliminated for use as representation features. The choice of stop words is not standard, though. Most research systems use a list of a few hundred; some commercial systems may use only a few stop words (Fox 1992).

PIRCS employs a list of about six hundred such stop words. In addition, words with too low or too high document frequencies—called "statistical stop words" in our work—are also eliminated in both documents and queries. Low document frequency words ($D_k < lo$, or in our system $lo = 3$) are either typographic errors or too rare to affect the average results, while ones with $D_k > hi$ would not be sufficiently discriminative for retrieval. In contrast to recommendations such as those offered in the *Introduction to Modern Information Retrieval* (Salton and McGill 1983), we found that to obtain good retrieval (especially for short queries), the high threshold hi needs to be set quite high, removing only a few words, as discussed in section 14.5.2 below. Yet eliminating high- and low-frequency words can bring more efficiency to a retrieval system in terms of time and space issues.

Word Stemming   Stemming may be viewed as having the effect of consulting a simple thesaurus without possessing one. Words like "computation," "computers," "compute," and "computing," irrespective of their parts of speech, are regarded as synonymous and treated as one single concept, "compute." We implemented Martin Porter's stemming algorithm (1980) in PIRCS. There are also studies on whether stemming brings about improvements in effectiveness (Harman 1991; Hull 1996). One can always find specific examples in which stemming should not be performed, but on average it appears to help. Moreover, it can lead to substantial savings in dictionary size.

Stop Phrases and "Not" Sentences in Queries   In long queries, one may encounter introductory phrases like "A relevant document would/should ..." or "To be relevant, a document must ..." that lead toward descriptions of conditions of relevance. These phrases are removed, as they have nothing to do with the information needs of the user and constitute noise for retrieval. In a similar vein, queries may also contain sentences describing what the user does not want, such as "Documents containing ... are not relevant (irrelevant)." In PIRCS, preprocessing of queries will remove such negation sentences as well. Empirically, our experience is that stop phrases are useful and often lead to small (1 to 3 percent) improvements in effectiveness. However it is not so clear-cut for removing "not" sentences since sometimes the negation sentences can contain useful related terms to augment the positive content terms. This is especially true for Chinese-language retrieval experiments.

Two-Word Phrases   To overcome the criticism of the simplicity of the bag-of-words approach, many systems including ours augment single-word representation by adjacent two-word phrases. These phrases may be compiled manually or obtained from a collection by enumerating all bigrams and keeping only those with a frequency above a set threshold. In PIRCS, we have a manually compiled phrase list of about 600 entries. These are augmented by an automatic list of about a 120,000 entries derived from newspaper collections—the *Wall Street Journal*, the Associated Press, and the *San Jose Mercury News*. Two-word phrases are much more specific than single words. Employing them also leads to longer query representation for very short queries. For simplicity, we regard them as single words for indexing. Yet because their phrase counts are quite different from words, their evaluated weights are reduced by a factor such as 0.5. We have found these phrases to be useful, especially for very short queries.

Subdocument Breakup   Previous to TREC, evaluated collections for IR experimentation (such as CACM, MED, CISI, NPL) contained abstracts or summaries typically of about a paragraph. In TREC, full-text documents are used. These documents can vary from a few words to over one megabyte in size. Some type of length normalization is needed in order to make statistical scoring more comparable between retrieval units. PIRCS employs subdocuments as retrieval units. Subdocuments are defined simply as nonoverlapping, contiguous sections of text of size n that ends on a paragraph boundary. We have variously used n as 360 words, 550 words, or 3,000 bytes. Subdocuments give more focused output with respect to a query; otherwise, a long document might have to be presented to the user as an answer. More important, subdocuments represent the more relevant portion of a long document. They can be more precise for pseudorelevance feedback. Our TREC-2 experiments (Kwok and Grunfeld 1994) showed that breaking documents into subdocuments is useful for long, verbose documents such as the *Federal Register*, and has small effects for those of normal sizes.

14.4.2 Factors Related to Retrieval

Aggregation of Subdocument RSVs   In PIRCS, subdocuments are ranked as retrieval units and for display. For evaluation, we further scan the retrieval list for subdocuments of the same document and aggregate their RSVs into a whole document RSV. Each subdocument in our system is enumerated with the original identification plus a two-character field. In aggregating the RSVs, we limit ourselves to the first document identification (with RSV_1) plus at most two-nearest, later-ranked subdocuments of the same identification (with RSV_2 and RSV_3) using the formula $RSV = RSV_1 + 0.25 * RSV_2 + 0.1 * RSV_3$. The rationale for doing this is that if several sections (subdocuments) of the same document are found to have a high RSV, the whole document should be influenced. This is a compromise of not aggregating or capturing all subdocuments (which may not be a good idea). This leads to a readjusting of the ranked list and has been found to improve MAP. This strategy has been employed in all of our experiments since TREC-2. Other researchers have dealt with varying document lengths such as the Okapi system (Robertson and Walker 1994) or the pivoted length normalization method (Singhal, Buckley, and Mitra 1996).

Term Weighting for Short Queries   Throughout the history of IR, it has been well-known that term weighting helps to discriminate among useful and less useful terms, and plays an important role for improving retrieval effectiveness (Salton and Buckley 1988). These term weights are usually defined using a retrieval model (such as vector, probabilistic, or language models), and are based on the occurrence statistics of terms in documents or queries and a collection. Our PIRCS model discussed in section 14.3 has its special formula for these weights. For the document-focused approach, totaling these weights in a document defines its relevance property and eventually reflects its ranked position in a retrieval list. One of the factors in this term weighting depends on its within-query frequency and query length—namely, $S(q_k/L_q)$ for term k of query q. This is reasonable for a long query where there is some variation of term frequency among terms. In a short item such as a query with a few words, q_k equals one for all terms and therefore is not useful for differentiating them.

Avtf weighting for short-query terms is a method where we try to restore some discrimination among these terms. Although there is no opportunity for a user to show which term is more important in a short query, one may look at the collection to deduce such information. This is the average term frequency (Kwok 1996) defined by F_k/D_k. This means that if a document uses this term k, then on average one would observe this much usage term frequency. The ratio F_k/D_k is the same as the average burstiness B1 formula that Slava Katz (1996) introduced to characterize content phrase behavior in texts, with B1 identified as "a combined measure of a word's propensity to be used topically.... [This] makes any phrase having B1 close to 1 a suspect, as far its terminological status is concerned" (p. 34). In reality, based on some experimentation, we have found the following formula more useful as the q_k factor for short-query terms:

$$\text{avtf} = (F_k/D_k)^a/\log\max(\text{constant}, D_k).$$

The rationale for this formula is that sometimes a widespread term with high document frequency D_k may also repeat more often within documents, giving it a high value for F_k/D_k. The log factor will act to depress these terms. The exponent $a \geq 1$ further allows a trade-off between the two effects.

Two-Stage Retrieval and Pseudorelevance Feedback   One of the most important advances during TREC has been the improvement of ad hoc retrieval using pseudorelevance feedback. This had been proposed before (Attar and Fraenkel 1977), but it was not found to be useful for the small abstract-based collections of the time. The idea behind pseudorelevance feedback is to employ a user's query statement to perform an initial retrieval and output n top-ranked documents. This set of documents is considered to define the topical domain of the query and is employed for relevance feedback as if all n of them have been judged relevant by the user. These feedback documents help to expand the initial query by m terms as well as reweigh the terms based on the retrieval model. A second retrieval is then performed using the expanded query, and the resultant ranked list of documents constitutes the answer. First used during TREC-2 (Evans and Lefferts 1994), pseudorelevance feedback has been shown time and time again in TREC experiments to improve retrieval effectiveness compared to the initial retrieval, sometimes by a large factor of 50 percent or more. This is true despite uncertainty concerning the parameters n and m. PIRCS has employed this strategy after TREC-2 and normally set n to between ten and forty, and m to between twenty and one hundred. The cost incurred is computer time to do a second retrieval with a long, expanded query. No user time or effort is involved.

If the user had really evaluated this set of n top-ranked documents from the initial retrieval, possibly only n' (which may be zero) of these n documents would have been judged relevant. The other set $n - n'$ would have contributed noise to the feedback operation. For some queries, the set $n - n'$ is truly irrelevant, and will cause topic drift (Mitra, Singhal, and Buckley 1998) and lead to a worse second retrieval. In many cases, however, even though the set $n - n'$ may not be directly relevant, it is sufficiently related to the topic so that the expanded query terms it helps to define are still useful and result in better second-stage retrieval.

Collection Enrichment   The pseudorelevance feedback described in the previous subsection can improve MAP in a second-stage retrieval, but not for all queries. As a rule of thumb, about two-thirds of a query set would be favorably affected. Pseudorelevance feedback works only if the n top-ranked documents chosen for feedback from an initial retrieval have a high percentage of relevant or closely related documents. For some queries, there are few good documents in the top-ranked ones—either because the original query is vague or badly constructed, or because there are genuinely few relevant documents in the collection for this query. Since we do not know how to set n, including setting $n =$ zero, we may run into problems for certain queries.

Collection enrichment (Kwok and Chan 1998) is a technique that tries to remedy this situation. Given a target collection, another collection of related content, time period, and similar genre is found, and it is added to the target for the first retrieval. The rationale is that enlarging the collection increases the probability that one will find documents sharing some common terms with the query as well as relevant to it. These documents would become part of the n top-ranked documents, thus enriching the signal-to-noise ratio in this set for finding good terms for query expansion. This is similar to pretranslation query expansion in cross-language retrieval (see section 14.6.2) where an external collection is used to suggest additional query terms to help hedge against translation failures.

Retrieved Document Local Statistics   In deriving probabilistic term-weight formulas such as PIRCSs (see section 14.3), a crucial requirement is that one has a sample of both a relevant set and an irrelevant set. Since most documents (and their components) in a large collection are irrelevant to a query, it is a good assumption to take the whole universe as the irrelevant sample and evaluate weights accordingly. This was done in section 14.3 above. Yet one may do better after an initial retrieval when the top-ranked one thousand documents for a query, for example, become available. These one thousand top-ranked documents share some common terms with, and are therefore related to, the query. In pseudorelevance feedback, we assumed that the top n was relevant. Likewise, one could reasonably assume that the bottom n' (for example, $n' = $ five hundred) is irrelevant. The technique of retrieved document local statistics (Singhal, Mitra, and Buckley 1997; Kwok and Chan 1998) means using this bottom n' set as the irrelevant set, and reevaluating term weights and RSV for this retrieved set of one thousand. The idea is that whole universe statistics for approximating the irrelevant part of term weights is reasonable during first-stage retrieval. During second-stage retrieval, it may be better to use a more related local irrelevant set to do this estimation.

Reranking of Retrieval List   The bag-of-words approach adopted by most IR systems has been criticized as not sufficiently accurate because the relationships of words that encode more precise concepts are ignored. On the other hand, the indexing and normalization of all possible concepts in free text documents, and resolving concepts in a query with those in a collection, seems to be a task not yet possible. A trade-off approach is to do document reranking after retrieval. The idea is to perform more detailed NLP processing on a subset of the n top-ranked documents, and promote those that have better conceptual matching or more closely satisfy the query's requirements—and thus may result in better precision for the top-ranked set. Reranking can be done at the initial retrieval stage to obtain a better pseudorelevance feedback set of the top n, and hence may favorably affect the second-stage retrieval. It can be performed after the second-stage retrieval to report higher precision results in the top-ranked documents.

We have applied reranking by matching query phrases with words occurring within small text windows from top-ranked documents. Many contingencies need to be considered (Kwok 2000; our TREC-7 report). Some of these include the text window size, out-of-order word matching, partial phrase matching, multiple matching in a sentence or document, the scale of matching values, and the relationship between retrieval RSV and phrase-matching values. Another knotty problem is the matching of similar concepts expressed by different surface terms.

Combination of Retrieval Lists   One could produce multiple retrieval ranked lists from one query and a collection. Circumstances where multiple lists may arise include retrieval using different indexing methods, multiple retrieval models, variations of parameter settings within a model, different sections of the same query or document, and others. Each list ranks documents differently with different evidence. A simple way to account for two retrieval lists with RSV_1 and RSV_2 is by linear combination:

$$RSV(d_i) = a * RSV_1(d_i) + (1 - a) * RSV_2(d_i), \quad 0 <= a <= 1.$$

If relevant documents occur in these lists more consistently in early positions while irrelevant ones occur more randomly, the above combination will tend to promote relevant ones toward the top-ranked positions and will result in a more effective retrieval than the individual component lists.

14.5   Summary of English Ad Hoc Retrieval

Table 14.1 lists the techniques discussed in section 14.4 in a slightly different way, and gives a chronological order of when which technique was used for which TREC year of our submissions and some of the parameter values. For example, under "query size" for TREC-4, S: 6.2 means short queries were used, averaging 6.2 terms per query. TREC-1 experiments were category B and not shown. This table can be coordinated with figures 14.1–14.4, where our experimental results are tabulated. Each year, the retrieval environment may have some special characteristics. For example, TREC-2 topics have the concept section with precise terminology while later ones do not. In TREC-6, the definition section of a topic (which are used to derive short queries) may not contain words from the title section. Readers should consult chapter 2, this volume, for these properties.

14.5.1   Results Submitted with PIRCS

We follow TREC convention to use MAP as a measure of retrieval effectiveness. Figure 14.1 contains a plot of our ad hoc *blind* results that were submitted over the years. All experiments were automatic unless otherwise indicated. The graph for "long" queries covers all years except TREC-4, which experimented only with "short" queries. We take short to mean four to about ten terms in a query after stop-word removal and stemming, typically coming from the description section of a TREC topic. "Very-short" means an average of one to four terms, coming from the title section only. These shorter queries were given more emphasis since TREC-4. (It should be mentioned

Table 14.1
Factors affecting ad hoc retrieval

TREC → / Year	2 / 1993	3 / 1994	4 / 1995	5 / 1996	6 / 1997	7 / 1998	8 / 1999	9 / 2000	10 / 2001
Query set	101–150	151–200	202–250	251–300	301–350	351–400	401–450	451–500	501–550
Query size (L = long, S = short, VS = very short)	L + concept	L	S: 6.2	L: 22.0 S: 6.3	L: 21.3 *S: 7.1 VS: 2.6	L: 17.2 S: 7.0 VS: 2.6	L: 12.8 S: 6.1 VS: 2.5	L: 9.1 S: 5.3 VS: 2.2	VS: 3.4
Document genre	Newspaper, magazine ———→							Web	Web
Stop-word removal	Performed for all years ———→								
Porter's stemming	Performed for all years ———→								
Stop phrases; "not relevant" sentence removal	Performed in queries for all years ———→								
Two-word phrases	14K	56K	56K	80K	125K	125K	125K	125K	125K
Subdocument breakup	360W	550W	550W	550W	550W	550W	550W	3KB	3KB
First retrieval									
Special weight				avtf	avtf	avtf	avtf	avtf	
Collection enrichment					√	√	√	√	
Query term variety				√		√	√		
Local term statistics						√	√		
Rerank					S, VS	L	L		
Second retrieval									
PRF parameters	no	6d30t	40d50t	40d50t	40d60t	24d40t	24d60t	L: 24d60t S: 24d30t	L: 24d60t VS: 24d30t
Rerank					L				
Retrieval list combination						S: t + td L: td + a	S: t + td L: td + a		

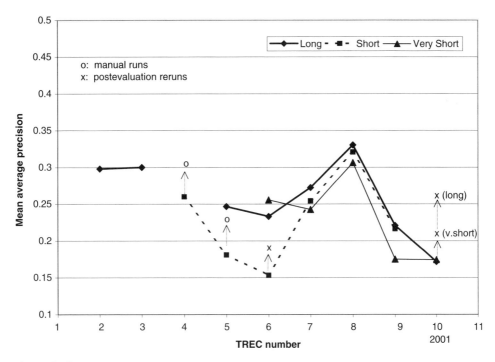

Figure 14.1
PIRCS ad hoc effectiveness: A decade of experimentation with varying TREC environment

that we have labeled short queries as "medium-length queries" and very short queries as "short queries" in our yearly TREC papers.) The following are some salient observations.

TREC-2 and TREC-3 results appear quite similar with a MAP value of about 0.3. In fact, TREC-3 represents major improvements because long queries that year had no concept section. Our TREC-3 improvement was due to the use of pseudorelevance feedback with limited query expansion.

TREC-4 and TREC-5 witnessed our manual ad hoc (in addition to automatic) experiments. Our manual procedures were simple: words in short queries were selected manually for double weighting by repeating them. This operation is fast and not burdensome. Additionally, one to three words related to a topic—often chosen from the other sections of a topic—were manually inserted. These operations were quite successful. Their MAP values, depicted as "o" in figure 14.1, are 18 to 40 percent better than the automatic short query results. The manual TREC-5 MAP value, however, was still below that of the automatic long query by about 7 percent (0.2298 versus 0.2466), showing the effectiveness of more user-composed wordings.

TREC-6–8 made use of practically the same collections for retrieval (the *Congressional Record* collection was used in TREC-6 only), but different query sets. Except for

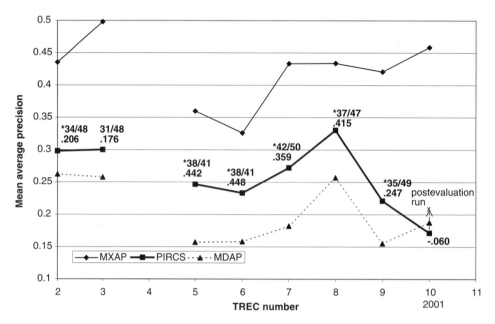

Figure 14.2
Long queries effectiveness: PIRCS versus overall performance (see section 14.5.2 for x:y and G values attached to each point)

TREC-6, long queries consistently provided better results than shorter ones in MAP values. TREC-6 had several topics with very precise single-word title sections such as "hydroponics" (#312), "agoraphobia" (#348), and so on. They formed the very short queries and provided the best MAP, and any terms added to define longer queries served only as noise to depress results. Short queries derived from the definition section in that year sometimes lacked the title words. This coupled with a run error led to exceptionally bad results. After correcting the error, MAP for short queries in our TREC-6 would have been 0.1928 (shown as "*x*") instead of the 0.1533 plotted.

In TREC-8, retrieval list combination was studied. For example, the short query result was the combination of very short (*t*) and a run that used both title and description sections (*td*) to form queries. The long query result was the combination of a run with all sections (*a*) as query and the (*td*) run. The former combination led to 6 percent and the latter 2 percent improvement compared with no combination.

For TREC-9 and TREC 2001, the target collections were changed to ten gigabytes of noisy Web pages—a five-fold size increase compared to previous news collections. We handled this by removing over 40 percent of the data from the collection such as HTML tags, heading and paragraph attributes, consecutive strings of characters over thirty-two bytes long, and so forth. Otherwise, the methodology followed that of TREC-8. The very short query result included seven queries with zero MAP value. These

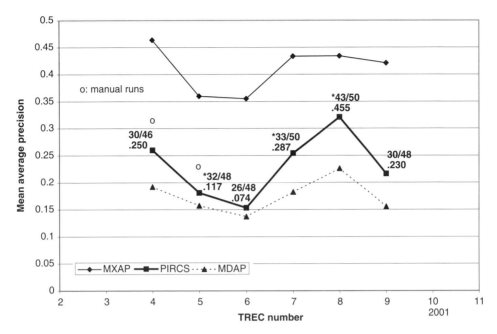

Figure 14.3
Short queries ad hoc effectiveness: PIRCS versus overall performance (see section 14.5.2 for x:y and G values attached to each point)

were due to three misspelled single-word titles (our system has no spell-checking), and other topics having only high-frequency words that we thresholded out (leaving empty queries). Adding other sections of the topic to form short and long queries removed this difficulty and improved results by 24 percent (MAP values of ~0.22 versus 0.1750 for very short). This points to the importance of spelling checks for operational systems.

The TREC 2001 Web results were not up to expectation. Our system had used a Zipf threshold (180,000) to screen out too many high-frequency terms. In postevaluation experimentation with a much higher Zipf threshold of 500,000, MAP values improved to .2039 for very short queries and .2546 for long based on this change (shown as *x* in figure 14.1). It seems the basic PIRCS approach still works for Web pages.

A general observation is that longer queries provide better MAPs most of the time (except for highly specific single-word topics).

14.5.2 Comparing PIRCS Retrieval with Overall Results
How does PIRCS performance compare with other systems? We choose two overall bases as references for comparison with our results. They are the mean of median

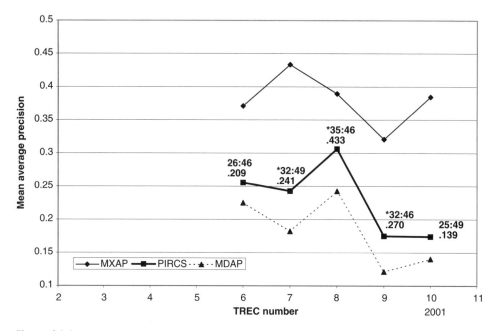

Figure 14.4
Very short queries ad hoc effectiveness: PIRCS versus overall performance (see section 14.5.2
for x:y and G values attached to each point)

average precision (MDAP) and the mean of maximum average precision (MXAP).
MDAP is obtained by averaging over all topics the median precision values (among all
participants) of each topic. This is in contrast to MAP, which refers to the mean average precision of all topics for one participant. MXAP would be the mean precision
obtained by a hypothetical "maxi-system" that returns the top average precision of
every topic. This is normally unattainable because it assumes a demon exists that
chooses correctly the top result among all systems for each query before evaluation is
known. (It is attainable only if one's system returns top performance for all queries.)
MXAP represents the best that can be achieved using the collective wisdom of all participants. These are plotted in figures 14.2–14.4 for long, short, and very short queries,
respectively.

For each year, two values are attached and displayed for a PIRCS's run. One
value compares our result with the median using the pair $x:y$, where x is the number
of topics better than, and y is the number of topics having average precision different
from, the median. This allows a two-tail sign test with respect to the median, and an
$^*x:y$ denotes those cases where the test is significant at the 5 percent level. Another
measure is G, the percentage of the gap between MDAP and the maximum MXAP
that this run has achieved that year, and shows how much our result closes onto the
maxi-system. $G > 0$ means it is above median. If many topics are above median, the

MAP would have a higher G value. This measure often can give an idea of how good that run was relative to others. It does not always work, especially with short and very short query experiments. One reason is because the bases available may not be obtained separately for each query length type; another is that in earlier years, manual results were also mixed in, which inflated the bases.

Using figure 14.2 long queries for discussion, it seems that the median precision (dashed) line may capture the notion of how difficult that year's task was with respect to the technologies employed. For example, we may consider that TREC-5 (median MAP ~ 0.16) was more difficult than TREC-2 or TREC-3 (median MAP ~ 0.26). The TREC-5 queries were much less elaborate than those of TREC-2 and TREC-3. From TREC-6–8, the target collection was stable and the median improved sequentially each year. This suggests that participants successively tuned their systems to meet the difficulty. TREC-9 used the new WT10g data, and the learning process started all over again. We observe that when a run attains a G value of about 40 percent or more (when the bases are correctly formed), it indicates good results close to or at the top among participants for that year. For example, our TREC-5 ($G = .442$), TREC-6 (.448), and TREC-8 (.415) results were of this nature. TREC-3 had a much better result than that implied by $G = .176$. This may be because the median and maximum values included many better-performing manual systems and shifted both bases up, depressing the G value comparison.

For short queries in figure 14.3, the G values for TREC-4 and TREC-5 were low also because the bases included results of manual runs or a mixture of query lengths. The TREC-4 and TREC-8 results shown were among the top. Similarly, figure 14.4 shows very short query comparisons. For TREC-6, the bases were correctly formed using very short query runs. Our MAP was among the top, but this was not reflected by the $x{:}y$ ratio or the G value. The TREC-6 very short query had several quite specific queries (some single word) with very high MAP. It seems our run behaved well with these specific queries, but overall only slightly above median. The G value of 0.209 and $x{:}y$ ratio 26:46 appear to convey this additional information. Since TREC-2, and except for the long query result of TREC 2001, our ten years' participation had above median performance and many were significantly better than median.

14.6   Summary of Chinese Ad Hoc and English-Chinese CLIR

NIST also initiated foreign-language retrieval experiments (see chapter 7, this volume), including TREC-5 and TREC-6 Chinese ad hoc and TREC-9 English-Chinese cross-language, in which we also participated. The former involved special processing for the Chinese language, and the latter required additional translation of English queries to Chinese, or Chinese documents to English. Afterward, retrieval was similar to monolingual ad hoc. The following subsections summarize our investigations in these tasks.

14.6.1   Monolingual Chinese Ad Hoc Retrieval
Chinese written text consists of strings of consecutive characters separated by punctuation, and does not have word boundaries. Word segmentation therefore seems crucial

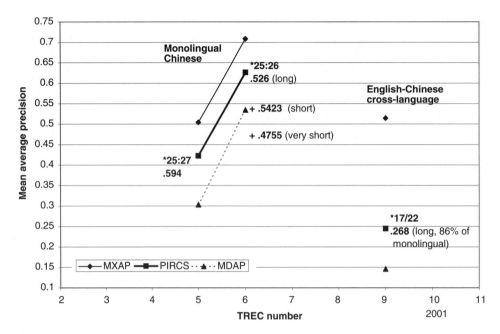

Figure 14.5
Chinese retrieval and CLIR: PIRCS versus overall performance (see section 14.5.2 for x:y and G values attached to each point)

to define content terms to be indexed for retrieval (see, for example, Sproat and Shih 1991; Wu and Tseng 1995; Gao et al. 2002). Word segmentation often results in long words (four or more characters, depending on the segmentation dictionary, for example). It is often ambiguous as to whether a long Chinese string is a word or a phrase. Longer words in a document may also be expressed as shorter or abbreviated versions in queries, which would raise the knotty issue of partial matching between index terms. Our approach to Chinese indexing for retrieval is based on the following assumptions:

1. Short words (two or three characters and four character names) are good indexing features for retrieval.
2. Segmentation consistency is as important as segmentation accuracy.
3. Single characters are also useful as index terms and may ameliorate segmentation errors.

Assumption 2 considers indexing features for retrieval rather than human understanding. So long as the query and document texts are segmented consistently, the resulting index terms will bring about matching between query and document. To further guard against "no match," assumption 3 considers using single characters as well. This leads to our "short word with single character" indexing based on an approximate segmentation methodology.

Our preprocessing of Chinese documents and queries involves the following steps:

1. Start with a small seed segmentation dictionary of short words.
2. Segment incoming texts using maximum forward matching.
3. Leftover unsegmented long strings are segmented by approximate rules.
4. Resulting index terms greater than a preset occurrence frequency threshold define new entries in a segmentation dictionary.
5. Repeat step 1 until there is no change.

For example, starting with a segmentation dictionary of about two thousand entries in TREC-5 and using one iteration, a final dictionary size of sixteen thousand was obtained. In TREC-6, we started with a much larger initial dictionary of approximately twenty-seven thousand and ended up with a final one of about forty-three thousand.

As verification that assumption 2 is reasonable, we also experimented in TREC-6 using consecutive overlapping bigrams as indexing units (see also Kwok 1997; Chen et al. 1997). This process is simple and does not need a segmentation dictionary. Over 70 percent of Chinese words are two characters in length. Bigram indexing will therefore cover these Chinese words, (as well as many spurious ones), exhaustively and correctly. Longer words will be broken up into multiple bigrams. In addition, we combined the retrieval lists from short word and bigram indexing.

The strategy has been quite successful. Results of the two Chinese ad hoc experiments are shown in figure 14.5. The long queries have a description section with a conceptlike content. The MAP values of 0.5 to over 0.6 are exceptionally high, and the G value lies between 0.5 to 0.6.

14.6.2   English-Chinese CLIR

CLIR has been a hot topic in recent years because of the prevalence of Web searching and the easy access of foreign-language documents via the World Wide Web. In particular, English-Chinese CLIR uses an English query to retrieve Chinese documents and is of special importance because of the sheer number of users of these two languages. In general, one can have three approaches to CLIR, as Gregory Grefenstette (1998) notes: translate the Chinese documents to English and do retrieval matching in English; translate the English query to Chinese and do matching in Chinese; or translate both to an intermediate representation. The advantage of the first approach is that the documents will be in (translated) English and presumably readable by the user after retrieval (McCarley and Roukos 1998; Oard and Hackett 1998). The wholesale translation of a large collection is a daunting task, however. Another difficulty is that the document collection may not be under a user's control, but available for retrieval purposes only. This makes document translation to the query language (or to an intermediate one) not suitable. A more flexible approach is to translate a query to Chinese and do retrieval in Chinese. This has been the more popular method to use for CLIR when NIST initiated the task during TREC-9 (see chapter 7, this volume).

We employed the query translation method, and our approach to CLIR is based on the following assumptions:

• Translation for retrieval is more forgiving than translation for human consumption. Good translation of content terms will be adequate to give reasonable retrieval.
• Multiple methods of translation for a query can improve retrieval by hedging for translation errors or by alleviating "no matching" due to variants of term usage.

Since the bag-of-words approach is still the most effective in IR, good content term translation would tailor well with IR. A problem is that the translation output for a query term may be correct, but inadequate because the same concept was expressed differently in documents, leading to "no matching." Using multiple and different translation output can diminish such problems, but can also lead to noise terms. Experiments seem to bear out the fact that the former advantage outweighs the latter disadvantage (Kwok 2001a).

For evaluations such as TREC or NTCIR, CLIR experiments usually also involve the corresponding monolingual retrievals. The monolingual experiments are done with a good manual translation of the English topics that are also provided. Thus, CLIR experiments can be evaluated by comparison both with other participants' results and with monolingual results within the same site. This assumes that the site would use the same retrieval methodology for both types of retrieval.

In general, one can perform query translation for IR via commercial machine translation (MT) software, dictionary-based mapping, or corpus-based methods such as (Xu and Weischedel 2000). We rely on a combination of the first two methods: a commercial off-the-shelf (COTS) translation package called HuaJian (⟨http://www.altlan.com⟩) that was developed on mainland China; and an English-to-Chinese phrase- and word-mapping approach using a Chinese-English bilingual dictionary (later called ldc2ce) of about 120,000 words from the Linguistic Data Consortium (⟨http://www.morph.ldc.edu/Projects/Chinese⟩).

The HuaJian software alone brought about 75 or 68 percent of the monolingual results in TREC-9 depending on whether pretranslation query expansion was used or not. In order to boost CLIR performance, researchers have employed pre- and post-translation query expansion. Pretranslation expansion means using an English query to do retrieval with an external, topically related English collection so as to bring in relevant or highly related terms to expand the original query before translation. Because more related terms are present, translation of this expanded query can hedge against insufficient coverage or wrong translations similar to the effect of multiple translations. This has been shown to be quite effective (Ballesteros and Croft 1997). Post-translation expansion is used to do similar query expansion on the translated query utilizing the target or a related collection before the retrieval of Chinese documents, and is also quite effective. Post-translation query expansion using the target Chinese collection is our default procedure, unless stated otherwise.

COTS MT software functions like a black box. Dictionary mapping, however, is more under user control. For each English word, there are usually quite a number of Chinese candidates, and disambiguation procedures are necessary to narrow down the choices. We employed several techniques for this purpose (Kwok 2001a,b):

• Dictionary-structure based. The ldc2ce format is employed to select the more correct Chinese candidates among multiple mappings by promoting entries that have only the exact English query word.
• Phrase based. ldc2ce can also be searched as if it were a phrase dictionary by matching query substrings with English explanations of Chinese terms, giving much more accurate phrase translations than individual word mappings.
• Corpus-frequency based. This promotes translation terms that have higher occurrence frequency in the target collection. Higher frequency usually means a higher probability of being correct.
• Weight based. A Chinese term set translated for one English word can be weighted as a synonym set that is more effective for retrieval (Pirkola 1998).
• Co-occurrence-data based. Translated candidate term sets from adjacent English words are selected pairwise based on the mutual information measure between the Chinese term pairs. The calculation is based on the target collection statistics. This may lead to more accurate term selection than single-term selection using corpus frequency.

It has been shown (Ballesteros and Croft 1997) that phrase translation, if available, is much more accurate and effective than individual component-word translations. Tested on TREC-5 and TREC-6 collections and topics, this dictionary approach alone can bring about 75 percent of monolingual effectiveness (Kwok 2001a).

PIRCS was used in the TREC-9 English-Chinese CLIR experiments, and the results are also shown in figure 14.5. We employed each of the two translations individually to do retrieval and later combined their retrieval lists. The run also involved pre- and post-translation methodology as well as collection enrichment. Our result was significantly better than median (seventeen out of twenty-two above median), and the G value of .268 showed it was not close to the top. Internal comparison showed that its MAP of 0.2447 achieved about 86 percent of the monolingual result. Further postevaluation studies on the TREC-9 CLIR experiment showed that a large improvement in MAP value to 0.3206 was achievable by using better pseudorelevance feedback parameters, concatenating the translation software and the dictionary-mapping outputs into one single query and perform retrieval with this query, and by using both short-word and bigram indexing for retrieval and then later combining these two retrieval lists (Kwok 2002).

14.7   Conclusion and Discussion

14.7.1   Recommended Techniques

Ad hoc retrieval is a fundamental problem in IR. It is particularly difficult because a system has only a user's impromptu query to work with. Relying on this crude clue, the system has to be able to filter out large amounts of irrelevant documents and return only the relevant ones. We experimented with a number of techniques in addition to our PIRCS retrieval model that provide probabilistic term weighting as their bases. It is probably true that none of these techniques will be effective for all topic types against all document types. For example, highly specific single-term or two-word queries do not need weighting; simple coordinate matching is sufficient. Stop-word removal and word stemming are practically standard practices in IR that buy efficiency in space and time, and can lead to better effectiveness in most circumstances. One can also make up special cases where these practices will fail. Nevertheless, considering the experience over the ten years of TREC and the varied types of queries we have encountered (which is actually a small sample), we may be able to point to the following techniques as useful more often than not within PIRCS and perhaps for others:

Term Weighting   The concept of "$tf * idf$" term weighting—which many retrieval models reduce to—is probably the most important factor to bring better effectiveness. It allows a system to differentiate one feature from another based on their importance for retrieval by considering a term's representation and discrimination values. Each retrieval model may have a different manifestation of the forms for "tf" or "idf," and ours are given in equations (1) and (2). A refinement of the tf factor is the "avtf" weighting (see the "Term Weighting for Short Queries" section under 14.4.2 above), which we have found to be useful for short queries.

Pseudorelevance Feedback and Query Expansion   This is probably one of the most important factors confirmed during TREC experimentation that is effective for all query types and full-text documents: expansion, and the reweighting of query terms based on the top-ranked documents of an initial retrieval. It does not work for every query, but on average it can bring improvements of a few percent to over 50 percent in MAP values.

Adjacent Two-Word Phrases and Query Preprocessing   Two-word phrase indexing has been found to be quite useful for very short queries and moderately so for long ones. Removing introductory, noncontent-bearing strings in a query has been found to improve precision and MAP value a small amount—say, 1 to 3 percent.

Subdocument Breakup for Long Documents and Aggregating Subdocument RSVs
When a document gets too long, space becomes an issue. For example, if word and/or sentence positions were captured in a posting file, the field width for these entries will grow with a document size. Breaking long documents into subdocuments remove this

implementation issue. For initial retrieval, this strategy is quite useful for truly long documents such as those from the *Federal Register*. For the newspaper genre, its effect is indifferent or very small either way. The true advantage of subdocuments lies in pseudorelevance feedback when shorter, more focused subdocuments can provide better feedback terms for second-stage retrieval (Kwok and Grunfeld 1994).

Zipf Thresholds   The use of Zipf thresholds grows out of our network implementation of PIRCS. When more terms are accounted for, our network grows substantially to the point where it cannot fit into memory and leads to a large time penalty for execution. We had used variable Zipf thresholds before (Kwok and Chan 1998). Recently, when more memory was available, we have found that including all but a few of the highest frequency terms improves MAP performance, sometimes substantially for very short queries, as in TREC 2001. Frequency one and two terms (low Zipf threshold) are still ignored.

Combination of Retrieval Lists   From the same topical need, one can define multiple queries (for instance, long, short, Boolean queries, and so on) that lead to multiple retrieval lists. Combining them has been shown to improve MAP values by a few percentage points. It is our experience, however, that this may not work if the two lists are substantially different in performance—in this case, the resultant MAP value may be the average of the two instead of improving both. One does not know before evaluation whether the lists are substantially different or not.

For Chinese retrieval, one could use bigram or short-word indexing as representation, also leading to two retrieval lists. Combining in this case has worked quite often; when it does not work, the negative effect is usually small. For cross-language, combining retrieval lists from translation software and dictionary mapping has also been shown to improve effectiveness.

Pretranslation Expansion and Collection Enrichment   Employing external collections to help translation or retrieval have been found to improve results. The collections need to be topically related to the task at hand.

14.7.2   Future Trends
Looking to the future, what might be a good strategy to improve retrieval? The first thing that comes to mind is naturally to involve the user (to select potentially useful terms or perform real relevance feedback), who knows what their information needs are. But this rightly belongs to the area of interactive retrieval. If we limit ourselves to one-shot ad hoc, which is a fundamental retrieval problem, the following might be useful as general directions for discussion:

Representation Improvement   The current bag-of-words independent feature approach has long been recognized as too naive. It seems that new representation methods that account for the relationship of terms ought to bring us closer to more precise conceptual retrieval. Together with new representation, one generally needs to consider new weighting methods.

More Individualized Approaches   Currently, most techniques and models are designed to apply uniformly to all situations. For example, TREC experiments have shown that short queries may behave differently from longer ones. Perhaps one could classify queries by some properties so that more individualized approaches can be employed for different query requirements, so as to maximize effectiveness.

Pseudorelevance Feedback Improvements   Pseudorelevance feedback has been found to be one of the most effective techniques for ad hoc retrieval during TREC experimentation. So far, it has been used without much theoretical guidance as to what parameter values to choose. For example, the number of top feedback documents (n) to use, and the number of terms (m) to expand a query are unknown parameters. As a rule of thumb, pseudorelevance feedback works about two-thirds of the time. Can individualized parameters be discovered for different query types so as to improve this ratio?

External Resources   As the Web has been developed to be a viable and stable information resource, it is time to consider whether it can be utilized to help general ad hoc retrieval, such as from internal or private collections. QA investigators have used the Web to help locate correct answers to questions. The Web has also been employed for translation to facilitate CLIR. Can the Web be useful as a source for collection enrichment, for example? How does one reduce the noise? (Other external resources that have been studied before include thesauri and WordNet—but so far they do not seem to have much effect.) For a recent work in this direction, see Grunfeld et al. 2003.

New Retrieval Models   History has shown that a field evolves with better and better models for the task at hand, and IR is no exception. We have seen the Boolean model develop into more advanced soft Boolean models, the coordinate matching model evolve to the vector model, and then to the probabilistic model, logical models (Crestani et al. 1998) and the currently popular language model (Ponte and Croft 1998; Lafferty and Zhai 2001). These developments will certainly not be the last, as we still do not understand how humans do conceptual matching, or how one understands sentences and queries, for instance. In the future, models closer to our cognitive ability will probably be necessary to make a quantum leap in retrieval effectiveness.

Acknowledgments

This work was partially supported by the Space and Naval Warfare Systems Center, San Diego, under grant number N66001-00-1-8912. The author would like to thank the many colleagues and past students who helped and participated in our TREC efforts. In particular, Laszlo Grunfeld contributed to the ad hoc experiments during the early years, and Norbert Dinstl helped upgrade and maintain PIRCS.

References

Attar, R., and R. Fraenkel. 1977. Local feedback in full text retrieval system. *Journal of the Association for Computing Machinery* 24, no. 3:397–417.

Ballesteros, L., and W. B. Croft. 1997. Phrasal translation and query expansion techniques for cross-language information retrieval. In *Proceedings of the twentieth annual international ACM SIGIR conference*, 84–91.

Campos, J., and A. D. de Figueriedo. 2001. Searching the unsearchable: Inducing serendipitous insights. In *Proceedings of the workshop program at the fourth international conference on case-based reasoning*. Technical note AIC-01-003. Washington, D.C.: Naval Research Laboratory, Navy Center for Applied Research in Artificial Intelligence.

Cerami, E. 1998. *Delivering push*. New York: McGraw-Hill.

Chen, A., J. He, L. Xu, F. C. Gey, and J. Meggs. 1997. Chinese text retrieval without using a dictionary. In *Proceedings of the twentieth Annual International ACM SIGIR Conference*, 42–49.

Cove, J. F., and R. C. Walsh. 1988. Online text retrieval via browsing. *Information Processing and Management* 24, no. 1:31–37.

Crestani, F., M. Lalmas, and C. J. van Rijsbergen, eds. 1998. *Information retrieval, uncertainty and logics: Advanced models for the representation and retrieval of information*. Dordrecht: Kluwer Academic Publishers.

Evans, D. A., and R. G. Lefferts. 1994. Design and evaluation of the CLARIT—TREC-2 system. In *TREC-2*, 137–150.

Fox, C. 1992. Lexical Analysis and Stoplists. In *Information retrieval: Data structures and algorithms*, ed. W. B. Frakes and R. Baeza-Yates, 102–130. Englewood Cliffs, NJ: Prentice Hall.

Gao, J., J. Goodman, M. Li, and K.-F. Lee. 2002. Towards a unified approach for statistical language model for Chinese. *ACM Transactions on Asian Language Information Processing* 1:3–33.

Garfield, E. 2001. A retrospective and prospective view of information retrieval and artificial intelligence in the twenty-first century. *Journal of American Society for Information Science* 52, no. 1:18–21.

Grefenstette, G. 1998. *Cross Language Information Retrieval*. Dordrecht: Kluwer Academic Publishers.

Grunfeld, L., K.-L. Kwok, N. Dinstl, and P. Deng. 2003. *TREC 2003 robust, HARD, and QA track experiments using PIRCS*. In *TREC 2003*, 510–521.

Harman, D. 1991. How effective is suffixing? *Journal of American Society for Information Science* 42:7–15.

Hull, D. 1996. Stemming algorithms: A case study for detailed evaluation. *Journal of American Society for Information Science* 47:70–84.

Katz, S. 1996. Distribution of content words and phrases in text and language modelling. *Natural Language Engineering* 2, no. 1:15–59.

Kwok, K.-L. 1995. A network approach to probabilistic information retrieval. *ACM Transactions on Office Information System* 13:324–353.

Kwok, K.-L. 1996. A new method of weighting query terms for ad-hoc retrieval. In *Proceedings of the nineteenth annual international ACM SIGIR conference*, 187–195.

Kwok, K.-L. 1997. Comparing representations in Chinese information retrieval. In *Proceedings of the twentieth annual international ACM SIGIR conference*, 34–41.

Kwok, K.-L. 2000. Improving English and Chinese ad-hoc retrieval: A TIPSTER text phase three project report. *Information Retrieval* 3:313–338.

Kwok, K.-L. 2001a. Exploiting the LDC Chinese-English bilingual wordlist for cross language information retrieval. *International Journal of Computer Processing of Oriental Languages* 14:173–191.

Kwok, K.-L. 2001b. NTCIR-2 Chinese and cross language experiments using PIRCS. In *Proceedings of the second NTCIR workshop on research in Chinese and Japanese text retrieval and summarization*, 111–118. Tokyo: National Institute of Informatics.

Kwok, K.-L. 2002. An analysis of the TREC-9 CLIR experiments. In *Proceedings of IEEE 2002, International Conference on Systems Man and Cybernetics*, 2, 443–448. Piscataway, NJ: IEEE.

Kwok, K.-L., and M. Chan. 1998. Improving two-stage ad-hoc retrieval for short queries. In *Proceedings of the twenty-first annual international ACM SIGIR conference*, 250–256.

Kwok, K.-L., and L. Grunfeld. 1994. Learning from relevant documents in large-scale routing retrieval. In *Proceedings of ARPA human language technology workshop*, 358–363. San Francisco: Morgan Kaufmann Publishers.

Lafferty, J., and C. Zhai. 2001. Document language models, query models, and risk minimization for information retrieval. In *Proceedings of the twenty-fourth annual international ACM SIGIR conference*, 111–119.

McCarley, J. S., and S. Roukos. 1998. Fast document translation for cross-language information retrieval. In *Proceedings of the Third Conference of the Association for Machine Translation in the Americas*. Lecture Notes in Computer Science 1529, 150–157. Heidelberg: Springer-Verlag.

Mitra, M., A. Singhal, and C. Buckley. 1998. Improving automatic query expansion. In *Proceedings of the twenty-first annual international ACM SIGIR conference*, 206–214.

Oard, D. W., and P. Hackett. 1998. Document translation for cross-language text retrieval in the University of Maryland. In *TREC-6*, 687–696.

Pirkola, A. 1998. The effects of query structure and dictionary setups in dictionary-based cross-language information retrieval. In *Proceedings of the twenty-first annual international ACM SIGIR conference*, 55–63.

Pitkow, J., H. Schutze, T. Cass, R. Cooley, D. Turnbull, A. Edmonds, E. Adar, and T. Breuel. 2002. Personalized search. *Communications of the ACM* 45:50–55.

Ponte, J. M., and B. W. Croft. 1998. A language modeling approach to information retrieval. In *Proceedings of the twenty-first annual international ACM SIGIR conference on research and development in information retrieval*, 275–281. New York: ACM Press.

Porter, M. F. 1980. An algorithm for suffix stripping. In *Readings in information retrieval*, ed. K. Sparck Jones and P. Willett, 313–316. San Francisco: Morgan Kaufmann.

Robertson, R. E., and K. Sparck Jones. 1976. Relevance weighting of search terms. *Journal of American Society for Information Science*, 129–146.

Robertson, S. E., and S. Walker. 1994. Some simple effective approximations to the two-Poisson model for probabilistic weighted retrieval. In *Proceedings of the seventeenth annual international ACM SIGIR conference*, 232–241.

Salton, G., and C. Buckley. 1988. Term-weighting approaches in automatic text retrieval. *Information Processing and Management* 24:513–523.

Salton, G., and M. J. McGill. 1983. *Introduction to modern information retrieval*. New York: McGraw-Hill.

Singhal, A., C. Buckley, and M. Mitra. 1996. Pivoted document length normalization. In *Proceedings of the nineteenth annual international ACM SIGIR conference*, 21–29.

Singhal, A., M. Mitra, and C. Buckley. 1997. Learning routing queries in a query zone. In *Proceedings of the twentieth annual international ACM SIGIR conference*, 25–32.

Sproat, R., and C. Shih. 1991. A statistical method for finding word boundaries in Chinese text. *Computer Processing of Chinese and Oriental Languages* 4:336–351.

Wu, Z., and G. Tseng. 1995. An automatic Chinese text segmentation system for full text retrieval. *Journal of American Society for Information Science* 46:83–96.

Xu, J., and R. Weischedel. 2001. TREC-9 cross-lingual retrieval at BBN. In *TREC-9*, 106–115.

15 MultiText Experiments for TREC
Gordon V. Cormack, Charles L. A. Clarke, Christopher R. Palmer, and Thomas R. Lynam

15.1 Introduction

MultiText has been a TREC participant since TREC-4 in 1995 [4; 1; 11; 14; 10; 6; 7; 5]. The MultiText project was founded at the University of Waterloo in 1993 to develop large-scale, distributed document retrieval technologies for deployment on clusters of workstations. The text-searching component of our initial research addressed the problem of efficient feature-oriented retrieval from structured text, such as SGML, as opposed to the traditional document-ranking problem targeted by TREC.

The MultiText search system is therefore dissimilar to the other information retrieval systems participating in TREC. It has a federated client/server architecture with a novel intermediate query language, GCL [3]. The server is not constrained to retrieve predefined units of text such as documents, paragraphs, or sentences. Instead, the client may, in GCL, specify the unit of retrieval to be an arbitrary contiguous fragment of the corpus. For example, in GCL it would be possible to retrieve "the titles of documents containing *Knuth* in the author field and *Cormack* in the references" provided that documents, titles, and references were delimited by some markup known to the client. Or the same client could retrieve "fragments containing both *space* and *telescope* within five words of one another."

The primary TREC tasks, routing (see chapter 5, this volume) and ad hoc (see chapter 4) retrieval, required that the system return the "most relevant" documents for a particular topic, ranked by the likelihood of relevance. GCL's semantics embody no notion of relevance; they specify exactly what fragments of the corpus are to be retrieved in response to any given query. It was necessary to invent some mechanism for relevance ranking in order to participate in TREC.

Shortest substring ranking was developed for TREC-4 and continues to be the foundation of our system. The central idea is that if query words are found close together in the text, that area of text is more likely to be relevant than an area of text where the query words are far apart. For example, if we issue the second query above on the hundred gigabytes TREC VLC-II corpus, the first eight fragments returned from the query all mention the Hubble space telescope. On the other hand, if the query is "documents containing both *space* and *telescope*," only five of eight mention the Hubble. The documents that have no mention contain the words from unrelated contexts; for instance, "accessible only through a telescope. Nebulae exist far out in space, where dust . . ."

Shortest substring ranking is useful only in conjunction with a GCL query containing appropriate terms. From TREC 4–10, our approach has progressed through various methods of manual and automatic query generation and ranking, culminating in *cover density ranking*—our best automatic method for retrieving high-precision fragments from a set of candidate query terms.

A major strength of the MultiText system, not initially harnessed for TREC, is the ability to both support interactive retrieval through very fast response times and extract small fragments relevant to the client's information need. Starting with TREC-5, we used this facility to create better manual queries, create and evaluate a parallel set of relevance judgments, and participate in the *high-precision* track, which specifically evaluated this ability. Starting with TREC-6, we used this facility as a mechanism for *pseudorelevance feedback*, in which query terms are augmented by those found in fragments returned from an initial, automatically generated query.

We were able to demonstrate and enhance the efficiency and precision of our system through our participation in the *very large corpus* (VLC) and later *large Web* tracks (see chapter 9, this volume). A key observation from these efforts was that we could take advantage of corpus size to achieve extremely good precision (as well as response times) for automatically generated queries.

The question-answering task (QA) (see chapter 10) afforded us a further opportunity to demonstrate and refine our query generation and ranking process. Starting with TREC-8, we used the VLC method to retrieve fragments, which were used as answer passages, with good results. For TREC-9, we employed a simple parser to generate better GCL queries and exploited redundancy within a larger set of retrieved fragments to select those most likely relevant. For TREC-10, based on our observation that very good precision can be achieved with huge corpora, we extracted fragments from the Web as well as the QA corpus and used these fragments as input to the redundancy computation. Each year's performance significantly improved on the previous year's.

This chapter details the development of our retrieval, query generation, and feedback systems as summarized above. We describe the MultiText system prior to our participation in TREC, the development of shortest substring ranking in TREC 4–6, the development of automatic query generation and feedback techniques in TREC 6–8, and the application of these methods to QA in TREC 8–10.

15.2   1994: Schema-Independent Retrieval from Structured Text

The MultiText architecture has four components (figure 15.1): text servers, index servers, a marshaler/dispatcher, and client applications. Data to be searched are loaded into the text and index servers.

Retrieval is a two-step process. First, a GCL query, generated by a client application, is dispatched to the index servers, where it is executed. The results are marshaled and returned to the client as one. The result of a GCL query identifies a set of locations within the corpus where fragments of text satisfying the query are found. To retrieve the actual text associated with these fragments, the client issues a second query, which is sent through the marshaler/dispatcher to the appropriate text servers, which return the text.

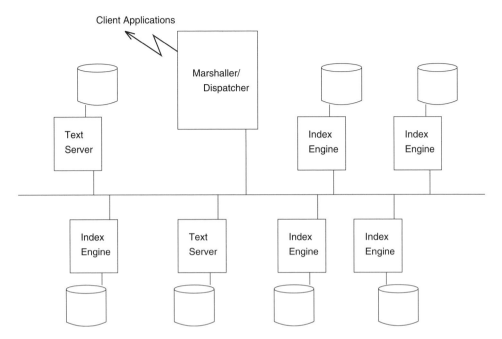

Figure 15.1
Architecture of the MultiText system

To be handled by the system, data must be represented as a sequence of tokens. For text, these tokens typically consist of words and markup symbols. In this chapter, we use XML-style tags to denote markup. It is important to note, however, that these tags have no particular meaning to the servers. They are tokens like any other. On the other hand, the tags may have significant meaning to the client application. The system is schema-independent in the sense that the servers store sequences of tokens without applying any interpretation; structure is harnessed through queries that reflect the client's interpretation of some tokens as structural cues.

Text stored by the system is treated as a single long string of tokens, with tags representing document boundaries treated in the same way as any other token. Starting at the beginning of the corpus, each token is assigned a consecutive integer address. Pairs of these addresses, specifying start and end positions, are used to specify fragments or intervals of text within the corpus.

The first major MultiText application, deployed in November 1994, was an online Usenet news server. The corpus contained two weeks of Usenet news articles (about four gigabytes of text) updated continuously to include new articles and to exclude older ones. Figure 15.2 shows the user interface to the client application giving the result of a search for the words "japan" and "baseball" within ten words.

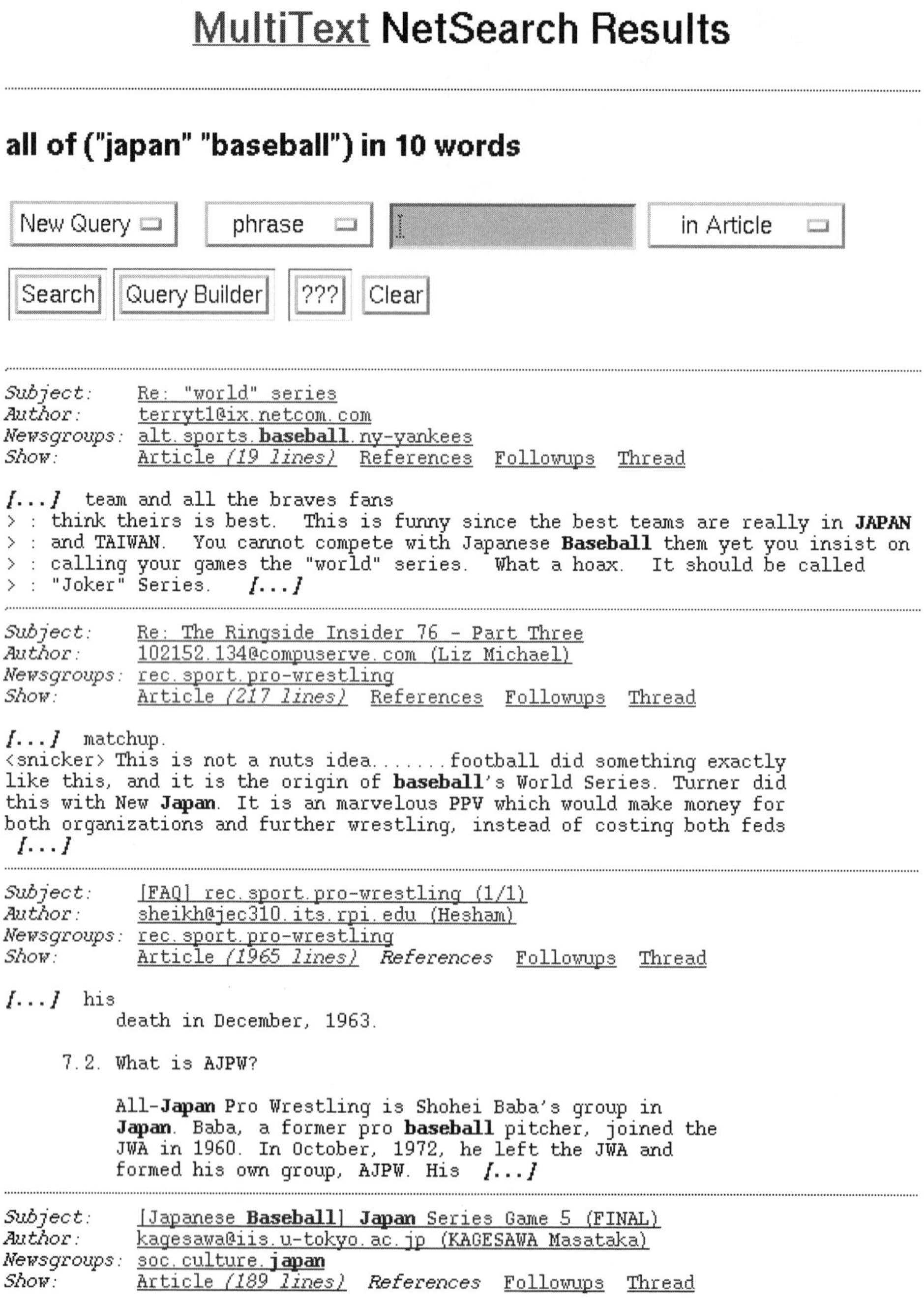

MultiText NetSearch Results

---

all of ("japan" "baseball") in 10 words

```
New Query ▭     phrase  ▭   [              ]        in Article   ▭

Search  Query Builder  ???  Clear
```

Subject: Re: "world" series
Author: terryt1@ix.netcom.com
Newsgroups: alt.sports.**baseball**.ny-yankees
Show: Article *(19 lines)* References Followups Thread

[...] team and all the braves fans
> : think theirs is best. This is funny since the best teams are really in **JAPAN**
> : and TAIWAN. You cannot compete with Japanese **Baseball** them yet you insist on
> : calling your games the "world" series. What a hoax. It should be called
> : "Joker" Series.   *[...]*

Subject: Re: The Ringside Insider 76 - Part Three
Author: 102152.134@compuserve.com (Liz Michael)
Newsgroups: rec.sport.pro-wrestling
Show: Article *(217 lines)* References Followups   Thread

[...] matchup.
<snicker> This is not a nuts idea.......football did something exactly
like this, and it is the origin of **baseball**'s World Series. Turner did
this with New **Japan**. It is an marvelous PPV which would make money for
both organizations and further wrestling, instead of costing both feds
 [...]

Subject: [FAQ] rec.sport.pro-wrestling (1/1)
Author: sheikh@jec310.its.rpi.edu (Hesham)
Newsgroups: rec.sport.pro-wrestling
Show: Article *(1965 lines)* References Followups   Thread

[...] his
        death in December, 1963.

    7.2. What is AJPW?

        All-**Japan** Pro Wrestling is Shohei Baba's group in
        Japan. Baba, a former pro **baseball** pitcher, joined the
        JWA in 1960. In October, 1972, he left the JWA and
        formed his own group, AJPW. His *[...]*

Subject: [Japanese **Baseball**] **Japan** Series Game 5 (FINAL)
Author: kagesawa@iis.u-tokyo.ac.jp (KAGESAWA Masataka)
Newsgroups: soc.culture.**japan**
Show: Article *(189 lines)* References Followups   Thread

Figure 15.2
The MultiText news server (1994)

To form the corpus, the articles were concatenated to form a single sequence bracketed by the markup tokens <news> and </news>. Individual articles were bracketed by <article> and </article> while the header was separated from the body by <body>. The header was stored in its native RFC 821 format. To facilitate structured retrieval based on this line-oriented format, we included <br> at the end of each line in the header. Figure 15.3 shows a much-elided example of the contents of the servers supporting the Usenet application.

15.2.1   GCL

A syntax-directed definition for a GCL query Q is:

```
Q ::= quoted-string            a specific string of one or more tokens
  ::= n WORDS                  any sequence of tokens of length n
  ::= Q1 AND Q2                sequence containing solutions to Q1 and Q2
  ::= Q1 OR Q2                 sequence containing solution to Q1 or Q2
  ::= Q1 .. Q2                 solution to Q1 through solution to Q2
  ::= Q1 CONTAINED IN Q2       solution to Q1 contained in solution to Q2
  ::= Q1 CONTAINING Q2         solution to Q1 containing Q2
  ::= Q1 NOT CONTAINED IN Q2   solution to Q1 not contained in solution to
                               Q2
  ::= Q1 NOT CONTAINING Q2     solution to Q1 not containing solution to Q2
  ::= n of (Q1,..., Qm)        sequence containing solutions to n of Q1,
                               Q2,...
```

To the definitions above, we apply the *shortest match* restriction. The result of a query Q is defined to be the set of intervals in the text that satisfy the syntax-directed definition, but do not properly contain an interval that also satisfies the syntax-directed definition. Consider, for example, the GCL query "japan" AND "baseball". In figure 15.2, the syntax-directed definition is met by any number of intervals, but only the interval containing exactly

```
"baseball's World Series. Turner did this with New Japan"
```

satisfies the shortest match criterion and is therefore the result. This definition of Boolean conjunction, which is independent of a containing structural element such as a document or paragraph, represents a key idea behind the ranking techniques pioneered by MultiText.

The query "TEN WORDS" has as its result every interval in the corpus of length ten. The compound query

```
("japan" AND "baseball") CONTAINED IN (10 WORDS)
```

finds all solutions to the first contained in the second. As it happens, the result of the ("japan" AND "baseball") is nine words long, so it is contained in two ten-word

<news>

...

<article>
From: 102152.134@compuserve.com (Liz Michael) *
*
Subject: Re: The Ringside Insider 76 - Part Three *
*
Date: 1996/10/26 *
*
Message-ID: <54sdro$htv@nnrp1.news.primenet.com> *
*
references: <961016175001_100517.156_JHB84-4@CompuServe.COM> *
*
organization: Mary Flash Productions *
*
x-posted-by: @204.212.59.106 (judges) *
*
reply-to: 102152.134@compuserve.com *
*
newsgroups: rec.sport.pro-wrestling *
*
<body>

...

It would be much better, if Turner and McMahon wanted to feud, to let
them do it in an annual World Series of Wrestling or something. Let
the tag champs wrestle each other, the World Champs wrestle each
other, the US champ wrestle the IC Champ, and 4 other matches, one of
which should be a War Games. I'd throw in a women's match but at this
point it would be that ever exciting Bull Nakano vs. Sable matchup.
<snicker> This is not a nuts idea.......football did something exactly
like this, and it is the origin of baseball's World Series. Turner did
this with New Japan. It is an marvelous PPV which would make money for
both organizations and further wrestling, instead of costing both feds
all these legal fees.

And let Turner and McMahon have a fair one in the ring! <snicker>

...

</article>

...

</news>

Figure 15.3
Text representation

sequences and is therefore a result of this query. On the other hand, had the query been (10 WORDS) CONTAINING ("japan" AND "BASEBALL"), the result would have been the two overlapping intervals containing the ten-word sequences:

```
of baseball's World Series. Turner did this with New Japan,
baseball's World Series. Turner did this with New Japan. It
```

For the Usenet application, GCL was used not only to satisfy user queries but as the basis for the hyperlinks offered in the user interface. For example, the link Newsgroups: rec.sport.pro-wrestling simply finds articles satisfying the GCL query

```
"alt.sport.pro-wrestling" CONTAINED IN ("<br> Newsgroups" .. "<br>").
```

Similarly, the link Followups, which finds articles that refer to this article, uses a GCL query to locate articles whose *references* field contain this article's unique identifier, as specified in RFC 822:

```
"54sdro$htv@nnrp1.news.primenet.com" CONTAINED IN ("<br> References" .. "<br>").
```

In the same manner, all of the navigation and search facilities of the news server were effected through GCL, with no special server support for retrieval by article identifier, author, newsgroup, or thread.

We found these structured search and navigation facilities to be useful in the course of our participation in TREC, but they did not directly address the fundamental problem of relevance ranking for information retrieval. Only one rather coarse tool for this purpose was present in the original system—that is, the aforementioned ability to specify the CONTAINED IN (n WORDS). By manually choosing queries with different n we were able to trade off precision and recall: queries with small values of n were observed to yield fewer results, but those results were more likely to be relevant.

15.3   1995–1998: Shortest Substring Ranking

The TREC ad hoc and routing tasks differ from those for which the system was originally designed in two ways:

1. Input to the retrieval process consists of a free-text *information need statement* characterizing relevance criteria, as opposed to a feature-oriented query.
2. Entire documents, rather than fragments of text, are to be retrieved and ranked according to their estimated likelihood of relevance.

For our initial participation in TREC, at TREC-4 in 1995, we addressed the first problem by having an expert read the information need statements and compose a sequence of

GCL queries considered likely to yield relevant text fragments. The second problem—ranked document retrieval—was addressed by shortest substring ranking, an automatic method for ranking documents containing solutions to a particular GCL query Q. Shortest substring ranking is occasioned by the following assumptions:

1. A document containing a smaller text fragment satisfying Q is more likely to be relevant.
2. A document containing many fragments satisfying Q is more likely to be relevant.

Each of these assumptions is intuitively reasonable and borne out by empirical observations. Assumption 1 suggests that documents should be ranked by the size of fragments satisfying Q that they contain. Assumption 2 suggests that documents should be ranked by the number of fragments satisfying Q that they contain.

Our basic approach is to use a weighted sum of a function of the lengths of the (potentially overlapping) fragments contained in a document. Let D be a document containing fragments $f_1, f_2, \ldots f_n$, labeled so that $|f_1| \leq |f_2| \leq \cdots \leq |f_n|$, where $|f_i|$ is the length of fragment f_i. We define a fragment scoring function $S(f_i)$ such that $S(f_i) > S(f_j) \Rightarrow |f_i| < |f_j|$; that is, the score is larger for more likely relevant documents. We chose

$$S(f_i) = \begin{cases} A/|f_i| & \text{if } |f_i| \geq A \\ 1 & \text{otherwise,} \end{cases}$$

where A is a constant fragment length below which assumption 1 did not appear to be hold. For TREC-4 and TREC-5, we used $A = 16$; in later experiments we found that $A = 4$ was more appropriate.

The document score $S(D)$ was computed as:

$$S(D) = \sum_{i=1}^{n} W(i)S(f_i),$$

where $W(i)$ is a weighting factor between 0 and 1. For TREC-4 and TREC-5, we implicitly used $W(i) = 1$ for all i. The notion of $W(i)$ as an explicit formula originated with our participation in the TREC-6 VLC track, where we used

$$W(i) = \begin{cases} 0.5^{(i-1)} & (i \leq 10) \\ W(i) = 0 & (i > 10). \end{cases}$$

For the QA tracks of TREC-8 and beyond we used

$$W(i) = \begin{cases} 1 & (i = 1) \\ W(i) = 0 & (i > 1), \end{cases}$$

which gives a nonzero weight only to the highest-scoring passage in each document. For other experiments we used

$$W(i) = d^{(i-1)}$$

for some $0 < d \leq 1$ or

$$W(i) = i^{-k}$$

for some $k \geq 0$, which both give progressively lower weights to the less likely relevant passages in D. The overall effects of varying A and $W(i)$ were observable but not pronounced [2].

15.3.1   TREC-4

The MultiText project participated in both the routing and ad hoc tasks. Queries were developed manually; the procedure differed only slightly for the two tasks. The queries were created manually by two of the investigators (Clarke and Cormack) working in conjunction. Approximately fifteen to forty-five minutes was spent developing a query for each topic. During the creation of the routing (but not ad hoc) queries, relevant documents were sometimes pulled and used as a source of possible terms, but this practice was not uniformly followed. Besides the personal knowledge of the investigators, the only external resources used were an online dictionary (*Webster's*); the Unix `spell` program; an online list of country, state, and city names and state postal abbreviations; and in some few cases, current issues of newspapers.

The final query developed for each topic was a query consisting of an ordered list of one or more subqueries or *tiers*. On average, each query contained 2.05 tiers. Results for each tier were determined separately using the ranking techniques described in the previous section. These results were then combined into a final solution set according to the ordering of the subquery list, with results of a particular tier ranked before the results of subsequent tiers. Documents given a nonzero score by one tier were eliminated from the results of subsequent tiers before this final ranking.

This approach reflects a trade-off between a desire for precision and an artificial need to produce one thousand ranked documents. The first tier is intended to be a precise expression of the requirements underlying the topic. Subsequent tiers are "weaker" and are intended to pick up a large number of possibly relevant documents.

Figure 15.4 shows topic 246 and figure 15.5 gives our query in the internal format presented to the system and forwarded to NIST. In this format, a terse syntax is used for operators and phrases are expanded into term queries. Some explanation of the syntax is required: "^" and "+" are equivalent to "AND" and "OR," respectively; "< >" is equivalent to the ordering operator ".."; and the expression "[2]" is equivalent to "2 WORDS," representing all two-word intervals in the text. The "@output" command sets the output file name for the query. The "@rank" command takes a topic number and a tiered query as arguments and executes the ranking procedure.

```
<top>

<num> Number:   246

<desc> Description:

What is the extent of U.S. arms exports?

</top>
```

Figure 15.4
Topic 246

```
@output "246.output"

arms0 = "arms" + "gun" + "guns" + "tanks"
arms1 = "firearm" + "firearms" + "weapon" + "weapons" + "rifle" + "rifles"
arms2 = (("fighter" <> ("jet" + "jets")) <  [2]) + "bomber" + "bombers"
arms = arms0 + arms1 + arms2

export0 = "export" + "exports" + "trade" + "sale" + "sales"
export1 = "tariff" + "tariffs"
export = export0 + export1

q = arms^export^USbroad

@rank 246 q
```

Figure 15.5
MultiText TREC-4 query for topic 246

The topic number is used by the @rank command only for formatting the output. In this case there is only a single tier, which has been assigned the name "q."

The query of figure 15.5 is essentially a Boolean expression in conjunctive normal form, consisting of three "facets," each built from several named pieces for convenience. The first facet ("arms") is a disjunction of terms and phrases related to military weapons. The second facet ("export") is a disjunction of terms related to trade. The final facet ("USbroad") is a disjunction of 150 geographic place names and abbreviations related to the United States. The definition of this last facet is not included in figure 15.5; its definition is global in scope and it is used whenever a topic concerns only the United States.

Several other global definitions of this type were used in developing the queries, and these definitions contributed significantly to the size of the queries. For the ad hoc task, queries contained an average of sixty-seven terms. For the routing task, queries contained an average of fifty-three terms. The variance was fairly high: for some topics the query consisted of hundreds of terms, and for other topics the query consisted of a single two-term phrase. Overall, about half of the query terms resulted from the expansion of global definitions, overwhelmingly from the expansion of the USbroad definition. Expansion of phrases into terms and the manual construction of morphological term variants also contributed to the large number of terms per query.

Our results for the ad hoc task are quite reasonable (average precision: 0.2994; R-precision: 0.3347). For over 65 percent of the topics, our average precision is above the median average precision for all groups. Mean average precision over all topics was the third best among manually generated queries (and overall). Our results for the routing task are relatively poor (average precision: 0.1188; R-precision: 0.1649). Post hoc analysis showed that this poor score was attributable to an error in loading the data; a significant fraction had been omitted.

15.3.2   TREC-5

For TREC-5, we focused on the development of interaction methods for manual query creation. As queries were formulated, they were tested against the corpus (ad hoc) or the training data (routing) using a graphical user interface adapted from our Usenet news system (figure 15.2). Interaction was used in four principal ways:

1. To discard ineffective queries and query terms
2. To gather new terms and features associated with relevant documents to aid in the composition or expansion of queries
3. To gather terms and features associated with nonrelevant documents
4. To test the effect of combining queries with OR or AND

In general, terms leading to relevant documents were included in the query and terms leading to nonrelevant documents were excluded. In some significant cases, however, information leading to nonrelevant documents was included in a negative query term. For example, if we are searching for information on the efficiency of storm windows, the expression `"windows" NOT CONTAINED IN (10 WORDS CONTAINING "microsoft")` is much more effective than `"windows"` by itself.

As in TREC-4, each query used in the MultiText runs consisted of a tiered query of one or more GCL subqueries. The first tier was intended to be a "high-precision" query, an accurate expression of the user requirements embodied in the topic. The additional tiers were intended to increase overall recall.

Our official run achieved a mean average precision over all topics of 0.3087; this was the second-best score of all manual participants. Thus, our score and our rank both improved from TREC-4 to TREC-5. In their overview of TREC-5, Ellen M. Voorhees and Donna K. Harman present evidence that the TREC-5 topics were considerably harder than those of TREC-4. Our slight improvement in TREC-5 therefore provides evidence, albeit weak, that our interactive process did generate better queries.

15.3.3   TREC-6

MultiText participated in five TREC-6 tracks. In the routing task, we derived quantitative estimates of the probability of relevance as a function of $S(D)$ for various queries, and used these estimates to formulate tiered queries. In the high-performance and ad hoc tasks, we explored the limits of user interaction and manually formulated queries. The Chinese track showed that our TREC-5 techniques were effective in another domain. The new VLC track afforded us the opportunity to test the efficiency and scalability of our architecture, and also the impetus to explore techniques for constructing very small, high-precision queries. TREC-6 saw the birth of our efforts in automated query construction, which are detailed in the next section. Details of our TREC-6 experiments have appeared elsewhere [13; 11].

TREC-6 Routing   The goal of our routing effort was to determine how best to combine the results of a number of GCL queries to produce the best-ranked result. To this end, we performed two runs. The baseline run used the same methodology as we had employed for TREC-5: tiered GCL queries were created through manual searching and interaction with the training data. Our experimental run took small queries that retrieved some of the relevant documents and combined their results automatically to form the run.

Figure 15.6 shows recall as a function of the number of documents returned for each of five candidate queries, $q1$ through $q5$. The slope of the curve approximates the instantaneous probability of relevance. Consistent with our objective that documents be ranked by likelihood of relevance, the slope, for the most part, diminishes as more documents are retrieved. Notice that no query is uniformly better than the rest: $q5$ has the highest slope—about 0.6 overall and 0.8 for the first hundred relevant documents—but has low recall; $q3$ has a lesser slope—about 0.5—but greater recall; and $q1$'s slope is as high as $q3$'s, but only for the first hundred relevant documents. In fact, many of the curves appear as piecewise combinations of nearly linear segments.

With this in mind, we split the queries into multiple subqueries, each returning approximately the documents corresponding to one of the linear segments. For example, $q5$ is split into two pieces: $q5a$, which returns the first hundred documents; and $q5b$, which returns the remainder. The other queries—except for $q4$, which is best approximated by a single segment—are split into two pieces. The split queries are constructed using GCL's length constraint; for example,

```
q5a = q5 CONTAINED IN n WORDS
q5b = q5 NOT CONTAINED IN q5a,
```

where n is chosen so that q5a returns a hundred documents. (We learned later that n is nearly always in the range 32–128, and 64 is a reasonable approximation.) The net effect is that each query returns documents with a common probability of relevance; a

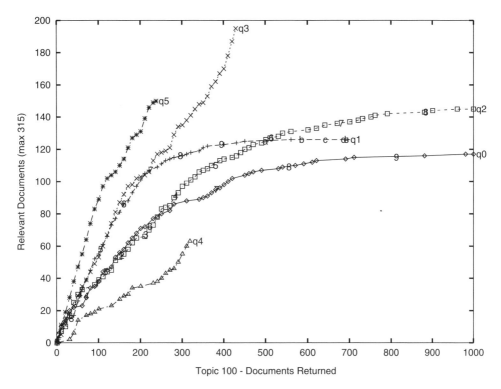

Figure 15.6
Slope estimation

tiered query is constructed in which queries yielding a higher probability of relevance are used before those yielding a lower probability of relevance. In order to improve robustness and efficiency, tiers yielding nearly equal probabilities are combined. For the example above, the tiered routing query that we generate is:

```
q5a
q3a OR q1a OR q5b
q3b
q2a OR q0a
q4
q2b OR q1b OR q0b
```

In our official run, this approach of splicing together queries yielded a modest improvement over our best manually constructed queries (an average precision of 0.3326 versus 0.3111). It should be noted that the baseline queries were constructed

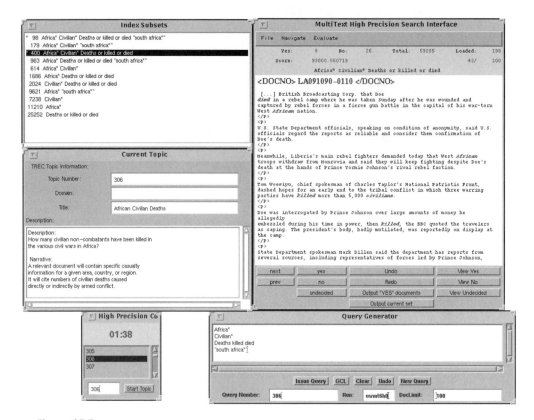

Figure 15.7
User interface for TREC-6 high-precision track

with much manual effort, and that the approach described here may be applied to blend the results of less carefully constructed (or automatically generated) queries.

The same general technique was later used to produce exceptionally good queries for our TREC-6 VLC run, and for our TREC-7 manual ad hoc and manual VLC-II runs.

TREC-6 High Precision   TREC-6 saw the introduction of the high-precision track, in which expert users were given five minutes per topic to find ten relevant documents. We used a Java client interface (see figure 15.7) similar to the one we used for manual ad hoc, but augmented it with a timer, a method to retrieve the information need statement, a semiautomatic query generator, and an interface for managing judged documents. The experiment was performed by three of the authors, who found an average of 5.68 relevant documents per topic. This performance was essentially the same as that reported for the other two top systems.

TREC-6 Manual Ad Hoc   For the manual ad hoc task, we explored the limits of user interaction by using a process similar to that of the high-precision track to find one thousand documents per topic as required for the ad hoc task. We judged some thirteen thousand documents based on passages retrieved using the original MultiText user interface, augmented to provide ranked results and radio buttons to record relevance judgments of *relevant, not relevant,* or *iffy* for each retrieved document (figure 15.8). No limit was placed on interaction time; four people spent a total of 105 hours over eight days (an average of 2.1 hours/topic) creating queries and making judgments for the fifty topics. We also recorded the time at which each judgment was recorded so that we could measure retrieval effectiveness as a function of interaction time. Our overall objective was to set a *gold standard* as to what results might reasonably be achieved with considerable human/computer interaction. Given that the aim of the task is to retrieve a thousand potentially relevant documents, 7.2 seconds per document seems a small fraction of the overall effort expended in reading or otherwise handling them.

In the end, we did not find one thousand documents that we considered relevant per topic. Our run thus consisted of several tiers for each topic: (1) the judgments we marked as relevant, (2) the judgments we marked as iffy, and (3) documents returned by a tiered query derived from the queries recovered from the logs of our judging process. We excluded from the third tier any documents judged not relevant; this decision was a mistake as it turns out that documents we examined and judged not relevant were more likely to be judged relevant by the NIST assessors than documents we did not examine. The process by which we derived this tiered query was similar to that used for our routing effort. This tiered query was also used in our VLC run. Not surprisingly, our ad hoc submission yielded by far the best results for this task and was much emulated in TREC-7.

The judgments gleaned from our TREC-6 participation were compared to official relevance judgments rendered by NIST and found to yield similar performance rankings among the systems participating in TREC. We further used these results to evaluate more efficient means of creating relevance judgments for test collections [13].

TREC-6 Chinese Track   TREC-6 also saw our participation in the Chinese track. For this track, we used exactly the same methodology as for the TREC-5 ad hoc task, and achieved the second-best average precision over all submissions. We treated each Chinese symbol as a token in the MultiText servers—no attempt was made to *segment* the text into units resembling words, as is usually done for Chinese information retrieval. Recall that GCL admits phrase queries, so the client was at liberty to juxtapose sequences of characters with special meaning. Queries were generated manually and refined using the TREC-5 user interface, modified to display Chinese characters.

TREC-6 VLC   The TREC-6 VLC track explored the scalability of information retrieval from two to twenty gigabytes. The federated architecture of MultiText was ideally suited to this task; we simply distributed the data among four commodity personal

"ferry" and "sink*"

New Query ▭   gcl ▭   all ▭   Topic: 326 docs: 100

Search | Rank | Query Builder | ??? | Clear

FT944-5773
<PROFILE> AN-ELBDWAADFT</PROFILE>
<DATE>941202
</DATE>
<HEADLINE>
FT 02 DEC 94 / World News in Brief: Manila **ferry sinks**
</HEADLINE>
<TEXT>
A **ferry** carrying 488 people collided with a cargo ship and sank off Manila.
At least 275 people were rescued and ships were still picking up survivors
early today.
</TEXT>
<XX>
Countries:-
</XX>
<CN>PHZ Philippines, Asia.
[...]

[326 ◇rel ◇not ◇iffy]

FT944-1600
<PROFILE> AN-ELSDLAFTFT</PROFILE>
<DATE>941219
</DATE>
<HEADLINE>
FT 19 DEC 94 / Survey of Sweden (14): A remarkable comeback - Profile:
Stena Line
</HEADLINE>
<BYLINE>
   By CHRISTOPHER BROWN-HUMES
</BYLINE>
<TEXT>
For a company that was in crisis and making

[...]
 extensive collaboration with P&O,
although this would have to meet with the approval of the relevant
competition authorities. In any case, it expects the overall market to grow,
helped by economic growth in both Britain and France.
Nordic **ferry** traffic has been hit hard by the **sinking** of the **ferry**
Estonia,
which capsized in heavy seas in September with the loss of more than 900
lives. Stena has suffered less than other shipping groups, partly because it
does not operate in the Baltic Sea where the tragedy occurred. The company'
[...]

[326 ◆rel ◇not ◇iffy]

FT944-5248
<PROFILE> AN-ELECYABLFT</PROFILE>

Figure 15.8
TREC-6 interactive search and judging (1997)

computers, each with four four-gigabyte EIDE hard drives. A total of sixteen index servers and text servers were deployed—one per hard drive. This deployment gave nearly perfect CPU/IO overlap and constant response time (at the expense of a linear increase in hardware cost) from two to twenty gigabytes.

The VLC queries were derived from the manual ad hoc queries using techniques akin to those for the routing task. Further interaction with the ad hoc data was used to simplify the queries and in some cases to create new queries. Execution efficiency was a primary concern in constructing the queries; this concern was addressed by limiting to 5.5 the average number of terms per query and by applying the length restriction CONTAINED IN 128 WORDS to each query. 5.5 terms per query represents a tenfold reduction over our previous ad hoc efforts. The length restriction eliminates few relevant documents and frees the server from having to process many spurious matches. Post hoc analysis showed that these restrictions did not compromise precision: when run on the ad hoc task, these restricted queries yielded a strong average precision of 0.3334.

Retrieval performance for VLC was measured by precision at twenty documents (P@20). MultiText achieved a P@20 of 0.498 for two gigabytes and 0.643 for twenty gigabytes, considerably higher than the next-best systems' scores of 0.356 and 0.530. The comparison is not fair, however, as ours was the only run that used manually constructed queries.

All participants showed a dramatic increase in precision from two to twenty gigabytes. Many participants expressed surprise that precision increased with size. Yet it is not unexpected that the number of high-scoring documents should be larger in a larger corpus. Hence, if we draw twenty, or any fixed number, of the highest-scoring documents, we would expect their average score to increase with corpus size. And if score truly reflects the likelihood of relevance, the expected number of relevant documents, and hence the P@20, should rise. We later built on this observation in a number of ways—specifically, in constructing an automatic query generation system for VLC, in developing pseudorelevance feedback systems for ad hoc retrieval, and in developing boosting techniques for question answering.

15.3.4   TREC-7

TREC-7 saw our final efforts in manual query formulation. In the manual ad hoc task, as for TREC-6, we employed interactive search and judging to build a set of relevance judgments. But we did not use the relevance judgments directly to form our runs. Instead, we focused on the formulation of succinct Boolean queries that were used to generate queries for our ad hoc and VLC-II runs. We also generated automatic tiered queries consisting of exactly the title words in various combinations; the method we used is elaborated in the next section. Queries comprising a single conjunction, averaging 1.86 terms, achieved high precision (average precision = 0.2983 on ad hoc; P@20 = 0.574 on VLC-II), with 100 GB retrieval time of 0.88 seconds per query, running on a pair of 350 MHz Pentium systems. Compound queries averaging 6.42 terms achieved precision competitive with the best runs (average precision = 0.359; P@20 = 0.598), and 100 GB retrieval time of 1.51 seconds per query. In contrast, the automatically generated queries consisting of exactly the title words averaged 2.84 terms, and achieved mediocre precision (average precision = 0.187; P@20 = 0.442) and an execution time of 0.71 seconds per query. MultiText was awarded the ACSys medal for its VLC-II results.

As for TREC-6, we observed that P@k for any given k increases with collection size c. This increase offsets the decrease in P@k that may be observed as k is increased while c is held constant. We are able to generalize this relationship between precision and collection size by the observation that P@k remains constant when k and c are both increased (or decreased) by the same factor. For example, our automatic VLC-II run achieves P@2 = 0.320 on the one gigabyte corpus and P@20 = 0.320 on the ten gigabyte corpus; also P@2 = 0.444 on the ten gigabytes corpus and P@20 = 0.442 on the hundred gigabyte corpus. In both cases, we see that increasing both k and c by a factor of ten leaves the precision unchanged. Thus, we may expect that P@k is a function of the ratio k/c regardless of corpus size. Figure 15.9 shows that when P is plotted

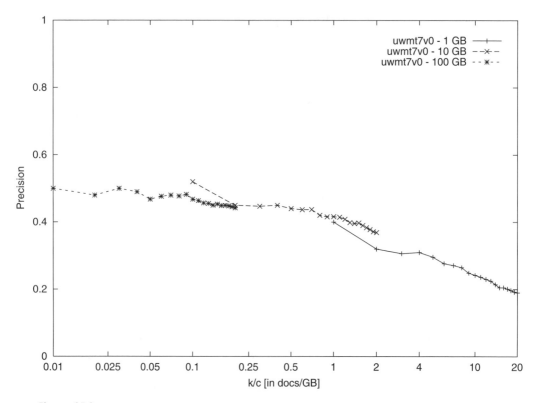

Figure 15.9
Relationship between corpus size (c) and P@k

as a function of k/c, the results of the three runs ($c = 1$ GB, $c = 10$ GB, $c = 100$ GB) form a common curve. This observation enables us to use the retrieval results from a sample of a corpus to predict results on the whole corpus [12].

15.4   1997–1999: Cover Density Ranking (CDR)

CDR refers to a family of techniques for automatically deriving high-performance tiered queries from a small number of search terms. It was first developed prior to TREC-6 [9] as a method to answer the search requests that arise in interactive settings. Experience with our Usenet and TREC interactive systems showed that typical users are impatient, usually issuing search requests consisting of three or fewer terms and seldom retrieving more than a handful of the highest-ranked documents. The design objectives for CDR are derived from these observations: *fast, automatic, high-precision retrieval from a small number of search terms*.

15.4.1   CDR Chronology

In TREC, our first application of CDR was to the TREC-6 *title-only* ad hoc task. We found that the longest title contained four words and that the average title length was less than three. Applying CDR to these titles we achieved an average precision of 0.217, comparable to our implementation of the Okapi measure on the same terms, which achieved an average precision of 0.215. We also used CDR to retrieve passages from which we extracted 24 feedback terms—these feedback terms formed the input to a second Okapi run. Our official submission blended the results of the three runs—CDR, Okapi (on the title terms), and Okapi (on the feedback terms)—to achieve an average precision of 0.239, the fourth best of all title-only runs.

For the compulsory *description-only* run, we used only the feedback strategy described above. That is, we used CDR to retrieve passages from which we extracted feedback terms and submitted the Okapi run on these terms. The average precision was 0.191, the third best of all participants.

From TREC 6–8, our VLC participation was the primary vehicle for developing CDR. We wished to explore the speed and the precision that could be achieved by automatically generated queries on huge corpora. Although our TREC-6 VLC effort was classified as manual, we developed query construction and tiering methods that were the basis for our TREC-7 and TREC-8 efforts. For TREC-7 we used CDR, with a new tiering method, on the title terms. This method provided high speed and reasonable precision. For TREC-8 we refined the tiering method, yielding the best precision of any TREC-8 participant (P@20 = 0.572).

15.4.2   CDR Method

Given a set of n search terms $t_1, t_2, \ldots t_n$, CDR generates a tiered query that is then evaluated using shortest substring ranking. Under the tiering strategy used prior to and during TREC-6, the tiers are constructed using *coordination level*: the first tier uses all of the terms, while the second tier uses all but one of the terms, and so on:

n OF $(t_1, t_2, \ldots t_n)$

$n - 1$ OF $(t_1, t_2, \ldots t_n)$

$\ldots$

1   OF $(t_1, t_2, \ldots t_n)$.

 A shortcoming of this approach is that it takes no account of the relative quality of the search terms. For example, consider the set of terms: "hubble," "space," and "telescope." The tiered query for this set of terms is:

```
3 OF {"hubble", "space", "telescope"}
2 OF {"hubble", "space", "telescope"}
1 OF {"hubble", "space", "telescope"}
```

The first tier is the strongest; fragments containing all of the terms are most likely to be relevant, provided the fragments are not too big (an issue that we have mentioned previously and will revisit). The second tier matches fragments that contain "hubble" and "space," "hubble" and "telescope," or "space" and "telescope." By luck or good fortune, it turns out that fragments containing any of these pairs are about equally likely to be relevant. On the other hand, the third tier matches any fragment containing "hubble," "space," or "telescope." While fragments containing "hubble" have a reasonable chance of being relevant, fragments containing "space" or "telescope" alone are unlikely to refer to the Hubble.

 Our general approach to this shortcoming is to consider each nonempty subset of the terms, joined as a conjunction, to be a candidate query. The candidate queries are then combined, using techniques similar to those for routing, into a common tiered query. For the current example, the candidate queries would be:

```
"hubble" AND "space" AND "telescope"
"hubble" AND "space"
"hubble" AND "telescope"
"space" AND "telescope"
"hubble"
"space"
"telescope."
```

The process by which we derive the tiered query is:

1. Apply a length restriction CONTAINED IN n WORDS to each candidate
2. Estimate the precision for each candidate
3. Order the candidates by precision
4. Combine candidates with similar precision to form tiers
5. Apply Boolean simplification to each tier

For the example, the final tiered query might be:

```
("hubble" AND "space" AND "telescope") CONTAINED IN 128 WORDS
("hubble" AND ("space" OR "telescope")) CONTAINED IN 128 WORDS
("space" AND "telescope") CONTAINED IN 128 WORDS
("hubble") CONTAINED IN 128 WORDS
("space" OR "telescope") CONTAINED IN 128 WORDS
```

Precision cannot be estimated using training data, as for routing. Instead, we assume that candidates containing a common set of terms are less likely to be relevant than candidates containing uncommon ones.

Method 1 estimates the commonality of a set of terms by the number of times they co-occur within n words in the corpus. To compute this quantity, we simply count the number of fragments in the corpus that satisfy the candidate query, with the length restriction applied.

Method 1 was first deployed in the user interface for the TREC-6 high-precision track (figure 15.7). The candidate queries are shown in the top-left corner, ordered by their commonality. Initially, the candidates were constructed from the title words; these were augmented by any terms typed in by the user in the lower-right pane. (Note that the user has entered the term "South Africa*" and expanded "Deaths" to "Deaths [or] killed [or] died.") No evaluation of the precision of the approach was done at this time; instead, the user manipulated the terms and examined the results until ten relevant documents were found, or the time limit elapsed.

Method 1 was used for our TREC-7 title-only ad hoc and VLC-II runs. In both cases, the commonality of passages was measured using the ad hoc corpus, so the queries were identical. The results were an average precision of 0.19 for ad hoc and a P@20 of 0.442 for VLC. Method 1 appears to give some improvement over coordination level ranking, but the overall results are not spectacular.

Method 2 estimates the commonality of a set of terms by the probability that they would co-occur in a random fragment of n words, assuming that the individual term occurrences were uniformly and independently distributed throughout the corpus. Let $t_{1,2},\dots t_k$ be the terms in a candidate query. Let N_i be the number of occurrences of term t_i in the corpus. Let S be the corpus size. Assuming that all terms are uniformly distributed, the probability that any particular term is t_i is $f_i = N_i/S$. Assuming that all term probabilities are independent, the probability that any particular fragment of length n contains t_i is $1 - (1 - f_i)^n$ or approximately nf_i. The probability that all of t_1 through t_k occur by chance in a fragment of length n is therefore approximately

$$P = \prod_{i=1}^{k} nf_i = n^k \prod_{i=1}^{k} f_i.$$

Method 2 was used for our TREC-8 VLC-II runs, which outscored all others (P@20 = 0.5720). For this run, we used $n = 128$ and grouped together candidates whose commonality (P) differed by less than a factor of two. Because method 2 was not developed in time, one of our official ad hoc runs used method 1 and achieved an average precision of 0.214. Later, we applied method 2 in an unofficial run and achieved an average precision of 0.223. Our other two ad hoc runs used feedback as described for TREC-6. Our title-only run achieved an average precision of 0.2673 while our title plus description run achieved 0.2671.

15.5   1999–2002: Passage Retrieval for QA

The QA tracks from TREC 8–10 required that each system, given a factual question written as a sentence, automatically return five fragments likely to contain an answer to the question. For TREC-8 two tasks were specified: one in which the fragments were 250 bytes long, and one in which the fragments were 50 bytes long. For TREC-9 the 50-byte task was compulsory, and for TREC-10 the 250-byte task was eliminated. In the paragraphs below, we outline the contribution of techniques derived from CDR to these tasks. Details of our QA results appear elsewhere [8].

15.5.1   TREC-8

For TREC-8, we used a simple application of the MultiText retrieval system to solve only the 250-byte task. The words from each question, less stop words, were taken as search terms. Intervals of text were found that contained subsets of the terms that would be unlikely to occur together by chance. The underlying assumption in this choice is that if the words occur for some reason other than chance, that reason is likely to be that they pertain to the subject of the question. The intervals containing the five least likely to occur subsets were truncated or padded as necessary to form the 250-byte answer passages.

Our measure of commonality is essentially the same as that used for CDR method 2; that is, the probability that a set of terms $t_1, t_2, \ldots t_k$ occurs by chance in an interval of length n is

$$P = \prod_{i=1}^{k} nf_i = n^k \prod_{i=1}^{k} f_i.$$

The only difference is that rather than fixing n, we compute P for every fragment f_i in the corpus containing a subset of the terms, with $n = |f_i|$. It is convenient to recast P above as its self-information

$$S = -\log P = -k \log n - \sum_{i=1}^{k} \log f_i.$$

For TREC-8, we simply returned the five passages (from distinct documents) with the highest S, ordered by S. Despite its simplicity, this technique achieved a mean reciprocal rank of 0.471, the sixth highest of the forty-one runs.

15.5.2 TREC-9

For TREC-9, we incorporated two significant new components to our QA process. The first component was a probabilistic context-free parser that was applied to each question. From the parse, we derived a superior set of GCL search terms, which were used with CDR method 2 to find the highest-scoring passage within each of the highest-scoring d documents. (For TREC-9, $d = 20$.) From the parse, we also derived a *category* for each question.

The passages and the question category were passed to the second new component: *answer selection*. The answer selection component uses the answer category to identify uncommon candidate answer terms within the passages. Each candidate answer term that occurs in d passages is assigned a score based on the probability that it would occur k times in d random passages.

The candidate scores are used to select a b-byte answer as follows. Each b-byte fragment from each passage is examined; its score is a combination of the scores of the candidate terms that it contains. The fragment with the highest score is taken as the first answer. Then, the scores of all candidate terms contained within the fragment are set to zero, and the process repeats until five answers are returned.

Overall, we achieved mean reciprocal ranks of 0.321 and 0.456 for the 50- and 250-byte tasks, respectively the second and third best of all runs for each task. Post hoc experiments showed that for the 250-byte task, the parser alone netted a 12 percent improvement, while the two components together netted 21 percent.

15.5.3 TREC-10

For TREC-10, we took advantage of our observation that precision increases with corpus size. We used the same parser to generate GCL queries and tiered them using CDR method 2. Each tier was translated into (somewhat weaker) queries suitable for each of two Web search engines, and for each question several thousand documents were retrieved from the Web and entered into a MultiText server. For each question, we used a tiered query to retrieve the best forty documents from each of three sources—the QA corpus and each of the Web-derived databases.

These 120 passages were given as input to the answer selection component, where the corpus and Web passages were treated in an identical manner for the scoring of candidate terms. During selection of the fragments, consideration was restricted to those passages originating with the QA corpus, as the track rules state that the answer must be justified by a document in this corpus.

Overall, we achieved a 25 percent improvement by using passages from the Web; we achieved a mean reciprocal rank of 0.379 without the Web passages, and 0.483 with the Web passages.

15.6 Summary

We have shown through our participation in TREC that retrieval based on the proximity of a few search terms can yield outstanding performance in information retrieval. CDR is a novel method for fast, automatic, high-precision retrieval from a small number of search terms. This chapter traces the evolution of CDR from its roots in shortest substring ranking through the development of method 2, which is applied to yield exceptional speed, scalability, price performance, and precision in the large Web and QA tracks.

Acknowledgments

The research described in this chapter was supported by Communications and Information Technology, Ontario, and by the Natural Sciences and Engineering Research Council of Canada.

References

[1] Clarke, C. L. A., and G. V. Cormack. Interactive substring retrieval. In *TREC-5*, 295–304.

[2] Clarke, C. L. A., and G. V. Cormack. Shortest substring retrieval and ranking. *ACM Transactions on Information Systems* 18, no. 1 (January 2000): 44–78.

[3] Clarke, C. L. A., G. V. Cormack, and F. J. Burkowski. Schema-independent retrieval from heterogeneous structured text. In *Fourth annual symposium on document analysis and information retrieval*, 279–289. Las Vegas: April 1995.

[4] Clarke, C. L. A., G. V. Cormack, and F. J. Burkowski. Shortest substring ranking. In *TREC-4*, 295–304.

[5] Clarke, C. L. A., G. V. Cormack, G. Kemkes, M. Laszlo, T. R. Lynam, E. L. Terra, and P. L. Tilker. Statistical selection of exact answers. In *TREC 2002*.

[6] Clarke, C. L. A., G. V. Cormack, D. Kisman, and T. R. Lynam. Question answering by passage selection. In *TREC-9*, 673.

[7] Clarke, C. L. A., G. V. Cormack, T. R. Lynam, C. M. Li, and G. L. McLearn. Web reinforced question answering. In *TREC 2001*, 673–679.

[8] Clarke, C. L. A., G. V. Cormack, T. R. Lynam, E. L. Terra, and M. Laszlo. Question answering by passage selection. In *Advances in open domain question answering*, ed. T. Strzalkowski and S. Harabagiu. Boston: Kluwer Academic Publishers, 2004.

[9] Clarke, C. L. A., G. V. Cormack, and E. A. Tudhope. Relevance ranking for one to three term queries. *Information Processing and Management* 36, no. 2 (2000): 291–311. A version of this paper was presented at the fifth RIAO conference, Montreal, Quebec, June 1997.

[10] Cormack, G. V., C. L. A Clarke, and D. Kisman. Fast automatic passage ranking. In *TREC-8*, 735–741.

[11] Cormack, G. V., C. L. A. Clarke, C. R. Palmer, and S. S. L. To. Passage-based query refinement. *Information Processing and Management* 36, no. 1 (2000): 133–153. A version of this paper was presented at TREC-6.

[12] Cormack, G. V., O. Lhotak, and C. R. Palmer. Estimating precision by random sampling. In *Proceedings of the twenty-second annual international ACM SIGIR conference*, 273–274.

[13] Cormack, G. V., C. R. Palmer, and C. L. A. Clarke. Efficient construction of large test collections. In *Proceedings of the twenty-first annual international ACM SIGIR conference*, 282–289.

[14] Cormack, G. V., C. R. Palmer, M. Van Biesbrouck, and C. L. A. Clarke. Deriving very short queries for high precision and recall. In *TREC-7*, 121–132.

16 A Language-Modeling Approach to TREC
Djoerd Hiemstra and Wessel Kraaij

16.1 Introduction

Started in 1996, the European Union–funded Twenty-One project originally intended to build a prototype cross-language information retrieval system. This led to a number of fruitful TREC participations, in which we evaluated the use of a probabilistic modeling approach known as *language modeling*. This chapter describes the Twenty-One language-modeling experiments on a variety of TREC tasks.

The term *language models* originates from probabilistic models of language generation developed for ASR systems in the early 1980s (see, for example, Rabiner 1990). Language models assign a probability to a piece of text. For instance, "how are you today?" would be assigned a higher probability than "cow barks moo soufflé" because the words in the former phrase (or word pairs or word triples if so-called *n*-grams are used) occur much more frequently in English than the words in the latter phrase. Automatic speech recognizers use language model probabilities to improve recognition performance. Language models were applied to information retrieval by a number of research groups in the late 1990s (Ponte and Croft 1998, Hiemstra and Kraaij 1999; Miller, Leek, and Schwartz 1999; Berger and Lafferty 1999; Ng 2000). For information retrieval, language models are built for each document. By following this approach, the language model of the book you are reading now would assign an exceptionally high probability to the word "TREC," indicating that this book would be a good candidate for retrieval if the query contains this word.

16.1.1 Probabilistic Models and IR: An Overview
Interestingly, probabilistic modeling has been around in information retrieval for much longer than the late 1990s, or even the 1980s, and in a way, the language-modeling approach builds directly on many of the ideas of the more traditional probabilistic models for information retrieval.

It is fair to say that the approach to information retrieval presented in this chapter was originally introduced by M. E. Maron and J. L. Kuhns (1960). At a time when manual indexing was still guiding the field, they suggested that an indexer, which runs through the various index terms q that possibly apply to a document D, might assign a probability $P(q|D)$ to a term given a document instead of making a yes/no decision. Using Bayes' theorem and a document prior $P(D)$, they then suggest ranking the documents by the probability that the document is relevant $P(D|q)$. Maron and Kuhns described how $P(D)$ could be inferred automatically, but they were not really looking for automatic ways to infer $P(q|D)$, or if they were, they did not know how the probabilities $P(q|D)$ could be defined.

Keith van Rijsbergen (1986) introduced an idea quite similar to that of Maron and Kuhns: modeling information retrieval as documents "implying" the query terms with some probability $P(q|D)$. Again, the definition of the probabilities $P(q|D)$ was not easily found, hampering its application to practical retrieval problems. Lacking such a definition, the INQUERY system (Turtle and Croft 1992) used some ad hoc combination of $tf \cdot idf$ weights to define the probabilities $P(q|D)$.

But there are alternatives to $tf \cdot idf$ weighting. The well-known probabilistic model developed by Stephen Robertson and Karen Sparck Jones (1976) is built around the probability of relevance. This model can be seen as a discriminative one—that is, it tries to separate the relevant documents from the nonrelevant ones by following the well-known "naive Bayes" assumption (Duda and Hart 1973): the terms in the document (usually restricted by some query terms) are conditionally independent given relevance (or nonrelevance). We might look at this as a mechanism to generate an unseen relevant, or nonrelevant, document. Yet a substantial set of relevant documents is needed to estimate the probabilities for a single query, making it hard to apply the model to practical retrieval situations like the TREC ad hoc task.

Another interesting probabilistic modeling approach is suggested by Abraham Bookstein and Fred Swanson (1974) and Stephen Harter (1975). They assume that documents are created by a random stream of term occurrences. For each term, the collection can be divided into two subsets, where one subset treats a subject represented by a term to a greater extent than the other. The number of term occurrences tf may then be modeled by a mixture of two Poisson distributions, one for each subset. Unfortunately, as with relevance, it is unknown as to which subset each document belongs, making it hard to apply the model to practical situations. The two-Poisson model, however, did inspire the Okapi BM25 weighting algorithm (Robertson and Walker 1994).

Knowing what we know now from the language-modeling approach, and looking back at the history of probabilistic modeling for information retrieval, we might observe that we are actually using many of the early ideas. We will use different TREC tasks to illustrate different aspects of the language-modeling approach. Where appropriate, we will refer to the classics of probabilistic modeling for information retrieval.

16.1.2 A Language Model for Every Task

Different tracks in TREC call for different approaches to information retrieval. Some tasks, like the ad hoc topic search task, might already be served quite well by a basic retrieval approach, but many other TREC tasks call for including some special "non-content" information. CLIR obviously needs to deal with some form of automatic translation, adaptive filtering needs to deal with the user's feedback on the selected documents, and the Web entry page search task might benefit from, for example, counting the number of inlinks to a document.

This chapter will introduce a language-modeling approach for four TREC subtasks. Every model is built around the basic query-generation language model, but each model has its own little twist. In section 16.2, we introduce the basic model and show how document priors can improve performance on the TREC ad hoc task. Section 16.3 elaborates on the use of document priors by applying them to the TREC Web entry page task. Section 16.4 extends the model by including a statistical translation model for application to the TREC cross-language retrieval task. Finally, section 16.5 presents a relevance feedback method, which is applied to the TREC adaptive filtering task.

16.2   The Basic Language Model and the TREC Ad Hoc Task

We believe that many of the early probabilistic models failed as general models for diverse retrieval tasks because they failed to answer a few quite fundamental questions about the use of probabilistic models in general. What justifies the use of probabilistic models? What probability mechanisms are involved? And how do these mechanisms fit the reality of information retrieval?

The use of probability theory might be justified by modeling the process of a user formulating a query Q while that user has a relevant document D in mind. Imagine picking a word at random from this page by pointing at the page with your eyes closed. Such a process would define a probability $P(Q|D)$, which might be used as van Rijsbergen's (1986) "logical implication." Is this really how users formulate queries? A pragmatic answer to that question would be, if such a model achieves good performance on a real retrieval task, then the model fits reality well. Test collections, like those developed at TRECs, can be used to measure a model's performance on realistic retrieval tasks in a controlled setting.

Actually, the answer to the above question is, No, such a model does not work well in practice because of the so-called sparse data problem (Manning and Schütze 1999). The mechanism above suggests that terms that do not occur in a document are assigned zero probability, but the fact that a term is never observed in a document does not mean this term is never entered in a query for which the document is relevant. The reality of information retrieval is that users are not very good at formulating queries. Many query terms do not seem to come from relevant documents at all; they seem to come from some general vocabulary. These might be words like "Find documents about" (which are often found in TREC topic descriptions; see chapter 2, this volume), but it might be any other query term that seems plausible yet does not contribute to retrieval performance.

We will call query terms that presumably were generated from the relevant document the *important* terms, and the terms that presumably were generated from the user's general vocabulary the *unimportant* terms. Given a document collection C and a relevant document D, the process of generating a query term q_i might be modeled by a mixture of two probability measures: $P(q_i|D)$ for the important terms, and $P(q_i|C)$ for the unimportant ones. Of course, just from looking at the query it is unknown which terms are important and which are unimportant. Therefore, the mixture parameter λ

defines the unknown probability of term importance. Equation (16.1) defines our basic language model if we assume that each term is generated independently from previous terms given the relevant document:

$$P(q_1, q_2, \ldots, q_n | D) = \prod_{i=1}^{n} (\lambda P(q_i | D) + (1 - \lambda) P(q_i | C)). \tag{16.1}$$

The basic language model addresses both the sparse data problem—all terms are generated with a nonzero probability—and the fact that queries consist of content words and query jargon (Zhai and Lafferty 2001). Interestingly, like Maron and Kuhns (1960), we take the document/query (term) implication $P(Q|D)$ as the basis of our model. Like Harter (1975), we assume an explicit probability mechanism that defines a mixture model.

Ideally, we would like to train the probability of an unimportant term on a large corpus of queries. In practice, however, we will use the document collection C to define these probabilities—hence, the notation $P(q_i|C)$. Whenever we use the TREC topic descriptions, a small number of words like "Find documents about" will be removed from the query to compensate for the lack of a query corpus. We use Bayes' theorem as shown in equation (16.2) to define the posterior probability of the document D being relevant given the query $Q = q_1, \ldots, q_n$:

$$P(D|q_1, q_2, \ldots, q_n) = \frac{P(q_1, q_2, \ldots, q_n | D) P(D)}{P(q_1, q_2, \ldots, q_n)}. \tag{16.2}$$

Note that the denominator on the right-hand side does not depend on the document. It might therefore be ignored when a document ranking is needed. The prior $P(D)$, though, should only be ignored if we assume a uniform prior—that is, if we assume that all documents are equally likely to be relevant in the absence of a query. Some noncontent information, like the source of a document, its age, and so on, might contain some hints on whether it is likely to be relevant or not. Stephen Robertson and Stephen Walker (1994) and Amit Singhal and his colleagues (1995) argued that on the ad hoc task, the length of a document already contains some clues. The longer the document, the more likely it is to be relevant.

Figure 16.1 shows the probability of relevance given the document length for the TREC ad hoc task. We divided the document length, which varies from documents containing only one or two words to documents containing over ten thousand words, into sixteen bins on a log scale. Each point on the plot marks the probability of relevance of the documents in one of these bins. The sixteen bins and the corresponding probabilities define a discrete probability measure $P(D)$, which takes one of sixteen different values based on the bin in which D falls. As such, it can be used directly in equation (16.2). Alternatively, looking at the plot, one could make the general modeling

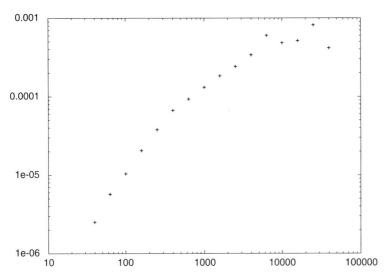

Figure 16.1
Prior probability of relevance $P(D)$ given document length on the ad hoc task

Table 16.1
Results of TREC-7 ad hoc runs

Run name	Description	Average precision
tno7cbm25	BM25 weighting	0.232
tno7tw3	Language model	0.241
tno7tw4	Language model with doclen prior	0.251

assumption that the a priori probability of relevance is taken as a linear function of the document length, so

$$P_{\text{doclen}}(D) = c \cdot doclen(D),\tag{16.3}$$

where $doclen(D)$ is the total number of words in document D, and c is a constant that can be ignored in the ranking formula.

Table 16.1 lists the results of TREC-7 ad hoc experiments using the title, the description, and the narrative of the topics (see chapter 4, this volume), with one run using the BM25 algorithm (implemented as in Singhal et al. 1995), and one run using the language-modeling algorithm with a document length prior.[1] As mentioned above, the language model has an unknown parameter λ that defines the mixture of local and global frequency information. We used $\lambda = 0.15$ based on experiments on the TREC-6 ad hoc collection (Hiemstra and Kraaij 1999).

16.3   Prior Probabilities and the TREC Entry Page Task

An application where the prior information component of the basic model (compare with equation [16.2]) is even more important is the TREC entry page task, which was run as a new task of the Web track of TREC-10 in 2001. Earlier issues of the Web track had already targeted the issue of integrating information about link-structure with traditional IR models for ad hoc retrieval. Since these attempts had shown no significant benefit for link-based approaches and it was realized that links played an important role in commercial search engines like Google (Brin and Page 1998), a special task was created to investigate the crucial subclass of searching for the entry page of an organization. This decision readjusted TREC's focus to "real-life" search tasks, which were no longer limited to the classical information-seeking queries modeled by the initial ad hoc and routing tasks.

For an elaborate description of the entry page task, see chapter 9, this volume, and Kraaij, Westerveld, and Hiemstra (2002). The basic idea is that each organization has an entry page on the Web, functioning as a portal to its information. An entry page search differs in two ways from an ad hoc search: there is only one (sometimes a few) entry page(s) for a particular organization, so high precision is important; and Web data are different from news data, the main difference being link structure. We could thus formulate the challenge of the entry page task as follows: to integrate knowledge about the external properties and the context of a document with our basic model in order to improve high precision.

We will show that the generative probabilistic approach we have presented in section 16.2 can easily accommodate information derived from these knowledge sources. In equation (16.4), l refers to the event when a user likes a document, given a certain task. In the context of an entry page search, a user is interested in an entry page as specified by the query Q. Equation (16.4) decomposes the posterior probability that a document is liked given the query and a specific document by applying Bayes' theorem:

$$P(l|D, Q) = \frac{P(Q|l, D)P(l|D)}{P(Q|D)}.$$

(16.4)

We include l here to relate the language-modeling approach to the Robertson and Sparck Jones model (Lafferty and Zhai 2003), and to show that estimating priors is not really different from estimating the probability of relevance (that is, the probability that the user "likes" the document), as demonstrated by Robertson and Sparck Jones (1976). Since our aim is to rank documents by their posterior probability, we can apply any convenient order-preserving transformation. It is customary to work with the log odds of being liked instead of the pure probability since it is difficult to estimate the normalizing probability $P(Q|D) = P(Q, l|D) + P(Q, \bar{l}|D)$. We further approximate the probability of the query given a document that is not relevant by generating it from the background collection:

$$\log \frac{P(l|D, Q)}{P(\bar{l}|D, Q)} = \log \frac{P(Q|l, D)}{P(Q|\bar{l}, D)} + \log \frac{P(l|D)}{P(\bar{l}|D)} = \log \frac{P(Q|l, D)}{P(Q|C)} + \log \frac{P(l|D)}{P(\bar{l}|D)} \tag{16.5}$$

Assuming term independence and applying smoothing by linear interpolation with a background model leads to:

$$\log \frac{P(l|D, Q)}{P(\bar{l}|D, Q)} = \sum_{q_i \in Q} \left(\log \frac{\lambda P(q_i|l, D) + (1 - \lambda) P(q_i|C)}{P(q_i|C)} \right) + \log \frac{P(l|D)}{P(\bar{l}|D)} \tag{16.6}$$

This model can be interpreted as a Bayesian update process. The prior log odds of being liked is initially purely determined by the document properties itself and subsequently updated with the additional knowledge of the likelihood of the query given the fact that the document is liked versus the likelihood of the query given a background model. As we will see, unlike the ad hoc task, prior knowledge is of utmost importance for entry page search.

We investigated three properties of Web pages in order to provide an initial estimate of the prior probability of a Web page: document length, the number of documents pointing to the document via a hyperlink (inlinks), and the form of the URL. It is well-known that longer documents have a higher probability of relevance for ad hoc search, but it is not clear whether long documents have a higher probability of being an entry page. The conjecture that a high number of incoming links indicates that the page pointed to is an entry page is already much more intuitive. Finally, most Web users, even with little search experience, know that entry pages usually have short URLs. There are probably some simple explanations for this fact: entry pages benefit from being short since they can be memorized more easily, and because information on the Web is often stored in a hierarchical file system, entry pages are usually located at the top of or at least high in the directory hierarchy.

We measured the informativeness of each of the three features in the following way: for each feature x_i, we divided the document set in disjunct classes v_{ij} and directly estimated $P(l|x_i = v_{ij})$ on a training set. This set consisted of a hundred training topics and the corresponding entry pages of the TREC 2001 Web track entry page task. The probability of being an entry page given the information that a document belongs to a certain bin is defined by:

$$P(l|x_i = v_{ij}) = \frac{c(EP, v_{ij})}{c(v_{ij})}, \tag{16.7}$$

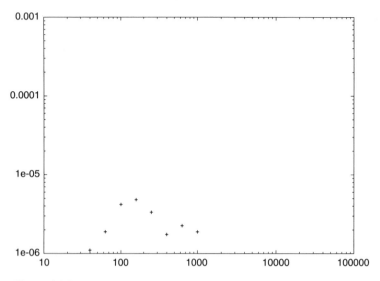

Figure 16.2
Prior probability of relevance given document length on the entry page task (P (*entry page*|*doclen*))

where $c(v_{ij})$ is the cardinality of class v_{ij} and $c(EP, v_{ij})$ is the number of entry pages in class v_{ij}. The training set is small, but probably sufficient to estimate probabilities for a small number of classes. Size and the number of classes are chosen such that a class contains at least five home pages of the training set, while trying to maximize the number of classes in order to reduce variance. The goal of this procedure is to define a partitioning of the data set, by means of feature restrictions, which correlates well with being an entry page.

16.3.1 Document Length
For the document-length feature, we created classes by quantization into sixteen bins on a log scale. Section 16.2 showed that document-length priors are useful in an ad hoc search task. Here, we investigate whether the length of a document is also a useful indicator of the probability that a document is an entry page. Figure 16.2 shows a plot of the probability of relevance versus page length, calculated on the training data provided for the entry page task of TREC 2001's Web track. Note that the probability of relevance is also plotted on a log scale; therefore, bins with zero probability of relevance do not appear.

Indeed, document length can predict the relevance of a page since the distribution is not uniform. Pages with a medium length (sixty to one thousand words) have a higher probability, with a maximum around one to two hundred words. The differences are much less marked than for ad hoc search, however.

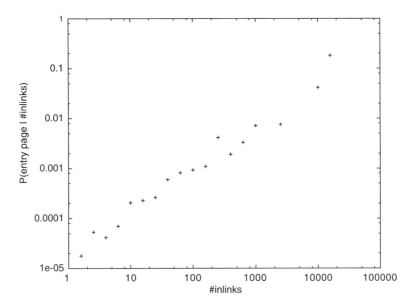

Figure 16.3
Prior probability of relevance given number of inlinks on the entry page task (P (*entry page*|*#inlinks*))

16.3.2 Number of Inlinks
For the inlinks feature, we created classes by quantization into nine bins on a log scale. The number of inlinks is a much better predictor of being an entry page, as is shown in figure 16.3 (which is based on eighteen bins). The prior could probably also be modeled as a linear function.

16.3.3 URL Depth
For the URL attribute of the Web pages, we defined four classes in the following way:

Root: a domain name, optionally followed by "index.html" (for example, ⟨http://trec.nist.gov⟩)

Subroot: a domain name, followed by a single directory, optionally followed by "index.html" (for instance, ⟨http://trec.nist.gov/publications/⟩)

Path: a domain name, followed by an arbitrarily deep path, but not ending in a file name other than "index.html" (say, ⟨http://trec.nist.gov/publications/trec8/system-descriptions/⟩)

File: anything ending in a file name other than "index.html" (for example, ⟨http://trec.nist.gov/resources.html⟩)

Table 16.2
Prior probabilities for different URL types, estimated on the training data

Document type	$P(EP)$
Root	$6.44 \cdot 10^{-3}$
Subroot	$3.95 \cdot 10^{-4}$
Path	$9.55 \cdot 10^{-5}$
File	$3.85 \cdot 10^{-6}$

The resulting probabilities for the different URL types are listed in table 16.2. Note that the prior probabilities differ several orders of magnitude; a root page has an almost two thousand times larger probability of being an entry page than any other page.

16.3.4 Generalizing to a Combination of Features

We have identified several noncontent features that seem promising in discriminating between relevant and nonrelevant Web pages. To estimate the prior on a combination of these features, we investigated the following. Let's assume each document D is described by a number of features $x_1, x_2, \ldots, x_n$, where x_1 represents the URL depth, x_2 represents the number of inlinks, and so on. The problem can be formalized as follows: we want to estimate

$$\log \frac{P(l|D)}{P(\bar{l}|D)} = \log \frac{P(l|x_1, x_2, \ldots, x_n)}{P(\bar{l}|x_1, x_2, \ldots, x_n)}. \tag{16.8}$$

A combined inlinks/URL-depth prior would already need $9 \times 4 = 36$ model parameters. Because the training set of one hundred entry pages is too small to reliably estimate this many parameters, we assume conditional independence of the features given relevance, giving:

$$\log \frac{P(l|D)}{P(\bar{l}|D)} = \sum_{i=1}^{n} \log \frac{P(x_i|l)}{P(x_i|\bar{l})} + \log \frac{P(l)}{P(\bar{l})}. \tag{16.9}$$

Some readers might recognize the above definition as the probabilistic model of information retrieval developed by Robertson and Sparck Jones (1976). An important difference from the Robertson/Sparck Jones model is the fact that the features are *not* the index terms but some noncontent information about the document. As a consequence, we are able to use relevance information over a hundred entry page queries of our training set and reliably estimate the probability of relevance. In practice, the training set did not contain labeled *non*entry pages, which made it difficult to estimate $P(x_j|\bar{l})$. Instead we used $P(x_j)$, which might be a good approximation as there are many more Web pages than entry pages in the training data.

Table 16.3
Distribution of entry pages and WT10g over different document types

Document type t_i	No. of entry pages	No. of WT10g		$P(EP)$
Root with 0–1 inlinks	11 (10.1%)	1484	(0.0%)	0.0074
Root with 2–4 inlinks	14 (12.9%)	3431	(0.2%)	0.0041
Root with 5–9 inlinks	14 (12.9%)	2446	(0.1%)	0.0057
Root with 10–19 inlinks	8 (7.4%)	1404	(0.0%)	0.0057
Root with 20–49 inlinks	12 (11.1%)	1110	(0.0%)	0.011
Root with 50–99 inlinks	5 (4.6%)	412	(0.0%)	0.012
Root with 100–199 inlinks	6 (5.5%)	205	(0.0%)	0.029
Root with 200–999 inlinks	5 (4.6%)	175	(0.0%)	0.028
Root with 1,000+ inlinks	4 (3.7%)	38	(0.0%)	0.11
Subroot	15 (13.9%)	37959	(2.2%)	0.00043
Path	8 (7.4%)	83734	(4.9%)	0.00010
File	6 (5.6%)	1557719	(92.0%)	0.000038

Table 16.4
Results for different priors

Ranking method	MRR	Description
$P(Q|D)$	0.3375	No prior
$P(Q|D)P_{inlinks}(D)$	0.5064	Inlinks prior (analytic)
$P(Q|D)P_{URL}(D)$	0.7705	URL-depth prior (four bins)
$P(Q|D)P_{inlinks+URL}(D)$	0.7504	Combined inlinks/URL depth prior assuming conditional independence
$P(Q|D)P_{inlinks+URL}(D)$	0.7832	Combined inlinks/URL-depth prior using direct estimation (twelve classes)

Instead of assuming conditional independence between inlinks and URL depth, we might also merge some of the thirty-six classes. We only partitioned the root URL class by the number of inlinks since most entry pages have root URLs, so a further division based on inlinks can still yield reasonably reliable parameter estimates. Table 16.3 shows the statistics of the twelve classes.

Table 16.4 shows the mean reciprocal rank (MRR) for runs on the TREC 2001 test collection in combination with different priors. Both inlinks and URL depth help to increase search effectiveness, especially the URL-depth is highly effective. The combination of the inlinks prior and the URL prior based on a conditional independence assumption shows somewhat lower performance than the run based on only the URL. This might indicate that the independence assumption does not hold. The setup based on twelve disjoint classes as defined in table 16.3 yielded an MRR of 0.7832, which is a small improvement with respect to the run based on just the content and URL-depth information. We think results could be improved even more with a larger training set and a more principled way to define classes—for example, using methods proposed by James Dougherty, Ron Kohavi, and Mehran Sahami (1995).

16.4   The Translation Model and the TREC Cross-Language Task

Our work on CLIR in TREC and the closely related CLEF evaluation is another good example that the basic language model can be easily extended for a new task. The CLIR problem deals with the retrieval situation where the query is formulated in a different language than the documents (for more information, see chapter 7, this volume). A simple approach is to use a machine translation (MT) system to translate either the query or all of the documents, such that the problem is reduced to a monolingual problem. There are several caveats and disadvantages to this approach. First, full MT is not available for all language pairs. There are also reasons to believe that an MT-based approach is not optimal since it provides just one translation. The fact that multiple translations could be helpful to find relevant documents (we assume a query translation approach since it is more efficient) is similar to a monolingual situation, where the searcher tries to enhance recall by providing synonyms for salient terms. Professional searchers use faceted queries (Pirkola, Keskustalo, and Järvelin 1999) for this purpose, where alternatives for each concept are specified as a disjunction and these disjunctions themselves are connected by a conjunction operator. The idea to use some kind of Boolean structure for CLIR was first proposed by David Hull (1997). For TREC-7 and TREC-8, we designed a probabilistic version of this idea by realizing that a conjunction can be modeled by summing over probabilities of translation alternatives.

We reformulate our basic model here to show the derivation of the extended model. Suppose we have an English document D_E and a French query Q_F consisting of n different words (types) f_i, each occurring $tf_q(f_i)$ times in Q_F, then we can reformulate equation (16.1) as follows:

$$\log P(Q_F|D_E) = \sum_{i=1}^{n} tf_q(f_i) \log(\lambda P(f_i|D_E) + (1 - \lambda)P(f_i)). \tag{16.10}$$

Estimation of $P(f_i|D_E)$—that is, a word in the source language given a document in the target language—is of course more difficult than its monolingual counterpart. By introducing a variable for a word in the target language, we can reduce $P(f_i|D_E)$ to two simpler estimation problems:

$$P(f_i|D_E) = \sum_{j=1}^{N_E} P(f_i, e_j|D_E) = \sum_{j=1}^{N_E} P(f_i|e_j, D_E)P(e_j|D_E) \approx \sum_{j=1}^{N_E} P(f_i|e_j)P(e_j|D_E), \tag{16.11}$$

where N_E is the size of the English target vocabulary. The approximation $P(f_i|e_j, D_E) \approx P(f_i|e_j)$ assumes that translation is independent of the document context. $P(f_i)$ can either be directly estimated on a corpus in the source language, but also—by the same derivation—on a corpus in the target language. The latter has the advantage that both estimates stem from corpora from the same size and domain, which makes the estimates more comparable. After substitution, equation (16.10) can be rewritten as:

$$\log P(Q_F|D_E) = \sum_{i=1}^{n} tf_q(f_i) \log \sum_{j=1}^{N_E} (P(f_i|e_j)(\lambda P(e_j|D_E) + (1-\lambda)P(e_j|C_E))), \qquad (16.12)$$

where n is the number of different terms in the query. Although often referred to as query translation, we think that this is actually a model for document (model) translation since the language model representing the document is first "mapped" to the source language before the actual matching process takes place. The approach is different from what is usually referred to as document translation in CLIR, though, since in that case a document model is estimated on a translated document, instead of translating the document model. We will refer to this model as the "document model translation" (dmt).

An alternative approach is to match in the target language and to use the reverse translation model $P(e_j|f_i)$. We actually first normalized the basic ranking equation (16.1) by taking the geometric mean of $P(Q|D)$, yielding:

$$\log P(Q|D)^{1/ql} = \log \frac{P(Q|D)}{ql} = \sum_{i=1}^{n} \frac{tf_q(q_i)}{\sum_{k=1}^{n} tf_q(q_k)} \log(\lambda P(q_i|D) + (1-\lambda)P(q_i|C))$$

$$= \sum_{i=1}^{n} P(q_i|Q) \log(\lambda P(q_i|D) + (1-\lambda)P(q_i|C)). \qquad (16.13)$$

Note that the query length ql is defined as follows: $ql = \sum_{k=1}^{n} tf_q(q_k)$. We can restate this as a CLIR model where the event space is defined over the vocabulary in the target language:

$$\log P(Q_F|D_E)^{1/ql} = \sum_{i=1}^{n} P(e_i|Q_F) \log(\lambda P(e_i|D_E) + (1-\lambda)P(e_i|C_E)). \qquad (16.14)$$

In this case, $P(e_i|Q_F)$ can be estimated with the aid of a reverse translation model and a derivation similar to (16.11):

$$\log P(Q_F|D_E)^{1/ql} = \sum_{i=1}^{n} \sum_{j=1}^{N_E} P(e_j|f_i)P(f_i|Q_F) \log(\lambda P(e_j|D_E) + (1-\lambda)P(e_j|C_E)). \qquad (16.15)$$

In equation (16.15), the query is first mapped to a probability distribution in the target language by assuming word-by-word context-insensitive translation. We will refer to this model as the "query model translation" (qmt). Since $P(e_j|f_i)$ is zero for all English words e_j that are not translations of a query term f_i, the model is just as efficient as the dmt model.

16.4.1   Related Work

A similar model has been developed for the Chinese and Arabic track by BBN (Xu, Weischedel, and Nguyen 2001). Our model is also quite similar to the IR model proposed by Adam Berger and John Lafferty (1999), who view monolingual IR as a translation process. These models have a different approach to smoothing since $P(f_i)$ is estimated on a source language corpus. Another related approach is the use of structured queries, as advocated by Ari Pirkola (1998). Here, translations of a term form an equivalence class by using INQUERY's synonym operator. This approach is similar to a special instantiation of the translation probability matrix—namely, the case where $P(f_i|e_j) = 1$ for each translation of a source term f_i. We will refer to this model as syn.

Our model assumes context-independent word-by-word translation, which is clearly too simplistic to reflect real-world translation problems. Recently, new language model–based approaches for CLIR have been proposed that start from weaker assumptions. In particular, the immediate context is taken into account by using a bigram model (Federico and Bertoldi 2002) or document-aligned corpora are exploited to estimate cross-lingual relevance models (Lavrenko, Choquette, and Croft 2002). Nevertheless, the gain in effectiveness of these models is relatively small and their efficiency is unfortunately much lower.

16.4.2   Comparison of Different CLIR Model Variants

We will illustrate the relative performance of the models on the CLEF 2000 data set for forty English queries on the French subcollection (*Le Monde*, 87,191 documents) and forty French queries on the English subcollection (*Los Angeles Times*, 113,005 documents). Documents and queries were lemmatized using the Xelda morphological tool kit from Xerox Grenoble.

We will compare the three systems discussed above (qmt, dmt, and syn), complemented with monolingual runs—a run based on query model translation with equal probabilities qmt-eq, a run where we took just the best translation in a query model translation setting (qmt-bt), and a run where the queries were translated using the Web-based MT service Babelfish MT.

We estimated the translation models $P(f_i|e_j)$ and $P(e_j|f_i)$ on a parallel Web corpus constructed at RALI (Nie et al. 1999; Kraaij, Nie, and Simard 2003). The translation models were pruned by taking the 100,000 best translation relations according to an entropy criterion.

As an illustration, we present the French translation of the word "drugs" taken from query C003 about drug policy, tuned for several CLIR models in table 16.5. It is clear that the dmt has a query expansion potential. Yet it expands both the medical

Table 16.5

Example translations of the word "drugs." The numbers at the top part of the table are the translation probabilities $P(f_i|e_j)$ and the numbers at the bottom part of the table are the reverse translation probabilities $P(e_j|f_i)$

Run identification	Translation
MT	⟨drogues⟩
qmt	⟨drogue, 0.44; medicament, 0.36; consommation, 0.06; relier, 0.01; consommer, 0.02; drug, 0.01; usage, 0.01; toxicomanie, 0.01; substance, 0.01; antidrogue, 0.01; utilisation, 0.01; lier, 0.01; therapeutique, 0.01; actif, 0.01; pharmaceutique, 0.01⟩
qmt-eq	⟨drogue, 0.06; medicament, 0.06; consommation, 0.06; relier, 0.06; consommer, 0.06; drug, 0.06; usage, 0.06; toxicomanie, 0.06; substance, 0.06; antidrogue, 0.06; utilisation, 0.06; lier, 0.06; therapeutique, 0.06; actif, 0.06; pharmaceutique, 0.06⟩
qmt-bt	⟨drogue, 1.0⟩
dmt	⟨médicament, 0.79; drogue, 1.0; toxicomane, 0.23; drug, 1.0; alcoolisme, 0.24; drugs, 0.70; stupéfiant, 0.34; antidrogue, 1.0; médicamenteux, 0.36; droguer, 1.0; pharmacorésistance, 0.47; pharmacothérapie, 0.25; assurance-médicaments, 0.33; relargage, 0.53; pharmacorésistants, 0.28; anti-inflammatoire, 0.17; surdose, 0.28; stéroïdiens, 0.35; drogué, 0.61; pharmacodépendance, 0.27; narcotrafiquants, 0.57; anticancéreux, 0.22; escherichia, 0.14; pharmacovigilance, 0.49; selby, 0.16; homelessness, 0.14; bounce, 0.23; anti-drogues, 0.14; antidiarrhéique, 0.12; imodium, 0.12; surprescription, 0.10⟩
syn	⟨drogue; medicament; consommation; relier; consommer; drug; usage; toxicomanie; substance; antidrogue; utilisation; lier; therapeutique; actif; pharmaceutique⟩

and the narcotic sense. We will see that the dmt model is able to take advantage of this query expansion effect, even if the expansion set is noisy.

Table 16.6 lists the results for the different CLIR models. The bottom of the table shows a few statistics about the translation models: #fw is the average number of translations in the forward translation model (source language to target language), which is used for all the qmt-based runs; #rev is the average number of translations of the model used for the dmt run; and the %missed statistic refers to the percentage of query terms, for which no translations were found.

There are several effects that can be observed from this table. First of all, translations based on a noisy parallel Web corpus outperform the high-quality lexica used by Babelfish. We think that this is due to the fact that our model is able to exploit multiple translations. Second, we see that both the qmt and dmt models are well able to deal with many translations: the translation models provide around ten translations per term on average. It is clear that a lot of those "translations" are probably highly

Table 16.6
Mean average precision and translation statistics (best 100,000 parameters)

Run identification	EN-FR		FR-EN	
mono	0.4489	(100.0%)	0.4323	(100.0%)
MT	0.3141	(69.9%)	0.3908	(90.4%)
qmt	0.3525	(78.5%)	0.4207	(97.3%)
qmt-eq	0.2698	(60.1%)	0.3777	(87.4%)
qmt-bt	0.3336	(74.3%)	0.3834	(88.7%)
dmt	0.3732	(83.1%)	0.3693	(85.4%)
syn	0.2445	(54.5%)	0.2352	(54.4%)
%missed fw	11.43		13.42	
#fw	8.82		8.39	
%missed rev	10.74		15.45	
#rev	12.16		14.59	

related terms, so one could argue that we actually do some form of query expansion on a parallel corpus. Comparing the several variant qmt runs shows that using the translation weighting is important. If we replace the corpus-based estimates by a uniform probability $(1/n)$, the retrieval effectiveness is significantly reduced. Using the best translation only is even better, which also offers evidence that weighting translations is crucial. The importance of weighting translations (or proper embedding of translation into the model) is also illustrated in a direct comparison of the (unweighted) synonym run following Pirkola (syn) and the run based on document model translation. The approach based on unweighted synonyms is clearly not able to handle the noisy translations from the Web corpus in a robust way.

Finally, there is no single-best CLIR model for the two CLIR tasks: for the EN-FR task the dmt model has the best retrieval effectiveness, and for the FR-EN model it is the qmt model. This actually correlates well with the percentage of terms for which a translation is found in the respective models. In other words, the $P(e|f)$ model is better than the $P(f|e)$ one. Since the models were trained on exactly the same sentence-aligned data set, using the same techniques, this asymmetry is surprising. Perhaps it could be due to the differences in verbosity of the French and English language. A French translation of an English text is approximately 10 percent longer. This means that it is more difficult to align an English word to a French word than a French word to an English word in a sentence-aligned corpus.

16.5   Relevance Feedback and the TREC Adaptive Filtering Task

The TREC adaptive filtering task evaluates systems that actively disseminate personalized information to the user. A filtering system receives a constant stream of news—for example, from Usenet—and alerts the user only if a news item matches the user's profile. The user is able to control the system by giving feedback, either *yes*, I like this item, or *no*, I do not like this item. (For more information, see chapter 5, this volume.)

In this section, our special interest lies in the development of a relevance feedback algorithm for the language-modeling approach. In principle, reasoning about relevance feedback for a query-generation language model is problematic, although some rather ad hoc solutions have been proposed by David Miller, Tim Leek, and Richard Schwartz (1999) and Jay Ponte (2000). The problem is the following. We assumed in section 16.2 that queries have been generated from one (and only one) relevant document. So it is easy to reason about multiple queries (one might argue that we reasoned about multiple queries when we used the translation models in section 16.4), but it is not as easy to reason about multiple relevant documents (Sparck Jones et al. 2003). A possible solution is to "reverse" the language model by assuming that documents are generated by a profile or a "relevance model," as done by Hubert Jin and his colleagues (1999) and Martijn Spitters and Wessel Kraaij (2000). The query-generation model and the document-generation model might be combined as well to model two-staged retrieval (or pseudorelevance feedback) as suggested by Lavrenko and Croft (2001).

In this section, we present a relevance feedback approach for the query-generation language models by introducing a term-specific smoothing parameter λ_i for each term q_i in the query. Term-specific smoothing models provide some characteristics of practical retrieval systems that are often left "outside" the retrieval model, like stop words and mandatory terms (Hiemstra 2002): From equation (16.16), it is easy to verify that if $\lambda_i = 0$, then the term does not affect the ranking (like a stop word), and that if $\lambda_i = 1$, then the term is mandatory—all documents that do not contain the term are assigned zero probability:

$$P(q_1, q_2, \ldots, q_n | D) = \prod_{i=1}^{n} (\lambda_i P(q_i | D) + (1 - \lambda_i) P(q_i | C)). \tag{16.16}$$

What is the probability mechanism behind such a model? Query generation is much like coin tossing. For each query term, imagine one first throws a coin. If the coin comes up heads, then we take the general model. If it comes up tails, then we take the relevant document's model. We might think of a mechanism for which there is a different (unfair) coin for each query term. Each document that is relevant for a query gives some independent evidence on which coin is used on each draw.

The EM-algorithm (Dempster, Laird, and Rubin 1977) of figure 16.4 iteratively maximizes the probability of the query $q_1, q_2, \ldots, q_n$ given r independently observed relevant documents $D_1, D_2, \ldots, D_r$. Before the iteration process starts, the importance weights λ_i are initialized to their default values $\lambda_i^{(0)}$, where i is the position in the query. Each iteration p estimates a new $\lambda_i^{(p+1)}$ by first doing the E-step and then the M-step until the value of the weight does not change significantly anymore. We added a little

$$
\text{E-step}: \quad m_i = \sum_{j=1}^{r} \frac{\lambda_i^{(p)} \cdot P(q_i|D_j)}{\lambda_i^{(p)} P(q_i|D_j) + (1 - \lambda_i^{(p)}) P(q_i|C)}
$$

$$
\text{M-step}: \quad \lambda_i^{(p+1)} = \frac{m_i + 1.5}{r + 3}
$$

Figure 16.4
Relevance feedback algorithm: EM-algorithm

constant, equivalent to three documents, to the M-step, because a small number of relevant documents should not radically change the initial weights.

At first, when no information on relevant documents is available, each term in the profile will get the same importance weight $\lambda_i = 0.5$. So initially we assume that the profile is best explained if on average half of the profile terms are sampled from relevant documents and the other half are sampled from the general model. If a relevant document is available, it might be possible to explain the profile better. The EM-algorithm for reestimation of importance weights λ_i will make sure that terms that occur often in the relevant documents that are selected so far get a high importance weight λ_i. Profile terms that do not occur (often) in the relevant documents are more likely to be sampled from the background model and get a low importance weight λ_i.

Six strategies were tried on the TREC-8 adaptive filtering tasks—three optimized for LF_1, and three optimized for LF_2:

$LF_1 = 3r - 2(n - r)$ r: number of relevant documents selected
$LF_2 = 3r - (n - r)$ n: number of documents selected
$LF_3 = 2r - (n - r)$ R: total number of relevant documents

The utility measures LF_1, LF_2, and LF_3 assign a value or cost to each document based on whether it is relevant or not. The measures do not use the total number of relevant documents R, representing the fact that users are not especially interested in recall as long as they do not get too much irrelevant items. The first measure represents a user for which a relevant selected document has a value of three, and a nonrelevant selected document has a cost of two. This user needs to see at least two relevant documents in each five selected. So the system should select the document if its probability of relevance is greater than $2/5 = 0.4$. The second measure represents a user whose costs of reading a nonrelevant document are twice as low. Two versions of the prototype system will be tested—one optimized for LF_1, and one optimized for LF_2. The systems are evaluated by the measures for which they are optimized. The higher the utility score of a system for a user profile, the better the system is performing. (The LF_3 measure was used in TREC-9 and TREC-10.) For both utility functions, the same three experiments were done:

Table 16.7
Adaptive filtering results averaged over topics

Run	LF_1	LF_2	Precision	Recall
LF_1 optimized	−9.30	4.86	0.242	0.240
LF_1 optimized; profile reweighting	−7.28	7.10	0.243	0.251
LF_1 optimized; high initial threshold	−1.20	2.46	0.216	0.105
LF_2 optimized	−12.96	4.80	0.232	0.254
LF_2 optimized; profile reweighting	−9.12	6.60	0.237	0.254
LF_2 optimized; high initial threshold	−5.54	1.34	0.199	0.127

1. A baseline run that only uses the initial threshold setting and threshold adaptation routines
2. The same run as experiment 1, but with relevance weighting of profile terms
3. The same run as experiment 1, but using a high initial threshold

The high initial threshold experiments were done to check whether a conservative threshold algorithm could possibly be more beneficial than a query reweighting technique. The threshold adaption algorithm is described by Wessel Kraaij, Renée Pohlmann, and Djoerd Hiemstra (2000).

Table 16.7 lists the evaluation results of the runs using four evaluation measures: LF_1, LF_2, precision, and recall averaged over topics. The utility scores reported are averaged over the fifty test profiles. Precision and recall were averaged over the profiles by assigning 0 percent recall to topics with no relevant documents and assigning 0 percent precision to topics with empty retrieved sets.

Both baseline runs show a consistent improvement in the average utility, average precision, and average recall when applying the relevance feedback algorithm. Interestingly, relevance feedback has a different impact on the two systems. It causes improved recall for the LF_1 system and improved precision for the LF_2 system: the LF_1 system selected 5 percent more documents after query reweighting, but the LF_2 system selected 8 percent fewer documents. Note, however, that it is better to ignore the LF_1 altogether because it did not beat the baseline of not selecting any document at all (which would result in zero utility).

16.6   Conclusions and Future Work

In this chapter we approached the TREC ad hoc, entry page, cross-language, and adaptive filtering tasks by using language models for information retrieval. Each TREC task illustrates a different aspect of the language-modeling approach. The ad hoc task shows the need for a basic retrieval model; the entry page tasks demonstrates the possibility of integrating noncontent information with the basic model; the cross-language task portrays the use of structured queries; and finally, the adaptive filtering task highlights the possibility of optimizing the basic model using relevance feedback.

Looking back at more than forty years of probabilistic modeling for information retrieval, it is interesting to see that many of the ideas that we presented here under the term language models have been out there for at least twenty-five years now. As noted earlier, Maron and Kuhns (1960) presented the basis for the models in this chapter: adding a linear combination of two probability models, as in Harter's two-Poisson model, is enough to make their model work. Robertson's probability of relevance estimation might be seen as the basis for estimating document priors.

But maybe there are different ways to give the language-modeling approach a place in information retrieval history. There are still major challenges for the language-modeling approach to information retrieval—for instance, how to include document structure, like author name, title, year, and so on, into the model; or how to model multiple relevant documents generating one query. The evaluation of new models and ideas will be of the utmost importance, and evaluation conferences like TREC are invaluable for the progress of the field.

Acknowledgments

Our first participations in TREC were partly funded by the European Union project Twenty-One on CLIR (⟨http://twentyone.tpd.tno.nl⟩). Later participations were funded by the DRUID project (⟨http://dis.tpd.tno.nl/druid⟩). Many people helped us during the TREC experiments that form the basis of this chapter; we especially want to thank Rudie Ekkelenkamp, Renée Pohlmann, and Thijs Westerveld. Thanks also to Richard Schwartz of BBN Technologies for helpful comments and discussions about generative-language models. Furthermore, we would like to thank Michel Simard (RALI, Université de Montréal) for assisting with the construction of aligned corpora and building translation models. We also thank George Foster and Jian-Yun Nie (also from RALI) for general discussions about the application of statistical translation models to cross-language retrieval.

Note

1. The runs were redone based on the official Twenty-One experiments.

References

Berger, A., and J. Lafferty. 1999. Information retrieval as statistical translation. In *Proceedings of the twenty-second ACM SIGIR conference*, 222–229.

Bookstein, A., and D. Swanson. 1974. Probabilistic models for automatic indexing. *Journal of the American Society for Information Science* 25, no. 5:313–318.

Brin, S., and L. Page. 1998. The anatomy or a large-scale hypertextual Web search engine. *Computer Networks and ISDN Systems* 30, 107–117.

Dempster, A., N. Laird, and D. Rubin. 1977. Maximum likelihood from incomplete data via the EM-algorithm plus discussions on the paper. *Journal of the Royal Statistical Society* 39, B:1–38.

Dougherty, J., R. Kohavi, and M. Sahami. 1995. Supervised and unsupervised discretization of continuous features. In *Proceedings of the twelfth international conference on machine learning*, 194–202. Morgan Kaufmann.

Duda, R., and P. Hart. 1973. *Pattern classification and scene analysis*. Wiley-Interscience.

Federico, M., and N. Bertoldi. 2002. Statistical cross-language information retrieval using n-best query translations. In *Proceedings of the twenty-fifth ACM SIGIR conference*, 167–174.

Harter, S. 1975. An algorithm for probabilistic indexing. *Journal of the American Society for Information Science* 26, no. 4:280–289.

Hiemstra, D. 2002. Term-specific smoothing for the language modeling approach to information retrieval: The importance of a query term. In *Proceedings of the twenty-fifth ACM SIGIR conference*, 35–41.

Hiemstra, D., and W. Kraaij. 1999. Twenty-One at TREC-7: Ad hoc and cross-language track. In *TREC-7*, 227–238.

Hull, D. 1997. Using structured queries for disambiguation in cross-language information retrieval. In *AAAI symposium on cross-language text and speech retrieval*, ed. D. Hull and D. W. Oard, 84–98. Stanford: American Association for Artificial Intelligence. ⟨http://raven.umd .edu/dlrg/filter/sss/papers/⟩.

Jin, H., R. Schwartz, S. Sista, and F. Walls. 1999. Topic tracking for radio, TV broadcast, and newswire. In *Proceedings of the second topic detection and tracking workshop (TDT-2)*. ⟨http:// www.nist.gov/speech/publications/darpa99/⟩.

Kraaij, W., J. Y. Nie, and M. Simard. 2003. Embedding Web-based statistical translation models in cross-language information retrieval. *Computational Linguistics* 29, no. 3:381–419.

Kraaij, W., R. Pohlmann, and D. Hiemstra. 2000. Twenty-One at TREC-8: Using language technology for information retrieval. In *Proceedings of the eighth text retrieval conference (TREC-8)*, NIST special publication 500-246, 285–300.

Kraaij, W., T. Westerveld, and D. Hiemstra. 2002. The importance of prior probabilities for entry page search. In *Proceedings of the twenty-fifth ACM SIGIR conference*, 27–34.

Lafferty, J., and C. Zhai. 2003. Probabilistic relevance models based on document and query generation. In *Language Modeling for Information Retrieval*, ed. W. B. Croft and J. Lafferty, 1–10. Dordrecht: Kluwer Academic Publishers.

Lavrenko, V., M. Choquette, and W. Croft. 2002. Cross-lingual relevance models. In *Proceedings of the twenty-fifth ACM SIGIR conference*, 175–182.

Lavrenko, V., and W. Croft. 2001. Relevance-based language models. In *Proceedings of the twenty-fourth ACM SIGIR conference*, 120–128.

Manning, C., and H. Schütze. 1999. *Foundations of Statistical Natural Language Processing*. Cambridge: MIT Press.

Maron, M., and J. Kuhns. 1960. On relevance, probabilistic indexing, and information retrieval. *Journal of the Association for Computing Machinery* 7:216–244.

Miller, D., T. Leek, and R. Schwartz. 1999. A hidden Markov model information retrieval system. In *Proceedings of the twenty-second ACM SIGIR conference*, 214–221.

Ng, K. 2000. A maximum likelihood ratio information retrieval model. In *TREC-8*, 483–492.

Nie, J. Y., M. Simard, P. Isabelle, and R. Durand. 1999. Cross-language information retrieval based on parallel texts and automatic mining of parallel texts from the Web. In *Proceedings of the twenty-second ACM SIGIR conference*, 74–81.

Pirkola, A. 1998. The effects of query structure and dictionary setups in dictionary-based cross-language information retrieval. In *Proceedings of the twenty-first ACM SIGIR conference*, 55–63.

Pirkola, A., H. Keskustalo, and K. Järvelin. 1999. The effects of conjunction, facet structure, and dictionary combinations in concept-based cross-language retrieval. *Information Retrieval* 1, no. 3:217–250.

Ponte, J. 2000. Language models for relevance feedback. In *Advances in information retrieval*, ed. W. Croft, 73–95. Dordrecht: Kluwer Academic Publishers.

Ponte, J., and W. Croft. 1998. A language modeling approach to information retrieval. In *Proceedings of the twenty-first ACM SIGIR conference*, 275–281.

Rabiner, L. 1990. A tutorial on hidden Markov models and selected applications in speech recognition. In *Readings in speech recognition*, ed. A. Waibel and K. Lee, 267–296. San Francisco: Morgan Kaufmann.

Robertson, S., and K. Sparck Jones. 1976. Relevance weighting of search terms. *Journal of the American Society for Information Science* 27:129–146.

Robertson, S., and S. Walker. 1994. Some simple effective approximations to the two-Poisson model for probabilistic weighted retrieval. In *Proceedings of the seventeenth ACM SIGIR conference*, 232–241.

Singhal, A., G. Salton, M. Mitra, and C. Buckley. 1995. *Document length normalization*. Technical report TR95-1529, Cornell University.

Sparck Jones, K., S. Robertson, D. Hiemstra, and H. Zaragoza. 2003. Language modeling and relevance. In *Language modeling for information retrieval*, ed. W. B. Croft and J. Lafferty, 57–72. Dordrecht: Kluwer Academic Publishers.

Spitters, M., and W. Kraaij. 2000. A language modeling approach to topic tracking. In *Proceedings of the third topic detection and tracking workshop (TDT-3)*. ⟨http://www.nist.gov/speech/tests/tdt/tdt2000/Papers-n-slides/⟩.

Turtle, H., and W. Croft. 1992. A comparison of text retrieval models. *Computer Journal* 35, no. 3:279–290.

van Rijsbergen, C. J. 1986. A non-classical logic for information retrieval. *Computer Journal* 29, no. 6:481–485.

Xu, J., R. Weischedel, and C. Nguyen. 2001. Evaluating a probabilistic model for cross-lingual information retrieval. In *Proceedings of the twenty-fourth ACM SIGIR conference*, 105–110.

Zhai, C., and J. Lafferty. 2001. A study of smoothing methods for language models applied to ad hoc information retrieval. In *Proceedings of the twenty-fourth ACM SIGIR conference*, 334–342.

17 IBM Research Activities at TREC

Eric W. Brown, David Carmel, Martin Franz, Abraham Ittycheriah, Tapas Kanungo, Yoelle Maarek, J. Scott McCarley, Robert L. Mack, John M. Prager, John R. Smith, Aya Soffer, Jason Y. Zien, and Alan D. Marwick

17.1 Introduction

Several groups in IBM's Research Division have participated in TREC, with differing goals.[1] This chapter summarizes some of their activities and the conclusions they reached. It should be emphasized that there was no central plan in these activities—individual groups decided to participate in the way that made sense to them at the time. In effect, participation in TREC was a tool they used to further their diverse research interests. In some cases, groups participated once or twice in order to explore some issue; in other cases, regular participation in certain TREC tracks has been a central component of a group's research agenda.

In this chapter, we will first describe IBM Research's participation in the TREC tracks most relevant to the classic document retrieval task, and in the tracks related to user interfaces for search and cross-language document retrieval. Then we will outline the extensive series of submissions made to the QA track, and finally discuss IBM Research's activities in multimedia retrieval at TREC.

17.2 Document Retrieval

IBM has had text search engines as part of its product line for many years. Many of IBM's business customers have large collections of documents or have text fields within structured data records. This has led to the incorporation of text search features in software products for data management, portals, collaboration, and other markets. In the early 1990s, as uses of text search evolved beyond bibliographic Boolean queries, some IBM Research groups studied the issues involved in searching where the users were untrained and used the kind of free-form natural-language query that has become the norm. At roughly the same time, several groups began to use TREC as a forum for evaluating their approaches. Some of these projects worked with systems that were either already in product at that time or were subsequently productized, while other projects were simply exploring new approaches.

The GURU [31] information retrieval system, first developed by Maarek during her doctoral work at the Technion [30], and then significantly extended at IBM, after she joined the T. J. Watson Research Lab, has been the basis for several TREC submissions from IBM Research groups. Different versions of GURU have emerged as the original code has been rewritten and adapted. The two following sections describe work done with one such version, which retained the original name, and was used in submissions to the ad hoc track and the very large corpus (VLC) track. Then, a submission to the Web track using a Java version, called JURU, is described, followed by a discussion of a submission to the home page–finding track, using a different system. Finally, the IR system used by the Natural Language Systems group is briefly described.

17.2.1 GURU at TREC-5 and TREC-6

Parts of the GURU code base had been incorporated into IBM's then product search engine in the early 1990s. The evolution of TREC provided an opportunity to further improve and tune the implementation of the algorithms, and to compare their performance to the state of the art at the time. It should be noted, however, that one well-known performance-boosting technique, automatic relevance feedback, was not explored in these submissions, as further discussed below. This was because it was considered to reduce the search speed to an unacceptable degree.

GURU was used in submissions to the ad hoc tracks of TREC-5 and TREC-6, and to the VLC track of TREC-6 (see the next subsection). The motivation for participating in these tracks was to evaluate the probabilistic text retrieval algorithms in this version of GURU on a large, standard test collection, to explore issues of scale and performance, and to verify that GURU provided a sufficient level of retrieval effectiveness to support other research systems in which it was used as a component.

The version of GURU used in this work may be run as a stand-alone system or in a client/server configuration. The GURU indexer performs minimal case and hyphen normalization, but otherwise indexes all words (including stop words) in their original form. The index includes document, paragraph, sentence, and word-in-sentence positional information for each word occurrence in the document collection. At search time, queries are input to GURU in a free-text format. Stop words are eliminated from the query and morphological variants for each query term are automatically generated and added as synonyms to the query term. Syntax is provided that allows the user to control morphological expansion and stop-word elimination. GURU ranks documents using a probabilistic algorithm that considers the frequency statistics of the query terms in individual documents and the collection as a whole. GURU also considers *lexical affinities* (LAs) as multiple-word indexing units in addition to regular single words. LAs were first introduced by Saussure in 1947 to represent the correlation between words co-occurring in a given language and then restricted to a given document for IR purposes [31]. LAs are identified by looking at pairs of words found in close proximity to each other. Documents that contain LAs that occur in a query receive an increment in their relevance score. This has the effect of picking out phrases, for example, without the user having to mark them explicitly.

The Ad Hoc Track at TREC-6 Our participation in TREC-5 served mainly as a learning experience for the group concerned with how to handle a relatively large (for 1996) text collection and follow the TREC experimental methodology. Here, we limit our discussion to TREC-6 results [6].

Our focus in the TREC-6 ad hoc task was to evaluate the performance of our core ranking algorithm. Our TREC-5 results [41] suggested that GURU was using LA scores in a suboptimal fashion. Most of our presubmission work involved determining

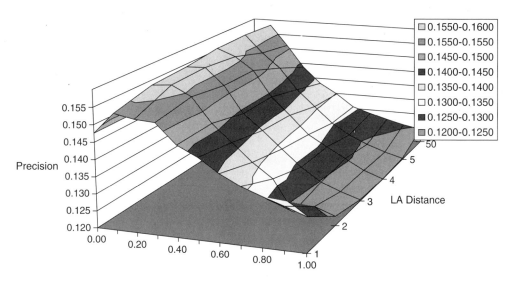

Figure 17.1
Average precision as a function of LA weight and distance

more appropriate settings for the LA distance and the weight of LAs' contribution to the overall document score. We ran a series of experiments on the TREC-5 data over which these parameters were varied. Figure 17.1 shows the average noninterpolated precision obtained by varying the LA distance from 1 to 5 words, and the weight given to LAs in the ranking algorithm from 0 to 1. The plot indicates that our probabilistic ranking formula should give LA terms a weight of 0.1 relative to single terms and the LA distance should be 5. Note, however, that performance is more sensitive to LA weight than LA distance, and the difference in performance between LA distances 1 and 5 is marginal. This is a useful result since a larger LA distance yields more LA terms for scoring, increasing the processing required to evaluate a query. If similar effectiveness can be obtained with a shorter LA distance, then the system will run faster.

For TREC-6 we submitted two runs, both in the automatic query construction category. One run (ibmg97a) was generated using the topic description field only, while the second run (ibmg97b) was generated from the topic description plus topic title. The script used to generate the queries extracts text from the appropriate topic fields, strips out certain stop phrases and words (based on previous TREC topics), removes punctuation, and produces a query suitable for input to GURU. Most stop words are left in the query at this stage since they are counted in the LA distance when identifying LA terms. GURU ultimately removes stop words from the query using a list of approximately 250 stop words. The queries were run with an LA weight of 0.1 and an LA distance of 5. Note that GURU performed no automatic query expansion or relevance feedback, for the reasons already mentioned.

Table 17.1
Ad hoc automatic category A results (a = short, b = long)

Interpolated precision

Recall	ibmg97a	ibmg97b	
0.00	0.5709	0.6659	(+16.6)
0.10	0.3557	0.4516	(+27.0)
0.20	0.3080	0.3842	(+24.7)
0.30	0.2578	0.3191	(+23.8)
0.40	0.2180	0.2614	(+19.9)
0.50	0.1716	0.2255	(+31.4)
0.60	0.1331	0.1929	(+44.9)
0.70	0.0642	0.1404	(+118.7)
0.80	0.0283	0.0613	(+116.6)
0.90	0.0086	0.0383	(+345.3)
1.00	0.0071	0.0234	(+229.6)
Average precision (noninterpolated)	0.1727	0.2309	(+33.7)

The results from our two submitted runs are summarized in table 17.1. Combining the topic title with the topic description yielded a significant improvement over using the topic description alone. A quick analysis of the query topics indicated that a number of the topics (for example, 308, 311, 312, 316, and 328) have significant keywords, phrases, or unique morphological variations that appear in the title but not in the description. Including these words in the query was usually beneficial. Of the sixteen participants in the ad hoc automatic category A long-topics task, GURU produced the best average precision (noninterpolated) for seven of the fifty topics. GURU performed above the median average precision on twenty-nine topics, and below the median average precision on twenty-one topics.

Overall, we felt that this was a satisfactory result considering that the submitted runs did not use query expansion or relevance feedback. The results we obtained by participating in TREC allowed us to obtain the information we were seeking as to the optimum LA weight and length for the version of GURU we were using.

The VLC Track at TREC-6 The VLC track gave us an opportunity to evaluate an approach to using a distributed system to search large collections of text that was being considered in our group at the time. We can attack the execution performance issues associated with large text collections at a variety of levels. Low-level techniques—such as those developed by Alan Smeaton and van Rijsbergen [44], Chris Buckley and Alan Lewit [8], and Eric Brown [5]—use thresholds and constrained candidate document sets to reduce the amount of work performed in the core ranking algorithm. Higher-level techniques—such as those developed by Craig Stanfill [47], Anthony Tomasic and Hector Garcia-Molina [48], and Brendan Cahoon and Kathryn McKinley [11]—use parallel or distributed architectures to scale IR system performance. We opted for a high-level approach in the VLC track.

We ran our VLC track tests using an experimental distributed search system that performs collection fusion across distributed document collections. Our system can distribute queries to an arbitrary number of search servers in parallel and merge the results into a single hit list. Result merging was performed without rank normalization, working under the assumption that the documents were distributed in such a way that collection-wide term statistics were approximately consistent across all search servers. GURU was used as the search server in all cases, with an LA weight of 0.1 and an LA distance of 1.

For our VLC runs, we used the same queries as were utilized to produce our ad hoc ibmg97a run (automatically generated from topic descriptions only with no automatic feedback or query expansion). Our baseline run was conducted on a single RS/6000 43P/140. The full VLC run was conducted on a network of six workstations, including four RS/6000 43P/140s, one RS/6000 C20, and one RS/6000 42T connected by a 16 Mbit token ring. The data for the full run were stored on only four of the six workstations due to disk space limitations on two of the machines. Figure 17.2 shows the distributed architecture and the distribution of the data.

Our VLC results are summarized in table 17.2. The batch time reported is the time to process all fifty queries in a single batch. Note that our Full VLC results were obtained on an incomplete VLC collection. Our indexer was unable to parse the long Web server log files contained in the AUNI collection on DAT3, causing that collection-indexing run to fail. Also, a large portion of the NEWS08 collection on DAT4 failed to unload from our tape and was not indexed. Unfortunately, these errors were not detected in time to make the necessary corrections before the runs had to be submitted.

Our results were generally encouraging. The average precision at twenty documents actually improved from the Baseline to the Full VLC. Our system found an average of seven relevant documents in the top twenty documents returned. This was six fewer than the best-performing system in the track, which found an average of thirteen. We note, however, that our queries did not include the topic titles. As discussed earlier, adding topic titles to the queries significantly improved performance.

The execution performance of our system was satisfactory. Under ideal circumstances, we would expect that using nine machines configured similarly to the baseline machine (each searching data stored on a local disk) would allow us to search 18 GB in approximately the same amount of time as required to search the baseline data. This ideal architecture was not available, though, forcing us to distribute the full VLC data such that the largest individual collection searched was over 4 GB, two of the six servers accessed their index data from a remote disk, and two of the six servers had to additionally act as file servers. This allowed the scalability of a single search server to limit the performance improvement obtainable in the distributed architecture. In spite

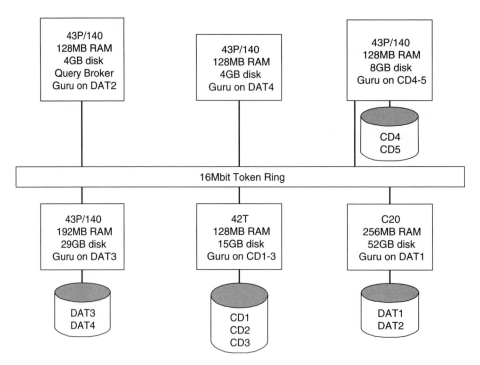

Figure 17.2
VLC system architecture, showing the distribution of data and processing

Table 17.2
VLC results

Collection	Search servers	Batch time (minutes)	Average precision @ 20
Baseline (2.02GB)	1	16.5	0.275
Full VLC (17.8GB)	6	47.2	0.361

of this, we achieved execution speeds that scale well with collection size. The single machine (baseline) system requires 9.6 milliseconds/megabyte/query, while the six-machine distributed (full VLC) system requires 3.1 milliseconds/megabyte/query.

Although the absolute performance times reported here pale in comparison to the performance achieved by modern Web search engines, our results at the time demonstrated that a distributed search system (in particular, a network of workstations) was a viable approach to achieving a scalable search on large text collections.

17.2.2   JURU in the Web Track

JURU at TREC-10   JURU is a full text search engine purely written in Java. It was developed at IBM's research lab in Haifa and is based on the GURU search engine [31]. A version of JURU is incorporated into some current IBM products. JURU participated in TREC for the first time in 2001 (TREC-10) [12].

Following the classic inverted index approach, JURU creates an index by associating terms with the documents that contain them and then storing this mapping in inverted files for efficient retrieval. For Web data, JURU uses a description database that provides for each page p in the collection a set of descriptions extracted from other pages that cite (that is, link to) p. JURU indexes every page based on its content as well as its set of descriptions. Simulations showed that using descriptions as indexing units for HTML pages improved precision by about 20 percent. JURU's query evaluation is based on the ranking process of the SMART system [9]. JURU makes use of LAs in order to improve search precision (see section 17.2.1).

The main goal of our experiments was to validate a novel pruning method, first presented at SIGIR (2001) [13], that significantly reduces the size of the index with little influence on the system's precision. By reducing the index size, it becomes feasible to index large text collections such as the Web track's data on low-end machines. Furthermore, using our method, Web search engines can significantly decrease the burden of storing, caching, or backing up extremely large indexes by discarding entries that have almost no influence on search results. For the TREC-10 experiments, we used a lossy pruning method that prunes the index at the posting level. The idea is to remove those postings whose potential contribution to the relevance score of a document is so small that their removal will have little effect on the accuracy of the system.

Our experiments in TREC-10 tested the impact of pruning on the search results. We created a sequence of pruned indexes using several variations of our pruning algorithms. For each index, we ran fifty queries, constructed automatically from the titles of topics 501–550. Our first experiment tested the effect of pruning on the precision of the results. Figure 17.3 shows the impact of pruning on precision as measured by mean average precision (MAP) and precision at 10 documents (P@10). From these tests, it is apparent that P@10 remains more or less stable up to 40 percent pruning. Although there is a slight decrease in MAP at 30 percent pruning, a significant loss of MAP occurs only at 40 percent pruning.

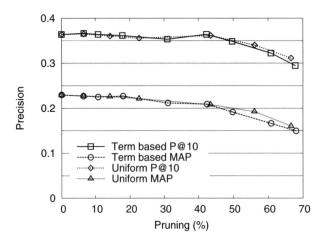

Figure 17.3
The impact of pruning on precision as measured by MAP and P@10

In addition to validating the pruning methods, the web track results also demonstrated the overall high quality of the JURU search engine. JURU achieved excellent results, ranking first in P@10 and second in MAP. Especially interesting in the context of the index-pruning experiments is the fact that JURU's four runs that included up to 35 percent pruning ranked one to four in terms of P@10.

JURU at TREC 2002 For TREC 2002, a new topic distillation task was proposed for the Web track. Topic distillation involves finding a list of key resources for a particular topic. According to the Web track guidelines, a key resource is a page that would be included if someone were to build a short list of key pages in a topic area. Our main goal [2] was to experiment with the knowledge agent (KA) technology [3], previously developed at our lab, for this particular task. The KA approach was designed to enhance Web search results by utilizing domain knowledge and link analysis. We experimented with two type of agents: the H&A agent, which uses hub and authority computation [29]; and the PR agent, which uses page-rank computation [34] for link analysis. The set of top ten results returned by the agent was further distilled by a set of filters:

• Site compression (SC) filter: ensure that the top ten results of each query will indeed be diverse
• Title filter (TF): the similarity of a page title to the topic title is used as another relevance filtering mechanism
• Duplicate elimination filter (DE): invoked to filter out duplicate results

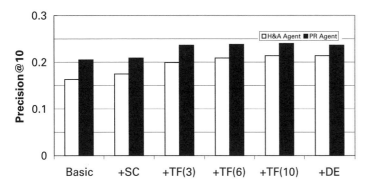

Figure 17.4
Filter contribution to Juru's P@10 at TREC 2002

Our experiments tested the specific contribution of the various distillation filters. Figure 17.4 presents the average P@10 for each run. For the Basic run, no filter was invoked. For the +SC run, the SC filter was invoked on the results of the Basic run. For the +TF(k) runs, the TF filter was invoked on the results of the +SC run, varying parameter k—the number of titles to filter. Finally, for the +DE run, the DE filter was invoked on the results of the TF(10) run. We performed the experiments using both the original KA algorithm (H&A agents) and the static-ranking algorithm (PR agents). We can clearly see the contribution of the SC and TF filters. From these results, it is apparent that the PR agent with maximal TF filtering ($k = 10$) indeed achieved the best results; it was ranked fourth among all participants.

17.2.3   Integrating Link Structure and Content Information for the Home Page–Finding Task

Web documents have an interesting feature that distinguishes them from other document data sets—they have interdocument links. TREC evaluations focused on the two most common modes in which a user utilizes a Web search tool to find information: information navigation, and content finding. In information navigation, the user would like to get to the home page that has links to the information the user is looking for. Thus, while the home page itself may not have the information the user is looking for, it has the links to the content pages. This was evaluated under the home page–finding task. The ad hoc evaluation task, on the other hand, focused on finding pages that actually contain the formation the user is looking for.

The IBM Almaden system that focused on the home page–finding task at TREC-10 combined both the link and content information in a unique way to score documents [28]. The system consists of three components: the indexer, the DocRanker, and the query engine. The indexer stems and tokenizes the documents, and records the presence of various attributes: capitalization, presence in title or bulleted lists, color, term, and document frequency, and so on. Furthermore, to take advantage of contextual cues on a page, we made use of heading and title information by giving more weight to term occurrences in those contexts. Next, the DocRanker ranks documents by extracting the link structure of the crawled pages, then computing the SameSite function [14], and finally computing the PageRank [34] on the graph. Our PageRank calculations use a weighted graph where the weight of a link was 1.0 if the link was composed of two pages from different sites, and 0.0001 if the links were on the same site, to deemphasize self-references. The query engine retrieves the filtered set of documents and ranks them using our integrated ranking function.

Although PageRank [34] provides useful information for scoring, it is unclear how this information should be combined into the page-content-based scoring function of Okapi/INQUERY [1]. We propose a new scoring function that augments the $TF * IDF$ model with document ranking. Let us examine the Okapi/INQUERY function's TF component in detail. The component $1.5|D_d|/A$ is the only portion of the function that contains document-related information. Here, $|D_d|$ is the size of the document and A is the average size of documents. This component provides a bias based on the importance (that is, size) of a document. We propose incorporating document rank (DocRank) ρ_d into this component—ρ_d is the scaled ordinal rank of a page. For instance, if the document is the third-ranked document in a collection of N documents, $\rho_d = 3/N$. Note that, in particular, the DocRank is not the actual PageRank value. Rather, the use of ordinal rank provides a smoother, more gradually changing value than the actual PageRank. Also, it is obvious that any algorithm that can generate an ordering of documents could be used in place of PageRank for our purposes. We experimented with two forms of combining DocRank with the document component of the score: multiplicative, $1.5\rho_d|D_d|/A$; and additive, $\alpha\rho_d + 1.5|D_d|/A$, where α is a user-specified constant. After experimentation, we found the additive form was more effective. We set $\alpha = 10.0$. The rest of the Okapi/INQUERY model was unchanged.

Results for the home page–finding task are shown in table 17.3. The results clearly show that when our DocRank scoring is used, both the average reciprocal rank and the top ten scoring method showed substantial improvement. Using linkage information was a clear win with home page–finding.

Table 17.3
Home page–finding results

Metric	Rank not used	Rank used
Average reciprocal rank over 145 topics	0.382	0.611
Number of topics for which entry pages were found in top 10	90 (62.1%)	113 (77.9%)
Number of topics for which no entry pages were found	17 (11.7%)	15 (10.3%)

In summary, we introduced a novel scoring function that combines TF $*$ IDF scoring with link-based ranking. Our experiments showed that this combined scoring method was exceptionally well suited to home page–finding.

17.3   The Interactive Track at TREC-6

In 1997, NIST initiated an interactive track aimed at evaluating the effectiveness of end-user interfaces (UIs) for search, and IBM Research participated. The goal of the interactive track was (and still is) to compare peoples' search behavior when using different search UIs built by participating institutions, and with a standard NIST search UI (and search engine). The rationale for the interactive track is that the usability of a search function depends not only on the quality of the underlying search technology (as measured in other tracks) but also on how these search capabilities are made available to end users in the search UI.

The interactive track specified an experimental design appropriate for behavioral evaluation using human participants. The design specified a corpus (*Wall Street Journal* news articles), a set of search scenarios, criterion for successful task completion, guidelines about the experience and background of participants, the experimental procedure (involving instructions), and so on. Within this framework, IBM Research's participation focused on search UI features that were of interest to internal IBM studies of IBM's external Web site as it was at that time. We were especially interested in obtaining evidence for the usefulness of emerging Web search conventions involving the use of "+" and "−" operators.

The overall track results are reported in detail in the TREC proceedings for 1998 [49], and IBM's quantitative performance on accuracy and completion rate for search tasks is reported in *The Sixth Text Retrieval Conference (TREC-6)* [43]. Although the reported rank of IBM's submission was near the bottom of twelve participants in this case, the differences between the twelve systems were not statistically significant. That is, the variability attributable to the experimental manipulation (search system and UI) was not sufficiently different from that due to "chance" (uncontrolled sources of variability, such as individual differences, differences in lab and experimenter context, and so forth). Thus, TREC-6 was a learning experience for the research community interested in behavioral issues for searches. Of more ultimate value for IBM was qualitative evidence for how people interpreted the Web search syntax. People's statements made spontaneously and in debriefing supported the interpretation we designed for the syntax. It also helped us to design online hints and tips for the search syntax of IBM's external search site at the time. IBM has not participated in subsequent interactive tracks, although this track has continued. The search goals and UI issues for IBM's internal and external Web sites are sufficiently different from the requirements of the TREC interactive track that we were not able to test those issues at TREC. Our participation in the first interactive track, however, was quite useful for helping us investigate questions relevant to IBM's Web search methods.

17.4 CLIR

The following subsections describe the activities of the Natural Language Systems group at the IBM T. J. Watson Research Laboratory in Yorktown Heights, New York, in TREC's Cross-Language Information Retrieval (CLIR) task. This task is motivated by scenarios in which a user can input a query in one language in order to retrieve documents written in another language.

17.4.1 Monolingual IR Techniques

Our monolingual IR system is a common subsystem for our multilingual IR, spoken-document retrieval, and QA systems; as a stand-alone system, it also performed strongly in the ad hoc tasks in TREC [16; 21; 22] and scaled to the VLC in TREC-6. The input to our system is prepared using several text preprocessing components including a decision-tree tokenizer, a part-of-speech tagger, and a morphological analyzer instead of the typical lexical stemmer. After removing stop words, word and bigram features were indexed for scoring. Query-document relevance scores were computed using a two-pass strategy. The first pass used an Okapi-like [42] $tf \cdot idf$ scoring formula. The second pass was based on a query expansion approach. We experimented with a variety of techniques for constructing expanded queries, including k–nearest neighbors [16], a probabilistic model of document generation [15], and an LCA-like [51] approach. The second-pass scoring was performed using either an Okapi-like [42] formula or the probabilistic model. Other techniques we experimented with included scoring with passage/document combination, sigmoidal adjustment factor for document length, "stop characters" instead of stop words in monolingual Chinese, and suppressing the scores of correlated features.

17.4.2 Multilingual IR: English, French, German, and Italian

For the TREC-7 and TREC-8 CLIR tasks, we constructed a system to retrieve English, French, German, and Italian documents given English or French queries. Building a multilingual (as opposed to a bilingual) system is an exercise in leveraging bilingual resources of varying quality and types [21; 22]. No single solution is ideal for all language pairs.

Between English and French, we trained statistical machine translation models (IBM Model 1, [7]) on the Canadian parliamentary proceedings. We captured local context by incorporating a trigram language model to produce a "fast MT" system [33] that could translate large document collections at high speed. We used this system to investigate the merits of query translation versus document translation. We expected query translation to be more fragile because queries are short and there is little opportunity for the IR system to recover from mistranslations. On the other hand, documents are longer and there is more opportunity for at least some instances of a word to be translated correctly. In practice, we found that a combination system outperforms either [32]. Thus, our TREC English-French system mixed the scores from a query translation system that translated English queries into the document language

(French) and performed Okapi-based scoring in French, and the scores from a document translation system that translated the document collection off-line from French into English and performed Okapi-based scoring in English. We combined the two systems with a linear combination of scores. Our system to retrieve English documents from French queries was identical, with French and English interchanged.

Incorporating German and Italian documents into the system posed a new challenge: we lacked a good parallel corpus for these languages, and an artificial German-English parallel corpus produced with a commercial MT system was found to be of little use. Yet the retrieval corpus itself contained a valuable trilingual resouce: the Schweizerischen Depeschenagentur (SDA) (a Swiss newswire agency) part of the corpus contained French, German, and Italian news stories that frequently reported the same events in different languages, even though the stories were not translations of each other. We did not know which stories in one language should be paired with which stories in another language. We refer to a corpus with this structure as a *comparable* corpus, to distinguish it from a parallel corpus. Although we did not know which pairs of articles referred to the same event, we used words with identical spellings in both languages (typically names) to find reasonable candidate pairs, and constrained the search by the dates of the article. We then trained a translation model based on these pairs and extracted a bilingual dictionary from this translation model. We then used the word pairs in this bilingual dictionary to find more candidate document pairs and repeated the entire process. This procedure produced translation models suitable for use in our French-German and French-Italian retrieval systems.

In order to handle English queries on German and Italian documents, we used French as a *pivot* language. We used the English query in the English-French retrieval system to find French documents, then used these French documents to formulate a French query that we issued to the French-German and French-Italian retrieval systems to find German and Italian documents. This approach worked better than approaches involving combined translation models, such as translating German documents to French and then translating the translations into English.

The TREC evaluation requires systems to output a single ranked list of documents across all four languages for each query. We converted retrieval scores to probabilities by observing that precision was approximately a linear function of log (rank) and estimating a straight line fit separately for each language pair.

We note that although English was the strongest query language of most of the contestants, our system produced strong performances with either English or French as the query language—in fact, our single-best run in TREC-8 was with French queries.

17.4.3   English-Chinese and English-Arabic CLIR

In order to explore Asian-language processing issues, the TREC-9 cross-language task switched from searching European languages to searching traditional Chinese documents with English queries. A particular difficulty with Chinese text is that words are not space delimited: some form of linguistic signal processing is essential before selecting the basic retrieval units. We built a Chinese segmenter that segmented the text into short words (< 5 characters). We also experimented with indexing overlapping bigrams of Chinese characters, without regard to whether the bigrams spanned word boundaries [23]. Both approaches yield reasonable performance (it varies from query set to query set which approach produces the better performance, so we used a linear mixture). An important lesson from this evaluation was how the quality of retrieval varies with the quality and quantity of the parallel corpus used as training data. We found that a system built with a moderate quantity of FBIS translations of news stories outperformed a system built with larger quantities of Hong Kong news and Hong Kong laws translations. Other differences in training data, such as mismatches between simplified and traditional Chinese, were found to have smaller effects.

The TREC-11 cross-language task searched Arabic documents with English queries. The challenge with Arabic is that it is a highly inflected language. We again built an Arabic stemmer and used the morphemes as the basic retrieval units. We confirmed earlier observations [52] that monolingual Arabic retrieval is highly sensitive to appropriate stemming and assorted character normalizations, whereas cross-lingual retrieval is much less so, apparently because many variations are seen in the English-Arabic United Nations parallel corpus that we use as training data [20].

17.5   Question Answering

When it was announced in 1998 that there would be a QA track in TREC-8, we were eager to participate due to a desire among some of us to develop search technology that would get closer to what the end user wanted, which in many cases was answers to fact-seeking questions. IBM groups have continued to participate in the QA track.

17.5.1   Predictive Annotation Approach

In this section, we describe an approach to the QA problem based on preannotation of the corpus and indexing; in the next section, a different approach will be discussed.

We realized, as did most or all other QA researchers, that the key to answering questions was identifying the answer type called for by natural-language questions and also recognizing instances of such types in text corpora. We already had the GURU search engine [41] as described above and a named-entity recognizer, Textract [50; 10]. For the work described in this section, we adapted both of these for the QA task and also developed other modules. The major innovation that came out of the first stages of this effort was Predictive Annotation [35].

With Predictive Annotation, we run Textract on the corpus prior to indexing, and then index not only the original corpus terms but also the semantic labels produced by the named-entity recognizer (for example, PERSON$, COUNTRY$, DATE$). This then enables us to include in the bag-of-words sent to the search engine the semantic label(s) representing the sought answer type. This approach was expected to greatly reduce the size of the hit list needed to retrieve documents with answers of the right type. With a smaller (but more precise) hit list, there would be less noise due to a smaller number of candidate answers. Indeed, subsequent experiments and modeling have both shown that for our system, an optimum hit-list size is around ten passages.

For QA, we adapted the GURU document retrieval engine by making some extensions that we felt would be particularly useful, and called it GURUQA. These modifications followed the intuition that unlike a typical ad hoc query for which one or more documents were to be sought, in QA the answers to questions (especially fact-based questions) would often be found in just one or a small number of sentences. Thus, GURUQA returns passages, not documents; to achieve this, the GURUQA query syntax requires the user to specify the number of sentences in the passages to be searched. Furthermore, unlike in the ad hoc track, where the strategy is to reward documents for having more occurrences of query terms, a sufficient answer sentence would likely only have a single instance of each query term. Hence, the ranking algorithm of GURUQA scored a passage by adding up the number of matching query terms in it (each term could only match once), multiplying the contribution of each term by a weight specified in the call. We used a simple approximation to idf weighting: common words (that is, nonproper names) had a relative weight of 1, proper names had a relative weight of 2, and the semantic labels indicating the sought answer type had a relative weight of 4. In addition, a density contribution to the score was computed, based on the reciprocal of the size of the subpassage spanning all of the matching query terms.

TREC-8   For TREC-8, we submitted two runs for each of the 50- and 250-byte tasks, although we had only trained our system on the 50-byte task. These runs differed in the answer-selection algorithm—namely, the algorithm to select candidate answers from the passages returned in the GURUQA hit list [40]. The ANSEL algorithm used straight linear regression based on features such as the search engine score, the number of words in a segment that were not in the query, the average distance of query words in the segment from the beginning of the segment, and so on. The WERLECT algorithm used similar features, but they were combined in a more ad hoc fashion. Our TREC-8 results [38] were as follows: the ANSEL runs were uniformly 10% better than WERLECT, and achieved an MRR of 0.319 in the 50-byte task and 0.430 in the 250-byte task (these scores positioned us at fourth out of twenty and tenth out of twenty-five, respectively).

TREC-9   Our TREC-9 entry used the same system as for TREC-8, but with a series of minor improvements. Using the TREC-8 data for training, we determined that a passage window size of one to three sentences and hit lists of ten documents gave optimal performance. We added more semantic classes and refined the recognition patterns for the existing ones. We noticed that in TREC-8, our system did particularly poorly with definition questions of the form "What is X," since with that kind of question we were unable to identify in advance the desired answer type, thus losing the advantages of predictive annotation. We remedied this to some degree by introducing the THING$ class for nouns, but to a greater extent by using the AT&T document set that NIST made available to QA participants who did not have their own search engine. Our use of this set was merely to boost scores for answer passages that GURUQA had found if they were from documents that were also in the AT&T set for that particular question [36]. The effect this had on the ultimate system performance was to boost the 50-byte task score by 13 percent and the 250-byte score by 8 percent, for the subset of questions (31 percent of the total) for which this technique was applied.

The TREC-9 questions are generally considered to be harder than TREC-8 because they were extracted from independent query logs, rather than being back formulated from the corpus. There was thus much more of a vocabulary-matching problem. Nevertheless, our scores were comparable to the previous year. Our MRR scores were 0.315 in the 50-byte task and 0.425 in the 250-byte task, putting us fourth out of thirty-five and fifth out of forty-three, respectively.

TREC-10 We continued the incremental improvements for TREC-10, but made a couple of qualitative changes in order to introduce more NLP. We replaced our answer-selection module with one that used fewer features, but with more reliance on linguistic relationships—a research area we have continued to work on up to the present. For definition questions, we developed a WordNet-based algorithm that we called Virtual Annotation [39], which found the most commonly used hypernym for the term in question and incorporated that into the search. Unfortunately, our reliance on this method was undercut by what in our view was inconsistent judging, especially in the area of granularity. For example, the assessors accepted "treatment" as an answer to "What is acupuncture?" and "tennis" for "What is Wimbledon?" but disallowed "disorder" for "What is cerebral palsy?" and "gland" for "What is a thyroid" (see [37]). A combination of this problem, and a bug that crept into the system just prior to the evaluation, caused us to get an MRR of 0.26 and 0.29 in two runs (in the 50-byte task; the 250-byte task was dropped). We also submitted a run in which we combined our results with that of the IBM Natural Language Systems group in a voting algorithm (weighting our answers relative to theirs in a 3:2 ratio). This combined run had an MRR of 0.36, which was an improvement over the prior year, but we slipped in rank to tenth out of ninety-two submitted runs.

TREC 2002 For TREC 2002, the task was made more difficult through limiting submissions to single answers rather than the top five, and a requirement that the answer string be "exact," rather than a text fragment that contained the answer. To address these challenges, we made significant improvements to the answer-selection module, which through parsing both the question and the hit-list passages, scored answers based on the strengths of syntactic relationships of terms, rather than their mere existence. We also began the task (still underway) of changing our system to perform question-specific processing when questions of certain classes were detected. One such specific process examined the question focus in "Where is X?" type questions: if X can be identified as a specific geographic entity (such as a city or a country, for example), then the set of allowable answer types would be restricted to those containing entities (state/country or continent/ocean/world region, respectively).

We began to centralize our ontological resources behind a service layer, and initially used it for answering questions whose answers would be most naturally found in a list or a table—for example, questions about capitals or the names of animal young. Due to the limited implementation of this mechanism at the time of the evaluation, it was unclear if it made any difference either way, but subsequent improvements have proven its utility.

The use of Cyc as part of our system was another addition whose benefit for the evaluation was limited due to the infancy of the implementation. We had observed in prior years that some of our candidate answers were ridiculous even though they were of the right type (for instance, an answer to "What is the diameter of the Earth?" was "four feet"). We had undertaken a relationship with Cycorp under the AQUAINT program and decided to use Cyc at first as a "sanity checker" to eliminate candidate answers that were clearly "insane." Our initial efforts in this direction were to have Cyc test that answers to numerical questions were within a reasonable range. Unfortunately, Cyc's coverage of such ranges at the time of the evaluation was insufficient to be of much help.

The final major change that we made for TREC 2002 was to extend the use of alternative corpora/answering agents. The first dimension explored here was to perform the search against alternative text indexes and the answer selection against the combined set of passages. A particular set of passages was denoted as "primary" if a final answer could be selected from it or as "support" if an answer found there could only boost the score of the same answer found in a primary passage. The primary corpus for this evaluation was the new AQUAINT corpus, while for support we used the old TREC QA corpus plus a subset of an encyclopedia. Our runs showed a 20 percent relative improvement in answers found and about 15 percent in average precision. Using the passages from our sister Statistical Machine Translation group instead of the encyclopedia, we achieved a slight improvement in these figures. The second dimension that we explored was to use the final answers from the Statistical Machine Translation group to recalculate the confidence in our answers and hence their position in the submitted ranking. Our results showed an improvement in average precision of a further 10 percent.

The average precision measure, also called *confidence-weighted score*, introduced for this evaluation was an attempt to grade systems for knowing what they know. Systems were to reorder their five hundred responses according to confidence, and correct answers nearer the head of the list would be given a greater weight than those following. This measure combines both a system's intrinsic QA ability with its confidence of its abilities; in [17], we separate out the latter contribution as *ranking ability*, for which one of our submissions scored second-best overall.

TREC 2003 Our work for TREC 2003 centered primarily on three aspects of our system:

1. Making engineering changes to enforce a more rigorous distinction between the different agents that we used, to allow easier switching on and off either by end users or automatically, depending on question type
2. A heavier use of Cyc and other external structured knowledge sources, particularly tables of facts downloaded from the Web, to aid with questions about popular culture
3. A new agent to implement our QA-by-dossier approach to answering definitional questions

In the dossier agent, the original question is transformed into a dozen or more subsidiary ones ("When was X born?" "What occupation did X have?" and so on), and the answers are collected, filtered by a machine-learned threshold, and then returned as a dossier or a profile of the subject of the original question.

17.5.2   Statistical QA

In TREC-9, IBM developed a statistical system for QA (SQA) [26; 27]; this was the first fully data-driven TREC QA system. The system used a pipeline architecture similar to other systems performing QA, but used maximum entropy to model both the answer tagging (classifying the answer phrase) and answer selection (selecting the best answer chunk from a list of answers). The system models the distribution $p(c|a,q)$, which attempts to measure the c (the correctness or more traditionally the relevance) of the answer to the question. Further, we introduced a hidden variable representing the class of the answer, e (answer tag/named entity), as follows:

$$p(c|q,a) = \sum_e p(c,e|q,a)$$

$$= \sum_e p(c|e,q,a)p(e|q,a). \tag{1}$$

These distributions are modeled using a maximum entropy formulation [4]. Human judgments of question-answer pairs form the training data. The answer-tag model is $p(e|q,a)$, which predicts from the question and proposed answers the entity that both satisfy. The training data for the answer-tag model is thirteen thousand questions that have been annotated with thirty-one categories. In this model, we make the assumption that the entity being sought by the question is independent of the answer.

The joint effect of the question and answer is modeled in the answer-selection model, $p(c|e,q,a)$. Given the question, the answer and an entity as predicted by the answer-tag model, we seek to model the correctness of the configuration. The answer-selection model is tractable because we have judgment data on 892 questions from TREC-8 and TREC-9 as well as 4,000 trivia questions. In formulating this model, note that there is no shortage of negative data, although the most useful question-answer pairs are those that are only nearly correct but need to be rejected. In order to generate the nearly correct data, a basic QA system (without the statistical answer-selection model) is used to propose answer candidates. The output is then judged by humans, and these judgments form the training data for the answer-selection algorithm.

The question is first analyzed by the answer-tag model, and the top answer tag is used by the answer-selection model. Simultaneously, the question is expanded using LCA [51] with an encyclopedia, and the top one thousand documents are retrieved. From these documents, the top one hundred sentences are chosen that maximize the question-word match, have the desired answer tag, minimize the dispersion of question words, and have similar syntactic structures as the question. From the top hundred sentences, named entity and parse chunks are extracted. The chunks are then ranked using the maximum-entropy answer-selection model and the best chunk is output as the answer.

Subsequent systems in TREC-10 and TREC-11 [25] explored richer features such as the machine-translation-based answer ranker, whether a candidate answer occured on the Web, and answer patterns for QA.

17.6 Multimedia Retrieval

IBM Research groups have participated in TREC tracks on spoken-document retrieval and video retrieval.

17.6.1 Spoken-Document Retrieval

In the TREC-6 spoken-document retrieval task, the documents to be retrieved were Voice of America broadcast recordings. IBM provided an automatic transcription of the broadcasts to other participants [18] in order to offer a standard baseline and encourage participation by other sites that did not have their own speech recognition systems. We used a large vocabulary research variant of the IBM ViaVoice speech recognizer to produce automatic transcripts of the audio. The IBM audio-indexing system was a combination of this automatic transcription and a text-based retrieval system. The audio-indexing system was also used as a platform to address the open vocabulary problem by developing a search-time phonetic fast match [19] that ran 2,400 times faster than the speaking rate. The intuition was that a significant fraction of news centers around newly important words unknown to the speech recognizer—for example, "Netanyahu" in the year of TREC-6. Unfortunately, the TREC queries contained fewout-of-vocabulary words so their effect on retrieval performance could not be addressed. The text retrieval system was based on the system that we used for the ad hoc track.

17.6.2 Video Retrieval at TREC-10

TREC-10 saw the first running of the video retrieval track. The benchmark consisted of a corpus of approximately eleven hours of video and seventy-four query topics. The challenge was to build a system capable of automatically analyzing and indexing the video, and of retrieving results for the seventy-four semantic queries. Example topics

included "retrieve video clips showing the lunar rover vehicle," "retrieve clips showing launch of the space shuttle," and "retrieve clips of beach scenes." The use of automatic speech recognition was not emphasized; rather, the track focused on the use of
content-based retrieval techniques.

The IBM Research team developed a system for automatic and interactive
content-based retrieval of video using visual features and statistical models [46]. The
system used automatic methods for shot boundary detection and key-frame selection
[24]. It indexed the key frames of the video shots using MPEG-7 visual descriptors
based on color histograms, color composition, texture, and edge histograms [45]. The
automatic searches were computed by matching descriptors of query content to those
of the target content. The system also used statistical models for classifying events (fire,
smoke, launch), scenes (greenery, land, outdoors, rock, sand, sky, water), and objects
(airplane, boat, rocket, vehicle, faces). The classifiers were used to generate labels and
corresponding confidence scores for each shot. The features and the models were then
used together for answering interactive searches where the user constructed query/filter
pipelines that cascaded content- and model-based searches. This allowed integration
of multiple searches using different methods for each topic—for example, to retrieve
"shots that have similar color to this image, have label 'outdoors,' and show a 'boat.'"

The overall results showed that the content-/model-based approach performed
relatively well compared to other systems. The team explored automatic speech recognition and text indexing as a baseline. In some cases, the speech provided better
results—for example, to retrieve "clips that deal with floods." In other cases, the
content-based retrieval was better—for instance, to retrieve "shots showing grass-
lands." In two cases, the best result was obtained by combining speech and content-/
model-based methods—say, to retrieve "clips of Perseus high-altitude plane." The
results show promise in particular for the approach based on statistical modeling
for video content classification. The overall results show that improvements are still
needed in terms of absolute retrieval effectiveness in order to deploy usable systems.
By creating the video retrieval benchmark, NIST is helping to accelerate the necessary
technology development.

17.7 Conclusions

The work by groups in IBM Research that has been surveyed here shows some of the
variety of scientific problems that were tackled and perhaps gives some insights into
the variety of motivations for participating in TREC as a way to tackle them. TREC
has proven to be a valuable forum in which IBM Research has contributed to an
improved understanding of search, while at the same time the insights obtained by
participating in TREC have helped to improve IBM's products and services. This fruitful
association looks likely to continue: TREC continues to play a central role in the research agendas of several groups, and IBM Research is a participant in new tracks,
such as genomics.

Acknowledgments

This work was supported in part by the Advanced Research and Development Activity's Advanced Question Answering for Intelligence (AQUAINT) Program under contract number MDA904-01-C-0988.

Notes

1. Alan D. Marwick, Eric W. Brown, Robert L. Mack, and John M. Prager are with the T. J. Watson Research Center, 19 Skyline Drive, Hawthorne, New York 10532; David Carmel, Yoelle Maarek, and Aya Soffer are with the Haifa Research Laboratory, University Campus, Carmel Mountains, Haifa, 31905, Israel; Martin Franz, Abraham Ittycheriah, and J. Scott McCarley are with the IBM T. J. Watson Research Center, P.O. Box 218, Yorktown Heights, New York 10598; and Tapas Kanungo and Jason W. Zien are with the Almaden Research Center, 650 Harry Road, San Jose, California 95120.

References

[1] Allan, J., M. Connell, W. B. Croft, F. F. Feng, D. Fisher, and X. Li. INQUERY and TREC-9. In *TREC-9*.

[2] Amitay, E., D. Carmel, A. Darlow, R. Lempel, and A. Soffer. Topic distillation with knowledge agents. In *TREC 2002*.

[3] Aridor, Y., D. Carmel, R. Lempel, Y. Maarek, and A. Soffer. Knowledge agents on the Web. In *Proceedings of the fourth international workshop on cooperative information agents, CIA 2000, (lecture notes in artificial intelligence LNAI 1860)*, ed. M. Klusch and L. Kerschberg, 15–26. Boston: Springer, July 2000.

[4] Berger, A. L., V. Della Pietra, and S. Della Pietra. A maximum entropy approach to natural language processing. *Computational Linguistics* 22, no. 1 (1996): 39–71.

[5] Brown, E. W. Fast evaluation of structured queries for information retrieval. In *Proceedings of the eighteenth international ACM SIGIR conference*, 30–38.

[6] Brown, E. W., and H. A. Chong. The GURU system in TREC-6. In *TREC-6*, 535–540.

[7] Brown, P., S. Della Pietra, V. Della Pietra, and R. Mercer. The mathematics of statistical machine translation: Parameter estimation. *Computational Linguistics* 19 (1993): 263–311.

[8] Buckley, C., and A. F. Lewit. Optimization of inverted vector searches. In *Proceedings of the eighth international ACM SIGIR conference*, 97–110.

[9] Buckley, C., A. Singhal, M. Mitra, and G. Salton. New retrieval approaches using SMART: TREC-4. In *TREC-4*, 25–48.

[10] Byrd, R., and Y. Ravin. Identifying and extracting relations in text. In *Proceedings of NLDB' 99*, eds. E. Métais and H. C. Mayr. Klagenfurt, Austria., 1999. *Data and Knowledge Engineering* 35, no. 2 (2000).

[11] Cahoon, B., and K. McKinley. Performance evaluation of a distributed architecture for information retrieval. In *Proceedings of the nineteenth international ACM SIGIR conference*, 110–118.

[12] Carmel, D., E. Amitay, M. Herscovici, Y. S. Maarek, Y. Petruschka, and A. Soffer. Juru at TREC-10: Experiments with index pruning. In *TREC-10*, 228–236.

[13] Carmel, D., D. Cohen, R. Fagin, E. Farchi, M. Herscovici, Y. S. Maarek, and A. Soffer. Static index pruning for information retrieval systems. In *Proceedings of the twenty-fourth international ACM SIGIR conference*, 41–50.

[14] Chakrabarti, S., B. Dom, D. Gibson, R. Kumar, P. Raghavan, S. Rajagopalan, and A. Tomkins. Spectral filtering for resource discovery. Presented at *SIGIR '98 workshop on hypertext information retrieval for the Web*. August 1998. Available at ⟨http://citeseer.ist.psu.edu/chakrabarti98spectral.html⟩.

[15] Chan, E. P., S. Garcia, and S. Roukos. Probabilistic modeling for information retrieval with unsupervised training data. In *Proceedings of the fourth international conference on knowledge discovery and data mining (KDD–98)*, ed. R. Agrawal and P. Stolorz, 159–163. AAAI Press, 1998.

[16] Chan, E. P., S. Garcia, and S. Roukos. TREC-5 ad hoc retrieval using k-nearest neighbors re-scoring. In *TREC-5*, 415–426.

[17] Chu-Carroll, J., J. Prager, K. Czuba, C. Welty, and D. Ferrucci. A multi-strategy and multi-source approach to question answering. In *TREC 2002*, 281–288.

[18] Dharanipragada, S., M. Franz, and S. Roukos. Audio indexing for broadcast news. In *TREC-7*, 115–120.

[19] Dharanipragada, S., and S. Roukos. A multi-stage algorithm for spotting new words in speech. *IEEE Transactions on Speech and Audio Processing* 10 (2002): 542–550.

[20] Franz, M., and J. S. McCarley. Arabic information retrieval at IBM. In *TREC 2002*.

[21] Franz, M., J. S. McCarley, and S. Roukos. Ad hoc and multilingual information retrieval at IBM. In *TREC-7*, 157–168.

[22] Franz, M., J. S. McCarley, and R. T. Ward. Ad hoc, cross-language, and spoken document information retrieval at IBM. In *TREC-8*, 223–234.

[23] Franz, M., J. S. McCarley, and W.-J. Zhu. English-chinese information retrieval at IBM. In *TREC-9*, 223–224.

[24] *IBM CueVideo Toolkit Version 2.1.* ⟨*http://www.almaden.ibm.com/cs/cuevideo/*⟩. Download at ⟨http://www.ibm.com/alphaworks⟩.

[25] Ittycheriah, A. Trainable question answering systems. PhD diss., Rutgers University, 2001.

[26] Ittycheriah, A., M. Franz, W.-J. Zhu, A. Ratnaparki, and R. Mammone. IBM's statistical question answering system. In *TREC-9*, 60–65.

[27] Ittycheriah, A., M. Franz, W.-J. Zhu, A. Ratnaparki, and R. Mammone. Question answering using maximum entropy components. In *The second meeting of the North American chapter of the association of computational linguistics*, 33–39. Pittsburgh. Morgan Kaufmann Publishers, 2001.

[28] Kanungo, T., and J. Y. Zien. Integrating link structure and content information for ranking Web documents. In *TREC-10*, 237–239.

[29] Kleinberg, J. M. Authoritative sources in a hyperlinked environment. In *Proceedings of the ninth annual ACM–SIAM symposium on discrete algorithms*, 25–27:668–677. Philadelphia, PA: Society for Industrial and Applied Mathematics, January 1998.

[30] Maarek, Y. S., D. M. Berry, and G. E. Kaiser. An information retrieval approach for automatically constructing software libraries. *Transactions on Software Engineering* 17, no. 8 (August 1991): 800–813.

[31] Maarek, Y. S., and F. A. Smadja. Full text indexing based on lexical relations. In *Proceedings of the twelfth international ACM SIGIR conference*, 198–206.

[32] McCarley, J. S. Should we translate the documents or the queries in cross-language information retrieval? In *Twenty-seventh annual meeting of the association for computational linguistics*, 208–214. Morristown, NJ: Association for Computational Linguistics, 1999.

[33] McCarley, J. S., and S. Roukos. Fast document translation for cross-language information retrieval. In *Machine translation and the information soup*, ed. D. Farwell, E. Hovy, and L. Gerber, 150–157. London: Springer Verlag, 1998.

[34] Page, L., S. Brin, R. Motwani, and T. Winograd. *The PageRank citation ranking: Bringing order to the Web*. Technical report. Stanford, CA: Stanford University, November 1999. Available at ⟨http://dbpubs.stanford.edu/pub/1999–66⟩.

[35] Prager, J., E. Brown, A. Coden, and D. Radev. Question answering by predictive annotation. In *Proceedings of the twenty-third annual international ACM SIGIR conference*, 184–191.

[36] Prager, J., E. Brown, D. Radev, and K. Czuba. One search engine or two for question-answering. In *TREC-9*, 235–256.

[37] Prager, J., J. Chu-Carroll, and K. Czuba. Use of WordNet hypernyms for answering what-is questions. In *TREC-10*, 250–257.

[38] Prager, J., D. Radev, E. Brown, A. Coden, and V. Samn. The use of predictive annotation for question answering in TREC. In *TREC-8*, 399–410.

[39] Prager, J., D. Radev, and K. Czuba. Answering what-is questions by virtual annotation. In *Proceedings of the human language technology conference*. San Diego, 2001.

[40] Radev, D., J. Prager, and V. Samn. Ranking suspected answers to natural language questions using predictive annotation. In *Sixth conference on applied natural language processing*, 150–157. Seattle: May 2000.

[41] Ravin, Y. The GURU system in TREC-5. In *TREC-5*, 427.

[42] Robertson, S. E., S. Walker, S. Jones, M. M. Hancock-Beaulieu, and M. Gatford. Okapi at TREC-3. In *TREC-3*, 109–126.

[43] Schmidt-Wesche, B., R. Mack, C. Lenz Cesar, and D. Van Esselstyn. IBM search UI prototype evaluation at the interactive track of TREC-6. In *TREC-6*, 517–534.

[44] Smeaton, A. F., and C. J. van Rijsbergen. The nearest neighbour problem in information retrieval: An algorithm using upperbounds. In *Proceedings of the fourth international ACM SIGIR conference*, 83–87.

[45] Smith, J. R. MPEG–7 standard for multimedia databases. In *ACM international conference on the management of Data (SIGMOD)*. Santa Barbara, May 2001, 627. Tutorial. New York: ACM Press, 2001.

[46] Smith, J. R., S. Basu, C.-Y. Lin, M. Naphade, and B. Tseng. Integrating features, models, and semantics for content-based retrieval. In *Proceedings of the multimedia content-based indexing and retrieval (MMCBIR) workshop*. Rocquencourt, France, September 2001.

[47] Stanfill, C. *Parallel computing for information retrieval: Recent developments*. Technical report TR-69 DR88-1. Cambridge, MA: Thinking Machines Corporation, January 1988.

[48] Tomasic, A., and H. Garcia-Molina. *Performance of inverted indices in distributed text document retrieval systems*. Technical report STAN-CS-92-1434. Stanford, CA: Stanford University Department of Computer Science, 1992.

[49] Voorhees, E. M., and D. K. Harman, eds. *The fifth text retrieval conference (TREC-5)*.

[50] Wacholder, N., Y. Ravin, and M. Choi. Disambiguation of proper names in text. In *Proceedings of the fifth conference on applied natural language processing*, ed. P. Jacobs, 202–208. Morgan Kaufmann Publishers, March 1997.

[51] Xu, J., and W. B. Croft. Query expansion using local global document analysis. In *Proceedings of the nineteenth annual international ACM SIGIR conference*, 4–11.

[52] Xu, J., A. Fraser, and R. Weischedel. TREC 2001 cross-lingual retrieval at BBN. In *TREC 2001*, 68–77.

Epilogue: Metareflections on TREC

Karen Sparck Jones

1 Introduction

TREC has been the largest evaluation program in the natural-language and information processing (NLIP) field, as the collective proceedings of TREC-1 to TREC 2002 (see *TREC* 1993–), make clear. In previous papers (Sparck Jones 1995, 2000a) I reviewed TREC in detail, considering it primarily from the point of view of "classical," or traditional, IR concerns and methodologies. Thus, my focus there was on what the TREC tests and their results had shown us about indexing approaches, strategies, and devices—for example, about the best form of indexing language—bearing in mind the generic evaluation framework within which these tests had been done. In general, the TREC evaluation has been within the paradigm established by the Cranfield experiments (Cleverdon 1967) and consolidated by the Cornell SMART research (Salton 1968, 1971; Salton and McGill 1983), of experiments designed to distinguish and determine the effects of specific system *performance factors* by controlled laboratory tests.

The TREC program has added a great deal to our understanding of retrieval system behavior within this bounded framework. In my second review, after TREC-6, I raised the question of whether it was not merely desirable but necessary for TREC to extend its horizons. There have been five further completed TREC cycles since then, up to 2002, so the immediate question is whether these have introduced significant changes in the TREC style. There have clearly been new developments within TREC in the last five cycles, which have introduced "more modern" types of data (that is, Net and Web documents as well as video) and "more current" tasks (that is, QA). But these have been handled in the same spirit as before. The aim of this chapter is therefore to address the questions: Does TREC need a radical shake-up? Should it adopt new goals and move in new directions? If so, what should these goals be, and how should it move toward them?

The reason for asking these questions is quite obvious. In what is, or is perceived to be, the rapidly changing world of information provision, search, and use associated with the astonishing growth of the World Wide Web, it is necessary to raise the issue loud and clear: How relevant is TREC? Thus on the one hand, how far have, should, or can TREC findings be exploited for Web-based IR? On the other hand, what are the problems of Web-based IR that a presumably continuing TREC ought to address? The TREC program has manifestly (and successfully) evolved by both changing task form in detail and introducing new tasks. Can it continue to do this, pertinently and usefully—that is, tackle whatever IR issues the Web and networked information systems generally present?

In its most obvious form, this is a question about relations between TREC and Web engines. Here, one possible view is that IR system development and provision on the Web is so fast moving, and so intensely competitive, that whatever is helpful will emerge from the marketplace itself, give or take a few brave spirits willing to invest in an idea or pick up and apply some accidentally encountered suggestion, without any need for a prior classical evaluation program—Google is the obvious example. A well-known economic theory suggests that the Web itself is the perfect environment for IR product evaluation, and certainly much better because it is more fast moving and global than any of the older forms of IR service context like libraries or online biblio-graphic search services.

Yet there is more to the Web than a vast and challenging arena for gladiatorial search engines. The Web and network connections are the enabling infrastructure for a much larger information world including, for example, bibliographic service sites, and database sites covering a wide range of information types and supporting users with varied needs. Thus, where Web engines may focus on precision, other services may address recall, and where on Web pages anything goes quality wise, with other information bases quality control is paramount. Some of these areas fall under the "digital library" heading, but there are other information situations also of potential relevance—for example, those associated with corporate intranets, where particular data types such as financial reports may loom large. This larger information scene is rapidly developing, and the question is whether and how TREC can connect with it, even whether TREC, with its paradigm of carefully controlled and hence time-consuming scientific research could keep up with such a changing world.

In this chapter, then, I will concentrate on TREC lessons (or perhaps the lack of them) for the future. I will begin in section 2 with a brief summary, for reference, of the TREC program itself and its major findings, and note key points about its approach to evaluation. Section 3 considers the messages that TREC conveys for how to do IR and how to evaluate it in rather more detail, in relation to previous research. This leads in sections 4 and 5 to a review of the strengths and weaknesses of the TREC approach first, and relatively briefly, in the context of conventional types of IR system and *setup*—that is, computational system plus functional context involving the system's users (Sparck Jones and Galliers 1996), and second, in the new Web-based and Web-driven IR context. My main focus will be an attempt to characterize key IR properties of the Web world and the broader type of networked setup, and to assess how far the traditional mode of evaluation to which TREC has subscribed can be applied in the new situation.

Because the Web's page data and search engines are the obvious initial point of entry to this world from TREC, and indeed TREC has already done some Web data eval-uation, my initial assessment of TREC's lessons will be from this point of view. But this then leads to a consideration of other modern information environments. There have already been comparative reviews of Web engine performance (see, for example, Gor-don and Pathak 1999), and I would not wish to claim that the Web, as an information management environment, is totally different from any previous one (though many assume it is). But it is clear that it is novel in important ways, and the question is therefore whether and how traditional IR research concerns and evaluation methodologies, as so successfully applied on a larger and more varied scale than ever before in TREC, can be applied in this new environment. My analysis in section 5 suggests that the traditional (and TREC) mode of evaluation that keeps users at arm's length may have more legitimacy in the hands-on Web world than appears at first sight. This implies, therefore, that TREC's substantive findings should also be examined for their Web applicability. But the analysis also leads to the conclusion that the information-seeking and information-management tasks that TREC addresses should change: it is time to move on, more quickly, from document retrieval as *the* IR research task. Looking further than the immediate comparison with the Web as the primary retrieval context leads to the same general conclusion: TREC has wide potential pertinence, but much more work is needed, even for the retrieval task, on varied data types and ranges of needs as well as, beyond retrieval, on appropriate forms of other tasks and modes of connection between tasks.

To declare my interests: I have been a member of both individual TREC participating teams and the TREC standing Program Committee for much of its life. This has been an exciting and valuable experience. But I trust that it has not biased my judgment so that the points I make about TREC for the future here are invalid.

I shall refer to individual TREC evaluation cycles as follows: TREC-3, and to the corresponding proceedings, *TREC-3* (for full details, see *TREC* 1993–).

2   Reference Summary of the TREC Program

2.1   Design Properties
For the present purposes, the key design features of the TREC program have been that it has:

• Addressed a range of tasks, essentially of a mainstream IR kind, notably one-off (*ad hoc*) searching and filtering, but also, especially more recently, tasks that have not hitherto figured in mainstream IR systems—in particular, QA
• Concentrated on retrieval from full texts of various sorts
• Worked on a large (document) file scale, intended to be realistic in ensuring that undesirable volume effects are overcome by selective retrieval
• Encouraged full automation in indexing and searching, though the manual construction of resources like thesauri has always been allowed, and explicit manual (and interactive) searching has normally been a possible option, for good reasons, and very instructively
• Sought and applied well-founded evaluation protocols in terms of test collection design and data gathering, especially for the necessary *answer data*—that is, relevance assessments

• Used a range of formal performance measures chosen to present results from different points of view
• Once the program became established, adopted a test-cycle model with annual task specifications aimed at clear-cut and well-controlled experiments in any one cycle, and a cumulative attack on a task area over several cycles
• Planned for reusable resources and results to provide a platform for future experiments, both within and outside the program

2.2   Contingent Features

Since the attractions of the TREC program rapidly became apparent to the IR research community, and there were no formal barriers to entry and relatively low participation costs (given that data provision, assessment, and program management were centrally funded), TREC became a popular success with many participating teams, which in many cases undertook several tasks. This has had both first- and second-order advantages for TREC and IR research, in each case stemming from critical mass.

The first-order benefits were:

• More sets of results, and so more informative performance comparisons
• More contributions to the assessment *pool*, and so more reliable test data
• More strategies and devices explored
• More confirmatory consolidation of results, promoting technology convergence (an effect noted in other government-sponsored evaluations, say, of information extraction [see Cardie 1997])

The second-order benefits were:

• More thorough discussion of task specifications and evaluation designs by more interested and informed participants
• More capacity to sustain evaluation over several cycles, with data variation or fine-grained task modification encouraging a better understanding of task requirements and appropriate strategies for meeting them
• More ability to address more issues, contributing to the evolution of the program as a whole, initially on the hub-and-spokes model with the specified ad hoc task as hub and others branching out from it, but later more as a set of *tracks*, each with their distinctive characteristics and variously related to one another

Altogether, to summarize these aspects of TREC, the program has involved increasingly large (and real) data sets. The ad hoc task involved at least 1.5 million regular documents altogether (so even subsets, sometimes used within TREC or chosen to meet specific needs outside it, can be substantial). The Web track has used 18.5 million Web pages in some experiments, the filtering track has included tests with some 870 thousand documents, the 2002 CLIR track used 380 thousand Arabic documents, and the 2002 QA track over 1.3 million news stories. The ad hoc task totaled 550 substantial topic requests (though in subsets of 50), and the Web track, spectacularly, has done tests with 10,000 queries drawn from Web engine logs (though only 150 of these had output assessed). There have also been input sets for other user-need types including Web home page queries and about 2,000 questions to be answered. There have been hundreds of thousands of relevance assessments, often on pools of more than 1,000 for an individual request, as well as candidate answer assessments for the QA track and sentence-level relevance and novelty assessments for the novelty track.

Taking the ad hoc and track specifications as defining distinct *problems*, by 2002 TREC had addressed 18 generic problems, the main ad hoc one 8 times, others on average 3; with 2 official runs per team as the default, there were at least 80 sets of results for an ad hoc cycle and about 20 for other earlier tracks, allowing in the former case for 80 individual performance comparisons for one system against others, or 6,400 distinct paired comparisons. The growth in participation in recent years has increased the number of runs, to about 40 per track on average in 2002. The program has also—a far from trivial point—published all the participants' submitted run performance figures and their papers reporting their work, and has made the test data available for future research.

This is clearly a huge mountain of material effort: it has certainly brought forth more than a mouse. But has it brought forth more than an unknown quantity of prairie dogs?

2.3 Major Findings

This chapter is explicitly not a detailed review, as would be required to do justice to all the individual TREC tracks. But since there are close relationships between many tracks, primarily because they address the same generic ad hoc retrieval task, and since TREC has been imbued with the some common aims, it is possible to list some general findings about IR that emerge from the work as a whole.

These still, however, refer only to the type of evaluation test that has characterized TREC—that is, they are heavily constrained in relation to the realities of information management at large. The TREC tests are primarily, though not exclusively, about *core* IR system objectives and contextual functionality of an immediate and narrow kind (Sparck Jones 2001). They are also, in general, for the kind of user request that has been taken as the norm for IR systems—namely, the *topic* search: finding documents about X (even if the actual formulation may suggest something more like a direct question). This has been routine for the main ad hoc task, and typical of the others, with a particular form in routing and filtering. The main exceptions have been home page searching in the Web track, and more important, the recent topic distillation task in the Web track, the sentence set identification in the novelty track, and the yet more distinctive requirements represented by the QA track. The video track introduced in TREC 2001 has also covered other forms of search specification.

Subject to these qualifications, the TREC evaluations have confirmed that:

· Fully automated systems can deliver reasonable retrieval performance
· They can do this for full text
· They can do it for languages, documents, and requests, with quite different properties
· They can do it with robust, simple strategies
· They can do as well as minimal manual searching, though not as well as with heavy-duty manual query development

In other words TREC appears to endorse, after exhaustive, large experimentation, the modern approach to retrieval—that is, the approach that is motivated, explicitly or implicitly, by statistical models, that starts from simple natural-language terms, that relies on weighting and feedback strategies, and that delivers ranked output. This is the approach that the research community has developed over several decades and, during that period, has consistently advocated in the face of the "Boolean thesaurus/keyword" approach entrenched in conventional bibliographic search systems, and has now shown can scale up satisfactorily (though TREC has not made significant, direct Boolean/ranking comparisons).

2.4   Evaluation Methods

As the foregoing suggests, the TREC evaluation methodology has followed a well-established protocol. It has continued to apply the laboratory experiment paradigm and performance criteria, focused on controlled system comparisons and hard output measures, that have been the mainstays of IR research. That is, in characterizing IR systems for evaluation purposes, and in concomitant performance measures, TREC has engaged in:

· Heavy abstraction from system *environments*, so user properties (background, purpose, and so on) are represented only by the facts of their expressed information requests and independent relevance assessments
· Aggressive reduction of information management and its varied elements to the "search loop"
· Narrow concentration in performance assessment on precision and recall, and their siblings and derivatives, especially MAP

Even with manual searching, the usual style has been that of a trained intermediary or deeply committed searcher. The interactive track has naturally used "ordinary," or at least pseudo-ordinary (that is, library school student), users, but still within a relatively controlled laboratory setting, and with test designs typically encouraging energetic and extended searching. The routing and filtering tracks have presupposed professional needs as starting points. The main exceptions to this model of users as both fairly dedicated and fairly skilled have been those where queries have been straightforwardly derived from Web engine logs, notably in the Web track. Within the ad hoc track, however, increasing attention was also paid to very short queries deemed similar to ordinary user Web engine ones.

3   TREC Messages

3.1   TREC and How to Do IR

It could be said that TREC has reprised the old research tune to the beat of a bigger drum. The main novelty is that the older claims hold when tremendously scaled up. Thus, what TREC says about how to do IR is what it says about how to build a respectable *core retrieval system*, particularly a general-purpose system where there can be little presumption about user experience or long-term commitment, in relation either to individual search sessions or to repeated or regular usage over a long period of time. However this focus on building robust general-purpose systems also has implications, because of the strategies these systems embody, for many particular specialized applications. Hence, the types of term-weighting, query formation, and iterative feedback procedures that have become established within TREC are ones that can deliver reasonable outputs even when supplied with rather poor inputs—for example, as requests. They can therefore be expected to work well when supplied with better-quality inputs, as indeed tests with the TREC-1 and TREC-2 topics showed.

TREC has, secondly, not merely confirmed previous research lines about how to do automatic indexing and searching, and in ways that can do without significant manual assistance either through the provision of support resources like thesauri or in the search process itself. It has also, primarily through being the first sustained series of IR experiments with full text, developed and honed the statistically based techniques of earlier research. These are directly usable specific tools (even if they are not always appropriately used in practice).

As mentioned in the introduction, these techniques are the products of lines of work long familar from the Cornell SMART research (Salton 1968, 1971; Salton and McGill 1983; Salton and Buckley 1988), the City University probabilistic model and Okapi system research (Okapi 1997), and the INQUERY system (Croft 2000). General ideas suggested in the 1950s and 1960s (see Stevens 1965), yet that could not be fully evaluated then, have now been significantly tried and tested within TREC, not only by the teams just mentioned but also, for instance, by Kui-Lam Kwok (Kwok 1995; Kwok and Chan 1998). TREC trials of latent semantic analysis (Dumais 1995) and, more recently, so-called language modeling—that is, Markov modeling—methods drawn from speech research (Ponte and Croft 1998; Miller, Leek, and Schwartz 1999; Croft and Lafferty 2003) fall under the same broad heading. This generic, statistically based class of methods "fits" the IR problem and performs in an appropriate, resilient way.

At the same time, and somewhat surprisingly, the TREC experiments have not shown that more refined indexing with complex terms is especially advantageous, even though this might seem necessary for bulk files of full text. The automated natural-language processing (NLP) systems required to test this on a large scale have only become available in the last decade. But the New York University/General Electric results (Perez-Carballo and Strzalkowski 2000) did not do better, compared with much cruder approaches, than their manual analogues in Cranfield (Cleverdon 1967) or automated predecessors (Fagan 1987). Thus, insofar as phrases may be of modest use, "statistical phrases" are good enough (Mitra et al. 1997).

These are all points about natural language directly as the indexing vehicle, with only light normalization (notably by stemming). The other long-standing research issue has been the relative merits of controlled and natural languages for IR. Many TREC participants have made use of any thesauri or other lexical resources that they have been able to find (for example, WordNet), though these have not usually been thesauri of the conventional bibliographic kind that supply controlled subject labels. But the heterogeneous test collections used for TREC (as much as proprietary rights) have meant that there have been no controlled languages with adequate coverage to apply for any systematic comparative evaluations. In many cases, thesauri have also been exploited for the manual-searching option, making it difficult to assess their independent contribution (see, for example, Adi, Ewell, and Adi 2000; Mahesh, Kud, and Dixon 2000). The TREC tests have shown that reasonable performance can be obtained without conventional types of vocabulary control and search aid, but have not been able to make comparisons between index language types that have long been of interest.

The strategies most commonly used in TREC, and in particular term weighting, have had another important consequence for comparisons with earlier work. These strategies deliver a genuinely ranked output. Many studies in the past, and especially those related to conventional search services, delivered Boolean outputs. Comparing these different types of output is like comparing chalk and cheese, and leads to the difficulties encountered in Gerard Salton's work (1972), though for a TREC study see Lu, Holt, and Miller 1996. Modern approaches to IR are based on good theoretical arguments for ranking, and with very large and full-text systems, Boolean query constraints tend to be treated as filters before ranking rather than simple output determiners. TREC here is thus reflecting a more general shift, as most obviously seen in Web engines.

These remarks are for the mainstream ad hoc case. The ad hoc test findings have in many cases been paralleled by track results, most obviously where the track task is the same but under other conditions, as for the Spanish and Chinese, confusion, database merge, NLP, spoken-document retrieval, cross-language, and Web tracks. Yet there are few, if any, significant earlier tests for these other conditions with which to compare the TREC results. The main point of note is some (albeit gratified) surprise that methods tried and tested have carried over with little hiccup to the other conditions. Scaling up to the large Web collection (18.5 million pages) was found less stressful than expected (Hawking 2001). With the high-precision and very large collection tracks, the task was the same, though the detailed performance measures differed, and the same generalizations apply.

The non–ad hoc tracks have therefore been only the routing/filtering, novelty, and QA ones as well as, in a complicated way, the interactive one. There have been evaluations of the routing/filtering (that is, selective dissemination of information) task in the past—see, for example, Barker, Wyatt, and Veal 1972—but nothing on the TREC comparative scale. Getting novel information, rather than only relevant information, has long been recognized as a matter of interest, but is hard to investigate without large files offering multiple relevant documents and a heavy investment in assessment. The nearest connection is probably with the recent topic detection and tracking evaluation program (see Allan 2002). With QA, apart from some initial investigations by, for instance, John O'Connor (1973), there are no precedents for the scale of the TREC comparative evaluations, not even for the cruder task of selective passage retrieval. These tracks have, however, been approached, like the others, with their focus on automation and hence *system* requirements and behavior.

The interactive track has necessarily been different (see *IP&M* 2001; Over 2001). The task is again ad hoc searching, but to meet particular requirements—for example, associated with particular forms of request—implying appropriately tailored performance measures. Although human searchers are involved, however, the whole exercise is under laboratory conditions, not natural-usage ones, for instance in having set tasks. This is more constraining than laboratory observation experiments of the kind reported by Micheline Beaulieu (1997) and Michael Sullivan, Christine Borgman, and Dorothy Wippern (1990), though even these were far from unconstrained. Nevertheless, the new 2003 HARD track was intended to take richer user requirements into account, like the search purpose and desired output genre, and also to allow for subdocument retrieval. (Unfortunately, the data obtained by monitoring real user behavior through logging Web engine searches is a less rich source of information about users than one would wish, even with very large search samples.)

3.2 TREC and How to Do IR Evaluation

The TREC evaluation methodology, aimed at system performance comparisons under (relatively) careful control and with a high degree of abstraction from the contexts in which systems are actually used, has an obvious motivation in the interest of automation itself: Can good-quality retrieval performance be obtained with fully automated indexing and searching? The TREC form of evaluation can, moreover, be justified by the fact that since it is impossible to evaluate IR systems without requests, and hardly helpful to evaluate them without relevance assessments, the key properties of real retrieval situations are preserved by the use of soundly designed and constructed test collections. The TREC collections have been formed with care, to obtain realistic document files and requests as well as extensive relevance assessments. Moreover, with several different collections and broadly based relevance pools, the results obtained should be free from hidden biases and usefully general or generalizable.

These are good arguments for the TREC approach. The care about test collections helps to offset the abstraction, and to protect TREC from claims that the emphasis on generic *technology* development, which has been characteristic of DARPA-sponsored programs in NLIP since the 1980s, has sometimes thrown the task baby out with the specific application waters (Sparck Jones 2001). NLIP is not an end in itself: NLIP systems are for tasks that are (directly or indirectly) of human interest.

These tasks have their different distinctive—that is, *core* characteristics and requirements—so systems, on the one hand, and the criteria and the measures used to evaluate systems, on the other, have to properly address this core. In the TREC case (for documents, setting aside QA), the core is clearly covered. Whatever else it should do, an IR system should deliver documents that are relevant rather than ones that are irrelevant, and performance is measured by the ability to do this, not only in one, but in several different ways. Thus, the information supplied by MAP (aka AvP), a single-number measure, can be enriched by, for example, precision figures at different document-level output ranks. Indeed, the core technology is required not only by the important retrieval task in itself but also by the need for it to underpin more selective tasks—for example, by supplying material from which to draw a resource set, as in the Web topic distillation task, or to extract sentences, as in the novelty task and full-blown QA.

The TREC methodology continues that of earlier laboratory research from Cranfield onward (see Sparck Jones 1981), with some gains from working with much larger test collections. Maintaining this laboratory paradigm can be justified by the nature both of the detailed run results and the broader TREC findings. Though we have learned a great deal from TREC, we often do not really know what works or fails to work, and why. On the one hand, TREC has repeatedly shown that plausible ideas do not work, and on the other, that different strategies and devices deliver similar performance. There is thus plenty of scope for further specific comparative analysis like those promoted by the query track, and for new experiments in the same style, especially in environmental conditions not so far represented by the TREC test collections that can throw further light on the environmental factors determining performance and hence leading to one choice of system strategy rather than another. There is also scope for more detailed analysis in relation to individual document and query properties, as pursued in the 2003 robust track.

Moreover, though TREC has worked, for these good reasons, within a traditional research evaluation framework, it has not been completely static. It has worked with new types of documents, particularly news material and Web data, spoken documents, and most recently video (though the problem of adequate evaluation is well illustrated with the novelty tests, where sentence recall and precision can only feasibly be computed if all participants started with the same ranked list of documents, rather than from their own varied lists). TREC has also developed specific new evaluation methods, notably for the routing/filtering and QA tasks. It has carried the analysis of test data and methods itself further, as in Justin Zobel's (1998) and Ellen Voorhees's (2000) relevance pool and reliability studies. Thus, insofar as controlled experiments are intrinsically desirable, TREC has helped to ensure that these are properly done for large data sets and NLIP tasks of current concern as well as long-established ones.

It is therefore not difficult to make a case for TREC as a distinguished modern representative of an old and eminent family, adding new lustre to its name. The question is whether TREC is moving in the right circles. What does TREC have to say to operational systems and their real users with their requests, as illustrated in Derr 1984, for example, or behaviors, as illustrated in Carmel, Crawford, and Chen 1992? How does TREC relate to information retrieval on the Web? Who cares in the Web context, for instance, about performance measured by computing by MAP over a thousand ranks? Again, what does TREC have to say to users of the rapidly growing specialist information sites—for example, genome ones—that cover both databases in the orthodox sense, specialized "catalog" records, and conventional text? Further, interpreting information management broadly, how important is document or text retrieval compared with other information-seeking tasks like QA, or in relation to other information-processing tasks like summarizing? Thus, especially, but not only, in the Web context, even if topic-based retrieval is important both as a task in its own right and a precursor to others like summarizing, it may be that we have now learned enough about retrieval from TREC and need to move on. But in that case, what is the best direction to move in, given that it is clearly more sensible to try to apply what we have already learned from TREC than to simply begin anew on some wholly independent task, however interesting and critical that may be?

4   TREC and Operational Systems

Conventional bibliographic systems, from DIALOG and ORBIT in the 1960s onward, have subscribed largely to the controlled language paradigm and have consistently adhered to the Boolean paradigm. Operational systems adopted natural-language searching, for titles and abstracts, primarily for practical reasons rather than because research suggested it would work as well as anything more elaborate; and they remained wedded to Boolean searching and hence eschewed weighting as a major element in indexing. Early systems for full text searching, particularly in the legal field, also endorsed the Boolean model, often at substantial performance cost (Blair and Maron 1985). Operational services only began to adopt the ranking model, derived from the previous decades of research, to any noticeable extent during the 1990s (Tenopir and Cahn 1994).

It is not surprising that what may be called the "Boolean thesaurus" model has remained a major force, and even more so the "Boolean (key)word" one. Past research, on small test collections, seemed irrelevant to large operational systems and was essentially ignored. Service organizations like Chemical Abstracts and Inspec deal in vast technical literatures calling for, and getting, skilled and informed searching that can deliver high-quality output with these tools. When a thesaurus is lacking, the Boolean keyword natural-language model can be as effective in experienced hands, and also seems the natural strategy for newer services like ScienceDirect to offer end users. Changing big, entrenched systems is extremely expensive, and systems based on the research paradigm have been new ones—for instance, WAIS and now the Web engines. Even with new services, straying from conventional models for established literature types, like scientific journals, seems unnecessarily rash.

The scale of the TREC evaluations, compared with those of earlier research, should make the results more pertinent to the conventional services. As the early

TREC ad hoc cycles demonstrated, with carefully formulated initial requests, automated system performance using only statistically based natural-language techniques, without invoking thesauri or subject classification schemes, can be very good indeed. It is true that TREC has not addressed retrieval in challenging technical subject areas with complex specialist terminology like chemistry, but this has been due to the difficulty of getting the necessary test data. Running TREC ad hoc and filtering cycles for, say, a biochemistry text collection in a way that would allow some proper comparisons with conventional service operations is thus something potentially worthwhile for future TRECs. In the meantime, the TREC genomics track introduced in 2003 was a welcome first effort in this area, with a restricted type of query. Yet the difficulty of obtaining "mainstream" scientific/technical literature test sets means that it is still impossible, though nearly half a century after modern methods promoting the use of natural language were first adumbrated by pioneers like Hans Peter Luhn (Schultz 1968), to carry out the large-scale performance comparisons between natural-language approaches and the use of controlled language subject indexing that continues to play a major role in modern bibliographic services.

My performance synopses over TREC cycles (Sparck Jones 1999, 2000b) show clearly that performance levels decline with request "quality" (brevity, ill definition, and so on). But this applies as much to conventional services. The TREC results suggest that where users are willing to supply initial requests formulated with moderate care, the research model may be applied to conventional services. The natural route for this, already adopted by Web engines, is to use some Boolean constraints as initial filters and rank the selected documents using statistically based weighting. This may not be formally optimal, but may be perfectly satisfactory in practice. Nevertheless, this depends on the setup within which a conventional service is used.

With few exceptions (see, for example, Saracevic et al. 1988), evaluation within the research paradigm that TREC adopted has ignored setup characteristics beyond those encapsulated by given documents, requests and assessments. For example, there has been no concern with why the documents are wanted, whether particular forms of documents are sought, whether other kinds of search keys are available, whether users are occasional or habitual, whether there are other retrieval resources available as well, not to mention a host of economic factors.

In part, this has been through failures to document collection formation properly, or because users are out of the reach of researchers. But this abstraction has a more fundamental rationale. The emphasis on the system itself has been justified by the "core assumption" mentioned earlier; by the associated assumption that the more the core can do, the better because it reduces the need to pay attention to the consequences of individual setups for system design; and by what has been an article of faith in IR research—namely, that the less the user has to do, the better. Thus, one of the attractions of blind relevance feedback is that the user is not even asked to make any actual relevance judgments to develop search queries. Again, one of the attractions of ranked output is that where the system is not pushed toward a precision or recall preference, users can make their own choice of rank cutoff in their specific situation. Other points that may be of importance for users—for instance, not delivering already-seen documents or avoiding content overlap in the output set—have been assumed to be either matters of mere mechanism (though identifying duplicate documents is far from trivial and is a concern for Web system engineers) or far too difficult and dangerous to tackle. Trying to make inferences from the semantic content of a request about performance preferences (say, for precision at the expense of recall) and what search strategies to apply is an extremely hard problem. Solving it is a motivation for the TREC query track, but there are serious difficulties about obtaining appropriate test collections with large request and accompanying relevance assessment sets, not to mention the user context data that is needed to support performance analysis. The interactive track has focused more on the role of user interaction as part of the search process than on user properties per se.

Overall, in the research context within which TREC has placed itself, it has been assumed that requests reflect typical user needs, so if the system can deliver some relevant documents, especially at top ranks, it will ipso facto meet those needs, without any further concern with setup detail or differences between setups. The system generality that IR research seeks should be either immediately hospitable to setup differences as embodied in requests or at any rate automatically adaptive to them, so there is no need for researchers to pay any explicit attention to contextual factors and notably human users. Thus, all of the concern for the information-seeking context and the properties of users that the information science literature at large exhibits, and to which conventional information services pay a good deal of attention, can be legitimately ignored. The precise point about the core assumption is that unless setup properties that might determine system design can be specified in such a (concrete) way that they can be taken into account in system design—and of course, this may be the case—everything that matters about the setup happens either *before* the request is submitted or *after* the documents have been delivered. The 2003 HARD track specifically makes this assumption: hence, *if* some additional information about the user can be gathered beforehand, can the system exploit it effectively in addition to the type of collection data (including past query data) that it already has?

All this does not mean that there is no rationale to investigations, using systems as black boxes, that might lead to different system design specifications. On the view just taken, that is someone else's concern, not TREC's. But it can be argued that TREC has not addressed some rather obvious specifications and thus has limited itself unduly. For example, though TREC evaluations have measured recall, this has been in an extremely abstract way, and the TREC evaluations so far have not said much about meeting high-recall needs in a humanly acceptable way (without, as in Web engines, relying on page hopping as one way of improving recall, for instance).

But whether or not this is a reasonable attitude to take to long-standing, conventional systems and services, it is at least as important to ask what TREC has to do with the Web, not just as an access route to conventional resources, but as a resource in its own right. Then, further, what has TREC to do with the varied types of other information resource that are appearing, enabled by the Web or networking more generally. What are the banners that TREC should be marching into this new world with? This is a pressing question, and not just because there are a good many who think that the Web in particular is the only action in town. One possibility is that though IR may be fundamentally the same on the Web as off it, it may be less easy to relegate setup issues to outer darkness. The other possibility is that IR on the Web is *not* fundamentally the same. So the questions to address now are:

• Is IR on the Web the IR task that the research community has long known and continued to love in TREC?
• If not, what is the Web IR task that TREC, if it believes in trying to solve real-world problems, ought to tackle?
• And then, further, are there new types of information resource facilitated by system connectivity that require new approaches to retrieval, or other tasks, that TREC should address?

5 TREC and the Web

5.1 Current Web Engines

The facilities a good many Web engines offer suggest that IR on the Web is in fact the task we know. Some engines, like Yahoo!, have indeed brought historical ideas about subject classification to market on the Web. But many engines have adopted research ideas. AltaVista, for example, was built right from the start to apply statistical weighting and ranking algorithms.

This might imply that TREC has no message for the Web. Perhaps, moreover, the boot is on the other foot. Searching for simple sentence or term list requests with engines that use the familiar statistical kind of weighting often does not work well. Precision is low, and users are invited to apply all the conventional apparatus of compulsory terms (and hence some Boolean constraints) as well as quoted phrases, say, to improve it.

Why don't these Web engines based on long-standing IR research work better? Setting aside problems like the one that page-header "spamming" presents, there are good reasons for this unsatisfactory performance. One is that the files are shatteringly large. At least one engine indexed over two *billion* pages in June 2002, and since relevant documents will always be few, they have to compete with a lot of noise. The second is that the file is amazingly heterogeneous. Lecture slides, for instance, often have few words yet a high proportion of good content words; they may therefore rank high compared with other short or much longer documents, but are often depressingly insubstantial, mere bullet lists. It is hard for uniform statistical methods to respond appropriately not only to variation in document length but to variation in discourse structure and genre. The Web engines' user needs, however, are too varied for systems to categorize document types as useless and ignore them. The third reason is indeed that partly because there is so much "information" available and partly because access is free, the Web engine user community is gigantic, the range of request and need types the engines have to serve is large, and the range of individual requests and needs is enormous.

Having a vast *reference library* at one's fingertips is of course what the Web is all about, and what the Web engines are intended to provide. The issue here is how the model of the IR task to which much IR research—and to a considerable extent, conventional search services—has been bound, fits that underlying the Web. Is the *literature access* model the same as the *reference data* model?

Of course the two overlap. One may use a reference library to find out about, say, elephants. But many Web engine searches are not for documents about something at all. They are what may be called "location" searches—that is, means to the end of finding, for example, "Where is there a university that runs a course on elephant training?" There are "definition" searches: "[What does] hermeneutic [mean]?" Again, many are not intended to be selective—for instance, "[Find me some] elephant pictures [that is, any ones will do]." Many are naked direction seeking—say, "What's the way to the Elephant House?" None of these fit the "classical" IR research paradigm model of a request, as in "Give me documents about the manufacture of wastepaper bins from elephant feet."

The Web engines have nevertheless in general sought to apply the classical topic request model to all these (and other) varied types of need, or at least have retained it as a substrate, taking some combination of user-friendly Boolean structure and data-reflective statistical weighting as their basic retrieval strategy. They have then added all kinds of elaborations and modifications designed to help users gain precision in topic searching or to adjust query expression to need type—for example, by using compulsory terms, applying category constraints, and so on—but also to refine back-end matching in ways that can both aid topic precision and satisfy some other types of query—for example, by emphasizing term matching on page titles or preferring pages that say "home page." At the same time, the engine builders have recognized that document searching is only one element in a user's complex information management activities, and so have imported other capabilities like translation or summarizing on demand. They have also sought to enhance retrieval itself for the user by, for example, routinely providing minimum, query-oriented "snippet" summaries. The Web engines have of course been able to take advantage of general interface developments—for instance, having multiple windows, which facilitates browsing and can compensate for a lack of retrieval accuracy.

But there have also been more radical departures. One, developed by Google, has been to wholeheartedly exploit the information supplied by page links, not just individually, but collectively—that is, to write the old idea of citation indexing new and large. When compared with "ordinary" citation indexing, Google takes advantage, on the one hand, of the fact that there may naturally be a much denser supply of connectivity data in Web page links than in conventional bibliographic citation, and on the other, that these links are better grounded and hence more likely to be useful for retrieval than simple lexical overlap between pages. This strategy also has the substantial advantage of characterizing documents that may well not make or get the usual kind of bibliographic citation.

The other, rather more substantial departure from the document retrieval model has been that on which Ask Jeeves is based—that is, to start from the presumption that when users seek information, they already have a specific question they want answered. Users are not in a rather general anomalous state of knowledge about some topic, so more specific questions only arise, and are answered, when they read the texts on the topic they have retrieved. With any luck, moreover, given a large user population, many user questions will in fact be frequently asked questions, or at any rate will instantiate familiar generic question templates, so the user can be served by preprocessing the incoming data to extract potential question answers.

The engine builders' holy grail is to be able to learn enough about individual users, or rather individual needs, to be able to target material to them. But it is hard to get direct feedback (as in relevance feedback for the individual request), and even with a good deal of log data, it is hard to make reliable inferences about users (certainly in legally or ethically acceptable ways). The problem is compounded by the way users fall over the edge, out of the engine and into individual sites, taking their further information management operations and the user data these might provide with them. The only real weapon the engine builders have is that they can get such an enormous amount of log data that some reliable patterns may be observed, even if any individual search does not provide much information at all.

Indeed, the main challenges for both Web engine developers and researchers hoping to offer good ideas and tools for practical use is that user queries are typically extremely short, averaging 2.6 terms per query in a large Excite sample, for instance. It is hard to get any leverage at all from such a minimal starting point, when it may also not be possible to draw on the user's "off-engine" working on actual pages, and when it is not certain that a sequence of submitted queries is actually part of a user's search to meet a single need.

Thus, though Web engines may seem, by being used online with nice friendly interfaces, to involve the close interaction between system and user that IR research ought on some views to cover, the relation is in reality much less close than it appears. Interaction with the Web engine is only part of the user's whole online activity, just as the user's interaction with the card catalog in a regular library was only one part of the getting and using of information. Hence, if one seeks to apply TREC findings to the Web, there appears to be less of a requirement than might have been expected to modify the core orientation, with its narrow view of the system environment, that has been characteristic of IR research and has been maintained through the TREC program. The fact that it is difficult for anyone building a public Web engine to really *integrate* their systems with the user's own information management environment as a whole, as opposed to simply supplying one or more tools among many for the user to choose from, seems only to imply that there is scope for developing more tools for a bigger and better toolbox—that is, for following the traditional IR research path.

Important generic ideas developed in earlier IR research, notably statistically based weighting, have long been deployed in Web engines; as mentioned earlier, the first Web engine, AltaVista, explicitly applied these, (indirectly) encouraged by TREC results. Exploiting hyperlinks, as in Google, is another form of statistical processing, making use of a type of information, citations, long recognized as of value. Anchor text is just a piece of text, albeit perhaps an especially useful one, with words in it open to statistical weighting like other text. At the same time, while links and their anchor text may seem to supply especially well-focused and hence rich forms of index information, experiments with these in TREC-9 and TREC 2001 found that they were of no special value for topic searches, though they were helpful for the rather particular home page–finding task (Hawking 2001; Hawking and Craswell 2002).

Some research-derived strategies, like statistically based relevance feedback, have proved difficult to deploy on the Web because they do not fit the modus operandi of Web engine users, even though they have been clearly shown to be effective off-line (Sparck Jones, Walker, and Robertson 2000) and also in filtering. Thus, though they may not always work online (see Koenemann and Belkin 1996), there is no reason to suppose they *cannot* work on the Web. But this is not a central issue for TREC Web pertinence. For the primary task, ad hoc search, the issue is different: given that there has already been a VLC/Web track in TREC that has had large Web document sets to work on (Hawking, Craswell, and Thistlethwaite 1999; Bailey, Craswell, and Hawking 2003; Craswell and Hawking 2003), along with a very large log-derived query set, and given that the Web track results have been those just mentioned, what more is there for TREC to do to get closer to the Web world and its needs? The Web track results might rather imply a "been there, done that" status for TREC in relation to the Web.

But this is a dubious conclusion, as consideration of the current lead engine, Google, suggests. Google is a complex beast, with indexing emphasizing links and, it seems, anchor text, but also using term-frequency information and document structure. Queries are handled on a Boolean filter with output ranking basis. In addition, matching is apparently phrasally "oriented" or proximity "biased." The overall thrust is toward precision, with little or no reference to recall. All of this is a response, given the file data realities, to short queries that are often phrasal, especially with names, and users wanting a few good hits early on.

It can be argued that TREC has essentially failed to come to grips with the realities that an actual engine like Google has to deal with. Thus, while the Web track has sought to address at least the most significant issues for Web retrieval, it has been subverted by the need to sample the Web; this has reduced linkage and, probably, the impact of varied data types. In TREC in general, both topics and files have not been Weblike, and are puny by comparison with the Web. With all its collections and the forms of performance measure that have been applied, TREC has perhaps underestimated what a precision focus requires as well as what can be done with Boolean queries, proximity constraints, document structure, or the like.

So how could or should TREC develop in relation to the Web?

5.2   Web Directions for TREC

The obvious, perhaps most obvious, direction for TREC is to engage, much more fully than hitherto, with the heterogeneity of Web documents and requests, and with their all-too-common inadequacy as levers to move the information world. The miscellaneous additional (indexing and) searching devices that the engines have adopted forcefully suggests that the statistically based strategies familiar from TREC research are too weak in the face of the Web's characteristic messiness, its string-bag mix of really useful lengths of stout cord, odd pieces of string, and little bits too short or frayed for much of anything. Again, there is more to investigate in links and, especially, anchor text (as, for example, Westerveld, Hiemstra, and Kraaij 2002 implies). At the same time, it would be instructive as well as useful for retrieval research to engage more fully with capturing and using document structure; this is a practical and theoretical challenge, for instance, for weighting formulas. It might also be useful, though this has not been neglected in TREC (see, for example, Rose and Stevens 1997), to reconsider Boolean and proximity-based matching.

But really tackling these issues, and particularly exploring "words versus links," presents enormous challenges, most obviously in establishing adequate test collections or environments. "Lifting" test collections from the Web presents all sorts of practical and formal difficulties; staying inside the Web presents complementary ones. But without larger-scale experiments and a fuller engagement with Web data properties at the very least, but also ideally Web users, it may not be possible to demonstrate that what look like counterintuitive results about the value of links really hold or that current retrieval research can contribute to improving Web search performance.

Since research done in the past, though in less taxing system environments, has provided some of the foundations for many Web engines, so new research, undertaken within more taxing environments characteristic of the Web, might in turn supply better-grounded strategies and devices to replace the ad hoc assemblies of gadgets that current engines have put together on top of their system foundations. The fact that the engines continue, indeed are obliged to continue, to seek general techniques that will work across a range of cases representing many actually different types of request, implies that there is further research in the traditional style on better retrieval methods to do. In particular, while it is not clear how to replicate Web query sequencing within a single search activity, the number of past queries that Web engines accumulate offers the opportunity to explore the value of query clustering. This is an old idea (see, for instance, Worona 1971), which can now be much more thoroughly investigated; and Falk Scholer and Hugh Williams's (2002) study suggests that with sufficient queries, the weakness of the inferences that can be drawn about relevance from single query-document matches can be overcome. Along similar lines, there appears to be much more to investigate in relating the TREC filtering as well as ad hoc technology to the Web data and their clientele. While so-called intelligent agents may already figure on the Web, there is much more scope for principled approaches to filtering related to Web engines.

Simply comparing the output for the same request obtained by searching Alta-Vista, Google, and other engines (also including Ask Jeeves) is extremely instructive: the results may overlap in some cases and be quite distinct in others. But the output from any one engine is not consistently superior to that of any other: the most striking point in many cases is that when different engines deliver good output, it is also complementary output; indeed, there are distinctive glittering nuggets in each system's dross. So the crucial issue for TREC is how to scale its work up and out, to get the test data and task specifications that are required to satisfy both operational pertinence and scientific propriety needs.

6   Going beyond the Web

6.1   Other Webs

The "ordinary" public Web, significant though it is, is not the only arena for retrieval research. There is the world of corporate intranets, of Usenet (the original stimulus for AltaVista). Research-based systems may be more helpful in such dedicated environments than in the general Web as, for example, Autonomy Corporation claims (Autonomy 2004). But this, of course, raises the problem of getting public test collections. The same problem arises with other manifestations of the hidden Web—for instance, the large conventional document databases being made available by journal publishers.

6.2   New Data Types

Both the public Web, as a directly accessible information resource, and these other information worlds raise the issue of data types other than text in more or less conventional and familiar forms.

The spoken-document retrieval track in TREC has already explored, albeit on a small scale, retrieval from speech data; and it has shown that good performance can be obtained, though transcription is far from perfect, using standard text retrieval techniques. The recently introduced video track, addressing the image retrieval task that is increasingly important both on and off the Web, draws attention not only to the need to rethink the notion of index key but also that of what a query looks like. What sort of thing can a video query be: "Find me a sequence showing a horse race," "Find me a striking closeup of a horse," or "Show me some cool panning"? There is much more challenging work on image retrieval to do, not just on its own, but in applying and using language keys related to images, and for many image types including, for example, those in scientific image databases.

In the same way, the range of resource types available on the Web emphasizes the need to develop hybrid or multifunction search techniques able to search different types of files—including conventional structured databases, semistructured data, and text—from a single starting point in, say, a natural-language request and to integrate the results. Effective combinations of search methods, from simple statistical ones to those properly requiring natural-language processing, are a necessary precursor for Web data mining (see *AI* 2000) and also a good line forward for TREC work. The main immediate challenge is devising suitable test environments and obtaining appropriate test data for meaningful evaluations; but the new genomics track is a natural starting point for this.

The genomics track draws attention to the opportunities more generally with networks for multifaceted information bases. This is not a new notion, or even an actuality, but the ease with which connections between one base and another can be made, both by the system and the user, emphasizes the challenge for future TRECs of dealing with information requests that are single entry points to a range of resource types—for example, textual and numerical—or in unstructured and structured databases, and require a retrieval mechanism able to develop a set of query types from this one starting point. This is an area that goes far beyond the visible Web.

6.3   New Tasks

Pursuing a more orthogonal line, the question is what new tasks rather than data types TREC ought to address. TREC has already taken a major step forward here in introducing the QA track. While many Web engine queries are topic ones or, like home page searches, approximate to "known-item recovery," it is quite clear that many users would like specific questions answered. The TREC QA tests so far have shown that when longer answer passages—that is, passages hopefully embedding answers—are allowed, established text retrieval methods can be quite competitive with only modest elaboration. Yet when only brief answer snippets are permitted, and even more when exact answers are required as in TREC 2002 (Voorhees 2003), a significant ramp-up in analysis and search techniques exploiting natural-language processing, to at least a nontrivial extent, is needed.

The QA track, challenging though it is, has been a success, with an animating effect on TREC as a whole. It has served to emphasize the fact that while document retrieval is a valid task in its own right, it is also part of a spread of information-seeking, modification, and presentation tasks. From this point of view, TREC has been a standard-bearer outside the retrieval world. The level of performance that has been obtained with a difficult task has been impressive (see, for instance, Moldovan et al. 2003). But it is also significant that while explicit natural-language processing appears to be essential, it can be materially enhanced with statistical learning (as illustrated by Yang and Chua 2003). There is manifestly much more, very hard research to do to support online, user-specific QA. This means not only being able to handle a range of question types but also being able to accommodate the many intrinsic uncertainties about what the user's question is, and to degrade gracefully when direct answering cannot be done. This is clearly a line of work that TREC can grow further with, though it clearly also raises the issue of interactive QA and a system's ability to extract pertinent contextual information.

Even here, however, traditional retrieval has a contributory role in selecting long passages, potentially containing answers, for more detailed analysis. Text retrieval has similar natural roles in relation to other tasks—for example, in supplying likely text for detailed information extraction, selecting documents pertinent to specific topic tracking (as in following news stories), and delivering key documents to be summarized. It may not be appropriate for TREC to extend itself to one or more of these other tasks simply as a matter of course—some already have their own evaluation programs, such as the so-called Document Understanding Conference, addressing summarization (DUC 2003). TREC needs to move into task areas either where there is a natural issue as to whether current IR methods are applicable or can be extended to be applicable, or whether the connection between the retrieval subtask and the other task(s) is particularly close. QA illustrates the former, and topic tracking and summarizing, especially extractive summarizing, could illustrate the latter. TREC thus needs to monitor other evaluation initiatives, taking advantage of the road mapping exercises that these may involve, and the changing opportunities for research partitioning or collaboration that they offer, as already illustrated with the two QA programs running respectively under TREC and ARDA's AQUAINT initiative (AQUAINT 2003).

6.4   New Resources

The relation between TREC and the Web is not a one-way street. The Web is also a source of resources for those engaged with retrieval and similar tasks. This is not only in the obvious sense, as in supplying, say, parallel texts as a source of translation equivalents for cross-language retrieval or handy dictionaries. The Web is also, as a huge text base, a source of information about word usage and discourse forms. It was thus used, for instance, to supply additional forms of QA patterns for searching the target file for the QA task (Brill et al. 2002). Opportunities like this imply that just as modern information retrieval began by recognizing the value of direct text clues, its indexing and searching tools can be further refined by exploiting the vast quantities of text the Web makes available. Of course, the same applies to off-Web resources, as Autonomy's corporate applications imply.

7   The Future: Multitasking

TREC can naturally, and valuably, continue along its existing lines, primarily by:

· Pushing ad hoc retrieval and its variations for new types of need or material
· Tackling other individual information-seeking tasks

There is plenty here to occupy the research community in collection building and evaluation design as well as system development and testing. There are problems about just continuing with more of the same, however.

As noted earlier, TREC has implications for retrieval in general, not only for retrieval on the Web. At the same time, Web engines illustrate major constraints on the core retrieval system that has been the main focus of TREC so far. First, Web engines deal successfully with the "quasi" known-item searches that figure so largely in Web usage, but to which TREC's topic-based search model can contribute very little. Second, Web users can remain, as they seem to be, lacking in search enterprise because there are so many pages out there on virtually any topic that even the most minimal search specification can usually retrieve something useful, but where the richer search strategies that IR research offers cannot get much leverage. Third, Web engines have been driven, by the quantity and heterogeneity of the material they are dealing with, to adopt "everything including the kitchen sink" approaches to indexing and searching that fall far outside IR research practice so far, as illustrated by TREC, even if more all-embracing yet still principled approaches could be developed through research study. Fourth, as noted earlier, most users' information-seeking behavior on the Web takes place beyond the scope of its engines, even further from the core system focus that TREC has had.

There are therefore good reasons for taking a more radical approach to TREC in the future. Continuing with the "one task at a time" approach, even if over a wider range of separate tasks than hitherto, would not be pursuing the capability that information management under Web conditions especially, but also under modern information technology conditions in general, should really offer—namely, providing a properly *integrated* information management service subsuming different tasks that can be executed, as occasion demands, in any particular user situation. This is, of course, the "integrated solutions" mantra that business system vendors invoke, though in practice to rather limited effect; much more real power is needed. The Web services have already begun to move in this direction. They already take in one another's washing as document retrieval engines, and in some cases point to one another within the broader framework of response to inquiry, by referring to QA as well as document retrieval. More important, they have also begun to offer other task capabilities, like translation and summarization on request.

But a vision of what a Web (or other modern) information management should be like has a larger task range—for example, including information extraction, new text derivation, and translation and summarization—and looks for more integration than the superficial one represented by a collection of buttons in a menu. Being able to invoke different task facilities at the press of a button in a single menu is much better than nothing as a convenience that information technology has brought us. But proper integration, allowing the user to move effectively from one task to another at will, implies a truly common information environment where pertinent, user-specialized detail can be moved between tasks and exploited as required. The current multiple task options that the engines offer are only superficially related, and hence not as productive as they should be. They do not maintain and use current context properly, and so do not take proper advantage of the information about the user that is in principle available to make the execution of any particular task more helpfully personalized.

There are beginning to be operational systems that offer integrated multitasking —for example, MiTAP (Damianos et al. 2002). MiTAP draws on the know-how developed in TREC and its companion evaluation programs. But there is much more to explore here, especially in how far general, statistically based methods can provide a common platform across tasks.

8   Rethinking TREC from the Bottom Up

TREC has been hugely successful in four different ways:

1. It has been a major IR research program that has delivered many important results.
2. It has built a large community (around eighty teams took part in TREC 2001, for example) and has fostered links with other, hitherto separate communities, importing participants and ideas—for example, from speech and natural-language processing.
3. It has stimulated, and will continue to stimulate, retrieval research outside TREC by reporting findings for comparison and supplying test data, and by encouraging other programs, as in the cross-language retrieval CLEF and NTCIR evaluations (see CLEF 2003; NTCIR 2003).
4. It has encouraged the application of statistical methods of information processing in task areas outside retrieval—for example, by exporting $tf * idf$-type word weighting.

It would indeed also have been nice to point to clear evidence that TREC findings have been taken up by commercial systems, especially Web ones. But though individual researchers link TREC with the operational world, so one hopes there has been some carryover, those responsible for Web engines and the like do not publish details of how the engines work.

There are areas within IR that TREC has not significantly addressed, such as retrieval from large files of full-text scientific material, primarily because it is difficult to get suitable test collections. Since the proprietors of large journal data files continue to maintain conventional approaches, not being able to challenge this conventional wisdom in sound evaluations is unfortunate.

But this is not the critical future direction for TREC. After a decade's solid work on document retrieval, it is time for TREC to enter a radically new phase. This can be expressed by saying it is necessary to relate TREC more fully to the Web than hitherto. But it means more, however, than focusing on the Web because it is there, or taking advantage of thinking about IR and the Web to review what we suppose information *retrieval* is all about. Relating TREC more fully to the Web and beyond the Web to information environments generally implies that we have to think again about what TREC's foundation, on some principled view of what information *management* is, should be.

The natural development is still to start from the notion of text, as with the first decade of TREC, albeit viewing this notion quite broadly; but it is also, now, to start from *interpretation*, not just retrieval. This means moving upward and outward from texts to cover a range of tasks, some crude and some complex, that are all related in doing something, in some way, with some information from some text(s), and are also in operation *dependent on one another* because they are invoked in common contexts. Studying the way common methods of processing text can be applied to different QA requirements, notably for long or short extracts, in the TREC QA track has been a modest move in the new direction. Other work, such as on summarizing (Mani and Maybury 1999; DUC 2003), has long explored extractive techniques with much in common with those used for retrieval. The fact that tasks currently only rather contingently related to the TREC program, like information extraction, topic detection and tracking, and summarization, share technologies with retrieval is thus one good reason to think about developing TREC to make connections with them. But the much more important reason for TREC to make these connections is that we want future information management systems to be able to carry out their tasks as subtasks supporting the users' information management activities. This implies a common, multipurpose evaluation framework so that, for example, if we take summaries as surrogates for full texts as inputs to QA, we can relate QA effectiveness to summarizing effectiveness. The evaluation experience that TREC has gained in the last decade makes TREC well placed to tackle more evaluation scenarios for more ambitious information management situations, and also justifies the argument that it should advance in this direction, tough though this will be.

Acknowledgment

I am grateful to my referees for comments.

References

Adi, T., O. K. Ewell, and P. Adi. 2000. High selectivity and accuracy with READWARE's automated system of knowledge organisation. In *TREC-8*, 493–498.

AI. 2000. Special issue on intelligent Internet systems. *Artificial Intelligence* 118, nos. 1–2:1–275.

Allan, J., ed. 2002. *Topic detection and tracking: Event-based information organization.* Boston: Kluwer.

AQUAINT. 2003. ⟨http://www.ic-arda.org/InfoExploit/aquaint/⟩ (visited August 2003).

Autonomy. 2004. ⟨http://www.autonomy.com/⟩ (visited April 2004).

Bailey, P., N. Craswell, and D. Hawking. 2003. Engineering a multi-purpose test collection for Web retrieval experiments. *Information Processing and Management* 39:853–871.

Barker, F. H., B. K. Wyatt, and D. C. Veal. 1972. Report on the evaluation of an experimental computer-based current-awareness service for chemists. *Journal of the American Society for Information Science* 23:85–99.

Beaulieu, M. M. 1997. Experiments on interfaces to support query expansion. *Journal of Documentation* 53:8–19.

Blair, D. C., and M. E. Maron. 1985. An evaluation of retrieval effectiveness for a full-text document retrieval system. *Communications of the ACM* 28:289–299.

Brill, E., et al. 2002. Data-intensive question answering. In *TREC 2001*, 393–400.

Cardie, C. 1997. Empirical methods in information extraction. *AI Magazine* 18, no. 4:65–79.

Carmel, E., S. Crawford, and H. Chen. 1992. Browsing in hypertext: A cognitive study. *IEEE Transactions on Systems, Man, and Cybernetics* 22:865–884.

CLEF. 2003. ⟨http://clef.iei.pi.cnr.it/⟩ (visited August 2003).

Cleverdon, C. W. 1967. The Cranfield tests on index language devices. *Aslib Proceedings* 19:173–194.

Craswell, N., and D. Hawking. 2003. Overview of the TREC 2002 Web track. In *TREC 2002*, 86–95.

Croft, W. B., ed. 2000. *Advances in information retrieval*. Dordrecht: Kluwer.

Croft, W. B., and J. Lafferty, eds. 2003. *Language modeling for information retrieval*. Dordrecht: Kluwer.

Damianos, L., et al. 2002. MiTAP for biosecurity: A case study. *AI Magazine* 23, no. 4 (Winter): 13–29.

Derr, R. L. 1984. Information seeking expressions of users. *Journal of the American Society for Information Science* 35:124–128.

DUC. 2003. ⟨http://www-nlpir.nist.gov/projects/duc/⟩ (visited August 2003).

Dumais, S. T. 1995. Latent semantic indexing (LSI): TREC-3 report. In *TREC-3*, 219–230.

Fagan, J. L. 1987. Experiments in automatic phrase indexing for document retrieval: A comparison on syntactic and non-syntactic methods. PhD diss., Cornell University.

Gordon, M., and P. Pathak. 1999. Finding information on the World Wide Web: The retrieval effectiveness of search engines. *Information Processing and Management* 35:141–180.

Hawking, D. 2001. Overview of the TREC-9 Web track. In *TREC-9*, 87–102.

Hawking, D., and N. Craswell. 2002. Overview of the TREC 2001 Web track. In *TREC 2001*, 61–67.

Hawking, D., N. Craswell, and P. Thistlethwaite. 1999. Overview of TREC-7 very large collection track. In *TREC-7*, 91–103.

IP&M. 2001. Special issue on interactivity at the text retrieval conferences (TREC). *Information Processing and Management* 37:365–541.

Koenemann, J., and N. J. Belkin. 1996. A case for interaction: A study of interactive information retrieval behavior and effectiveness. In *Proceedings of CHI 1996*, ed. R. Bilger, S. Guest, and M. J. Tauber, 205–212. New York: Association for Computing Machinery.

Kwok, K. L. 1995. A network approach to probabilistic information retrieval. *ACM Transactions on Office Information Systems* 13:325–353.

Kwok, K. L., and M. Chan. 1998. Improving two-stage ad-hoc retrieval for short queries. In *Proceedings of the twenty-first annual international ACM SIGIR conference*, 250–256.

Lu, X. A., J. D. Holt, and D. J. Miller. 1996. Boolean system revisited: Its performance and its behavior. In *TREC-4*, 459–473.

Mahesh, K., J. Kud, and P. Dixon. 2000. Oracle at TREC-8: A lexical approach. In *TREC-8*, 207–216.

Mani, I., and M. T. Maybury, eds. 1999. *Advances in automatic text summarization.* Cambridge, MA: MIT Press.

Miller, D. R. H., T. Leek, and R. M. Schwartz. 1999. A hidden Markov model information retrieval system. In *Proceedings of the twenty-second annual international ACM SIGIR conference*, 214–221.

Mitra, M., et al. 1997. An analysis of statistical and syntactic phrases. In *Proceedings, RIAO-97, computer-assisted information searching on the Internet*, 200–214. Paris: Centre de Hautes Etudes Internationales d'Informatique Documentaires.

Moldovan, D., et al. 2003. LCC tools for question answering. In *TREC 2002*, 388–397.

NTCIR. 2003. ⟨http://research.nii.ac.jp/ntcir/⟩ (visited August 2003).

O'Connor, J. 1973. Text searching retrieval of answer-sentences and other answer passages. *Journal of the American Society for Information Scientists* 24:445–460.

Okapi. 1997. Papers on Okapi. Special issue, *Journal of Documentation* 33:3–87.

Over, P. 2001. The TREC interactive track: An annotated bibliography. *Information Processing and Management* 37:369–381.

Perez-Carballo, J., and T. Strzalkowski. 2000. Natural language information retrieval: Progress report. *Information Processing and Management* 36:155–178.

Ponte, J. M., and W. B. Croft. 1998. A language modelling approach to information retrieval. In *Proceedings of the twenty-first annual international ACM SIGIR conference*, 275–281.

Rose, D. E., and C. Stevens. 1997. V-Twin: A lightweight engine for interactive use. In *TREC-5*, 279–290.

Salton, G. 1968. *Automatic information organisation and retrieval.* New York: McGraw-Hill.

Salton, G. 1972. A new comparison between conventional indexing MEDLARS and automatic text processing (SMART). *Journal of the American Society for Information Science* 23:75–84.

Salton, G., ed. 1971. *The SMART retrieval system.* Englewood Cliffs, NJ: Prentice Hall.

Salton, G., and C. Buckley. 1988. Term weighting approaches to automatic text retrieval. *Information Processing and Management* 24:513–523.

Salton, G., and M. J. McGill. 1983. *Introduction to modern information retrieval.* New York: McGraw-Hill.

Saracevic, T., et al. 1988. A study of information seeking and retrieving: I. Background and methodology; II. Users, questions, and effectiveness; III. Searchers, searches, and overlap. *Journal of the American Society for Information Science* 39:161–176, 177–196, 197–216.

Scholer, F., and H. E. Williams. 2002. Query association for effective retrieval. In *Proceedings of the ACM international conference on information and knowledge management,* 324–331. New York: Association for Computing Machinery.

Schultz, C. K., ed. 1968. *H. P. Luhn: Pioneer of information science.* New York: Spartan.

Sparck Jones, K. 1995. Reflections on TREC. *Information Processing and Management* 31:291–314.

Sparck Jones, K. 1999. Summary performance comparisons, TREC-2 through TREC-7. In *TREC-7,* B1–B6.

Sparck Jones, K. 2000a. Further reflections on TREC. *Information Processing and Management* 36:37–85.

Sparck Jones, K. 2000b. Summary performance comparisons, TREC-2 through TREC-8. In *TREC-8,* B1–B5.

Sparck Jones, K. 2001. Automatic language and evaluation processing: Rethinking evaluation. *Natural Language Engineering* 7:1–18.

Sparck Jones, K., ed. 1981. *Information retrieval experiment.* London: Butterworths. Available at ⟨http://www.nist.gov/itl/div894/894.02/projects/irlib⟩.

Sparck Jones, K., and J. R. Galliers. 1996. *Evaluating natural language processing systems.* Lecture notes in artificial intelligence 1083. Berlin: Springer.

Sparck Jones, K., S. Walker, and S. E. Robertson. 2000. A probabilistic model of information retrieval: Development and comparative experiments, parts 1 and 2. *Information Processing and Management* 36, no. 6:779–808, 809–840.

Stevens, M. E. 1965. *Automatic indexing: A state of the art report.* Monograph 91. Washington, DC: National Bureau of Standards.

Sullivan, M. V., C. L. Borgman, and D. Wippern. 1990. End-users, mediated searches, and front-end assistance programs on Dialog: A comparison of learning, performance, and satisfaction. *Journal of the American Society for Information Science* 41:27–42.

Tenopir, C., and P. Cahn. 1994. TARGET and FREESTYLE: DIALOG and MEAD join the relevance ranks. *Online* 18, no. 3:31–47.

Voorhees, E. M. 2000. Variations in relevance judgments and the measurement of retrieval effectiveness. *Information Processing and Management* 36:697–716.

Voorhees, E. M. 2003. Overview of the TREC 2002 question answering track. In *TREC 2002,* 57–68.

Westerveld, T., D. Hiemstra, and W. Kraaij. 2002. Retrieving Web pages using content, links, URLs, and anchors. In *TREC 2001*, 663–672.

Worona, S. 1971. Query clustering in a large document space. In *The SMART retrieval system*, ed. G. Salton, 298–310. Englewood Cliffs, NJ: Prentice Hall.

Yang, H., and T.-S. Chua. 2003. The integration of lexical knowledge and external resources. In *TREC 2002*, 486–491.

Zobel, J. 1998. How reliable are the results of large-scale information retrieval experiments? In *Proceedings of the twenty-first annual international ACM SIGIR conference*, 307–314.

List of Contibutors

James Allan
University of Massachusetts Amherst

Nicholas J. Belkin
Rutgers University

Eric W. Brown
IBM T. J. Watson Research Center

Chris Buckley
Sabir Research, Inc.

Jamie Callan
Carnegie Mellon University

David Carmel
IBM Haifa Research Laboratory

Charles L. A. Clarke
University of Waterloo

Gordon V. Cormack
University of Waterloo

Nick Craswell
CSIRO

W. Bruce Croft
University of Massachusetts Amherst

Susan T. Dumais
Microsoft Research

Martin Franz
IBM T. J. Watson Research Center

John S. Garofolo
National Institute of Standards and Technology

Donna K. Harman
National Institute of Standards and Technology

David Hawking
CSIRO

Djoerd Hiemstra
University of Twente

Abraham Ittycheriah
IBM T. J. Watson Research Center

Tapas Kanungo
IBM Almaden Research Center

Wessel Kraaij
TNO

Kui-Lam Kwok
City University of New York

Thomas R. Lynam
University of Waterloo

Yoelle Maarek
IBM Haifa Research Laboratory

Robert L. Mack
IBM T. J. Watson Research Center

Alan D. Marwick
IBM T. J. Watson Research Center

J. Scott McCarley
IBM T. J. Watson Research Center

Christopher R. Palmer
Vivisimo Inc.

John M. Prager
IBM T. J. Watson Research Center

Stephen Robertson
Microsoft Research, Cambridge, and City University, London

John R. Smith
IBM T. J. Watson Research Center

Aya Soffer
IBM Haifa Research Laboratory

Karen Sparck Jones
University of Cambridge

Ellen M. Voorhees
National Institute of Standards and
Technology

Jason Y. Zien
IBM Almaden Research Center

Index